A Life in Letters

Also by George Orwell

FICTION

Burmese Days
A Clergyman's Daughter
Keep the Aspidistra Flying
Coming Up for Air
Animal Farm
Nineteen Eighty-Four

NON-FICTION

Down and Out in Paris and London
The Road to Wigan Pier
Homage to Catalonia
A Kind of Compulsion (1903–36)
Facing Unpleasant Facts (1937–39)
A Patriot After All (1940–41)
All Propaganda Is Lies (1941–42)
Keeping Our Little Corner Clean (1942–43)
Two Wasted Years (1943)
I Have Tried to Tell the Truth (1943–44)
I Belong to the Left (1945)
Smothered Under Journalism (1946)
It Is What I Think (1947–48)
Our Job Is to Make Life Worth Living (1949–50)
Critical Essays
Narrative Essays
Diaries

George Orwell

A LIFE IN LETTERS

SELECTED AND ANNOTATED

BY

Peter Davison

Harvill
Secker

Published by Harvill Secker 2010

2 4 6 8 10 9 7 5 3

First published in Great Britain in 2010 by
HARVILL SECKER
Random House
20 Vauxhall Bridge Road
London SW1V 2SA

www.rbooks.co.uk

Addresses for companies within The Random House Group Limited can be found at:
www.randomhouse.co.uk/offices.htm

The Random House Group Limited Reg. No. 954009

Letters collected from *The Complete Works of George Orwell*, edited by Peter Davison, OBE,
published in Great Britain in 1998 by Secker & Warburg

A CIP catalogue record for this book is available from the British Library

ISBN 9781846553554

The Random House Group Limited supports The Forest Stewardship
Council (FSC), the leading international forest certification organisation.
All our titles that are printed on Greenpeace approved FSC certified paper carry the FSC logo.
Our paper procurement policy can be found at www.rbooks.co.uk/environment

Mixed Sources
Product group from well-managed
forests and other controlled sources
www.fsc.org Cert no. TT-COC-2139
© 1996 Forest Stewardship Council
FSC

Typeset in Monotype Dante by Dinah Drazin
Printed and bound in Great Britain by
Clays Ltd, St Ives plc

Contents

List of Illustrations

Sketches within the body of the text are Orwell's own drawings and are copyright The Estate of Sonia Brownell Orwell.

Introduction

George Orwell 'is in the peculiar position of having been a by-word for fifty years'. No, not Orwell of course, but Rudyard Kipling as described by Orwell. However, it is not far off the mark for Orwell himself. Orwell also wrote of Kipling, 'before one can even speak about Kipling one has to clear away a legend that has been created by two sets of people who have not read his works'. This may be a little further from the mark but many of those who refer to Orwell seem not to have read much more than *Animal Farm* and *Nineteen-Eighty-Four*, if those. The millions who have heard of *Big Brother* and *Room 101* know nothing of their progenitor. Ignorance of Orwell is also to be found in academic circles and in what would regard itself as the higher reaches of journalism. When Professor Raymond B. Browne of Bowling Green University died he was credited by the *Daily Telegraph* with having launched 'popular culture' into the mainstream. Browne's *Journal of Popular Culture* was published in 1967, but Orwell was writing most intelligently about popular culture over twenty-five years earlier. Indeed, when *Critical Essays* was published in the United States in 1946 as *Dickens, Dali and Others* it was given the subtitle *Studies in Popular Culture*. At one extreme Orwell is canonised – hence the sub-title, *The Making and Claiming of 'St. George' Orwell*, of John Rodden's excellent study analysing *The Politics of Literary Reputation* (1989). At the other he is subjected to the vigorous wielding of the hatchet, something Scott Lucas does 'with remarkable efficiency' in his *Orwell* (2003) according to Terry Eagleton in the *London Review of Books*, 19 June 2003. Where does poor old George stand? Professor Eagleton in his review of the three biographies of 2003, aptly titled, 'Reach-Me-Down Romantic', suggests that Orwell 'combined cultural Englishness with political cosmopolitanism, and detested political personality cults while sedulously cultivating a public image of himself'. Despite world-wide acclaim, Orwell saw himself as dogged by 'Failure, failure, failure'. 'Failure', as Eagleton says, 'was his forte.'

I am inclined to think that Orwell had within his deepest self an unresolved conflict that made him so contradictory a character. He was ever in arms against organised religion, especially the Roman Catholic Church. He thought there was no afterlife. Yet he was married in church, had his adopted son Richard baptised, and wished to be buried, not cremated, according to the rites of the Church of England. For so rational a man it was strange that he should ask Rayner Heppenstall to cast a horoscope for Richard (21 July 1944); that he should believe he saw a ghost in Walberswick churchyard (16 August 1931); and discuss poltergeists with Sir Sachaverell Sitwell (6 July 1940), not to mention the quasi-religious conclusion to *A Clergyman's Daughter* (but that, after all, is 'only a novel'). Perhaps most telling is Sir Richard Rees recalling that Orwell had told him that it 'gave him an unpleasant feeling to see his real name in print': 'how can you be sure your enemy won't cut it out and work some kind of black magic on it?' Was this mere whimsy, or was it deeply felt? Not 'some enemy or other' but 'your enemy'. Who was that? The title of Rees's study sums up his subject perfectly: *George Orwell: Fugitive from the Camp of Victory* (1961). He fled from triumph and sought refuge in 'Failure, failure, failure'.

Orwell was born Eric Arthur Blair in Motihari, Bengal, on 25 June 1903. His father, Richard Walmsley Blair was born in 1857 in Milborne St Andrew, Dorset, where his father was the Vicar. Orwell's father served in the Opium Department of the Indian Civil Service. His mother, Ida Mabel Limouzin, was born in 1875 at Penge, Surrey but her family had a long association with Burma. Indeed, there seems to be a curious survival of the Limouzin family in Moulmein, Myanmar, to this day, as Emma Larkin discovered a year or two ago. She found not only that Orwell was well (if covertly) remembered, but she noticed a street called *Leimmaw-zin*, 'the nearest Burmese pronunciation for "Limouzin"'. However, when she asked a passer-by to interpret the name, he confidently offered, 'Orange-Shelf Street' (*Secret Histories*, pp. 145–6).

Orwell's parents married in the intriguingly-named church of St John in the Wilderness at Naini Tal on 15 June 1897. Orwell would surely have found that appropriate. Their first child, Marjorie, was born at Gaya, Bengal, on 21 April 1898. Ida Blair returned with her two children to live in England at Henley-on-Thames, in 1904. In 1907 Richard Blair took three months' leave at Henley. On 6 April 1908, Orwell's younger sister, Avril, was born. From 1908–11, Orwell attended a Roman Catholic day-school run by Ursuline nuns. He then boarded at St Cyprian's, a private preparatory school in Eastbourne where he would meet Cyril Connolly, who was to feature significantly in his later life. Orwell's essay, 'Such, Such Were the Joys' is based (sometimes loosely) on his experiences at St Cyprian's, but the school educated him well enough for him to enter Eton as a King's Scholar in May 1917.

A letter that has only very recently come to light gives an account of his life thereafter from Orwell's point of view. The letter has not previously been published and I am very grateful to its owner (who wishes to remain anonymous) for permission to include it here. Orwell had been asked by Richard Usborne, the editor of the *Strand*, a monthly literary periodical published from January 1891 to March 1950, to contribute to the journal and to give some account of his life. As Orwell's last paragraph indicates, he felt far too busy to contribute – he was writing *Nineteen Eighty-Four* – but despite that went to some trouble to respond to Mr Usborne. It was typical of Orwell, as some of the letters in this selection show, that he would go to great trouble to respond to correspondents whom he hardly knew – if at all. The letter to Richard Usborne was written from Barnhill, Jura, on 26 August 1947:

Dear Mr Usborne,*

Many thanks for your letter of the 22nd. I will answer your queries as best I can. I was born in 1903 and educated at Eton where I had a scholarship. My father was an Indian civil servant, and my mother also came of an Anglo-Indian family, with connections especially in Burma. After leaving school I served five years in the Imperial Police in Burma, but the job was totally unsuited to me and I resigned when I came home on leave in 1927. I wanted to be a writer, and I lived most of the next two years in Paris, on my savings, writing novels which no one would publish and which I subsequently destroyed. When I had no more money I worked for a while as a dishwasher, then came back to England and did a series of ill-paid jobs usually as a teacher, with intervals of unemployment and dire poverty. (That was the period of the slump.) Nearly all the incidents described in *Down and Out* actually happened, but at different times, and I wove them together so as to make a continuous story. I did work in a bookshop for about a year in 1934–5, but I only put that into *Keep the Aspidistra Flying* to make a background. The book is not, I think, autobiographical, and I have never worked in an advertising office. In general my books have been less autobiographical than people have assumed. There are bits of truthful autobiography in *Wigan Pier*, and, of course, *Homage to Catalonia*, which is straight reporting. Incidentally *Keep the A.F.* is one of several books which I don't care about and have suppressed.

As to politics, I was only intermittently interested in the subject until about 1935, though I think I can say I was always more or less 'left.' In *Wigan Pier* I first tried to thrash out my ideas. I felt, as I still do, that there are huge deficiencies in the whole conception of Socialism, and I was still wondering whether there was any other way out. After having a fairly good look at British industrialism at its worst, ie. in the mining areas, I came to the conclusion that it is a duty to work for Socialism even if one is not emotionally drawn to it, because the continuance of present conditions is simply not tolerable, and no solution except some kind of collectivism is viable, because that is what the mass of the people want. About the same time I became infected with a horror of totalitarianism, which indeed I already had in the form of hostility towards the Catholic Church. I fought for six months (1936–7) in Spain on the side of Government, and had the misfortune to be mixed up in the internal struggle on the Government side, which left me with the conviction that there is not much to choose between Communism and Fascism, though for various reasons I would choose Communism if there were no other choice open. I have been vaguely associated with Trotskyists and Anarchists, and more closely with the left wing of the Labour Party (the Bevan-Foot end of it). I was literary editor of *Tribune*, then Bevan's paper, for about a year and a half (1943–5), and have written for it over a longer period than that. But I have never belonged to a political party, and I believe that even politically I am more valuable if I record what I believe to be true and refuse to toe a party line.

Early last year I decided to take a holiday, as I had been writing 4 articles a week for 2 years. I spent 6 months in Jura, during which time I did not do any work, then came back to London and did journalism as usual during the winter. Then I returned to Jura and started a novel which I hope to finish by the spring of 1948. I am trying not to do anything else while I get on with this. I do very occasionally write book reviews for the *New Yorker*. I mean to spend the winter in Jura this year, partly because I never seem to get any continuous work done in London, partly because I think it will be a little easier to keep warm here. The climate is not quite so cold, and food and fuel are easier to get. I have a quite comfortable house here, though it is in a remote place. My sister [Avril] keeps house for me. I am a widower with a son aged a little over 3.

I hope these notes will be of help. I am afraid I cannot write anything for the *Strand* at present, because, as I have said, I am trying not to get involved in outside work. We have only 2 posts a week here and this letter won't go until the 30th, so I shall address it to Sussex.

Yours sincerely
George Orwell

Although Orwell says he was never a member of a political party, he had either forgotten, or is glossing over, that for a short time he was a member of the Independent Labour Party. He wrote about joining in 'Why I Join the I.L.P.', 24 June 1938. He left when war broke out because it retained its pacifist stance. His forgetting might have been a wish for disassociation.

Orwell makes only the briefest, indirect, reference in his letter to his first wife, Eileen. Typically for a man of his character and time, he does not harp on her loss in his letters, though there is no doubt he felt it keenly. Eileen O'Shaughnessy was born in South Shields in 1905. He and Eileen met at a party given by Mrs Rosalind Obermeyer at 77 Parliament Hill, London, in March 1935. For Orwell it was love at first sight. On leaving the party he told a friend, 'The girl I want to marry is Eileen O'Shaughnessy', something he also said to Mrs Obermeyer. Eileen was at the time reading for a master's degree in psychology at University College London. Despite the hard fact that Orwell was earning very little and his obvious prospects limited, they were married from Orwell's cottage in Wallington in the adjacent parish church on 9 June 1936. She died under anaesthetic at Newcastle upon Tyne on 29 March 1945.

There is a very curious link between Orwell and Eileen that quite possibly neither may have realised. Both 'celebrated' the year 1984. The title of Orwell's novel, only chosen shortly before he sent his typescript to his publisher, Fredric Warburg, could obviously not have been known to Eileen, but did he know that she had written a poem to celebrate the centenary of her school, Sunderland High, called 'End of the Century: 1984'? It has three fourteen-line stanzas, entitled 'Death', 'Birth', and 'The Phoenix' and seems to have no obvious link with anything Orwell was to write. Her poem celebrates the past; Orwell's novel warns of the future.

Over 1,700 letters by George Orwell are included in Vols X–XX of *The Complete Works of George Orwell* and in *The Lost Orwell*. This figure does not include the many letters he wrote in reply to readers of *Tribune*, nor the many dozens of internal memoranda he wrote making programme booking arrangements whilst working for the Indian Section of the BBC Overseas Service, 1941–43. *The Complete Works* and *The Lost Orwell* also include many letters written to Orwell or about him and, most particularly, letters by his wife, Eileen. This compilation is, therefore, only a small proportion of what is available.

In making this selection I have had two principles in mind. Firstly, that the letters chosen should illustrate Orwell's life and hopes; and secondly that each one should be of interest in its own right. Most of the letters are given in full, but I have cut the lengthier passages that repeat what is printed elsewhere. As Orwell's horizons narrowed in his last couple of years as a result of increasing illness and confinement to hospitals and Jura, even though his circle of friends grew rather than narrowed, there is more repetition and hence more excisions.

It is surprising how many people saved letters that Orwell wrote to them. Inevitably what has survived varies over the years and sometimes, in order to tell the story of Orwell's life, one must rely on letters sent *to* Orwell. A notable example of this last is the important correspondence with Ihor Szewczenko regarding the publication of the Ukrainian version of *Animal Farm* from 11 April 1946 onwards. Even if one wished to include an equal number of letters from each year of Orwell's adult life, mere survival defines what can be chosen for inclusion. Thus, and most obviously, there are no extant letters from the five years Orwell spent in Burma.

Despite exhaustive searches by Ian Angus and the editor in the preparation of *The Complete Works*, material about Orwell, including valuable letters, still comes to light – hence, of course, *The Lost Orwell*. It has been gratifying to be able to include here a few letters – and important ones – for the first time. I am especially grateful to the owners of the 'new' letters for allowing their inclusion. I am also grateful to those who have acquired already published letters for permission to include them here; their names are given in the notes to their letters. Rumours abound that a further batch of letters to Eleanor Jaques was initially offered for sale by Bonhams in 2009 and then withdrawn.

Orwell's letters tend to be businesslike. This applies equally to friends as to his literary agent. He is quick to apologise if he feels he has been slow in explaining some action or has neglected some social pleasantry – such as on 24 December 1934 when he regrets not writing earlier to send Christmas greetings to Leonard Moore, adding 'Please remember me very kindly to Mrs Moore'. Even the letters that have come to light to Eleanor Jaques, Brenda Salkeld, and Lydia Jackson are short on endearments although his wish for a loving relationship is plain. The deaths of Eileen, his father and mother, and his sister Marjorie were all deeply felt by him, but he is reticent about expressing his pain. This is not a mark of coldness of character but how those brought up in the first half of the twentieth century expected to be seen to behave, at least publicly. Pain and suffering were thought to be relative and given that experienced by millions in the two 'Great' wars, personal loss, especially natural loss, was felt in context. One suffered in silence. Orwell can strike the casual observer as dour. His close friends likened him to his creation Benjamin, the donkey of *Animal Farm*. But, as David Astor told the editor, when he was depressed or troubled he would telephone Orwell and ask him to meet him in a local pub because he knew Orwell would make him laugh, would cheer him up. One can almost put this dourness into financial terms. Orwell was often poor – see his letters responding to Jack Common's pleas for even small sums of money when Orwell was in French Morocco. He even speaks of making do for much of 1936 at The Stores by living on potatoes. *Animal Farm* earned him good royalties but when he died, and before the huge royalties that flooded in from *Nineteen Eighty-Four*, at his death he was shown to have £9,909 at probate – perhaps some £250,000 today, the cost of a modest house. But, at the time, he was owed £520 that he had lent to friends: George Kopp £250; Paul Potts £120; Sonia £100; Inez Holden £75; and Jack Common £50.

It is apparent how hard he worked on his correspondence. It is easy to forget nowadays, when using a personal computer with its facility to copy, paste, and save, that typing letters on a mechanical machine could be hard physical work, especially if, as for Orwell, he had to type when ill in bed. There was a limit as to how many copies could be typed at a time. Thus, if he or Eileen wanted to pass on the same information to more than one person, each one would receive a separate letter and each of those would have to be typed afresh. (See the conclusion to Eileen's letter to Mary Common, 5

December 1938.) Yet Orwell would patiently type and retype his news in letters to different friends.

One very significant characteristic of Orwell's letter-writing, telling something of his generosity of character, is how he would write at length to those he did not know, may never have met, and to whom he owed nothing. The letter above to Richard Usborne, and that to Jessica Marshall written from Hairmyres Hospital on 19 May 1948 are both letters on which he spent considerable time although a brief acknowledgement would have sufficed for most of us.

Eileen's letters are completely different in content and style. It is to Eileen we must turn to discover what it was like staying with her husband's parents at Southwold, what it was like living in their almost primitive cottage at Wallington, and it is to Eileen we turn for irony. She had a fine sense of humour and although both she and Orwell were self-deprecatory, in Eileen this is put with delicious wit.

Because so much has been published of Orwell's work and because so many of his letters have survived, we know (or think we know) what to expect. Eileen so often comes as a surprise. There are the lovely letters written to her husband (then working as a war correspondent on the Continent) telling him how their little boy was developing and also her hopes for their future away from London (which Orwell would realise on Jura) and her anxieties about the operation which we now know would bring an end to her life. Eileen also lived a life that we did not know about until the batch of letters to Norah Myles was published in *The Lost Orwell* and reproduced here. It was known that she went to Chapel Ridding at Windermere in July 1938 but we have never known why – and still do not know. Something of this other side of Eileen is revealed in her letters. One thing that is certain from them is that she had a very affectionate nature.

A small handful of letters by others than Orwell and Eileen have been included. Each one – such as Jennie Lee's letter to Miss Goalby on page 68 – illuminates Orwell's character or his medical condition (as does that from Dr Bruce Dick to David Astor on page 433). These few letters help to develop further our picture of Orwell – for example, the unforgettable image of his arrival in Spain just after Christmas 1936: 'This was George Orwell and his boots arriving to fight in Spain.' As Jennie Lee explains, 'He knew he could not get boots big enough' in Spain and he had come with a spare set hanging round his neck. The problem of getting footwear large enough for his feet came back to haunt him towards the end of his life.

Taken together, this volume and its companion volume, Orwell's *Diaries*, go some way to offering the autobiography that Orwell did not write.

Peter Davison

This edition

Most letters are reproduced in full but their layout has been regularised. I have made a few cuts to avoid repeating what is readily available elsewhere in the selection (for example, Orwell's instructions for making the journey from London to Barnhill, Jura). Where a cut is made, this is indicated within square brackets. A complete record with the original styling is available in *The Complete Works*. Addresses from which letters are sent are often shortened and standardised. After each letter is an inconspicuous reference to its source in *Complete Works*. Such explicatory notes to letters are provided as are deemed to be helpful in a volume of this kind. They are not exhaustive – but, again, *Complete Works* can usually be consulted for further information.

Over ninety much-abbreviated biographies of many of those to whom letters were written are given in the Biographical Notes. This will save too-frequent repetition of biographical information and the need to search for such notes where the individuals are first mentioned. Those for whom biographical notes are given are indicated by asterisks after their names in the body of the book. 'George Orwell' as we tend to call him, was born Eric Blair. He continued to use his birth names throughout his life. Some of his friends knew him as 'Eric', some as 'George'. His first wife, Eileen, was always Eileen Blair and his son is Richard Blair. In this book, 'the Blairs' refers to Orwell's parents and family and 'the Orwells' to George and Eileen as a couple.

The sources of these letters together with full notes are to be found in *The Complete Works of George Orwell* and its supplementary volume, *The Lost Orwell*. The first nine volumes of *The Complete Works* comprise Orwell's books. These were published by Secker & Warburg in 1986–1987 and have been printed in paperback since by Penguin Books. Volumes X–XX were published in 1998 and then in paperback (with some supplementary material) in 2000–2002. The supplementary volume was published by Timewell Press in 2006. The facsimile of the extant manuscript of *Nineteen Eighty-Four* was published in 1984 by Secker & Warburg in London and M&S Press, Weston, Massachusetts. These volumes were edited by Peter Davison and amount to 9,243 pages. It will be evident that this present volume offers only a small proportion of what is to be found in the whole edition to which, of course, further reference might, if necessary, be made.

In the main the texts of letters are printed as Orwell wrote them. Slight oversights are silently corrected and titles of books and magazines and foreign-language expressions are italicised (something Orwell could not do on a typewriter). Occasionally (as in *Complete Works*) Orwell's typical misspellings are retained but indicated by a superior degree sign (°). References to the *Complete Works* are given as Volume number in roman figure + item number + page(s), e.g., XIX, 3386, pp. 321–2. References to letters from *The Lost Orwell* are given similarly but preceded by *LO* + page numbers; their position in *Complete Works* follows. References to books listed in 'A Short List of Further Reading' are given by the author's name + page number – e.g. Crick, p. 482, except for *Orwell Remembered* and *Remembering Orwell*, which are so designated followed by their page numbers.

Initials such as ILP, sometimes appear with and sometimes without stops after each letter, e.g., ILP and I.L.P. Orwell's practice is followed. Many are defined when used. Those that are not but which might be unfamiliar to some readers are:

ARP:	Air Raid Precautions
CB:	Commander of the Bath
CBE:	Commander of the Order of the British Empire
CH:	Companion of Honour
CP:	Communist Party
FDC:	Freedom Defence Committee
GPU:	Gosudarstvennoye Politicheskoye Upravlenye (Soviet Secret Police)
IB:	International Brigade
ILP:	Independent Labour Party
IRD:	Information Research Department
KG:	Knight of the Order of the Garter
Kt:	Knight(ed)
LCC:	London County Council
NCCL:	National Council for Civil Liberties
NKVD:	Narodniy Kommissariat Vnutrennykh Dyel (Soviet Secret Police)
NL:	*New Leader*
NYK:	Nippon Yusen Kaisha (Japanese Mail Steamer Co.)
OBE:	Officer of the Order of the British Empire
OUP:	Oxford University Press
PAS:	para-amino-salycylic acid
PEN:	International Association of Poets, Playwrights, Editors, Essayists and Novelists
POUM:	Partido Obrero de Unificación Marxista (Revolutionary (anti-Stalinist) Communist Party – under whose aegis Orwell fought in Spain)
PR:	*Partisan Review*

RAMC: Royal Army Medical Corps
TUC: Trades Union Congress
YCL: Youth Communist League

It is difficult to give precise equivalents of value with today's prices because individual items vary considerably. However, a rough approximation can be gained if prices in the 1930s are multiplied by forty; by thirty-five during the war; and by thirty between then and Orwell's death. In pre-decimal coinage there were 12 pence to a shilling and twenty shillings to £1 – so 240 pence to a £. Sixpence in old coinage = 2½p; one shilling (12 pennies) = 5p; 10 shillings (10/-) = 50p. For the Orwells' time in Morocco it might be convenient to refer to R.L. Bidwell's *Currency Conversion Tables* (1970). He records the French franc as being 165 to the £ (39.8 to the $) in March 1938. In January 1939 he gives 176.5 to the £ (39.8 to the $). Thus, the Orwells' rent for their cottage – 7s 6d per week – is approximately £1.50 for four weeks in 1930s equivalences and, say, £60 per month at current values. The rent for the villa in Morocco was 550 francs per month, approximately £3.25 then but, say, £130 at today's values.

Grateful thanks are due to The Orwell Estate, in particular Richard Blair and Bill Hamilton, and to Gill Furlong, Archivist, and Steven Wright, UCL Special Collections Library, for enabling these letters to be published. I am indebted to my grandson, Tom, for much technical support. The Orwell Estate and the publishers expressed thanks to copyrights holders of letters published in the *Complete Works* and *The Lost Orwell* and that gratitude is renewed here. Thanks are also due to those who have allowed letters not previously published, or for which the originals have changed hands, to be reproduced. I am immensely grateful to Myra Jones for her careful proofreading (once again) and to Briony Everroad of Harvill Secker for her courtesy and her splendid support.

Peter Davison

An asterisk after a correspondent's name indicates that that person
will be found in the Biographical Notes. Cross references to
other letters are emphasised in bold.

From Pupil to Teacher to Author

1911–1933

Orwell left Eton in December 1921. He had applied to join the Indian Imperial Police and was coached for the competitive entrance examination. The results were published on 23 November 1922. He had come seventh of twenty-nine successful applicants obtaining 8,464 marks out of a possible 12,400, the pass mark being 6,000. His strongest subjects were Latin, Greek, and English. He just passed the horse-riding test and scored 174 out of 400 for Freehand Drawing (so he had advanced from the little drawings with which he embellished his letters to his mother from St Cyprian's).

He arrived in Burma on 27 November 1922. He learned Hindi, Burmese, and Shaw Karen and could converse in fluent 'very high-flown Burmese' with Burmese priests. He served in a number of stations and he did see a hanging and did shoot an elephant, about both of which he wrote important essays. For shooting the elephant (which had killed a coolie) he was despatched by an angry commanding officer to Katha on 23 December 1926, the basis for Kyauktada of *Burmese Days*.

He left Burma on 12 July 1927 to take the six months' leave he was due. Whilst on leave he resigned from the Police. He had evidently saved a fair amount of his pay and went to Paris where he attempted to earn a living as a writer. He did have six articles published in Paris in French and one that was published in England, but he failed to get short stories or a novel accepted and they were all destroyed. When he ran out of money he worked for a few weeks as a kitchen hand in a luxury hotel, either the Crillon or the Lotti. For a short while he was a patient in the Cochin Hospital with 'une grippe', an experience about which he also wrote.

Orwell returned to England and, using the family home in Southwold as a base, made forays tramping and hop-picking. He began to get articles accepted (for very little money) and from April 1932 to July 1933 taught boys aged ten to sixteen at The Hawthornes, a private school in Hayes, Middlesex. He did not return for the autumn term at The Hawthorns, which had, in any case, run into financial difficulties, but went to teach at Frays College, a private school for boys and girls, in Uxbridge, Middlesex; it is illustrated in Thompson, p. 40. On 9 January 1933 Victor Gollancz published *Down and Out in Paris and London*.

From Orwell's letter to his mother, 15 October 1911

To Ida Blair*

2 December 1911
St Cyprian's School
Eastbourne

My dear Mother, I hope you are alright,

It was Mrs: Wilkes[1] birthday yesterday, we had aufel fun after tea and played games all over the house. We all went for a walk to Beachy-Head.

I am third in Arithmatick.

'Its' very dull today, and dosent look as if its going to be very warm.

Thank you for your letter.

It is getting very near the end of term, there are only eighteen days more.

On Saturday evening we have dncing, and I am going to say a piece of poetry, some of the boys sing.

Give my love to Father and Avril. Is Togo alright, We had the Oxford and Cambridge Matches yesterday. Cambridge won in the first and third, and the second did not have a Match. I am very glad Colonel Hall[2] has given me some stamps, he said he wold last year but I thought he had forgotten. Its a beastly wet day today all rain and cold.

I am very sorry to hear we had those beastly freaks of smelly white mice back. I hope these arnt smelly one. if they arnt I shall like them.

From your loveing son,
E.A.Blair.

[X, 8, p. 10; handwritten with original spelling and errors]

1. Mrs Vaughan Wilkes, wife of the headmaster and owner of St Cyprian's.
2. Colonel Hall was a neighbour of the Blairs at Shiplake.

To Steven Runciman *

[?] August 1920
Grove Terrace
Polperro RSO[1]
Cornwall

My dear Runciman,

I have a little spare time, and I feel I *must* tell you about my first adventure as an amateur tramp. Like most tramps I was driven to it. When I got to a wretched little place in Devonshire, — Seaton Junction, Mynors,[2] who had to change there, came to my carriage & said that a beastly Oppidan who had been perpetually plaguing me to travel in the same compartment as him was asking for me. As I was among strangers, I got out to go to him where-upon the train started off. You need two hands to enter a moving train, & I, what with kit-bag, belt etc had only one. To be brief, I was left behind. I despatched a telegram to say I would be late (it arrived next day), & about 2½ hours later got a train: at Plymouth, North Rd, I found there were no more trains to Looe that night. It was too late to telephone, as the post offices were shut. I then made a consultation of my financial position. I had enough for my remaining fare & 7½d over. I could therefore either sleep at the Y.M.C.A. place, price 6d, & starve, or have something to eat but nowhere to sleep. I chose the latter, I put my kit-bag in the cloak-room & got 12 buns for 6d: half-past-nine found me sneaking into some farmer's field, — there were a few fields wedged in among rows of slummy houses. In that light I of course looked like a soldier strolling round, — on my way I had been asked whether I was demobilized yet, & I finally came to anchor in the corner of a field near some allotments. I then began to remember that people frequently got four-teen days for sleeping in somebody else's field & 'having no visible means of support', particularly as every dog in the neighbourhood barked if I ever so much as moved. The corner had a large tree for shelter, & bushes for con-cealment, but it was unendurably cold; I had no covering, my cap was my pillow, I lay 'with my martial cloak (rolled cape) around me'.[3] I only dozed & shivered till about 1 oc, when I readjusted my puttees, & managed to sleep long enough to miss the first train, at 4.20. by about an hour, & to have to wait till 7.45 for another. My teeth were still chattering when I awoke. When I got to Looe I was forced to walk 4 miles in the hot sun; I am very proud of this adventure, but I would not repeat it.

Yours sincerely,
E. A. Blair.

[X, 56, pp. 76–7; handwritten]

1. Railway Sorting Office, which acted as poste restante. Polperro had no station. The nearest was at Looe, three miles to the east. The Blair family spent most of its summer holidays in Cornwall at either Looe or Polperro. On this particular journey Orwell was returning from an Eton Officers' Training Corps exercise and was therefore in uniform.

2. Roger Mynors (1903–1989; knighted 1963) was a member of Orwell's Election. He and Orwell produced the school journal, *Election Times*. He was a leading classical scholar; he became a Fellow of Balliol in 1926 and later a Professor at Cambridge and Oxford. He married Lavinia, daughter of Cyril Allington, Headmaster of Eton in his and Orwell's time.

3. From stanza 3 of 'The Burial of Sir John Moore after Corunna' by Charles Wolfe, a poem parodied by Orwell at Eton in *College Days* (X, p. 69).

Extract from letter to Cyril Connolly*

Easter 1921

The original and the complete text of this letter are lost. What survives does so because Cyril Connolly quoted part of Orwell's letter when writing to Terence Beddard at Easter 1921; Connolly copied out this section for the Orwell Archive in June 1967.

Another version, with interspersed ironic comments by Connolly, exists at Tulsa University, and that is given in Michael Shelden's biography of Orwell (pp. 75–76). In a note added to the copy made for the Archive, Connolly explained that this extract was part of a letter to Beddard which Connolly printed in Enemies of Promise *(1938), pp. 256–59. Beddard was dead by the time Connolly made this copy. It is impossible to be sure how reliable is Connolly's copy. Beddard was a King's Scholar in the Election before Orwell's; he left Eton exactly a year before Orwell and was no longer there when Connolly wrote to him. Christopher Eastwood is described by Connolly in his notes as 'an attractive boy with a good voice & rather a prig'.[1] He went on: 'The point of the letter is that Eastwood, being in my election, was bound to see much more of me than of Blair, in the election above us.' E. A. Caröe[2] was in Blair's Election, and Redcliffe-Maud[3] two Elections below Connolly's. For something of the background to this letter, see chapters 20 and 21 of* Enemies of Promise. *Michael Shelden remarks that it would be unwise to assume that Orwell's 'adolescent affections for other boys ever reached an advanced stage of sexual contact. He may well have been as chaste in his relationships with boys as he was in his relationship with Jacintha. As his letter to Connolly reveals, he was awkward in romantic matters and was slow to assert himself.'*

I am afraid I am gone on Eastwood. This may surprise you but it is not imagination I assure you. The point is that I think you are too, at any rate you were at the end of last half. I am not jealous of you. But you though you aren't jealous are apt to be what I might call 'proprietary'. In the case of Maud & Caroe° you were quite right but what I want you to do is not regard me as another Caroe whatever points of resemblance there may be. Don't suspect me of any ill intentions either. If I had not written to you, about 3 weeks into next half you would notice how things stood, your proprietary instincts would have been aroused & having a lot of influence over Eastwood you would probably have put him against me somehow, perhaps even warned him off me. Please dont° do this I implore you. Of course I dont° ask you to resign your share in him only dont° say spiteful things.

[X, 60, pp. 79–80]

Connolly's copy in the Orwell Archive concludes: 'Rather a revelation . . . Anyhow Eastwood has noticed it and is full of suspicion as he hates Blair.'

1. Christopher Eastwood (1905–1983) became a senior civil servant. See *Remembering Orwell*, 16–18, for his reminiscences of Orwell at Eton.
2. Einar Athelstan Caröe (1903–1988) became a grain merchant and broker, associated with Liverpool. According to Connolly's notes, he was unpopular at Eton.
3. Baron Redcliffe-Maud (1906–1982) became a particularly distinguished civil servant, and he later became High Commissioner, then Ambassador, to South Africa, 1959–63; Master of University College, Oxford, 1963–76.

A letter from Jacintha Buddicom*

This letter seeks to comfort a relative. It looks back on the writer's own history and, in particular, her relationship in her youth with Eric Blair long before he became George Orwell. Its full background is explained in the Postscript by Dione Venables to Jacintha Buddicom's Eric & Us, *2006. I have omitted one or two personal names not relevant to Orwell. I am deeply grateful to Dione Venables and Jacintha's relatives for permission to publish this letter and to Mrs Venables for providing background notes and the two photographs reproduced in the plates.*

4 May 1972
'Dragons'
John Street
Bognor Regis

I have just finished reading your sad letter and hasten to answer it. I cannot believe that the same miserable tragedy has struck twice in the same family but I CAN give you my total understanding and sympathy which might help a little. Strangely, your letter comes at a time when my mind and concentration are centred on similar events that took place in my life also some time ago.

After the publication last year of *The World of George Orwell* for which I wrote the opening essay, I am now writing a short monograph of my own on the subject (they edited out most of the important bits) in the hope of ridding myself of a lifetime of ghosts and regrets at turning away the only man who ever really appealed on all levels.

Your experience has many similarities, but the difference is that you briefly carried Xxxxx's child and then refused his proposal. The loss of the first was your decision (I did not have the option and the result has been the cross I have had to bear ever since). But your integrity and courage in refusing the proposal of such a high profile figure makes me feel very proud [*a few words omitted*]. Such a union in 1958 would certainly have ended in tears, especially as he died so young. How I wish I had been ready for betrothal when Eric asked me to marry him on his return from Burma. He had ruined what had been such a close and fulfilling relationship since childhood by trying to take us the whole way before I was anywhere near ready for that. It took me literally years to realise that we are all imperfect creatures but that Eric was less imperfect than anyone else I ever met. When the time came and I was ready for the next step it was with the wrong man and the result haunts me to this day.

You were absolutely right to reject marriage with a man who you know will be constantly unfaithful because that is the way he is made. What credit that decision did you, even though you are still plagued by it. Memories of the joys and fun that Eric and I shared, knowing each others' minds so totally ensured that I would never marry unless that 'oneness' could be found again.

You are still an extremely beautiful woman, even if you feel that this has been your downfall. The men in your life have not wanted your very great intelligence and so it has caused you to drift from relationship to relationship, looking for something you never find. A tragedy which you simply *must* take control of, or life will begin to depend on the bottle rather than the fascination of other lives and situations. At least you have not had the public shame of being destroyed in a classic book as Eric did to me. Julia in *Nineteen Eighty-Four* is clearly Jacintha, of that I feel certain. He describes her with thick dark hair, being very active, hating politics – and their meeting place was a dell full of bluebells. We always wandered off to our special place when we were at Ticklerton which was full of bluebells. They die so quickly if you pick them so we never did but lay amongst them and adored their heavy pungent scent. That very bluebell dell is described in his book and is part of the central story but in the end he absolutely destroys me, like a man in hob nailed boots stamping on a spider. It hurt my mother so much when she read that book that we always thought it brought on her final heart attack a few days later. Be glad that you have not been torn limb from limb in public.

Gather yourself together, my Dear. Our family is well blessed with looks and brains and you have both in liberal quantities. You are an extremely elegant communicator so enjoy what you have instead of looking at the past. [*sentence omitted*] You have the finest of minds which outstrips your physical attributes. Make both work for *you*. Look ahead. What is past is gone. It is the only way I manage to keep my reason. . . . . .

What the writer and recipient of this letter had in common was that both had conceived children outside marriage, at that time a matter of shame. The recipient terminated her pregnancy; the writer, Jacintha, gave birth to the child she was carrying but it was adopted by her uncle and aunt, Dr and Mrs Noel Hawley-Burke. A street photographer caught the moment when Jacintha, her uncle and her aunt left the solicitor's office after she had signed over her six-month-old baby to them. The contrast in the body language, even in such a poor quality photograph, perfectly captures her pain and their joy.

Dione Venables, in her Postscript to Jacintha Buddicom's Eric & Us, *gives a graphic account of the occasion that led to Jacintha's break with Orwell before he went to Burma. He had 'attempted to take things further and make SERIOUS love to Jacintha. He had held her down (by that time he was 6' 4" and she was still under 5') and though she struggled, yelling at him to STOP, he had torn her skirt and badly bruised a shoulder and her left hip'. The assault went no further and Orwell stayed with the family for the rest of the holiday but he and Jacintha kept apart (p. 182). It will be recalled that in* A Clergyman's Daughter *Orwell was required by Gollancz's libel lawyer to tone down the first line of p. 41 and Orwell responded to the lawyer's concerns by saying he had 'altered the statement that Mr Warburton "tried to rape Dorothy".'*

As Dione Venables goes on to explain, on Orwell's return from Burma, he 'lost no time in contacting the Buddicoms and was invited to join Prosper and Guiny [Jacintha's brother and sister] at Ticklerton. There was no Jacintha – and the family were evasive and embarrassed on the subject so that Eric must have assumed that, even after all this time, she was still angry with him and would never forgive his momentary fall from grace. The tragedy is that in fact, Jacintha had just, in May 1927, given birth to her daughter Michal Madeleine. . . . The father escaped abroad as soon as her condition was discovered' (p. 183). Michal emigrated to Canada. She had six children and was killed in a car crash in 1997. As Jacintha's sister, Guinever, later observed, Orwell 'might well have welcomed the little girl as his own child' (p. 186).

Because Jacintha was not at Ticklerton on his return, Orwell persuaded Prosper to give him her London telephone number. He rang begging her to meet him, but in vain. He tried again a fortnight later, but she still could not face meeting him. He was desperate to patch up the past; she was distressed over the imminent adoption of her baby yet still felt unable to tell Orwell of Michal's existence. Orwell had gone so far as to bring her an engagement ring from Burma. They never again met. Jacintha did not *know that Eric was Orwell until 8 February 1949 when her Aunt Lilian wrote from Ticklerton to tell her. She asked his publisher for his address and wrote to him at Cranham Sanatorium. He immediately replied with two letters on 14 **and** 15 February 1949. He hoped she would visit him but she felt she could not. So, there was a kind of reconciliation but, alas no meeting. So much was lost for both of them. Although Jacintha might not be Orwell's only inspiration, it is clear that many of his female characters as well as Julia in* Nineteen Eighty-Four *owed much to Jacintha.*[1]

1. A forthcoming study by William Hunt, *Orwell's Demon: The Lonely Rebellion of Eric Blair*, explores in much greater detail than is possible here the links between Orwell and many of those he knew and the places where they met. (The title draws on 'Why I Write', XVIII, 3007, p. 320.)

To Max Plowman*

1 November 1930
3 Queen St
Southwold, Suffolk

Dear Mr Plowman,

Thank you very much for the copy of the *Adelphi,* which I found an interesting one. I see that Mr Murry* says in his article, 'Because orthodox Christianity is exceedingly elaborate, it presents a greater appearance of unity than (childish superstition)'. I know this is so, but the *why* is beyond me. It is clear that the thicker the fairy tales are piled, the more easily one can swallow them, but this seems so paradoxical that I have never been able to understand the reason for it. I don't think Roger Clarke in his article on Sex & Sin gets to [the] very bottom of the question. He says rightly that the 'spiritual love' stuff fixes the desires on something unattainable, & that this leads to trouble. The point he doesn't bring out is that the 'sinful lust' stuff also fixes it on something unattainable, & that attempts to realise the impossible *physical* desire are even more destructive than attempts on the spiritual side. Of course it is important to teach boys that women like Esther Summerson[1] don't exist, but it is just as important, & far harder, to teach them that women like the *Vie Parisienne* illustrations[2] don't exist. Perhaps the writer had not the space to bring this out thoroughly. You will, I know, forgive my troubling you with my reflections, as I was interested by the questions raised.

Thanks very much for the books. I find the novel[3] well enough, the Cayenne book[4] interesting, though it is almost certainly exaggerated. The book on Bodley is more solid stuff, but I don't know that it is the kind of thing you would care to use much space on. What I suggest is doing about 1000 words altogether on the three, either in one article or separately as you prefer. I think they are worth mentioning, but not worth more than 1000 words between them. Would this do? If so, I can let you have the review in about 10 days. If you don't think it worthwhile, I will send the books back.

I enclose the other article, reduced to 3,500 words.[5] Thank you for giving my M.S° to Mr Murry. I hope he understands that there is no hurry & I don't want to be a nuisance to him.

Yours sincerely
Eric A. Blair

[X, 100, pp. 189–90; handwritten]

1. The docile heroine and pseudo part-author of *Bleak House* by Charles Dickens (1882–3).
2. Highly glamorised pictures of showgirls.
3. In the April 1931 issue, Orwell reviewed *Hunger and Love* by Lionel Britton and *Albert Grope* by F O. Mann (X, 105, pp. 203–5). Neither may be referred to here, though Britton's book is a possibility.
4. Reviewed December 1930 (X, 101, pp. 190–1).
5. From its length and timing, this is probably 'The Spike,' April 1931 (X, 104, pp. 197–203).

To Dennis Collings*

16 August 1931
At 1B Oakwood Road
Golders Green NW[1]

Dear Dennis,

I said I would write to you. I haven't anything of great interest to report yet about the Lower Classes, & am really writing to tell you about a ghost I saw in Walberswick cemetery. I want to get it on paper before I forget the details. See plan below.

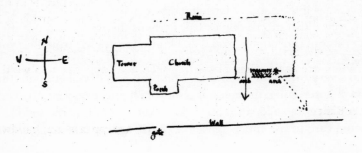

Above is W'wick church as well as I can remember it. At about 5.20 pm on 27.7.31 I was sitting at the spot marked *, looking out in the direction of the dotted arrow. I happened to glance over my shoulder, & saw a figure pass along the line of the other arrow, disappearing behind the masonry & presumably emerging into the churchyard. I wasn't looking *directly* at it & so couldn't make out more than that it was a man's figure, small & stooping, & dressed in lightish brown; I should have said a workman. I had the impression that it glanced towards me in passing, but I made out nothing of the features. At the moment of its passing I thought nothing, but a few seconds later it struck me that the figure had made no noise, & I followed it out into the churchyard. There was no one in the churchyard, & no one within possible distance along the road—this was about 20 seconds after I had seen it; & in any case there were only 2 people in the road, & neither at all resembled the figure. I looked into the church. The only people there were the vicar, dressed in *black*, & a workman who, as far as I remember, had been sawing the whole time. In any case he was too tall for the figure. The figure had therefore vanished. Presumably an hallucination.

I have been up in town since the beginning of the month. I have made arrangements to go hop-picking, but we shan't start till the beginning of September. Meanwhile I've been busy working. I met recently one of the editors of a new paper[2] that is to start coming out in October, & I hope I shall be able to get some work from them—not enough to live on, of course, but enough to help. I've been making just a few enquiries among the tramps. Of the three friends I had before, one is believed to have been run over & killed, one has taken to drink & vanished, one is doing time in Wandsworth. I met a man today who was, till 6 weeks ago, a goldsmith. Then he poisoned his right forefinger, & had to have part of the top joint removed; that means he will be on the road for life. It is appalling what small accidents can ruin a man who works with his hands. Talking of hands, they say hop-picking disables your hands for weeks after—however, I'll describe that to you when I've done it.

Have you ever looked into the window of one of those Bible Society shops? I did today & saw huge notices 'The cheapest Roman Catholic Bible 5/6d. The cheapest Protestant Bible 1/–', 'The Douay° version *not* stocked here' etc. etc. Long may they fight, I say; so long as that spirit is in the land we are safe from the R.C.'s—this shop, by the way, was just outside St Paul's. If you are ever near St Paul's & feel in a gloomy mood, go in & have a look at the statue of the first Protestant bishop of India, which will give you a good laugh. Will write again when I have news. I am sending this to S'wold.

Yours
Eric A Blair

[X, 109, pp. 211–212; handwritten]

1. In 1930–31 Orwell lived with his parents in Southwold but made forays tramping and writing what would become *Down and Out in Paris and London*. When he visited London he would stay with Francis and Mabel Sinclair Fierz in Golders Green. Mrs Fierz reviewed for *The Adelphi* and her husband was a Dickens enthusiast. It was Mrs Fierz who was instrumental in getting *Down and Out* published and having Orwell taken on by Leonard Moore as his literary agent. She died in 1990 aged 100.

2. *Modern Youth*. Orwell submitted two stories but the publication evidently went bankrupt and the printers seized Orwell's stories with the journals assets. They have not been identified.

To Leonard Moore*

26 April 1932
The Hawthorns [School]
Station Rd
Hayes, Middlesex

Dear Mr Moore,

Thank you for your letter. The history of the ms. 'Days in London and Paris' is this. About a year and a half ago I completed a book of this description, but shorter (about 35000 words), and after taking advice I sent it to Jonathan Cape. Cape's said they would like to publish it but it was too short and fragmentary (it was done in diary form), and that they might be disposed to take it if I made it longer. I then put in some things I had left out, making the ms. you have, and sent it back to Capes,° who again rejected it. That was last September. Meanwhile a friend who was editor of a magazine had seen the first ms., and he said that it was worth publishing and spoke about it to T. S. Eliot, who is a reader to Faber and Faber. Eliot said the same as Cape's— i.e. that the book was interesting but much too short. I left the ms. you have with Mrs Sinclair Fierz and asked her to throw it away, as I did not think it a good piece of work, but I suppose she sent it to you instead. I should of course be very pleased if you could sell it, and it is very kind of you to take the trouble of trying. No publishers have seen it except Faber's and Cape's. If by any chance you *do* get it accepted, will you please see that it is published pseudonymously, as I am not proud of it. I have filled up the form you sent, but I have put in a clause that I only want an agent for dealings with publishers. The reason is this. I am now very busy teaching in a school, and I am afraid that for some months I shan't be able to get on with any work except occasional reviews or articles and I get the commissions for these myself. But there is a novel[1] that I began some months ago and shall go on with next holidays, and I dare say it will be finished within a year: I will send it to you then. If you could get me any French or Spanish books to translate into English I would willingly pay you whatever commission you think right, for I like that kind of work. There is also a long poem describing a day in London which I am doing, and it *may* be finished before the end of this term. I will send you that too if you like, but I should not think there is any money for anybody in that kind of thing. As to those stories[2] you have I should shy them away, as they are not really worth bothering with.

Yours truly
Eric A Blair

P.S. I tried to get Chatto & Windus to give me some of Zola's novels to translate, but they wouldn't. I should think somebody might be willing to translate Zola—he has been done, but atrociously badly.[3] Or what about Huysmans? I can't believe *Sainte Lydwine de Schiedam* has been translated into English. I also tried to get Faber's to translate a novel called *A la Belle de Nuit*, by Jacques Roberti. It is very good but apallingly° indecent, & they refused it on that ground. I should think somebody might take it on—do you know anybody who isn't afraid of that kind of thing? (The book isn't pornographic, only rather sordid.) I could get hold of the copy I had & send it if necessary. I could also translate old° French, at least anything since 1400 A.D.

[X, 124, pp. 243–3; typewritten; handwritten postscript]

1. *Burmese Days*.
2. These stories do not appear to have survived.
3. Zola's novels had been published in England by Henry Vizetelly (1820–1894), who also established the Mermaid Series of Dramatists and published translations of Dostoevsky, Flaubert, and Tolstoy. The publication in English of Zola's *La Terre* (though 'amended') led to Vizetelly's being fined and in 1889 jailed on the charge of obscenity. British publishers, and Gollancz in particular, feared expensive legal costs if charged with defamation, libel or obscenity. (See **14.11.34**, n.2.)

To Eleanor Jaques*

Tuesday [14 June 1932]
The Hawthorns

Dear Eleanor,

How do things go with you? I hope your father is better, & that you have got your garden into shape. I have been teaching at the above foul place for nearly two months. I don't find the work uninteresting, but it is very exhausting, &

apart from a few reviews etc. I've hardly done a stroke of writing. My poor poem, which was promising not too badly, has of course stopped dead. The most disagreeable thing here is not the job itself (it is a day-school, thank God, so I have nothing to do with the brats out of school hours) but Hayes itself, which is one of the most godforsaken places I have ever struck. The population seems to be entirely made up of clerks who frequent tin-roofed chapels on Sundays & for the rest bolt themselves within doors. My sole friend is the curate—High Anglican but not a creeping Jesus & a very good fellow. Of course it means that I have to go to Church, which is an arduous job here, as the service is so popish that I don't know my way about it & feel an awful B.F.[1] when I see everyone bowing & crossing themselves all round me & can't follow suit. The poor old vicar, who I suspect hates all this popery, is dressed up in cope & biretta & led round in procession with candles etc., looking like a bullock garlanded for sacrifice. I have promised to paint one of the church idols (a quite skittish-looking B.V.M.[2], half life-size, & I shall try & make her look as much like one of the illustrations in La Vie Parisienne as possible) & to grow a marrow for the harvest festival. I would 'communicate' too, only I am afraid the bread might choke me. Have you read anything interesting lately? I read for the first time Marlowe's Faustus, & thought it rotten, also a mangy little book on Shakespeare trying to prove that Hamlet = Earl of Essex,[3] also a publication called The Enemy of Wyndham Lewis (not the professional R.C[4]), who seems to have something in him, also something of Osbert Sitwell, also some odes of Horace, whom I wish I hadn't neglected hitherto—otherwise nothing, not having much time or energy. Mrs. Carr[5] sent me two books of Catholic apologetics, & I had great pleasure in reviewing one of them[6] for a new paper called the New English Weekly. It was the first time I had been able to lay the bastinado on a professional R.C. at any length. I have got a few square feet of garden, but have had rotten results owing to rain, slugs & mice. I have found hardly any birds' nests—this place is on the outskirts of London, of course. I have also been keeping a pickle-jar aquarium, chiefly for the instruction of the boys, & we have newts, tadpoles, caddis-flies etc. If when you are passing, if you ever do, the pumping station at the beginning of the ferry-path, you see any eggs of puss-moths on the poplar trees there, I should be awfully obliged if you would pick the leaves & send them me by post. I want some, & have only been able to find one or two here. Of course I don't mean make an expedition there, I only mean if you happen to be passing. What is Dennis[7] doing these days? I want to consult him about an extraordinary fungus that was dug up here, but of course he never answers letters. I may or may not come back to S'wold for the summer holidays. I want to get on with my novel[8] and if possible finish the poem I had begun, & I think perhaps it would be best for me to go to some quiet place in France, where I can live cheaply & have less temptation from the World, the Flesh

& the Devil than at S'wold. (You can decide which of these categories you belong to.) By the way, if you are ever to be in London please let me know, as we might meet, that is if you would like to. Please remember me to your parents, also to Mr and Mrs Pullein[9] if you see them.

Yours
Eric A Blair

P.S. In case you see Dennis, you might tell him the fungus was like this (below.) It was dug up underground.

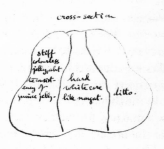

About this size & very like an apple in shape, but dead white, & flabby to the touch.

cross-section

stiff colourless jelly, about the consistency of quince jelly

hard white core like nougat.

ditto

P.P.S. I trust this adress° is all right.

[X, 129, pp. 249–50; handwritten; dated from postmark[10]]

1. B.F.: Bloody Fool
2. B.V.M.: Blessed Virgin Mary
3. Probably *The Essential Shakespeare* by J. Dover Wilson (1932)
4. D. B. Wyndham Lewis (1891–1969), a Roman Catholic and a *bête noire* of Orwell's. He was one of the contributors to a jokey column in the *Daily Express* under the pseudonym, 'Beachcomber'.

5. A Southwold friend of Orwell and Eleanor Jaques.
6. *The Spirit of Catholicism* by Karl Adam. Orwell's review appeared in *New English Weekly*, 9 June 1932 (X, 127, pp. 246–8).
7. Dennis Collings.
8. *Burmese Days*.
9. Collett Cresswell Pulleyne, a Yorkshire barrister and his mother. He was a friend of both Orwell and Collings. Orwell had some difficulty spelling his name.
10. Published by kind permission of Richard Young.

In addition to Orwell's letters to Brenda Salkeld which have been published in the Complete Works, *he wrote at least nineteen others to her, seventeen of them between 13 May 1931 and 25 June 1940. These letters survive in private hands. Gordon Bowker was permitted to read them for his biography,* George Orwell *(2003) and summaries of the letters derived with permission from his biography are given in* The Lost Orwell, *pp. 92–8. Many of the letters described events in Orwell's life but there is a thread running through them indicating his wish to have an affair with Brenda. She refused such attentions but they remained friends throughout his life. In his penultimate letter of 15 February 1946 he invited her to high tea at 27b Canonbury Square to see Richard. She accepted, as she did an invitation by Orwell's sister, Avril, to stay at Barnhill, Jura. In the last of these letters, 30 June 1946, Orwell sent Miss Salkeld instructions for the journey.*

To Brenda Salkeld*

Sunday [September 1932]
The Hawthorns

Dearest Brenda

I am writing as I promised, but can't guarantee an even coherent letter, for a female downstairs is making the house uninhabitable by playing hymn-tunes on the piano, which, in combination with the rain outside & a dog yapping somewhere down the road, is rapidly qualifying me for the mental home. I hope you got home safely & didn't find the door barred against you. I reached home just on the stroke of midnight. It was ever so nice seeing you again & finding that you were pleased to see me, in spite of my hideous prejudice against your sex, my obsession about R.C.s, etc.

I have spent a most dismal day, first in going to Church, then in reading the *Sunday Times*, which grows duller & duller, then in trying to write a poem which won't go beyond the first stanza, then in reading through the rough draft of my novel,[1] which depresses me horribly. I really don't know which is the more stinking, the *Sunday Times* or the *Observer*. I go from one to the other like an invalid turning from side to side in bed & getting no comfort whichever way he turns. I thought the *Observer* would be a little less dull when Squire[2] stopped infesting it, but they seem deliberately to seek out the dullest people they can get to review the dullest books. By the way, if you are by any chance wanting to impose a penance upon yourself, I should think you might try Hugh Walpole's recent 800-page novel.[3]

I hope you will read one or two of those books I mentioned to you.[4] By the way, I forgot to mention, what I think you told me before you had not read, Dr Garnett's (not Richard or Edward Garnett) *The Twilight of the Gods*.[5] If you haven't read that, it's a positive duty to do so. The story the title is taken from is far from being the best, but some of the others, such as 'The Purple Head' are excellent. I suppose you have read Mark Twain's *Life on the Mississippi*? And J. S. Haldane's *Possible Worlds*? And Guy Boothby's *Dr Nikola*? And Mrs Sherwood's *The Fairchild Family*? All these are in different ways a little off the track (*Dr Nikola* is a boy's sixpenny thriller, but a first rate one) & I can recommend all of them. H. L. Mencken's book *In Defence of Women* would probably be amusing, but I haven't read it. I see Wyndham Lewis (*not* D. B. Wyndham Lewis, a stinking RC) has just brought out a book called *Snooty Baronet*, apparently a novel of sorts. It might be interesting. All I've ever read of his was a queer periodical called *The Enemy*, & odd articles, but he's evidently got some kick in him—whether at all a sound thinker or not, I can't be sure without further acquaintance. The copy of *The Enemy* I read was all a ferocious attack, about the length of an average novel, on Gertrude Stein—rather wasted energy, one would say.

Well, au revoir, for I have really no news. I will write again in a week or so & hope I shall then be in a more cheerful mood. I hope you will not have too unbearable a term—

With much love
Eric

[X, 142, pp. 268–9; handwritten]

1. *Burmese Days*.
2. John C. Squire (1884–1958; Kt., 1933), journalist, essayist, poet, and literary editor of the *New Statesman and Nation*, 1913–19, founded the *London Mercury* and edited it, 1919–34. He also edited the English Men of Letters series.
3. *The Fortress*.
4. For books Orwell recommended to Brenda Salkeld in the 1930s, as reported to Howard Fink, see X, pp. 308–9. *The Twilight of the Gods* and *Dr Nikola* are included in his list.
5. Dr Richard Garnett (1835–1906) was a librarian and author. His *Twilight of the Gods and Other Tales* was published in 1888 and augmented in 1903; the stories were described as 'cynical apologues'.

To Eleanor Jaques*

Wed. night [19 October 1932]
The Hawthorns

Dearest Eleanor,

I am glad to hear you had a nice time on the broads, even tho' the motor boat was not too docile. I have been unutterably busy & am half exhausted already. I am going up to town for a night or two on the 28th—intend going out on to the Embankment that night to see how the sleepers-out get on at this time of year. Is there any chance of your being up in town by then? And when you *are* coming up, what will your adress° be? We simply must meet if it can be managed.

The papers this morning report quite serious rioting in Lambeth round the City Hall.¹ It was evidently *food*-rioting, as the bakers' shops were looted. That points to pretty serious conditions & there may be hell to pay in the winter if things are as bad as that already. I expect, tho', just enough will be done to prevent anything violent happening. I know the quarter where it happened so well—I dare say some of my friends took part in it.

I was sorry to hear about poor old Crick² being run in over the entertainment tax tickets—another sign of the bad times of course. I hope people in the town aren't being beastly to him about it? I heard from Denis Collings the other day, asking me to go & stay with him at Cambridge at the half term. I would have liked to, but it is hard for me to get away, & there are, tho' I did not tell him so, two or three people at Cambridge whom I'm not anxious to meet. By the way, if you see the Pulleynes (*do* they spell their name like that? I'm never sure) any time, I would be awfully obliged if you would get from them a ms. of mine they have describing some adventures last Xmas. It's not very interesting but Brenda Salkeld is anxious to see it & I'd take it very kindly if you would send it to her—I hope it would not be too much trouble? Don't let your parents see the ms.,³ as it has bad words in it. My novel⁴ is making just a little progress. I see now more or less what will have to be done to it when the rough draft is finished, but the longness° & complicatedness are terrible. I've done no other writing, except part of a mucky play the boys are to act later.⁵ I am told that there was a letter in the *New Statesman* some weeks back, attacking me for an article I'd written for them.⁶ So annoying—I never saw it, & not to reply to an attack looks as tho' one admitted being wrong, which I'm sure I wasn't there in any major fact. I take in the *Church Times* regularly now & like it more every week. I do so like to see that there is life in the old dog yet—I mean in the poor old C. of E. I shall have to go to Holy Communion soon, hypocritical tho' it is, because my curate friend is bound to think it funny if I always go to Church but never communicate. What is the procedure? I have almost forgotten it. As far as I remember you go up to the rail & kneel down, but I don't remember whether there are any responses to make. You have to go fasting, do you not? And what about being in mortal sin? I wish you would prompt me. It seems rather mean to go to H.C. when one doesn't believe, but I have passed myself off for pious & there is nothing for it but to keep up the deception.

Dearest Eleanor, it was so nice of you to say that you looked back to your days with me with pleasure. I hope you will let me make love to you again some time, but if you don't it doesn't matter, I shall always be grateful to you for your kindness to me. Write soon & let me know your news, & above all if & when you are coming up to town. By the way, the other day I saw a man— Communist, I suppose—selling the *Daily Worker*,[7] & I went up to him & said, 'Have you the *D.W.*?'—He: 'Yes, sir.' Dear old England!

With love
Eric

[X, 145, pp. 270–1; handwritten]

1. Should be County Hall. The extensive rioting in the Lambeth area of London on Tuesday, 18 October 1932, was described in the *Brixton Free Press* of 21 October under the headline 'Police Charge Riotous Unemployed.' (See Thompson, p. 34.) Shops were looted, police were attacked, and dozens of rioters were arrested. There were also demonstrations near St Thomas's Hospital, at St George's Circus, and in Murphy Street, a march from Brixton to the Public Assistance Commission in Brook Street on Thursday, 20 October and from 27 to 30 October there were serious clashes in central London to protest against unemployment.

2. Crick was the proprietor of the local cinema at Southwold, where Orwell's father attended every new film (see letter to Brenda Salkeld, **late August 1934**). Entertainment tax was first levied on 1 August 1918 as a wartime measure, but it was continued thereafter.

3. 'Clink', X, 135, pp. 254–60. It describes Orwell's deliberate and successful attempt to get himself sent to prison in order to enlarge his experience. It was unpublished in his lifetime.

4. *Burmese Days*.

5. *King Charles II*, performed by the boys of The Hawthorns, Christmas 1932. The text is to be found at X, 154, pp. 277–94. It is anything but 'mucky': this is simply Orwell typically denigrating his work. A 40-page, lavishly-illustrated edition of the play was published by the Bellona Press, Warsaw, in 2000, translated by Dr Bartek Zborski.

6. The article was 'Common Lodging Houses' (X, 141, pp. 265–7). The letter was from Theodore Fyfe who described himself as an architect who had worked for

the London County Council on the construction of lodging houses. He thought the L.C.C. was 'worthy of all praise'.

7. The *Daily Worker* represented Communist Party views and policies, 1 January 1930 to 23 April 1966; incorporated in the *Morning Star* from 25 April 1966. It was suppressed by government order 22 January 1941 to 6 September 1942.

To Leonard Moore*

Sat.[1] [19 November 1932]
The Hawthorns

Dear Mr Moore,

Many thanks for your letter. I sent off the proof with the printer's queries on it yesterday. I made a few alterations & added one or two footnotes, but I think I arranged it so that there would be no need of 'over-running'.[2] I will send on the other proof as soon as possible.

As to a pseudonym, the name I always use when tramping etc. is P. S. Burton,[3] but if you don't think this sounds a probable kind of name, what about

Kenneth Miles,
George Orwell,
H. Lewis Allways.

I rather favour George Orwell.[4]

I would rather not promise to have the other book[5] ready by the summer. I could certainly do it by then if I were not teaching, but in this life I can't *settle* to any work, & at present particularly I am rushed off my feet. I have got to produce a school play, & I have not only had to write it, but I have got to do all the rehearsing &, worst of all, make most of the costumes.[6] The result is that I have practically no leisure.

I should like very much to come out & see you & Mrs Moore some time. I can get to Gerrard's Cross quite easily from here, but I have unfortunately forgotten your home adress°. Perhaps you could let me know it? I could come over some Sunday afternoon—Sunday the 4th Dec.,[7] for instance, if you would be at home then?

Yours sincerely
Eric A. Blair

P.S. [*at top of letter*] As to the *title* of the book. Would 'The Confessions of a Dishwasher' do as well? I would *rather* answer to 'dishwasher' than 'down and out', but if you and Mr G[ollancz] think the present title best for selling purposes, then it is better to stick to it.

[X, 148, p. 274; handwritten]

1. This undated letter, as for a number of others, can be placed from the receipt stamp used in Moore's office. The use of this evidence is not again mentioned.
2. Before electronic setting with its automatic re-lineation, print was set in lead type and changes affecting lineation were troublesome and very time-consuming – hence, expensive.
3. In 'Clink' Orwell writes that he had the name Edward Burton put down on the charge sheet. He also used the name Burton for a character in his play *King Charles II*.
4. In the BBC radio broadcast about the magazine *The Adelphi*, 6 July 1958, produced by Rayner Heppenstall, Sir Richard Rees recalled Orwell's fear of his real name appearing in print. In *George Orwell: Fugitive from the Camp of Victory*, Rees elaborated on this: Orwell had told him that it 'gave him an unpleasant feeling to see his real name in print because "how can you be sure your enemy won't cut it out and work some kind of black magic on it?" Whimsy, of course; but even Orwell's genuine streak of old-fashioned conventionality sometimes bordered on whimsy and you could not always be quite certain if he was serious or not' (p. 44).
5. *Burmese Days*.
6. Compare Dorothy in *A Clergyman's Daughter*.
7. In a letter to Eleanor Jaques of 30 November he said he was going to 'see some people at Gerrard's Cross'.

To Brenda Salkeld*

Saturday [? June 1933]
The Hawthorns

Dearest Brenda

I sent you about two thirds of the rough draft of my novel[1] yesterday. I would have sent it earlier, but it has been with my agent all this time. He is quite enthusiastic about it, which is more than I am; but you are not to think that when finished it will be quite as broken-backed as at present, for with me almost any piece of writing has to be done over and over again. I wish I were one of those people who can sit down and fling off a novel in about four days. There is no news here. I am frightfully busy, suffering from the heat, and exercised about the things in my garden, which are going to dry up and die if this cursed weather doesn't change. I am growing, among other things, a pumpkin, which of course needs much more careful treatment than a marrow. I have read nothing, I think, except periodicals, all of which depress me beyond words. Do you ever see the *New English Weekly*? It is the leading Social Credit[2] paper. As a monetary scheme Social Credit is probably sound, but its promoters seem to think that they are going to take the main weapon out of the hands of the governing classes without a fight, which is an illusion. A few years ago I thought it rather fun to reflect that our civilisation is doomed, but now it fills me above all else with boredom to think of the horrors that will be happening within ten years—either some appalling calamity, with revolution and famine, or else all-round trustification and Fordification, with the entire population reduced to docile wage-slaves, our lives utterly in the hands of the bankers, and a fearful tribe of Lady Astors[3] and Lady Rhonddas[4] *et hoc genus* riding us like succubi in the name of Progress. Have you read *Ulysses* yet? It sums up better than any book I know the fearful despair that is almost normal in modern times. You get the same kind of thing, though only just touched upon, in Eliot's poems. With E, however, there is also a certain sniffish 'I told you so' implication, because as the spoilt darling of the *Church Times* he is bound to point out that all this wouldn't have happened if we had not shut our eyes to the Light. The C[hurch] T[imes] annoys me more and more. It is a poor satisfaction even to see them walloping the Romans, because they do it chiefly by descending to their level. I wonder whether it is true, as I have been told, that the *CT* advertisement columns are full of disguised abortion advertisements? If so it is pretty disgusting in a paper which is in constant pursuit of Bertrand Russell, Barney the Apostate,[5] etc because of their birth control propaganda. By the way did you see Barney's recent pronouncements at the Conference on I forget what, about the undesirable multiplication of the lower classes. His latest phrase is 'the social problem class', meaning all those below a certain income. Really you sometimes can't help thinking these people are doing it on purpose, Write soon. I wish you were here now. Have you been bathing yet? I keep putting it off.

With love
Eric A. Blair

[X, 176, pp. 316–18; handwritten]

1.   *Burmese Days.*
2.   The Social Credit movement, based on the ideas of Major C. H. Douglas, claimed that prosperity could be achieved through a reform of the monetary system.
3.   Nancy Witcher Astor (1879–1964), wife of the first Viscount Astor, born in Virginia, society and political hostess at Cliveden, the Astor estate on the Thames, was the first woman to take her seat in the House of Commons, 1919–45. She was an eloquent advocate of temperance and women's rights. In the first edition of *Coming Up for Air* (1939), Orwell included Lady Astor's name among a 'fearful tribe' of 'soul-savers and Nosey Parkers'. Though that name was set for the Secker & Warburg 1948 edition – as the 1947 proof witnesses – it was marked for omission in proof and has not been included (VII, p. 183). The omission sign does not appear to be Orwell's, but it might follow his instructions. Since the name Lord Beaverbrook

in this same list was allowed to stand, fear of an action for libel or defamation could hardly be responsible for the omission. Perhaps Orwell removed the name out of his friendship with David Astor; he did not know of the change.

4. Margaret Haig Thomas (1883–1958), second Viscountess Rhondda, was a highly successful businesswoman and ardent believer in the equality of the sexes. She actively edited her own independent weekly, *Time and Tide*, 1928–58.

5. Ernest William Barnes (1874–1953) was a mathematician and modernist church-man, and Bishop of Birmingham, 1924–53. His writings include *Should Such a Faith Offend?* and *Scientific Theory and Religion*.

To Eleanor Jaques*

7 July 1933
The Hawthorns

Dearest Eleanor,

It seems so long since that day I went out with you—actually, I suppose, about a month. This 'glorious' weather has been almost the death of me. However, I occasionally manage to get over to Southall & have a swim at the open-air baths, & my garden has done pretty well considering the drought. The only failures I have had were shallots & broad beans, both I fancy due to having been planted too late. I have had enormous quantities of peas, & I am a convert forever to the system of sinking a trench where you are going to grow a row of peas. I hope I shall be in S'wold for part of the summer holidays, but I am afraid it won't be long, because I am going to a new school at Uxbridge next term & they may want me to do some tutoring during the holidays. God send I'll be able to drop this foul teaching after next year. I do hope you'll be in Southwold during the holidays & perhaps we can go & picnic as we did last year. I am so pining to see the sea again. Do try to be in S'wold if you can, & keep some days free for me during the first fortnight in August. I think I shall get home about the 28th of this month. My novel will be about finished by the end of this term, but I don't like large sections of it & am going to spend some months revising it. Please write & tell me what your plans are, & remember me to your parents.

With much love
Eric

[X, 178, p. 319; handwritten¹]

1. Published by kind permission of Richard Young.

To Eleanor Jaques*

Thursday [20 July 1933]
The Hawthorns

Dearest Eleanor,

Do write & tell me if you will be in S'wold during the summer holidays. I am going to be there I think from the 29th inst. to the 18th August, & am so wanting to see you. If you are to be there, try & keep some days free for me, & it would be so nice if we could go & bathe & make our tea like we used to do last year along the W'wick[1] shore. Let me know.

The heat here is fearful, but it is good for my marrows & pumpkins, which are swelling almost visibly. We have had lashings of peas, beans just beginning, potatoes rather poor, owing to the drought I suppose. I have finished my novel,[2] but there are wads of it that I simply hate, & am going to change. They say it will be soon enough if it is done some time at the end of the year. Please G. I get a little spare time in my next job. I went over to see the prize-giving at the school & it looked pretty bloody—the girls' section of the school (which I shall have nothing to do with—perhaps it is for the best) sang the female version of Kipling's 'If.' I am told that there is also a female version of 'Forty years on', which I would give something to get hold of.[3] I have been reading *in* D. H. Lawrence's collected letters. Some of them very interesting—there is a quality about L. that I can't define, but everywhere in his work one comes on passages of an extraordinary freshness, vividness, so that tho' I would never, even given the power, have done it quite like that myself, I feel that he has seized on an aspect of things that no one else would have noticed. In another way, which I can still less explain, he reminds me of someone from the Bronze Age. I think there are some scraps of mine in the August *Adelphi*[4]—a poem, but I am not sure it is not one you have seen. *Au revoir*, & write soon.

Much love from
Eric

[X, 179, pp. 319–20; handwritten[5]]

1. Walberswick is about two miles south of Southwold.
2. *Burmese Days*.
3. 'Forty Years On,' the Harrow school song, written in 1872 by John Farmer, was also sung by many girls' schools; in *Great Days and Jolly Days* (1977), Celia Haddon lists a wide range of such girls' schools (p. 21). It was also sung by such coeduca-

tional state schools as Eccles Grammar School. (Orwell reverted to this topic in a letter to Brenda Salkeld, **7.5.35**.)

4. There was no poem by Orwell in the August issue of *The Adelphi*, though his review of Enid Starkie's *Baudelaire* appeared.

5. Published by kind permission of Anthony Loudon.

Publishing, Wigan and Spain

1934 - 1938

This was a productive period for Orwell. *Burmese Days, A Clergyman's Daughter, Keep the Aspidistra Flying,* and *The Road to Wigan Pier* were published and, although Orwell dismissed the second and third of these as potboilers which he did not wish to see reprinted unless they would bring in his heirs a shilling or two, they are not wholly unrewarding. His experiences in the 'Distressed Areas' – he travelled around far more than solely to Wigan, of course – and in Spain were formative both to his character and outlook, social and political. He also contributed reviews and essays to literary journals, notably 'Shooting an Elephant', which says as much about the decline of the Raj as the collapse of an elephant.

Having delivered the typescript of *The Road to Wigan Pier* to Victor Gollancz just before Christmas Day 1936, he made his own way to Spain to fight for the Government against Franco. He had intended to join the International Brigade but, as he told Gollancz, partly by accident he enrolled in the POUM – the Partido Obrero de Unificación Marxista. This he described as 'one of those dissident Communist parties which have appeared in many countries in the last few years as a result of the opposition to "Stalinism"; i.e. to the change, real or apparent, in Communist policy. It was made up partly of ex-Communists and partly of an earlier party, the Workers' and Peasants' Bloc. Numerically it was small, with not much influence outside Catalonia . . . [where] its strongold was Lérida' (*Homage to Catalonia*, pp. 202–3). He would probably not have joined had he known that, long before he left England, the Soviet Communists were determined to eliminate it. In October 1936, Victor Orlov, head of the NKVD in Spain, assured his Headquarters that 'the Trotskyist organization POUM can easily be liquidated' (Christopher Andrew and Vasili Mitrokhin, *The Mitrokhin Archive* (1996), p. 95). Thus the description of Orwell and Eileen as 'trotzquistas pronunciados' (confirmed Trotskyists) in the Report on them to the Tribunal for Espionage and High Treason in Valencia (a document Orwell knew nothing about) was to damn them utterly. Had they been in Spain at the time of the trial of such colleagues as Jordi Arquer* it could have led to their imprisonment or even execution.

Orwell was on leave in Barcelona during 'the May Events' when the Communists attempted to eliminate the revolutionary parties (including the POUM). He returned to the Huesca front and, on 20 May 1937, he was shot through the throat. He and Eileen escaped from Spain and they returned to their Wallington Cottage where Orwell wrote *Homage to Catalonia*. In March 1938 he was taken seriously ill with a tubercular lesion and spent over five months in Preston Hall Sanatorium, Kent. On 2 September, he and Eileen left for French Morocco, believing it would restore him to health.

From Orwell's letter to his mother, 2 December 1911

To Brenda Salkeld*

Tuesday night [late August? 1934]
36 High St
Southwold, Suffolk

Dearest Brenda

Many thanks for your letter. I hope you are enjoying yourself more in Ireland than I am in England. When are you coming back? I am going up to town as soon as I have finished the book I am doing,[1] which should be at the end of October. I haven't settled yet where I am going to stay, but somewhere in the slums for choice. A friend wrote offering me the lease of part of a flat in Bayswater, but it would choke me to live in Bayswater. No, I have never seen a tortoise drinking. Darwin mentions that when he was in the Galapagos Is. the big tortoises there which lived on cactuses & things on the higher ground used to come down into the valley once or twice in the year to drink, & the journey took them a day or two. They stored water in a kind of sack in their bellies.[2] I have been reading some books by Lafcadio Hearn— tiresome stuff, & he idolises the Japanese, who always seem to me such a boring people.[3] I also tried to read Lord Riddell's diary of the Peace Conference & After.[4] What tripe! It is amazing how some people can have the most interesting experiences & then have absolutely nothing to say about them. I went to the pictures last week and saw Jack Hulbert in *Jack Ahoy* which I thought very amusing, & a week or two before that there was quite a good crook film, which, however, my father ruined for me by insisting on telling me the plot beforehand. This week *The Constant Nymph* is on. I haven't been to it, of course, but even when I see the posters it makes me go hot all over to think that in my youth—I think I must have been about 23 when it was published in book form—I was affected by it almost to tears *O mihi prae-teritos* etc.[5] I should think that any *critic* who lives to a great age must have many passages in his youth that he would willingly keep dark. There must be, for instance, many critics who in the 'nineties went all mushy over Hall Caine or even Marie Corelli—though M.C. isn't so absolutely bad, judging by the only book of hers I ever read. It was called *Thelma* & there was a very licentious clergyman in it who wasn't half bad. Did you, by the way, give me back those books of Swift? It doesn't matter, only I don't want to lose them. Yes, *Roughing It.*[6] does 'date' a bit, but not enough—because anything worth reading always 'dates.' Do come back soon. I am so miserable all alone. I have practically no friends here now, because now that Dennis & Eleanor are married & Dennis has gone to Singapore,[7] it has deprived me of two friends at a single stroke. Everything is going badly. My novel about Burma made me spew when I saw it in print, & I would have rewritten large chunks of it, only that costs money and means delay as well. As for the novel I am now completing, it makes me spew even worse, & yet there *are* some decent passages in it. I don't know how it is, I can write decent passages but I can't put them together. I was rather pluming myself on having a poem[8] in the *Best Poems of 1934*, but I now learn that there are several dozen of these anthologies of the so called best poems of the year, & Ruth Pitter[9] writes to tell me that she is in 4 of this year's batch, including one called *Twenty Deathless Poems*. We are getting delicious French beans from the garden, but I am concerned about the pumpkin, which shows signs of ripening though it is not much bigger than an orange. All my fruit has been stolen by the children next door, as I forsaw° it would. The little beasts were in such a hurry to get it that they didn't even wait till it was half ripe, but took the pears when they were mere chunks of wood. Another time I must try a dodge Dr Collings told me, which is to paint a mixture of vaseline & some indelible dye, I forget what, on a few of the fruit that are likely to be taken first & then you can spot who has taken it by the stains on their hands. The town is very full & camps of Girl Guides etc. infesting all the commons. I nearly died of cold the other day when bathing, because I had walked out to Easton Broad not intending to bathe, & then the water looked so nice that I took off my clothes & went in, & then about 50 people came up & rooted themselves to the spot. I wouldn't have minded that, but among them was a coastguard who could have had me up for bathing naked, so I had to swim up & down for the best part of half an hour, pretending to like it. Do come back soon, dearest one. Can't you come & stay with somebody before the term begins? It is sickening that I have to go away just after you come back. Write soon.

With much love
Eric

[X, 204, pp. 346–8; handwritten]

1. *A Clergyman's Daughter.*
2. Orwell had recommended Brenda read *The Voyage of the Beagle* some eighteen months earlier. His dramatised account of the voyage was broadcast by the BBC on 29 March 1946 (XVIII, 2953, pp. 179–201).
3. Lafcadio Hearn (1850–1904), writer and translator. Born at Levkás in the Ionian

Islands. Lived in the USA, 1869–90, then in Japan, where he became a citizen. Served with distinction as Professor of English at Imperial University, Tokyo. Wrote several books on Japanese life and culture. Three of his ghost stories were made into the Japanese film, *Kwaidon*, 1965.

4. George Riddell (1865–1934; cr. Baron 1920), *Intimate Diary of the Peace Conference and After, 1918–23* (1934). He owned, among other newspapers, the *News of the World*.

5. *O mihi praeteritos referat si Iuppiter ° annos:* 'O would Jupiter restore me the years that are fled!', Virgil, *Aeneid*, viii, 560.

6. By Mark Twain (1872): it describes the author's experiences with silver miners in Nevada a decade earlier. An unsigned review in *Overland Monthly*, June 1872, said its humour was such that it 'should have a place in every sick-room, and be the invalid's chosen companion'.

7. Dennis Collings and Eleanor Jaques married in 1934; he had been made assistant curator at the Raffles Museum in Singapore.

8. 'On a Ruined Farm near the His Master's Voice Gramophone Factory (X, 196, pp. 338–9).

9. Ruth Pitter, CBE (1897–1992) had known Orwell since World War I, and he had stayed in her house from time to time in 1930. He later reviewed two of her books of poetry. In 1937 she won the Hawthornden Prize for Literature and in 1955 was awarded the Queen's Medal for Poetry. Her *Collected Poems* appeared in 1991. She ran the Walberswick Peasant Pottery Co. Ltd in the 1930s, illustrated in Thompson, p. 23.

To Brenda Salkeld*

Wed. night [early September? 1934]
36 High St
Southwold

Dearest Brenda

As you complain about the gloominess of my letters, I suppose I must try and put on what Mr Micawber called the hollow mask of mirth, but I assure you it is not easy, with the life I have been leading lately. My novel[1] instead of going forwards, goes backwards with the most alarming speed. There are whole wads of it that are so awful that I really don't know what to do with them. And to add to my other joys, the fair, or part of it, has come back and established itself on the common just beyond the cinema, so that I have to work to the accompaniment of roundabout music that goes on till the small hours. You may think that this is red ink I am writing in, but really it is some of the bloody sweat that has been collecting round me in pools for the last few days. I am glad to hear you enjoyed yourself in the peninsular, as you are

pleased to call it. I shall send this to the London address you gave me, hoping they will keep it for you. The garden isn't doing badly. We had so many
cauliflowers that we couldn't eat them up fast enough, so about twenty have
run to seed. I have one marrow—the eighth so far—that is almost Harvest
Festival size, and I am letting it get ripe to make jam out of. I managed to get
my copy of *Ulysses* through safely this time.[2] I rather wish I had never read
it. It gives me an inferiority complex. When I read a book like that and then
come back to my own work, I feel like a eunuch who has taken a course in
voice production and can pass himself off fairly well as a bass or a baritone,
but if you listen closely you can hear the good old squeak just the same as
ever. I also bought for a shilling a year's issue of a weekly paper of 1851,
which is not uninteresting. They ran among other things a matrimonial
agency, and the correspondence relating to this is well worth reading. 'Flora
is twenty one, tall, with rich chestnut hair and a silvery laugh, and makes
excellent light pastry. She would like to enter into correspondence with a
professional gentleman between the ages of twenty and thirty, preferably
with auburn whiskers and of the Established Church.' The interesting thing
to me is that these people, since they try to get married through a matrimonial agency, have evidently failed many times elsewhere, and yet as soon
as they advertise in this paper, they get half a dozen offers. The women's
descriptions of themselves are always most flattering, and I must say that
some of the cases make me distinctly suspicious—for of course that was
the great age of fortune-hunting. You remember that beautiful case in *Our
Mutual Friend*, where both parties worked the same dodge on each other. I
wish you could come back here. However, if you can't it can't be helped. I
could not possibly have come to Haslemere. I most particularly want to get
this novel done by the end of September, and every day makes a difference.
I know it sounds silly to make such a fuss for so little result, but I find that
anything like changing my lodging upsets my work for a week or so. When
I said that I was going to stay in a slummy part of London I did not mean
that I am going to live in a common lodging house or anything like that. I
only meant that I didn't want to live in a respectable quarter, because they
make me sick, besides being more expensive. I dare say I shall stay in Islington. It is maddening that you cannot get unfurnished rooms in London, but
I know by experience that you can't, though of course you can get a flat or
some horrible thing called a maisonette. This age makes me so.sick that
sometimes I am almost impelled to stop at a corner and start calling down
curses from Heaven like Jeremiah or Ezra or somebody — 'Woe upon thee,
O Israel, for thy adulteries with the Egyptians' etc etc. The hedgehogs keep
coming into the house, and last night we found in the bathroom a little tiny
hedgehog no bigger than an orange. The only thing I could think was that it

was a baby of one of the others, though it was fully formed—I mean, it had its prickles. Write again soon. You don't know how it cheers me up when I see one of your letters waiting for me.

  With love
  Eric

                                        [X, 205, pp. 348–9; typewritten in red]

1. *A Clergyman's Daughter*.
2. *Ulysses*, which was printed in Paris, was liable to be seized by Customs & Excise.

To Brenda Salkeld*

                              Tuesday night [11? September 1934]
                                                    36 High St
                                                    Southwold

Dearest Brenda,

Many thanks for your letter. I am so glad to hear you have been having such an interesting time, and only wish I could reciprocate, but the most exciting things I have been doing are to plant out cabbages and make hurried trips into Lowestoft and Norwich in search of bulbs. Last time we were in Lowestoft we saw some Jews selling alarm clocks at sixpence each! Even if they had gone for a month you would have fairly good value for your money. My novel is due to come out in New York tomorrow—I don't know that it actually will, but that is the day it is scheduled for.[1] Please pray for its success, by which I mean not less than 4000 copies. I understand that the prayers of clergyman's° daughters get special attention in Heaven, at any rate in the Protestant quarter. I suppose I shall get some copies in about 10 days and some reviews in about 10 days after that. I hope they haven't put quite such a bloody jacket on it as they did last time. I hope to finish the other one[2] about the end of the month, and then I must sit down and plan out my next before going up to London. I am pleased with parts of this one I am doing, and other parts make me spew. I don't believe anyone will publish it or if they do it won't sell, because it is too fragmentary and has no love-interest. When exactly are you coming back to Southwold? Be sure and let me know so that I can keep Sunday free for you, and *please* don't go and tie yourself up with engagements for the whole of the first fortnight so that I never get a chance to see you. I have just been reading Huc's *Travels in Tartary and Thibet*,[3] which I can reccommend.° The garden is now looking very bare, as we have taken nearly everything up, but we are putting in bulbs etc. I have started taking snuff, which is very nice and useful in places where you can't smoke. Please write soon and let me know when you are coming. Don't forget what you are to tell me when you come back.

With much love
Eric

P.S. Don't forget to bring back my *Roughing It*,[4] will you? I want it to look up some quotes.

[X, 207, pp. 350–1; typewritten]

1. *Burmese Days* was not published until 25 October 1934.
2. *Keep the Aspidistra Flying*.
3. Published in French 1850 and in English in 1851, by the French missionary Abbé Évariste Régis Huc (1813–60).
4. See letter to Brenda Salkeld, **late August 1934**.

The following is one of twenty letters and postcards exchanged between Orwell and René-Noël Raimbault regarding the translation of Down and Out in Paris and London *into French. Three more will be found at* **29.11.34, 3.1.35,** *and* **22.12.35**. *All but two of the letters are in French. English translation only is provided here. The sequence gives a fascinating insight into Orwell's approach to his writing and into his translator's concerns and reactions to Orwell's writing (for example his contrast between a novel he has just translated and Orwell's* Burmese Days*). The letters not reproduced here and the French originals will be found in* The Lost Orwell.

To R. N. Raimbault*

9 October 1934
36 High Street
Southwold, Suffolk
Angleterre

Cher Monsieur Rimbault,°

I will reply to you in French, hoping that you will forgive my grammatical errors.

It has been a few years since I lived in France and although I tend to read French books I am not able to write your language very accurately. When I was in Paris people always said to me 'You don't talk too badly for an Englishman, but you have a fantastic accent'. Unfortunately I have only kept the accent. But I will do my best.

I give below answers to the questions you asked me, and of the dashes on page 239, which represent words which it is forbidden to print in England, but which will not cause, we can hope, any scandal in France. As for the preface, I will be very happy to write it – in English of course – and will send it to you in ten or fifteen days' time. I am unable to finish it any earlier because I am about to go to London and I will be very busy during the next week.

I am sending you at the same time as this a copy of *Down and Out*, which I have signed with my pen name, 'George Orwell'. This is a copy of the American edition. I don't have a copy of the English edition and given that the book was published eighteen months ago, it would probably be impossible to obtain one without some delay. When the French version is published, I shall, of course, send you a copy.

You must have faced many difficulties in translating a book such as *Down and Out* and it is very kind of you to propose a translation of my next novel. It is called *Burmese Days*, and it is about to be published by Harper's in New York. It is a novel which deals with the lives of the English in Burma (in India) and it is being published in New York because my publisher (Gollancz) would not dare publish it in England owing to the observations I made regarding English imperialism. I hope, however, to find an English publisher soon who has more courage. It doesn't seem very likely that such a book would interest the French public, but in any case I will tell my literary agent to let you see a copy as soon as we receive some from New York. You will be able to judge for yourself whether a translation might have any success in France.[1] By the way, you told me that Mr. André Malraux wrote the preface to a book by William Faulkner that you had translated. If I am not mistaken, Mr. Malraux wrote novels which deal with China, India etc. In this case it is possible that *Burmese Days* would interest him and if he would also be so kind as to write a preface for me, that would without doubt ensure the success of a book that bore the name of such a distinguished writer.[2] But you will be able to judge better after having seen a copy of *Burmese Days*.

In conclusion, it only remains for me to thank you for the great service you have done me by translating my book into French and to hope that, when the book is published, you will receive recompense appropriate to your efforts. I also hope that in writing in French I have not imposed on you an even worse translation task than the other!

Recevez, cher Monsieur, l'expression de mes meilleurs sentiments.

Eric Blair ('George Orwell')

For Orwell's notes the identical paginations of Complete Works I *and the Penguin Twentieth-Century editions are given within square brackets after each reference.*

Page 228 [170, line 7]: '…tum – a thing to make one shudder' etc. In Hindustani [3] there are two words for 'you' – 'ap' and 'tum.' 'Ap' is the more respectful word. 'Tum' is only used between close friends or from a superior to an inferior. To say 'tum' is nearly the same thing as addressing someone by 'tu'. An Englishman in India would therefore be very angry if a Hindu addressed him with 'tum.'

Page 159 [118, 4 lines up] and 240–241 [179, 6 lines up]: 'Bahinchut' etc. 'Bahinchut' is a Hindustani word that one should never address to a Hindu but which, unfortunately, one uses rather often. It is quite difficult to translate. 'Bahin' means 'sister' and 'chut' means the sexual organ. By saying 'Bahinchut' to a man, you are saying 'I am very familiar with the sexual organs of your sister' – in other words, I have slept with her. One would perhaps be able to translate 'bahinchut' as 'brother-in-law.' The English soldiers brought this word home from India in the form 'barnshoot', which has been accepted as quite an innocent word in England.

Pages 238–239 [178, lines 12–13]: 'The current London adjective' etc. This adjective is 'fucking.' 'Fuck' means 'to fuck,' and 'fucking' is the present participle.

Page 239, line 19 [178, lines 27–28]: 'For example -----.' The word is 'fuck.' The English no longer use this word in the sense of 'fornicating,' which was its original meaning, but simply as an expletive.

Page 239, line 23 [178, line 31]: 'Similarly with----.' The word is 'bugger'.

Page 239 line 25 [179, lines 1–2]: 'One can think etc.' These words are 'fuck' and 'bugger.' 'Fuck' which takes its origin from the Latin 'futuo' originally meant 'to fornicate,' but workers use it as a simple expletive in such expressions as 'I will fuck the lot of them,' 'we're fucked' etc. etc. The word 'bougre' is the same as 'bugger,' both being derived from 'Bulgare' or 'Bulgar,' because in the sixteenth century the Bulgarians, or even the Cathars, were suspected of practising sins against nature. But although the Parisian workers sometimes use the word 'bugger,' they do not know, according to my observation, what it originally meant.

Page 256 [191, 4 lines up]: 'The one bite law.' According to the English law, if a dog bites two men, its owner is obliged to kill it. The first time the dog is forgiven. This is where the expression 'one bite law' comes from.

Page 259 [194, line 7]: 'Bull shit' is an expression which means bulls' excrement. A man says to another 'you are talking bull shit;' in other words, 'You are talking nonsense.' It is a very impolite expression

[*LO,* pp. 8–13; X, 210A, p. 353; typewritten]

1. *Burmese Days* was published in France by Nagel, Paris, as *Tragédie Birmane* on 31 August 1946. The translation was made by Guillot de Saix. Orwell was paid a royalty of £5 17s 9d on 29 September 1945.

2. André Malraux (1901–76). Novelist and leftist intellectual. He left Paris for Indochina and China when he was 21 and became involved with the revolutionary movements then stirring. Founding the Young Annam League, he later travelled to Afghanistan and Iran and returned to Indochina in 1926. His experiences led to the novels, *Les Conquérants* (1928), *La Voie royale* (1930), and then, and most successfully, *La Condition humaine* (1933). He did not write an introduction for *Down and Out,* nor for *Burmese Days.* It was later suggested that he might write a preface to *Homage to Catalonia* but, despite his having served in Spain, did not do so, perhaps because he moved to the Right, later becoming Minister of Information and then of Culture in General de Gaulle's government after the war. From 1928 he was a member of Gallimard's Reading Committee and, from 1929, its Artistic Director.

3. Orwell had passed Indian Police examinations in Hindi, Burmese and Shaw-Karen.

To Leonard Moore*

14 November 1934
3 Warwick Mansions
Pond St
Hampstead NW3

Dear Mr Moore,

Many thanks for your letter—I hope you can read my handwriting—I have left my typewriter down in the shop.

I knew there would be trouble over that novel.[1] However, I am anxious to get it published, as there are parts of it I was pleased with, & I dare say that if I had indicated to me the sort of changes that Mr Gollancz wants, I could manage it. I am willing to admit that the part about the school, which is what seems to have roused people's incredulity, is overdrawn, but not nearly so much so as people think. In fact I was rather amused to see that they say 'all that was done away with 30 or 40 years ago' etc, as one always hears that any particularly crying abuse was 'done away with 30 or 40 years ago.' As to this part, it is possible that if Mr Gollancz agrees, a little 'toning down' might meet the bill. I dont° want to bother you with details about this, however.

As to the points about libel, swearwords etc., they are a very small matter & could be put right by a few strokes of the pen. The book does, however, contain an inherent fault of structure[2] which I will discuss with Mr Gollancz, & this could not be rectified in any way that I can think of. I was aware of it when I wrote the book, & imagined that it did not matter, because I did not intend it to be so realistic as people seem to think it is.

I wonder if you could be kind enough to arrange an interview for me with Mr Gollancz?[3] I should think it would take quite an hour to talk over the various points, if he can spare me that much time. I don't particularly mind what day or time I see him, so long as I know a day beforehand so as to let them know at the shop.

I have seen one review of *Burmese Days* in the *Herald Tribune*. Rather a bad one, I am sorry to say—however, big headlines, which I suppose is what counts.

Yours sincerely
Eric A Blair

P.S. [at top of letter] If you should have occasion to ring up about the interview, my number is Hampstead 2153.[4]

[X, 215, p. 358.; handwritten]

1. Orwell had sent the manuscript of *A Clergyman's Daughter* to Moore on 3 October. Victor Gollancz must have read it quickly for on 9 November he wrote to Moore about his reservations. On 13 November Moore wrote to Gollancz to tell him that 'in view of what you say I think you may like to know that when sending the manuscript to me the author pointed out that "in case the point should come up, the school described in chapter IV is totally imaginary, though of course I have drawn on my general knowledge of what goes on in schools of that type."' Moore must have sent Orwell details of this and other objections to the novel; this letter is Orwell's response. For problems posed by *A Clergyman's Daughter*, see III, Textual Note and Crick, pp. 256–8.

2. This may refer to Dorothy's sudden loss of memory, which is implicitly a belated result of Warburton's assault on her (p. 41), leading to her finding herself in the New Kent Road, London (Chapter 2). Rape was a taboo subject in the 1930s. The long section about the school where Dorothy taught would have caused Gollancz anxiety because he had published a fictional account of a school in Kensington in Rosalind Wade's *Children Be Happy* which had led to a libel action. (See **26.4.32**, n. 3.)

3. Annotated in Moore's office: '3.30 Geo Orwell,' presumably for 19 November 1934.

4. The telephone number of Booklovers' Corner (see **20.11.34**, n. 1).

To Leonard Moore*

20 November 1934
Booklovers' Corner
1 South End Road
Hampstead NW 3[1]

Dear Mr Moore,

Thanks for your letter. I had a talk with Gollancz yesterday, & we decided that it lay between cutting out or 'toning down' the part objected to. The former would be easier, but it would I think make the ending of the book too abrupt, so I am going to rewrite that chapter, which will take about a month. I told Gollancz I would send it to him direct.

I am glad M. Raimbault likes *Burmese Days*. No, I shouldn't think it would be much use trying it elsewhere. I did, however, hear that Wishart (a publisher I had never heard of)[2] will publish books that other people are afraid of. No pressing°-cuttings yet from New York, I suppose?[3]

Yours sincerely
Eric A Blair

[X, 216, p. 359; handwritten]

1. This is written on paper with a printed letterhead. It gives the telephone number (Hampstead 2153), and 'Francis G. Westrope, Bookseller, &c.' with a framed line drawing captioned 'South End Green in 1833, now the Tram Terminus.'
2. Lawrence & Wishart is still active. Ernest Edward Wishart (1902–1987) founded the publishing house of Wishart & Co shortly after completing a degree in history and law at Cambridge. He published Nancy Cunard's *Negro* and books by Geoffrey Gorer, Roy Campbell, E. M. Forster, Aldous Huxley and Bertrand Russell; from 1925 to 1927 Wishart published *The Calendar of Modern Letters*, edited by Edgell Rickword. Despite his Marxist sympathies, Wishart refused to join the Communist Party. In 1935 he merged with Martin Lawrence. They published the complete works of Marx, Lenin, and Stalin.
3. Annotated in Moore's office: 'Some have crossed this letter.'

To R. N. Raimbault*

29 November 1934
3 Warwick Mansions
Hampstead NW [3]

Cher Monsieur Raimbault,

I would have replied earlier to your very kind letter, but I have had a terrible cold for a few days, thanks to the poor weather that we have had recently. The fog was sometimes so thick that you could not see from one side of the road to the other. Princess Marina,[1] who has just arrived to marry Prince George, must have a very bad impression of the weather of her adopted country. But now, thankfully, it is a bit better, and I feel well enough to write letters.

I was, as you can believe, very flattered by your opinion of *Burmese Days*. Let's hope that Mr Malraux will be of the same opinion. Regarding *La Vache Enragée*,[2] if Mr Francis Carco agrees to write an introduction, I shall, naturally, be extremely grateful. When you told me that you had translated William Faulkner's books, I thought you must be 'the nonpareil,' among translators, as Shakespeare put it.[3] Personally, I cannot imagine a more difficult author for a foreigner to translate; but of course, his style, however complicated, is truly distinguished. It seems likely to me that after a century, or even fifty years, English and American will no longer be the same language[4] – which will be a shame because the Australians and Canadians etc. will probably prefer to follow the Americans.

Having thanked you for your letter, what I should like to do is ask if you would be interested in seeing an article on Mr Malraux which appeared two months ago in the *Adelphi* (a monthly journal to which I contribute now and again). I can send you a copy without any difficulty. Also, the other day whilst I was looking through my books I found by chance a collection, *Nursery Rhymes*, and the idea came to me that it might interest you, assuming you don't already possess such a collection. Nursery Rhymes are usually total nonsense, but they are so well known in England that they are quoted almost unconsciously when writing and they have exerted a big influence on some modern poets such as Robert Graves and T. S. Eliot.[5] If you think that the book would interest you, I will be very happy to send it to you.

If you have occasion to write to me, my address will be as above. At the moment I am working in a bookshop. It is a job that suits me much better than teaching.[6]

Veuillez agréer, Monsieur, l'expression de mes meilleurs sentiments.

Eric A Blair

[*LO*, pp.22–4; X, 216B, p. 359; typewritten]

1. Princess Marina of Greece married Prince George, Duke of Kent, on 29 November 1934. She proved with the public a gracious and very popular member of the Royal Family.

2. The title of the French translation of *Down and Out*. (See **22.12.35**, n. 2.)

3. Shakespeare uses the word 'nonpareil' in five plays: *Twelfth Night*, 1.5.254; *Macbeth*, 3.4.18; *Antony and Cleopatra*, 3.2.11; *Cymbeline*, 2.5.8; and *The Tempest*, 3.2.100. The play to which Orwell refers is unclear. In three the reference is to a woman who is, as in *Twelfth Night*, 'the nonpareil of beauty'. Macbeth refers to one of the murderers as a nonpareil and Enobarbus so describes Caesar.

4. For English adopting American practices, see Orwell's complaint of the use in English of 'the American habit of tying an unnecessary preposition on to every verb' (XVII, 2609, p. 31).

5. Orwell continued to be interested in nursery rhymes and fairy tales. His dramatisation of 'Little Red Riding Hood' was broadcast in the BBC's *Children's Hour* programme on 9 July 1946. Writing to Rayner Heppenstall* on 25 January 1947 he described Cinderella as 'the tops so far as fairy stories go' (XIX, 3163, p. 32). And, of course, *Animal Farm* is subtitled by Orwell, 'A Fairy Story'.

6. Orwell had taught at Frays College, Uxbridge, Middlesex until December 1933, when he developed pneumonia. He then gave up teaching.

To R. N. Raimbault*

3 January 1935
3 Warwick Mansions
Hampstead NW 3

Dear Monsieur Raimbault,

I wonder if you will forgive my writing in English this time, as I want to make sure that I do not make any misstatements?

Before anything else, I want to thank you very much for making such an extraordinarily good job of the translation of *Down and Out*. Without flattering you I can truthfully say that I am not only delighted but also greatly astonished to see how good it seems when translated. As to the Paris part, I honestly think it is better in French than in English, and I am delighted with the way you have done the conversations. Allowing for the fact that there are, naturally, a good many slang words that I don't know, that is exactly how I imagined the characters talking. Let's hope that the book will have a success proportionate to your efforts, and that we shan't get into too much trouble with the hotel fraternity – for we must expect at any rate some trouble from them, I am afraid. If I am challenged to fight a duel by any hotel proprietor, perhaps you will second me.[1]

I have been through the proofs with great care and have made my corrections in pencil, as you asked. I have made alterations or suggestions [*references omitted here*]. As to the quarrel between the stevedore and the old age pensioner, I enclose herewith a copy of it with the blanks filled in and the words explained.[2] You will be able to use your judgement if you wish to rewrite that speech. In the one or two instances where I have written in the margin 'it would be better to write so and so,' I mean, of course, 'something to that effect,' as I know that what I suggest is not likely to be in perfect French. I have made my proof-corrections, by the way, in French. I hope you will be able to read and understand them.

I spoke to my agent, Mr Moore, about handing over the Italian rights of *Down and Out* and *Burmese Days*. He says that Mr. Amato may certainly have the Italian rights, only, in case of his finding any publisher willing to commission their translation into Italian, will he please communicate with Messrs. Christy and Moore Literary Agents 222 Strand London W.C. By the terms of my contract with him, I have to make all business arrangements through Mr Moore.

Thanking you again, and wishing all success to the book when it appears, I am

Yours very sincerely
Eric A Blair

P. S. I will send the proofs under a separate cover.

[LO, pp. 38–40; X, 221C, p. 367; typewritten
with handwritten PS at head of letter]

1.   Orwell was taken to task by M. Umberto Possenti, of the Hotel Splendide, 105 Piccadilly, London, in a letter to *The Times* (X, 159, pp. 301–2).
2.   This does not appear to have survived. However, the French edition has a number of abusive readings which can be found in I, p. 226 at 138/11–16.

To Victor Gollancz [Ltd?]*

10 January 1935
3 Warwick Mansions
Hampstead NW 3

Dear Sir,

I am returning the MS. of *A Clergyman's Daughter* herewith. I think there is now nothing in it that could possibly be made the subject of an action for libel. None of the characters are intended as portraits of living individuals, nor are any of the names those of actual persons known to me. As to the localities described, they are imaginary. 'Knype Hill' is an imaginary name and so far as I know no place of that name exists; in the story it is mentioned as being in Suffolk, but that is all. In the hop-picking part (chapter 2) there is nothing whatever to indicate an exact locality. In Chapter 4 Southbridge is described as a suburb ten or a dozen miles of° London, but there is now nothing to show which side of London it was. As to the reference to a shop called 'Knockout Trousers Ltd.' in Chapter 2, so far as I know there is no shop of any such name, and the house mentioned in the same part as being a refuge of prostitutes is again totally imaginary. It is stated to be somewhere off Lambeth Cut. Lambeth Cut is a longish street, but if this is still considered dangerous, I can easily change Lambeth Cut to a fictitious street in the proof. I enclose a note on the alterations, together with Mr Rubinstein's letter, herewith.

Yours faithfully
Eric A. Blair[1]

[X, 223, pp. 367–8; typewritten]

1. Orwell's list of changes required is omitted here. They include 'Barclay's Bank' which becomes 'the local bank'; a reference to *The Church Times* is cut; 'Lambeth public library' is changed to 'the nearest public library'. Gollancz's libel lawyer, Harold Rubinstein (1891–1975), a perspicacious literary critic, playwright and author as well as a distinguished lawyer, crossed out the statement that *The High Churchman's Gazette* had a 'remarkable° small circulation'. Orwell said he was not aware there was such a journal but changed the offending passage to 'a small and select circulation'. (See II, pp. 299–302 for pre-publication revisions, 1934–35.) New information about these changes has emerged and is included here in the appendix New Textual Discoveries.

To Brenda Salkeld*

Tuesday [15 January 1935]
3 Warwick Mansions
Hampstead NW 3

Dear Brenda,

Thanks for your letter. No, I cannot say that Havelock Ellis's signature, as I remember it, struck me as being at all like what I expected.[1] I should have expected him to write a very fine hand and use a thinner nib. We bought recently a lot of books with the authors' signatures in, and some of them containing autograph letters as well, but they were all sold almost at once. One that pleased me was inscribed 'From Beverley Nicholls, in all humility.' There is a subtle humour in that. I often see autographed letters advertised among the lots at book-auctions. I remember distinctly that in one case a letter from Sheila Kaye-Smith was priced higher than one from Sarah, Duchess of Marlborough (the Queen Anne one.) You often see autographs of Napoleon advertised, but they are usually pretty expensive, and of course they are not letters, only documents signed by him. Towards the end of his life he never seems to have written anything except his signature with his own hand, and apparently his spelling was appalling. I haven't done much to my new novel,[2] but I have written a poem that is to be part of it.[3] Talking of choosing a new pseudonym, I think it would be rather amusing, as so many women writers have chosen male pseudonyms, to choose a female one. Miss Barbara Bedworthy or something like that. With portrait of the author on the jacket. I have been feeling horribly tired, as for a variety of reasons I have been keeping very bad hours lately. On Sunday night I came away from a friend's house late, found there were no sort of conveyances running, had to walk several miles through drizzling rain, and then, to crown all, found myself locked out and had to raise hell before I could wake anybody up and get in. Have you ever seen Fowler's *Modern English Usage*?[4] Fowler is the man who did, or at any rate contributed to, the small Oxford dictionary, and he is a great authority on syntax etc. He is very amusing about such things as the split infinitive. I was also reading a rather amusing pamphlet on Dr Watson, which proved among other things, from internal evidence, that Watson was married twice. Also one or two of D. H. Lawrence's short stories, also Max Beerbohm's *And Even Now*, also, for the I don't know how many-th time, Maupassant's *Boule de Suif* [5] and *La Maison Tellier*. I suppose you have read both of those? I must stop now. I hope this letter will be duly waiting for you when you arrive and that you will not be in too unbearably depressed a state. Try and come up to town some time during the term and we will meet. Good bye for the present.

Yours
Eric A. Blair

[X, 224, pp. 368–9; typewritten]

1. Salkeld was then collecting autographs and Orwell was finding them for her.
2. *Keep the Aspidistra Flying*.
3. 'St Andrew's Day, 1935', printed in *The Adelphi* in November 1935 and in *Keep the Aspidistra Flying*, pp. 167–8, with two word changes but untitled.
4. *A Dictionary of Modern English Usage*, by H. W. Fowler, was first published in April 1926 and is still not fully superseded.
5. In September 1946 Orwell proposed to the BBC that he dramatise this story (XVIII, 3059, p. 386). The proposal was rejected (XVIII, 3095, n. 2, p. 448).

To Brenda Salkeld*

16 February 1935
Booklovers' Corner

Dearest Brenda,

Isn't it sickening, I can't keep the room I am in at present for more than a few weeks.¹ It was let to me on the understanding that I should have to give it up if somebody offered to take it & another room that are° beside it together, & now somebody has done so. So I shall have fresh miseries of house-hunting, & probably shan't find another place where I shall be so comfortable & have so much freedom. My present landlady² is the non-interfering sort, which is so rare among London landladies. When I came she asked me what I particularly wanted, I said 'The thing I most want is freedom.' So she said, 'Do you want to have women up here all night?' I said, 'No,' of course, whereat she said, 'I only meant that I didn't mind whether you do or not.' Not much is happening here.

Gollancz, who has re-read *Burmese Days*, wrote enthusiastically about it & said he was going to have it thoroughly vetted by his lawyer, after which the latter was to cross-examine me on all the doubtful points. I hope the lawyer doesn't report against it as he did last time. You notice that all this happened a year ago, & I do not know what has made G. change his mind again. Perhaps some other publisher has wiped his eye by publishing a novel about India, but I don't seem to remember any this year. Rees* got me a lot more signatures for you, which I will send when I can find them, but at present I have mislaid them. I am living a busy life at present. My time-table is as follows: 7 am get up, dress etc, cook & eat breakfast. 8.45 go down & open the shop, & I am usually kept there till about 9.45. Then come home, do out my room, light the fire etc. 10.30 am—1 pm I do some writing. 1 pm get lunch & eat it. 2 pm—6.30 pm I am at the shop. Then I come home, get my supper, do the washing up & after that sometimes do about an hour's work. In spite [of] all this, I have got more work done in the last few days than during weeks before when I was being harried all day long. I hope G. *does* publish *Burmese Days*, as apart from the money (& my agent has tied him down with a pretty good contract) it will tide over the very long interval there is going to be between *A Clergyman's Daughter* & the one I am writing now.³ I want this one to be a work of art, & that can't be done without much bloody sweat. My mother writes me that she isn't going away after all, so I will come down to S'wold for a week-end as soon as I can, but it will have to be when my employer's wife is up & about again. Write soon.

> With much love
> Eric

[X, 235, pp. 374–5; typewritten]

1. By 'more than a few weeks' Orwell was not referring to a few weeks more, but to the total time he had been able to spend in the Westropes' flat.
2. Mrs Myfanwy Westrope, wife of the owner of Booklovers' Corner.
3. *Keep the Aspidistra Flying*.

To Brenda Salkeld*

7 May [1935]
77 Parliament Hill
Hampstead NW 3

Dearest Brenda,

I am afraid this will not reach St Felix¹ before you do, as I only got your letter this evening—I suppose the posts were late owing to the jubilee.² I went down to Brighton, for the first time in my life, for Sunday and Monday. I went there with disagreeable apprehensions, but consoling myself by thinking that sooner or later I was sure to want to mention a trip to Brighton in a novel. However, I was rather agreeably surprised, and I didn't, in any case, spend much time by the sea shore, but went inland and picked bluebells etc. I found a number of nests, including a bullfinch's with four eggs, and by the way about a week ago I found a tit's nest, but I couldn't get at it, though I saw the bird go off the nest, as it was in the middle of a thorn bush. The crowds in Brighton weren't so bad, but of course it was an awful business getting back on Sunday,³ the train being so packed that people were hanging out of the windows. On Saturday night I was down in Chelsea, and it took me two hours to get back to Hampstead, the whole centre of London was so blocked with taxis full of drunken people careering round, singing and bellowing 'Long live the King!' What surprised me was that most of them were very young—the last people whom you would expect to find full of patriotic emotion; but I suppose they just welcomed the excuse for making a noise. That night I had been to see Rees,* really to borrow some money off him,⁴ as I had forgotten Monday was a bank holiday and had not got any money out of the bank, but he was at some sort of Socialist meeting and they asked me in and I spent three hours with seven or eight Socialists harrying me, including a South Wales miner who told me— quite good-naturedly, however—that if he were dictator he would have me shot immediately. I have done quite a lot of work, but oh! what mountains there are to do yet. I don't know that I shall be able to let you have that piece⁵ to see in June after all, but I will some time—when it is fit to be seen, I mean. I am now getting to the stage where you feel as though you were crawling about inside some dreadful labyrinth. I don't know that I have read much. I read D. H. Lawrence's *Women in Love*, which is certainly not one of his best. I remember reading it before in 1924—the unexpurgated version that time—and how very queer it seemed to me at that age. I see now that what he was trying to do was to create characters who were at once symbolical figures and recognizable human beings, which was certainly a mistake. The queer thing is that when he concentrates on producing ordinary human characters, as in *Sons and Lovers* and most of the short stories, he gets his meaning across much better as well as being much more readable. I have also been glancing into some numbers of *The Enemy*, the occasional paper Wyndham Lewis used to run, which we have in the shop. The man is certainly insane. I have hit on a wonderful recipe for a stew, which is the following: half a pound of ox-kidney, chopped up small, half a pound of mushrooms, sliced; one onion chopped very fine, two cloves of garlic, four skinned tomatoes, a slice of lean bacon chopped up, and salt, the whole stewed very gently for about two and a half hours in a very little beef stock. You eat it with sphagetti° or rather coquillettes. It is a good dish to make, as it cooks itself while you are working. I have been deriving a lot of pleasure from some numbers of the *Girls'° Own Paper* of 1884 and 1885. In the answers to correspondents two questions crop up over and over again. One, whether it is ladylike to ride a tricycle. The other, whether Adam's immediate descendents° did not have to commit incest in order to carry on the human species. The question of whether Adam had a navel does not seem to have been agitated, however.

I must stop now, as I don't think I have any more news. As to your presentiment, or 'curious feeling' about me, you don't say when exactly you had it. But I don't know that I have been particularly unhappy lately—at least, not more than usual.

With much love and many kisses
Eric

P.S. [at top of first page] Near Brighton I passed Roedean School. It seemed to me that even in holiday time I could feel waves of snobbishness pouring out of it, & also aerial music to the tune of the female version of 'Forty Years On' & the Eton 'Boating Song.'⁶ Do you play them at hockey, or did they write to you 'St Felix, who are you?'

[X, 245, p. 385–7; typewritten; handwritten postscript]

1. St Felix School for Girls, Southwold, where Salkeld was the gym mistress.
2. The Silver Jubilee of King George V.
3. Orwell must mean Monday.
4. Although not a direct autobiographical contrast, compare Gordon refusing to borrow £10 from Ravelston, Keep the Aspidistra Flying, pp. 106–7, but sponging on him and taking his money, pp. 212–3.
5. Presumably a portion of Keep the Aspidistra Flying. In his letter to Moore of 14 May 1935 Orwell says he intended to write what became a novel as a book of essays; the 'piece' referred to was perhaps one of these essays in process of transformation into a different genre.
6. See 20.7.33, n. 3.

To Rayner Heppenstall*

Tuesday night [24 September 1935]
50 Lawford Rd
Kentish Town NW¹

Dear Rayner,

Many thanks for letter. I hope the enclosed MS. is what you wanted. I infer from what you would no doubt call your handwriting that you were taught script at school; the result is that I can't read a single word of the manuscript part of your letter, so I may not have followed your instructions exactly.

I am suffering unspeakable torments with my serial, having already been at it four days and being still at the second page. This is because I sat down and wrote what was not a bad first instalment, and then upon counting it up found it was 3500 words instead of 2000. Of course this means rewriting it entirely. I don't think I am cut out for a serial-writer. I shall be glad to get back to my good old novel where one has plenty of elbow room. I have three more chapters and an epilogue to do, and then I shall spend about two months putting on the twiddly bits.

Even if my serial doesn't come to anything, and I don't expect it to, I intend taking a week or so off next month. My people have asked me to come down and stay with them, and if I can get my sister to drive me over, as I don't think I can drive her present car, I will come over and see you. I don't know that part of the country, but if it is like ours it must be nice this time of year.

I forwarded a letter this evening which had urgent proofs on it. I hope it gets to you in time, but it had already been to your old address. You ought to let editors and people know that you have changed your address.

You are right about Eileen.[2] She is the nicest person I have met for a long time. However, at present alas! I can't afford a ring, except perhaps a Woolworth's one. Michael was here last night with Edna[3] and we all had dinner together. He told me he has a story in the anthology of stories that is coming out, but he seemed rather down in the mouth about something. I was over at the Fierz'[4] place on Sunday and met Brenda[5] and Maurice[6] whom no doubt you remember, and they were full of a story apparently current among Communists to the effect that Col. Lawrence[7] is not really dead but staged a fake death and is now in Abyssinia. I did not like Lawrence, but I would like this story to be true.

Au revoir. Please remember me to the Murrys.[8]

Yours
Eric A. Blair

[X, 253, pp. 393–5; typewritten]

1.   Orwell moved to this address from Booklovers' Corner. The flat is illustrated by Thompson, p. 47. It was rented in Orwell's name but he shared it with Rayner Heppenstall and Michael Sayers (1911–) who contributed short stories and reviews to *The Adelphi*. The relationship was not wholly satisfactory. On one occasion Orwell and Heppenstall came to blows (see *Orwell Remembered*, pp. 106–15). Orwell remained there until the end of January 1936 when he stopped working at Booklovers' Corner.

2.   Eileen O'Shaughnessy (1905–1945) was to marry Orwell on 9 June 1936. According to Lettice Cooper they met at a party given by Mrs Rosalind Obermeyer at 77 Parliament Hill in March 1935. Before George left the house he said to a friend, 'The girl I want to marry is Eileen O'Shaughnessy.' At the time she met Orwell she was

reading for a master's degree in psychology at University College London. For Lydia Jackson's reminiscences see *Orwell Remembered*, pp. 66–68. See also Eileen Blair*.

3. 'Michael' is Michael Sayers; Edna is Edna Cohen, Michael's cousin.

4. Francis and Mabel Fierz, at whose home in Golders Green Orwell often found refuge when he first came to London. Mabel Fierz introduced Orwell's writing to Leonard Moore, who, as a result, became his literary agent.

5. Brenda Eason Verstone (1911–) studied art at the Chelsea School of Art and then worked as a journalist for trade publications concerned with paper and packaging.

6. Maurice Oughton was a leading aircraftman in the Royal Air Force in 1942, when he published a slim volume of poems, *Out of the Oblivion*, which includes his picture.

7. T. E. Lawrence ('Lawrence of Arabia'), who had died as a result of a motor-cycle accident on 19 May 1935.

8. Heppenstall was staying with John Middleton Murry* in Norfolk.

On 9 November 1935, writing on black-bordered paper, M. Raimbault told Orwell that 'a terrible misfortune' had befallen his family. They had taken their summer holiday at Batz-sur-Mer: 'one of my twin daughters fell from a rock, hurt herself, near fatally, on her head, and rolled unconscious into the sea. The weather was bad, all the efforts to save her proved in vain. When it was possible to recover her two hours later nothing could be done to revive her. She was approaching seventeen years of age and was life and joy itself. I was in despair. I am still. I have great difficulty finding the courage to live.'

To R. N. Raimbault*

22 December 1935
50 Lawford Road
Kentish Town NW 5

Dear Raimbault,

I am sorry I have not written for so long. It is mainly because I have been so busy, first with struggling to get my novel finished, then with the extra Christmas work at the shop, that I have had very little time for letters.

I am writing in English this time because I am not certain of expressing myself adequately in French. I just want to tell you how terribly sorry I was to hear the sad news about the death of your daughter. There is not much one can say on these occasions, and the more so as I did not know your daughter myself, but I can imagine something of what your feelings must be, and I would like you to know that, for what they are worth, you have all my sympathies.

I am sorry that I have been rather discourteous to M. Jean Pons, because I have not done anything about his letter.[1] I am, however, writing to explain to him that it is on account of press[ure] of work that I have neglected him. I am sorry to hear that *La Vache Enragée*[2] didn't sell. For myself I hardly expected a large sale for it, as the interest is rather specialised, but it is disappointing for you after all the trouble you have had. You ask me whether I have any short stories which might be translateable°. I have made various attempts to write short stories and have always failed. For some reason or another it is a form I cannot manage. It occurs to me, however, that a descriptive sketch I wrote a few years ago might be worth looking at – it is a description of an execution in a jail in Burma and at the time I wrote it I was rather pleased with it. I will look out the copy of the magazine it was in, and send it to you. My novel is almost finished. I had promised to get it done by the end of the year, but I am behind time, as usual. I suppose it will come out some time in the spring.[3] I am afraid it is not the kind of thing that would be of any use to you for translation purposes, but I will send you a copy for yourself if you would like one. I forget whether I told you that a Frenchman wrote to me asking whether I would like *La Vache Enragée* translated into English! He had heard bits of it over the wireless but did not know it was already a translation.

Once again, all my sympathies for you in your sad loss. And my best wishes for Christmas and the New Year.

Yours
Eric A Blair

P.S. If you have occasion to write any time, would you write to 36 High Street, Southwold, Suffolk? I shall be changing my address shortly, but my parents will always forward letters.

[LO, pp. 60–1; X, 263A, p. 406; typewritten in English]

1. Mr Jean Pons, head of the Strand Palace Hotel Kitchens, The Strand, London, WC 2, had written to the French publishers to say that if Orwell would like 'supporting information' regarding his account of life in the kitchens of a large hotel, he would be happy to provide it (see *LO*, p. 56). No letter to or from M. Pons has survived.
2. *La Vache Enragée* was the French title of *Down and Out in Paris and London*. M. Raimbault explained to Orwell on 15 October 1934 that 'manger de la vache enragée . . . nearly enough corresponds to your expression "to go to the dogs".' It implies suffering great hardship. It was, though Orwell certainly did not know it, the title of a satirical journal published in Paris in 1896 for which Toulouse-Lautrec designed a fine poster. The contemporary French translation has changed the title to *Dans la dèche*, an expression Arnold Bennett uses to describe destitution in the Paris scenes of *The Old Wives' Tale* (1908): 'Is he also in the ditch?' (III, 6, iii).

3. *Keep the Aspidistra Flying* was published by Gollancz on 20 April 1936. No French edition appeared until 1960 when Gallimard published a translation by Yvonne Davet* as *Et Vive l'Aspidistra!*

To Leonard Moore*

24 February 1936
22 Darlington Street
Wigan
Lancs[1]

Dear Mr Moore,

Many thanks for your letter. I have made the alterations Gollancz asked for and sent back the proof and I trust it will now be all right. It seems to me to have utterly ruined the book, but if they think it worth publishing in that state, well and good. Why I was annoyed was because they had not demanded these alterations earlier. The book was looked over and O.K.'d by the solicitor as usual, and had they *then* told me that no reminiscence (it was in most cases only a reminiscence, not a quotation) of actual advertisements was allowable, I would have entirely rewritten the first chapter and modified several others. But they asked me to make the alterations when the book was in type and asked me to equalise the letters, which of course could not be done without spoiling whole passages and in one case a whole chapter. On the other hand to rewrite the whole first chapter when it was in type would have meant an immense addition to expenses, which obviously I could not ask Gollancz to bear. I would like to get this point clear because I imagine the same trouble is likely to occur again. In general a passage of prose or even a whole chapter revolves round one or two key phrases, and to remove these, as was done in this case, knocks the whole thing to pieces. So perhaps another time we could arrange with Gollancz that all alterations are to be made while the book is in typescript.[2]

If you manage to get an American publisher to accept the book, I wonder whether you could see to it that what he prints is the version first printed, without these subsequent alterations? I should like there to be one unmutilated version of it in existence.

The above address will find me till Saturday.

Yours sincerely
Eric A Blair

[X, 284, pp. 434–5; handwritten]

1. Orwell was in Lancashire studying conditions. One result would be *The Road to Wigan Pier*. (See *Orwell: Diaries* (2009).)

2. Orwell had been rightly exasperated by the many changes required for fear of actions for libel and defamation despite the text having been approved by the libel lawyer. These had to be made to the printed text and changes were restricted to the same number of letters as the original. (See IV, Textual Note, pp. 279–86.) *Keep the Aspidistra Flying* was not published in the United States until 1956 and it followed the corrupt text. Further details of these changes are included here in the appendix New Textual Discoveries.

To Jack Common*

17 March 1936
4 Agnes Terrace
Barnsley, Yorks

Dear Common,

Would you like a short review of Alec Browne's° book *The Fate of the Middle Classes*? Or is someone else doing it for you? I have scrounged a free copy and it seems not an uninteresting book, at any rate it is on an important subject and I thought I might, eg., do a few lines for the *Adelphi Forum*[1] on it.

I have been in these barbarous regions for about two months and have had a very interesting time and picked up a lot of ideas for my next book[2] but I admit I am beginning to pine to be back in the languorous South and also to start doing some work again, which of course is impossible in the surroundings I have been in. My next novel[3] ought to be out shortly. It would have been out a month ago only there was one of those fearful last-minute scares about libel and I was made to alter it to the point of ruining it utterly. What particularly stuck in my gizzard was that the person who dictated the alterations to me was that squirt Norman Collins.[4] Do you want a copy sent to the *Adelphi*? If you think you could get it reviewed I will have them send a copy, but not if you haven't space to spare. I went to the *Adelphi* offices[5] in Manchester and saw Higginbottom°[6] several times, also Meade[7] with whom I stayed several days. I may tell you in case you don't know that there are fearful feuds and intrigues going on among the followers of the *Adelphi* and I will tell you about these when I see you. I didn't say anything of this to Rees* when I wrote, because I thought his feelings might be hurt.

What about the international situation? Is it war? I think not, because if the government have any sense at all they must realise that they haven't got the country behind them. I think things will remain uneasily *in statu quo* and the war will break out later, possibly this autumn. If you notice wars tend to break out in the autumn, perhaps because continental governments don't care to mobilise until they have got the harvest in.

I heard Mosley[8] speak here on Sunday. It sickens one to see how easily a man of that type can win over and bamboozle a working class audience. There was some violence by the Blackshirts, as usual, and I am going to write to the *Times* about it, but what hope of their printing my letter?[9]

I shall be at the above address till about the 25th, after that returning to London, by sea if I can manage it. Hoping to see you some time after that,

Yours
Eric A. Blair

[X, 295, pp. 458–9; typewritten]

1. *The Adelphi Forum* was described by its editor as being 'open for short topical comments and for the expression of opinion which may be entirely different from our own.'
2. *The Road to Wigan Pier.*
3. *Keep the Aspidistra Flying.*
4. Norman Collins (1907–82), writer, journalist and broadcaster. He was deputy chairman of Victor Gollancz Ltd., 1934–41, and then he joined the BBC Overseas Service. Orwell was to cross swords with him in each of his manifestations. Orwell reviewed his best-known novel, *London Belongs to Me* on 29 November 1945 (XVII, 2805, pp. 399–41). He became Controller of the BBC Light Programme in 1946 and was later a leading figure in commercial television.
5. On the initiative of some of Middleton Murry's northern admirers, the printing and publishing organisation of *The Adelphi* was taken over by the Workers' Northern Publishing Society in Manchester. In the early 1930s Murry* found himself at the head of a breakaway segment of the Independent Labour Party known as the Independent Socialist Party—a short-lived phenomenon. It was from these *Adelphi* supporters that Richard Rees gave Orwell contacts in the north.
6. Sam Higenbottam (1872–?) was a contributor to *The Adelphi*, a socialist, and author of *Our Society's History* (1939), an account of the Amalgamated Society of Woodworkers.
7. Frank Meade was an official of the Amalgamated Society of Woodworkers and ran the Manchester office of *The Adelphi*; he was also business manager of *Labour's Northern Voice*, an organ of the Independent Socialist Party.
8. Sir Oswald Mosley, Bt. (1896–1980), was successively a Conservative, Independent, and Labour MP In 1931 he broke away from the Labour Party to form the 'New Party'. Later he became fanatically pro-Hitler and turned his party into the British Union of Fascists. His followers were known as Blackshirts. He was interned early in the war.
9. He also wrote to the *Manchester Guardian*. His diary for 20.3.36 concludes, 'I hardly expected the *Times* to print it, but I think the M.G. might, considering their reputation.' Neither did.

Writing to Sir Richard Rees from Wigan on 22 February 1936 Orwell said, 'I am arranging to take a cottage at Wallington near Baldock in Hertfordshire, rather a pig in a poke because I have never seen it, but have trusted the friends who have chosen it for me, and it is very cheap, only 7s 6d a week' (CW, X, 288, p. 442). The friend (there was only one) was his aunt, Nellie Limouzin, who had, until very recently, lived in 'The Stores' as the cottage was called. The reasons for choosing this cottage were that its rent was low, it was a congenial place in which to write, the shop which was part of the cottage would earn him enough from the village's one hundred or so inhabitants to cover the rent without too many distractions, and that it had enough land for him to grow vegetables and keep hens and goats. However, it also came with disadvantages that might have put off anyone less hardy than Orwell. It dated from the sixteenth century and had seen very little modernisation. It was pokey; there were four small rooms, two up and two down, one doubling as the shop area taking up valuable space; the ceilings were very low and Orwell was very tall; there was no inside w.c.; it had a sink but poor drainage; no proper cooking facilities; no electricity – lighting was by oil lamps (see Eileen's letter to Norah, **New Year's Day**, 1938); and a corrugated-iron roof. One might say, without being facetious, it suited Orwell down to the ground.*

To Jack Common*

Thursday [16? April 1936]
The Stores
Wallington, Nr. Baldock[1]
[Herts]

Dear Common,

Thanks for yours. I have now seen my landlord and it is O.K. about the rent, so I have definitely decided to open the shop and have spread the news among the villagers to some extent. I should certainly be very obliged if you would find out about the wholesalers. I didn't know you had your shop still. I believe there are some wholesalers of the kind at Watford, Kingford or Kingston or some such name. I don't know whether, seeing that I shall only want tiny amounts at a time (apart from the smallness of the village I haven't much storage room), they will make any trouble about delivery. I intend, at first at any rate, to stock nothing perishable except children's sweets. Later on I might start butter and marg. but it would mean getting a cooler. I am not going to stock tobacco because the pubs here (two to about 75 inhabitants!) stock it and I don't want to make enemies, especially as one pub is next door to me. I am beginning to make out lists, though whether any one wholesaler will cover the lot I am not certain. I suppose what I shall start off° will be about twenty quids' worth of stuff. Are these people good about giving credit? What I would like to do would be to give a deposit of about £5 and then pay quarterly. I suppose my bank would give me a reference. It is a pity in view of this that I have just changed my branch because the Hampstead branch were getting quite trustful and told me I could overdraw, though I never asked them. I shall want besides stock one or two articles of shop equipment, such as scales, a bell etc. There are some that go with this place but my landlord has them and he is the sort of person who takes a year before he hands anything over. I have got to tidy up the shop premises and repaint, but if I can click with the wholesalers I should be ready to open up in about 3 weeks.

Yes, this business of class-breaking is a bugger. The trouble is that the socialist bourgeoisie, most of whom give me the creeps, will not be realistic and admit that there are a lot of working-class habits which they don't like and don't want to adopt. E.g. the typical middle-class socialist not only doesn't eat with his knife but is still slightly horrified by seeing a working man do so. And then so many of them are the sort of eunuch type with a vegetarian smell who go about spreading sweetness and light and have at the back of their minds a vision of the working class all T.T.[1], well washed behind the ears, readers of Edward Carpenter[2] or some other pious sodomite and talking with B.B.C. accents. The working classes are very patient under it all. All the two months I was up north, when I spent my entire time in asking people questions about how much dole they got, what they had to eat etc., I was never once socked on the jaw and only once told to go to hell, and then by a woman who was deaf and thought I was a rate-collector. This question has been worrying me for a long time and part of my next book is to be about it.

I will get over when I have a bike or something. If you come over here, either let me know so that there shall be food, or take your chance—but there'll always be *something*, of course. The garden is still Augean (I have dug up twelve boots in two days) but I am getting things straight a little. It is awful to think that for nearly three months I have not done a stroke of work. Getting and spending we lay waste our powers.[3] However I have wads of notes which give me the illusion of not having wasted my time.

Yours
Eric A. Blair

[X, 300, pp. 470–1; typewritten]

1.   T.T.: teetotal.
2.   Edward Carpenter (1844–1929) was a socialist writer and social reformer whose works include *Towards Democracy* (1883) and *The Intermediate Sex: A Study of Some Transitional Types of Men and Women* (1908).

3.   Line 2 of Wordsworth's sonnet, 'The world is too much with us; late and soon'
     (1807).

To Geoffrey Gorer*

Sat. [23 May 1936]
The Stores
Wallington

Dear Gorer,

Many thanks for your kind offices re. *Time & Tide*. They gave me some novels to review. I would have written to you before only as usual I lost your
letter with the address & it didn't turn up till this morning. I have had the
shop open nearly a fortnight. I took 19/– the first week, this week will be
25/– or 30/–. That is turnover & the profit on it about pays the rent. I think
the business could be worked up to £3 or so. It is very little trouble & no
hanging about like in a bookshop. In a grocer's shop people come in to buy
something, in a bookshop they come in to make a nuisance of themselves.

I am getting married very shortly—it is fixed for June 9th at the parish
church here. This is as it were in confidence because we are telling as few
people as possible till the deed is done, lest our relatives combine against us
in some way & prevent it. It is very rash of course but we talked it over &
decided I should never be economically justified in marrying so might as well
be unjustified now as later. I expect we shall rub along all right—as to money
I mean—but it will always be hand to mouth as I don't see myself ever writing a best-seller. I have made a fairly good start on my new book.[1]

I was glad to see your book[2] got such good reviews. I saw a very good one
in the *Times*. The book itself I haven't seen yet. When you were in that part
of the world did you go to Singapore by any chance? I have a great friend
there at the Raffles Museum, Dennis Collings his name is, an anthropologist
& very gifted in various strange ways—for instance he can do things like
forging a medieval sword so that you can't tell it from a real one. I read
your Notes by the Way[3] with great interest. What you say about trying to
study our own customs from an anthropological point of view opens up a
lot of fields of thought, but one thing to notice about ourselves is that people's habits etc. are formed not only by their upbringing & so forth but also
very largely by books. I have often thought it would be very interesting to
study the conventions etc. of *books* from an anthropological point of view.
I don't know if you ever read Elmer Rice's *A Voyage to Purilia*. It contains a
most interesting analysis of certain conventions—taken for granted & never
even mentioned—existing in the ordinary film. It would be interesting & I

believe valuable to work out the underlying beliefs & general imaginative background of a writer like Edgar Wallace. But of course that's the kind of thing nobody will ever print.[4]

Thank God it has rained at last, after 3 weeks drought, & my vegetables are doing fairly well.

Yours
Eric A. Blair

[X. 311, pp. 481–2; handwritten]

1. *The Road to Wigan Pier.*
2. *Bali and Angkor.*
3. Properly, 'Notes on the Way,' *Time and Tide*, 23 May 1936.
4. In proposing study of this kind Orwell was well ahead of his time.

To Denys King-Farlow*

9 June 1936
The Stores
Wallington

Dear King-Farlow,

Of course I remember you. But have you changed your name back to King-Farlow? It was Nettleton most of the time you were at Eton. I only got your letter this morning. It was forwarded by Cyril Connolly*, who has been away. I'm afraid I can't possibly come along on the 11th, much as I would like to, first of all because it's always difficult for me to get away from here, secondly because like the chap in the N.T. I have married a wife & therefore I cannot come.[1] Curiously enough I am getting married this very morning—in fact I am writing this with one eye on the clock & the other on the Prayer Book, which I have been studying for some days past in hopes of steeling myself against the obscenities of the wedding service. When exactly I'll be up in Town I don't know. This place as you see by the address used to be the village 'general' shop, & when I came here I re-opened it as such—the usual little shop stocking groceries, sweets, packets of aspirins etc. It doesn't bring in much but it does pay my rent for me, & for a literary gent that is a consideration. On the other hand it makes it very difficult to get away from here. But if you are ever passing anywhere near, do drop in. It's not much off your track if you are going anywhere in a north-easterly direction or eg. to Cambridge. I should always be at home, except on Saturday afternoons & sometimes on Sundays, & should love to see you again.

I am not in touch with many of the Etonians of our time. Connolly came to see me once in town & he has been very kind in reviewing my books. I used to see Alan Clutton-Brock² in 1928—just recently his wife was killed in a motor smash. It was sad about poor Godfrey Meynell.³ I went & stayed at Cambridge with Gow* when I came back from Burma at the end of '27, but though he was very kind it seemed to me I had moved out of his orbit & he out of mine. I suppose most of the others we knew are dons, civil servants & barristers. I hear you have been in the U.S.A. a long time & are very rich & flourishing. I have had a bloody life a good deal of the time but in some ways an interesting one. Please excuse this untidy scrawl.

Yours
Eric A. Blair

[X, 316, p. 485; handwritten]

1. Gospel according to St Luke, xiii, 20.
2. Alan Clutton-Brock (c. 1903–1976), a contemporary of Orwell's at Eton. He became art critic of *The Times* and was Slade Professor of Fine Art, Cambridge, 1955–58.
3. Godfrey Meynell, a contemporary at Eton, had joined the army and was killed on the North West Frontier of India leading his native troops in action. He was posthumously awarded the Victoria Cross.

To Henry Miller*

26–27 August 1936
The Stores

Dear Miller,

Many thanks for your letter. It made me feel rather bad all the same, because I had been meaning for weeks to write to you and had been putting it off. Well, *Black Spring* arrived all right and I liked part of it very much, especially the opening chapters, but I do think, and shall say in reviewing it¹, that a book like *Tropic of Cancer*, dealing with events that happened or might have happened in the ordinary three-dimensional world, is more in your line. I liked *Tropic of Cancer* especially for three things, first of all a peculiar rhythmic quality in your English, secondly the fact that you dealt with facts well known to everybody but never mentioned in print (eg. when the chap is supposed to be making love to the woman but is dying for a piss all the while), thirdly the way in which you would wander off into a kind of reverie where the laws of ordinary reality were slipped just a little but not too much. You do this also in *Black Spring*, eg. I like very much your meditation beginning in a public urinal on pp. 60–64, but I think on the whole you have moved too much away from the ordinary world into a sort of Mickey Mouse universe where things and people don't have to obey the rules of space and time. I dare say I am wrong and perhaps have missed your drift altogether, but I have a sort of belly to earth attitude and always feel uneasy when I get away from the ordinary world where grass is green, stones hard etc. It is also, I know, pretty bloody when you have written one unusual book to be blamed for not writing another exactly like it. But I don't want you to think there wasn't a lot in *Black Spring* that I enjoyed. The quality of the prose is fine too, especially that passage I referred to before about the dung and the angels. When I read a piece like that I feel as you feel when you are galloping a really good horse over ground where you don't have to look out for rabbit holes. I will do what I can in the way of reviews. *The Adelphi* told me I could do a short bit on it, but they are soon going to become a quarterly, and I shall also do it for the *New English*, but they have shut up shop for August as they always do, so the reviews will be a bit late I expect, but I suppose in your case that doesn't matter so much as with the ordinary twopenny halfpenny novel that is genius for a week and then is sold off as a remainder. I have got to go and milk the goat now but I will continue this letter when I come back.

27.8.36. I am glad you managed to get hold of a copy of *Down and Out*. I haven't one left and it is out of print, and I was going to send you a copy of the French translation (I suppose it was the English version you saw) when I got your letter. Yes, it was published in America too but didn't sell a great deal. I don't know what sort of reviews it got in France—I only saw about two, either because the press-cutting people didn't get them or because I hadn't arranged to have copies sent out with flattering letters to leading critics, which I am told you should do in France. Some others of my books have also been published in America. My second book, *Burmese Days*, was published there before being published in England, because my publisher was afraid the India Office might take steps to have it suppressed. A year later my English publisher brought out a version of it with various names etc. altered, so the American edition is the proper one. That is the only one of my books that I am pleased with— not that it is any good *qua* novel, but the descriptions of scenery aren't bad, only of course that is what the average reader skips. My third book, *A Clergyman's Daughter* which came out in England about a year ago, was published in America last week. That book is bollox, but I made some experiments in it that were useful to me. My last book, *Keep the Aspidistra Flying*, won't, I imagine be published in America, because it is a domestic sort of story with an entirely English theme and the American public are getting restive about what I believe is called 'British sissy-stuff.' I noticed also when I worked in the bookshop that it is harder and harder to sell American books in England. The two languages are drifting further and further apart.

Yes, I agree about English poverty. It is awful. Recently I was travelling among the worst parts of the coal areas in Lancashire and Yorkshire—I am doing a book[2] about it now—and it is dreadful to see how the people have collapsed and lost all their guts in the last ten years. I reviewed Connolly's novel for the N[ew] E[nglish] W[eekly], but though it amused me I didn't think a lot of it[3]. It surprised me that he should be in such a stew about the book 'dating' as though every book worth reading didn't 'date!' I see from the blurb on *Black Spring* that you got a pretty good write-up from Eliot & Co, also that I am mentioned among them. That is a step up for me—the first time I have been on anybody else's blurb. So no doubt I shall be Sir Eric Blair yet.[3]

Write if or when you feel inclined.

Yours
Eric A. Blair

[X, 323, pp. 495–7; typewritten]

1. Orwell's review of Miller's *Black Spring* appeared in the *New English Weekly* in September 1936 (X, 325, pp. 499–501). Miller wrote to Orwell to thank him for his 'amazingly, sympathetic' review.
2. *The Road to Wigan Pier.*
3. *The Rock Pool* (X, 321, pp. 400–1).
4. See Gordon Comstock's (incorrect) sneering bestowal of a knighthood on John Drinkwater in *Keep the Aspidistra Flying* (IV, p. 138).

Eileen wrote six letters to a friend she had made at Oxford, Norah Symes. Norah also met her future husband, Quartus St Leger Myles, at Oxford. They became engaged when he returned to Clifton as a General Practitioner. They had no children. She died in 1994 and these letters were in her bequest to John Durant. They passed to Mrs Margaret Durant who allowed their inclusion in The Lost Orwell. *Recently, they were bought by Richard Young who has very kindly allowed them to be reproduced here. The letters give no indication to whom they were written, and, except for the initial 'E' at the end of the last letter, are always signed by the pet-name, 'Pig'. Possibly Norah's maiden name suggested the name for a character in* Nineteen Eighty-Four.

Only one of the letters is dated (New Year's Day, 1938) so dating is conjectural. Fuller notes are given in The Lost Orwell.

Eileen Blair* to Norah Myles*

3 or 10 November 1936
36 High Street
Southwold[1]

[*no salutation*]

I wrote the address quite a long time ago & have since played with three cats, made a cigarette (I make them now but not with the naked hand),[2] poked the fire & driven Eric (i.e George) nearly mad – all because I didn't really know what to say. I lost my habit of punctual correspondence during the first few weeks of marriage because we quarrelled so continuously & really bitterly that I thought I'd save time & just write one letter to everyone when the murder or separation had been accomplished. Then Eric's aunt[3] came to stay & was so dreadful (she stayed <u>two</u> <u>months</u>) that we stopped quarrelling & just repined. Then she went away & now all our troubles are over. They arose partly because Mother drove me so hard in the first week of June[4] that I cried all the time from pure exhaustion & partly because Eric had decided that he mustn't let his work be interrupted & complained bitterly when we'd been married a week that he'd only done two good days' work out of seven.[5] Also I couldn't make the oven cook anything & boiled eggs (on which Eric had lived almost exclusively) made me sick. Now I can make the oven cook a reasonable number of things & he is working very rapidly.[6] I forgot to mention that he had his 'bronchitis' for three weeks in July & that it rained every day for six weeks during the whole of which the kitchen was flooded & all food went mouldy in a few hours. It seems a long time ago now but then seemed very permanent.

I thought I could come & see you & have twice decided when I could, but Eric always gets something if I'm going away if he has notice of the fact, & if he has no notice (when Eric my brother arrives[7] & removes me as he has done twice) he gets something when I've gone so that I have to come home again. For the last few weeks we have been completely broke and shall be now until Christmas because the money we expected in October for *Keep the Aspidistra Flying* won't be paid until April and the next book won't earn its advance until December anyway and possibly January. But I must be in London for some days this month. Is there a chance of one of these Wednesdays? If so & if you tell me which I'll make my visit to fit it. I must see Eric (brother) a bit about his book, the proofs of which I'm now correcting, & also have some intelligence testing to do with Lydia.[8] Could you come either on the 18th or on the 25th? I think they're Wednesdays – anyway I mean Wednesdays. I want passionately to see you. Lydia must have a bit of notice

& indeed at any minute is going to descend on me in wrath (against Eric on social grounds not against me, for I am perfection in her eyes) & force me to go to London exactly when I don't want to. So if you were to send a post-card------[9]

This is our address for the rest of this week. We are staying with the Blairs & I like it. Nothing has surprised me more, particularly since I saw the house which is very small & furnished almost entirely with paintings of ancestors. The Blairs are by origin Lowland Scottish & dull but one of them made a lot of money in slaves & his son Thomas who was inconceivably like a sheep married the daughter of the Duke of Westmorland (of whose existence I never heard) & went so grand that he spent all the money & couldn't make more because slaves had gone out. So his son went into the army & came out of that into the church & married a girl of 15 who loathed him & had ten children of whom Eric's father, now 80, is the only survivor & they are all quite penniless but still on the shivering verge of gentility as Eric calls it in his new book which I cannot think will be popular with the family.[10] In spite of all this the family on the whole is fun & I imagine unusual in their attitude to me because they all adore Eric & consider him quite impossible to live with–indeed on the wedding day Mrs Blair shook her head & said that I'd be a brave girl if I knew what I was in for, and Avril the sister said that obviously I didn't know what I was in for or I shouldn't be there. They haven't I think grasped that I am very much like Eric in temperament which is an asset once one has accepted the fact

If I'd written this from Wallington it would have been about the real things of life–goats, hens, broccoli (eaten by a rabbit). But it would be better perhaps to tell you because this has got out of hand. Poor girl, miss it all out except the bit about the Wednesdays & say you can come on the 18th or the 25th to meet

Pig[11]

[LO, pp. 63–7 (with substantial additional notes); X, 331A, p. 515; handwritten]

1. Orwell's parents' home.

2. Orwell was able to roll his own cigarettes by hand. Evidently Eileen required a hand-roller.

3. Nellie Limouzin had lived in Paris with her husband, Eugène Adam, an ardent Esperantist, when Orwell was living there (1928–29). Adam left Nellie and went to Mexico where, in 1947, he committed suicide.

4. Eileen's mother, Marie O'Shaughnessy, evidently spent the week before the wedding with her daughter and Orwell, doubtless preparing for the event. Given the cramped and bare conditions, the lack of electricity, bathroom or indoor w.c.,

coupled with pre-wedding tensions, it is plain why Eileen was so distressed – and also why she found Aunt Nellie's long stay burdensome.

5. On 12 June Orwell submitted 'Shooting an Elephant' to John Lehmann, editor of *New Writing*. He published it in *New Writing*, 2, Autumn, 1936 (X, 326, pp. 501–6).

6. As well as sending off 'Shooting an Elephant', between his wedding and leaving for Spain, Orwell was very busy earning money from book reviewing and was writing *The Road to Wigan Pier*, which he completed just before he left for Spain about 23 December 1936. In this period he wrote twelve reviews of thirty-two books.

7. Confusingly, especially in letters Eileen was to write from Spain, her brother, Dr Laurence O'Shaughnessy* was also known in the family as Eric. The proofs to which she refers are her brother's and Sauerbruch's *Thoracic Surgery*.

8. Lydia Jackson.*

9. This is as written by Eileen: nothing has been left out.

10. The family background is well summarised by Sir Bernard Crick in *A Life*, pp. 46–7 and in the family bible. Orwell's mother, though born in Penge, South London, lived most of her early life in Moulmein, Burma. As Emma Larkin reports in *Finding George Orwell in a Burmese Teashop* (2004), there is a street sign, 'Leimmaw-zin', which means Orange-shelf Street but is a corruption of Limouzin Street (pp. 145–6). The phrase 'on the shivering verge of gentility' does not sound like Orwell; it does not appear in his 'new book', presumably *Keep the Aspidistra Flying*, pub-lished by Victor Gollancz on 20 April 1936, nor in the one he was writing, *The Road to Wigan Pier*. This may suggest it appeared in a draft read by Eileen. If so, that sug-gests a greater involvement by Eileen in Orwell's writing (other than for *Animal Farm*, where it is well established) than has been suspected.

11. It is ironical that Eileen's pet name should have been that of the animals Orwell pilloried in *Animal Farm*.

Jennie Lee* on Orwell's Arrival in Barcelona

Orwell saw Gollancz on the 21ˢᵗ December 1936 about the publication of The Road to Wigan Pier. *He arrived in Barcelona about the 26ᵗʰ (Crick, p. 315). After Orwell's death, Jennie Lee wrote on 23 June 1950 to a Miss Margaret M. Goalby of Presteigne, Radnorshire, who had asked her about Orwell. This is part of that letter.*

In the first year of the Spanish Civil War I was sitting with friends in a hotel in Barcelona when a tall thin man with a ravished° complexion came over to the table. He asked me if I was Jennie Lee, and if so, could I tell him where to join up. He said he was an author: had got an advance on a book from Gollancz,[1] and had arrived ready to drive a car or do anything else, prefer-ably to fight in the front line. I was suspicious and asked what credentials he had brought from England. Apparently he had none. He had seen no-one, simply paid his own way out. He won me over by pointing to the boots over his shoulder. He knew he could not get boots big enough for he was over six feet. This was George Orwell and his boots arriving to fight in Spain.

I came to know him as a deeply kind man and a creative writer. . . . He was a satirist who did not conform to any orthodox political or social pattern. . . . The only thing I can be quite certain of is, that up to his last day George was a man of utter integrity; deeply kind, and ready to sacrifice his last worldly possessions – he never had much – in the cause of democratic socialism. Part of his malaise was that he was not only a socialist but profoundly liberal. He hated regimentation wherever he found it, even in the socialist ranks.

[XI, 355A, p. 5]

1.   This advance was for *The Road to Wigan Pier*.

Eileen Blair* to Norah Myles*

[16 February 1937?]
24, Croom's Hill
Greenwich[1]

[*no salutation*]

A note to say that I am leaving for Spain at 9 a.m. tomorrow (or I think so, but with inconceivable grandeur people ring up from Paris about it, and I may not go until Thursday). I leave in a hurry, not because anything is the matter but because when I said that I was going on the 23rd, which has long been my intention, I suddenly became a kind of secretary perhaps to the I.L.P. in Barcelona. They hardly seem to be amused at all. If Franco had engaged me as a manicurist I would have agreed to that too in exchange for a *salvo conducto*,[2] so everyone is satisfied. The I.L.P. in Barcelona consists of one John McNair,*[3] who has certainly been kind at long distances but has an unfortunate telephone voice and a quite calamitous prose style in which he writes articles that I perhaps shall type. But theoretically George gets leave at the end of this month[4] and then I shall have a holiday, willy John nilly John. By the way, I suppose I told you George was in the Spanish Militia? I can't remember. Anyway he is, with my full approval until he was well in. He's on the Aragon front, where I cannot help knowing that the Government ought to be attacking or hoping that that is a sufficient safeguard against their doing so. Supposing that the Fascist air force goes on missing its objectives and the railway line to Barcelona is still working, you'll probably hear from there some day. But letters take 10-15 days as a rule, and if the railway breaks down

I can't think how long they'll take. Meanwhile it would be a nice gesture if you were to write a nice letter yourself, addressing it c/o John McNair, Hotel Continental, Boulevard de las Ramblas, Barcelona.[5] I am staying at the Continental too to begin with, but as we have now spent practically all the money we shall have until November, when the Left book Club wealth will be available,[6] I think I may be doing what the Esperantists call sleeping on straw – and as they are Esperantists they <u>mean</u> sleeping on straw. The I.L.P. of course is not contributing to my support, but the Spanish Government feeds George on bread without butter and 'rather <u>rough</u> food' and has arranged that he doesn't sleep at all, so he has no anxieties.

This is longer than I meant it to be – (that should be a long dash, but you have to move the carriage.) Write the letter, because I think it likely that I may loathe Barcelona, though I'd like to see some of the excitements that won't happen.[7] I don't know of course how long we'll be there. Unless George gets hurt I suppose he'll stay until the war *qua* war is over – and I will too unless I get evacuated by force or unless I have to come and look for some money. But to-day's news suggests that the war may not last very long – I doubt whether Mussolini or even Hitler would feel enthusiastic about trying to push Franco across Catalonia, and certainly they'd need a lot more men to do it.[8]

The dinner gong is going. Is it not touching to think that this may be the last dinner unrationed available for

Pig.

Give everyone my love – even yourself. Eric is lecturing at Bristol,[9] but I think not till May. Hey Groves[10] came to the heart lecture at the College of Surgeons and then invited him to talk to you, but the date isn't settled yet. He has some pretty pictures. I could have come with him – perhaps after all I shall come with him. If you meet Hey Groves tell him to make the date after the war is over.

Could you tell Mary[11] (not urgently) that I simply hadn't time to write separate letters to the two old Oxford Friends – which is simply true.

[*LO*, pp. 68–70; XI, 361A, p. 12; typewritten]

1. The O'Shaughnessy family home in London, SE 10.
2. *salvo conducto:* safe conduct.
3. John McNair* was a Tynesider so his 'unfortunate telephone voice' might have been his Geordie accent, with which Eileen, who came from South Shields, would have been familiar. She was probably being comically ironic.
4. Leave was not given.
5. No such letter survives.
6. It is a common mistake to believe that Orwell was commissioned to go to Wigan

and to write *The Road to Wigan Pier* by the Left Book Club. In fact the Club had not been formed when he left for Wigan and it was not decided by the Club to adopt the book until January 1937, well after Orwell had handed in his manuscript.

7. She tells her mother on 22 March, after her return from the front, 'I'm enjoying Barcelona again', so her worst fears were not realised though she would experience in all their pain the 'May Events' in Barcelona when their Communist 'allies' violently suppressed the POUM.

8. Orwell was shot through the throat (see note preceding **2.7.37**). Communist attacks on the POUM meant they had to leave surreptitiously on 23 June 1937 (with John McNair and the young Stafford Cottman).

9. Eric here is her brother Laurence, called Eric (from his middle name, Frederick) by his family.

10. Ernest William Hey Groves (1872–1944), was a distinguished surgeon specialising in reconstructive surgery of the hip; he developed the use of bone grafts.

11. Bertha Mary Wardell graduated with Eileen. She married Teddy (A.E.F.) Lovett, a Lieutenant in the Royal Navy. He was serving on HMS *Glorious* which, with her two escorting destroyers, *Ardent* and *Acasta*, was sunk off Norway on 8 June 1940, there being only 40 survivors from *Glorious*, two from *Ardent* and one from *Acasta*.

Eileen Blair* to her mother, Marie O'Shaughnessy

22 March 1937
Seccion Inglesa
10 Rambla de los Estudios
Barcelona[1]

Dearest Mummy,

I enclose a 'letter' I began to write to you in the trenches! It ends abruptly—I think I've lost a sheet—& is practically illegible but you may as well have a letter written from a real fighting line, & you'll read enough to get the essential news. I *thoroughly* enjoyed being at the front. If the doctor had been a good doctor I should have moved heaven & earth to stay (indeed before seeing the doctor I had already pushed heaven & earth a little) as a nurse—the line is still so quiet that he could well have trained me in preparation for the activity that must come. But the doctor is quite ignorant & incredibly dirty. They have a tiny hospital at Monflorite in which he dresses the villagers' cut fingers etc. & does emergency work on any war wounds that do occur. Used dressings are thrown out of the window unless the window happens to be shut when they rebound onto the floor—& the doctor's hands have never been known to be washed. So I decided he must have a previously trained assistant (I have one in view—a man). Eric did go to him but he says there is nothing the matter except 'cold, over-fatigue, etc' This of course is quite true. However, the weather is better now & of course the leave is overdue, but another section on the Huesca front made an attack the other day which had rather serious results & leave is stopped there for the moment. Bob Edwards[2] who commands the I.L.P. contingent has to be away for a couple of weeks & Eric is commanding in his absence, which will be quite fun in a way. My visit to the front ended in a suitable way because Kopp* decided I must have 'a few more hours' & arranged a car to leave Monflorite at 3:15 a.m. We went to bed at 10 or so & at 3 Kopp came & shouted & I got up & George[3] (I can't remember which half of the family I write to) went to sleep again I hope. In this way he got 2 nights proper rest & seems much better. The whole visit's unreality was accentuated by the fact that there were *no* lights, not a candle or a torch; one got up & went to bed in black dark, & on the last night I emerged in black dark & waded knee deep in mud in & out of strange buildings until I saw the faint glow from the Comité Militar where Kopp was waiting with his car.

On Tuesday we had the only bombardment of Barcelona since I came. It was quite interesting. Spanish people are normally incredibly noisy & pushing but in a° emergency they appear to go *quiet*. Not that there was any real emergency but the bombs fell closer to the middle of the town than usual & did make enough noise to excite people fairly reasonably. There were very few casualties.

I'm enjoying Barcelona again—I wanted a change. You might send this letter on to Eric & Gwen, whom I thank for *tea*. Three lbs of it has just come & will be much appreciated. The contingent is just running out, Bob Edwards tells me. The other message for Eric is that as usual I am writing this in the last moments before someone leaves for France & also as usual my cheque book is not here, but he will have the cheque for £10 within 2 weeks anyway & meanwhile I should be very grateful if he gave Fenner Brockway[4] the pesetas. (In case anything funny happened to the last letter, I asked him to buy £10 worth of pesetas & give them to Fenner Brockway to be brought out by hand. Living is very cheap here, but I spend a lot on the I.L.P. contingent as none of them have had any pay & they all need things. Also I've lent John [McNair]* 500 ps. because he ran out. I guard my five English pounds, which I could exchange at a fairly decent rate,[5] because I must have something to use when we—whoever we may be—cross the frontier again.)

I hope everyone is well—& I hope for a letter soon to say so. Gwen wrote a long letter which was exciting—even I fall into the universal habit of yearning over England. Perhaps the same thing happens in the colonies. When a waiter lit my cigarette the other day I said he had a nice lighter & he said 'Si, si, es bien, es *Ingles*!' Then he handed it to me, obviously thinking I should like to caress it a little. It was a Dunhill—bought in Barcelona I expect as a matter of fact because there are plenty of Dunhill & other lighters but a shortage of spirit for them. Kopp, Eric's commander, longed for Lea & Perrins° Worcester Sauce. I discovered this by accident & found some in Barcelona—they have Crosse & Blackwell's pickles too but the good English marmalade is finished although the prices of these things are fantastic.

After seeing George I am pretty confident that we shall be home before the winter—& possibly much sooner of course. You might write another letter to the aunt[6] some time. I have *never* heard from her & neither has Eric,[7] which worries me rather. I think she may be very sad about living in Wallington. By the way, George is positively urgent about the gas-stove—he wanted me to write & order it at once, but I still think it would be better to wait until just before our return, particularly as I have not yet heard from Moore about the advance on the book.[8] Which reminds me that the reviews are better than I anticipated, as the interesting ones haven't come through yet.

I had a bath last night—a great excitement. And I've had 3 superb dinners in succession. I don't know whether I shall miss this café life. I have coffee about three times a day & drinks oftener, & although theoretically I eat in a rather grim pension at least six times a week I get headed off into one of about four places where the food is really quite good by any standards though limited of course. Every night I mean to go home early & write letters or something & every night I get home the next morning. The cafés are open till 1.30 & one starts one's after-dinner coffee about 10. But the sherry is *undrinkable*—& I meant to bring home some little casks of it!

Give Maud[9] my love & tell her I'll write some time. And give anyone else my love but I shan't be writing to them. (This letter is to the 3 O'Shaughnesseys[10] who are thus 'you' not 'they'.) It is a dull letter again I think. I shall do this life better justice in conversation—or I hope so.

Much love
Eileen

[XI, 363, pp. 13–15; handwritten]

1. Offices of the POUM journal *The Spanish Revolution*.
2. Robert Edwards (1905–90), unsuccessful Independent Labour Party parliamentary candidate in 1935, was a Labour and Co-operative MP from 1955 to 1987. In January 1937 he was Captain of the ILP contingent in Spain, linked to the POUM. He left Spain at the end of March to attend the ILP conference at Glasgow. In 1926 and 1934 he led delegations to the Soviet Union meeting Trotsky, Stalin and Molotov; was General Secretary of the Chemical Workers' Union, 1947–71; National Officer, Transport and General Workers' Union, 1971–76; and member of the European Parliament, 1977–79. (See *Orwell Remembered*, pp. 146–48, and especially Shelden,

pp. 264–65, which demolishes Edwards's accusation that Orwell went to Spain solely to find material for a book.)

3. Eileen started to write 'Eric' but overwrote 'George.'

4. Fenner Brockway (1888–1988; Lord Brockway, 1964) was General Secretary of the ILP, 1928, 1933–39, and its representative in Spain for a time. A devoted worker for many causes, particularly peace, he resigned from the ILP in 1946 and rejoined the Labour Party, which he represented in Parliament, 1950–64.

5. In a footnote to *Homage to Catalonia* (p. 151), Orwell gives the purchasing value of the peseta as 'about fourpence' in pre-metric currency; 500 pesetas would be about £8 6s 8d – say £320 at today's values.

6. Orwell's aunt Nellie Limouzin, then living at The Stores, Wallington, the Orwells' cottage.

7. Eileen must here mean her husband.

8. *The Road to Wigan Pier*.

9. Possibly an aunt of Eileen's whose second name was Maud.

10. Eileen's mother, her brother, 'Eric' and his wife Gwen.

To Eileen Blair*

[5? April 1937]
[Hospital, Monflorite]

Dearest,

You really are a wonderful wife. When I saw the cigars my heart melted away. They will solve all tobacco problems for a long time to come. McNair* tells me you are all right for money, as you can borrow & then repay when B[ob] E[dwards] brings some pesetas, but don't go beggaring yourself, & above all don't go short of food, tobacco etc. I hate to hear of your having a cold & feeling run down. Don't let them overwork you either, & don't worry about me, as I am much better & expect to go back to the lines tomorrow or the day after. Mercifully the poisoning in my hand didn't spread, & it is now almost well, tho' of course the wound is still open. I can use it fairly well & intend to have a shave today, for the first time in about 5 days. The weather is much better, real spring most of the time, & the look of the earth makes me think of our garden at home & wonder whether the wallflowers are coming out & whether old Hatchett[1] is sowing the potatoes. Yes, Pollitt's review[2] was pretty bad, tho' of course good as publicity. I suppose he must have heard I was serving in the POUM militia. I don't pay much attention to the *Sunday Times* reviews[3] as G[ollancz] advertises so much there that they daren't down his books, but the *Observer* was an improvement on last time. I told McNair that when I came on leave I would do the *New Leader* an article, as they wanted one, but it will be such a come-down after B.E's that I don't expect they'll print it. I'm afraid it is not much use expecting leave before about the 20th April. This is rather annoying in my own case as it comes about through my having exchanged from one unit to another—a lot of the men I came to the front with are now going on leave. If they suggested that I should go on leave earlier I don't think I would say no, but they are not likely to & I am not going to press them. There are also some indications—I don't know how much one can rely on these—that they expect an action hereabouts, & I am not going on leave just before that comes off if I can help it. Everyone has been very good to me while I have been in hospital, visiting me every day etc. I think now that the weather is getting better I can stick out another month without getting ill, & then what a rest we will have, & go fishing too if it is in any way possible.

As I write this Michael, Parker & Buttonshaw⁴ have just come in, & you should have seen their faces when they saw the margarine. As to the photos, of course there are lots of people who want copies, & I have written the numbers wanted on the backs, & perhaps you can get reproductions. I suppose it doesn't cost too much—I shouldn't like to disappoint the Spanish machine-gunners etc. Of course some of the photos were a mess. The one which has Buttonshaw looking very blurred in the foreground is a photo of a shell-burst, which you can see rather faintly on the left, just beyond the house.

I shall have to stop in a moment, as I am not certain when McNair is going back & I want to have this letter ready for him. Thanks ever so much for sending the things, dear, & do keep well & happy.⁵ I told McNair I would have a talk with him about the situation when I came on leave, & you might at some opportune moment say something to him about my wanting to go to Madrid etc. Goodbye, love. I'll write again soon.

With all my love
Eric

[XI, 364, pp. 15–17; handwritten]

1. Old Hatchett was a neighbour at Wallington who often helped Orwell in his garden.
2. Harry Pollitt (1890–1960), a Lancashire boiler-maker and founder-member of the Communist Party of Great Britain in 1920, became its general secretary in 1929. With Rajani Palme Dutt (1896–1974, expelled from Oxford in 1917 for disseminating Marxist propaganda; member of the Executive Committee of the Communist Party and from 1936–38 editor of the *Daily Worker*) he led the party until his death. He was, however, removed from leadership in the autumn of 1939 until Germany's invasion of Russia in July 1941 for his temporary advocacy of a war of democracy

against fascism. His review of *The Road to Wigan Pier* appeared in the *Daily Worker*, 17 March 1937.

3. *The Road to Wigan Pier* was reviewed by Edward Shanks in the *Sunday Times* and by Hugh Massingham in the *Observer*, 14 March 1937.

4. Michael Wilton (English), also given as Milton, Buck Parker (South African), and Buttonshaw (American) were members of Orwell's unit. Douglas Moyle, another member, told Ian Angus, 18 February 1970, that Buttonshaw was very sympathetic to the European left and regarded Orwell as 'the typical Englishman—tall, carried himself well, well educated and well spoken'.

5. Orwell would not have realised the irony in his use of 'happy'. Sir Richard Rees wrote in his *For Love or Money* (1960), p. 153, of the strain of Eileen's experience in Barcelona: 'In Eileen Blair I had seen for the first time the symptoms of a human being living under a political Terror.'

Eileen Blair* to Dr Laurence ('Eric') O'Shaughnessy*

1 May 1937
10 Rambla de los Estudios
Barcelona

Dear Eric,

You have a hard life. I mean to write to Mother with the news, but there are some business matters. Now I think of these, they're inextricably connected with the news so Mother must share this letter.

George is here on leave. He arrived completely ragged, almost barefoot, a little lousy, dark brown, & looking really very well. For the previous 12 hours he had been in trains consuming anis, muscatel out of anis bottles, sardines & chocolate. In Barcelona food is plentiful at the moment but there is nothing plain. So it is not surprising that he ceased to be well. Now after two days in bed he is really cured but still persuadable so having a 'quiet day'. This is the day to have on May 1st. They were asked to report at the barracks, but he isn't well enough & has already applied for his discharge papers so he hasn't gone. The rest of the contingent never thought of going. When the discharge is through he will probably join the International Brigade.[1] Of course we—perhaps particularly I—are politically suspect but we told all the truth to the I.B. man here & he was so shattered that he was practically offering me executive jobs by the end of half an hour, & I gather that they will take George. Of course I must leave Barcelona but I should do that in any case as to stay would be pointless. Madrid is probably closed to me, so it means Valencia for the moment with Madrid & Albacete in view but at long distance. To join the I.B. with George's history is strange but it is what he thought he was doing in the first place & it's the only way of getting to Madrid. So there it is. Out of this arises a further money crisis because when I leave Barcelona I shall leave all my affiliations—& my address & even my credit at the bank; & it will take a little time to get connected again perhaps. Meanwhile we spend immense sums of money for Spain on new equipment etc. I did write to you about getting money through banks—i.e. your bank buys pesetas with your pounds & instructs a bank in Barcelona to pay me the number of pesetas you bought. If this can be done will you do it (about another 2000 pesetas I should think), & will you ask the bank to cable. Probably I shall be here for a couple of weeks but I'm not *sure* where I shall go next & I want if possible to have some money in hand before leaving. If the bank business can't be done I frankly don't know what can—i.e. I must use the credit at 60 to the £. before leaving here & find some method of getting money through my new friends, whoever they may be (I have met the *Times* correspondent at Valencia).

The other business is the cottage. I gather & hear from Mrs Blair that the aunt is not only tiring but tired, & I have written to her suggesting evacuation with all the arrangements under headings. You take over in a manner of speaking. If she shows you the letter it may alarm you, but twenty minutes will settle most of the problems. There are several things to be paid, but they're all matters of shillings & the shop may have—should have—a few pounds in hand. The shop will be closed. I've said you can buy any perishables. It is not of course suggested that you should *pay* for these, except in the aunt's eyes, but she will never give anything away so you might dump doubtful stuff in the car & dispose of it anyhow you like. If Mother is at Greenwich she might perhaps go over *after* the aunt is out & see that there is nothing to attract *mice*. There is a chance that Arthur Clinton,[2] who was wounded, may go & recuperate in the cottage. He is perhaps the nicest man in the world & I hope he may be able to use it. He'll return to England unfit, ineligible for dole & penniless. If he wants the cottage he'll ask you about it of course.

We shall owe you money. We *have* money in our sense of the word, but I haven't much fancy for sending cheques if they get lost in the post.

I must take this to the office now—one of the contingent is going home tomorrow & will take it. I have in progress an immense letter to mother, started two or three weeks ago, which will arrive in due course. I am very well.

About the L.C.C. pay I fully agree that there must be no *sessional* payment—it is a vicious system.[3]

My love to Gwen. By the way, I gather from the correspondence that she isn't coming. If this is wrong & she is coming of course I'll wait in Barcelona.

Yours
Eileen.

For the bank's information my name is Eileen Maud Blair & my passport number 174234.

I really am sorry for you—but what can I do?

[XI, 367, pp.20–2; handwritten]

1. The International Brigade was composed of foreign volunteers, mostly Communist, and played an important part in the defence of Madrid. Its headquarters was at Albacete where the Brigade's prison was sited. George Woodcock commented that Orwell 'would not long have survived the attention of Marty's political commissars if he had joined the International Brigade'. André Marty (1886–1956) a leading member of the French Communist Party, was known as Le Boucher d'Albacete. He claimed to have executed some 500 brigaders – and there were slightly fewer than 60,000 foreigners in the International Brigade.

2. A member of the ILP contingent. He was with Orwell in the Sanatorium Maurín (see *Homage to Catalonia*, VI, p. 153).

3. Eileen was objecting to payment by the London County Council of a fee for each session worked instead of at an annual rate. If one was booked for a session but not required, time had been set aside for no financial recompense.

To Victor Gollancz*

9 May 1937
Hotel Continental
Barcelona

Dear Mr Gollancz,

I didn't get an opportunity earlier to write & thank you for the introduction you wrote to *Wigan Pier*, in fact I didn't even see the book, or rather the L[eft] B[ook] C[lub] edition of it, till about 10 days ago when I came on leave, & since then I have been rather occupied. I spent my first week of leave in being slightly ill, then there was° 3 or 4 days of street-fighting in which we were all more or less involved, in fact it was practically impossible to keep out of it. I liked the introduction very much, though of course I could have answered some of the criticisms you made. It was the kind of discussion of what one is really talking about that one always wants & never seems to get from the professional reviewers. I have had a lot of reviews sent on to me, some of them very hostile but I should think mostly good from a publicity point of view. Also great numbers of letters from readers.

I shall be going back to the front probably in a few days & barring accidents I expect to be there till about August. After that I think I shall come home, as it will be about time I started on another book. I greatly hope I come out of this alive if only to write a book about it. It is not easy here to get hold of any facts outside the circle of one's own experience, but with that limitation I have seen a great deal that is of immense interest to me. Owing partly to an accident I joined the P.O.U.M. militia instead of the International Brigade, which was a pity in one way because it meant that I have never seen the Madrid front; on the other hand it has brought me into contact with Spaniards rather than Englishmen & especially with genuine revolutionaries. I hope I shall get a chance to write the truth about what I have seen. The stuff appearing in the English papers is largely the most appalling lies—more I can't say, owing to the censorship. If I can get back in August I hope to have a book ready for you about the beginning of next year.

Yours sincerely,
Eric A. Blair

[XI, 368, pp. 22–3; handwritten]

Orwell was shot through the throat by a sniper at 5.00 a.m. on 20 May 1937. He discusses the incident in Homage to Catalonia, *VI, pp. 137–39. Eileen sent a telegram from Barcelona at noon on 24 May 1937 to Orwell's parents in Southwold. This read: 'Eric slightly wounded progress excellent sends love no need for anxiety Eileen.' This reached Southwold just after 2.00 p.m. Orwell's commandant, George Kopp,* wrote a report on his condition on 31 May and 1 June 1937. When this report was lost, Kopp wrote another, for Dr Laurence O'Shaughnessy, Orwell's brother-in-law, dated 'Barcelona, the 10*[th]* of June 1937'. It differs slightly from the version given in* Orwell Remembered, *pp. 158–61. Kopp illustrated his report with a drawing of the bullet's path through Orwell's throat:*

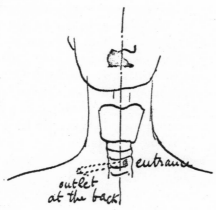

Bert Govaerts, who uncovered details of Kopp's life, suggests that this shows his training in engineering drawing. (See XI, 369, pp. 23–6.)

To Sergei Dinamov,* Editor, *International Literature*, Moscow

Professor Arlen Blyum of the St Petersburg Academy of Culture, in 'An English Writer in the Land of the Bolsheviks' (The Library, December 2003) records the fascinating exchange of letters between Dinamov and Orwell. International Literature *was allowed considerable leeway and introduced such writers as John Steinbeck, Ernest Hemingway, Thomas Mann, and John Dos Passos to its readers, so creating 'a favourable image of the Land of the Soviets'. The editor wrote to Orwell on 31 May 1937 saying he had read reviews of* The Road to Wigan Pier *and asked for a copy so that it could be introduced to the journal's readers. This is Orwell's reply, found in the Russian State Archive of Literature and Art.*

2 July 1937
The Stores
Wallington

Dear Comrade,

I am sorry not to have answered earlier your letter dated May 31st, but I have only just got back from Spain and my letters have been kept for me here, rather luckily, as otherwise some of them might have been lost. I am sending separately a copy of *The Road to Wigan Pier*. I hope parts of it may interest you. I ought to tell you that parts of the second half deal with subjects that may seem rather trivial outside England. I was preoccupied with them at the time of writing, but my experiences in Spain have made me reconsider many of my opinions.

I have still not quite recovered from the wound I got in Spain, but when I am up to writing again I will try and write something for you, as you suggested in your earlier letter. I would like to be frank with you, however, and therefore I must tell you that in Spain I was serving in the militia of the P.O.U.M., which as you know° doubt know, has been bitterly denounced by the Communist Party and was recently suppressed by the Government; also that after what I have seen I am more in agreement with the policy of the P.O.U.M. than with that of the Communist Party. I tell you this because it may be that your paper would not care to have contributions from a P.O.U.M. member[1], and I do not wish to introduce myself to you under false pretences.

The above is my permanent address.

Yours fraternally,
George Orwell

[*LO*, pp. 99–100; XI, 374B, p. 37; typewritten]

1.   The journal responded that Orwell's association with the POUM ensured that *International Literature* could 'have no relations' with him (XI, 362, p. 12).

To Rayner Heppenstall*

31 July 1937
The Stores
Wallington

Dear Rayner,

Thanks so much for your letter. I was glad to hear from you. I hope Margaret[1] is better. It sounds dreadful, but from what you say I gather that she is at any rate up and about.

We had an interesting but thoroughly bloody time in Spain. Of course I would never have allowed Eileen to come nor probably gone myself if I had foreseen the political developments, especially the suppression of the P.O.U.M., the party in whose militia I was serving. It was a queer business. We started off by being heroic defenders of democracy and ended by slipping over the border with the police panting on our heels[2] Eileen was wonderful, in fact actually seemed to enjoy it. But though we ourselves got out all right nearly all our friends and acquaintances are in jail and likely to be there indefinitely, not actually charged with anything but suspected of 'Trotskyism.' The most terrible things were happening even when I left, wholesale arrests, wounded men dragged out of hospitals and thrown into jail, people crammed together in filthy dens where they have hardly room to lie down, prisoners beaten and half starved etc., etc. Meanwhile it is impossible to get a word about this mentioned in the English press, barring the publications of the I.L.P., which is affiliated to the P.O.U.M. I had a most amusing time with the *New Statesman* about it. As soon as I got out of Spain I wired from France asking if they would like an article and of course they said yes, but when they saw my article was on the suppression of the P.O.U.M. they said they couldn't print it. To sugar the pill they sent me to review a very good book which appeared recently, *The Spanish Cockpit*,[3] which blows the gaff pretty well on what has been happening. But once again when they saw my review they couldn't print it as it was 'against editorial policy,' but they actually offered to pay for the review all the same— practically hush-money. I am also having to change my publisher, at least for this book.[4] Gollancz is of course part of the Communism-racket, and as soon as he heard I had been associated with the P.O.U.M. and Anarchists and had seen the inside of the May riots in Barcelona, he said he did not think he would be able to publish my book, though not a word of it was written yet. I think he must have very astutely foreseen that something of the kind would happen, as when I went to Spain he drew up a contract undertaking to publish my fiction but not other books. However I have two other publishers on my track and I think my agent is being clever and has got them bidding against one another. I have started my book but of course my fingers are all thumbs at present.

My wound was not much, but it was a miracle it did not kill me. The bullet went clean through my neck but missed everything except one vocal cord, or rather the nerve governing it, which is paralysed. At first I had no voice at all, but now the other vocal cord is compensating and the damaged one may or may not recover. My voice is practically normal but I can't shout to any extent. I also can't sing, but people tell me this doesn't matter. I am rather glad to have been hit by a bullet because I think it will happen to us all in the near future and I am glad to know that it doesn't hurt to speak of. What I saw in Spain did not make me cynical but it does make me think that the future is pretty grim. It is evident that people can be deceived by the anti-Fascist stuff exactly as they were deceived by the gallant little Belgium stuff, and when war comes they will walk straight into it. I don't, however, agree with the pacifist attitude, as I believe you do. I still think one must fight for Socialism and against Fascism, I mean fight physically with weapons, only it is as well to discover which is which. I want to meet Holdaway⁵ and see what he thinks about the Spanish business. He is the only more or less orthodox Communist I have met whom I could respect. It will disgust me if I find he is spouting the same defence of democracy and Trotsky-Fascist stuff as the others.

I would much like to see you, but I honestly don't think I shall be in London for some time, unless absolutely obliged to go up on business. I am just getting going with my book, which I want to get done by Xmas, also very busy trying to get the garden etc. in trim after being so long away. Anyway keep in touch and let me know your address. I can't get in touch with Rees*. He was on the Madrid front and there was practically no communication. I heard from Murry* who seemed in the weeps about something. *Au revoir.*

Yours
Eric

[XI, 381, pp. 53–4; typewritten]

1. Mrs Rayner Heppenstall.
2. In *Homage to Catalonia*, Orwell tells how his hotel room was searched by six plain-clothes policemen, who took away 'every scrap of paper we possessed', except, fortunately, Eileen's and his passports and their cheque-book. He learned later that the police had seized some of his belongings, including a bundle of dirty linen, from the Sanatorium Maurín (see VI, p. 164). More than fifty years later, a

document was discovered by Karen Hatherley in the National Historical Archive, in Madrid, that precisely confirmed this (XI, 374A, pp. 30–7).

3.   Orwell's review of *The Spanish Cockpit* by Franz Borkenau appears in XI, 379, pp. 51–2. When reviewing his *The Communist International* in 1938 he wrote that he still thought the former 'the best book on the subject'. Dr Borkenau (1900–57) was an Austrian sociologist and political writer. From 1921–29 he was a member of the German Communist Party. He emigrated to Britain in 1933 when the Nazis came to power. Orwell greatly admired him and his work.

4.   *Homage to Catalonia.*

5.   N.A. Holdaway was a schoolmaster and Marxist theorist, a member of the Independent Socialist Party, contributor to *The Adelphi*, and Director of the Adelphi Centre.

To Charles Doran*

2 August 1937
The Stores
Wallington

Dear Doran,

I don't know your address, but I expect they will know it at the I.L.P. summer school, where I am going on Thursday. I was also there yesterday, to hear John McNair* speak.

I was very relieved when I saw young Jock Branthwaite,[1] who has been staying with us, and learned that all of you who wished to had got safely out of Spain. I came up to the front on June 15th to get my medical discharge, but couldn't come up to the line to see you because they kept sending me about from hospital to hospital. I got back to Barcelona to find that the P.O.U.M. had been suppressed in my absence, and they had kept it from the troops so successfully that on June 20th as far down the line as Lérida not a soul had heard about it, though the suppression had taken place on the 16th–17th. My first intimation was walking into the Hotel Continental and having Eileen and a Frenchman named Pivert,[2] who was a very good friend to everyone during the trouble, rush up to me, seize me each by one arm and tell me to get out. Kopp* had just recently been arrested in the Continental owing to the staff ringing up the police and giving him away. MacNair°, Cottman* and I had to spend several days on the run, sleeping in ruined churches etc., but Eileen stayed in the hotel and, beyond having her room searched and all my documents seized, was not molested, possibly because the police were using her as a decoy duck for MacNair° and me. We slipped away very suddenly on the morning of the 23rd, and crossed the frontier without much difficulty. Luckily there was a first class and a dining car on the train, and we did our best to look like ordinary English tourists, which was the safest thing to do. In Barcelona one was fairly safe during the daytime, and Eileen and I visited Kopp several times in the filthy den where he and scores of others, including Milton,[3] were imprisoned. The police had actually gone to the length of arresting the wounded P.O.U.M. men out of the Maurín [Hospital], and I saw two men in the jail with amputated legs; also a boy of about ten. A few days ago we got some letters, dated July 7th, which Kopp* had somehow managed to send out of Spain. They included a letter of protest to the Chief of Police. He said that not only had he and all the others been imprisoned for 18 days (much longer now, of course) without any trial or charge, but that they were being confined in places where they had hardly room to lie down, were half starved and in many cases beaten and insulted. We sent the letter on to McNair, and I believe after discussing the matter Maxton[4] has arranged to see the Spanish ambassador and tell him that if something is not done, at any rate for the foreign prisoners, he will spill the beans in Parliament. McNair also tells me that there is a credible report in the French papers that the body of Nin,[5] also I think other P.O.U.M. leaders, has been found shot in Madrid. I suppose it will be 'suicide,' or perhaps appendicitis again.[6]

Meanwhile it seems almost impossible to get anything printed about all this . . . [Here Orwell repeats what he had written to Rayner Heppenstall* on **31 July 1937** about the reactions of the *New Statesman* and Gollancz.*]

I went up to Bristol with some others to take part in a protest meeting about Stafford Cottman* being expelled from the Y.C.L.[7] with the words 'we brand him as an enemy of the working class' and similar expressions. Since then I heard that the Cottmans' house had been shadowed by members of the Y.C.L. who attempt to question everyone who comes in and out. What a show! To think that we started off as heroic defenders of democracy and only six months later were Trotsky-Fascists sneaking over the border with the police on our heels. Meanwhile being a Trotsky-Fascist doesn't seem to help us with the pro-Fascists in this country. This afternoon Eileen and I had a visit from the vicar, who doesn't at all approve of our having been on the Government side. Of course we had to own up that it was true about the burning of the churches, but he cheered up a lot on hearing they were only Roman Catholic churches.

Let me know how you get on. Eileen wishes to be remembered.

Yours
Eric Blair

P.S. [*handwritten*] I forgot to say that when in Barcelona I wanted greatly to write to you all & warn you, but I dared not, because I thought any such letter would simply draw undesirable attention to the man it was addressed to.

[XI, 386, pp. 64–6; typewritten]

1. Jock Branthwaite (d. 1997) was the son of a miner. He served with Orwell in Spain. He remembered copies of *The Road to Wigan Pier* arriving at the Front and said the book did not offend his working-class sensibilities. He told Stephen Wadhams that Orwell was not a snob: 'I thought he was a wonderful man.' He got out of Spain on the last refugee boat from Barcelona to Marseilles. (See *Remembering Orwell*, pp. 83–4, 93, 99.)

2. Marceau Pivert was a contributor to *Controversy*.

3. Harry Milton was the only American serving with Orwell's unit. He and Orwell were talking when Orwell was shot through the throat (*Homage to Catalonia*, p. 138). He was Trotskyist and regarded Orwell as 'politically virginal' on arrival in Spain. They spent hours together discussing politics. Orwell was 'as cool as a cucumber' and 'a very disciplined individual' (see *Remembering Orwell*, pp. 81, 85, 90).

4. James Maxton (1885–1946), Independent Labour Party MP, 1922–46; Chairman of the ILP, 1926–31, 1934–39.

5. Andrés Nin (1892–1937), leader of the POUM; he had once been Trotsky's private secretary in Moscow, but broke with him when Trotsky spoke critically of the POUM. He was murdered by the Communists after the customary Soviet interrogation in May 1937. (See Thomas, p. 523.)

6. This refers to Bob Smillie, thrown into jail in Valencia where according to his captors he died of appendicitis. (See *Homage to Catalonia*, p. 149.)

7. Young Communist League.

Orwell and The Road to Wigan Pier *were subjected to vicious attacks by Communists and the extreme Left Press. Ruth Dudley Edwards describes Orwell as being 'blackguarded' by Harry Pollitt, leader of the Communist Party of Great Britain in the* Daily Worker, *17 March 1937 (Victor Gollancz (1987), p. 248). Pollitt wrote: 'Here is George Orwell, a disillusioned little middle-class boy who, seeing through imperialism, decided to discover what Socialism had to offer . . . a late imperialist policeman . . . . If ever snobbery had its hallmark placed upon it, it is by Mr Orwell. . . . I gather that the chief thing that worries Mr Orwell is the "smell" of the working-class, for smells seem to occupy the major portion of the book. . . . One thing I am certain of, and it is this – if Mr Orwell could only hear what the Left Book Club circles will say about this book, then he would make a resolution never to write again on any subject that he does not understand.' Attacks on Orwell continued during the summer and finally Orwell sought Gollancz's help.*

To Victor Gollancz*

20 August 1937
The Stores
Wallington

Dear Mr Gollancz,

I do not expect you will have seen the enclosed cutting, as it does not refer to anything you published for me.

This (see underlined words) is the—I think—third reference in the *Daily Worker* to my supposedly saying that the working classes 'smell.' As you know I have never said anything of the kind, in fact have specifically said the opposite. What I said in Chapter VIII of *Wigan Pier*, as you may perhaps remember, is that middle-class people are brought up to *believe* that the working classes 'smell,' which is simply a matter of observable fact. Numbers of the letters I received from readers of the book referred to this and congratulated me on pointing it out. The statement or implication that I think working people 'smell' is a deliberate lie aimed at people who have not read this or any other of my books, in order to give them the idea that I am a vulgar snob and thus indirectly hit at the political parties with which I have been associated. These attacks in the *Worker* only began after it became known to the Communist Party that I was serving with the P.O.U.M. militia.

I have no connection with these people (the *Worker* staff) and nothing I said would carry any weight with them, but you of course are in a different position. I am very sorry to trouble you about what is more or less my own personal affair, but I think perhaps it might be worth your while to intervene and stop attacks of this kind which will not, of course, do any good to the books you have published for me or may publish for me in the future. If therefore at any time you happen to be in touch with anyone in authority on the *Worker* staff, I should be very greatly obliged if you would tell them two things:

1. That if they repeat this lie about my saying the working classes 'smell' I shall publish a reply with the necessary quotations, and in it I shall include what John Strachey[1] said to me on the subject just before I left for Spain (about December 20th). Strachey will no doubt remember it, and I don't think the C.P. would care to see it in print.

2. This is a more serious matter. A campaign of organised libel is going on against people who were serving with the P.O.U.M. in Spain. A comrade of mine, a boy of eighteen whom I knew in the line,[2] was recently not only expelled from his branch of the Y.C.L. for his association with the P.O.U.M., which was perhaps justifiable as the P.O.U.M. and C.P. policies are quite

incompatible, but was also described in a letter as 'in the pay of Franco.' This latter statement is quite a different matter. I don't know whether it is libellous within the meaning of the act, but I am taking counsel's opinion, as, of course, the same thing (ie. that I am in Fascist pay) is liable to be said about myself. Perhaps again, if you are speaking to anyone in authoritative position, you could tell them that in the case of anything actionable being said against me, I shall not hesitate to take a libel action immediately. I hate to take up this threatening attitude, and I should hate still more to be involved in litigation, especially against members of another working-class party, but I think one has a right to defend oneself against these malignant personal attacks which, even if it is really the case that the C.P. is entirely right and the P.O.U.M. and I.L.P. entirely wrong, cannot in the long run do any good to the working-class cause. You see here (second passage underlined) the implied suggestion that I did not 'pull my weight' in the fight against the Fascists. From this it is only a short step to calling me a coward, a shirker etc., and I do not doubt these people would do so if they thought it was safe.

I am extremely sorry to put this kind of thing upon you, and I shall understand and not be in any way offended if you do not feel you can do anything about it.[3] But I have ventured to approach you because you are my publisher and may, perhaps, feel that your good name is to some extent involved with mine.

Yours sincerely
Eric Blair

[X, 390, pp.72–4; typewritten]

1. John Strachey (1901–63), political theorist, Labour MP, 1929–31, then stood unsuccessfully for Parliament for Oswald Mosley's New Party (of Fascist inclination), then supported Communism. He was Labour Minister of Food, 1945–50 and Secretary of State for War, 1950–51.
2. Stafford Cottman.*
3. Gollancz told Orwell he was passing his letter on 'to the proper quarter'. That proved to be the Communist Party's offices in King Street, London. To Pollitt, he wrote, 'My dear Harry, you should see this letter from Orwell. I read it to John [Strachey] over the telephone and he assures me that he is quite certain that he said nothing whatever indiscreet.' What Strachey said is not known. However, the attacks did, for the moment, cease.

To Geoffrey Gorer*

15 September 1937
The Stores
Wallington

Dear Geoffrey,

Thanks so much for your letter. I am glad you are enjoying yourself in Denmark, though, I must admit, it is one of the few countries I have never wanted to visit. I rang you up when I was in town, but of course you weren't there. I note you are coming back about the 24th. We shall be here till the 10th October, then we are going down to Suffolk to stay at my parents' place for some weeks. But if you can manage it any time between the 24th and the 10th, just drop us a line and then come down and stay. We can always put you up without difficulty.

What you say about not letting the Fascists in owing to dissensions between ourselves is very true so long as one is clear what one means by Fascism, also who or what it is that is making unity impossible. Of course all the Popular Front stuff that is now being pushed by the Communist press and party, Gollancz and his paid hacks etc., etc., only boils down to saying that they are in favour of British Fascism (prospective) as against German Fascism. What they are aiming to do is to get British capitalist-imperialism into an alliance with the U.S.S.R. and thence into a war with Germany. Of course they piously pretend that they don't want the war to come and that a French-British-Russian alliance can prevent it on the old balance of power system. But we know what the balance of power business led to last time, and in any case it is manifest that the nations are arming with the intention of fighting. The Popular Front boloney boils down to this: that when the war comes the Communists, labourites etc., instead of working to stop the war and overthrow the Government, will be on the side of the Government provided that the Government is on the 'right' side, ie. against Germany. But everyone with any imagination can foresee that Fascism, not of course called Fascism, will be imposed on us as soon as the war starts. So you will have Fascism with Communists participating in it, and, if we are in alliance with the U.S.S.R., taking a leading part in it. This is what has happened in Spain. After what I have seen in Spain I have come to the conclusion that it is futile to be 'anti-Fascist' while attempting to preserve capitalism. Fascism after all is only a development of capitalism, and the mildest democracy, so-called, is liable to turn into Fascism when the pinch comes. We like to think of England as a democratic country, but our rule in India, for instance, is just as bad as German Fascism, though outwardly it may be less irritating. I do not see how one can oppose Fascism except by working for the overthrow of capitalism, starting, of course, in one's own country. If one collaborates with a capitalist-imperialist government in a struggle 'against Fascism,' ie. against a rival imperialism, one is simply letting Fascism in by the back door. The whole struggle in Spain, on the Government side, has turned upon this. The revolutionary parties, the Anarchists, P.O.U.M. etc., wanted to complete the revolution, the others wanted to fight the Fascists in the name of 'democracy,' and, of course, when they felt sure enough of their position and had tricked the workers into giving up their arms, re-introduce capitalism. The grotesque feature, which very few people outside Spain have yet grasped, is that the Communists stood furthest of all to the right, and were more anxious even than the liberals to hunt down the revolutionaries and stamp out all revolutionary ideas. For instance, they have succeeded in breaking up the workers' militias, which were based on the trade unions and in which all ranks received the same pay and were on a basis of equality, and substituting an army on bourgeois lines where a colonel is paid eight times as much as a private etc. All these changes, of course, are put forward in the name of military necessity and backed up by the 'Trotskyist' racket, which consists of saying that anyone who professes revolutionary principles is a Trotskyist and in Fascist pay. The Spanish Communist press has for instance declared that Maxton is in the pay of the Gestapo. The reason why so few people grasp what has happened in Spain is because of the Communist command of the press. Apart from their own press they have the whole of the capitalist anti-Fascist press (papers like the *News Chronicle*) on their side, because the latter have got onto the fact that official Communism is now anti-revolutionary. The result is that they have been able to put across an unprecedented amount of lies and it is almost impossible to get anyone to print anything in contradiction. The accounts of the Barcelona riots in May, which I had the misfortune to be involved in, beat everything I have ever seen for lying. Incidentally the *Daily Worker* has been following me personally with the most filthy libels, calling me pro-Fascist etc., but I asked Gollancz to silence them, which he did, not very willingly I imagine. Queerly enough I am still contracted to write a number of books for him, though he refused to publish the book I am doing on Spain before a word of it was written.

I should like to meet Edith Sitwell[1] very much, some time when I am in town. It surprised me very much to learn that she had heard of me and liked my books. I don't know what° I ever cared much for her poems, but I liked very much her life of Pope.

Try and come down here some time. I hope your sprue[2] is gone.

Yours
Eric

[XI, 397, pp. 80–81; typewritten]

1. Edith Sitwell (1887–1964; DBE, 1954), poet and literary personality. Her first book of poems was published at her own expense in 1915, and she continued to write throughout her life. She achieved lasting and widespread recognition for *Façade*, which was read in a concert version, with music by William Walton, in January 1922. She encouraged many young artists and was greatly interested in Orwell's work. Her *Alexander Pope* was published in 1930.

2. Here, a throat infection.

To H. N. Brailsford*

10 December 1937
The Stores
Wallington

Dear Mr Brailsford,

I cannot exactly claim your acquaintance, though I believe I did meet you for a moment in Barcelona, and I know you met my wife there.

I have been trying to get the truth about certain aspects of the May fighting in Barcelona. I see that in the *New Statesman* of May 22nd you state that the P.O.U.M. partisans attacked the Government with tanks and guns 'stolen from Government arsenals.' I was, of course, in Barcelona throughout the fighting, and though I cannot answer for tanks I know as well as one can be certain about such a thing that no guns were firing anywhere. In various papers there occurs a version of what is evidently the same story, to the effect that the P.O.U.M. were using a battery of stolen 75 mm. guns on the Plaza de España. I know this story to be untrue for a number of reasons. To begin with, I have it from eye-witnesses who were on the spot that there were no guns there; secondly, I examined the buildings round the square afterwards and there were no signs of gunfire; thirdly, throughout the fighting I did not hear the sound of artillery, which is unmistakeable if one is used to it. It would seem therefore that there has been a mistake. I wonder if you could be kind enough to tell me what was the source of the story about the guns and tanks? I am sorry to trouble you, but I want to get this story cleared up if I can.

Perhaps I ought to tell you that I write under the name of George Orwell.

Yours truly
Eric Blair

[XX, 413A, pp. 309–10; typewritten]

To H. N. Brailsford*

18 December 1937
The Stores
Wallington

Dear Mr Brailsford,

Thank you very much for your letter.[1] I was very interested to know the source of the story about tanks and guns. I have no doubt the Russian ambassador told it you in good faith and from what little I know myself I should think it quite likely it was true in the form in which he gave it you. But because of the special circumstances, incidents of that kind are apt to be a little misleading. I hope it will not bore you if I add one or two more remarks about this question.

As I say, it is quite conceivable that at some time or other the guns *were* stolen, because to my own knowledge, though I never actually saw it done, there was a great deal of stealing of weapons from one militia to another. But people who were not actually in the militia do not seem to have understood the arms situation. As far as possible arms were prevented from getting to the P.O.U.M. and Anarchist militias, and they were left only with the bare minimum that would enable them to hold the line but not to make any offensive action. There were times when the men in the trenches actually had not enough rifles to go round, and at no time until the militias were broken up was artillery allowed to get to the Aragon front in any quantity. When the Anarchists made their attacks on the Jaca road in March–April they had to do so with very little artillery support and had frightful casualties. At this time (March–April) there were only about 12 of our aeroplanes operating over Huesca. When the Popular Army attacked in June a man who took part in the attack tells me that there were 160. In particular, the Russian arms were kept from the Aragon front at the time when they were being issued to the police forces in the rear. Until April I saw only one Russian weapon, a submachine gun, which quite possibly had been stolen. In April two batteries of Russian 75 mm. guns arrived—again possibly stolen and conceivably the guns referred to by the Russian ambassador. As to pistols and revolvers, which are very necessary in trench warfare, the Government would not issue permits to ordinary militiamen and militia officers to buy them, and one could only buy them illegally from the Anarchists. In these circumstances the outlook everyone had was that one had to get hold of weapons by hook or by crook, and all the militias were constantly pilfering them from one another. I remember an officer describing to me how he and some others had stolen a field gun from a gun-park belonging to the P.S.U.C.,[2] and I would have done the same myself without any hesitation in the circumstances. This kind of thing always goes on in war-time, but, coming together with the newspaper stories to the effect that the P.O.U.M. was a disguised Fascist organisation, it was easy to suggest that they stole weapons not to use against the Fascists but to use against the Government. Owing to the Communist control of the press the similar behaviour by other units was kept dark. For instance there is not much doubt that in March some partisans of the P.S.U.C. stole 12 tanks from a Government arsenal by means of a forged order. *La Battalia*, the P.O.U.M. paper, was fined 5000 pesetas and suppressed for 4 days for reporting this, but the Anarchist paper, *Solidaridad Obrera*, was able to report it with impunity. As to the guns, if stolen, being kept in Barcelona, it seems to me immensely unlikely. Some of the men at the front would certainly have heard of it and would have raised hell if they had known weapons were being kept back, and I should doubt if you could keep two batteries of guns concealed even in a town the size of Barcelona. In any case they would have come to light later, when the P.O.U.M. was suppressed. I do not, of course, know what was in all the P.O.U.M. strongholds, but I was in the three principle° ones during the Barcelona fighting, and I know that they had only enough weapons for the usual armed guards that were kept on buildings. They had no machine guns, for instance. And I think it is certain that there was no artillery-fire during the fighting. I see that you refer to the Friends of Durruti[3] being more or less under P.O.U.M. control, and John Langdon-Davies[4] says something to the same effect in his report in the *News Chronicle*. This story was only put about in order to brand the P.O.U.M. as 'Trotskyist.' Actually the Friends of Durruti, which was an extremist organisation, was bitterly hostile to the P.O.U.M. (from their point of view a more or less right-wing organisation) and so far as I know no one was a member of both. The only connection between the two is that at the time of the May fighting the P.O.U.M. are said to have published approval of an inflammatory poster which was put up by the Friends of Durruti. Again there is some doubt about this—it is certain that there was no *poster*, as described in the *News Chronicle* and elsewhere, but there may have been a handbill of some kind. It is impossible to discover, as all records have been destroyed and the Spanish authorities would not allow me to send out of Spain files even of the P.S.U.C. newspapers, let alone the others. The only sure thing is that the Communist reports on the May fighting, and still more on the alleged Fascist plot by the P.O.U.M., are completely untruthful. What worries me is not these lies being told, which is what one expects in war-time, but that the English left-wing press has refused to allow the other side a hearing. Eg. the papers made a tremendous splash about Nin[5] and the others being in Fascist pay, but have failed to mention that the Spanish Government, other than the Communist members, have denied that there was any truth in the story. I suppose the underlying idea is that they are somehow aiding the Spanish Government by allowing the Communists a free hand. I am sorry to burden you with all this stuff, but I have tried to do all I can, which is not much, to get the truth about what has happened in Spain more widely known. It does not matter to me personally when they say that I am in Fascist pay, but it is different for the thousands who are in prison in Spain and are liable to be murdered by the secret police as so many have been already. I doubt whether it would be possible to do much for the Spanish anti-Fascist prisoners, but some kind of organised protest would probably get many of the foreigners released.

My wife wishes to be remembered to you. Neither of us suffered any ill-effects from being in Spain, though, of course, the whole thing was terribly distressing and disillusioning. The effects of my wound passed off more quickly than was expected. If it would interest I will send you a copy of my book on Spain when it comes out.

Yours sincerely
Eric Blair

[XX, 413B, pp. 310–12; typewritten]

1. Brailsford replied on 17 December 1937 (XI, 424, p. 119). He said he had the information from the Soviet Consul General, Vladimir Antonov-Ovsëenko (1884–1937) in Barcelona. He 'has since been purged'. He and his wife, Sofia, were recalled to the USSR after the 'May Events' and arrested in October 1937 with their daughter, Valentina (aged 15). The parents were shot on 8 February 1938. For the daughter's future life, see Orlando Figes, *The Whisperers* (2007; Penguin 2008), pp. 336–8.

2. Partido Socialists Unificado de Cataluña (The United Catalan Socialist Party, a communist party).

3. The Friends of Durruti was an extreme anarchist group within the Federación Anarquista Ibérica. (See *Homage to Catalonia*, pp. 219, 220, and 237, and Thomas, p. 656, n. 1.) It was named after Buenaventura Durruti (1896–1936) who had been mortally wounded fighting in Madrid and thereafter became a 'legendary anarchist warrior' (see Thomas, p. 36).

4. John Langdon-Davies (1897–1971), journalist and author. He wrote for the *News Chronicle* in Spain and was joint secretary with the Communist lawyer Geoffrey Bing of the Comintern-sponsored Commission of Inquiry into Alleged Breaches of the Non-Intervention Agreement in Spain (see Thomas, pp. 397–8). Orwell's refusal to 'accept the politics of liquidation and elimination' led to sneering by 'harder Communists', of which Langdon-Davies was one (see Valentine Cunningham, *British Writers of the Thirties*, 1988, p. 4). Following his experiences in Barcelona, he wrote *Air Raid* (1938), advocating large-scale evacuation and underground highways.

Eileen* to Norah Myles*

The Stores had no electricity. This letter, because seemingly typed by the light of a candle, which towards the end is guttering, has a small number of typographical errors. These have been silently corrected.

New Year's Day 1938
The Stores, Wallington

[*no salutation*]

You see I have no pen, no ink, no glasses and the prospect of no light, because the pens, the inks, the glasses and the candles are all in the room where George is working and if I disturb him again it will be for the fifteenth time tonight. But full of determined ingenuity I found a typewriter, and blind people are said to type in their dark.

I have also to write to a woman who has suddenly sent me a Christmas present (I think it may be intended for a wedding present after an estrangement of five or ten years, and in looking to see whether I had any clues to her address I found a bit of a letter to you, a very odd hysterical little letter, much more like Spain than any I can have written in that country. So here it is. The difficulty about the Spanish war is that it still dominates our lives in a most unreasonable manner because ~~Eric~~ George (or do you call him Eric?) is just finishing the book about it and I give him typescripts the reverse sides of which are covered with manuscript emendations that he can't read, and he is always having to speak about it and I have returned to complete pacifism and joined the P.P.U.[1] partly because of it. (Incidentally, you must join the P.P.U. too. War is fun so far as the shooting goes and much less alarming than an aeroplane in a shop window, but it does appalling things to people normally quite sane and intelligent – some make desperate efforts to retain some kind of integrity and others like Langdon-Davies make no efforts at all but hardly anyone can stay reasonable, let alone honest.) The Georges Kopp*[2] situation is now more Dellian[3] than ever. He is still in jail but has somehow managed to get several letters out to me, one of which George opened and read because I was away. He is very fond of Georges, who indeed cherished him with real tenderness in Spain and anyway is admirable as a soldier because of his quite remarkable courage, and he is extraordinarily magnanimous about the whole business – just as Georges was extraordinarily magnanimous. Indeed they went about saving each other's lives or trying to in a way that was almost horrible to me, though George had not then noticed that Georges was more than 'a bit gone on' me. I sometimes think no one ever had such a sense of guilt before. It was always understood that I wasn't what they call in love with Georges – our association progressed in little leaps, each leap immediately preceding some attack or operation in which he would almost inevitably be killed,[4] but the last time I saw him he was in jail waiting, as we were both confident, to be shot, and I simply couldn't explain to him again as a kind of farewell that he could never be a rival to George. So he has rotted in a filthy prison for more than six months with nothing to do but remember me in my most pliant moments. If he never gets out, which is indeed most probable, it's good that he has managed to have some thoughts in a way pleasant, but if he does get out I don't know how one reminds a man immediately he is a free man again that one has only once missed the cue for saying that nothing on earth would induce one to marry him. Being in prison in Spain means living in a room with a number of others (about fifteen to twenty in a room the size of your sitting-room) and never getting out of it; if the window has steel shutters, as many have, never seeing daylight, never having a letter; never being charged, let alone tried; never knowing whether you will be shot tomorrow or released, in either case without explanation; when your money runs out never eating anything but a bowl of the worst imaginable soup and a bit of bread at 3 p.m. and at 11 p.m.

On the whole it's a pity I found that letter because Spain doesn't really dominate us as much as all that. We have nineteen hens now – eighteen deliberately and the other by accident because we bought some ducklings and a hen escorted them. We thought we ought to boil her this autumn so we took it in turns to watch the nesting boxes to see whether she laid an egg to justify a longer life, and she did. And she is a good mother, so she is to have children in the spring. This afternoon we built a new henhouse – that is we put the sections together – and that is the nucleus of the breeding pen. There is probably no question on poultry-keeping that I am not able and very ready to answer. Perhaps you would like to have a battery (say three units) in the bathroom so that you could benefit from my advice. It would be a touching thing to collect an egg just before brushing one's teeth and eat it just after. Which reminds me that since we got back from Southwold, where we spent an incredibly family Christmas with the Blairs, we have eaten boiled eggs almost all the time. Before we had only one eggcup from Woolworths' – no two from Woolworths' and one that I gave George with an Easter egg in it before we were married (that cost threepence with egg). So it was a Happy Thought dear, and they are such a nice shape and match your mother's butter dish and breadboard, giving tone to the table.

We also have a poodle puppy. We called him Marx to remind us that we had never read Marx[5] and now we have read a little and taken so strong a personal dislike to the man that we can't look the dog in the face when we speak to him. He, the dog, is a French poodle, supposed to be miniature and of prize-winning stock, with silver hair. So far he has black and white hair, greying at the temples, and at four and a half months is rather larger than his mother. We think however he may take a prize as the largest miniature. He is very appealing and has a remarkable digestion. I am proud of this. He has never been sick, although almost daily he finds in the garden bones that no eye can have seen these twenty years and has eaten several rugs and a number of chairs and stools. We weren't going to clip him, but he has a lot of hairs which are literally dripping mud on the driest day – he rolls on every cushion in turn and then drips right through my lap – so we thought we would clip him a little. But now we shall never get him symmetrical till we shave him. Laurence[6] (it is a dreadful thing that you have never seen Laurence) bears with him in a remarkable way and has never scratched even his nose.

I went to stay with Mary.[7] You will have heard about the domestic changes. She went to stay with that pregnant cousin and read a book on infant feeding, from which she discovered that everything Nanny did was wrong. So of course she had to come home and tell her so, because otherwise she would have killed the children. Now they have a Norwegian nurse. I think she is better but it's bad luck for David who was hopelessly spoilt by fat Nanny and is not approved of by the Norwegian – who never raises her voice but puts him in the corner. Mary herself has become a good mother – when the children are there, I mean. She is perfectly reasonable with them. I don't know what happened. David is very intelligent and makes me slightly jealous because I should like a son and we don't have one. Mary and I summed up human history in a dreadful way when I was there – I was in the throes of pre-plague pains, which had happened so late that I was wondering whether I could persuade myself that I felt as though I were not going to have them, and Mary wasn't having any pre-plague pains at all and was in a fever and going to the chemist to try to buy some ergot or other corrective. We had two parties – we went to see Phyl Guimaraens and the MAMMETT CAME TO TEA.[8] She might just as well have been in Girl Guide uniform but now she organises play-readings, when all the old St. Hugh's girls go to her house and read *Julius Caesar*. Mary went once but she thought they would be given something to eat and they weren't, not even a bun or a cup of tea, so she is embittered and not being a good old girl any more. David and the Mammett had a nice conversation. David had told me earlier in the day that she was coming to tea and he knew her very well, so I repeated this to her and she was delighted. When he was brought into the room this happened:

'Well, little David (holding out the hand), and do you think you know who I am?'

'Yes – you're granny' (with complete confidence, allowing his hand to be held and stroked).

'No (ever so kindly), I'm not <u>granny.</u>'

'Oh? What are you then?'

Phyl is just the same as she used to be in her most charming moments. It was fun seeing her again. I think perhaps we might have a proper reunion some day. Couldn't you come and stay with her and while she is at the office eat potato crisps at the Criterion (Mary and I did this as much for old times' sake as because it was cold)? It seems to me superlatively clever for anyone to keep herself on the Stock Exchange, as she says she does. I wonder about it all the time I'm with her.

The last candle is guttering, and there isn't any good way out of this letter. But perhaps it has broken a spell. Does yours mean that June is at Oxford? I just didn't know. Anyway she can't be more than fifteen. Norman? John? Elisabeth? Jean? Ruth? Your mother? Your father?[9] I don't think I want any news of you and Quartus because I am quite sure I know all about you and it would be so dreadful to hear something quite different. The only thing I can do is to come and see. I am supposed to be having a holiday when the book is finished, as it will be this month, only we sha'n't have any money at all, and we were so rich.[10] When are you coming to the sales? Or are you? I don't know whether I can get away even for a day because the book is late and the typescript of the final draft is not begun and Eric is writing a book in collaboration with a number of people including a German and I keep getting his manuscript to revise and not being able to understand anything at all in it[11] – but if you <u>were</u> coming to the sales these things would all be less important to

Pig.

Did I wish you a happy new year?

Please wish all your family a happy new year from me.

Eric (I mean George) has just come in to say that the light is out (he had the Aladdin lamp because he was Working) and is there any oil (such a question) and I can't type in this light (which may be true, but I can't read it) and he is hungry and wants some cocoa and some biscuits and it is after midnight and Marx is eating a bone and has left pieces in each chair and which shall he sit on now.

[*LO*, pp. 70–5; XI, 415A, p. 109; typewritten]

1. Peace Pledge Union. Orwell has been said to have been a member but this is almost certainly not so. Orwell bought some of their pamphlets and a receipt, no. 20194, exists in the Orwell Archive for 2s 6d, dated 12 December 1937, from Mrs E. Blair – Eileen. That was thought to be a receipt for pamphlets but it seems to have been her subscription.

2. George(s) Kopp* was Orwell's commander in Spain. They were then very close friends but their friendship cooled in the late 1940s. It was Kopp who did much to

care for Orwell after he was wounded in the throat. Eileen's opening her heart to Norah here tells us much more than has previously been conjectured about their supposed relationship.

3. Either Dellian *for* Delian, related to the Greek island of Delos, home of an oracle who posed obscure and convoluted responses to questions put to it; or an ironic reference to the romantic novels of Ethel M. Dell about whom Orwell is scathing in *Keep the Aspidistra Flying*, p. 3.

4. Such operations give an impression of greater activity on the Huesca front than Orwell himself modestly suggested.

5. There has been disagreement as to when Orwell first read Marx (see XI, pp. 65–6, n. 1). Richard Rees records in *George Orwell: Fugitive from the Camp of Victory* (1961) that everyone at the Adelphi Summer School in 1936 was astonished by his knowledge of Marx (p. 147). (See Crick, p. 629, n. 49.)

6. This must be Eileen's brother, Laurence O'Shaughnessy. Laurence's son, also called Laurence, was not born until 13 November 1938.

7. Presumably Bertha Mary Wardell who had graduated with Eileen. (See **16.2.37** n. 11.)

8. Phyllis Guimaraens read Modern Languages at St Hugh's. Her father was a shipper of port wine; they lived at Petridge Wood, Redhill, Surrey. She married Harold Gabell 5 June 1926 at St Peter's, Eaton Square, London. Jenny Joseph suggested privately that The Mammett was a one-time tutor at St Hugh's or connected with the Senior Members' Association.

9. Norah had two sisters, Jean and Ruth. Jean married Maurice Durant and was the mother of John, Margaret Durant's husband.

10. Orwell took a second, carbon, copy of *Homage to Catalonia* to his agent, Leonard Moore, on 10 February 1938. Eileen's reference to their being so rich may be ironic but could refer to royalties received for the Left Book Club edition of *The Road to Wigan Pier* – some £600 though much of that must have been spent in Spain. The 'holiday' to which Eileen refers might have been delayed because of Orwell's illness and then spent at Chapel Ridding, Windermere, about the middle of July. Whom she went to stay with there is not known.

11. There is possibly confusion of Eric/husband and Eric/brother here. Eileen may well be referring to the latter and a medical book on which he was collaborating.

On 5 February 1938 Orwell wrote to the editor of Time and Tide, *which had published his review of Franz Borkenau's* The Spanish Cockpit, *regarding its rejection on political grounds by 'another well-known weekly paper'. Raymond Mortimer, critic and literary editor of the* New Statesman and Nation *wrote to Orwell on 8 February 1938 in protest, saying: 'It is possible of course that the "well known weekly paper" to which you refer is not the* New Statesman *but I take this as reference to us, and so no doubt will the majority of those who read your letter.' The offices of the* New Statesman *were bombed during the war, so all the correspondence of that time has been lost, but among his papers Orwell kept the originals of letters from Kingsley Martin, editor of the* New Statesman *and Raymond Mortimer and a carbon copy, reprinted here, of his reply to Mortimer.*

To Raymond Mortimer*

9 February 1938
The Stores
Wallington

Dear Mortimer,

With reference to your letter of February 8th. I am extremely sorry if I have hurt your or anybody else's feelings, but before speaking of the general issues involved, I must point out that what you say in it is not quite correct. You say 'Your review of *The Spanish Cockpit* was refused, because it gave a most inadequate and misleading description of the book. You used the review merely to express your own opinions and to present facts which you thought should be known. Moreover, last time I saw you you acknowledged this. Why then do you now suggest, quite mistakenly, that the review was refused because it "controverted editorial policy"? Are you confusing the review with the previous refusal of an article, which you submitted, and which the editor turned down because we had just printed three articles on the same subject'

I attach a copy of Kingsley Martin's letter[1]. You will see from this that the review *was* refused because it 'controverts the political policy of the paper' (I should have said 'political policy' not 'editorial policy'.) Secondly, you say that my previous article had been turned down 'because we had just printed three articles on the same subject'. Now, the article I sent in was on the suppression of the P.O.U.M., the alleged 'Trotsky-Fascist' plot, the murder of Nin, etc. So far as I know the *New Statesman* has never published any article on this subject. I certainly did and do admit that the review I wrote was tendentious and perhaps unfair, but it was not returned to me on those grounds, as you see from the letter attached.

Nothing is more hateful to me than to get mixed up in these controversies and to write, as it were, against people and newspapers that I have always respected, but one has got to realise what kind of issues are involved and the very great difficulty of getting the truth ventilated in the English press. So far as one can get at the figures, not less than 3000 political prisoners (ie. anti-Fascists) are in the Spanish jails at present, and the majority of them have been there six or seven months without any kind of trial or charge, in the most filthy physical conditions, as I have seen with my own eyes. A number of them have been bumped off, and there is not much doubt that there would have been a wholesale massacre if the Spanish Government had not had the sense to disregard the clamour in the Communist press. Various members of the Spanish Government have said over and over again to Maxton, McGovern, Felicien Challaye[2] and others that they wish to release these people but are unable to do so because of Communist pressure. What happens in Loyalist Spain is largely governed by outside opinion, and there is no doubt that if there had [been] a general protest from foreign Socialists the anti-Fascist prisoners would have been released. Even the protests of a small body like the I.L.P. have had some effect. But a few months back when a petition was got up for the release of the anti-Fascist prisoners, nearly all the leading English Socialists refused to sign it. I do not doubt that this was because, though no doubt they disbelieved the tale about a 'Trotsky-Fascist' Plot, they had gathered a general impression that the Anarchists and the P.O.U.M. were working against the Government, and, in particular, had believed the lies that were published in the English press about the fighting in Barcelona in May 1937. To mention an individual instance, Brailsford* in one of his articles in the *New Statesman* was allowed to state that the P.O.U.M. had attacked the Government with stolen batteries of guns, tanks etc. I was in Barcelona during the fighting, and as far as one can ever prove a negative I can prove by eye-witnesses etc. that this tale was absolutely untrue. At the time of the correspondence over my review I wrote to Kingsley Martin to tell him it was untrue, and more recently I wrote to Brailsford to ask him what was the source of the story. He had to admit that he had had it on what amounted to no authority whatever. (Stephen Spender* has his letter at present, but I could get it for you if you wanted to see it). Yet neither the *New Statesman* nor Brailsford has published any retraction of this statement, which amounts to an accusation of theft and treachery against numbers of innocent people. I do not think you can blame me if I feel that the *New Statesman* has its share of blame for the one-sided view that has been presented.

Once again, let me say how sorry I am about this whole business, but I have got to do what little I can to get justice for people who have been imprisoned without trial and libelled in the press, and one way of doing so is to draw attention to the pro-Communist censorship that undoubtedly exists. I would keep silent about the whole affair if I thought it would help the Spanish Government (as a matter of fact, before we left Spain some of the imprisoned people asked us *not* to attempt any publicity abroad because it might tend to discredit the Government), but I doubt whether it helps in the long run to cover things up as has been done in England. If the charges of espionage etc. that were made against us in the Communist papers had been given a proper examination at the time in the foreign press, it would have been seen that they were nonsense and the whole business might have been forgotten. As it was, the rubbish about a Trotsky-Fascist plot was widely circulated and no denial of it was published except in very obscure papers and, very half-heartedly, in the [*Daily*] *Herald* and *Manchester Guardian*. The result was that there was no protest from abroad and all these thousands of people have stayed in prison, and a number have been murdered, the effect being to spread hatred and dissension all through the Socialist movement.

I am sending back the books you gave me to review. I think it would be better if I did not write for you again, I am terribly sorry about this whole affair, but I have got to stand by my friends, which may involve attacking the *New Statesman* when I think they are covering up important issues.

Yours sincerely

[XI, 424, pp. 116-20; typewritten with handwritten addition]

Handwritten on a separate sheet is a note by Orwell which, because there is no salutation, was almost certainly sent to Raymond Mortimer with the typewritten letter above. Orwell enclosed the letter from H. N. Brailsford which he said Spender had. (See XI, p.118.)

1. Basil Kingsley Martin (1897–1969), left-wing writer and journalist, was editor of the *New Statesman and Nation*, 1931–60.
2. John McGovern (1887–1968), ILP MP, 1930–47; Labour MP, 1947–59, led a hunger march from Glasgow to London in 1934. Félicien Challaye, French left-wing politician, member of the committee of La Ligue des Droits des Hommes, a liberal, anti-Fascist movement to protect civil liberty throughout the world. He resigned in November 1937, with seven others, in protest against what they interpreted as the movement's cowardly subservience to Stalinist tyranny.

Raymond Mortimer quickly sent Orwell a handwritten note saying, 'Dear Orwell, Please accept my humble apologies. I did not know Kingsley Martin had written to you in those terms. My own reasons for refusing the review were those that I gave. I should be sorry for you not to write for us, and I should like to convince you from past reviews that there is no premium here on Stalinist orthodoxy.' On 10 February, Kingsley Martin wrote to Orwell: 'Raymond Mortimer has shown me your letter. We certainly owe you an apology in regard to the letter about The Spanish Cockpit. *There is a good deal else in your letter which suggests some misunderstanding and which, I think, would be better discussed than written about. Could you make it convenient to come and see me some time next week? I shall be available on Monday afternoon, or almost any time on Tuesday.' It is not known whether Orwell accepted Martin's invitation, but he probably did. Orwell's review of Galsworthy's* Glimpses and Reflections *was published in the* New Statesman *on 12 March 1938, and he contributed reviews to the journal from July 1940 to August 1943. However, as is recorded in conversation with friends, he never forgave Martin for his 'line' on the Spanish civil war.*

To Cyril Connolly*

14 March 1938
The Stores
Wallington

Dear Cyril,

I see from the *New Statesman & Nation* list that you have a book coming out sometime this spring.[1] If you can manage to get a copy sent me I'll review it for the *New English*, possibly also *Time & Tide*. I arranged for Warburg to send you a copy of my Spanish book[2] (next month) hoping you may be able to review it. You scratch my back, I'll scratch yours.

I am writing this in bed. I may not be going to India after all & any way not before the autumn. The doctors don't think I ought to go. I've been spitting blood again, it always turns out to be not serious, but it's alarming when it happens & I am going to a Sanatorium in Kent[3] to be X rayed.° I've no doubt they'll find as before that I am O.K. but any way it's a good excuse for not going to India, which I never wanted to.[4] This bloody mess-up in Europe has got me so that I really can't write anything. I see Gollancz has already put my next novel[5] on his list tho' I haven't written a line or even sketched it out. It seems to me we might as well all pack our bags for the concentration camp. King Farlow* was here the other day & I am going to stay next week-end with him after leaving the Sanatorium. When in town I'll try & look you up. Could you be kind enough to write me a line to 24 Croom's Hill, Greenwich S.E. 10,[6] to let me know your telephone address, which of course I've lost again, & then if occasion arises I can ring you up. Please remember me to your wife.

Yours
Eric Blair

[XI, 431, p. 127; handwritten]

1. *Enemies of Promise* (see Orwell's letter to Connolly of **14.12.38**).
2. *Homage to Catalonia.*
3. Orwell's Preston Hall Sanatorium records show he coughed blood when ill in 1929, 1931, and 1934; that he had pneumonia in 1918, 1921, 1933, and 1934; and dengue fever when in Burma.
4. Orwell had been invited to write leaders and book reviews, and sub letters for *The Pioneer*, Lucknow in Pakistan. (See XI, 426, pp. 120–2.)
5. *Coming Up for Air.* Orwell is not being quite fair here: he had suggested that this be done (see his letter to Leonard Moore, 6 December 1937, XI, 412, pp. 100–1).
6. Home of Eileen's brother.

The sequence of events leading to Orwell's admission to Preston Hall Sanatorium is uncertain and complicated by doubts about the dating of Eileen's letter to Jack Common. Orwell's Case Record (found by Michael Shelden) shows that Orwell was admitted to Preston Hall on Tuesday, 15 March, and discharged that same day; and that he was re-admitted on Thursday, 17 March, and remained until 1 September 1938. The records also include an analysis of X-rays of Orwell's lungs dated 16 March. It might reasonably be assumed that he was rushed to the hospital on 15 March; that the heavy bleeding described by Eileen was then stopped, and that X-rays were taken; after these were examined on the following day, he was admitted for treatment. This involved complete rest, colloidal calcium injections and vitamins A and D until pulmonary tuberculosis could be definitely excluded.

Preston Hall Sanatorium, Aylesford, Kent, was a mile or two north of Maidstone. It was a British Legion hospital for ex-servicemen (hence the name of Orwell's ward, after the World War I Admiral, Jellicoe). Initially Orwell was given a single room; this aroused comments about preferential treatment, but he insisted on mixing with the others and got on easily with them. (See Crick, 358–60; Shelden, 316–19, and for a fuller note, XI, 432, pp. 127–8.)

Eileen Blair* to Jack Common*

> Monday [and Tuesday, 14–15 March 1938]
> 24 Croom's Hill
> Greenwich

Dear Jack,

You'll probably have heard about the drama of yesterday. I only hope you didn't get soaked to the skin in discovering it.[1] The bleeding seemed prepared to go on for ever & on Sunday everyone agreed that Eric must be taken somewhere where really active steps could be taken if necessary—artificial pneumothorax to stop the blood or transfusion to replace it. They got on to a specialist who visits a smallish voluntary hospital near here & who's very good at this kind of thing & he also advised removal, so it happened in an ambulance like a very luxurious bedroom on wheels. The journey had no ill-effects, they found his blood pressure still more or less normal—& they've stopped the bleeding, without the artificial pneumothorax. So it was worth while. Everyone was nervous of being responsible for the immediate risk of the journey, but we supported each other. Eric's a bit depressed about being in an institution devised for murder, but otherwise remarkably well. He needn't stay long they say,[2] but the specialist has a sort of hope that he may be able to identify the actual site of haemorrhage and control it for the future.

This was really to thank you for being so neighbourly from such a distance, & in such weather. One gets hysterical with no one to speak to except the village who are not what you could call soothing.

I'll let you know what happens next. I have fearful letters to write to relations.

Love to Mary & Peter,[3]

Eileen

[XI, 432, pp. 127–9; handwritten]

1.   Although Common lived only some half-dozen miles from Wallington, the journey was awkward and he had no car.
2.   He did not leave the sanatorium until 1 September 1938.
3.   Jack Common's wife and son.

Orwell wrote to Spender on 2 April. Spender, in an undated reply told him that he had arranged to review Homage to Catalonia *for the* London Mercury. *He then broached the matter of Orwell's attitude to him. Knowing nothing of Spender, Orwell had, he said, attacked him, but he was 'equally puzzled as to why when still knowing nothing of me, but having met me once or twice, you should have withdrawn those attacks', and wanted to discuss this. In the meantime, saying how sorry he was to hear Orwell was ill, he sent him his play,* Trial of a Judge, *which he thought Orwell might care to read if he had little else to do: 'If you can't bear the thought of it, don't look at it: I won't be offended.'*

To Stephen Spender*

Friday [15? April 1938]
Jellicoe Pavilion
Preston Hall
Aylesford, Kent

Dear Spender,

Thank you so much for your letter and the copy of your play. I waited to read the latter before replying. It interested me, but I'm not quite sure what I think about it. I think with a thing like that one wants to see it acted, because in writing you obviously had different scenic effects, supplementary noises etc. in mind which would determine the beat of the verse. But there's a lot in it that I'd like to discuss with you when next I see you.

You ask how it is that I attacked you not having met you, & on the other hand changed my mind after meeting you. I don't know that I had ever exactly attacked you, but I had certainly in passing made offensive remarks about 'parlour Bolsheviks such as Auden & Spender' or words to that effect. I was willing to use you as a symbol of the parlour Bolshie because *a.* your verse, what I had read of it, did not mean very much to me, *b.* I looked upon you as a sort of fashionable successful person, also a Communist or Communist sympathiser, & I have been very hostile to the C.P. since about 1935, & *c.* because not having met you I could regard you as a type & also an abstraction. Even if when I met you I had not happened to like you, I should still have been bound to change my attitude, because when you meet anyone in the flesh you realise immediately that he is a human being and not a sort of caricature embodying certain ideas. It is partly for this reason that I don't mix much in literary circles, because I know from experience that once I have met & spoken to anyone I shall never again be able to show any intellectual brutality towards him, even when I feel that I ought to, like the Labour M.Ps. who get patted on the back by dukes & are lost forever more.

It is very kind of you to review my Spanish book. But don't go & get into trouble with your own Party—it's not worth it. However, of course you can disagree with all my conclusions, as I think you would probably do anyway, without actually calling me a liar. If you could come & see me some time I would like it very much, if it's not much of an inconvenience.[1] I am not infectious. I don't think this place is very difficult to get to, because the Green Lines°[2] buses stop at the gate. I am quite happy here & they are very nice to me, but of course it's a bore not being able to work and I spend most of my time doing crossword puzzles.

Yours
Eric Blair

[XI, 435, pp. 132–3; handwritten]

1.   Spender did visit Orwell at Aylesford. Others who made what was often a long and difficult journey were former comrades from the Spanish contingent, who hitchhiked there, Jack Common, Rayner Heppenstall, and Max and Dorothy Plowman, who brought the novelist L. H. Myers.
2.   Green Line buses were long-distance, limited stop, buses that ran from one suburban or country district to another on the outer limits of London proper.

Homage to Catalonia *was published on 25 April 1938, but, as is customary, review copies had been sent out in advance. On a Saturday before Orwell's letter to Gorer, probably 16 April, Gorer sent him a short note to say how 'absolutely first-rate' he thought* Homage to Catalonia, *as well as a carbon copy of his review for* Time and Tide, *'in case they object to its inordinate length', and so that Orwell could let him know before the proof arrived if there were any errors. The review appeared on 30 April.*

To Geoffrey Gorer*

18 April 1938
Jellicoe Pavilion
Aylesford

Dear Geoffrey,

I must write to thank you for your marvellous review. I kept pinching myself to make sure I was awake, but I shall also have to pinch myself if *T. & T.* print it—I'm afraid they'll think it's too long & laudatory. I don't think they'll bother about the subject-matter, as they've been very good about the Spanish war. But even if they cut it, thanks ever so for the intention. There were just one or two points. One is that you say the fighting in Barcelona was started by the Assault Guards. Actually it was Civil Guards.¹ There weren't any Assault Guards there then, & there is a difference, because the Civil Guards are the old Spanish Gendarmerie dating from the early 19ᵗʰ century & in reality a more or less pro-Fascist body, ie. they have always joined the Fascists where it was possible. The Assault Guards are a new formation dating from the Republic of 1931, pro-Republican & not hated by the working people to the same extent. The other is that if you are obliged to shorten or otherwise alter the review, it doesn't particularly matter to insist, as you do now, that I only took part in the Barcelona fighting to the extent of doing sentry. I did, as it happens, but if I had been ordered to actually fight I would have done so, because in the existing chaos there didn't seem anything one could do except obey one's own party & immediate military superiors. But I'm so glad you liked the book. Various people seem to have received review copies, but I haven't had any myself yet & am wondering uneasily what the dust-jacket is like. Warburg talked of decorating it with the Catalan colours, which are easily mistaken for *a.* the Spanish royalist colours or *b.* the M.C.C.²

Hope all goes well with you. I am much better, in fact I really doubt whether there is anything wrong with me.³ Eileen is battling with the chickens etc. alone but comes down once a fortnight.

Yours
Eric Blair

[XI, 436, pp, 133–4; handwritten]

1. Orwell was wrong about this. He was later to ask that if a second edition of *Homage to Catalonia* were published – there was only one English edition in his lifetime and the US and French editions did not appear until after his death – this error should be rectified. The correction has been made in the *Complete Works*

edition (see VI, p. 253 and p. 257, note 102/15).

2. Marylebone Cricket Club, the then ruling cricket authority. Its tie has broad red and yellow stripes.

3. According to Orwell's Blood Sedimentation Test on 27 April (and on 17 May), his disease was 'moderately active'. It was not until 4 July that it became 'quiescent'. It is never shown as normal.

Eileen Blair* to Leonard Moore*

30 May 1938
[The Stores] Wallington

Dear Mr. Moore,

I promised Eric I would write and tell you the news about him, which is that he is to go abroad for the winter, staying at Preston Hall until he leaves England—that is, probably until August or September. After that we hope he will be able to come home, though not to this house. We think of trying to find somewhere to live in Dorset. All this does not of course mean that he is worse, but only that the position has been made clearer to him. As a matter of fact, the original diagnosis was wrong: he had bronchiectasis and probably no phthisis.[1] Apparently there is no point in treating bronchiectasis by the absolute rest that sometimes cures phthisis, and I think he is going to be allowed up as soon as the weather is reasonable.[2] He ought also to be able to do some gentle work on the novel in July or August. Of course it's not easy to work in a sanatorium, where people constantly walk about and impose a timetable that probably interferes with the work timetable, but the book seethes in his head and he is very anxious to get on with it. I ought to have written to you some time ago about this novel, when Eric first realised that he couldn't finish it by October, but he then wanted Gollancz to be told that it would be ready anyway before Christmas. Now he thinks that it will be ready in the spring and this seems quite probable. I should be very grateful if you could give Gollancz a message about it in whatever terms you think proper.

I hear there is a wonderful review of *Homage to Catalonia* in the *Observer*,[3] but I haven't seen it yet. On the whole the reviews have really been very good don't you think? It's interesting that the C.P. have decided not to be rude— and extremely clever of them to be reticent in the definitely Communist press and to say their little piece anonymously in the *T.L.S.* and the *Listener*.[4] By the way, do you know when Warburg proposes to pay an advance? We thought he was to pay £75 in January and £75 on publication, but perhaps that's wrong.

Eric is still being extraordinarily amenable and placid about everything, and everyone is delighted with his general condition.

Yours sincerely,
Eileen Blair

[XI, 447, pp. 154–5; typewritten]

1.   Bronchiectasis: chronic viral disease affecting the bronchial tubes; phthisis: tuberculosis.

2.   Orwell was allowed up for one hour a day from 1 June and for three hours a day a week later.

3.   The review, on 29 May 1938 was by Desmond Flower (1907–97; MC), author, editor, publisher. He was Director of Cassell & Co in 1931, then Literary Director, 1938, and Chairman, 1958–70. He was also founder/editor, with A. J. A. Symons, of *Book Collector*.

4.   The *Times Literary Supplement*. *The Listener* was published by the BBC and, amongst other things, printed talks it had broadcast (often shortened). Orwell reviewed for *The Listener* and it published some of his talks. (See letter of **16.6.38** regarding the review in *The Listener*.)

To the Editor, *The Listener*

16 June 1938
Aylesford

Review of *Homage to Catalonia*

Your reviewer's[1] treatment of facts is a little curious. In his review of my book *Homage to Catalonia* in *The Listener* of May 25 he uses about four-fifths of his space in resurrecting from the Communist Press the charge that the Spanish political party known as the P.O.U.M. is a 'fifth column' organisation in the pay of General Franco. He states first that this accusation was 'hyperbolical', but adds later that it was 'credible', and that the leaders of the P.O.U.M. were 'little better than traitors to the Government cause'. Now, I leave on one side the question of how it can be credible that Franco's 'fifth column' could be composed of the poorest of the working class, led by men most of whom had been imprisoned under the regime Franco was trying to restore, and at least one of whom was on Franco's special list of 'persons to be shot'. If your reviewer can believe in stories of that kind, he is entitled to do so. What he is not entitled to do is to repeat his accusation, which is incidentally an accusation against myself, without even indicating from whom it came or that I had had anything to say about it. He leaves it to be inferred all through that the absurd charges of treachery and espionage originated with the Spanish Government. But, as I pointed out in great detail (Chapter XI of my book), these charges never had any footing outside the Communist Press, nor was any evidence in support of them ever produced. The Spanish Government has again and again repudiated all belief in them, and has steadfastly refused to prosecute the men whom the Communist newspapers denounced. I gave chapter and verse from the Spanish Government's statements, which have since been repeated several times. Your reviewer simply ignores all this, no doubt hoping that he has so effectually put people off reading the book that his misrepresentations will pass unnoticed.

I do not expect or wish for 'good' reviews, and if your reviewer chooses to use most of his space in expressing his own political opinions, that is a matter between him and yourself. But I think I have a right to ask that when a book of mine is discussed at the length of a column there shall be at least some mention of what I have actually said.

George Orwell

[XI, 452, pp. 160–2]

Orwell's complaint drew this response from The Listener's *reviewer:*

We have sent the above letter to our reviewer, who replies:

'Mr. Orwell's letter ignores the major fact that conditions in Barcelona at one time became so bad that the Spanish Government was forced to send in armed police to put down what amounted to an insurrection. The leaders of that insurrection were the extreme anarchist elements allied with the P.O.U.M. It is not a question of "resurrecting" charges from the Communist Press, but of historic fact. I have spent a considerable part of the Spanish war in Spain, and have not relied upon newspaper reports for my information.

'As I made clear in my review, it was not the intention of the rank and file of the P.O.U.M. to do other than fight against Franco. Being poor and ignorant men, the complexities of the revolutionary situation were beyond them; their leaders were to blame. As for being part of Franco's fifth column, there is no doubt that whoever declined to co-operate with the central government and to abide by the law was, in fact, weakening the authority of that government and thus aiding the enemy. I submit that in time of war ignorance is as reprehensible as malicious sabotage. It is effect that matters, not the reasons for action.

'I am sorry if Mr. Orwell thinks that I wanted to put readers off a magnificently written book: I didn't: I want people to read it even if, in my opinion, his analysis is wrong. It is the essence of a democracy in peace time that all views should be available to everybody'.

We are bound to say, in printing our reviewer's reply, that we consider it hardly meets the points made by Mr. Orwell, to whom we express our regrets.—Editor, THE LISTENER[2]

1.   Philip Furneaux Jordan (1902–1951), journalist, novelist, and reviewer. He was on the staff of the Paris *Daily Mail* and edited the Riviera edition of the *Chicago Tribune*. In 1936 he joined the *News Chronicle* and served as its correspondent in Spain, 1936–37. He later became its features editor and then its foreign correspondent. In 1946–47 he was First Secretary at the British Embassy, Washington, and thereafter Public Relations Adviser to Prime Minister Clement Attlee.

2.   J. R. Ackerley (1896–1967) was literary editor, 1935–59. His support for Orwell despite his reviewer's explanation is telling. (See *Ackerley* by Peter Parker (1989).)

Eileen Blair* to Denys King-Farlow*

22 June 1938
[The Stores] Wallington

Dear Denys,

When I told you on the telephone that I was more or less writing to you it was quite true. But I was also having flu, although at that time incredulously because the time even of this year seems so odd.

I hadn't *forgotten* this money: indeed I have thought of it often with growing appreciation as the 'advance' on the Spanish book went on not coming. Eventually it was extracted by instalments! Poor man—I mean poor publisher. I hope it was time that you didn't need. As a matter of fact I shouldn't have kept the cheque if I'd had any doubt about repaying it almost at once. Or I think not.

Eric isn't so ill as they thought, as you'll have gathered. He of course has never believed that he was 'ill', but for the first two months or so he appeared to have phthisis in both lungs which could have been pretty hopeless. Now it turns out to be bronchiectasis, which people *do* go on having more or less indefinitely under really favourable conditions. I suppose he told you that we can probably go abroad for the winter together instead of his going to a sanatorium, & after that we have to find a perfect cottage in one of the southern counties at an inclusive rental of about 7/6. I shall come back early to do this— They even think that he might leave Preston Hall in August & spend a month or so under normal conditions in England—he must of course be very 'careful' but the treatment really only consists in resting a great deal & eating a lot. We might perhaps stay on a farm somewhere. By that time this cottage will be handed over either to the landlord or to an unfortunate old uncle of Eric's who is suggested as a tenant.[1]

I'm so glad you went to see Eric & took him out. I think it's really more depressing for him to be in this semi-confinement than to be in bed, & he loved having a party.[2] It was particularly nice of you to send that money instead of offering to.

With many thanks,

Yours sincerely,
Eileen Blair

[XI, 455A, pp. 164–5; handwritten]

1. Although Orwell's parents had seventeen brothers and sisters between them, the only uncles to whom Eileen could be referring were Charles Limouzin, at one time secretary of a golf club at Parkstone, Bournemouth; George Limouzin, who was married to Ivy; and Eugène Adam, who was married to Nellie Limouzin. None took the cottage.

2. If the party was to celebrate anything, it might have been for the publication of *Homage to Catalonia* on 25 April; or a party slightly ahead of Orwell's thirty-fifth birthday, 25 June.

To Jack Common*

5 July 1938
New Hostel
Preston Hall
Aylesford, Kent

Dear Jack,

You know I have to go abroad for the winter, probably for about 6 months starting about end of August. Well, would you like to have our cottage rent free & in return look after the animals? I'll tell you all the facts & you can work out the pros & cons for yourself.

i. The doctors say I must live somewhere further south. That means giving up the cottage when we come back at latest. But I don't want to scrap the livestock, because we have now worked the flock of fowls up to about 30, which can be worked up to about 100 next year, & it would also mean selling the hen-houses, which cost a lot but which you don't get much for if you sell them. We have therefore the choice of getting someone to inhabit the cottage, or of paying someone to look after the animals, which plus storage of furniture works out at about the same expense as keeping on the rent of the cottage.

ii. You know what our cottage is like. It's bloody awful. Still it's more or less livable. There is one room with a double bed & one with a single, & I fancy there is enough linen etc. to do for 2 people & a kid. When there is sudden rain in winter the kitchen tends to flood, otherwise the house is passably dry. The living room fire, you may remember, smokes, but I think the chimney will have been seen to before we leave—anyway it doesn't need anything very drastic doing to it. There is water laid on, but no hot, of course. There is a Calor Gas stove, which is expensive (the gas, I mean), but there is also a little oil oven that can be resuscitated. As to produce, there won't be many vegetables, as of course Eileen alone couldn't cope with all of the garden, but at any rate there will be potatoes enough to see you through the winter. There'll also be milk, about a quart a day, as the goat has just kidded. A lot of people are prejudiced against goats' milk but really it's no different from cow & is said to be good for kids.

iii. As to the looking after animals. This means feeding etc. about 30 fowls & feeding & milking the goats. I'll leave careful instructions about food etc. & arrange for the corn merchant to deliver supplies & send the bill on to me. You could also sell the eggs (the butcher who calls twice a week buys any quantity) & put the money aside for us. There won't be many eggs at first, as most of the birds are young pullets hatched this year, but by early spring they should be laying about 100 a week.

Let me know would you whether you would like to take this on. It would suit us, & for you at any rate I dare say it would be a quiet place to work in.[1]

All the best to Mary & Peter.

Yours
Eric Blair

[XI, 461, p. 171; handwritten]

1.   They did take the cottage

From Morocco to the BBC

1938 – 1941

It was thought that the climate of North Africa would be beneficial for Orwell's health. That, however, was chiefly illusory although the relative rest probably helped him. He still managed to grow a few vegetables and keep one or two hens and goats. His time in Morocco was plagued by anxiety that he had borrowed more than he could easily repay although, unbeknownst to him, the novelist L.H. Myers had advanced the cost, £300, as a gift. Orwell harped on this 'debt' on many occasions and eventually repaid what he thought he owed to an intermediary, Dorothy Plowman.

Whilst in Morocco, the Orwells spent a few days in the Atlas Mountains and he wrote *Coming Up for Air*, the typescript of which he delivered to Leonard Moore, his agent, for Gollancz immediately on his return to England on 30 March 1939. On 28 June 1939, Orwell's father died of cancer and Orwell wrote movingly about wandering the seafront at Southwold pondering what to do with the pennies that had weighted down his father's eyes at his death. He eventually threw them into the sea.

The outbreak of war on 3 September 1939 began a period of great frustration for him. He could obtain no work to advance the Allied cause and was far too unfit for the Army. Eileen was engaged at first in (ironically) a Whitehall Censorship Office. Even more ironic was that later one of her notebooks used to record censored mail was used by Orwell to record his earnings so that he could declare them to the Inland Revenue. He reviewed books, plays and films and in May 1940, after Dunkirk, he joined what would become the Home Guard, serving actively as a Sergeant. The photograph included in this volume of Orwell with the Home Guard shows the composition of his section. On the right is his publisher, Fredric Warburg. He had served as a lieutenant at Passchendaele. Other's in Orwell's section included two wholesale grocers, the owner of a large garage and his son, a Selfridge's van-driver, Denzil Jacobs (a chartered accountant who later served as an RAF navigator) and his father, both of whom visited Orwell in University College Hospital in 1949. Denzil Jacobs told the editor that to Orwell, 'commitment was everything'.

Orwell's *The Lion and the Unicorn* was published on 19 February 1941. He made a few broadcasts for the BBC including four for its Overseas Service. Then, on 18 August 1941, he was appointed a Talks Assistant in the BBC Overseas Service at £640 per annum. After attending a short training course (called rather unfairly 'The Liars' School' – it was, in fact, very straightforward and practical), he began two years of hard, intensive work. Although he would come to regard these as 'two wasted years', they were, in fact, more valuable than he realised. By now, Eileen had moved from the soul-destroying Censorship Department to more enjoyable work in the Ministry of Food, working on such programmes as 'The Kitchen Front', advising the population on how to make the most and best of such food as was available at a time of severe rationing.

From Orwell's letter to his mother, 25 February 1912

Eileen* to Orwell's mother, Ida*

Dearest Mrs Blair,

I think Eric sent postcards today, explaining that I'd been 'upset' as he says. We could both be said to have been upset, partly I expect by the climate & partly by the horror we conceived for this country. My additional achievement was some kind of fever, possibly from food poisoning but more probably from mosquitoes—Eric has eaten the same things but hasn't been bitten to any extent whereas I look as though I were made of brioches.

The journey until we left Tangier was so pleasant that we were spoilt. It's true that we went to Gib by mistake & then got held up at Tangier because the boats to Casablanca were full, but Gib was quite interesting & Tangier enchanting. Eric's stuff for seasickness worked even on the crossing from Gib. to Tangier, which was rough (he walked round the boat with a seraphic smile watching people being sick & insisted on my going into the 'Ladies' Cabin' to report on the disasters there), & the Continental Hotel in Tangier was very good indeed. If we could have come here by sea as we intended we should probably like Morocco better but we had to come by train which meant having breakfast at 5 a.m., going through endless agonies to satisfy police & customs authorities of all nations before getting into the train at all & then having more police & customs interrogations a) before the train left the International Zone, b) before entering the Spanish zone & c) before entering the French zone. The Spaniards were very pleasant & careless which was as well because at the last minute a man came round & collected the French newspapers that most people had & that were not allowed in Spanish territory. We had in our suitcases a collection of about 20 newspapers, Fascist & anti-Fascist. The French were in character, absolutely refusing to believe that we were not coming to Morocco to break the law. However, they agreed to let the Morocco police do the arresting & we got as far as the junction where we were to change into a train with a restaurant car. By this time it should have been 11 a.m. & was 11.45. Everyone fled across the station surrounded by hordes of Arab porters, aged 10–70, & the train started before we were well in it. Our junior porter, who was about 3' 6", had not unnaturally put the two cases he was carrying down on the platform so that he could catch us to get his tip (he said they were in the dining-car), but to establish this took us hours & to get the cases at Casablanca took two days. Then we came to Marrakech, again leaving at 7 a.m., & went to the Hotel Continental which had been recommended to us & which may have been quite good once. Lately it has changed hands & is obviously a brothel. I haven't much direct knowledge of brothels but as they offer a special service they can probably all afford to be dirty & without any other conveniences. However we stayed for one day, partly because Eric didn't notice anything odd about it until he tried to live in it & partly because my temperature was by that time going up about one degree an hour & I only wanted to lie down, which was easy enough, & to get drinks, which were brought me by a limitless variety of street Arabs who looked murderous but were very kind. Eric of course ate out & this is very expensive in Morocco so we moved here as soon as possible. This is the second most expensive hotel in Marrakech but it's much cheaper to have full pension here (95 fr. a day for two)[1] than to go to restaurants.

Sunday.
Eric made me go to bed at that point, & since then we've been busy. He has written to you this morning while I unpacked, so you'll know about Mme Vellat & the villa in prospect. I think the villa will be fun from our point of view. It's entirely isolated except for a few Arabs who live in the outbuildings to tend the orange grove that surrounds it. We're going to buy enough furniture to camp with. As it will be the cheapest French furniture obtainable the aesthetic effect may be unfortunate, but we hope to get some decent rugs as we want them to take home. There is a large sitting room, two bedrooms, a bathroom & a kitchen. No provision for cooking but we'll have some little pots with charcoal in them & a Primus. The country is practically desert but may look different after the rains. Anyway we can have a goat & Eric will really get the benefit of the climate. In Marrakech itself he couldn't. The European quarter is intolerable with a second-rate respectability, & very expensive. The native quarter is 'picturesque' but the smells are only rivalled by the noises. Eric was so depressed that I thought we should have to come home but he is now quite excited about the villa & I think will be happy there. According to Dr. Diot (who was recommended by a friend of my brother's in Paris) the climate is ideal for him, or will be in a few weeks when it's cooler. And the villa has a sort of observatory on its roof which will be good to work in.
    The second bedroom is of course Avril's when she wants it. If she went to Tangier by sea the fare would be about £12 return. At Tangier one can stay at

the Continental for 10/– a day all in. The fare from Tangier to Marrakech by train is 155 fr. second class. Unfortunately the train gets into Casablanca at 3 p.m. or so & the next one to Marrakech leaves at 8 & takes all night. It would be better to stay one night at Casablanca, which I suppose would cost another 10/– altogether, & get the morning train here. It only takes 4 hours & one sees the country such as it is. We loathed it but that was largely because we were sentenced to live in it for six months. As one approaches Marrakech camels become more & more common until they're as ordinary as donkeys, & the native villages are extraordinary collections of little thatched huts about 5 feet square (but generally round), sometimes surrounded by a kind of hedge of dead wood or possibly a mud wall. We don't know what the walls are for; they aren't strong enough or high enough to keep anything out. Marrakech itself was largely built of mud & has enormous mud ramparts. The earth dries a reddish colour which is very beautiful *in earth* but unfortunate when approximately reproduced in paint by the French, who like to call Marrakech 'la rouge'. Some of the native products are lovely, especially the earthenware pots & jugs they use.

Dr. Diot hasn't really examined Eric yet but intends to. He is not particularly sympathetic but he must be a good doctor & through him we'll be able to know that the chest really is reacting properly.

Please give my love to Mr Blair & Avril. I do hope Mr Blair is getting out & that Avril will get out as far as Morocco. It's said to be a wonderful light here for photography. From her point of view it might have been more interesting to stay in Marrakech but one can walk one way (about 3 miles) in cooler weather & a taxi will cost about 2/6 I think. She might be able to hire a car if she liked to do her International driving test before coming. Anyway there are buses from Marrakech to all the other places.

With love
Eileen.

[XI, 481, pp. 198–200; handwritten]

1.   At a rate of exchange of 170 francs to the pound, about 11s 2d (about £22 at current values).

Eileen* to Marjorie Dakin*

27 September 1938
Chez Mme Vellat
rue Edmond Doutte Medina
Marrakech
French Morocco

My dear Marjorie,

We've just had our first letter—from Mrs Blair. It was full of good news. I'm so glad you have a well family & that Marx appreciates his good fortune.[1] I only hope he behaves as they say.

Yesterday we were rather hysterically writing semi-business letters in the hope that they'd be delivered before war broke out. Today the papers are somewhat calmer, but it's maddening to see none except those published in Morocco (we can get others but 4 to 8 days late & those at the moment might as well be years old). The extraordinary thing is that no one here seems interested. We were in a cafe when the evening paper arrived yesterday & only one other person bought one & he didn't open it. Yet there are many young Frenchmen here who would be mobilised for service in France I suppose. The general idea is that Morocco would be very safe, anyway inland. The Arabs don't seem ripe to make trouble & if they did make it the poor wretches would have 15,000 regular troops to contend with in Marrakech alone, complete with artillery & all. So long as we're allowed to stay here, & that will probably be as long as we have any money, we probably have a better chance than most of keeping alive. Though what we should be keeping alive for God knows. It seems very unlikely that Eric will publish another book after the outbreak of war. I was rather cheered to hear about Humphrey's* dugout.[2] Eric has been on the point of constructing one for two years, though the plans received rather a check after he did construct one in Spain & it fell down on his & his companions' heads two days later, not under any kind of bombardment but just from the force of gravity. But the dugout has generally been by way of light relief; his specialities are concentration camps & the famine.

He buried some potatoes against the famine & they might have been very useful if they hadn't gone mouldy at once. To my surprise he does intend to stay here whatever happens. In theory this seems too reasonable & even comfortable to be in character; in practice perhaps it wouldn't be so comfortable. Anyway I am thankful we got here. If we'd been in England I suppose he must have been in jail by now & I've had the most solemn warnings against this from all the doctors though they don't tell me how

I could prevent it. Whatever the solution I do still desperately hope that there won't be war, which I'm sure would be much worse for the Czechs. After all political oppression, though it gets so much publicity, can make miserable only a small proportion of a whole nation because a political regime, especially a dictatorship, has to be popular. We keep seeing & being exasperated by pictures of London crowds 'demonstrating' when we don't know what they're demonstrating for, & there are occasional references to 'extremists' who are arrested but whether the extremists are Communists demonstrating against Chamberlain's moderation or Fascists or socialists or pacifists we don't know. Eric, who retains an extraordinary political simplicity in spite of everything, wants to hear what he calls the voice of the people. He thinks this might stop a war, but I'm sure that the voice would only say that it didn't want a war but of course would have to fight if the Government declared war. It's very odd to feel that Chamberlain is our only hope, but I do believe he doesn't want war either at the moment & certainly the man has courage.[3] But it's fantastic & horrifying to think that you may all be trying on gas masks at this moment.[4]

You'll probably have heard that we don't like Marrakech. It's interesting, but at first anyway seemed dreadful to live in. There are beautiful arches with vile smells coming out of them & adorable children covered in ringworm & flies. I found an open space to watch the sunset from & too late realised that part of the ground to the west of us was a graveyard; I really couldn't bear Eric's conversation about the view as dominated by invisible worms & we had to go away without seeing the sunset. On the whole, however, I get acclimatised & I thought Eric was moving in the same direction, but he says he isn't. But when we have our villa (we move in on the 15th) he is going to be happy. He is even buying things for the house, including a copper tray four feet across that will dominate us for the rest of our lives. We also have two doves. Here they live in a cage but at the villa they are to go free. One can't have any tame animals because on the whole they have dreadful lives here & six months' spoiling would only make the future worse for them. Otherwise we'd have some donkeys—you can buy a donkey for 100 francs.[5]

I expect you can't read a word of this. We only have one table & Eric is typing diary notes on it. He sends his love to everyone, including Marx. So do I.

Eileen.

If there *is* a war I don't know what Bristol,[6] or indeed anywhere, will be like. But if at any time you wanted some place more remote for the children it's quite possible that the cottage will be empty. I don't know what the Commons would do but we've suggested to my brother that the cottage might anyway be kept *in statu quo*. It could be almost as safe as anywhere in England, & comparatively self-supporting, so we thought someone might be glad of it. Of course the Commons may all stay. Someone at my brother's house (24 Croom's Hill, S.E.10) will know. My brother himself would be mobilised at once I suppose as he's in the RAMC.[7]

[*At top of letter*] There's no actual news yet about E's health. The doctor says we must allow 3 or 4 weeks for 'acclimatisation' before expecting much.

[XI, 487, pp. 205–7; handwritten]

1. Marx, the Orwells' black poodle, was being cared for by Marjorie and her husband, Humphrey Dakin.
2. An air-raid shelter dug into the back garden. Such a shelter – not much more than a corrugated steel shell covered by earth – was introduced in November 1938 by the Home Secretary, Sir John Anderson, and was named after him. Over two million were erected, or dug out. They were free to those earning £250 a year or less and cost £7 for those earning more. Though subjected to a fair amount of ridicule, and inclined to flood, they probably saved lives.
3. Early in September 1938, Sudeten Germans, led by Konrad Henlein (1898–1945, by suicide), organised rallies demanding the reunification of Czech border areas with Germany. By 14 September, the Czech government had declared martial law in the Sudetenland, the French had reinforced the Maginot Line, and on 26 September mobilisation of the Royal Navy was ordered. The French and British governments urged the Czechs to accede to German demands, but on 23 September the Czech government ordered general mobilisation, and war seemed inevitable. The day after Eileen wrote, Hitler called a conference of the Czechs, French, and British; Prime Minister Neville Chamberlain flew to Munich to attend. For the sake of a short breathing space, the Czechs were forced to accept German demands, and annexation of the Sudetenland began on 1 October. Poland seized the opportunity to take over Czech Silesia. In the light of Chamberlain's much criticised statement in a radio broadcast on 1 October that he believed 'it is peace in our time . . . peace with honour', Eileen's comment is particularly telling, and probably reflects what many people, without the benefit of hindsight, felt at the time.
4. Gas masks were distributed in late September 1938.
5. Then about 11s 2d equivalent to perhaps £22 today.
6. Where Marjorie and her family were living.
7. Royal Army Medical Corps. Laurence O'Shaughnessy was called up as soon as war was declared one year later.

To Jack Common*

29 September 1938
Chez Madame Vellat
Marrakech

Dear Jack,

I wrote yesterday making suggestions as to what you should do in case of war, then this morning received your letter in which you didn't sound as though war were really likely, so write now in a more normal mood. At this end of the world I can't make out about this war business. The troops are standing by more or less in full kits, the artillery is trained on the proletarian end of the town 'in case of trouble' and this afternoon we had some kind of air-raid practice which I couldn't get the hang of, but meanwhile the French population is utterly uninterested and evidently doesn't believe that war is coming. Of course they are out of all danger here, except for the young ones who will be mobilised, and perhaps that affects their attitude. The whole thing is so utterly insane that it just sickens me. One thing I am certain of. Unless there is some tremendous loss of prestige, such as Hitler seizing the whole of Czechoslovakia while England and France do nothing, and perhaps at the same time painting the British ambassador's arse green and sending him back to England, Chamberlain is safe to win the next election with a big majority. The so-called left parties have played straight into his hands by their idiotic policy.

I'm sorry to hear the cockerels don't fetch anything We crossed the hens with a Leghorn because they're good layers and it's much more paying to go in for eggs than for table birds. The best thing to do really is to eat them. They['re] all right to eat, only they're so light they fetch nothing. The earliest pullets ought to lay this month and the others I suppose about November. Try giving them a spot of Karswood, which is quite cheap, to bring them on. I hope Muriel¹ is behaving. I still can't remember what arrangement was made about her food. Are Clarke's delivering the stuff? If so, ask them about their bill. They know I am good to pay, and they could make some suggestion, whether to send the bills on to me here or what not. Yes, have the telephone disconnected if it hasn't been done. I thought my brother in law had had it done. Could you drop him a line about it? I gave you his address in the last letter. I wonder if there are any apples on the tree in the kitchen garden. It gives 30 or 40 pounds some years. They're very good cookers but you want to use them up because they don't keep.

It makes me sad to hear you say you've never been out of England, especially when I think of the bastards who do travel, simply going from hotel to hotel and never seeing any difference anywhere except in the temperature. At the same time I'm not sure how much good travel does to anyone. One thing I have always believed, and that is that one really learns nothing from a foreign country unless one works in it, or does something that really involves on[e] with the inhabitants. This trip is something quite new to me, because for the first time I am in the position of a tourist. The result is that it is quite impossible, at any rate at present, to make any contact with the Arabs, whereas if I were here, say, on a gun-running expedition, I should immediately have the entrée to all kinds of interesting society, in spite of the language difficulty. I have often been struck by how easy it is to get people to take you for granted if you and they are really in the same boat, and how difficult otherwise. For instance, when I was with the tramps, merely because they assumed that I was on the bum it didn't make a damn's worth of difference to them that I had a middle-class accent and they were willing to be actually more intimate than I wanted. Whereas if, say, you brought a tramp into the house and tried to get him to talk to you it would just be a patron-client relationship and quite meaningless. I am as usual taking careful notes of everything I see, but am not certain what use I shall be able to make of them afterwards. Here in Marrakech it is in some ways harder to find out about conditions in Morocco than it would be in a less typical Arab town. In a town like Casablanca you have a huge French population and a white proletariat, and consequently local branches of the Socialist Party and so forth. Here with not very important differences it is very like Anglo-Indian society and you are more or less obliged to be a pukka sahib or suffer the consequences. We're staying in the town itself for another two or three weeks, then we're taking a villa outside. That will be slightly more expensive but quieter to work in and I simply have to have a bit of garden and a few animals. I shall also be interested to see a little of how the Arab peasants live. Here in the town conditions are pretty frightful, wages generally work out at about 1d or 2d an hour and it's the first place I've seen where beggars do literally beg for bread and eat it greedily when given it. It's still pretty hot but getting better and we're both pretty well in health. There's nothing wrong with me really, but much as I resent the waste of time it's probably done me good to lay off work for seven months. People who don't write think that writing isn't work, but you and I know the contrary. Thank God I've just begun to work again and made a start on my new novel, which was billed for this autumn but might appear in the spring perhaps. Of course if war comes God knows if the publishing of books will even continue. To me the idea of war is a pure nightmare. Richard Rees* was talking as though even war couldn't be worse than the present conditions, but I think what this really means is that he doesn't see any peace-time activity for himself which he feels to be useful. A lot of intellectuals feel like this, which I think is one explanation of why the so-called left-wingers are now the jingoes. But

I personally do see a lot of things that I want to do and to continue doing for another thirty years or so, and the idea that I've got to abandon them and either be bumped off or depart to some filthy concentration camp just infuriates me. Eileen and I have decided that if war does come the best thing will be to just stay alive and thus add to the number of sane people.

The above address will find me for a bit. I'll give you the new one when I have it—probably a poste restante address, as I don't think they will deliver letters where we are going to. Best love to Mary and Peter. Eileen also sends love.

Yours
Eric

P.S. [*handwritten at top of first page*] Yes, I did once just meet Alec Henderson[2] at a party. The village people are really very nice, especially the Hatchetts, Mrs Anderson, Titley, Keep, Edie (Mrs Ridley's daughter) & her husband Stanley, & Albert, Mrs R's other son in law. I don't know what one can really do for old H[atchett] except occasionally to give him eggs when his hens don't lay. He is a dear old man. Tell them all you've heard from me & I wanted to be remembered to them.

[XI, 489, pp. 210–12; typewritten]

1. Orwell's goat, with whom he is to be seen in a very familiar picture (see Crick, plate 19). Also the name of the goat in *Animal Farm*.
2. Possibly this was a neighbour at Wallington, but since he is separated from the 'village people' he may not be local. 'Alec' could be an error for 'Arthur', Arthur Henderson, Sr (1863–1935). His son (1893–1966), like his father, was a Labour MP, 1923–24, 1929–31, and 1935–66.

Marjorie Dakin* to Eileen Blair* and Orwell

3 October 1938
166 St Michael's Hill
Bristol

My dear Eileen and Eric,

Thanks very much for your letters, and the £1 enclosed. Marx is being perfectly good except for such natural wickedness as will never be eradicated. He is very obedient out of doors, and comes directly when called, also is learning to keep on pavements, as we let him off the leash in quiet roads to train him. He has simply terrific games with the children, especially on the downs. A sword of Damocles has been hanging over his head, he was threatened with being made into sausages if there was a food shortage, also Tor, though he is getting a bit tough.

As you will have gathered there has been complete wind-up about war, everybody thought it had really come this time, as indeed it may yet. All preparations are being pushed on just the same. I took the children down to get their gas-masks the other day, not that I have much faith in them, but still it is the correct thing to do. I have heard that the A.R.P. is a farce so far, if there was a really bad bombing raid, there would be practically nobody who knew what to do.[1] I also heard that all the warning that Bristol would get would be four minutes, and London only 25 seconds, but I don't know if this is true.[2] If it is it hardly seems worth while to do anything, as I don't see myself getting the children into gasmasks and shelter in four minutes.

Humph has been transferred *pro. tem.* into the Ministry of Transport, and has been sent off to Salisbury, but I imagine he will be back quite soon now. As far as he could make out all the high officials in London (in transport) moved out in a body to the south of England with their wives and families. The head man took over the Truro district. Humph as the only outsider was given Salisbury, it being the most dangerous place.

Everything here was perfectly calm, no meetings of any kind. All the parks and gardens have been dug up into shelters, and England is swept clean of corrugated iron and sand bags. I believe the grocers have done a roaring trade 'better than Christmas'. I didn't go in for a food hoarding myself except to buy a sack of potatoes, which the grocer offered me.

Devon and Cornwall are simply packed, there is not a house or rooms to be had for love or money, people who went up to London on Friday said it was practically empty, Hyde Park and Kensington Gardens have miles of trenches in them. The bill has now to be paid.

I hope Chamberlain rounds off the thing properly, and offers to give back Germany her mandated colonies, also tries to do something about removing tariffs. Otherwise I think we shall have everything to be ashamed of, in saving our skins at the expense of the Czechs. But I bet he won't. It looks as if poor France has had a kick in the pants, to be vulgar, agreements being signed without reference to her. Personally I think there is going to be a most awful row over the whole thing, when the hysteria has died down a bit. One school of thought says that we shall not be ready for war for another two years and that the Govt. will do anything to put it off till then,[3] others, that now that the great ones of the earth realise that it is really going to be a 'free for all' and that is not just a case of 'giving' one's son it puts a different complexion on things.

I think if there is another war, I shall have Humph in a lunatic asylum in two twos,[4] his nerves are in an awful state, I was really quite glad when he went off to Salisbury poor dear, as he was adding to the horrors of the situation very considerably and of course the children[5] didn't care two hoots, and were enjoying the whole thing, Hen[ry] went round and really had his fill of looking at searchlights and machine guns, and Jane was perfectly indifferent, except that she hoped they wouldn't turn the Art School into a Hospital.

My heart goes out to you over the four-foot tray, I have one of the same ilk, but I had a trestle made to go under it and use it as [a] table. I have had some pretty B.[6] furniture landed on me from Dr. Dakin's[7] house, things I have loathed from my childhood, but I am hoping to be able to discreetly jettison them soon. Excuse typing faults, I am doggedly practising on all my friends and relations.

Have you read any books by a man called R. C. Hutchinson.[8]

I have just read a book of his called *Shining Scabbard* which I thought was awfully good. I believe his latest one *Testament* is even better.

Thanks very much for the offer of the cottage, but if things become really desperate, I expect we should try to get up to Middlesmoor,[9] the cottage there is still furnished, a friend of mine took it over, and I daresay we could all fit in, as it is a magic cottage, and will hold an unlimited amount of people.

Best love to you both
Marge.

[XI, 492, pp. 215–7; typewritten]

1. In January 1938 the government decreed that children be issued gas masks and in April 1938 the rest of the population be measured for them, many months before the Munich crisis. A.R.P. = Air Raid Precautions (which were more effective than Marjorie feared).
2. It was not correct: there was generally adequate time to seek shelter. Bristol would be severely bombed.
3. This was a reasonable approximation of the position.
4. In the 1930s this meant the brief time necessary to add dabs of rouge and powder to each cheek before dashing out. In the nineteenth century it referred to an over-rouged overpowdered street woman.
5. Marjorie and Humphrey Dakin had three children: Jane, born 1923; Henry, 1925; and Lucy, 1930.
6. Bloody.
7. Humphrey's father. Both he and Humphrey served in World War I, and were on the Somme together. Humphrey was wounded and lost an eye. His father, who was a captain in the Royal Army Medical Corps, patched him up.
8. Ray Coryton Hutchinson (1907–1975). *Shining Scabbard* was published in 1936 and *Testament* had just appeared.
9. In his Wigan Pier Diary for 9 March 1936 Orwell writes that he had gone to stay there with Marjorie and Humphrey.

Eileen Blair* to Geoffrey Gorer*

4 October 1938
Chez Mme Vellat
Marrakech

Dear Geoffrey,

Your letter has just arrived. Of course *we* are blameworthy. I thought Eric had written to you & now I see he can't have done so. For myself I don't remember the last few weeks in England except that they were spent almost entirely in trains. People had to be said good-bye to & things (including Eric) collected from all over the country & the cottage had to be handed over furnished but nakedly to the Commons who are spending the winter there & mustering the goats etc. We were thrust out of England very hurriedly partly in case war broke out & partly because Eric was getting rebellious & I had rebelled. As it turns out this was rather a pity. Marrakech is the *dernier cri* of fashionable medicine. Certainly it is dry. They've had three years' drought, including 17 months entirely without rain. But the climate doesn't get tolerable in any year until the end of September & this year the hot weather still persists. We are both choosing our shrouds (the Arabs favour bright green & don't have coffins which is nice on funeral days for the flies who leave even a restaurant for a few minutes to sample a passing corpse¹), but have now chosen instead a villa. It's in the middle of an orange-grove in the palm-tree country at the foot of the Atlas from which the good air comes. I think Eric really will benefit when we get there but it isn't available until the 15ᵗʰ. We've bought the furniture—for about £10. I've only seen the place once for five minutes & I wasn't allowed to open the shutters & there was no artificial light, but I believe it could be very attractive. Garnished with us & our ten pounds' worth it may be odd to the eye but will be comforting to the spirit. We shall even have goats who will be physically as well as emotionally important because fresh milk is otherwise unobtainable. It's five kilometres from Marrakech.

Do you know Morocco? We found it a most desolate country—miles & miles of ground that is not technically desert, i.e. it could be cultivated if it were irrigated but without water is simply earth & stones in about equal proportions with not even a weed growing. We got all excited the other day because we found a dock. The villa is in one of the more fertile bits. Marrakech itself is beautiful in bits. It has ramparts & a lot of buildings made of earth dug up about five feet below ground level. This dries a soft reddish colour so the French call Marrakech 'la rouge' & paint everything that isn't earth a dreadful salmon-beige. The best thing is the native pottery. Unfortunately it generally isn't glazed (except some bits painted in frightful designs for the tourist trade) but we're trying to get some things made watertight. There are exquisite white clay mugs with a very simple black design inside. They cost a franc & it seems to us that people here generally earn about a franc to two francs an hour.

Eric is going to write to you & I shall leave him the crisis. I am determined to be pleased with Chamberlain because I want a rest. Anyway Czecho-Slovakia ought to be pleased with him; it seems geographically certain that that country would be ravaged at the beginning of any war fought in its defence. But of course the English Left is always Spartan; they're fighting Franco to the last Spaniard too.

I hope the old book & the new go well.[2] Are you going to America? If you happen to come to the south of Europe, call on us. It isn't very diffi-cult—indeed there's an air service from Tangier—& we have a spare room (quite spare I should say, not even furniture in it) & we could go & look at the country on donkeys & possibly at the desert on camels, & we should enjoy it very much.

I'd better send love from us both in case Eric's letter gets delayed. He has begun his novel[3] & is also carpentering—there is a box for the goats to eat out of & a hutch for the chickens though we have no goat yet & no chickens.

Yours ever
Eileen.

The villa is not in any postal district & I think we have to have a 'box'. We'll let you know the proper address when we discover it.

[XI, 493, pp. 217–8; handwritten]

1. Compare the first paragraph of Orwell's essay, 'Marrakech'(published Christmas 1939; XI, p. 416); 'As the corpse went past the flies left the restaurant table in a cloud and rushed after it, but they came back a few minutes later.' (See also **14–17.12.38**, n. 6.)
2. Probably *Hot Strip Tease and Other Notes on American Culture* (1937) and *Himalayan Village: An Account of the Lepchas of Sikkim* (1938; US, 1967).
3. *Coming Up for Air.*

To Jack Common*

12 October 1938
Chez Madame Vellat
Marrakech

Dear Jack,

Thanks for yours. There were several important items I wanted to talk to you about but they were chased out of my mind by the European situation. The first is, I think we forgot to warn you not to use thick paper in the WC. It sometimes chokes the cesspool up, with disastrous results. The best to use is Jeyes paper which is 6d a packet. The difference of price is negligible, and on the other hand a choked cesspool is a misery. Secondly, if you find the sitting room fire smokes intolerably, I think you can get a piece of tin put in the chimney, which is what it needs, for a very small sum. Brookers in Hitchin would tell you all about it. Or you could probably do it yourself. I was always meaning to but put it off. Thirdly, I enclose cheque for £3. Could you some time get this cashed and pay £2 to Field, the postmaster at Sandon, for the rent of the field. It's a lot overdue as a matter of fact but F. never remembers about it. Field goes past in his grey car, which he uses to carry cattle in, every Tuesday on his way to Hitchin Market, and one can sometimes stop him if one jumps into the middle of the road and waves. As to the remaining £1, could you some time in the winter get some or, if possible, all of the ground in the vegetable garden dug over? Old H[atchett] is getting so old that I don't really like asking him to do that kind of work, but he's always glad of it and, of course, willing to work for very low rates. There's no hurry, it's just a question of getting the vacant ground turned over some time in the winter and preferably some manure (the goat's stuff is quite good if there isn't too much straw in it) dug in. The official theory is that we are to give up the cottage next spring, so I suppose on good business principles one ought to exhaust the soil by taking an enormous crop of Brussels off it and then let it go to hell. But I hate starving soil and in addition I'm not so certain of giving up the cottage. As I expect you've discovered by this time it's truly a case of be it never so humble, but the fact is that it's a roof and moving is so damned expensive besides being a misery. I think I would rather feel I had the cottage there to move into next April, even if when the time comes we don't actually do it, because I don't know what my financial situation will be next year. I don't believe my book on Spain sold at all, and if I have to come back to England and start on yet another book with about £50 in the world I would rather have a roof over my head from the start. It's a great thing to have a roof over your head even if it's a leaky one. When Eileen and I were first married, when I was writing *Wigan Pier*, we had so little money that sometimes we hardly knew where the next meal was coming from, but we found we could rub along in a remarkable manner with spuds and so forth. I hope the hens have begun laying. Some of them have by this time, I expect, at any rate they ought to. We've just bought the hens for our house, which we're moving into on Saturday. The hens in this country are miserable little things like the Indian ones, about the size of bantams, and what is regarded as a good laying hen, ie. it lays once a fortnight, costs less than a shilling. They ought only to cost about 6d, but at this time of year the price goes up because after Yom Kippur every Jew, of whom there are 13,000 in this town, eats a whole fowl to recompense him for the strain of fasting 12 hours.

Well, the mortal moon hath her eclipse endured[1] till 1941, I suppose. I don't think one need be surprised at Chamberlain's stock slumping a bit after the danger is over. Judging from the letters I get from home I should say people feel as you feel when you are just going to dive off the springboard and then think better of it. The real point is what will happen at the election, and unless the Conservative Party splits right up I prophecy they will win hands down. Because the other bloody fools can't produce any policy except 'We want war', and however ashamed people may feel after we've let down Czechoslovakia, or whoever it may be, they'll shy away from war when it comes to a show-down. The only hope of Labour getting in is for some downright disaster to happen, or alternatively, for the elections to be held a year hence with another million unemployed. I think now we're in for a period of slow fascisation°, the sort of Dollfuss-Schussnig Fascism[2] which is what Chamberlain and Co would presumably introduce, but I would sooner have that than have the Left parties identified in the public mind as the war party. The only hope is that if Chamberlain wins and then begins seriously to prepare for war with Germany, as of course he will, the L[abour] P[arty] will be driven back to an anti-war policy in which they will be able to exploit the discontent with conscription etc. The policy of simultaneously shouting for a war policy and pretending to denounce conscription, rearmament etc. is utter nonsense and the general public aren't such bloody fools as not to see it. As to the results if war comes, although *some* kind of revolutionary situation will no doubt arise, I do not see how it can lead to anything except Fascism *unless* the Left has been anti-war from the outset. I have nothing but contempt for the fools who think that they can first drive the nation into a war for democracy and then when people are a bit fed up suddenly turn round and say 'Now we'll have the revolution.' What sickens me about left-wing people, especially the intellectuals, is their utter ignorance of the way things actually happen. I was always struck by this when I was in Burma and used to read anti-imperialist stuff. Did you see Kingsley Martin's ('Critic') article in last week's N[ew] S[tatesman] about the conditions on which the L.P. should support the Government in war? As though the Government would allow any conditions. The bloody fool seems to think war is a cricket match. I wish someone would print my anti-war pamphlet I wrote earlier this year,[3] but of course no one will.

All the best. Love to Mary and Peter. E. sends love.

Yours
Eric

P.S. [*handwritten at top of first page*] This address will find us.

[XI, 496, pp. 221–2; typewritten]

1. 'The mortal moon hath her eclipse endur'd, / And the sad augurs mock their own presage', Shakespeare, Sonnet 107.
2. Engelbert Dollfuss (1892–1934) was Chancellor of Austria, 1932–34. He was largely responsible for the establishment of a quasi-fascist regime on the Italian pattern, which brought to an end parliamentary government in Austria, but not without bloodshed. He was assassinated by members of the Nazi Party. Kurt von Schuschnigg (1897–1977), Austrian Minister of Justice and later of Education, then became chancellor and attempted to maintain Austria's independence. After annexation by Germany in 1938, he was imprisoned until the end of World War II. (See his *The Brutal Takeover* (1969).)
3. 'Socialism and War'. Orwell told Leonard Moore on 28 June that he was in the process of writing this 5,000–6,000-word article (XI, 458, p. 169). It was not published.

To John Sceats*

26 October 1938
Boite[1] Postale 48
Guéliz
Marrakech
French Morocco

Dear Sceats,[2]

I hope all goes well with you. I had meant to look you up before leaving England, but as it turned out I went almost straight from the sanatorium to the boat and only had one day in London, which of course was pretty full. I'm writing to you now for some expert advice. The chap in the novel I'm writing[3] is supposed to be an insurance agent. His job isn't in the least important to the story, I merely wanted him to be a typical middle-aged bloke with about £5 a week and a house in the suburbs, and he's also rather thoughtful and fairly well-educated, even slightly bookish, which is more plausible with an insurance agent than, say, a commercial traveller. But I want any mention that is made of his job to be correct. And meanwhile I have only very vague ideas as to what an insurance agent does. I want him to be a chap who travels round and gets part of his income from commissions, not merely an office employee. Does such a chap have a 'district' and a regular round like a commercial traveller? Does he have to go touting round for orders, or just go round and sign the people up when they want to be insured? Would he spend all his time in travelling or part of it in the office? Would he have an office of his own? Do the big insurance companies have branch offices all over the place (this chap lives in a suburb which might be Hayes or Southall) or do they only have the head office and send all the agents out from there? And would such a man do valuations of property, and would the same man do life insurance and property insurance? I'd be very glad of some elucidation on these points. My picture of this chap is this. He spends about two days a week in the branch office in his suburb and the rest of the time in travelling round in a car over a district of about half a county, interviewing people who've written in to say that they want to be insured, making valuations of houses, stock and so forth, and also touting for orders on which he gets an extra commission, and that by this he is earning round about £5 a week after being with the firm 18 years (having started very much at the bottom). I want to know if this is plausible.

Well, 'The mortal moon hath her eclipse endured and the sad augurs mock their own presage'⁴ and some of them are very sad indeed to judge by the *New Statesman*. However, I suppose they'll get the war they're longing for in about two years. The real attitude of the governing class to this business is summed up in the remark I overheard from one of the Gibraltar garrison the moment I set foot there: 'It's pretty clear Hitler's going to have Czechoslovakia. Much better let him have it. We shall be ready in 1941.' Meanwhile the net result will be a sweeping win for the Conservatives at the General Election. I judge from letters from more or less conservative relatives at home that now that it is all over people are a bit fed up and saying 'What a pity we didn't hold on a bit longer and Hitler would have backed down' And from this the bloody fools of the L[abour] P[arty] infer that after all the English people *do* want another war to make the world safe for democracy and that their best line is to exploit the anti-fascist stuff. They don't seem to see that the election will revive the spirit of the crisis, the word will be Chamberlain and Peace, and if the L.P. go round saying 'We want war', which is how ordinary people, quite rightly, interpret the firm line with Hitler stuff, they will just be eaten up. I think a lot of people in the last two years have been misled by phenomena like the Left Book Club. Here you have about 50,000 people who are willing to make a noise about Spain, China etc., and because the majority of people are normally silent this gives the impression that the Left Bookmongers are the voice of the nation instead of being a tiny minority. No one seems to reflect that what matters is not what a few people say when all is quiet but what the majority do in moments of crisis. The only hope is that if the L.P. gets a knock at the election, as it's almost certain to do, this will gradually force them back to their proper policy. But I am afraid it may be a year or two years before this happens.

I've got to go down to a meal that's getting cold, so *au revoir*. I'd be enormously obliged if you'd let me know about those points some time, but there's no immediate hurry.

Yours
Eric Blair

[XI, 498, pp. 226–8; typewritten]

1. Orwell had no accents on his typewriter and always spells 'Boîte' as 'Boite'. His French was very good so he would have been well aware of the correct spelling. It is silently corrected hereafter.

2. John Sceats only met Orwell once, at Preston Hall Sanatorium probably in May or June 1938: 'We talked chiefly of politics and philosophy. I remember he said he thought *Burmese Days* his best book (excluding, *sans dire*, the latest). At the time he was reading Kafka. Despite his recent association with POUM, he had already decided he was not a Marxist, and he was more than interested in the philosophy of Anarchism. [...] He was of course anti-Nazi, but could not (at the time) stomach the idea of an anti-German war: in fact, talking to Max Plowman* (who called in the afternoon) he implied that he would join him in opposition to such a war with whatever underground measures might be appropriate.' Sceats marked the last sentence with an asterisk and added a footnote: 'Indeed, it was Max who put the views of common sense.'

3. *Coming Up for Air*.

4. Shakespeare, Sonnet 107; also quoted in part in Orwell's letter to Jack Common, **12.10.38** (and see its n. 1).

To John Sceats*

24 November 1938
Boîte Postale 48
Marrakech

Dear Sceats,

Thanks so much for your letter with the very useful information about insurance offices. I see that my chap will have to be a Representative and that I underrated his income a little. I've done quite a lot of work, but unfortunately after wasting no less than a fortnight doing articles for various papers fell slightly ill so that properly speaking I've done no work for 3 weeks. It's awful how the time flies by. What with all this illness I've decided to count 1938 as a blank year and sort of cross it off the calendar. But meanwhile the concentration camp looms ahead and there is so much one wants to do. I've got to the point now when I feel I could write a good novel if I had five years peace and quiet, but at present one might as well ask for five years in the moon.

This is on the whole rather a dull country. Some time after Xmas we want to go for a week into the Atlas mountains which are 50 or 100 miles from here and look rather exciting. Down here it's flat dried-up country rather like a huge allotment patch that's been let 'go back', and practically no trees except olives and palms. The poverty is something frightful, though of course it's always a little more bearable for people in a hot climate. The people have tiny patches of ground which they cultivate with implements which would have been out of date in the days of Moses. One can get a sort of idea of the prevailing hunger by the fact that in the whole country there are practically no wild animals, everything edible being eaten by human beings. I don't know how it would compare with the poorer parts of India, but Burma would seem like a paradise compared to it, so far as standard of living goes. The French are evidently squeezing the country pretty ruthlessly. They absorb most of the fertile land as well as the minerals, and the taxes seem fairly heavy considering the poverty of the people. On the surface their administration looks better than ours and certainly rouses less animosity in the subject race, because they have very little colour-prejudice. But I think underneath it is much the same. So far as I can judge there is no anti-French movement of any size among the Arabs, and if there were one it would almost certainly be nationalist rather than Socialist, as the great majority of the people are at the feudal stage and the French, I fancy, intend them to remain so. I can't tell anything about the extent of the local Socialist movement, because [it] has for some time only existed illegally. I asked the

I.L.P. to get the French Socialist party to put me in touch with any Socialist movement existing here, if only because I could thus learn more about local conditions, but they haven't done so, perhaps because it's too dangerous. The local French, though they're quite different from the British population in India, mostly petty traders and even manual workers, are stuffily conservative and mildly pro-Fascist. I wrote two articles on local conditions for the *Quarterly* which I hope they'll print[1] as they were I think not too incorrect and subtly Trotskyist. I hope by the way that *Controversy* has not succumbed.[2] It would be a disaster if it did, and still more if the *N.L.*[3] had to turn into a monthly. As to *Controversy* I'm sure the sale could be worked up with a little energy and a certain willingness to distribute back numbers, and I'll do what I can in my nearest town when I get back.

Have you heard any rumours about the General Election? The only person I can make contact with here who might conceivably know something is the British consul, who thinks the Government are going to defer the election as long as possible and that attempts may also be made to resuscitate the old Liberal party. Personally I don't think anything can prevent Chamberlain winning unless there is some unforeseen scandal. Labour may win a few by-elections, but the general election will be fought in a completely different emotional atmosphere. The best one can hope is that it may teach Labour a lesson. I only get English papers rather intermittently and haven't seen the results of some of the by-elections. I see Labour won Dartford but gather the Conservatives won Oxford.[4]

Let me have a line some time to hear how things are going.

Yours
Eric Blair

[XI, 504, pp. 237–8; typewritten]

1. Despite a thorough search, these have not been traced.
2. It did survive, but became *Left Forum* in June 1939.
3. *The New Leader.* It depended on voluntary contributions in order to survive. It recorded in November 1938 the results of two appeals in which £63 and £51 6s 7d were raised, averaging 6s 11d for each contribution. Orwell's was 5s 7d.
4. In its issue for 9 December 1938, *The New Leader* reported what it described as 'Amazing Stories' of how Labour candidates had been 'ousted' at selection meetings for the constituencies of Bridgwater and Oxford by 'Independent Progressives'. At Bridgwater, the 'alleged Independent candidate' was introduced to the constituency by Sir Richard Acland (1906–1990; Bt.), a Liberal MP from 1935 and very active in the popular front campaign from 1936. Orwell wrote a Profile of him for the *Observer*, 23 May 1943 (XV, 2095, pp. 103–6). There was also intervention by 'the new political party, the Left Book Club'. At Oxford, academics were

blamed for manipulating the selection of an Independent Progressive. The report concluded: 'These "intelligentsia" and their Left Book Clubs are the new instrument of the Communist Party.' This manoeuvring was to little effect, because the Conservative, Quintin Hogg, took the seat.

To Charles Doran*

26 November 1938
Boîte Postale 48
Marrakech

Dear Charlie,

Thanks so much for your letter with the copy of *Solidarity* and the too kind review of my book. I see from the front page of *Solidarity* that those bloody liars in the *News Chronicle* reported the result of the P.O.U.M. trial under the heading 'spies sentenced' thus giving the impression that the P.O.U.M. prisoners were sentenced for espionage. *The Observer* also did something of the kind, though more circumspectly, and the French press of this country, which is in the main pro-Franco, reported the act of accusation against the P.O.U.M., stated that it had been 'all proved' and then failed to report the verdict at all! I admit this kind of thing frightens me. It means that the most elementary respect for truthfulness is breaking down, not merely in the Communist and Fascist press, but in the bourgeois liberal press which still pays lip-service to the old traditions of journalism. It gives one the feeling that our civilization is going down into a sort of mist of lies where it will be impossible ever to find out the truth about anything. Meanwhile I've written to the I.L.P. asking them to send me a copy of the issue of *Solidaridad Obrera*[1] which reported the case, so that if necessary I can write to the press, that is to say such papers as would print my letter, stating quite clearly what the P.O.U.M. prisoners *were* sentenced for. I trust, however, that someone has already done so. It's difficult for me to get hold of foreign papers here, especially a paper like *Solidaridad Obrera*, which I couldn't get nearer than Gibraltar and there only with difficulty.

As perhaps you know I was told to spend the winter here for the sake of my lungs. We've been here nearly three months now and I think it has done me a certain amount of good. It is a tiresome country in some ways, but it is interesting to get a glimpse of French colonial methods and compare them with our own. I think as far as I can make out that the French are every bit as bad as ourselves, but some what better on the surface, partly owing to the fact that there is a large indigenous white population here, part of it proletarian or near-proletarian. For that reason it isn't quite possible to keep up the sort of white man's burden atmosphere that we do in India, and there is less colour-prejudice. But economically it is just the usual swindle for which empires exist. The poverty of most of the Arab population is frightful. As far as one can work it out, the average family seems to live at the rate of about a shilling a day, and of course most of the people are either peasants or petty craftsmen who have to work extremely hard by antiquated methods. At the same time, so far as one can judge, there is no anti-French movement on any scale. If one appeared it would I think be merely nationalist at the beginning, as the great majority of the people are still at the feudal stage and fairly strict Mahommedans. In some of the big towns such as Casablanca there is a proletariat, both white and coloured, and there the Socialist movement just exists. But as for the Arab Socialist parties, they were all suppressed some time ago. I feel reasonably sure that unless the working class (it really depends on them) in the democracies change their tactics within a year or two, the Arabs will be easy game for the Fascists. French opinion here is predominantly pro-Franco, and I should not be greatly surprised to see Morocco become the jumping-off place for some French version of Franco in the years to come. I don't altogether know what to think about the crisis, Maxton etc. I think Maxton put his foot in it by being too cordial to Chamberlain, and I also think it would be absurd to regard Chamberlain as really a peace-maker. I also quite agree with what anybody chooses to say about the way in which the Czechs have been let down. But I think we might face one or two facts. One is that almost anything is better than European war, which will lead not only to the slaughter of tens of millions but to an extension of Fascism. Certainly Chamberlain and Co. are preparing for war, and any other government that is likely to get in will also prepare for war; but meanwhile we have got perhaps two years' breathing space in which it *may* be possible to provoke a real popular anti-war movement in England, in France and above all in the Fascist countries. If we can do that, to the point of making it clear that no government will go to war because its people won't follow, I think Hitler is done for. The other fact is that the Labour Party are doing themselves frightful harm by getting stamped in the public mind as the war party. In my opinion they can't now win the general election[2] unless something very unforeseen turns up. They will therefore be in the position of an opposition pushing the government in the direction in which it is already going. As such they might as well cease to exist, and in fact it wouldn't surprise me in the next year or two to see Attlee and Co. cave in and take office in some new version of a national government.[3] I admit that being anti-war probably plays Chamberlain's game for the next few months, but the point will soon come when the anti-wars, of all complexions, will have to resist the fascising° processes which war-preparation entails.

I hope things are prospering with you. After all the frightful waste of time due to being ill I got started on my novel, which I suppose will be ready to come out about April. Eileen sends love.

Yours
Eric Blair

P.S. [*at top of letter*] Thanks so much for your good offices about my Spanish book. That's what sells a book—getting asked for in libraries.

[XI, 505, pp. 238–40; typewritten]

1. A Spanish Anarchist daily newspaper of the time.
2. A largely Conservative government—with National Liberal and National Labour adherents—had assembled on 16 November 1935, with a majority of 247, for a maximum five-year term. Orwell is expecting a general election in 1939 or 1940, but because of the outbreak of war none was held until 1945.
3. With the fall of Neville Chamberlain and the appointment of Winston Churchill as Prime Minister in May 1940, Labour joined a genuinely national government, Clement Attlee becoming deputy prime minister. The Labour Party would win the 1945 election with a majority of 146.

To Leonard Moore*

28 November 1938
Boîte Postale 48
Marrakech

Dear Mr. Moore,

I have just had a letter from Allen Lane, who apparently runs the Penguin Series.[1] He says:

'I am writing to you to know whether it would be possible to include some of your work in my series. As a matter of fact I was very much impressed by one of your stories which I published some time ago in *New Writing* when I was at the Bodley Head.[2] If it is not possible for us to get one of your novels have you a collection of short stories sufficient for one volume?'

I think we ought to cash in on this if possible. Of course I haven't any short stories for them. I simply can't write short stories. But I gather from this that they would prefer one of my novels, and I have replied suggesting *Down and Out*,[3] *Burmese Days*[4] and *Keep the Aspidistra Flying*. I don't know which if any of these they'd be likely to choose. But I have asked Mr Lane to get in touch with you if he is interested, and said you would supply him with copies of any book he wanted. If it is a question of *Down and Out*, I haven't a copy and I believe you have not either. The only person I know has one is my mother. If there should be a demand for one, could you write and ask for it from her, which would save time? Her address is Mrs R W Blair, 36 High Street, Southwold, Suffolk. I am writing to her asking her to hand it over if she hears from you. If the Penguin people *do* seem inclined to take one of these books, I don't in the least know on what terms they deal. But I think it would be well worth letting them have one on not very advantageous terms for us, if necessary, because it is first-rate publicity.

Please don't give yourself any more trouble with that wretched pamphlet.[5] I am sorry you have had so much already. As you say, there is no sale for pamphlets, and in any case the Hogarth Press is in the hands of Communists (at any rate Lehmann is one)[6] who won't publish my work if they can help it.

The weather has got a lot cooler and I think the climate is doing me good. The novel is going pretty well. I think I can promise it for the beginning of April, which perhaps you could tell Gollancz if he makes further enquiries. If he does, tell him I was very sorry to let him down about the time, but I suppose he knows I was actually in the sanatorium till the end of August.

I hope Miss Perriam[7] is making some progress. My wife sends all the best.

Yours sincerely
Eric Blair

[XI, 506, pp. 241-2; typewritten]

1. Allen Lane (1902-1970; Kt., 1952), one of the most influential British publishers of the twentieth century, was apprenticed to his uncle, John Lane, at the Bodley Head Press in 1919. He resigned in 1936 and founded Penguin Books, which revolutionised paperback publication in Britain – and, indeed, more widely.

2. *New Writing* had published 'Shooting an Elephant' in its second number, Autumn 1936. Orwell's 'Marrakech' appeared in the Christmas 1939 issue, and 'Shooting an Elephant' was reprinted in the first number of *Penguin New Writing*, November 1940.

3. Published by Penguin Books in December 1940.

4. Published by Penguin Books in May 1944.

5. 'Socialism and War'. The pamphlet was never published.

6. John Lehmann was probably not, at least formally, a Communist, but he had been associated with Lawrence & Wishart briefly and he reviewed for the *Daily Worker*.

7. Miss Periam was Moore's secretary and had been seriously ill.

To Richard Walmsley Blair*

2 December 1938
Boîte Postale 48
Marrakech

Dear Father,

I am glad to hear from Mother that you have been a little better and getting up occasionally. If your appetite is very bad, did you ever think of trying Haliborange? I have taken it occasionally, and it is not at all unpleasant to take, nourishing in itself and seems to improve one's appetite after a while. I should think Doctor Collings would approve of it. It's only halibut's liver oil flavoured with orange and a few other things.

The weather here has got a lot cooler and is rather like the cold weather in Upper Burma, generally fine and sunny but not hot. We have a fire most days, which one doesn't actually need till the evening, but it is nice to have it. There is no coal in this country, all the fires are wood and they use char-coal to cook on. We have tried to do a bit of gardening but not been very successful because it's hard to get seed to germinate, I suppose because it is generally so dry. Most English flowers do pretty well here once they are established, and at the same time there are tropical plants like Bougainvillea. The peasants are just getting in their crops of chilis,° like the ones they used to grow in Burma. The people here live in villages which are surrounded by mud walls about ten feet high, I suppose as a protection against robbers, and inside they have miserable little straw huts about ten feet wide which they live in. It is a very bare country, parts of it almost desert, though it's not what is considered true desert. The people take their flocks of sheep, goats, camels and so forth out to graze on places where there seems nothing to eat at all, and the wretched brutes nose about and find little dried up weeds under the stones. The children seem to start work when they are five or six. They are extraordinarily obedient, and stay out all day herding the goats and keeping the birds off the olive trees.

I think the climate is doing me good. I was a little unwell last week, but on the whole feel much better and am putting on a little weight. I have done quite a lot of work. We are going to take some more photographs, including some of the house, and will send them to you when developed.¹ Look after yourself and get well soon.

With love
Eric

[XI, 509, pp. 247–8; typewritten]

1 See plates 9, 10 and 11.

Eileen Blair* to Mary Common*

5 December 1938
Boîte Postale 48
Marrakech

Dear Mary,

We have just got back from a Christmas shopping. It began by my bicycle having a puncture. The next stage was my arrival in Marrakech, entirely penniless, two minutes after the bank had shut. By the time Eric arrived for lunch I had scoured the town (in which we know no one) for succour and had succeeded in cashing a cheque and in collecting a retinue of guides, porters etc., all of whom had most charmingly waited for money so long that they might be said to have earned it. After lunch we began to shop and we went on for two and a half hours, surrounded by as many as twenty men and boys, all shouting and many of them weeping. If either of us tried to speak, long before we had mentioned what we were talking about everyone present cried 'Yes, yes. I understand. The others don't understand.' We bought a lot of things in one shop because the people there will post to England—at least so they say. The things are being sent in three lots, to three key recipients who are to distribute them. You are a key recipient, and you ought to get a dish for Mrs. Hatchett, a brass tray for Mrs. Anderson, and a 'couverture' for yourself (and Jack). You may of course get something quite different, or nothing at all. A porter is engaged if he succeeds in laying hands on any piece of property, and as I put each thing on its appropriate pile it was instantly seized by one to four helpers and put somewhere else, or the pieces in several different places. Supposing you do get something, there may be duty to pay. I don't think it can be more than three or four shillings and I hope it will be nothing. We have sent a few things home already without trouble (by which I mean paying money) and they should be kind at Christmas, but it is perfectly probable that they put on for Christmas a special staff to be unkind. Anyway if there is duty of course we'll refund it when we get back or before by proxy, but meanwhile we can't think of any better arrangement than that Peter[1] should pay it. Peter, like all our younger friends, is having money for Christmas because we can't get anything here for children unless we pay about thirty francs for something that Woolworth makes better. Money means 5/–. I hope that will arrive, but naturally we are doing all this much too late. We should have done it too late in any case, but in fact Eric was ill and in bed for more than a week and as soon as he was better I had an illness I'd actually started before his but had necessarily postponed. I enjoyed the illness: I had to do all the cooking as usual but I did it in a dressing-gown and firmly carried my tray back to bed. Now we are both very well, or I remember thinking that we were very well last night. This evening we are literally swaying on our feet and the menu for supper, which once included things like a mushroom sauce and a souffle, has been revised to read: Boiled eggs, bread, butter, cheese; bread, jam, cream; raw fruit. The servant goes home after lunch. He was supposed to sleep here in a kind of stable, but he prefers to cycle the five or six miles to Marrakech morning and evening. I like it much better. There is nothing for him to do in the evening except wash up the supper things, and until they were dirty he used to sit on the kitchen step, often in tears, getting up every ten minutes or so to tidy the kitchen and put away (generally in the cellar) the things I was just about to use for the cooking. It is customary, among the French as well as among the Arabs, to get up at five o'clock at the latest, and he arrives here about seven with fresh bread and milk for breakfast. It is early enough for us. We come to understand each other fairly well, though I seldom know whether he is speaking French or Arabic and often talk to him myself in English. The weather has got quite cold, which is delightful. Indeed it's a good climate now and I think we sha'n't die of it, which until recently seemed probable in my case and certain in Eric's. His illness was a sort of necessary stage in getting better; he has been worse here than I've ever seen him. The country is, or was anyway, almost intolerably depressing, just not desert. Now it's better because a few things are growing, and according to the guide books by February or so the whole land will be covered with a carpet of wild flowers. We found a wild flower the other day with great excitement and as it was a kind of lilyish thing without any stalk we suppose it was the first shred of the carpet. In our own garden we have had heartrending experiences. I suppose we have sowed about twenty packets of seed and the result is a few nasturtiums, a very few marigolds and some sweet peas. They take about three or four weeks to germinate and either grow at the same pace or don't grow higher than half an inch. But generally of course they don't germinate. The two goats are more satisfactory now because they went right out of milk and that saves trouble. Until recently they were milked twice a day, with Mahjroub[2] holding head and hind leg, Eric milking and me responding to cries of agony while some good cows' milk boiled over; and the total yield of the two per day was well under half a pint. The hens however have become very productive—they've laid ten eggs in four days. We started with twelve hens but four died immediately, so if you like you can do the sum I was thinking of doing but find too difficult. I hope all those great hens at Wallington will be ashamed. They really ought to be laying pretty well (i.e. about four each a week) now. Last Christmas we had great numbers of eggs and sent quite a lot away, with the result that all the lucky recipients got letters from the P.M.G.[3] who regretted that a parcel addressed to them had had to be destroyed because it was offensive. I must write some Christmas letters, which is why I go on typing this. I get intolerably melancholy if I have to say exactly the same thing twice, so at about the tenth or fifteenth Christmas letter I am sending people the most surprising greetings, but by the twentieth I am resigned to intolerable melancholy and wish the rest a happy Christmas. That's what I wish you, and a bright New Year of course. And Eric, I am sure, does the same. And we both send our love.

Yours,
Eileen.

[XI, 510, pp. 248–50; typewritten]

1. Son of Mary and Jack Common.
2. The Orwells' servant, Mahdjoub Mahommed. For Orwell and Mahdjoub milking a goat see plate 10.
3. Postmaster-General.

To Cyril Connolly*

14 December 1938
Boîte Postale 48
Marrakech

Dear Cyril,

I see your book¹ is out. Send me a copy, won't you? I can't get English books here. The *New English* [*Weekly*] were going to send it to me to review, but they haven't done so, perhaps haven't had a copy. I have been in this place about three months, as it is supposed to do my lungs good to spend the winter here. I have less than no belief in theories about certain climates being 'good for' you, on enquiry they always turn out to be a racket run by tourist agencies and local doctors, but now I am here I suppose I shall stay till about April. Morocco seems to me a beastly dull country, no forests and literally no wild animals, and the people anywhere near a big town utterly debauched by the tourist racket and their poverty combined, which turn them into a race of beggars and curio-sellers. Some time next month we are going into the Atlas for a bit, which may be more interesting. I am getting on with my novel which was listed to come out in the autumn but, owing to this bloody illness, didn't get started till two or three months ago. Of course I shall have to rush it as I must get it done in time for the spring. It's a pity, really, as it's a good idea, though I don't think you'll like it if you see it. Everything one writes now is overshadowed by this ghastly feeling that we are rushing towards a precipice and, though we shan't actually prevent ourselves or anyone else from going over, must put up some sort of fight. I suppose actually we have about two years before the guns begin to shoot. I am looking forward to seeing your book, I gather from the reviews that a lot of it is about Eton, and it will interest me very much to see whether the impressions you retain are anything like my own. Of course you were in every way much more of a success at school than I, and my own position was complicated and in fact dominated by the fact that I had much less money than most of the people about me, but as far as externals go we had very much the same experiences from 1912 to 1921. And our literary development impinged at certain points, too. Do you remember one or other of us getting hold of H. G. Wells's *Country of the Blind* about 1914, at St. Cyprian's, and being so enthralled with it that we were constantly pinching it off each other? It's a very vivid memory of mine, stealing along the corridor at about four o'clock on a midsummer morning into the dormitory where you slept and pinching the book from beside your bed. And do you remember at about the same time my bringing back to school a copy of Compton Mackenzie's *Sinister Street*, which you began to read, and then that filthy old sow Mrs Wilkes found out and there was a fearful row about bringing 'a book of that kind' (though at the time I didn't even know what 'sinister' meant) into the school. I'm always meaning one of those days to write a book about St. Cyprian's. I've always held that the public schools aren't so bad, but people are wrecked by those filthy private schools long before they get to public school age.

Please give all the best to your wife. I hope I'll see you when I get back.

Yours
Eric Blair

P.S. [*handwritten*] I suppose the Quintin Hogg [2] who won the Oxford election was the little squirt who was a fag when I left school.

[XI, 512, pp. 253–4; typewritten]

1. *Enemies of Promise*. Although primarily concerned with aspects of life that work against the creative writer, it also describes life at St Cyprian's (called St Wulfric's) and Eton. Connolly was at both schools with Orwell, who is quite frequently mentioned. Orwell and Christopher Isherwood are described 'as the ablest exponents of the colloquial style among the young writers'. Mrs Wilkes was the headmaster's wife.

2. Quintin Hogg (1907–2001; 2nd Viscount Hailsham; peerage disclaimed for life, 1963; created life peer, Baron Hailsham of St Marylebone, 1970; PC, 1956; KG, 1988; CH, 1974), lawyer, Conservative Party politician, and writer, had entered Eton shortly after Orwell. He was elected to the House of Commons for Oxford City in 1938. Edward Hulton's *Picture Post* reported that Hogg's platform was 'Unity: solid behind Chamberlain.'

Eileen* to Norah Myles*

14–17 Dec 1938
Boîte Postale 48
Marrakech

[no salutation]

I know my dear girl will receive a New Year Gift just as gladly as she would have done a Xmas Present. Whether she will guess what to do with it afterwards I do not know. They say it's to put money in & indeed if one does that it sits erect in an appealing way. But that's just as you like dear. Only I would like to hope that it will be full of money all through 1939 & that you will have other riches too, the better kind.

The news is that I feel very happy now. So far as I can judge the happiness is the direct result of yesterday's news, which was a) that Mr Blair is dying of cancer, b) that Gwen's baby Laurence[1] had to be taken to Great Ormond Street (he is 4½ weeks old, or 5), c) that George Kopp* proposes to come & stay with us in Morocco (he has no money & we had heard the day before by cable that he was out of jail & Spain;[2] Eric's reaction to the cable was that George must stay with us & his reaction to George's letter announcing his arrival is that he must not stay with us, but I think the solution may be that George won't find anyone to lend him the necessary money). Eric however is better. I protested a lot about coming here at the beginning of September & I like to be right but I did feel too right. The weather was practically intolerable. I had a temperature of 102 before I'd been in the place twenty-four hours & Eric, without any actual crisis, lost 9lbs in the first month & coughed all day & particularly all night so that we didn't get thirty minutes' consecutive rest until November. He has put on about five of the pounds again now & doesn't cough much (though still more than in England) so I think he may not be much worse at the end of the winter abroad than he was at the beginning. I expect his life has been shortened by another year or two but all the totalitarians make that irrelevant. One reason for my unwillingness to come when we did was that I'd made all the arrangements to come to Bristol, bringing Marx the poodle (who is wintering with Eric's sister there) but staying with you. Of course you hadn't heard but you know how pleased you would have been. We were hurled out of the country largely because Eric defied brother Eric to the extent of going to see his father who was already ill though cancer hadn't been thought of. Brother Eric was unable to think of any more lies about the disease (they'd kept him in Preston Hall on a firm and constantly repeated diagnosis of phthisis for two months after they knew he hadn't got it & I discovered in the end that on the very first X-rays the best opinions were against even a provisional diagnosis of phthisis) so turned his attention to Morocco. Of course we were silly to come but I found it impossible to refuse & Eric felt that he was under an obligation though he constantly & justly complains that by a quite deliberate campaign of lying he is in debt for the first time in his life[3] & has wasted practically a year out of the very few in which he can expect to function. However, now that we're hardened to the general frightfulness of the country we're quite enjoying it & Eric is writing a book that pleases both of us very much.[4] And in a way I have forgiven Brother Eric who can't help being a Nature's Fascist & indeed is upset by this fact which he realises.[5]

If you would like some news about Morocco I'll send you a picture postcard. The markets are fascinating if you smoke (preferably a cigar) all the time & never look down. At first we lived in Marrakech itself, *en pension* (after the first night which we spent in a brothel owing to Cooks' lists being a bit out of date). Marrakech crawls with disease of every kind, the ringworm group, the tuberculosis group, the dysentery group; & if you lunch in a restaurant the flies only show themselves as flies as distinct from black masses when they hurry out for a moment to taste a corpse on its way to the cemetery.[6] Now we live in a villa several kilometres out. It is furnished with grass & willow chairs made to order for six francs (armchairs they are, rather comfortable), two rugs & a praying mat, several copper trays, a bed & several camel-hair 'couvertures', three whitewood tables, two charcoal braziers for cooking, about a third of the absolutely essential crockery & some chessmen. It looks rather attractive. The house stands in an orange grove & everything belongs to a butcher who cultivates the orange-grove but prefers to live with his meat. The only neighbours are the Arabs who look after the oranges. We have an Arab too, called Mahjroub[7] His life history is 'Moy dix ans et dooje ans avec Francais – soldat.' He says a lot of good things, sort of biblical. 'Dire gaz' means 'If you put oil in the methylated spirits cup of a Primus it make fumes' – which you could hardly tell apart from Mizpah.[8] He has been worried lately because he never can remember the French for fish but this week he's really learnt it – it's oiseau[9]. We understand each other very nicely now (he often calls me Mon vieux Madame) though I seldom know whether he is talking French or Arabic & myself often speak English. He does the shopping & pumps the water & washes the floors (Moy porty sack chitton) & I do the cooking & curiously enough the washing. The laundries are very expensive (10 francs for a sheet, 11 francs for a shirt, 14 francs for a dress) & generally take two or three weeks. I think probably no one uses them except me so they have to engage a staff every time I send anything. We have two goats who used to give half a pint a day between them at two milkings (the milking being done by Eric while Mahjroub holds head & hind leg) but now their yield has fallen off. Our hens however lay very well. We bought 12, 4 died immediately & the remainder have laid 10 eggs in three days; the answer is a Record for a Moroccan Hen. We have people at the back door wanting to buy them. We also have two doves. They don't lay eggs but if they think of it will doubtless nest in our pillows as they spend most of the day <u>walking</u> about the house – one behind the other.

A thing I must remember is Eric's sister. I was going to Put you in Touch during that weekend. They only came to Bristol about July. Their name is Dacombe:[10] Marjorie *aetat* 40, Humphrey rather older I suppose, Jane 15, Henry 10, Lucy 7. They live in St. Michael's Hill – 166 I think. Deep in my heart I dislike Marjorie who isn't honest but I always enjoy seeing her. We all spent Christmas together & Humphrey wanted to tell me a story that wasn't fit for the children. It was a very long story, lasting through every passage & always converging on the larder which was colder than any place I remember. I never knew what the story was about, though the children explained several bits to me, but it was a good story. The children are nice children. If you were to call on them it would be kind & you might like them. Humph rather reminds me of Frank Gardner[11] but it's libellous because he hasn't the same habits. I'm really fond of him. If you don't call the meeting shall take place when I fetch Marx in the spring but the call would be better for my reputation. The whole family by the way is generally in a state of absolute penury. Of course the <u>nicest</u> Blair is Mr Blair who's dying but the poor old man is 82 & he doesn't have any pain which is something.

Choosing your mother's Christmas card is always one of my treats but this year I've missed it. Partly because of the Christmas cards. Partly because a fortnight ago I suddenly got violent neuralgia & a fever. Normally I go into Marrakech on a red bicycle made in Japan for someone with very short legs & the biggest hands in the world, but for this occasion I had a taxi to go for an X-ray. It seemed obvious that I had another cyst – indeed I even packed a bag in case I had to go into hospital again. There was nothing whatever the matter with my jaws & the fever just went away two or three days ago & today I went out for the first time with a handkerchief round my head. I sent off two parcels & filled in 12 forms & paid more for the postage than I had for the contents. But it's too late for Christmas cards so give your mother my love instead for the moment, & your father, & Ruth, Jean, Billy, Maurice, June, Norman, John, Elizabeth. Even Quartus, & yet uniquely Norah is loved by

Pig.

[*LO*, pp. 75–9; XI, 512A, p. 254; handwritten]

1. Laurence O'Shaughnessy Jnr was born on 13 November 1938; 4½ weeks thereafter would be about 14 December and five weeks thereafter about the 17 December.

2. Writing to Frank Jellinek on 20 December 1938 (*CW*, XI, 513, p. 257), Orwell says 'I have heard today from George Kopp,* who was my commandant at the front, and who has just got out of Spain . . .' but Orwell initially typed 'jail' before 'Spain' and then crossed it through. There may have been slight confusion between Orwell's and Eileen's understanding of precisely when Kopp left jail and Spain.

3. Orwell thought he was in debt because he considered he had financed the stay in French Morocco by £300 borrowed from the novelist, L. H. Myers*. In fact, it was a gift from Myers, but that was kept concealed from Orwell; indeed, he did not even know the name of his benefactor because the money was transferred via Max Plowman, whom he had known from his time writing for *The Adelphi*. When Orwell had sufficient money (from the sales of *Animal Farm*) he repaid the gift via Max Plowman's widow, Dorothy (see **19.2.46**).

4. *Coming Up for Air*, published by Gollancz on 12 June 1939.

5. Eileen's description of her dearly-loved brother as 'a Nature's Fascist' suggests that, doubtless for the best of reasons, Laurence attempted to deceive Orwell as to his condition.

6. Compare the opening of Orwell's essay, 'Marrakech' (and see **4.10.38**, n. 2).

7. Also known as Mahdjoub Mahommed. In his Morocco Diary for 22 November 1938, Orwell says Mahdjoub served in an Arab line regiment for about fifteen years and received a pension of about Frs 5 a day – roughly 3p in today's coinage but perhaps very roughly £1.20 at today's values.

8. Mizpah: A Palestinian place-name referred to in Genesis 31.49 and used as a word or token expressing close association: 'The Lord watch between me and thee', often inscribed on brooches or rings exchanged between lovers.

9. Mahdjoub has confused *oiseau* (bird) with *poisson* (fish).

10. It was actually Dakin. Jenny Joseph suggests that Eileen mistakenly gave the surname of a contemporary at St Hugh's, Ursula Dacombe. The Dakins* though not well off on a civil servant's salary, were hardly 'in a state of absolute penury'.

11. Unidentified.

To Jack Common*

26 December 1938
Boîte Postale 48
Marrakech

Dear Jack,

Thanks so much for yours. I'm really frightfully sorry about these blasted hens. We seem to have saddled you with a herd of white elephants. I can't think what it can be. It seems to me that if it were any definite illness they would die off and not merely stop laying. As to its being the ground, I don't think there can be anything in that. To begin with, wherever they are in the field they must be on ground they ranged over before with good results. The hens of old Desborough, who had the field up to end of 1935 or so, died of coccidiosis, but I doubt to start with whether the disease germs would remain in the ground so long, secondly why haven't they developed it before, thirdly you probably wouldn't mistake coccidiosis, which makes the fowls weak and droopy even when they don't die, as most of them do. The thing I really don't understand is why the old fowls (there are a few, aren't there?) don't lay. As to the pullets, it does sometimes happen that they just miss coming into lay in August–September, and then what with the moult and the cold weather don't start till spring. But meanwhile you are being saddled with the food-bills. In a few days I'll try and send you a few quid (I'm afraid at best it'll have to be a few) towards ex[pens]es. I've written recently to my bank to know whether I've got any money left, and I'll get their reply in a few days. Of course this journey, which at any rate was made on borrowed money, has been very expensive and I don't think I'll have any money to speak of coming in for three or four months. The novel ought to be done beginning of April. It's really a mess but parts of it I like and it's suddenly revealed to me a big subject which I'd never really touched before and haven't time to work out properly now. I can't tell you how deeply I wish to keep alive, out of jail, and out of money-worries for the next few years. I suppose after this book I shall write some kind of pot-boiler, but I have very dimly in my mind the idea for an enormous novel in several volumes and I want several years to plan it out in peace. Of course when I say peace I don't mean absence of war, because actually you can be at peace when you're fighting, but I don't think what I mean by peace is compatible with modern totalitarian war. Meanwhile the Penguin people are making moves towards reprinting one or other of my books, and I hope they'll do so, because though I don't suppose there's much dough in it it's the best possible advert. Besides it's damned annoying to see your books out of print. One of mine, *Down and Out*, is so completely out of print that neither I nor anyone else known to me except my mother possesses a copy—this in spite of the fact that it was the most-taken-out book in the library at Dartmoor. I'm glad Warburg* has struck it lucky with at any rate one book. I must say for him that he has enterprise and has published a wider range of stuff than almost anyone. My Spain book sold damn all, but it didn't greatly matter as my agent had got the money out of him in advance and the reviews were O.K.

God knows when that parcel will turn up. From what I know of French post offices it wouldn't surprise me if it was just in time for Xmas 1939. Actually I left it and a lot of others to be sent off by the shopkeeper, because I was fatigued by a long afternoon of shopping, which is really tiring in this country as in most oriental countries. Arabs are even greater bargainers than Indians and one is obliged to conclude that they like it. If the price of an article is a shilling, the shopman starts by demanding two shillings and the buyer starts by offering threepence, and they may well take half an hour to agree on the shilling, though both know from the start that this is the right price. One thing that greatly affects one's contacts in foreign countries is that English people's nerves are not so durable as those of some other races, they can't stand noise, for instance. I like the Arabs, they're very friendly and, considering their position, not at all servile, but I've made no real contact, partly because they mostly speak a kind of bastard French and so I've been too lazy to learn any Arabic. The French in this country seem dull and stodgy beyond all measure, far worse than Anglo-Indians. I doubt whether there's any real political movement among the Arabs. The left-wing parties have all been suppressed (by the Popular Front) but I don't think they can ever have amounted to much. The people are entirely in the feudal stage and most of them seem to think they are still ruled by the Sultan, which by a fiction they are. There've been no echoes of the Tunis business except in the French press. If a big Arab movement ever arises I think it's bound to be pro-Fascist. I am told the Italians in Libya treat them atrociously, but their main oppressors have been the democracies, so-called. The attitude of the so-called left wing in England and France over this imperialism business simply sickens me. If they went on in the same vein they would end by turning every thinking coloured person into a Fascist. Underlying this is the fact that the working class in England and France have absolutely no feeling of solidarity with the coloured working class.

You asked where Marrakech was. It's somewhere near the top left hand corner of Africa and immediately north of the Atlas Mountains. Funnily enough we've been having the cold snap even here and on Xmas eve there was a heavy frost—don't know whether that is usual here, but judging by the vegetation I don't think it can be. I had the queer and rather pleasant experience of seeing the oranges and lemons on the trees frosted all over, which apparently didn't damage them. The effects of the frost were very curious. Some nasturtiums I had sown earlier were withered up by it, but the cactuses and the Bougainvillea, which is a tropical plant from the South Pacific, weren't affected. The mountains have been covered with snow even on their lower slopes for some time past. As soon as I've done the rough draft of my novel we're going to take a week off and go into the mountains. The Romans thought they were the end of the world, and they certainly look as if they might be. It's generally fine and bright in the day time, but we have fires all the time. The only fuel is olive wood, because there simply isn't a wild tree for miles and miles. This is one of those countries which are very nearly desert and which just exactly support a small population of men and beasts who eat every eatable thing and burn every burnable thing on the surface, so that if there were one more person there'd be a famine. And to think that in Roman times North Africa was full of magnificent forests full of lions and elephants. There are now practically no wild animals bigger than a hare, and I suppose even the human population is smaller. I've just been reading about approximately these parts in Flaubert's *Salammbô*, a book which for some reason I'd always steered clear of but which is simply stunning.

I'm not surprised at J.M.M[urry]* entering the Church. But he won't stay in it long. I suppose in the near future there will be a book called 'The Necessity of Fascism.'¹ But I think it's really time someone began looking into Fascism seriously. There must be more to it than one would gather from the left press. Mussolini has been 'just about to' collapse ever since 1926.

The French hardly celebrate Xmas, only the New Year. The Arabs probably celebrate the New Year, but it may not be the same as ours. They are pretty strict Mahomedans, except that owing to poverty they are not over-scrupulous about what they eat. We simply haven't celebrated Xmas yet, but shall when we get a pudding that is coming from England. Eileen was ill on Xmas day and I actually forgot till the evening what day it was. It's all very gloomy, because my father is very ill and my sister who was to come out here consequently can't. Two friends have just got back from Spain. One is a chap called Robert Williams² who has come out with his guts full of bits of shell. He says Barcelona is smashed out of recognition, everyone is half starved and you can get 900 pesetas for a £. The other is George Kopp,* a Belgian, whom there is a lot about in my book. He has just escaped after 18 months in a G.P.U.³ jail, in which he lost seven stone in weight. They were bloody fools to let him go after what they have done to him, but I suppose they couldn't help themselves. It's evident from several things that the Communists have lost most of their power and the GPU only exists unofficially.

My love to Mary and Peter. Eileen sends love and thanks Mary for the letter. I'll write again when I hear from the bank. I hope the cold will let up. It can be bloody in a small cottage. About February we'll have to think of getting Muriel mated, but there's no hurry. Whatever happens don't let her go to that broken-down old wreck of Mr Nicholls's,⁴ who is simply worn out by about twenty years of fucking his own sisters, daughters, granddaughters and great-grand-daughters.

Yours
Eric

PS. Were you giving the pullets a forcing mash? Clarke's stuff is pretty good.

[XI, 516, pp. 259–63; typewritten]

1. Murry had a predilection for such titles: *The Necessity of Art* (with others) (1924), *The Necessity of Communism* (1932; New York, 1933), and *The Necessity of Pacifism* (1937).
2. A fellow member of the POUM militia.
3. Secret police of the USSR.
4. A neighbour at Wallington.

To Herbert Read*

4 January 1939
Boîte Postale 48
Marrakech

Dear Read,

Thanks for your letter and the manifesto.[1] Funnily enough I'd already seen it in *La Flèche* and had thought of making further enquiries. I'll certainly sign it, though if you merely want a few names to represent England you could get some much better-known people. But any way use my name for anything it is worth. You asked if I wanted to suggest any changes in the manifesto. The only point I am a bit doubtful about, though I don't press it, is this. On p. 2 you say 'To make Russia safe for bureaucracy, first the German workers, then the Spanish workers, then the Czechoslovakian workers, have been left in the lurch.' I've no doubt this is true, but is it strategically wise for people in our position to raise the Czech question at this moment? No doubt the Russians *did* leave the Czechs in the soup, but it does not seem to me that they behaved worse or very differently from the British and French Governments, and to suggest by implication that they ought to have gone to war to defend the Czechs is to suggest that Britain and France ought to have gone to war too, which is just what the Popular Frontiersmen would say and what I don't believe to be true. I don't press this point, I merely suggest it and any way add my name to the manifesto.

I am spending the winter here for the sake of my lungs, which I think it is doing a little good to. Owing to this blasted health business I have had what is practically a wasted year, but the long rest has done me good and I am getting on with a new novel, whereas a year ago, after that awful nightmare in Spain, I had seriously thought I would never be able to write a novel again. Meanwhile, curiously enough, I had for some time past been contemplating writing to you about a matter which is much on my mind. It is this:—

I believe it is vitally necessary for those of us who intend to oppose the coming war to start organising for illegal anti-war activities. It is perfectly obvious that any open and legal agitation will be impossible not only when war has started but when it is imminent, and that if we do not make ready *now* for the issue of pamphlets etc. we shall be quite unable to do so when the decisive moment comes. At present there is considerable freedom of the press and no restriction on the purchase of printing presses, stocks of paper etc., but I don't believe for an instant that this state of affairs is going to continue. If we don't make preparations we may find ourselves silenced and absolutely helpless when either war or the pre-war fascising° processes begin. It is difficult to get people to see the danger of this, because most English people are constitutionally incapable of believing that anything will ever change. In addition, when one has to deal with actual pacifists, one generally finds that they have a sort of lingering moral objection to illegality and underground work. I quite agree that people, especially people who have any kind of notoriety, can get the best results by fighting in the open, but we might find it extremely useful to have an underground organisation *as well*. It seems to me that the commonsense thing to do would be to accumulate the things we should need for the production of pamphlets, stickybacks etc., lay them by in some unobtrusive place and not use them until it became necessary. For this we should need organisation and, in particular, money, probably 3 or 4 hundred pounds, but this should not be impossible with the help of the people one could probably rope in by degrees. Would you drop me a line and let me know whether you are interested in this idea? But even if you are not, don't speak of it to anyone, will you?

I enclose the manifesto, which I have signed.

Yours
Eric Blair

P.S. [*handwritten*] I'm keeping the leaflet of *Clé* ² & will send in a subscription as soon as I can get into Marrakech & buy a money-order.

[XI, 522, pp. 313–4; typewritten]

1 . *Towards a Free Revolutionary Art*. This called for the formation of an International Federation of Independent Revolutionary Art. It was signed by André Breton, founder and leader of the Surrealist movement, and Diego Rivera, painter of the Mexican revolution, when they rejected the Third International politically and culturally.

2. *La Clé*: monthly bulletin of the International Federation of Independent Revolutionary Art.

To Francis Westrope*

15 January 1939
Boîte Postale 48
Marrakech

Dear Frank,

I wonder if you could be kind enough to send us the following:

Thackeray's *Pendennis* (Nelson Double Vol. 2/–).
Trollope's *Eustace Diamonds* (World's Classics).
H. James' *Turn of the Screw* (Everyman No. 912.)
J. S. Mill's *Autobiography* (World's Classics.)

I think that about exhausts our credit, but if we owe you anything, let me know, won't you?

I am afraid it is a long time since I have written, and I never answered the letter Mrs Westrope¹ wrote me about the time we left England. We have been in this country about four months now and expect to be here till about the beginning of April. [*Summary of descriptions of life in French Morocco as in 24.11.38, 26.11.38, and 26.12.38.*]

I must say I was very thankful to be out of Europe for the war crisis. Here the people paid very little attention to it, partly I think because they did not want to excite the Arabs but also because they evidently didn't believe war was coming. I think one of the determining factors of the situation is that the French people can't be got into war unless France is invaded, and their politicians are aware of this. I suppose the next bit of trouble will be over the Ukraine, so perhaps we may get home just in time to go straight into the concentration camp if we haven't been sunk by a German submarine on the way. I hope and trust it won't be so. I have just finished the rough draft of my novel, and then we are going into the Atlas mountains for a week before I begin the revision, which will take till about the beginning of April. I think the climate has done me good. I cough very little now and I have put on a bit of weight, about half a stone already. It does seem so infuriating to be interrupted all the time by these wars and things.

I don't think by the way I ever thanked you for very kindly sending me that book of Arabic. I'm sorry to say Eileen and I have learned practically no Arabic, except the few words one can't help learning, because all the Arabs speak a kind of pidgin French, at any rate if they are at all in contact with Frenchmen. They also, of course, in these parts, speak a kind of dialect with Berber and even Spanish words mixed up in it. A lot of the people round here are Chleuh, a race the French only conquered quite recently, and there is also a certain amount of negro blood. We had to pass through Spanish Morocco coming down here. I didn't of course get more than glimpses, but I saw a few Franco troops, who looked indistinguishable from the Government troops I used to see a year earlier. The French here are mainly pro-Franco, and I think when all is known it will come out that they have given Franco a good deal of help, direct and indirect. There is a huge Jewish population here and in consequence a lot of anti-Jewish feeling, though most of the Jews are terribly poor and live much the same life as the Arabs. I hadn't realised before that much of the characteristic Moroccan work, coppersmithing and so forth, is done by Jews. Most of the native work is lovely and, of course, extremely cheap, though unfortunately many of the best things aren't portable.

Please give all the best to everyone. I trust when we next meet it won't be behind the barbed wire.

Yours
Eric Blair

[XI, 527, pp. 319–20; typewritten]

1. Myfanwy Westrope, wife of Francis Westrope, proprietor of Booklovers' Corner, where Orwell had worked as a part-time shop assistant, 1934–35. Orwell mistakenly addresses Francis Westrope by the first name of another bookseller, Frank Simmonds.

To Lady Rees

23 February 1939
Boîte Postale 48
Marrakech

Dear Lady Rees,[1]

I do so hope all is well with Richard.* The last I heard from the Plowmans some months back was that he was still in Barcelona, but since the retreat I have had no news of him, of course. I hope and trust he got out all right and isn't too overcome by all he must have been through. If he is home and cares to write, our address is the above until about the end of March. I think my wife told you I had been ill with what they finally decided after a lot of X-raying was not tuberculosis but something with a long name. I spent about six months in a sanatorium and then they told me I should spend the winter here. I don't know how much good it has done me, but I have no doubt it was as well to be out of England for this winter, which seems to have been a very severe one. Of course this business has set my work back a lot, however I have nearly finished another novel and we are going to come home as soon as it is done, about the beginning of April. They said I ought to live further south, so I dare say we shall settle in Dorset or somewhere like that when we can find another cottage.

It is very quiet and peaceful here. We have a little house a few miles out of Marrakech and we don't see any other Europeans except when some of the soldiers from the Foreign Legion come and see us. A short while back we spent a week about 5,000 feet up in the mountains, where the Berber race called the Chleuh live. They are rather interesting people, very simple, all free and equal, very dirty but splendid to look at, especially the women. They have beautiful little pastures with grass almost like England, and you can lie about on the snow in blazing sunshine. Down here the country is flat and very dried up, with no natural trees, much like northern India, I should think. The Arabs are terribly poor and most of the people work for about a penny an hour. For Europeans living isn't very cheap, not so cheap as France, I should say, though certain things are fantastically cheap, for instance you can buy a camel for three hundred francs, supposing that you wanted one. The brass & copper work that they do here is beautiful, but the most attractive thing of all is the very cheap native pottery, which unfortunately it is almost impossible to bring away.

We were most thankful to be out of England during the war crisis, and I trust we shan't get back just in time to meet another. The idea of war is just a nightmare to me, and I refuse to believe that it can do the slightest good or even that it makes much difference who wins. If Richard is back and doesn't feel up to writing, could you give him all our love and say we hope to see him when we get back?

Yours sincerely
Eric Blair

[XI, 532, pp. 329–30; typewritten]

1.   Sir Richard Rees's mother. Rees was serving as an ambulance driver in Spain.

To Jack Common*

23 February 1939
Boîte Postale 48
Marrakech

Dear Jack,

Did you write to Miss Woods about Muriel's mating? If not, could you be good enough to drop her a card? I don't remember the exact address, but I think it's Woods, Woodcotes, Nr. Sandon, and any way they'll know at the pub. [*Orwell was anxious that Mr Nicholls's 'old wreck' should not be mated*

*with Muriel (see **26.12.38**) and on 12.1.39 had asked him to contact Miss Woods.*]
Incidentally I hope there's no foot and mouth this year. I suppose they are
right in not letting animals be moved about while it is on, though they don't
stop men and dogs, but it is really time they stopped that insane business of
slaughtering a whole flock of cattle because of one case.

I don't know exactly when we'll be back, but some time in April, and will
let you know the exact date later. I've got to finish the novel, which has been
set back because I have again been ill and was in bed a fortnight, though I'm
all right now, and then there's the question of a boat. If possible we want to go
all the way from Casablanca by boat, but there's only one a month and I can't
obtain the date yet. After we get back I must go straight down to Southwold
and see my father, and Eileen as soon as possible is going to look for a new
house. This is all supposing war hasn't broken out by then, because if it has I
don't want to be caught with my pants down and shall keep the cottage. But if
it would suit you to stay on at the cottage till about the end of April, it would
suit us. On the other hand if you wished to leave a bit earlier we could fit that
in as well, because in any case either E. or I will have to come down to Wallington to superintend moving the stuff. We shall take the hens, of course, in
spite of their failure to make good, but shall probably dump the fowl houses
and buy new ones, which would not be dearer than transporting and less fag.
I wonder if anything is coming up in the garden. There ought to be a few
snowdrops and crocuses soon.

I don't know whether the world situation is better or worse. I look at it
now simply with a meteorological eye, is it going to rain or isn't it?, though
I suppose once it's started one will fail as usual to keep out of it. If I was
biologically a good specimen and capable of founding a new dynasty I would
devote all my energies during the war to keeping alive and keeping out of
sight. I haven't heard of or from Richard [Rees], but I've just written to his
mother to know what the news is. I suppose he got out all right. It's all a
ghastly mess, and if one is not personally involved the most ghastly thing of
all will be the complete failure of left-wingers to learn anything from this
disaster, the awful sterile controversies which will go on for years, everyone
laying the blame on everybody else.

I wonder if Murry's* ordination is going through all right? I suppose as
he's got a degree already he won't have to study for very long. But is he
quite sound on the 39 articles[1] etc.? I shouldn't have thought so. It would
be comic if he ended up as a bishop. By the way, have you run across the
rector of Rushden cum Wallington, Mr Rossborough. Although not very
prepossessing he's a nice little man and has a very nice son. The son, Rob, is
at Haileybury and he joined the P.P.U.[2] and refused to enter the O.T.C.[3] What
impressed me was not so much this as that his father after thinking it over
decided to back him up. He has been a missionary in Africa and seen the way
the natives are treated, and this has given him slightly heterodox views on

some questions, as often happens with missionaries. His wife though very nice impresses me as being a bit off her rocker. By the way her praying circle pray regularly for my health (don't tell anyone this as it's supposed to be a secret even from me, Mrs R. having told Eileen in confidence).

Best love to Mary and Peter. Eileen sends love.

Yours
Eric

[XI, 533, pp. 330–1; typewritten]

1. Those ordained as priests of the Church of England must assent to the Thirty-nine Articles. These encapsulate the doctrinal position of the church following the Reformation.

2. Peace Pledge Union, founded 1934. Max Plowman* was its General Secretary, 1937–38. It published *Peace News*, for which Orwell wrote a review of F.J. Shead's *Communism and Man*, 27 January 1939 (XI, 529, pp. 322–4). .

3. Officers' Training Corps, formed by Lord Haldane, Lord Chancellor, 1912–15, before World War I as a means of training a pool of officers; it is chiefly to be found in public schools.

To Lydia Jackson*

Lydia Jackson had visited Orwell at Aylesford Sanatorium in 1938 and she gave this account of her visit:

I found George fully dressed sitting in a deck chair outside; on my arrival, he got up and suggested we should go for a walk in the park. We did not go very far. When we were out of sight of the buildings, we sat on the grass and he put his arms around me. It was an awkward situation. He did not attract me as a man and his ill health even aroused in me a slight feeling of revulsion. At the same time, the fact that he was a sick man, starved of intimacy with his wife, made it difficult for me to repulse him. I did not want to behave like a prude or to treat the incident as a serious matter. Why should I push him away if kissing me gave him a few minutes of pleasure? I was convinced that he was very fond of Eileen and I was in no sense a rival to her (A Russian's England, 1976, p. 419).

1 March 1939
Boîte Postale 48
Marrakech

Dear Lydia,

I am afraid it is a very long time since I have written to you & I don't think you have written to me either, have you? I hope all is going well with you. We are in all probability leaving this country on the 23rd March, in which case we should get back about the 30th. I suppose I shall be in London for a bit before going down to see my people etc. So looking forward to seeing you! So try & keep a date or two open a few days after the 1st of April. How is your work getting on? I hope to get my novel finished before we sail, though it will hardly be typed before then. Parts of it I am quite pleased with, others not. Eileen is well though she has had one or two spells of being a little off colour. I was recently quite ill & in bed for a fortnight with what was evidently flu, however I'm all right again now. I don't believe in the alleged marvellous qualities of this climate which I think is neither better nor worse than any other. All our spending the winter here has really meant is that we have spent immense quantities of borrowed money, however, we were out of England for the war-crisis & that was a blessed relief. Let's hope we aren't going to bump into another just when we get back.

I wonder who your young man is now?[1] I have thought of you so often—have you thought about me, I wonder? I know it's indiscreet to write such things in letters, but you'll be clever & burn this, won't you? I am so looking forward to seeing you & having a good talk with you. Eileen too is longing to get back to England. We'll have to give up the Wallington cottage, I suppose, but if possible we're going to get one in Dorset or somewhere. Take care of yourself. Hoping to see you early in April.[2]

    With love
    Eric

                           [XI, 534A, pp. 335–7; handwritten]

1.   This was Karl Schnetzler, but Lydia says although they were friends neither was in love with the other. She thought, however, he was in love with Eileen (*A Russian's England*, p. 417). (See **9.4.46 to Inez Holden**, n. 2.)

2.   In *A Russian's England*, which reproduces a few lines of this letter, Lydia Jackson says she read this letter with mixed feelings: 'I was looking forward to seeing Eileen again, but not George, especially as the tone of his letter suggested a renewal of the amorous behaviour I had been too soft-hearted to repel at the Maidenhead hospital' (that is, Aylesford Sanatorium, near Maidstone). Further, 'I had several men friends at the time whom I found more attractive than George, and his masculine conceit annoyed me. Least of all did I want to disturb his relationship with Eileen, or have anything to conceal from her' (p. 430).

To Jack Common*

5 March 1939
Boîte Postale 48
Marrakech

Dear Jack,

Hope all goes well with you. About our arrangements. If the bank sends us the money in time we're going to take a boat which sails from Casablanca on the 22nd or 23rd and ought to get to London about the end of March. After that I've got to go down to Southwold and see my people and there will be other odds and ends to see to. After much thought we've decided to go on living in the cottage for the rest of the summer and not move till the autumn. Apart from anything else we shall have no money at any rate till my book comes out, which would make it very awkward to move, and in any case one can find a better place if one takes one's time looking for it. Barring war we shall no doubt move, as they say I oughtn't to spend the winter there and by going further afield one could get a much more sanitary cottage at not much more rent, but we might as well spend the summer there as anywhere else. Also if we go in the autumn we can take certain fruit bushes etc. which we have put in. So, any work you've done or had old Hatchett to do won't have been wasted, rather a barren consideration for you, I'm afraid.

Meanwhile can you do us a great favour, which might, however, ease things up if there happened to be an interval between your finding somewhere else to go to and our coming in. You may remember reading in my book on the Spanish war about Georges Kopp,[1] who was commander of my brigade for a while. He's been for some time staying with Eileen's brother at Greenwich, but we can't ask them to have him stay there indefinitely, because they've got the house full already and it's awkward for them. So if necessary could you put him up at Wallington? I don't mean in the cottage, he can stay at Mrs Anderson's, but could you see about his meals? Gwen O'Shaughnessy, Eileen's sister in law, will see about the money for his grub etc., so that you shan't be out of pocket, and perhaps it wouldn't be so much trouble for Mary to have one extra person at meals? You'll find him very easily satisfied. I think you'll like him also. Of course this might turn out not to be necessary, some job might turn up for him in the mean while, but I doubt whether he's fit to work yet after being 18 months in jail and starved and so forth. Then if it so happened that you wanted to clear out before we could move in, he could keep the place warm for us. But in any case he'd be there till we come and could then stay for a while until he can get a job, which I expect he can ultimately. If this *should* turn out to be necessary, I hope it won't put you out too much.

I'm longing to see England again. It's starting to get hot here. This is the only time of the year when there's a bit of greenness, and all the camels, donkeys etc. are gorging themselves while the going's good. Quite a lot of the wildflowers are the same as in England. The cherry trees are in flower and the apple trees just coming into leaf. It's nice that we shall see this over again in England. I wonder if there were any snowdrops and crocuses in the garden. I think I shall just finish my novel before we board the boat, but it will probably have to be typed on the sea. There's about 100 pages I'm pleased with, the rest is a failure. I haven't heard any more about the Penguin business² and hope it hasn't fallen through.

Did you drop a card to Miss Woods about Muriel?³ I haven't heard a word about Richard [Rees]* but I wrote to his mother to ask about him. If writing, don't send any letter later than the 15th, as it might miss us. Love to Mary and Peter,

Yours
Eric

P.S.⁴ Eileen sends love—& the postscript, really to Mary. I think you might find George Kopp* quite an asset, especially if you can bear to be separated from the gas oven. He is quite handy in the house & *adores* cooking. But the thing is this: if you can have him will you write & ask him to come? Without of course mentioning that anyone is going to pay for his food. We feel Gwen may be getting a bit down as she's just had a baby & the house is full of it & its nurse & the locum it necessitates (Gwen is a doctor). On the other hand she can't suggest that George should go somewhere else; but she could let him accept our invitation. It could be given on the grounds that he'd be staying with us if we were in England & he might like to see our village (he would). He's the sort of man who's happy anywhere if people are pleased to see him & you'd find him interesting to talk to—he speaks English quite fluently. If you don't want to write to George but don't mind having him, write to Gwen & she can pass on the invitation. The only important thing is that he should be allowed to think that you're inviting him spontaneously.

[*Eileen wrote at the top of the letter*:] Gwen's address: Dr. Gwen O'Shaughnessy, 24 Crooms Hill, Greenwich, London S.E.10

[XI, 535, pp. 337–8; typewritten]

1. Among Orwell's papers were three issues of *Independent News*: a special number of, probably, late November or early December 1938 devoted to 'The P.O.U.M. Trial in Barcelona'; No. 59, 16 December 1938, with an article titled 'After the P.O.U.M. Trial'; and No. 60, 23 December 1938, which included a report on George Kopp's imprisonment and release. Orwell and Eileen visited him in prison. (For

full details, see XI, 359, pp. 338–9 and VI, pp. 171–78.)
2. See letter to Leonard Moore, **28.11.38**.
3. See **23.2.39** and **19.3.39** to Jack Common.
4. The postscript, apart from the first three words, is in Eileen's hand.

To Herbert Read*

5 March 1939
Boîte Postale 48
Marrakech

Dear Read,

Thanks so much for your letter. I am probably leaving this country about the 22nd or 23rd of March and should be in England by the end of the month. I shall probably be in London a few days and I'll try and arrange to come and see you. If I could help with *Revolt*[1] I'd like to, though till I've seen what kind of paper it is to be I don't know whether I could be any use. The trouble is that if I am writing a book as I generally am I find it almost impossible to do any other creative work, but on the other hand I *like* doing reviews, if they would want anything in that line. If we could keep a leftwing but non-Stalinist review in existence (it's all a question of money, really) I believe a lot of people would be pleased. People aren't all fools, they must begin soon to see through this 'antifascist' racket. A thought that cheers me a lot is that each generation, which in literature means about ten years, is in revolt against the last, and just as the Audens etc. rose in revolt against the Squires[2] and Drinkwaters,[3] there must be another gang about due to rise against the Audens.

About the press business. I quite agree that it's in a way absurd to start preparing for an underground campaign[4] unless you know who is going to campaign and what for, but the point is that if you don't make some preparations beforehand you will be helpless when you want to start, as you are sure to sooner or later. I cannot believe that the time when one can buy a printing press with no questions asked will last forever. To take an analogous case. When I was a kid you could walk into a bicycle-shop or ironmonger's and buy any firearm you pleased, short of a field gun, and it did not occur to most people that the Russian revolution and the Irish civil war would bring this state of affairs to an end. It will be the same with printing presses etc. As for the sort of thing we shall find ourselves doing, the way I see the situation is like this. The chances of Labour or any left combination winning the election are in my opinion nil, and in any case if they did get in I doubt whether they'd be better than or much different from the Chamberlain lot. We are therefore in either for war in the next two years, or for prolonged war-preparation, or possibly only for sham war-preparations designed to cover up other objects, but in any of these cases for a fascising° process leading to an authoritarian regime, ie. some kind of austro-fascism. So long as the objective, real or pretended, is war against Germany, the greater part of the Left will associate themselves with the fascising° process, which will ultimately mean associating themselves with wage-reductions, suppression of free speech, brutalities in the colonies etc. Therefore the revolt against these things will have to be against the Left as well as the Right. The revolt will form itself into two sections, that of the dissident lefts like ourselves, and that of the fascists, this time the idealistic Hitler-fascists, in England more or less represented by Mosley. I don't know whether Mosley will have the sense and guts to stick out against war with Germany, he might decide to cash in on the patriotism business, but in that case someone else will take his place. If war leads to disaster and revolution, the official Left having already sold out and been identified in the public mind with the war-party, the fascists will have it all their own way unless there is in being some body of people who are both anti-war and anti-fascist. Actually there will be such people, probably very great numbers of them, but their being able to do anything will depend largely on their having some means of expression during the time when discontent is growing. I doubt whether there is much hope of saving England from fascism of one kind or another, but clearly one must put up a fight, and it seems silly to be silenced when one might be making a row merely because one had failed to take a few precautions beforehand. If we laid in printing presses etc. in some discreet place we could then cautiously go to work to get together a distributing agency, and we could then feel 'Well, if trouble does come we are ready.' On the other hand if it doesn't come I should be so pleased that I would not grudge a little wasted effort. As to money, I shall probably be completely penniless for the rest of this year unless something unexpected happens. Perhaps if we definitely decided on a course of action your friend Penrose[5] might put up something, and I think there are others who could be got to see the necessity. What about Bertrand Russell,[6] for instance? I suppose he has some money, and he would fall in with the idea fast enough if he could be persuaded that free speech is menaced.

When I get back I'll write or ring up and try and arrange to meet. If you're going to be in town about the beginning of April, or on the other hand going to be away or something, could you let me know? But better not write to the above as the letter might miss me. Write to: AT: 24 Croom's Hill, Greenwich SE.10.

Yours
Eric Blair

[XI, 536, pp. 340–1; typewritten]

1. *Revolt!*, jointly edited by Vernon Richards* in London, ran for six issues, from 11 February to 3 June 1939. It aimed at presenting the Spanish civil war from an anti-Stalinist point of view.

2. John Squire (1884–1958; Kt.1933) literary editor *New Statesman and Nation*, 1913–19; founded the *London Mercury*, and edited it, 1919–34. He stood for Parliament for Labour in 1918 and for the Liberals in 1924, unsuccessfully both times. Among the many books he wrote and edited were *A Book of Women's Verse* (1921) and *The Comic Muse* (1925).

3. John Drinkwater (1882–1937), poet, playwright, and essayist, was evidently an object of particular scorn to Orwell; Gordon Comstock sneeringly refers to him as *Sir* John Drinkwater in *Keep the Aspidistra Flying* (*CW*, IV, p. 287), though he was not knighted.

4. See letter to Read, **4.1.39**.

5. Roland Penrose (1900–1984; Kt., 1966) was a painter and writer who used his independent means to support many painters and artistic and left-wing projects.

6. Bertrand Russell, 3rd Earl Russell (1872–1970), philosopher and Nobel Prize winner, was a prominent advocate for peace, and wrote and campaigned vigorously for it. Supported World War II and advocated threatening USSR with Atomic Bomb at start of Cold War. See also Orwell's review of his *Power: A New Social Analysis* (XI, 520, pp. 311–2).

To Jack Common*

19 March 1939
Marrakech

Dear Jack,

Thanks so much for your good offices re. George Kopp.* He wrote telling us you had invited him to go to Wallington & that he wasn't going, at which I dare say you were not unrelieved, though you'd have liked him, I think. It's all rather awkward, Gwen O'Shaughnessy, Eileen's sister in law, has been putting him up for about 2 months now & we can't ask her to do so indefinitely. Meanwhile I don't know if it is going to make difficulties about our moving in—there being no one there, I mean. If so be you wanted to move out before we could get back, ie. that some opportunity of another house arose, or something, I suppose it would be quite simple to arrange with old Hatchett to look after the creatures till we arrive. He knows we'll make it up to him, & anyway, he's very good & kind about undertaking anything like that. I don't think we'll reach London before April 2nd, & then I must go straight down & see my father, who I am afraid is dying, poor old man. It's wonderful how he's lasted through this winter, which must have been beastly cold in Suffolk, & he was too frail to be moved. He's 81, so he's had a pretty good innings, but what a hole it seems to leave when someone you have known since childhood goes. We can't get back earlier because the boat we were to have sailed on on the 23rd has been delayed at sea in some way. Of course if something like that didn't happen on any journey I take this wouldn't be my life. However there's a Japanese boat a few days later which has got to stop off at Casablanca to drop a cargo of tea & we are going to take that instead. I've never been on a Japanese boat before but I'm told they're very good. We could go the way we came, across Spanish Morocco to Tangier, but it is intolerable if one has much luggage. Coming down we lost most of our luggage & didn't get it back for weeks because at every station there is an enormous horde of Arabs all literally fighting for the job of porter, & whenever the train stops they invade it, grab all luggage they can see, carry it off & stow it away in any other trains that happen to be in the station, after which it steams away into various parts of Africa while you try to explain what has happened to people who don't speak anything but arabic. I like to go as far as possible by sea, because on a ship at any rate there's no question of getting out at the wrong station.

My novel's finished, which is why I'm writing in pen, as it is being typed. I've heard from Richard [Rees], who's at Perpignan & sounds pretty exhausted, as well he may be. I wonder if we can possibly get 5 years of respite before the next war. It doesn't look like it. Anyway, thank God for a roof over one's head & a patch of potatoes when the fun begins. I hope Muriel's mating went through. It is a most unedifying spectacle, by the way, if you happened to watch it. Love to Mary & Peter. Eileen sends love. Don't write because it would cross us. If any occasion to write, write to the Greenwich address.

Yours
Eric

P.S. Did my rhubarb come up, I wonder? I had a lot, & then last year the frost buggered it up. I don't know whether it survives that or not.

[XI, 539, pp. 344-5; handwritten]

To Lydia Jackson*

[30 March 1939]
postcard¹

Dear Lydia,

I knocked at the door of your flat & was very disappointed not to find you at home. I gathered from the hall porter that you weren't actually away from London. I've got tomorrow to go down & see my parents for the week-end, but hope to see you when I get back, about Tuesday. Meanwhile if clever I *may* be able to look in for an hour tomorrow morning, so try & stay at home in the morning will you?

Love
Eric

[XI, 542A, p. 348; handwritten]

1.   The postcard was of 'A Café in the Faubourg Montmartre' by Edgar Degas. It, and the next item, have been dated by reference to adjacent letters. This, and the other letters, are not quite accurately reproduced in her *A Russian's England*, pp. 430–31.

To Lydia Jackson★

Friday [31 March 1939]
36 High Street
Southwold

Dear Lydia,

You were mean not to stay at home this morning like I asked you. But perhaps you couldn't. I rang up 3 times. Are you angry with me? I did write to you twice from Morocco & I don't think you wrote to me. But listen. I am coming back to town Monday or Tuesday, & Eileen is going to stay down here a bit longer. I shall have to be in town several days to see to various things, so we can arrange to meet—unless you don't want to. I'll ring up.

Yours ever.
Eric.

[XI, 542B, p. 348; handwritten]

To Leonard Moore★

25 April 1939
The Stores
Wallington

Dear Mr Moore,

Many thanks for your letter. I am afraid you must be very overworked, with Miss Perriam away[1] and having been unwell yourself, and I am sorry to trouble you with all this stuff.

I thought Gollancz might show fight. The book is, of course, only a novel and more or less unpolitical, so far as it is possible for a book to be that nowadays, but its general tendency is pacifist, and there is one chapter (Chapter i. of Part III—I suppose you haven't seen the manuscript) which describes a Left Book Club meeting and which Gollancz no doubt objects to. I also think it perfectly conceivable that some of Gollancz's Communist friends have been at him to drop me and any other politically doubtful writers who are on his list. You know how this political racket works, and of course it is a bit difficult for Gollancz, or at any rate Lawrence and Wishart, to be publishing books proving that persons like myself are German spies and at the same time to be publishing my own books. Meanwhile how does our contract stand? I didn't see our last contract, which you may remember was drawn up while I was in Spain, but I understood from my wife that Gollancz undertook to publish my next three works of fiction and pay £100 in advance on each. He has also had this book in his advance lists three times, owing to the delay caused by my illness. But at the same time I think it would be much better not to pin him down to his contract if he is really reluctant to publish the book. To begin with he has treated me very well and I don't want to make unpleasantness for him, and secondly if he really objects to the book he could hardly be expected to push it once published. It might be better to have a quite frank explanation with him. If we are to go to another publisher, whom do you recommend? I suppose it would be better to go to one of the big ones if they will have me, but meanwhile there will I suppose be considerable delays. It is all a great nuisance. I have earned little or no money since last spring and am infernally hard up and in debt, and I was looking to this book to see me through the summer while I get on with my next. I am also not completely decided about my next book, I have ideas for two books which I had thought of writing simultaneously, and if we are going to change publishers it might be necessary to talk that over too. So perhaps the sooner this business is settled the better. I am sorry to be such a nuisance.

I hope you are quite over your flu. I am very well again and have been putting in some strenuous gardening to make up for lost time. My wife sends all the best.

Yours sincerely
Eric Blair

P.S. [*at top of letter*] If G. wants alterations in the book, I am willing to make the usual minor changes to avoid libel actions, but not structural alterations.

[XI, 546, pp. 352–3; handwritten]

1.　Miss Periam was Moore's secretary and had been ill for some months (see **28.11.38**, n. 7).

To Leonard Moore*

[4 July 1939?][1]
The Stores
Wallington

Dear Mr. Moore,

Many thanks for your letter. I called at your office yesterday and was sorry not to find you there. I am terribly behind with my book of essays[2] which I had hoped to finish by September at latest. These infernal illnesses have of course wasted months of time. Also I am sorry to tell you my father has just died. I was with the poor old man for the last week of his life, and then there was the funeral etc., etc., all terribly upsetting and depressing. However, he was 82 and had been very active till he was over 80, so he had had a good life, and I am very glad that latterly he had not been so disappointed in me as before. Curiously enough his last moment of consciousness was hearing that review I had in the *Sunday Times*. He heard about it and wanted to see it, and my sister took it in and read it to him, and a little later he lost consciousness for the last time.

About the book. I shan't be starting my novel till after I have done the book of essays, and unless something upsets my plans I intend doing next a long novel, really the first part of an enormous novel, a sort of saga(!) which will have to be published in three parts. I think I *ought* to finish the book of essays in October, but the novel will take a long time and even barring wars, illnesses etc. isn't likely to be finished before the late summer of 1940. Those at any rate are my plans. As to the book of essays, I don't know whether Gollancz will want them. They may be a bit off his track, and as they are sort of literary-sociological essays they touch at places on politics, on which I am certain to say things he wouldn't approve of. The subjects are Charles Dickens, boys' weekly papers (the *Gem*, *Magnet* etc.), and Henry Miller, the American novelist. I am finishing the rough draft of the Dickens one now, but the others probably won't take so long. I should say it will be a short book, 50–60 thousand words. I don't know whether this is at all the kind of thing to interest Gollancz, but if he wants to have the first refusal that is up to him and you. If he wants to take a chance on the book and put it in his lists I will think of a title, but I can't send a specimen, as it is all rather in a mess as yet.

I see *Coming up for Air* has gone into a second edition, so I suppose it's doing fairly well. It had some wonderful reviews, especially from James Agate. The Frenchwoman[3] who was translating *Homage to Catalonia* has finished it and is hawking it round various publishers, always unsuccessfully, as people are fed up with books on the Spanish war, which well they may be. She has an idea however that she may be able to induce someone to publish it or part of it unpaid. But she is afraid Warburg will kick against this, as he apparently did over some book of Freda Utley's.[4] In case of this coming to anything, I suppose we can get Warburg to agree.[5] It's always a bit of an advert., and in any case one never gets much out of a French publisher. Appropos° of this, can you tell me what if anything ever came of that Burmese translation of *Burmese Days* which those people wrote to me about? It was sometime last year.[6]

I hope all goes well. My wife sends all the best.

Yours sincerely
Eric Blair

[XI, 555, pp. 365–6; typewritten]

1. This letter is dated from its receipt in Moore's office; Orwell incorrectly dated it the 14th.
2. *Inside the Whale*.
3. Yvonne Davet★.
4. Presumably *Japan's Gamble in China*, mentioned in Orwell's letter to Yvonne Davet 19 June 1939.
5. From an annotation to this letter made in Moore's office, it appears that Warburg agreed to permit this for a 'Nominal fee of £1.'
6. Nothing came of the proposal, however it was 'published' in a pirated photocopied version of the Penguin Twentieth-Century Classics edition in the late 1990s. It could be bought on the approach to the Kuthodaw Pagoda for 600 Kyats (about US $2) in 1999.

To Leonard Moore★

4 August 1939
The Stores
Wallington

Dear Mr Moore,

Naturally I'm delighted about the Albatross business.[1] It was very clever of you to work it. I've always wanted to crash one of those continental editions. English people abroad always read the few English books they can get hold of with such attention that I'm sure it's the best kind of publicity.

Of course I've no objection to the alterations they want to make, but in two of the four cases I've suggested substituting another phrase instead of just leaving a blank. Of course they can do as they prefer, but in these two cases I felt that simply to cut the phrase out without inserting another would upset the balance of the paragraph. Also as they're going to set up the type anew they might correct two misprints which I let through. I've made notes on all this on the attached, and perhaps you could explain to them.

Yours
Eric Blair

[XI, 561, pp. 384–5; typewritten]

1.   The Albatross Modern Continental Library was a paperback series of books in English put out by John Holroyd-Reece (born Johann Herman Riess) for distribution on the Continent. Most were sold in Germany. Holroyd-Reece also later took over the Tauchnitz series. The entry records that the contract was between Orwell and The Albatross Verlag G.m.b.H. and was dated 31 August 1939. It stipulated that the book was to be issued no later than August 1940. Although the publishing house was German, the contract was issued from 12 rue Chanoinesse, Paris.

To Leonard Moore★

6 October 1939
The Stores
Wallington

Dear Mr Moore,

Can you tell me whether there is any channel through which one can find out the circulations of weekly papers? As I think I told you, one of the essays in the book I am doing deals with the boys' twopenny weeklies of the type of the *Gem*, *Wizard* etc, and I should like to know their circulations, but don't quite know how to find them out. I suppose if you write and ask the editor he won't necessarily tell you? I have a dozen papers on my list, and should be greatly obliged if you could help me to find this out.

My wife has already got a job in a government office.[1] I have so far failed to do so. I shall try again later, but for the time being I am staying here to finish the book[2] and get our garden into trim for the winter, as I dare say we shall be glad of all the spuds we can lay hands on next year. The book should be finished some time in November. It ought to have been done already, but of course this war put me right off my stride for some weeks.

Yours
Eric A Blair

[XI, 572, pp. 410–1; typewritten]

1. Eileen was working in the Censorship Department, War Office, Whitehall; see Crick, p. 382.
2. *Inside the Whale*, the book of essays described in a letter to Leonard Moore, 4.7.39.

To Leonard Moore*

Friday [8 December 1939]
The Stores
Wallington

Dear Mr Moore,

I have finished my book (the book of essays—the title is *Inside the Whale*) and have typed most of it but my wife is typing another portion in London. Meanwhile Cyril Connolly* and Stephen Spender*, who as perhaps you know are starting a new monthly called *Horizon* want to see the Ms. in case they would like to print one of the essays in their paper.¹ I don't know if any of them are really suitable for this, but if they do wish to use one of them, would that be all right with the publisher? Could one arrange things? As you may remember Gollancz wanted to see the book but whether he'll publish it I don't know, as there is at any rate one passage which politically won't appeal to him.² If Gollancz refuses it, what about trying Warburg again? I met him a little while back and he was very anxious to have my next non-fiction book, so perhaps we might get a good offer out of him for this, though no doubt it would be better to get the money in advance if possible. I am arranging with Connolly to keep the Ms. only a few days. I should think it would be best not to say anything to any publisher about this beforehand, because if Connolly and Co. don't want any of it, which they well may not, it might prejudice him against the book.

Do you know what has happened to the Albatross people?³ You may remember we signed up a contract with them for *Coming Up for Air* just before war broke out. Have they gone west, I wonder?

Yours sincerely
Eric Blair

[XI, 581, pp. 422–3; typewritten]

1. *Inside the Whale* consisted of the essay with that title, 'Charles Dickens,' and 'Boys' Weeklies'. An abridged version of the last was published in *Horizon* the same month as the book's publication, March 1940.
2. In fact, *Inside the Whale* appealed greatly to Victor Gollancz, who did publish it. He wrote to Orwell on 1 January 1940 (misdated 1939) to express his delight: 'It is, if I

may say so, first rate.' He was in complete sympathy with Orwell's general political point of view, 'though I fight against pessimism'. He suggested that the only thing worth doing was 'to try to find some way of reconciling the inevitable totalitarian economics with individual freedom'. Finally, he asked Orwell whether he could lend him a copy of Henry Miller's *Tropic of Cancer*, of which he had not heard. Exactly four weeks after Gollancz wrote, Orwell returned to him the page proofs of *Inside the Whale*. The collection of essays was published on 11 March 1940.

3. Although Albatross and Tauchnitz were German firms, the contract Orwell signed was from their Paris office. (See **4.8.39**.) William B. Todd and Ann Bowden in their *Tauchnitz International Editions in English* record a document in the Albatross archive that notes that the publisher still hoped in 1940 to publish *Coming Up for Air*. After Paris was occupied by the Germans, 14 June 1940, a decree was issued forbidding the sale of British books first published after 1870 (Todd and Bowden, item 5365), and that finally ended Orwell's hopes for an Albatross edition.

To Victor Gollancz*

8 January 1940
The Stores
Wallington

Dear Mr Gollancz,

I cannot *at this moment* lend you *Tropic of Cancer*, because my copy has been seized. While I was writing my last book two detectives suddenly arrived at my house with orders from the public prosecutor to seize all books which I had 'received through the post'. A letter of mine addressed to the Obelisk Press had been seized and opened in the post. The police were only carrying out orders and were very nice about it, and even the public prosecutor wrote and said that he understood that as a writer I might have a need for books which it was illegal to possess. On these grounds he sent me back certain books, eg. *Lady Chatterley's Lover*, but it appears that Miller's books have not been in print long enough to have become respectable. However, I know that Cyril Connolly has a copy of *Tropic of Cancer*. He is down with flu at present, but when I can get in touch with him again I will borrow the book and pass it on to you.

As to your remarks on my book. I am glad you liked it. You are perhaps right in thinking I am over-pessimistic. It is quite possible that freedom of thought etc. may survive in an economically totalitarian society. We can't tell until a collectivised economy has been tried out in a western country. What worries me at present is the uncertainty as to whether the ordinary people in countries like England grasp the difference between democracy and despotism well enough to want to defend their liberties. One can't tell until they see themselves menaced in some quite unmistakeable manner. The intellectuals who are at present pointing out that democracy and fascism are the same thing etc. depress me horribly. However, perhaps when the pinch comes the common people will turn out to be more intelligent than the clever ones. I certainly hope so.

Yours sincerely
Eric Blair

[XII, 583, p. 5; typewritten]

To Geoffrey Gorer*

10 January 1940
The Stores
Wallington

Dear Geoffrey,

It seems an age since I saw you or heard from you. I wonder what hemisphere you are in at this moment, but anyway I'll send this to Highgate trusting it'll be forwarded. I rang you up at about the beginning of the war & your brother answered & said you were in America.

We got back from Morocco in the Spring & I began on another book, then I'm sorry to say my father died, all very painful & upsetting but I was glad when the poor old man went because he was 82 & had suffered a lot his last few months. Then I got going on the book again & then the war threw me out of my stride, so in the end a very short book that was meant to take 4 months took me 6 or 7. It ought to come out in March & I think parts of it might interest you. I have so far completely failed to serve HM. government in any capacity, though I want to, because it seems to me that now we are in this bloody war we have got to win it & I would like to lend a hand. They won't have me in the army, at any rate at present, because of my lungs. Eileen has got a job in a government department, which as usual she got by knowing somebody who knew somebody, etc., etc. I also want a job because I want to lay off writing for a bit, I feel I have written myself out & ought to lie fallow. I am sort of incubating an enormous novel, the family saga sort of thing, only I don't want to begin it before I'm all set. It is frightfully bad for one, this feeling of the publisher's wingèd chariot hurrying near¹ all the time. Have you seen the new monthly magazine, *Horizon*, that Cyril Connolly & Stephen Spender are running? They are trying to get away from the bloody political squirrel-cage, & about time too. I saw Gollancz recently & he is furious with his Communist late-friends, owing to their lies etc., so perhaps the Left Book Club may become quite a power for good again, if it manages to survive. I believe there is going to be a bad paper-shortage some time next year & the number of books published will be curtailed. At the moment however the publishers are rather chirpy because the war makes people read more. Let me know how you are getting on, whether you're in England or when you're likely to be, & if you *can* indicate any wire I could pull to get a job, of course I'd be obliged. Eileen would send love if she were here.

Yours
Eric

[XII, 585, pp. 6–7; handwritten]

1. Orwell adapts line 22 of Marvell's 'To His Coy Mistress', where the chariot is Time's.

To Geoffrey Gorer*

3 April 1940
The Stores
Wallington

Dear Geoffrey,

I was very glad to get your letter & know you are at any rate fairly comfortable & congenially employed. All is very quiet on the Wallington front. Like nearly everyone else I have completely failed to get any kind of 'war work'. But I am trying very hard to join a Gov.t training centre & learn machine draughtsmanship, partly because I want a job, partly because I think it would interest me & as I fancy we are all going to be conscripted in one form or another within about a year I'd rather do something more or less skilled, & partly because I think it might be well to come out of the war having learned a trade. However I don't know whether it will go through yet. Eileen is still working in a Gov.t department but if we can possibly afford it when our affairs are settled I want to get her out of it, as they are simply working her to death besides its making it impossible for us to be together. I dare say we *could* get by if I stuck simply to writing, but at present I am very anxious to slow off & not hurry on with my next book, as I have now published 8 in 8 years which is too much. You didn't I suppose see my last (*Inside the Whale*) which came out a few weeks back. There is one essay in it that might interest you, on boys' weekly papers, as it rather overlaps with your own researches. You remember perhaps my saying to you some years back that very popular fiction ought to be looked into & instancing Edgar Wallace. This essay was published first in a slightly abridged form in Cyril Connolly's monthly paper *Horizon*, & now the editor of the *Magnet*, which you no doubt remember from your boyhood, has asked for space in which to answer my 'charges'. I look forward to this with some uneasiness, as I've no doubt made many mistakes, but what he'll probably pick on is my suggestion that these papers try to inculcate snobbishness.[1] I haven't a copy left to send you but you might be able to get it from the library. There is an essay on Dickens that might interest you too. I find this kind of semi-sociological literary criticism very interesting & I'd like to do a lot of other writers, but unfortunately there's no money in it. All Gollancz would give me in advance on the book was £20! With novels it's easier to be sure of a sale, but I've now got an idea for a really big novel, I mean big in bulk, & I want to lie fallow before doing it. Of course God knows what hope there is of making a living out of writing in the future or where we'll all be a few years hence. If the war really gets going one may get a chance of a scrap after all. Up to date I haven't felt greatly moved to join the army because even if one can get past the doctors they make all the older men into pioneers etc. It's ghastly how soon one becomes 'older'.

There is not much happening in England. As far as I can gather people are fed up with the war but not acutely so. Except for small sections such as Pacifists etc. people want to get it settled & I fancy they'd be willing to go on fighting for 10 years if they thought the sacrifices were falling equally on everybody, which alas isn't likely with the present Government in office. The Government seem to have done all their propaganda with the maximum of stupidity & there'll probably be hell to pay when people begin to grasp that fighting the war means a 12-hour day etc., etc. The new paper *Horizon* is going very well, sells about 6,000 or 7,000 already. Gollancz has grown a beard & fallen out with his Communist pals, partly over Finland[2] etc., partly because of their general dishonesty which he's just become alive to. When I saw him recently, the first time in 3 years, he asked me whether it was really true that the G.P.U. had been active in Spain during the civil war, & told me that when he tied up with the Communists in 1936 he had not known that they had ever had any other policy than the Popular Front one. It's frightful that people who are so ignorant should have so much influence. The food situation is quite O.K., & I think what rationing there is (meat, sugar, butter)[3] is actually unnecessary & done just to teach people a lesson. They've recently had to double the butter ration as they found the stocks going bad on them. I am busy getting our garden dug & am going to try & raise ½ ton[4] of potatoes this year, as it wouldn't surprise me to see a food shortage next winter. If I thought I was going to be here all the time I'd breed a lot more hens & also go in for rabbits.

Eileen would send love if she was here.

Yours
Eric

[XII, 607, pp. 137–8; handwritten]

1. 'Frank Richards' (= Charles Hamilton, 1876–1961), author of many of the stories (although not unaidedly as he claimed), responded in *Horizon*, May 1940 (see XII, 599, pp. 79–85). He did take up the matter of snobbishness among other things.
2. The Soviet Union invaded Finland on 30 November 1939. A peace treaty was signed on 13 March 1940, after a bitterly fought winter campaign.
3. Rationing of food started on 8 January 1940. Adults were allowed four ounces of butter a week; twelve of sugar; four of bacon or ham uncooked, and three and a half cooked. Meat was rationed from 11 March 1940 and clothes from 3 June 1941. As the war progressed, rationing became much more severe, and, indeed, worsened still more during the first years of peace.
4. An ambitious quantity (1,120 lbs.) which Orwell later reduced to 6 cwt (672 lbs.).

To Rayner Heppenstall*

16 April 1940
The Stores
Wallington

Dear Rayner,

Thousands of congratulations on the kid. I hope and trust both are doing well. Please give Margaret all the best and my congratulations. What a wonderful thing to have a kid of one's own, I've always wanted one so. But, Rayner, don't afflict the poor little brat with a Celtic sort of name that nobody knows how to spell. She'll grow up psychic or something. People always grow up like their names. It took me nearly thirty years to work off the effects of being called Eric. If I wanted a girl to grow up beautiful I'd call her Elizabeth, and if I wanted her to be honest and a good cook I'd choose something like Mary or Jane. The trouble is that if you called her Elizabeth everyone would think you'd done it after the queen, as she presumably will be some day.

Thanks for the photos but you didn't tell me what the negative etc. cost. I chose the ones marked 3 and 5 to send to the people. I thought the one marked 3 the best likeness, but naturally I know my own face best from the front. Let's hope the photo will have the desired effect. Seeing that it's for people at the other end of the world I don't know why one shouldn't send a photo of some nice-looking boy in the Air Force or something. I am afraid I definitely lack glamour, because I get quite a lot of letters from readers nowadays, but it's always from people snootily pointing out some mistake I've made and never from young women telling me I'm a sheik. I had some wonderful letters once from a midwife, and I wrote back not telling her I was married, but in the end to Eileen's great glee she turned out to be 35 and have 4 children.

I don't know when I'll be in town. I am buried under books I keep reviewing and not getting on with my own book. God knows whether it will ever
get written or whether such things as publishing novels will still be happening two years hence. All the best.

Yours
Eric

[XII, 612, pp.146–7; typewritten]

To Geoffrey Trease*

1 May 1940
As from The Stores
Wallington

Dear Mr Trease,

Please excuse this paper, which is far from being my own,[1] but I am on a sort
of hurried visit to London. I was very glad to get your letter. From what you
say I dare say you saw either my last book *Inside the Whale* or else the essay
from it that was printed in *Horizon*, & in connection with that two people
had written to me telling me of your *Bows against the Barons* etc. I'm going
to get hold of them, not only because I greatly enjoyed *It's Only Natural*[2] but
because there is no question that this matter of intelligent fiction for kids is
very important for I believe the time is approaching when it might be possible
to do something about it. I don't think it's unimaginable that some paper like
the *News Chronicle* might start a line of kids' papers or I suppose it's even conceivable that the T.U.C. might. Of course such a thing would be quite hopeless if done by the ultra-left political parties. *Boys of the Ogpu*, or, *The Young
Liquidators* etc, etc., but nobody would read them & it would be all the worse
if they did. But I do think there is a chance for papers just a little more 'left' &
also a little less out of date than the present ones. The immediate success of
papers like *Picture Post* & the *News Review*, which would certainly have been
considered 'Bolshevik' 20 years ago shows how opinion is swinging. Did you
by the way see in *Horizon* Frank Richards's reply to my article? I can't make up
my mind to what extent it was a fake, but it certainly wasn't *altogether* a fake,
& it's well-nigh incredible that such people are still walking about, let alone
editing boys' papers.

It makes me laugh to see you referring to me as 'famous' & 'successful'. I
wonder if you know what my books sell—usually about 2000. My best book,
the one about the Spanish war, sold less than 1000, but by that time people
were fed up with Spanish war books, as well they might be.

I'd like to meet some time[3]

Yours sincerely
George Orwell

[XII, 618, pp. 156–7; handwritten]

1. Orwell used Dr Laurence O'Shaughnessy's paper, headed 49 Harley Street, London, W.1.

2. The correct title is *Only Natural*. Orwell reviewed it on 26 April 1940 (XI, 616, p. 154).

3. Trease replied at some length on 5 May 1940 from Gosforth, Cumberland. He said that if Orwell did have time and inclination to take further any scheme of publications for children—'good vivid writing with the right slant'—he could count on Trease for anything he could do to help. He did not think the Trades Union Congress 'could ever assimilate such a new and interesting idea' but the Co-operative Movement was 'a more promising field'. He also suggested W. B. Curry, head of Dartington Hall (an experimental, independent school in Devon that placed great emphasis on the arts); he might tap some of the 'millions which lie behind *that* experiment'.

To the Editor, *Time and Tide*

22 June 1940

Sir: It is almost certain that England will be invaded within the next few days or weeks, and a large-scale invasion by sea-borne troops is quite likely. At such a time our slogan should be ARM THE PEOPLE. I am not competent to deal with the wider questions of repelling the invasion, but I submit that the campaign in France and the recent civil war in Spain have made two facts clear. One is that when the civil population is unarmed, parachutists, motor cyclists and stray tanks can not only work fearful havoc but draw off large bodies of regular troops who should be opposing the main enemy. The other fact (demonstrated by the Spanish war) is that the advantages of arming the population outweigh the danger of putting weapons into the wrong hands. By-elections since the war started have shown that only a tiny minority among the common people of England are disaffected, and most of these are already marked down.

ARM THE PEOPLE is in itself a vague phrase, and I do not, of course, know what weapons are available for immediate distribution. But there are at any rate several things that can and should be done *now*, i.e. within the next three days:

1. Hand grenades. These are the only modern weapon of war that can be rapidly and easily manufactured, and they are one of the most useful. Hundreds of thousands of men in England are accustomed to using hand grenades and would be only too ready to instruct others. They are said to be useful against tanks and will be absolutely necessary if enemy parachutists with machine-guns manage to establish themselves in our big towns. I had a front-seat view of the street fighting in Barcelona in May, 1937, and it convinced me that a few hundred men with machine-guns can paralyse the life of a large city, because of the fact that a bullet will not penetrate an ordinary brick wall. They can be blasted out with artillery, but it is not always possible to bring a gun to bear. On the other hand, the early street fighting in Spain showed that armed men can be driven out of stone buildings with grenades or even sticks of dynamite if the right tactics are used.

2. Shotguns. There is talk of arming some of the Local Defence Volunteer[1] contingents with shotguns. This may be necessary if all the rifles and Bren guns are needed for the regular troops. But in that case the distribution should be made *now* and all weapons should be immediately requisitioned from the gunsmiths' shops. There was talk of doing this weeks ago, but in fact many gunsmiths' windows show rows of guns which are not only useless where they are, but actually a danger, as these shops could easily be raided. The powers and limitations of the shotgun (with buckshot, lethal up to about sixty yards) should be explained to the public over the radio.

3. Blocking fields against aircraft landings. There has been much talk of this, but it has only been done sporadically. The reason is that it has been left to voluntary effort, i.e. to people who have insufficient time and no power of requisitioning materials. In a small thickly-populated country like England we could within a very [few] days make it impossible for an aeroplane to land anywhere except at an aerodrome. All that is needed is the labour. Local authorities should therefore have powers to conscript labour and requisition such materials as they require.

4. Painting out place-names. This has been well done as regards sign-posts, but there are everywhere shopfronts, tradesmen's vans, etc., bearing the name of their locality. Local authorities should have the power to enforce the painting-out of these immediately. This should include the brewers' names on public houses. Most of these are confined to a fairly small area, and the Germans are probably methodical enough to know this.

5. Radio sets. Every Local Defence Volunteer headquarters should be in possession of a radio receiving set, so that if necessary it can receive its orders over the air. It is fatal to rely on the telephone in a moment of emergency. As with weapons, the Government should not hesitate to requisition what it needs.

All of these are things that could be done within the space of a very few days. Meanwhile, let us go on repeating ARM THE PEOPLE, in the hope that more and more voices will take it up. For the first time in decades we have a Government with imagination, and there is at least a chance that they will listen.

[XII, pp. 192–3; typewritten]

1. Orwell attended a conference on the formation of the Local Defence Volunteers, which he joined, at Lord's Cricket Ground on 12 June 1940. This was later renamed the Home Guard. Orwell was soon promoted Sergeant in C Company, 5th County of London Battalion and proved a keen and innovative member. His lecture notes survive and are included in the *Complete Works*.

To Sacheverell Sitwell*

6 July 1940
18 Dorset Chambers
Chagford Street
Ivor Place NW 1

Dear Mr. Sitwell,

I had your book on poltergeists to review for *Horizon* and was very interested by it. I could only do a review of about 600 words and I don't know whether they'll print all of that, as they haven't much space. When I read that very creepy incident you describe of the girl medium dressing dummies or arranging clothes about the room, it brought back to me a memory of 10 years ago which I thought you might like to hear, as I believe it has a remote bearing on your subject.

About ten years ago I was out for a walk on Walberswick common, near Southwold, in Suffolk, with a backward boy I was tutor to at the time.[1] Under a gorse bush the boy noticed a neatly tied-up parcel and drew my attention to it. It was a cardboard box about 10" by 6" by 3" deep. Inside we found that it was lined with cloth and made up like a little room, with tiny furniture made of matchwood and scraps of cloth glued together. There were also (for the sake of complete accuracy I must say that I am not sure whether these were in the same box or another) some tiny female garments including underclothes. There was also a scrap of paper with 'This is not bad is it?' (or nearly those words) written on it in an evidently feminine hand. The neatness and flimsiness of the whole thing made me feel sure it had been made by a woman. What chiefly impressed me was that anyone should go to the trouble of making this thing, which would have meant some hours' work, then carefully tie it up in a parcel and thrust it away under a bush, and in a rather remote spot at that. For what such 'intuitive' feelings are worth, I may say that I felt convinced (a) that it had been put there with the intention that someone should find it, and (b) that it had been made by someone suffering from some kind of sexual aberration. Walberswick has a very small population and one could probably have deduced who was responsible with a little trouble. I may add that the boy I was with could have had nothing to do with it. He was not only very backward but was a cripple and so clumsy with his hands as to have been quite incapable of anything of the kind. The strange thing is that I do not remember what finally happened to the box. To the best of my recollection we put it back under the bush and on coming back some days later found it was gone. At any rate I didn't keep it, which would seem the natural thing to do. I have often puzzled over the incident since, and always with the feeling that there was something vaguely unwholesome in the appearance of the lit-tle room and the clothes. Then in your book you linked up the doll-dressing impulse in girls with definite mental aberration, and it struck me that this affair had a sort of bearing on the subject. The fact that I promptly remem-bered the incident when reading that passage in your book seems to establish a kind of connection.

I have ventured to write to you though not knowing you. Possibly you have seen some of my books however. I believe your sister at any rate knows of me as we have a common friend in Geoffrey Gorer.*[2]

Yours sincerely
George Orwell

[XII, 653, pp. 208–9; typewritten]

1. Bryan Morgan who had been crippled by polio. (See D.J. Taylor, p. 112.)
2. Sitwell replied on 22 July, saying he would have written earlier but was trying to finish a book. Orwell's story was, he said, 'most interesting—and decidedly weird. I wish one knew the secret of it.' He also wished they could meet sometime and said that his sister, Dame Edith Sitwell (1887–1964), was staying with him and had asked him to say that she had 'read with admiration nearly everything you have written'.

To Leonard Moore*

22 October 1940
18 Dorset Chambers
Chagford Street NW 1

Dear Mr Moore,

I have only just had your letter as I have been in the country for a week. I didn't get a previous letter you refer to in it. That is what the posts are like.

I have thought it over and I don't think I can do that thing for Hutchinson's.
I am sorry you have been to some trouble about it. But I don't really know
anything about the subject and it would mean doing research which is very
difficult at present, especially as I can't leave London for any length of time.
Please apologise to them for me, and accept my own apologies for yourself.[1]

I have nearly finished the short book I am doing for Warburg and shall
have it done in about 10 days° time. I would have finished it earlier only I
have been ill, which was why I went down to the country. The title is to be
The Lion and the Unicorn.[2]

Yours sincerely
Eric Blair

[XII, 699, p. 277; typewritten]

1.   It is not known what this proposal was.
2.   This was the first of the series of Searchlight Books. The series was planned by
Fredric Warburg, Tosco Fyvel and Orwell. The full title is *The Lion and the Unicorn:
Socialism and the English Genius*. It was published on 19 February 1941. The first run
comprised 7,500 copies and was followed by a second impression of 5,000 copies.
Unfortunately unsold stock and the type, with that for *Homage to Catalonia*, were
destroyed when the Mayflower Press in Plymouth was bombed. (See also Eileen's
letter to Norah, **5.12.40**.)

Eileen★ to Norah Myles★

[c. 5 December 1940?]
24 Croom's Hill SE 10

[no salutation]

This is to accompany a Charming Gift but I don't know what the gift is yet
because it will be bought this afternoon. Or so I hope. I have been ILL. Ever
so ill. Bedridden for 4 weeks & still <u>weak</u>. You know or Quartus does perhaps though it's more than all my local doctors do. They diagnosed cystitis
and then they diagnosed nephrolithiasis & then they diagnosed Malta fever[1]
with ovarian complications & then they went all hush-hush while they diagnosed a tuberculous infection so that I couldn't possibly guess what they were
testing for. They haven't yet diagnosed cancer or G.P.I.[2] but I expect they
will shortly. They're in a great worry because nothing can be found wrong
with my heart as that was assumed to be giving out very soon. Meanwhile
a perfectly sweet little pathologist like a wren did an ordinary blood count
& found the haemoglobin down to 57%. This is much despised by the clin-
icians but in fact they can find nothing else. So now I hear I'll be cured when

I weigh <u>9 stone</u>. As my present weight is 7st 12. with my clothes on I think perhaps they'll lose interest before the cure is complete. I went to Norfolk for a fortnight's convalescence and wanted to start work on Monday as all this is just silly, but I can't go back without a health certificate & the wretched man won't sign one. However I am now allowed to go shopping on medical grounds though the financial ones aren't so good.

How is your paint?[3] I hope for a Word at Christmas. Marjorie (née Blair) says they're quite O.K. but I don't know where S. Michael's Hill is[4] & have no inside information about the Bristol blitz. I may give up this job for a bit anyway & perhaps see for myself after all. I had arranged a long weekend (which I was going to spend with <u>you</u>) because the pain was worse but then it got a lot worse & the long weekend was merged in sick leave.

George has written a little book, no 1 in the Searchlight Books (Secker & Warburg 2/-), out next month, which please note. Explaining how to be a Socialist though Tory. It was going to cost 1/-, which would have been better, but Warburg changed at the last minute & the book had to have another 10,000 words inserted to give value for twice the money. Some of the later ones look like being good.

I hope you have a tolerable Christmas. We're having the Dinner on Boxing Day, theoretically for lonely soldiers but they are so lonely that we don't know them yet. Mother is still away of course. Now I shall go and shop. But can you send on an envelope to Mary, of whose address I have no idea[?] I also don't know whether she got any further news about Teddy though he was posted Missing in the *Times* months after the *Glorious* went down.[5] She was really magnificent about that. I have been assuming that it was hopeless but of course it's possible that he was taken prisoner. George Kopp,* whom I had also assumed dead, was captured with two bullets in his chest & part of his left hand shot off. Later he escaped to unoccupied France & he's now trying to get here[6] but his letters take about two months to come so one can't know much of what is happening.

By the way, where is Norman?[7] I hope not in Egypt.

Now I must go shopping being as ever a Devoted Pig.

Having walked twelve or fourteen miles to find mother <u>soft</u> slippers <u>with</u> heels, I had to buy everyone else hcfs[8] in a horrible shop. Last year's gift was identical I believe but you will have a nice stock of white hcfs for the cold days.

[*LO*, pp. 79–81; XII, 714A, p. 294; handwritten]

1. Nephrolithiasis: kidney stones; Malta Fever: undulant fever resulting in swelling of the joints and enlarged spleen. It was common in Malta, hence its name, and is an affliction especially suffered by goats.

2. G.P.I: General Paralysis of the Insane. Ill though Eileen certainly is, she can still be comically ironic.

3. Presumably Eileen (perhaps ironically) refers to superficial damage to the paint-work of the house arising from the air-raid.

4. St. Michael's Hill runs south-east to north-west, alongside the University of Bristol campus.

5. See Bertha Mary Wardell, **16.2.37** n. 11.

6. Kopp worked for much of the war in or near Marseilles as 'a sort of engineer' and eventually reached England. He helped Eileen make the journey north from King's Cross to Stockton-on-Tees shortly before she died under an anaesthetic.

7. Norman was the older brother of John Durant. (See headnote to **3.11.36**, and **1.1.38**, n. 8.)

8. hcfs = handkerchiefs. The gift had to be white, easily bought even in wartime, suitable for men and women, and ordinary to the point of being unimaginative. Clothes were not rationed until 1 June 1941, when, of the 66 coupons allowed per year for an adult, one would have been required for each handkerchief.

To Z. A. Bokhari*

17 March 1941
18 Dorset Chambers
Chagford Street NW 1

Dear Mr Bokhari,

I am sending you a rough synopsis of four broadcasts on literary criticism,[1] which I discussed with you a week or two back. I think they are full enough to give you an idea of whether they are the sort of thing you want, and, if they are, I can get on with the scripts. I really don't know whether this is the sort of thing an Indian audience is interested in, but you told me to talk on the lines along which my own interest lies, and naturally I am glad of an opportunity to do that.

Yours sincerely
George Orwell

[XII, 776, pp. 451–2; typewritten]

1. These were broadcast on 30 April and 7, 14, and 21 May 1941; they were published in *The Listener* on 29 May, and 5, 12, and 19 June 1941 (see XII, 792, 797, 800, and 804).

Orwell's review of General Wavell's biography of Field Marshal Allenby had been published in Horizon *in December 1940 and Orwell commented in his War-time Diary, 2 January 1941 that his criticism appeared when Wavell was successful in North Africa. Janus, in 'A Spectator's Notebook', 21 February, remarked it was ironical that the review appeared the day Sidi Barrani fell to the British, noting particularly Orwell's comment that Allenby was 'perhaps . . . the best of a bad lot . . . he remains totally uninteresting—a fact which also tells one a good deal about General Wavell.' This was followed, in* The Spectator *of 7 March 1941, by a letter from A. C. Taylor, who had noted Janus's remarks and drew attention to another interesting coincidence: the same issue of* Horizon *had contained Orwell's 'The Ruling Class', in which Orwell dismissed the bayonet as useless except for opening tins, at a time when Italian troops 'were surrendering in thousands the moment they saw this weapon in the hands of the charging enemy'.*

To *The Spectator*

21 March 1941

Sir,—The letter from Mr. A. C. Taylor raises the question of the value of bay-onets, and also refers back to 'A Spectator's Notebook' of the previous week. Perhaps I can answer both criticisms together. Of course I was wrong about General Wavell, and Heaven knows, I am glad to have been wrong. What I said in my review of his life of Allenby was that as General Wavell held one of the key commands in the present war, it was important for outsiders to try and gauge his intellect from the only evidence then available to them, *i.e.*, the book itself. I submit that it was a dull book, about a man who may have been an able soldier but was a dull personality. Where I was wrong was in supposing that General Wavell's literary shortcomings reflected in any way on his skill as a commander. I apologise to him, in case this should ever meet his eyes, but I doubt whether he will have been very seriously affected by anything I have said about him.

As to bayonets, Mr. Taylor states that Italian troops 'both in Libya and Albania, were surrendering in their hundreds and thousands the moment they saw this weapon in the hands of the charging enemy.' I suspect that the tanks, aeroplanes, &c, may also have had something to do with the Italian surrenders. One must use common sense. A weapon which will kill a man at hundreds of yards is superior to one which will only kill him at a distance of a few feet. Otherwise why have firearms at all? It is quite true that a bayonet is terrifying, but so is a tommy gun, with the added advantage that you can kill somebody with it. Certainly a soldier with a bayonet on the end of his rifle feels aggressive, but so he does with a haversack full of hand-grenades. In the last war exactly the same propaganda stories about the 'power of the bayonet' were current, in the German newspapers as much as in the British. There were tales of thousands of German prisoners who had received bayonet wounds, always in the hindquarters, and countless German cartoons showed British soldiers in flight with Germans prodding them, also in the hindquarters. The psycho-analysts can no doubt tell us why this fantasy of prodding your enemy in the backside appeals so deeply to sedentary civilians. But statistics published after the war was over showed that bayonet wounds accounted for about 1 per cent of total casualties. They will account for far less in this war, in which automatic weapons have grown more important.[1]

But why, in the book Mr. Taylor refers to, did I complain about the continuation of bayonet training? Because it wastes time which ought to be spent in training for things the infantryman will actually have to do, and because a mystical belief in primitive weapons is very dangerous to a nation at war. The experience of the last hundred years shows that whereas military opinion in England often becomes realistic after a defeat, in interim periods the belief always gains ground that you can somehow disregard the power of breach-loading° weapons if your morale is good enough. The majority of British commanders before 1914 'did not believe in' the machine-gun. The results can be studied in the enormous cemeteries of northern France. I am not saying that morale is not important. Of course it is. But for Heaven's sake let us not deceive ourselves into thinking that we shall defeat the German mechanised divisions with rifles and bayonets. The campaign in Flanders ought to have shown whether that is possible.

Yours faithfully.

[XII, 778, pp. 453–4; typewritten]

1. Orwell was proved correct; the bayonet was relatively rarely used for the purpose for which it was designed.

Eileen* to Norah Myles*

[March 1941?]

[no salutation]

The semi crest means that the paper was waste before it Flowered. The same is true of my time as a government servant. There is not much paper, so to sum up:

Physical condition – much improved by air raids, possibly because I now sleep several hours a night longer than ever in my life;

Mental condition – temporarily improved by air raids which were a change, degenerating again now that air raids threaten to become monotonous;

Events since the war – daily work of inconceivable dullness; weekly efforts to leave Greenwich always frustrated; monthly visits to the cottage which is still as it was only dirtier;

Future plans – imaginings of the possibility of leaving a furnished flat ('chambers') that we have at Baker Street[1] & taking an unfurnished flat north of Baker Street to remain in George's Home Guard district, with the idea that we might both live in this flat – probably to be frustrated by continued lack of five shillings to spend & increasing scarcity of undemolished flats & perhaps by our ceasing to live anywhere. But the last is unlikely because a shorter & no less accurate summing up would be

NOTHING EVER HAPPENS TO
Pig.

Please write a letter. The difficulty is that I am too profoundly depressed[2] to write a letter. I have many times half thought I could come to Bristol but it is literally years since a weekend belonged to me & George would have a haemorrhage. I suppose London is not a place to come to really but if you do ring NATIONAL 3318. My departmental head is almost as frightened of me as he is of taking any decision on his own & I can get Time off. Meanwhile give my love to everyone. E.[3]

[LO, pp. 81–2; CW, XII, 771A, p. 443; handwritten]

1.   Although Orwell was still spending some time at Wallington, which Eileen visited monthly, and Eileen was also sometimes at her late brother's house at Greenwich with his widow, Gwen O'Shaughnessy* (also a G.P.), they moved from Dorset Chambers (hence 'chambers' in this letter) to 111 Langford Court, Abbey Road, NW8 on 1 April 1941. This block is north of Baker Street. The date of this letter is not known but in Orwell's War-time Diary for 3 March 1941 he writes that he went with Gwen to see an air-raid shelter in the crypt under Greenwich church. Orwell records in his War-time Diary for 29 May 1940 that Eileen was working in the Censorship Department in Whitehall (hence the NATIONAL exchange for the telephone number and work of 'inconceivable dullness'). She later worked for the Ministry of Food where her environment was much friendlier, one of those also employed there becoming a good friend, Lettice Cooper*.

2. There were many reasons why Eileen should have felt depressed – the unsettled nature of where she should live, shortage of money, the war and the bombing, her own ill-health, but especially the serious effect upon her of the death of her brother Laurence during the retreat to Dunkirk. She never fully recovered from his loss.

3. E: This is the only occasion in her six letters to Norah that Eileen indicates her name.

To the Reverend Iorwerth Jones*

8 April 1941
111 Langford Court
Abbey Road
London NW 8

Dear Mr Jones,

Many thanks for your letter. Perhaps in one or two cases I expressed myself rather ambiguously [in *The Lion and the Unicorn*] and can make things clearer by answering some of your queries.

1. 'The U.S.A. will need a year to mobilise its resources even if Big Business can be brought to heel.' You comment that it is the strikers who are holding up production. That is so, of course, but I was trying to look deeper than the immediate obstruction. The sort of effort that a nation at war now needs can only be made if *both labour and capital* are conscripted. Ultimately what is needed is that labour should be as much under discipline as the armed forces. This condition practically obtains in the USSR and the totalitarian countries. But it is only practicable if *all* classes are disciplined alike, otherwise there is constant resentment and social friction, showing itself in strikes and sabotage. In the long run I think the hardest people to bring to heel will be the business men, who have most to lose by the passing of the present system and in some cases are consciously pro-Hitler. Beyond a certain point they will struggle against the loss of their economic freedom, and as long as they do so the causes for labour unrest will exist.

2. War aims. Of course I am in favour of declaring our war aims, though there is a danger in proclaiming any very detailed scheme for post-war reconstruction, in that Hitler, who is not troubled by any intention of keeping his promises, will make a higher bid as soon as our war-aims are declared. All I protested against in the book was the idea that propaganda *without* a display of military strength can achieve anything. Acland's book *Unser Kampf*, which I referred to, seemed to assume that if we told the Germans

we wanted a just peace they would stop fighting. The same idea is being put about, though in this case not in good faith, by the People's Convention[1] crowd (Pritt[2] and Co.)

3. A pro-Fascist rebellion in India. I wasn't thinking of a rebellion primarily by Indians, I was thinking of the British community in India. A British general attempting a Fascist *coup d'état* would probably use India as his jumping-off place, as Franco used Morocco. Of course it isn't a likelihood at this stage of the war, but one has got to think of the future. If an attempt to impose open naked Fascism upon Britain is ever made, I think coloured troops are almost certain to be used.

4. Gandhi and pacifism. Perhaps I ought not to have implied that pacifists are always people who *as individuals* have led sheltered lives, though it is a fact that 'pure' pacifists usually belong to the middle classes and have grown up in somewhat exceptional circumstances. But it is a fact that pacifism as a movement barely exists except in communities where people don't feel foreign invasion and conquest to be likely. That is why pacifist movements are always found in maritime countries (there is even I believe a fairly considerable pacifist movement in Japan). Government cannot be conducted on 'pure' pacifist lines, because any government which refused in all circumstances to use force could be overthrown by anyone, even any individual, who *was* willing to use force. Pacifism refuses to face the problem of government and pacifists think always as people who will never be in a position of control, which is why I call them irresponsible.

Gandhi has been regarded for twenty years by the Government of India as one of its right-hand men. I know what I am talking about—I used to be an officer in the Indian police. It was always admitted in the most cynical way that Gandhi made it easier for the British to rule India, because his influence was always against taking any action that would make any difference. The reason why Gandhi when in prison is always treated with such lenience,° and small concessions sometimes made when he has prolonged one of his fasts to a dangerous extent, is that the British officials are in terror that he may die and be replaced by someone who believes less in 'soul force' and more in bombs. Gandhi is of course personally quite honest and unaware of the way in which he is made use of, and his personal integrity makes him all the more useful. I won't undertake to say that his methods will not succeed in the long run. One can at any rate say that by preventing violence and therefore preventing relations being embittered beyond a certain point, he has made it more likely that the problem of India will ultimately be settled in a peaceful way. But it is hard to believe that the British will ever be got out of India by those means, and certainly the British on the spot don't think so. As to the conquest of England, Gandhi would certainly advise us to let the

Germans rule here rather than fight against them—in fact he did advocate just that. And if Hitler conquered England he would, I imagine, try to bring into being a nationwide pacifist movement, which would prevent serious resistance and therefore make it easier for him to rule.

Thank you for writing.

Yours sincerely
George Orwell

[XII, 785, pp. 465–7; typewritten]

1. The People's Convention was organised in January 1941 by the Communists, ostensibly to fight for public rights, higher wages, better air-raid precautions, and friendship with the USSR. Some historians maintain that its true purpose was to agitate against the war effort. In July 1941, after the Soviet Union's entry into the war, it immediately called for a second front. By 1942 its active work had ceased.
2. D. N. Pritt (1887–1972) was a Labour MP, 1935–40, then, on expulsion from the party for policy disagreements, Independent Socialist MP until 1950. Well known as a barrister, he was a fervent supporter of left-wing causes and the Soviet Union.

To Dorothy Plowman*

20 June 1941
111 Langford Court
Abbey Road   NW 8

Dear Dorothy,

I can't say much about Max's death. You know how it is, the seeming uselessness of trying to offer any consolation when somebody is dead. My chief sorrow is that he should have died while this beastly war is still going on. I had not seen him for nearly two years, I deeply disagreed with him over the issue of pacifism, but though I am sorry about that you will perhaps understand when I say that I feel that at bottom it didn't matter. I always felt that with Max the most fundamental disagreement didn't alter one's personal relationship in any way, not only because he was incapable of any pettiness but also because one never seems able to feel any resentment against an opinion which is sincerely held. I felt that though Max and I held different opinions on nearly all specific subjects, there was a sense in which I could agree with his vision of life. I was very fond of him, and he was always very good to me. If I remember rightly, he was the first English editor to print any writing of mine, twelve years ago or more.[1]

There is still the £300 which I borrowed through you from my anonymous benefactor.[2] I hope this doesn't embarrass you personally in any way. I can't possibly repay it at this moment, though I hope you understand that I haven't abandoned the intention of doing so. It is hard to make much more than a living nowadays. One can't write books with this nightmare going on, and though I can get plenty of journalistic and broadcasting work, it is rather a hand-to-mouth existence. We have been in London almost from the outbreak of the war. We have kept on our cottage, but we let it furnished and only manage to go down there very occasionally. For more than a year Eileen was working in the Censorship Department, but I have induced her to drop it for a while, as it was upsetting her health. She is going to have a good rest and then perhaps get some less futile and exasperating work to do. I can't join the army because I am medically graded as class D, but I am in the Home Guard (a sergeant!) I haven't heard from Richard Rees* for some time, but last time I heard from him he was a gunner on a coal boat.

Eileen sends her best love. Please remember me also to Piers[3] and everyone. I gather from your card that Piers is now in England. I hope you succeed in keeping him out of danger. This is a rotten time to be alive, but I think anyone of Piers's age has a chance of seeing something better.

Yours
Eric Blair

[XII, 817, pp. 514–5; typewritten]

1. *G. K.'s Weekly* published his first article in English, 'A Farthing Newspaper', 29 December 1928 (X, 80, pp.119–21). Max Plowman did much to further Orwell's writing in *The Adelphi*.
2. L. H. Myers.*
3. The Plowmans' son.

The BBC and the War

1941 – 1943

Orwell worked incredibly hard at the BBC. He wrote 105 English-language newsletters for India, and for occupied Malaya and Indonesia. He also wrote the originals for 115 newsletters for translation into Indian languages. We know some were heard in Japanese-occupied territories. A nun in Malaya, Sister Margaret, described to a WRAC officer, Barbara Rigby, how she and the Sisters risked their lives to listen in and walked many miles to give others the news. The nuns, she said, had been cheered by Orwell: 'we used to bless that good man'. Orwell's idea of propaganda was to broadcast educational and cultural programmes. Long before the Open University he organised courses based on Calcutta and Bombay University syllabuses on literature, science, medicine, agriculture and psychology, engaging speakers of outstanding distinction as varied as T.S. Eliot* and Joseph Needham. He arranged programmes on *The Koran* and *Das Kapital*, on music and poetry. There was a curious programme in which five distinguished writers, including E.M. Forster completed, independently, a story that Orwell had begun. And he made dramatic adaptations.

How effective was all this? Orwell thought he had wasted his time and listener research was not encouraging. Two documents might suggest otherwise. On 20 November 1945, Balraj Sahni* wrote to Orwell from Bombay sympathising on Eileen's death. Balraj and his wife, Damyanti, had worked with Orwell in a series on the mechanics of presenting drama, *Let's Act It Ourselves*. Balraj Sahni wrote, 'We saw little of you two but you endeared yourselves to us greatly, through your work and your sincerity.' They were working in the Indian People's Theatre, 'work which doesn't bring us money but a lot of happiness'. They had had nearly fifty new plays written which they had performed to audiences totalling more than a million people. Damyanti died very young in 1947. Balraj became a very famous film actor. Orwell also presented a series of Indian plays in abbreviated format such as the Sanscrit *Mrocchakatika* ('The Little Clay Cart'). When this was presented in London forty years later it was described as 'a first'.

Secondly, on 7 August 1943, the Director of the Indian Services, Rushbrook-Williams* wrote this in his confidential annual report on Orwell (reproduced by kind permission of the BBC Written Archives Centre): 'He has a great facility in writing and a literary flair which makes his work distinguished… He supports uncomplainingly a considerable burden of poor health. This never affects his work, but occasionally strains his nerves. I have the highest opinion of his moral, as well as of his intellectual capacity. He is transparently honest, incapable of subterfuge, and, in early days, would have either been canonised – or burnt at the stake! Either fate he would have sustained with stoical courage. An unusual colleague – but a mind, and a spirit, of real and distinguished worth.' His achievement was no less than to provide an inspiration for the Third Programme (now Radio 3) (see **19.9.46**, n.3).

In the midst of this, Orwell's mother, Ida, died on 19 March 1943 of bronchitis complicated by emphysema. Orwell was at her bedside, but, as Gordon Bowker points out, it failed to stop her son smoking his pungent roll-up cigarettes (p. 297).

From Orwell's letter to Mrs Laura Buddicom, 27 June 1920

This is an abstract from the sole surviving copy of a memorandum establishing the BBC Eastern Services Committee. It was written by R.A. Rendall, Director of the Empire Service at the time, and is the copy sent to R.W. Brock of the India Section of the Ministry of Information (situated in the University of London's Senate House, which would be the model for the Ministry of Truth in Nineteen Eighty-Four*).*

16 October 1941
[*no address: BBC internal memo*]

I think you are aware that in our endeavour to integrate and expand the Eastern Services of the B.B.C., we have decided to constitute an Eastern Services Committee, which will hold regular fortnightly sessions. On this Committee, which will be an internal organism of the Corporation, the India Office and the Ministry of Information will be represented. . . . The Committee will be presided over by Professor Rushbrook Williams,* our recently appointed Eastern Services Director. . . .

It is intended to hold the first meeting of the Committee at 2.30 p.m. in Room 101 at 55 Portland Place on <u>Wednesday, October 22nd</u>.

[XIII, 870, pp. 57–8]

An agenda was enclosed. Orwell was not invited to the first meeting (though his superior, Zulfaqar Ali Bokhari* attended). 55 Portland Place was a block of flats close to Broadcasting House which the Indian Section used until it moved to 200 Oxford Street. When it was returned to the BBC it was completely refashioned and the surviving plans do not show the layout of rooms at the time the BBC used them, so Room 101 cannot be identified. It was probably on the ground floor. It was certainly not in Broadcasting House itself. Orwell is known to have attended at least twelve meetings and on 14 October 1942 was listed as convenor of a sub-committee to explore the possibilities of organising drama and poetry competitions in India. By this time the BBC had moved to 200 Oxford Street and the meeting was held in Room 314.

In Nineteen Eighty-Four *O'Brien tells Orwell that the thing that is in Room 101 is the worst thing in the world (p. 296). The understandable impression is that this is something like drowning, death by fire, or impalement, but Orwell is more subtle: for many, and for him, the worst thing in the world is that which is the bureaucrat's life-blood: attendance at meetings.*

To E. Rowan Davies*

16 May 1942

Information Re Burma Campaign

The questions which I think could usefully be asked of the Burma government
are: —

i. What number of Burmese voluntarily evacuated themselves along
with British troops etc. leaving India, and what proportion of these were
officials.

ii. Attitude of Burmese officials when breakdown appeared imminent.
Whether there was a marked difference in loyalty between Burmese and
Indian officials. To what extent Burmese officials are known to be carrying
on under the Japanese occupation.

iii. Behaviour under fire of the Burma regiments and military police.
Whether any actual Burmese (not Kachins etc.) were fighting for the British.

iv. What difference appeared between political attitude of the Burmese
proper and the Karens, Shans, Chins, Kachins.[1]

v. What number of the Eurasian community, especially in Rangoon,
Moulmein, Mandalay evacuated with the British and how many stayed
behind under the Japanese occupation. Whether any who remained behind
are known to have changed their allegiance.

vi. Behaviour of the Burmese population under bombing raids. Whether
these produced resentment against the Japanese, admiration for Japanese air
superiority, or mere panic.

vii. The native Christians, especially Karens.[2] Whether interpenetrated to
any extent by nationalist movement.

viii. Number of shortwave sets known to have been in Burmese, Indian
and Eurasian possession before the invasion.

ix. Detailed information about the Burmese nationalist and leftwing political parties. The main points are:—

a. Numbers and local and social composition of the Thakin party.[3]

b. Extent to which Buddhist priests predominate.

c. What affiliations exist between the Burmese nationalist parties and the
Congress and other Indian parties.

d. Burmese Communists, if any, and what affiliations.

e. Extent of Burmese trade union movement and whether it has affiliations with trade unions in India or Europe.

x. Estimated number of Burmese actually fighting on side of Japanese.
Whether people of good standing or mainly dacoits etc. Whether they are
reported to have fought courageously.

xi. Extent of Japanese infiltration before the invasion. Whether many Japanese are known to speak local languages,[4] especially Burmese, and to what extent they are likely to be dependent on Burmans for monitoring and interpretation generally.

Eric Blair

[XIII, 1174, pp. 327–8; typewritten]

1.   In addition to Burmese people, the Burmese nation is composed of many ethnic groups, of which these four are among the most important. There were then more than a million Shans, 1.25 million Karens, half a million Chins, and 200,000 Kachens in a total population of approximately 17 million, many of them being hill peoples. By 1984 the population had doubled.

2.   Most Burmese are Buddhist, as are the Karens, but some 175,000 Karens are Christian.

3.   The Thakin movement developed among radicals in the Young Men's Buddhist Association schools (later the National Schools), who resented British rule. Two university students, Aung San and U Nu, who joined the movement after the student strike in 1936, were instrumental in leading Burma to independence. Aung San was among a number of Burmese politicians murdered in July 1947 at the instigation of a former prime minister, U Saw. When Burma became an independent republic, on 4 January 1948, U Nu became prime minister. Aung San's daughter, Suu Kyi, born shortly before his murder, has led a long fight against the military government of Burma (Myanmar). Her National League for Democracy won a landslide victory in 1990 but was not allowed to govern. She was awarded the Nobel Prize for Peace.

4.   Orwell, when serving in the Indian Imperial Police in Burma, passed the language examinations in Burmese and in Shaw-Karen.

On 27 June 1942, Picture Post *published 'the first article in an important new series', 'Britain's Silent Revolution' by J. B. Priestley. The series asked 'What is happening in Britain? What kind of a country is being shaped by the war?' At the head of Priestley's article was this statement in bold type: 'We are threatened with decay—but the war has saved us. Some of the old are uprooted; some of the new blessings are steadily growing. Here is our great chance to fashion a really healthy society.' On 4 July, Vernon Bartlett, MP, wrote on 'The Revolt Against Party Politics' and on 11 July, a column was run, 'What They Say About Bartlett and Priestley'. Two letters were printed in response to Priestley's article, one from the Bishop of Bradford and this from Orwell.*

To *Picture Post*

11 July 1942

I am in agreement with Mr. Priestley as to the general direction in which our society is moving, but do not share his apparent belief that things will *inevitably* happen fast enough to prevent the old gang getting their claws into us again. Two years ago I would have echoed his optimistic utterances more confidently than I would now. At that time an appalling disaster had brought this country to what looked like the first stage of revolution, and one could be excused for believing that class privilege and economic inequality would quite rapidly disappear under the pressure of danger. Obviously this has failed to happen. But I do agree with Mr. Priestley that the sort of society we knew before 1939 is not likely to return. I don't share the belief which some people still seem to hold, that 'this is a capitalist war,' and that if we win it we shall simply see the British ruling class in power again. What I should like to hear about in Mr. Priestley's next article is not 'What?' but 'How?'—just *how* we are to set about getting the truly democratic society we want.

George Orwell, Abbey Road, NW 8.

[XIII, 1269, p. 391; typewritten]

To Alex Comfort*

15 July 1942
10a Mortimer Crescent
London NW 6

Dear Mr Comfort,

The *Partisan Review* sent me a copy of the letter you had written them, along with some others. I believe they are going to print all the letters, or extracts from them, and my reply. But there was one point I didn't care to answer in print. You queried my reference to 'antisemitism' (by the way I didn't say antisemitism but Jew-baiting, a very different thing) in the *Adelphi*. Of course I was thinking of Max Plowman*, who hated Jews, and though he was aware of this tendency in himself and struggled against it, sometimes let it influence his editorship. I had two particular instances in mind. The first was when Macmurray's book *The Clue to History* was published in 1938. This was a rather unbalanced book and extremely pro-Jew in tendency. Max was infuriated by this and had the book reviewed by five separate people, including himself and myself, in one issue of the *Adelphi*. His own review (you could look it up—

round about December 1938) was definitely provocative in tone. Later on he got the *Adelphi* involved in a controversy with some Jew whose name I don't remember, Cohen I think, about the alleged warmongering activities of the Jews. Having got the Jew hopping mad and said his own say in a very snooty manner, Max suddenly declared the controversy closed, not allowing the Jew to reply. This would be some time in 1939. Since the war Murry has at least once referred with apparent approval to Hitler's 'elimination' of the Jews.

The reason why I don't care to print anything about this is because Max was a very old friend of mine and was very good to me, and his wife might hear about [it] and feel hurt if I actually name names. In my reply in the *Partisan Review* I put in a note to the effect that I was answering this privately, but I daresay they'll omit both this and your query,¹ as I have explained the circumstances to Dwight Macdonald.*

Yours truly
George Orwell

[XIII, 1282, pp. 405–6 (including Comfort's response); typewritten]

Alex Comfort replied on 16 July 1942:

Dear Mr. Orwell

Thank you very much for writing to me. I didn't know about Max in this connection, and you were entirely right. I shouldn't really have replied to you where the *Adelphi* was concerned, as I have only known it since the war: I rather took it that you meant that Jew baiting in it was a recent thing—a feature which had cropped up during the period you were reporting on. (I suppose Max's foible was of pretty long standing).

I thought some of the things you said should have been far more fully answered, but doubted if *P.R.* would have room for more than a squib-retort. I honestly don't think that the last lot of us are any more constructively pro-Fascist than our predecessors, but from the people I encounter, I would say they were nearer to Russian nihilism than any contemporary line of thought.

However, I often want to remonstrate with *Peace News*, not for being Fascist, but for trying, as you say, to get away with both ends of the same argument. I have written a commination to J.M. Murry but he did not print it. He needs another beginning 'cursed is the man who imagines one can assume opposite viewpoints and say that whichever turns out to be true, his main contention is right.'

I'd like an opportunity of congratulating you over that *Horizon* article on Donald McGill°. It was the best example of an analysis I think I ever read.

I'll be writing to the editor of *P.R.* and explain that I entirely agree with you, on seeing the references. I didn't want to put you on the spot over a personal question like that, and I apologize for my ignorance.

All good wishes and many thanks
Alex Comfort

I'd like to have started an argument over that review of yours,[2] but the *Adelphi* hadn't room to unleash me. Anyhow, thank you for doing it. It made me revise several ideas.

1.   *Partisan Review* omitted all reference to this topic.
2.   For Orwell's review of Comfort's novel, *No Such Liberty*, see XIII, 855, pp. 389–44.

To Routledge & Sons Ltd.

23 July 1942
The BBC
Broadcasting House
London W 1

Dear Sir,

My attention has just been drawn to a book published by you entitled *Victory or Vested Interests*, in which you have included a lecture of mine delivered last year for the Fabian Society. I submitted this lecture to you in type-written form, and, I believe, corrected the proofs. I now find that you have been through it and made the most unwarrantable alterations about which I was not even consulted—a fact which I should never even have discovered if I had not bought a copy of the book, as you did not even send me one. I am communicating with my literary agents to see what remedy I have against this treatment, but meanwhile, I should be glad to have an explanation from you. I shall be obliged by an early answer.[1]

Yours truly,
Geo. Orwell

[XIII, 1319, p. 424; typewritten]

1.   T. Murray Ragg, the Managing Director, replied on 24 July explaining that they had made no alterations and had delivered copies as instructed by the Fabian Society. He suggested that someone at the Society had made the alterations. (For a full account see XIII, 884, pp. 66–7.)

On 8 August 1942, Captain Basil Liddell Hart wrote to Orwell expressing surprise that someone of his penetration had been misled by Philippe Barrès's Charles de Gaulle, *which Orwell had reviewed in the* Observer *on 2 August (XIII, 1346, pp. 443–4), in so far as it discussed the evolution of mechanised warfare and the use of armoured divisions. He sent Orwell six pages of notes to show that it was not de Gaulle who had devised modern methods of tank warfare, which the Germans, rather than the French or British, had adopted, but a British officer, Colonel J. F. C. Fuller (1878–1966; CB, DSO) in 1927. (Fuller was identified by the security service as 'the military strongman willing to take part in, if not preside over, a British Vichy'.) Two years later, the British War Office had issued 'the first official manual on mechanized warfare . . . embodying the new conception'. This included the organisation and methods that were to become the foundation of Panzer attacks. General de Gaulle's book,* Vers L'Armée de Métier *(1934), had only ten of its 122 pages devoted to tactics, in the English translation. This, said Liddell Hart, was hardly surprising, since de Gaulle's 'first personal experience with tanks was not until three years later, in 1937'. Niall Ferguson in his* The War of the World *(2006) discusses the considerable influence Liddell Hart had on tank and aircraft strategy – alas, 'it was hugely influential not in Britain but in Germany', especially on Heinz Guderian, commander of the 19th German Army Corps (pp. 386–7).*

To B. H. Liddell Hart*

12 August 1942
10a Mortimer Crescent
NW 6

Dear Captain Liddell Hart,

Many thanks for your letter. I am sorry I accepted too readily the legend of the Germans having taken their tank theories from de Gaulle. The *Observer* had to compress my review of Barrès's book by cutting out a passage from de Gaulle's memorandum of early in 1940. I hadn't seen this memorandum till seeing it in Barrès's book, and it certainly did seem to me to foretell what happened a few months later with considerable prescience. The story of 'the man the Germans learned from' had already been built up elsewhere, and I had already more or less accepted it, not, of course, being much versed in military literature. I had read many of your own writings but didn't realise that the Germans had drawn on them to that extent. And I was more ready to accept de Gaulle as a revolutionary innovator because of the obviously old-fashioned nature of the French army as a whole. I was in French Morocco from the autumn of 1938 to the spring of 1939, and with war obviously imminent

I naturally observed the French colonial army as closely as I could, even to the point of getting hold of some of their infantry textbooks. I was struck by the antiquated nature of everything, though I know very little of military matters. I could if you wish write to the *Observer* and say that I was mistaken and had transferred some of your thunder to de Gaulle, but from a political point of view I don't like writing de Gaulle down. It was a misfortune that we didn't succeed in getting a leftwing politician of standing out of France, but since de Gaulle is the only figure we have at present to represent the Free French we must make the best of him.

No, I didn't write *Bless 'Em All.*[1] I am not in the army because I am not physically fit (Class IV!) but I have been in the Home Guard from the beginning and could write a rather similar booklet about that. I don't know who the author is except that he is an Australian. The book has had a fairly large sale, 15–20,000 copies, and has probably done a lot of good.

I should like to meet you some time when you are in London. I never get out of London as I am working in the BBC. I expect Humphrey Slater is a mutual friend of ours.

Yours sincerely
Geo. Orwell

[XIII, 1379, pp. 471–2; typewritten]

1.   Liddell Hart asked Orwell whether he had written *Bless 'Em All* because he so admired the book that he had 'distributed quite a number of copies . . . in quarters where I thought it might do some good'. The full title of the book, published pseudonymously by Boomerang, is *Bless 'Em All: An Analysis of the British Army, Its Morale, Efficiency and Leadership, Written from Inside Knowledge* (1942). 'Boomerang' was Alan W. Wood, an Australian who had worked on Beaverbook newspapers before the war and who, according to Fredric Warburg, 'died far too young'. It sold 37,625 copies in the first fifteen months.

To Tom Wintringham*

17 August 1942

Dear Wintringham,

I am in general agreement with the document you sent me,[1] and so are most of the people I know, but I think that from the point of view of [a] propaganda approach it is all wrong. In effect, it demands two separate things which the average reader will get mixed up, first, the setting up of a committee, and secondly, the programme which that committee is to use as a basis for discussion. I should start by putting forward boldly and above all with an eye to intelligibility a programme for India coupled with the statement that this is what the Indian political leaders would accept. I would *not* start with any talk about setting up committees; in the first place because it depresses people merely to hear about committees, and in any case because the procedure you suggest would take months to carry through, and would probably lead to an inconclusive announcement. I should head my leaflet or whatever it is RELEASE NEHRU—REOPEN NEGOTIATIONS and then set forth the plan for India in six simple clauses, viz:

1). India to be declared independent immediately.
2). An interim national government from the leading political parties on a proportional basis.
3). India to enter into full alliance with the United Nations.
4). The leading political parties to co-operate in the war effort to their utmost capacity.
5). The existing administration to be disturbed as little as possible during the war period.
6). Some kind of trade agreement allowing for a reasonable safe-guarding of British interests.

Those are the six points. They should be accompanied by an authoritative statement from the Congress Party that they are willing to accept those terms—as they would be—and that if granted these terms they would cooperate in crushing the pro-Japanese faction. Point 6 should carry with it a rider to the effect that the British and Indian Governments will jointly guarantee the pensions of British officials in India. In this way at small cost one could neutralise a not unimportant source of opposition in this country.

All I have said could be got on to a leaflet of a page or two pages, and I think might get a hearing. It is most important to make this matter simple and arresting as it has been so horribly misrepresented in the press and the big public is thoroughly bored by India and only half aware of its strategic significance. Ditto with America.

Yours,
[*No name/position*]

[XIII, 1391, pp. 479–80; typewritten]

1.   Tom Wintringham had sent Orwell a copy of the press release issued by the Common Wealth National Committee on 15 August 1942. This was issued over the names of J.B. Priestley (Chairman), Richard Acland (Vice-Chairman; see **24.11.38**, n. 4), and Tom Wintringham* (Vice-Chairman). The stature of the novelist, playwright, and commentator, J. B. Priestley (1894–1984) was considerable at this time and was further enhanced by his inspiring broadcasts, especially after Dunkirk. He was seen by many as akin to Churchill in his dogged determination; even in

the darkest days he was sure the war would end in Britain's favour. He also argued forcefully for a better Britain when peace came.

To Leonard Moore*

4 September 1942
10a Mortimer Crescent
NW 6

Dear Mr Moore,

Many thanks for the cheque for £10–17–1, and the accounts. I return the latter.

I am unfortunately far too busy to write anything except casual journalism. Besides being in the BBC I am in the Home Guard, and between the two I don't have many evenings to myself. However, during 1940–1941 I kept a diary, and when I had been keeping it some time it struck me that it might be publishable some time, though I felt it would be more likely to be of interest after a lapse of 5 or 10 years. But events have moved so fast that it might as well be 10 years since 1940 now, and I am not sure the thing is not worth trying on a few publishers. A friend who had also kept a diary had some idea of making a book out of the two, but this idea fell through.[1] At present my diary is being typed, but when that is done, in about 10 days, we might see what we can do with it. Gollancz did hear about [it] and said he would like to see it, but I am not certain whether people are not rather fed up with war diaries. I should think the best place for publishing a thing of this kind would be America, if one could connect with an American publisher and then get the Ms through the censorship. My books have never sold well in the USA, but I think I may have built myself up a small public there via the 'London Letters' I have done from time to time during the last 18 months in the *Partisan Review*. The editor told me some New York publisher said he thought the 'London Letters' might be worth reprinting in pamphlet form, and if so the diary might have a chance. It is about 25,000 or 30,000 words, an awkward length, and I shouldn't expect such a book to have more than a small sale, but I should think some publisher might think it worth risking a few pounds on.

I hope business is good. Everyone seems to be reading, when they can get hold of books.

Yours sincerely
Eric Blair

[XIV, 1443, p. 5; typewritten]

1. The friend was Inez Holden.* The joint publication was not realised.

To Mulk Raj Anand*

7 October 1942

Dear Mulk,

I am sending back your script on *War and Peace* because I wish you would re-write the later part, roughly speaking from page 4 onwards in order to deal more with the sociological aspect of *War and Peace*. I think it is quite true that Tolstoy marked the beginning of a new attitude towards the novel, but that in itself is not big enough to justify the title 'Books That Changed the World'. What I wanted was a talk on *War and Peace* as exemplifying the new attitude towards war. If not the first, it is certainly one of the first books that tried to describe war realistically and many modern currents of thought, probably including pacifism, derive from it to some extent. I do not of course want pacifist propaganda, but I think we might make valuable use of a comparison between Tolstoy's description of the battle of Oesterlitz[1] and for instance Tennyson's 'Charge of the Light Brigade'.

Gollancz has expressed interest in your idea for a book about India.[2] He says it would have to be done quickly, which however would be quite easy by the method we were projecting of doing it. He wants you, or failing you, me to go and see him today week, October 14th, at 11 a.m. at his office. Do you think you could see me between now and then so that we can draw up a synopsis of the book?

Yours sincerely,
George Orwell

[XIV, 1550, pp. 85–6; typewritten]

1. Austerlitz, where Napoleon gained a brilliant victory over the Austrians and Russians in 1805. Tolstoy's account is given in Book 3, chapters 14–19. The letter illuminates Orwell's attitude to his idea for broadcasting to India: far more educational and cultural than crudely propagandist.

2. In a letter to Orwell of 11 October 1942 (which discussed factual aspects of the broadcast), Anand added a postscript to say that he would telephone on Monday (presumably the next day) to discuss the book. He said that the only real basis for a symposium was a constructive plan for the defence of India. That might bring together different points of view and 'reveal the idiocy of reaction more strongly'. There is nothing else on file about this proposed book.

Laurence Brander* to L. F. Rushbrook Williams*

8 October 1942, with copy to Orwell

Saturday Weekly News Letter

In conversation with Mr. Eric Blair this morning, I discovered that he writes our Saturday Weekly News Letter which is read by some Indians. The audience in India supposes that the reader is the composer, and the present audience is small. As you know, the universal demand amongst our Indian audience is for well-known Englishmen. If, therefore, it could be arranged that this News Letter be no longer anonymous, but the known work of 'George Orwell' and read by him[1] instead of largely being ignored as at present, it would be looked forward to with the very greatest interest, as few names stand so high with our Indian audience at present as that of George Orwell.

[XIV, 1557, p. 89; typewritten]

1.   This was agreed. Orwell read his Newsletters from No. 48, 21 November 1942.

To the Editor of *The Times*

12 October 1942
10A Mortimer Crescent
NW 6

Sir,

May I be allowed to offer one or two reflections on the British Government's decision to retaliate against German prisoners, which seems so far to have aroused extraordinarily little protest?[1]

By chaining up German prisoners in response to similar action by the Germans, we descend, at any rate in the eyes of the ordinary observer, to the level of our enemies. It is unquestionable when one thinks of the history of the past ten years, that there *is* a deep moral difference between democracy and Fascism, but if we go on the principle of an eye for an eye and a tooth for a tooth we simply cause that difference to be forgotten. Moreover, in the matter of ruthlessness we are unlikely to compete successfully with our enemies. As the Italian radio has just proclaimed, the Fascist principle is two eyes for an eye and a whole set of teeth for one tooth. At some point or another public opinion in England will flinch from the implications of this statement, and it is not very difficult to foresee what will happen. As a result of our action the Germans will chain up more British prisoners, we shall have to follow suit by chaining up more Axis prisoners, and so it will continue till logically all the prisoners on either side will be in chains. In practice, of course, we shall become disgusted with the process first, and we shall announce that the chaining up will now cease, leaving, almost certainly, more British than Axis prisoners in fetters. We shall thus have acted both barbarously and weakly, damaging our own good name without succeeding in terrorising the enemy.

It seems to me that the civilised answer to the German action would be something like this: 'You proclaim that you are putting thousands of British prisoners in chains because some half-dozen Germans or thereabouts were temporarily tied up during the Dieppe raid. This is disgusting hypocrisy, in the first place because of your own record during the past ten years, in the second place because troops who have taken prisoners have got to secure them somehow until they can get them to a place of safety, and to tie men's hands in such circumstances is totally different from chaining up a helpless prisoner who is already in an internment camp. At this moment, we cannot stop you mal-treating° our prisoners, though we shall probably remember it at the peace settlement, but don't fear that we shall retaliate in kind. You are Nazis, we are civilised men. This latest act of yours simply demonstrates the difference.'

At this moment this may not seem a very satisfying reply, but I suggest that to anyone who looks back in three months' time, it will seem better than what we are doing at present and it is the duty of those who can keep their heads to protest before the inherently silly process of retaliation against the helpless is carried any further.

Yours truly,
George Orwell

[XIV, 1563, pp. 97–8; typewritten]

1. In his War-time Diary for 11 October 1942, Orwell recorded that following the unsuccessful raid on Dieppe, the Canadians had 'chained up a number of German prisoners equal to the number of British prisoners chained up in Germany'. (See *Diaries*, p. 367.) The letter was not published.

To R. R. Desai*

3 March 1943

Dear Desai

The Indian Government have cabled asking us to do something in Gujerati about the Beveridge report so we shall have to use your Gujerati period on Monday next for this. They evidently want to have the whole story, i.e. what the scheme proposes and also the history of the Parliamentary Debate. I need not tell you that the censorship would not allow through any comment, i.e. any comment on our part which amounted to a criticism of the Government for watering the Beveridge scheme down. On the other hand, the debate on the subject with the arguments brought forward for and against the report could be given, objectively. I should suggest simply setting out the provisions of the report, not going into too much detail, but emphasizing the more important clauses, especially family allowances, then mention the debate and then explain how much of the report the Government actually proposes to adopt. You can say, with safety, that whatever else goes out, family allowances on some scale or another are certain to be adopted. And it would be worth adding that this itself is an important advance and likely to raise the British birth-rate.[1] However, they evidently want an objective report on the Beveridge scheme rather than a propaganda statement. You can use the whole of your period on Beveridge or use about ten minutes and reserve about three minutes for the headline news of the week, just as you wish. I hope you will let us have your script in good time. We have already cabled our people in India that we're going to deal with Beveridge this week.

Yours
Eric Blair
Talks Producer
Indian Section.

P.S. If I could have this particular script on Saturday [6th] I shall be much obliged.

[XV, 1923, p. 10; typewritten]

1.   Orwell was proved right. Later, when the Labour Government of 1999 increased child benefits, the Institute of Fiscal Studies report, *Does Welfare Reform Affect Fertility?*, estimated that badly educated mothers had an additional 45,000 children in the year after the reforms were introduced (*Daily Telegraph*, 22 December 2008).

To Penguin Books

8 March 1943
10a Mortimer Crescent
NW 6

Dear Sir,

With reference to your letter dated 5.3.43. I am not absolutely certain without looking up my contracts how I stand about the rights in my books, but I am *almost* certain that if the publisher has issued no cheap edition two years after publication, the rights revert to me. I can verify this, but in any case neither of my publishers is likely to make trouble about the republication of books which appeared some time ago. The books of mine which might be worth reprinting are (I give date of publication with each):—

Burmese Days (1934–1935).
Homage to Catalonia (1938)
Coming Up for Air (1939)
Inside the Whale (1940).

I should say *Burmese Days* was much the most hopeful. It was first published by Harper's in the USA, then a year later in a slightly bowdlerised edition by Gollancz. The English edition sold 3000 to 4000, the American about 1000.[1] I think it deserves reprinting, and it has a certain topicality owing to the campaign in Burma. Gollancz's stock of it has come to an end and it is totally out of print, but I possess a copy of the American edition. *Inside the Whale* is also totally out of print, the stocks of it having been blitzed, but I have a proof copy. It didn't sell much but got a certain notoriety owing to parts of it being reprinted in magazines. *Homage to Catalonia* I think ought [to] be reprinted some time, but I don't know whether the present is quite the moment. It is about the Spanish civil war, and people probably don't want that dragged up now. On the other hand if Spain comes into the war I suppose it would be for a while possible to sell anything which seemed informative about Spanish internal affairs, if one could get it through the press in time.

I shall be happy to give you any further information you want.

Yours faithfully
George Orwell

[XV, 1942, pp. 18–19; typewritten]

1.   In the light of Orwell's later bitterness over the way Gollancz had 'garbled' *Burmese Days* (see II, p. 310), his comment that it was 'slightly bowdlerised' is surprising. The

US edition sold better than Orwell remembered. It was, in fact, reprinted. The first printing was of 2,000 copies. A Penguin edition was published in May 1944.

To Dwight Macdonald*

26 May 1943
10a Mortimer Crescent
NW 6

Dear Macdonald,

Many thanks for your letter (dated April 13 and arrived yesterday!) and cheque. I enclose a list of 15 people who° I should think would be possible subscribers to P[artisan] R[review].¹ Some of them I know are acquainted with the paper, and some may possibly be subscribers, but not to my knowledge. I am circularising all of them, telling them you can accept foreign subscriptions, and offering to lend copies so that they can have a look at it. Forster was interested when I showed him a copy some time back, so I am pretty certain he would subscribe if you prodded him, also Myers and Rees.

I am glad the last letter was a success and I will send another as soon as possible. As you see by the above address I didn't get the job I was trying for (in North Africa) and am still at the BBC. I enjoy very much doing these letters for *PR*, it is a tremendous relief every now and then to write what one really thinks about the current situation, and if I have occasionally shown signs of wanting to stop it is because I keep fearing that your readers will get tired of always hearing about affairs in England from the same person. My point of view isn't the only one and as you will have seen from the various letters from Alex Comfort* etc. there are some pretty vigorous opponents of it.² But within my own framework I have tried to be truthful and I am very happy to go on with the arrangement so long as you are.

We have shortly coming out a book made up from the broadcasts sent out to India by my department.³ I think some copies will be sent to the USA, and I will try to get a copy to *PR*. Of course all books of broadcasts are crashingly dull, but it might interest you to see some specimens of British propaganda to India.

I will send off my next letter probably in about a fortnight. In that case it should reach you before the end of July unless the mail service comes unstuck again.

All the best.

Geo. Orwell

[XV, 2098A, p. xxiv; typewritten]

1. For the list of names, see XV, pp. xxiv–xxv.
2. In his 'London Letter', 1 January 1942 (XIII, 913, pp. 107–14), Orwell attacked Comfort* and others. (See its n. 4 and 'Pacifism and War: A Controversy', XIII, 1270, pp. 392–400.)
3. *Talking to India*, edited by Orwell, published 18 November 1943 (XV, 2359, pp. 320–1).

To Alex Comfort*

Sunday [11?] July 1943
10a Mortimer Crescent NW 6

Dear Comfort,

Very many thanks for sending me the copy of *New Road*. I am afraid I was rather rude to you in our *Tribune* set-to,¹ but you yourself weren't altogether polite to certain people. I was only making a *political* and perhaps moral reply, and as a piece of verse your contribution was immensely better, a thing most of the people who spoke to me about it hadn't noticed. I think no one noticed that your stanzas had the same rhyme going right the way through. There is no respect for virtuosity nowadays. You ought to write something longer in that genre, something like the 'Vision of Judgement'.² I believe there could be a public for that kind of thing again nowadays.

As to *New Road*. I am much impressed by the quantity and the general level of the verse you have got together. I should think half the writers were not known to me before. Apropos of Aragon³ and others, I have thought over what you said about the reviving effect of defeat upon literature and also upon national life. I think you may well be right, but it seems to me that such a revival is only *against* something, ie. against foreign oppression, and can't lead beyond a certain point unless that oppression is ultimately to be broken, which must be by military means. I suppose however one might accept defeat in a mystical belief that it will ultimately break down of its own accord. The really wicked thing seems to me to wish for a 'negotiated' peace, which means back to 1939 or even 1914. I have written a long article on this for *Horizon* apropos of Fielden's book on India, but I am not certain Connolly will print it.⁴

I am going to try to get Forster to talk about *New Road*, together with the latest number of *New Writing*, in one of his monthly book talks to India. If he doesn't do it this month he might next.⁵ There is no sales value there, but it extends your publicity a little and by talking about these things on the air in wartime one has the feeling that one is keeping a tiny lamp alight somewhere. You ought to try to get a few copies of the book to India. There is a small public for such things among people like Ahmed Ali⁶ and they are starved for books at present. We have broadcast quite a lot of contemporary verse to India, and they are now doing it to China with a commentary in Chinese. We also have some of our broadcasts printed as pamphlets in India and sold for a few annas, a thing that could be useful but is terribly hard to organise in the face of official inertia and obstruction. I saw you had a poem by Tambimuttu. If you are bringing out other numbers, you ought to get some of the other Indians to write for you. There are several quite talented ones and they are very embittered because they think people snub them and won't print their stuff. It is tremendously important from several points of view to try to promote decent cultural relations between Europe and Asia. Nine tenths of what one does in this direction is simply wasted labour, but now and again a pamphlet or a broadcast or something gets to the person it is intended for, and this does more good than fifty speeches by politicians. William Empson[7] has worn himself out for two years trying to get them to broadcast intelligent stuff to China, and I think has succeeded to some small extent. It was thinking of people like him that made me rather angry about what you said of the BBC, though God knows I have the best means of judging what a mixture of whoreshop and lunatic asylum it is for the most part.

Yours sincerely
Geo. Orwell

[XV, 2185, pp. 168–9; typewritten]

1. See Orwell's verse-letter, 'As One Non-Combatant to Another (A Letter to "Obadiah Hornbrooke")', XV, 2138, pp. 142–5 (and Comfort's initial verse-letter, pp. 138–141).

2. When George III died, Robert Southey, the poet laureate, wrote a conventional elegy, *Vision of Judgement* (1821). To this, Byron wrote a devastating rejoinder, *The Vision of Judgement*. Its satire was so biting that John Murray refused to take the risk of publishing it, and when Leigh Hunt, editor of *The Liberal*, printed it in 1822, he was fined £100.

3. Louis Aragon came to the fore after the collapse of France, through his patriotic poems – *Le Crève-coeur* (1941) and *Les Yeux d'Elsa* (1942) among them. (See also **9.4.46** to Philip Rahv. n. 3.)

4. Lionel Fielden (1896–1974), after serving in World War I (including Gallipoli) and working for the League of Nations and the High Commission for Refugees in Greece and the Levant, joined the BBC in 1927. He served as a staff officer in Italy in 1943 and was Director of Public Relations for the Allied Control Commission in Italy, 1944–45. Orwell contributed a long review article to *Horizon*, September 1943 (XV, 2257, pp. 209–16), on Fielden's 'ironical attack on British imperialism in India', *Beggar My Neighbour*. Fielden responded with 'Toothpaste in Bloomsbury' (XV, 2258, pp. 216–21).

5. Orwell was as good as his word and Forster discussed *New Road* on 7 August 1943.

6. Ahmed Ali (1908–), author and academic, was at this time the BBC's Listener and Research Director in India.

7. William Empson (1906–84; Kt., 1979), poet and critic. He had been Professor of English Literature in Tokyo and Peking before the war and after at Sheffield University (1953–71). He achieved scholarly recognition with *Seven Types of Ambiguity* (1930). His *Times* obituary described him as 'the most famously over-sophisticated man of his time' who 'revolutionized our ways of reading a poem'.

On 28 August, Ivor Brown, on behalf of the Observer, *wrote to Orwell saying he had heard he was leaving the BBC and he wondered whether he would like to go to Algiers and Sicily, 'accredited' by the War Office, though not as 'a regular war correspondent'. It might mean writing for other newspapers as well as the* Observer, *in order to share costs, 'but primarily you would be* The Observer *man'.*

To Ivor Brown*

31 August 1943
10a Mortimer Crescent NW 6

Dear Mr Brown,

Many thanks for your letter. I would, of course, like very greatly to go to North Africa for you if it can be arranged. If it *can*, however, I wonder if it would be possible to have some idea of the date. I have not put in my formal resignation to the BBC but have informed my immediate chiefs that I intend to leave them, and when resigning formally I am supposed to give 2 months' notice. This however would not be insisted on so long as I could give at any rate a few weeks' notice. Meanwhile I have arranged to go on my annual holiday (for a fortnight) at the end of this week. Of course I would throw this up if the opportunity of going to North Africa occurred immediately, but otherwise I am not anxious to miss my holiday as I have not had one for 14 months and am rather in need of one. So I should be greatly obliged if you could give me some idea of when this scheme is likely to materialise, supposing that it does so.

Yours sincerely
Geo. Orwell

[XV, 2255, p. 208; typewritten]

To L. F. Rushbrook Williams*

24 September 1943
B.B.C.

Dear Mr Rushbrooke-Williams,[1]

In confirmation of what I said to you earlier in private, I want to tender my resignation from the BBC, and should be much obliged if you would forward this to the proper quarter.

I believe that in speaking to you I made my reasons clear, but I should like to put them on paper lest there should be any mistake. I am not leaving because of any disagreement with BBC policy and still less on account of any kind of grievance. On the contrary I feel that throughout my association with the BBC I have been treated with the greatest generosity and allowed very great latitude. On no occasion have I been compelled to say on the air anything that I would not have said as a private individual. And I should like to take this opportunity of thanking you personally for the very understanding and generous attitude you have always shown towards my work.

I am tendering my resignation because for some time past I have been conscious that I was wasting my own time and the public money on doing work that produces no result. I believe that in the present political situation the broadcasting of British propaganda to India is an almost hopeless task. Whether these broadcasts should be continued at all is for others to judge, but I myself prefer not to spend my time on them when I could be occupying myself with journalism which does produce some measurable effect. I feel that by going back to my normal work of writing and journalism I could be more useful than I am at present.

I do not know how much notice of resignation I am supposed to give.[2] The *Observer* have again raised the project of my going to North Africa. This has to be approved by the War Office and may well fall through again, but I mention it in case I should have to leave at shorter notice than would otherwise be the case. I will in any case see to it that the programmes are arranged for some time ahead.

Yours sincerely
Eric Blair

[XV, 2283, pp. 250–1; typewritten]

1. Rushbrook Williams signed his name over this misspelling of his name, without hyphen and 'e'; both errors were Orwell's.
2. On 29 September, Sir Guy Williams, Overseas Services Establishment Officer, wrote to Orwell, accepting his resignation 'with much regret'. Whilst recognising

that he should normally work his two months' notice, Sir Guy wrote: 'if, as you say, you may have to leave at shorter notice, the Corporation would be prepared to allow you to do so'; Orwell's resignation would take effect from 24 November 1943 'unless you inform me that you wish to leave at an earlier date'. On 7 October 1943, Brown wrote to Orwell saying he had heard he would be free at the end of November and he would be glad if he could come over to see him at *The Observer* to discuss the amount of reviewing and other writing he could do for that paper. He mentioned also that he much appreciated Orwell's review 'of Laski' (of *Reflections on the Revolution of Our Time*), 10 October 1943 (XV, 2309, pp. 270–2).

To S. Moos

16 November 1943
10a Mortimer Crescent NW 6

Dear Mr. Moos,

I hope you will forgive my long delay in commenting on and returning the enclosed manuscript, but I have been in poor health in recent weeks, and I am also very busy, as you can perhaps imagine.

I find what you say very interesting, but I have two criticisms of a general nature to make. The first is that I think you are concerned with 'what' a little too much to the exclusion of 'how'. It is comparatively easy to see the evils of modern industrialised society, and it is only one more step beyond that to see the inadequacy of the solutions put forward by Socialists etc. The real trouble begins when one wants to communicate these ideas to a large enough number of people to make some actual change in the trend of society. We certainly have to decide what kind of world we want, but I suggest that the greatest problem before intellectuals now is the conquest of power. You speak of forming a 'new elite' (which I think there probably must be, though I am inclined to shrink from the idea). But how to start forming that elite, how one can do such things *inside* the powerful modern state which is controlled by people whose interest is to prevent any such thing—that is another question. If you have seen anything of the innumerable attempts during the past 20 years to start new political parties, you will know what I mean.

Secondly, I think you overestimate the danger of a 'Brave New World'— i.e. a completely materialistic vulgar civilisation based on hedonism. I would say that the danger of that kind of thing is past, and that we are in danger of quite a different kind of world, the centralised slave state, ruled over by a small clique who are in effect a new ruling class, though they might be adoptive rather than hereditary. Such a state would not be hedonistic, on the contrary its dynamic would come from some kind of rabid nationalism and leader-worship kept going by literally continuous war, and its average standard of living would probably be low. I don't expect to see mass unemployment again, except through temporary maladjustments; I believe that we are in much greater danger of forced labour and actual slavery. And at present I see no safeguard against this except (a) the war-weariness and distaste for authoritarianism which may follow the present war, and (b) the survival of democratic values among the intelligentsia.

I don't know whether these cursory comments are much use to you. They might be worth thinking over. I should say that Faber's or somebody like that might publish your Ms as a pamphlet—at any rate it would be worth trying. But I would brush up the English a bit (rather involved and foreign-sounding in places) and get the Ms retyped before submitting it.

Once again, please forgive the delay.

Yours sincerely,
Geo. Orwell

[XV, 2356, pp. 308–9]

Journalism and the
Death of Eileen

1943-1945

Orwell began work as Literary Editor of *Tribune* immediately on leaving the BBC at the end of November 1943. The first of his eighty causeries, 'As I Please', was published on 3 December 1943 and on Christmas Eve *Tribune* published an article by 'John Freeman' – Orwell under an assumed name – 'Can Socialists Be Happy?'. For the next two years he was remarkably busy writing articles, reviews, columns, and journalism of every kind. He was, as he told Dorothy Plowman on 19 February 1946, 'smothered under journalism' and desperate to get away – to Jura. Nevertheless, smothered or not, some of his outstanding essays were published in this period – 'Raffles and Miss Blandish', 'Benefit of Clergy', 'In Defence of P.G. Wodehouse', 'Funny but not Vulgar', 'Good Bad Books', and 'The Sporting Spirit'.

Relatively few letters by Orwell have survived from autumn 1944 to spring 1945 other than brief business notes. On 15 February 1945 he went to Paris to begin a three-month stint as a war correspondent for the *Observer* and *Manchester Evening News*, contributing nineteen reports. These articles tend to be dismissed too easily, partly, perhaps, because they were entirely overlooked for so many years. One result of this experience was another fine essay, 'Revenge is Sour', 9 November 1945. During this time his contributions to *Tribune* and the *Manchester Evening News* were taken over by Jennie Lee⋆ for the former and the critic Daniel George for the latter.

It was a time of personal gain and loss for Orwell. In June 1944 he and Eileen adopted a son, Richard. On the 28th their flat was bombed and they had to move out, Orwell trundling his books four miles each lunchtime to the *Tribune* office in a wheelbarrow. Eileen had never fully come to terms with the death of her brother, Eric, during the retreat to Dunkirk. She was not well, was overworked, and depressed throughout the war (see her letter to Norah Myles, 5 December 1940, and her cryptic note – so unlike her – of March 1941). A medical examination arranged by Gwen O'Shaughnessy revealed tumours of the uterus. The operation was to take place in Newcastle upon Tyne. She awaited the operation at Greystone, the O'Shaughnessy family home near Stockton-on-Tees, where Gwen and her children had taken refuge when the flying-bomb raids started. Richard had also gone there when the Orwells were bombed out. He was cared for by the O'Shaughnessy nanny, Joyce Pritchard. Long and moving letters from Eileen to her husband have survived from this period, planning and looking forward to their future. Unfortunately she died under the anaesthetic on 29 March 1945. Orwell rushed back from Europe, settled Richard, and then returned to bury himself in work. VE-Day (8 May) followed shortly after. As a day it meant little to Orwell (the experience of many people). 'I was not in England for VE-Day, but I am told it was very decorous – huge crowds, but little enthusiasm and even less rowdiness – just as it was in France. No doubt in both cases this was partly due to the shortage of alcohol' ('London Letter', XVII, 2672, p. 163). For an excellent account of the day confirming this, see Chapter 1 of David Kynaston's, *Austerity Britain, 1945–51* (Bloomsbury, 2007).

From November 1943 to February 1944 he wrote *Animal Farm* and after many difficulties, some posed by a KGB agent working in the Ministry of Information, it was published by Fredric Warburg on 17 August 1945, two days after VJ-Day. Then, in September, when he stayed in a fisherman's cottage his love affair with Jura – his 'Golden Country' – began.

From Orwell's letter to his mother, 17 March 1912

Dwight Macdonald wrote to Orwell on 22 October 1943 telling him he had resigned from Partisan Review. *His letter of resignation, with, he said, 'a rather hot reply from my ex-colleagues', appeared in the July–August issue. He was starting a new journal and asked Orwell whether he had done any writing lately on 'popular culture' (Macdonald gives it quotations marks). He suggested something on British advertising since the war and also asked whether Orwell had ever written anything on the Spanish civil war.*

To Dwight Macdonald*

11 December 1943
10a Mortimer Crescent NW 6

Dear Macdonald,

Many thanks for your letter dated October 22nd (only just arrived!) I hope your new magazine will be a success. I'd like to write something for it, but I think I can't write anything of a strictly political nature while I have my arrangement with P[artisan] R[eview]. Apart from anything else, my periodical 'London Letters' so to speak use up anything I have to say about the current situation in this country. That article about the Spanish war that I spoke to you of I did finally write, but I sent it to *New Road* 1943, edited by Alex Comfort and Co, who somewhat to my annoyance printed it in a mutilated form.[1] Recently I did a short thing for a French magazine on the English detective story,[2] and it struck me that something interesting could be done on the change in ethical outlook in the crime story during the last 50 years or so. This subject is so vast that one can only attack corners of it, but how would you like an article on Raffles ('The Amateur Cracksman'), comparing him with some modern crime story, eg. something from one of the pulp mags? (I could only do this in a rather sketchy way as one can't buy the pulp mags in this country since the war, but I was a reader of them for years and know their moral atmosphere). Raffles, about contemporary with Sherlock Holmes, was a great favourite in England and I fancy in the USA too, as I remember he is mentioned in the O. Henry stories. And into the essay I could bring some mention of Edgar Wallace, who in my opinion is a significant writer and marks a sort of moral turning-point. Tell me whether you would like this, and if so, how many words about. I dare say I could turn the stuff in fairly soon after hearing from you, but how soon it would get to you I can't say.[3] You see what the posts are like nowadays.

I have left the BBC after wasting 2 years in it, and have become editor[4] of the *Tribune*, a leftwing weekly I dare say you know. The job leaves me a little spare time, so I am at last getting on with a book again, not having written one for nearly 3 years.

> Yours sincerely
> Geo. Orwell

[XVI, 2392, pp. 24–5; typewritten]

1. 'Looking Back on the Spanish War'; the headnote to which lists the cuts. (See XIII, 1421, pp. 497–511.)
2. 'Grandeur et décadence du roman policier anglais', *Fontaine*, 17 November 1943 [XV, 2357, pp. 309–20].
3. Orwell wrote 'Raffles and Miss Blandish', which appeared in *Horizon*, October 1944 (XVI, 2538, pp. 345–7); it was reprinted in Macdonald's new journal, *Politics*, the following month with a slightly extended title: 'The Ethics of the Detective story: from Raffles to Miss Blandish'.
4. Actually as literary editor.

To Leonard Moore*

9 January 1944
10a Mortimer Crescent NW 6

Dear Mr Moore,

Thanks for your letter. I think there might be the basis for a book of reprinted critical pieces when I have done one or two more which at present are only projected.[1] I don't think it is worth reprinting anything which has already been in print twice, but the other possible ones are:

> Charles Dickens. (about 12,000?)
> Wells, Hitler and the World State. (about 2000).
> Rudyard Kipling. (about 4000).
> W. B. Yeats. (about 2000).
> Gandhi in Mayfair. (about 3000).

The last 4 are all in *Horizon*. In addition, when I can get the books for it, I am going to do for an American magazine an essay on 'Raffles', probably about 3–4000. I also did one of about 2000 on Sherlock Holmes for the Free

French² magazine *Fontaine*. This I think could be put in but could do with some expansion. I would also like to put in an 'imaginary conversation' I did on the wireless with Jonathan Swift, and perhaps the substance of another talk I did on Gerrard° Manley Hopkins, if I can get hold of the script of the latter. In all this might make a book of about 30,000 words or more.

I can't see to this now because I am overwhelmed with work. I am getting on with my book and unless I get ill or something hope to finish it by the end of March.³ After that I have contracted to do one for the 'Britain in Pictures' series, but that shouldn't take long.⁴

This thing I am doing now will be very short, about 20,000 to 25,000 words. It is a fairy story but also a political allegory, and I think we may have some difficulties about finding a publisher. It won't be any use trying it on Gollancz nor probably Warburg, but it might be worth dropping a hint elsewhere that I have a book coming along. I suppose you know which publishers have paper and which haven't?

Yours sincerely
Eric Blair

[XVI, 2403, p. 59; typewritten]

1. The collection was published in England by Secker & Warburg on 14 February 1946 as *Critical Essays*, and in the United States by Reynal & Hitchcock, New York, on 29 April 1946 as *Dickens, Dali & Others: Studies in Popular Culture*. Of the essays mentioned, 'Gandhi in Mayfair' and those on Sherlock Holmes, Swift, and Hopkins are not included; not mentioned here, but included are 'Boys' Weeklies', 'The Art of Donald McGill', and those on Dali, Koestler, and P.G. Wodehouse.

2. Free French: those fighting with the Allies under General de Gaulle. Of some 100,000 French soldiers who were rescued from the beaches of Dunkirk with about a quarter of a million British, some 10,000 joined de Gaulle and about 90,000 returned to France.

3. *Animal Farm*.

4. *The English People*, belatedly published, with unauthorised changes, by Collins in 1947.

To Gleb Struve*

17 February 1944
10a Mortimer Crescent NW 6

Dear Mr Struve,

Please forgive me for not writing earlier to thank you for the very kind gift of *25 Years of Soviet Russian Literature* with its still more kind inscription. I am afraid I know very little about Russian literature and I hope your book will fill up some of the many gaps in my knowledge. It has already roused my interest in Zamyatin's *We*, which I had not heard of before. I am interested in that kind of book, and even keep making notes for one myself that may get written sooner or later.[1] I wonder whether you can tell if there is an adequate translation of Blok?[2] I saw some translated fragments about ten years ago in *Life and Letters*, but whether they were any good as a translation I do not know.

I am writing a little squib which might amuse you when it comes out, but it is so not O.K. politically that I don't feel certain in advance that anyone will publish it. Perhaps that gives you a hint of its subject.[3]

Yours sincerely
Geo. Orwell

[XVI, 2421, p. 99; typewritten]

1.   This would become *Nineteen Eighty-Four*.
2.   Alexander Blok (1880–1921), lyric poet much influenced by Symbolism. Although he welcomed the 1917 Revolution he quite quickly became disillusioned.
3.   *Animal Farm*.

To C. K. Ogden*

1 March 1944
Tribune

Dear Mr. Ogden

Very many thanks for the booklet. I was aware, of course, that you have much to put up with from the Esperanto people, and that that was why you drew attention to their very unfortunate choice for the verb 'to be' or whatever it is. We have had them on to us since mentioning Basic, but I have choked them off. Also the Ido[1] people.

As I told you when I was in the B.B.C. (I have left there now) there was great resistance against doing anything over the air about Basic, at any rate for India. I rather gathered that its chief enemies were the writers of English textbooks, but that all Indians whose English is good are hostile to the idea, for obvious reasons. At any rate it was with great difficulty that I got Miss Lockhart on to the air.[2]

I don't know a great deal about G. M. Young.[3] He is the ordinary silly-clever 'intelligent' conservative whose habitual manoeuvre is to deal with any new idea by pointing out that it has been said before. The only time I met him he struck me as ordinarily snobbish, talking about the terrible sacrifices the upper classes had made on account of the war etc. He was also trying to chase our little Indian Section of the B.B.C. for broadcasting 'unsound' ideas. I think he was a supporter of appeasement. That's about all I know about him.

Hope to see you some time.

Yours sincerely,
Geo. Orwell,
Literary Editor

[XVI, 2427, pp. 108–9; typewritten]

1. An artificial language based on Esperanto.
2. Leonora Lockhart was an assistant to C.K. Ogden. Orwell arranged for her to speak to India on Basic English. Basic was developed in the 1920s and attempted to provide a readily learned 'English' based on a strictly limited number of words.
3. George Malcolm Young (1882–1959), historian and essayist specialising in Victorian England. His *Charles I and Cromwell* was published in 1936, and he contributed *The Government of Britain* to the Britain in Pictures series in 1941.

To Roy Fuller*

7 March 1944
10a Mortimer Crescent NW 6

Dear Mr Fuller,

Since receiving your letter I have procured a copy of the *Little Reviews Anthology*[1] and read your story, 'Fletcher'. I must say that I myself cannot see anything anti-semitic in it. I imagine that what Cedric Dover[2] meant was that the central character was a Jew and also a not very admirable character, and perhaps that counts as anti-semitism nowadays. I am sorry about this, but you will understand that as Literary Editor I cannot read all the books sent out for review and have to take the reviewers' judgement for granted. Of course if he had made a bald-headed attack on you as an anti-semite I should have checked up on it before printing, but I think he only said 'subtly anti-semitic' or words to that effect.[3] I am sorry that you should have had this annoyance. I must add, however, that by my own experience it is almost impossible to mention Jews in print, either favourably or unfavourably, without getting into trouble.

Yours truly
Geo. Orwell

[XVI, 2431, pp. 116–7; typewritten]

1. *Little Reviews Anthology* was edited by Denys Val Baker (1917–1984), novelist, short-story writer, and editor. Five numbers appeared, in 1943, 1945, 1946, 1947–48, and 1949. Cedric Dover reviewed Baker's *Little Reviews, 1914–1943* at the same time ('a useful but pedestrian record'), *Tribune*, 18 February 1944. Orwell's review of three of T. S. Eliot's *Four Quartets*, which had first appeared in *Poetry (London)*, October–November 1942, was included in the *Anthology*.

2. Cedric Dover (1904–51), born in Calcutta and educated there and at the University of Edinburgh. He wrote books and articles and listed his special subjects as 'Race, Colour & Social Problems, India, Hybrids & Negro America'. He worked with Orwell at the BBC and it was he who had suggested to Orwell that it was racialist to print 'Negro' without a capital 'N' in *Talking to India*. See his 'As I Please,' 2, 10 December 1943 [XVI, 2391, pp. 23–24].

3. Dover had written: 'Roy Fuller's "Fletcher" is subtle and subtly anti-Semitic: a good example, in fact, of the growing anti-Semitism of which Alec° Comfort complains'—a reference to Alex 'Comfort's biting analysis of the "Social Conventions of the Anglo-American Film,"' which Dover had just mentioned. It is very difficult to understand how the story can be regarded as anti-Semitic. The only reference to Fletcher direct or indirect as Jewish is the statement, 'Fletcher, a middle-aged bachelor of Jewish ancestry and intellectual tastes. . . .' He is shown as sensitive and alone. Fuller's story is entirely from the point of view of those who attack the vulnerable, whether they be Jewish or women. (For further details see XVI, 2431, n. 4.)

To Leonard Moore*

19 March 1944
10a Mortimer Crescent NW 6

Dear Mr Moore,

I have finished my book[1] and will be sending you the Ms in a few days' time. It is being typed now. I make it about 30,000 words. To avoid wasting time I think we ought to decide in advance what to do about showing it to Gollancz. According to our contract he has the first refusal of my fiction books, and this would come under the heading of fiction, as it is a sort of fairy story, really a fable with a political meaning. I think, however, Gollancz wouldn't publish it, as it is strongly anti-Stalin in tendency. Nor is it any use wasting time on Warburg, who probably wouldn't touch anything of this tendency and to my knowledge is very short of paper. I suggest therefore that we ought to tell Gollancz but let him know that the book is not likely to suit him, and say that we will only send it along if he very definitely wants to see it. I am going to write to him in this sense now. The point is that if Gollancz and his readers get hold of it, even if they end by not taking it, they will probably hang onto the Ms for weeks. So I will write to him, and then he will know about it before you get the Ms.

As to what publisher to approach, I think Nicholson and Watson might be the best.[2] I told one of their men I had a book coming along and he seemed anxious to get hold of it. Or else Hutchinson, where I have a contact in Robert Neumann. Or anyone else who (a) has got some paper and (b) isn't in the arms of Stalin. The latter is important. This book is murder from the Communist point of view, though no names are mentioned. Provided we can get over these difficulties I fancy the book should find a publisher, judging by the stuff they do print nowadays.

I am going to send two copies. I think we might have a try at an American publication as well. About a year ago the Dial Press wrote asking me to send them the next book I did, and I think they might like this one.[3]

I am contracted now to do a 'Britain in Pictures' book, which I suppose will take me 6–8 weeks. After that I am arranging to do two longish literary essays, one on *No Orchids for Miss Blandish*, and one on Salvador Dali, for two magazines. When I have done those two we shall have enough stuff for the book of reprinted essays.

Yours sincerely
Eric Blair

[XVI, 2436, pp. 126–7; typewritten]

1. *Animal Farm*. Paper was in desperately short supply (except, of course, for government bureaucracy).
2. At the top of this letter to Moore someone has written the names of two more publishers: Eyre & Spottiswoode and Hollis & Carter.
3. In *Partisan Review*, 63 (1996), William Phillips claimed he was the first person in America to read *Animal Farm*; he then recommended it to the Dial Press.

To Leonard Moore*

23 March 1944
10a Mortimer Crescent NW 6

Dear Mr Moore,

Thanks for your letter. I sent off two copies of the Ms of the book yesterday and hope they reached you safely. I haven't heard from Gollancz and I dare say he will write direct to you.

We must *on no account* take this book to either Eyre & Spottiswoode or Hollis & Carter. They are both Catholic publishers and Hollis, in particular, has published some most poisonous stuff since he set up in business. It would do me permanent harm to be published by either of these. I don't know what the objections to Hutchinson's and N. & W.[1] are, but perhaps you could let me know. I should think Cape is another possibility. Or Fabers°. I have a contact in Faber's and a slight one at Cape's.[2] But let me know whom you are going to take it to. I should like it settled as early as possible.

Yours sincerely
Eric Blair

[XVI, 2440, pp. 130–1; typewritten]

1. Nicholson & Watson.
2. T.S. Eliot at Faber & Faber and Miss C. V. Wedgwood at Cape. Daniel George (who reviewed novels for *Tribune*) was chief reader at Cape.

To Leonard Moore*

15 April 1944
10a Mortimer Crescent NW 6

Dear Mr Moore,

Nicholson & Watson refuse to print *Animal Farm*, giving much the same reason as Gollancz, ie. that it is bad taste to attack the head of an allied government in that manner etc.[1] I knew we should have a lot of trouble with this book, at any rate in this country. Meanwhile I have taken the copy I had round to Cape's, as Miss Wedgwood[2] there had often asked me to let them see something, but I wouldn't be surprised if they made the same answer. I think Faber's is *just* possible, and Routledges rather more so if they have the paper. While Cape's have it I'll sound both Eliot and Herbert Read.[3] I saw recently a book published by Eyre and Spottiswoode and I think they must be all right—perhaps, as you say, I was mixing them up with Burns, Oates and Washburne. Failing all else I will try to get one of the small highbrow presses to do it, in fact I shouldn't wonder if that is the likeliest bet. I know of one which has just started up and has a certain amount of money to dispose of. Naturally I want this book printed because I think what it says wants saying, unfashionable though it is nowadays.

I hope the copy went off to the USA? I suppose you still have one copy, so perhaps you might send it me to show to Read if I can contact him.

How do my copyrights with Gollancz stand? When I have done the necessary stuff I want to compile that book of essays and I am anxious to include the Dickens essay which was printed by Gollancz. I suppose if I fixed up with some other publisher, eg. Cape, to do *Animal Farm* they might ask for my next book, which would be the essays. Have I the right to reprint the Dickens essay, since the book is out of print?

Your sincerely
Eric Blair

[XVI, 2453, pp. 155–6; typewritten]

1. In a letter to *The Observer*, 23 November 1980, Andre Deutsch, who was working for Nicholson & Watson in 1944, told how, having been introduced to Orwell in 1943 by George Mikes, he had occasionally been commissioned to write reviews for *Tribune* for a fee of £1. About Whitsun 1944, Orwell let him read the typescript of *Animal Farm*, and he was convinced that Nicholson & Watson would be keen to publish Orwell's book. Unfortunately, though they did not share Gollancz's political reservations, they lectured Orwell on what they perceived to be errors in *Animal Farm*. Orwell was calm but depressed; Deutsch, deeply embarrassed. Deutsch was even then hoping to start publishing in his own right, but though Orwell twice offered him *Animal Farm*, and he would dearly have loved to publish it, he felt himself still a novice and not yet able to start his own firm.

2. Veronica Wedgwood (1910–1997; DBE, 1968), the historian, was then working for Cape.

3. T.S. Eliot was working for Faber & Faber, and Herbert Read for Routledge.

To Noel Willmett

18 May 1944
10a Mortimer Crescent NW 6

Dear Mr Willmett,

Many thanks for your letter. You ask whether totalitarianism, leader-worship etc. are really on the up-grade and instance the fact that they are not apparently growing in this country and the USA.

I must say I believe, or fear, that taking the world as a whole these things are on the increase. Hitler, no doubt, will soon disappear, but only at the expense of strengthening (a) Stalin, (b) the Anglo-American millionaires and (c) all sorts of petty fuhrers° of the type of de Gaulle. All the national movements everywhere, even those that originate in resistance to German domination, seem to take non-democratic forms, to group themselves round some superhuman fuhrer (Hitler, Stalin, Salazar, Franco, Gandhi, De Valera are all varying examples) and to adopt the theory that the end justifies the means. Everywhere the world movement seems to be in the direction of centralised economies which can be made to 'work' in an economic sense but which are not democratically organised and which tend to establish a caste system. With this go the horrors of emotional nationalism and a tendency to disbelieve in the existence of objective truth because all the facts have to fit in with the words and prophecies of some infallible fuhrer. Already history has in a sense ceased to exist, ie. there is no such thing as a history of our own times which could be universally accepted, and the exact sciences are endangered as soon as military necessity ceases to keep people up to the mark. Hitler can say that the Jews started the war, and if he survives that will become official history. He can't say that two and two are five, because for the purposes of, say, ballistics they have to make four. But if the sort of world that I am afraid of arrives, a world of two or three great superstates which are unable to conquer one another, two and two could become five if the fuhrer wished it.[1] That, so far as I can see, is the direction in which we are actually moving, though, of course, the process is reversible.

As to the comparative immunity of Britain and the USA. Whatever the pacifists etc. may say, we have *not* gone totalitarian yet and this is a very hopeful symptom. I believe very deeply, as I explained in my book *The Lion and the Unicorn*, in the English *people* and in their capacity to centralise their economy without destroying freedom in doing so. But one must remember that Britain and the USA haven't been really tried, they haven't known defeat or severe suffering, and there are some bad symptoms to balance the good ones. To begin with there is the general indifference to the decay of democracy. Do you realise, for instance, that no one in England under 26 now has a vote and that so far as one can see the great mass of people of that age don't give a damn for this? Secondly there is the fact that the intellectuals are more totalitarian in outlook than the common people. On the whole the English intelligentsia have opposed Hitler, but only at the price of accepting Stalin. Most of them are perfectly ready for dictatorial methods, secret police, systematic falsification of history[2] etc. so long as they feel that it is on 'our' side. Indeed the statement that we haven't a Fascist movement in England largely means that the young, at this moment, look for their fuhrer elsewhere. One can't be sure that that won't change, nor can one be sure that the common people won't think ten years hence as the intellectuals do now. I *hope*[3] they won't, I even trust they won't, but if so it will be at the cost of a struggle. If one simply proclaims that all is for the best and doesn't point to the sinister symptoms, one is merely helping to bring totalitarianism nearer.

You also ask, if I think the world tendency is towards Fascism, why do I support the war. It is a choice of evils—I fancy nearly every war is that. I know enough of British imperialism not to like it, but I would support it against Nazism or Japanese imperialism, as the lesser evil. Similarly I would support the USSR against Germany because I think the USSR cannot altogether escape its past and retains enough of the original ideas of the Revolution to make it a more hopeful phenomenon than Nazi Germany. I think, and have thought ever since the war began, in 1936 or thereabouts, that our cause is the better, but we have to keep on making it the better, which involves constant criticism.

Yours sincerely,
Geo. Orwell

[XVI, 2471, pp. 190–2; typewritten]

1. and 2. Foreshadowings of *Nineteen Eighty-Four.*
3.   Compare *Nineteen Eighty-Four*, p. 72, 'If there is hope, wrote Winston, it lies in the proles'.

To Leonard Moore*

8 June 1944
10a Mortimer Crescent NW 6

Dear Mr Moore,

Many thanks for your letter.[1] It is awkward about Gollancz. I don't however remember anything in that contract about *full-length* novels. As I remember it, it simply referred to my next three works of fiction (you could verify that from the contract.) If so, *Animal Farm* which is certainly a work of fiction (and any way what is 'full-length') would be one of them. But even so there is one more novel to be accounted for. Do you think it would be possible to arrange with Cape that Gollancz had the refusal of my next novel (or two novels if *Animal Farm* doesn't count), on the understanding that all other works went to Cape, including novels after the Gollancz contract ran out? In that case I should only be going away from Cape for one or at most two books. (Incidentally, I don't know when I shall write another novel. This doesn't seem a propitious time for them.) I shouldn't in any case go to Gollancz again for non-fiction books. His politics change too fast for me to keep up with them. Could you find out what Cape thinks about that?

Meanwhile how do we stand about the book of reprints? Cape could have that too if he wants it. But the Dickens essay, which I should *like* to reprint, was in a Gollancz book. Has he the copyright of that, or have I? I have only one more essay to do, then I can start assembling the book.

I am sorry about *Keep the Aspidistra Flying*, but I don't think it worth reprinting a book I don't care about. If you tell Lane's I don't want that one done I dare say they'll be readier to close with *Coming up for Air*.[2]

I hope it will be O.K. with Cape and this book won't have to start on its rounds once again. I do want it to see the light this year if possible.

Yours sincerely
E. A. Blair

[XVI, 2485, pp. 250–1; typewritten]

1. Jonathan Cape wrote to Victor Gollancz on 26 May 1944 to say that he was inclined to publish *Animal Farm*, and to publish Orwell's future work. He wished to know whether that would be acceptable to Gollancz. On 1 June, Gollancz wrote to Moore, pointing out that he had a contract dated 1 February 1937 to publish three novels by Orwell, only one of which, *Coming Up for Air*, had been delivered. He argued that his rejection of *Animal Farm* did not affect that agreement. Moore then wrote to Orwell—his letter has not been traced—and this is Orwell's response.

2. Penguin Books did not publish *Coming Up for Air* in Orwell's lifetime. It was reprinted in the first of Secker's Uniform series in May 1948.

To Leonard Moore*

24 June 1944
10a Mortimer Crescent NW 6

Dear Mr Moore,

It is a pity about Cape's.[1] I rang up T. S. Eliot, telling him the circumstances, and shall give him the other copy of the MS on Monday. I have no doubt Eliot himself would be on my side in this matter, but, as he says, he might not be able to swing the rest of the board of Faber's.

About the contract with Gollancz. If 30,000 words is not 'full-length', what does amount to full-length? Is an actual amount of words named in our existing contract?[2] If not, could we get from Gollancz a definite statement as to what he considers a full-length work of fiction. It is clearly very unsatisfactory to have this clause in the contract without a clear definition of it.

Yours sincerely
Eric Blair

[XVI, 2494, pp. 265–6; typewritten]

1. Jonathan Cape wrote to Victor Gollancz on 26 May 1944 to say that he was inclined to publish *Animal Farm*. His principal reader, Daniel George, and C. V. Wedgwood, then working for Cape, both strongly urged publication. However, on 19 June 1944, Cape wrote to Leonard Moore to say he would not publish the book. He did have some anxiety about Orwell having to offer his next two works of fiction to Gollancz, but the basis for the rejection was the representation made to him by 'an important official in the Ministry of Information' whom he had consulted. He had come to the conclusion that it would be 'highly ill-advised to publish [it] at the present time', partly because it was not a generalised attack on dictatorships but was aimed specifically at the Soviets, and partly because the 'choice of pigs as the ruling caste' would be especially offensive. (Crick gives the full text of this letter, with background details, pp. 454–56.) Inez Holden, in a letter to Ian Angus of 27 May 1967, summarised Cape's reason for the rejection and Orwell's reaction: 'He said he couldn't publish that as he was afraid "Stalin wouldn't like it". George was amused at this. I will quote what he said on this: "Imagine old Joe (who doesn't know one word of any European language) sitting in the Kremlin reading *Animal Farm* and saying 'I don't like this'"'. It is now known that the 'important official in the Ministry of Information' was Peter Smollett, the alias for Peter Smolka, an Austrian who had come to England in the 1930s and was a Soviet spy, codename 'Abo'. Smollett's deception was so successful that he was not only appointed OBE by a grateful Britain, but the Soviets thought he had been turned and came to disregard him (see *The Lost Orwell*, pp. 207, 210–12).

2. Annotated in Moore's office: 'Agreement only states "full-length."'

To T. S. Eliot*

28 June 1944
10a Mortimer Crescent NW 6
(or *Tribune* CEN 2572)

Dear Eliot,

This Ms.[1] has been blitzed which accounts for my delay in delivering it & its slightly crumpled condition, but it is not damaged in any way.

I wonder if you could be kind enough to let me have Messrs. Faber's decision fairly soon. If they are interested in seeing more of my work, I could let you have the facts about my existing contract with Gollancz, which is not an onerous one nor likely to last long.

If you read this MS. yourself you will see its meaning which is not an acceptable one at this moment, but I could not agree to make any alterations except a small one at the end which I intended making any way. Cape or the MOI, I am not certain which from the wording of his letter, made the imbecile suggestion that some other animal than the pigs might be made to represent the Bolsheviks. I could not of course make any change of that description.

Yours sincerely
Geo. Orwell

Could you have lunch with me one of the days when you are in town?

[XVI, 2496, p. 269; handwritten]

1. Of *Animal Farm*. The Orwells' flat was bombed on the very day he dated his letter to Eliot.

To John Middleton Murry*

14 July 1944
Tribune

Dear Murry,

Thanks for your letter[1]. I have not the text by me, but you wrote in an article in the *Adelphi* something that ran more or less as follows:

'We are in the habit of describing the war between Japan and China as though it were a war in the European sense. But it is nothing of the kind, because the average Chinese expects to be conquered. That is what the history of thousands of years has taught him to expect. China will absorb Japan, and Japan will energise China. And so also with India.'

If this is not praise and encouragement of the Japanese invasion of China, and an invitation to the Japanese to go on and invade India, I don't know what it is. It takes no account of what has been happening in China since 1912 and uses exactly the same argument ('these people are used to being conquered') that was always brought forward to justify our own rule in India. In any case its moral is, 'don't help the Chinese'

As to the general charge of 'praising violence' which your correspondent refers to. Many remarks you have made in recent years seem to me to imply that you don't object to violence if it is violent enough. And you certainly seem or seemed to me to prefer the Nazis to ourselves, at least so long as they appeared to be winning.

If you'll send the book along I'll naturally be glad to give it a notice, but I *might* have to turn it over to someone else, though I'll do it myself if possible. I am smothered under work, and also I've been bombed out and we have a very young baby,[2] all of which adds to one's work.

Yours,
George Orwell

[XVI, 2509, p. 288; typewritten]

1. On 11 July 1945, Murry wrote to Orwell saying that a correspondent (possibly Dr Alfred Salter, 1873–1945, a sponsor of the Peace Pledge Union) had asked him to comment on Orwell's statement in a review that Murry had praised the Japanese invasion of China. Murry told Orwell that he was 'given to taking pot-shots' at him and suggested instead that he tackle him frankly by reviewing his latest book, *Adam and Eve*.

2. The Orwells had adopted Richard Blair (born 14 May 1944 in Greenwich) in June. Orwell reviewed *Adam and Eve* in the *Manchester Evening News* on 19 October 1944 (XVI, 2565, pp. 432–4). Although not without criticism it concludes, 'This is an interesting book and a good antidote to the current notion that we should all be perfectly happy if we could get rid of Hitler and then go back to 1939 with shorter working hours and no unemployment.'

To Rayner Heppenstall*

21 July 1944
Tribune

Dear Rayner,

Herewith that book.[1] About 600 words perhaps? I'd like you very much to draw little Richard's horoscope.[2] He was born on May 14th. I thought I had told you, however, that he is an adopted child. Does that make any difference to the horoscope? Don't forget to look me up if you do get to town. The above is the safest address for the time being.

Yours
Eric

[XVI, 2515, p. 295; typewritten]

1. Presumably *Stephen Hero*, to which Orwell refers, 17 July 1944 (XVI, 2511, pp. 290–1).
2. Heppenstall had offered to cast this horoscope and sent it on 14 October but said he seemed to have lost the technique and feeling for casting a horoscope (XVI, 2558, n. 2, p. 420).

When Richard was adopted in June, Eileen gave up her job at the Ministry of Food. Orwell told Leonard Moore that the flat in Canonbury Square, which the Orwells were to rent, would be theirs on 1 September but they would probably move in only on 9 September, although it proved to be later. In the following letter, Eileen writes, 'When and if Richard comes'; he was therefore not then living with them. It is possible that the reason for the journey north was to see Richard at the O'Shaughnessy family home near Stockton-on-Tees. Although Eileen had left the Ministry of Food when she wrote this letter, she evidently still had some of the Ministry's headed paper.

Eileen⋆ to Lydia Jackson⋆

Wednesday [9? August 1944]
Ministry of Food
Portman Court
Portman Square
London W 1

Dear Lydia,

I didn't know where to write to you and indeed I don't know whether this is a very good idea because one of Gwen's letters to Florrie took ten days in transit. However we'll *hope*.

So far as I can see the cottage is going to repeat its Disney act. *Two* babies are now supposed to be going into residence, one with a mother and father the other with a mother (fortunately the father is in Normandy or somewhere). I pity them but it's satisfactory to have the space so well used. Mrs. Horton[1] has seen the space now so it's her responsibility. And about that, I thought I might come down for an hour or two while you're there and pack away some of our oddments—papers chiefly. I've arranged that the old tin trunk can stay locked but I think it would be a good idea to put it in the bottom of the larder (if it'll go) and also that the linen chest will be used for our things or yours. They're providing their own linen of course and will bring it in something in which it can be kept. I expect they will move most of the furniture about and the two passage rooms will go into use again. By the way, do you . . .° (There was a long interruption on the telephone and I can't at all remember what this important enquiry was.)

But I have remembered what I really wanted to write to you about. It was a confession. Lettice Cooper* and her sister went down to the cottage for the week-end. Barbara the sister is in the act of recovering from a nervous breakdown and this life is not good for her. She won't go away without Lettice and Lettice couldn't free herself for the week-end until just before it came. Then she did but of course it was too late to make any ordinary arrangements. They had a *lovely* time they say. Mrs. Anderson[2] swore she would clean on Tuesday and I hope she did but Lettice has a curious liking for housewifery and doubtless did clean quite well herself; the real crisis was about the sheets as usual—they carried one but couldn't well do more than that. Anyway I hope you don't mind. It seemed a pity to have the place empty for the bank holiday and I couldn't contact you. Seeing how much they enjoyed it and how well they looked I rather hoped that all these babies wouldn't like the place after all. It would be fun to send people down all the time and I don't think it need have been empty for a night for the rest of the summer anyway. But of course it won't be *empty*!

Can I come to tea? It's a bit of a job because we are going North with Gwen on the 17th [August] to help with the luggage primarily. But I could manage Saturday or Monday—or Sunday I suppose but the travelling back is so ungodly. It'll have to be a compressed trip because we are also more or less in the act of moving. We have a flat in Canonbury Square—at least references are now being taken up and we shall have it unless the bombs beat us to the post which is rather likely. It's a top floor flat and there have been numbers of bombs in the vicinity though the square itself has lost nothing but a window or two. I rather like it, in fact in some ways I like it very much indeed. The outlook is charming and we have a flat roof about three yards by two which seems full of possibilities. Disadvantage is that to get to it you climb an uncountable number of stone stairs—to get to the flat I mean; to get to the roof you climb one of those fire-escape ladders with very small iron rungs. I don't know how Richard will be managed if the bombing ever stops. I thought we might have a crane and sling and transport him the way they do elephants in the films but George thinks this unsuitable.

Which day? With preference Saturday or Monday. No. Posts being as they are, I think I'll come on Saturday unless I hear to the contrary, and hope to see you. I expect I shan't get on the bus anyway but I'll come some time in the afternoon and leave in the late afternoon, having put away the papers and possibly collected one or two things. When and if Richard comes I'll be wanting a few things but probably the best thing to do will be to leave them for the moment in the linen chest so that they don't get bombed before they're used. I meant to brood on this when I went over with Mrs. Horton but she had to get back and we only had half an hour in the cottage which didn't leave much time for brooding.

See you on Saturday I hope.

With love
Eilee.[3]

[*Handwritten postscript*] (One thing I want to do *with* you is to check up on the things you want out of the garden. Kay wants you to have the crops of course but she'd better be forewarned so that the apple disaster isn't repeated the day they arrive.

Also I want to arrange to buy the coal and the Calor Gas.

[XVI, 2528A, pp.323–6; typewritten with handwritten postscript]

1. Mrs Horton was evidently the new tenant of The Stores at Wallington.
2. Mrs Anderson was one of the Orwells' neighbours at Wallington; she often looked after their affairs in their absence.
3. Eileen signs off with an indecipherable scrawl. She possibly writes 'With best wishes/Eilee.' but it is a little more likely that it is 'With love/Eilee.'—and the degree of scrawl is indicated by interpretations that see two and three words here. What is clear is that there is no final 'n' to 'Eilee', which may have been a name she was familiarly called at the Ministry of Food.

To Leonard Moore*

15 August 1944
Care of *The Tribune*

Dear Mr Moore,

Thanks for your letter of 14th August. Yes, it is O.K. about Gollancz retaining the rights of *Wigan Pier*.

I think Warburg is going to publish *Animal Farm*—I say 'I think', because although W. has agreed to do so there *may* be a slip-up about the paper. But so long as we can lay hands on the paper he will do it. So that will save me from the trouble of doing it myself.

I am now doing that essay I spoke to you of,[1] & I shall then be able to compile the book of essays, but I shall have to find someone to do the typing as I have not time to do it myself.

We are, I think, taking a flat in Islington at the end of this month, & I will let you have the address when we move in.

Yours sincerely
E. A. Blair

[XVI, 2533, p. 335; handwritten]

1.   'Raffles and Miss Blandish' was completed on 28 August 1944, according to Orwell's Payments Book. It was published in *Horizon*, October 1944 (XVI, 2538, pp. 345–58).

To Leonard Moore*

29 August 1944
Care of *The Tribune*

Dear Mr Moore,

I have just seen Warburg. He has definitely arranged to publish *Animal Farm* about March 1945, so perhaps you can get in touch with him about the contract. He is willing to pay an advance of £100, half of this to be paid about Christmas of this year. I shall give him an option on all my future books, but this can be arranged in such a way as not to tie me down if for some special reason I want to take a book elsewhere. I have finished the final essay for the book of essays, & as soon as possible I will get the whole thing typed & send you a copy. Warburg presumably won't be able to do it till some time next year, but meanwhile we should make an attempt at an American edition. The Dial Press have asked to see this book & I more or less promised to send it to them.

Yours Sincerely
E. A. Blair

P.S. My address as from Sept. 1st will be 27B Canonbury Square Islington London N. 1 but I probably shan't move in there till Sept. 8th, so *Tribune* is the safest address for the time being.

[XVI, 2539, p. 358; handwritten]

[Ivor Brown]* to Dr Thomas Jones*

14 October 1944

Dear T. J.,

I would be very grateful for your opinion on this review by George Orwell, which I held out of the paper this week.[1] It came in very late and there was not time to talk it over with him. It seems to me that the whole tone of it breathes a distaste for Christianity, which would be offensive to a great many of our readers and, almost certainly, to Lord Astor. I dont,° myself, complain as a member of the Faith who is pained, but simply as the Editor of a paper having a tradition of Protestant christianity, which I believe the Chairman of Directors is eager to maintain. That does not mean that a reviewer like Orwell need be barred from such topics, but it does mean that he should endeavour to express himself in a different way.

The effect his review had on me was this: I felt that the reader who is a churchman, or chapelman, would say to himself 'This man so dislikes us and our ideas that we will never get any justice out of him'. I may be quite wrong in feeling this and that is why I am asking your opinion. Do you think the review as a whole is likely to create the impression that I have suggested, and that a few minor alterations would put it right, or do you think that a few changes, such as I have pencilled in, would put the matter right?

I am sorry to trouble you, but this is a case where the atmosphere built up by a review is of great importance, and I very much want your sense of the atmosphere.

Yours ever,
[*unsigned*]

[XX, 2563B, pp. 557-8; typewritten copy]

1. This must refer to a review of *Beyond Personality* by C. S. Lewis, which the *Observer* did not publish. It was set in type and is published in XVI, 2567, pp. 437-9 from its galley-proofs.

Whilst waiting for her operation in Newcastle upon Tyne Eileen stayed at the O'Shaughnessy family home, Greystone. Meanwhile, Orwell had gone abroad as War Correspondent for the Observer *and the* Manchester Evening News, *reporting from France and later Germany and Austria. See the Chronology for details of his reports.*

Eileen Blair* to Leonard Moore*

2 March 1945
Greystone
Carlton
Near Stockton-on-Tees
Co. Durham[1]

Dear Mr. Moore,

Thank you very much for your letter and various press cuttings. I am sorry to have been so dilatory but I had to go to London to complete the adoption of the son that Eric may have told you about and was held up there by illness while my mail waited for me here.

I am afraid I can't sign the letter on his behalf. If I had been in London while he was getting ready to go I should probably have a power of attorney as before, but as it is I have only the most informal authority. So I have sent the letter on to him and I suppose it will be back in about three weeks. I have had one letter and that took eleven days. I have also written to Warburg about the letter—I know Eric spoke to Frederick° Warburg about it and I imagine there will be no trouble about it, though I quite see that from your point of view these loose ends are very unsatisfactory.

I have no real news from Eric. He wrote the day after arriving in Paris and had seen little except his hotel which seems to be full of war correspondents and quite comfortable—with central heating on. I expect the next letter will be more informative, though it will mostly concern this son we have adopted in whom Eric is passionately interested. The baby is now nine months old and according to his new father very highly gifted— 'a very thoughtful little boy' as well as very beautiful. He really is a very nice baby. You must see him sometime. His name is Richard Horatio.

Yours sincerely,
Eileen Blair

[XVII, 2630, p. 81; typewritten]

To Mrs Sally McEwan*

12 March 1945
Room 329
Hotel Scribe[1]
Rue Scribe
Paris 9e

Dear Sally,

I hope you are getting on O.K. I won't say without me but in my absence. I haven't had a copy of *Tribune* yet, thanks to the condition of the posts I suppose. I expect you also got via the *Observer* some frantic S.O.Ss for tobacco, but at the moment the situation isn't so bad because I got a friend who was coming across to bring me some. None has arrived by post, needless to say. Our Paris opposite number, *Libertés*, with whom I want *Tribune* to arrange a regular exchange, are never able to get the paper commercially but see copies at the Bibliothèque Nationale and frequently translate extracts. I went to a semi-public meeting of their readers and also to the paper's weekly meeting which was very like *Tribune*'s Friday meeting but on a higher intellectual level I thought. I don't know whether Louis Levy[2] came and saw Bevan and Strauss about his idea of a continental edition of *T.*, but if that can't be arranged it would certainly be a good idea if they could manage to send a few copies over here weekly, even say 50. A lot of British and American papers are sold regularly here, and there is a considerable public which would be glad to get hold of *T.*

I am trying to arrange to go to Cologne for a few days, or, if not Cologne, at any rate some where in occupied territory. After that I fancy I shall go to Toulouse and Lyons, then return to Paris and come back to England towards the end of April. By the time the posts seem to take, I don't think it would be worth forwarding any letters after about the 10th of April. Otherwise they are liable to arrive here after I have left and then will probably be lost for good. But it's all right forwarding letters while I am out of Paris because I should come back here to pick up my stuff in any case. I wonder whether you could be kind enough to do one thing for me. I only rather hurriedly saw, before leaving, Stefan Schimanski[3] who had had a war diary of mine from which he thought he might like to use extracts in some book or other. I wonder if you could ring him up (I think he is at Lindsay Drummonds°) and impress upon him that if he does want to use such extracts, he must in no case do so without my seeing them beforehand.

I dare say you heard that the court case went off all right and little Richard is now legally mine. I hear that he has 5 teeth and is beginning to move about a bit. I saw the other day a knitted suit in a shop that I thought would be nice for him, so I went in and asked the price and it was Frs. 2500, ie. about £12.10s.[4] That is what prices are like here. If you take two people out to lunch it costs at least Frs 1000 for the three. However it isn't me that is paying. I am glad I managed to bring a lot of soap and coffee across with me because you can produce a terrific effect by distributing small quantities of either, also English cigarettes. Luckily it isn't at all cold. I've taken to wearing a beret, you'll be glad to hear. Please give everyone my love and impress on them again not to expect any silk stockings because there just aren't such things here. The Americans bought them all up long ago.

Yours
George

P.S. Before being able to send this off, ie. before getting hold of some envelopes which aren't too plentiful here, I got your letter of March 6th and 2 *Tribunes*, 2nd and 9th March. It was nice to see *Tribune* again, and it seems so fat and heavy compared with French papers.

[XVII, 2634, pp. 88–90; typewritten]

1. Very many war correspondents were based at the appropriately named Hotel Scribe in Paris.
2. Louis Levy was editor of *Libertés*.
3. Stefan Schimanski (d. 1950), journalist and editor (for example, of the annual *Transformation*, with Henry Treece, 1943–47). He and Treece edited *Leaves in the Storm: A Book of Diaries* (published by Lindsay Drummond, 1947). Orwell's diaries were not included. Schimanski was killed when the plane in which he was travelling on an assignment to Korea for *Picture Post* to cover that war, exploded. (See Tom Hopkinson, *Of This Our Time* (1982), pp. 278–81.)
4. It was reported in the *Manchester Evening News*, 8 February 1945, that a pay award of £4 per week was made by the official Resettlement Committee to a soldier who had served for five years and was returning to a civilian job – the employer had offered £1 15s. Thus the knitted suit was the equivalent in cost to three weeks of his pay.

To Roger Senhouse*

17 March 1945
Room 329
Hotel Scribe
Rue Scribe
Paris 9e

Dear Roger,

Thanks so much for your letter, and for sending the copy of *Homage to Catalonia*. I didn't after all give it to André Malraux, who is not in Paris, but to, of all people, Jose Rovira, who was the commander of my division in Spain and whom I met at a friend's house here.

I don't know whether *Animal Farm* has definitely gone to press. If it has not actually been printed yet, there is one further alteration of one word that I would like to make. In Chapter VIII (I think it is VIII), when the windmill is blown up, I wrote 'all the animals including Napoleon flung themselves on their faces.' I would like to alter it to 'all the animals except Napoleon.' If the book has been printed it's not worth bothering about, but I just thought the alteration would be fair to J[oseph] S[talin], as he did stay in Moscow during the German advance.[1]

I hope Fred [Warburg]* will have a good long rest. I know how long it takes to get one's strength back. I am trying to arrange to go to Cologne for a few days, but there keep being delays. I shall be back in England at the end of April.

Yours
George

[XVII, 2635, p. 90; typewritten]

---

1. This change was made. The source of the correction is almost certainly Orwell's meeting in Paris with Joseph Czapski, a survivor of Starobielsk, and of the series of massacres of Polish prisoners carried out by the Russians and associated especially with that at Katyn. (See Orwell's letter to Arthur Koestler, **5.3.46**.)

Eileen Blair* to her husband

Wednesday 21 March 1945
Greystone [1]
Carlton

Dearest your letter came this morning—the one written on the 7th after you got my first one. I was rather worried because there had been an interval of nearly a fortnight, but this one took 14 days whereas the last one came in 10 so probably that explains it. Or one may have gone astray.

I am typing in the garden. Isn't that wonderful? I've only got a rug for myself and typewriter and the wind keeps blowing the paper down over the machine which is not so good for the typing but very good for me. The wind is quite cold but the sun is hot. Richard is sitting up in his pram talking to a doll. He has the top half of a pram suit on but he took off the rest some time ago and has nothing between himself and the sky below his nappies. I want him to get aired before the sun gets strong so that he'll brown nicely. That's my idea anyway. And he is enjoying the preliminaries anyway. I bought him a high chair—the only kind I could get. It sort of breaks in half and turns up its tail like a beetle if you want it to, and then you have a low chair attached to a little table, the whole on wheels. As a high chair it has no wheels and the usual tray effect in front of the chair. He loves it dearly and stretches out his hands to it—partly I'm afraid because what normally happens in the chair is eating. When it is being a low chair Laurence[2] takes him for rides round the nursery and down the passage—indeed Laurence wheeled the whole con-traption home from the station and I found it very useful myself on the way up as a luggage trolley. I came by night in the end so that George Kopp*[3] could see me off at King's X which was very nice, but there were no porters at all at Thornaby or Stockton—and only one at Darlington but I got him. There is no real news about Richard. He is just very well. I was sorry to be away from him for a week because he always stops feeding himself when I don't act as waiter, but today he did pick up the spoon himself from the dish and put it in his mouth—upside down of course, but he was eating rather adhesive pudding so he got his food all right. I bought him a truck too for an appalling sum of money. I had to forget the price quickly but I think it's important he should have one.

We're no longer in the garden now. In fact Richard is in bed and has been for some time. Blackburn[4] came and told me all about his other jobs and how Mr. Wilson fished and Sir John once had to go to his office on August 12th but the car went with him full of guns and sandwiches and they got to the moors by 1.30. And Blackburn's predecessor here shot himself. I think perhaps the general shooting standard was rather lower than at Sir John's, because this man shot a wood pigeon and tried to pull it out of the bush into which it had fallen with his gun (this might be better expressed but you can guess it). Naturally the bush pulled the trigger and there was another shot in the other barrel and the ass was actually holding the barrel to his belly, so he might as well have been an air raid casualty. This convinced me not that Richard must never have a gun but that he must have one very young so that he couldn't forget how to handle it.

Gwen rang up Harvey Evers[5] and they want me to go in for this operation at once. This is all a bit difficult. It is going to cost a terrible lot of money. A bed in a kind of ward costs seven guineas a week and Harvey Evers's operation fee is forty guineas. In London I would have to pay about five guineas a week in a hospital but Gwen says the surgeon's fee would be higher. The absurd thing is that we are too well off for really cheap rates— you'd have to make less than £500 a year. It comes as a shock to me in a way because while you were being ill I got used to paying doctors nothing. But of course it was only because Eric[6] was making the arrangements. I suppose your bronchoscopy would have cost about forty guineas too— and I must say it would have been cheap at the price, but what worries me is that I really don't think I'm worth the money. On the other hand of course this thing will take a longish time to kill me if left alone and it will be costing some money the whole time. The only thing is, I think perhaps it might be possible to sell the Harefield house[7] if we found out how to do it. I do hope too that I can make some money when I am well—I could of course do a job but I mean really make some money from home as it were. Anyway I don't know what I can do except go ahead and get the thing done quickly. The idea is that I should go in next week and I gather he means to operate quickly—he thinks the indications are urgent enough to offset the disadvantages of operating on a bloodless patient; indeed he is quite clear that no treatment at all can prevent me from becoming considerably more bloodless every month. So I suppose they'll just do a blood transfusion and operate more or less at once.

While I was in London I arranged to take Evelyn's[8] manuscript in to *Tribune*. I set off with it all right, broke the journey to go to the bank and was taken with a pain just like the one I had the day before coming North, only rather worse. I tried to have a drink in Selfridges' but couldn't and all sorts of extraordinary things then happened but after a bit I got myself into the Ministry. I simply could not do any more travelling, so Miss Sparrow[9] rang up Evelyn for me and they arranged between them about the transfer of the manuscript. People from *Tribune* then rang up in the *most* friendly way, offering to come and look after me, to bring me things and to *get you home*. I was horrified. But yesterday I had a phase of thinking that it was really outrageous to spend all your money on an operation of which I know you disapprove, so Gwen rang *Tribune* to know whether they had means of communicating with you quickly and could get your ruling. They hadn't but suggested she should ring the *Observer*, which she did and talked to Ivor Brown*. He said you were in Cologne now he thought and that letters would reach you very slowly if at all. He suggested that they would send you a message about me by cable and wireless, like their own. Gwen says he couldn't have been nicer. But I'm not having this done. It's quite impossible to give you the facts in this way and the whole thing is bound to sound urgent and even critical. I have arranged with Gwen however that when the thing is over she'll ask the *Observer* to send you a message to that effect. One very good thing is that by the time you get home I'll be convalescent, really convalescent at last and you won't have the hospital nightmare you would so much dislike. You'd more or less have to visit me and visiting someone in a ward really is a nightmare even to me with my fancy for hospitals—particularly if they're badly ill as I shall be at first of course. I only wish I could have had your approval as it were, but I think it's just hysterical. Obviously I can't just go on having a tumour or rather several rapidly growing tumours. I *have* got an uneasy feeling that after all the job might have been more cheaply done somewhere else but if you remember Miss Kenny's fee for a cautery, which is a small job, was fifteen guineas so she'd certainly charge at least fifty for this. Gwen's man might have done cheaper work for old sake's sake, but he's so very bad at the work and apparently he would have wanted me in hospital for weeks beforehand—and I'm morally sure I'd be there for weeks afterwards. Harvey Evers has a very high reputation, and George Mason[10] thinks very well of him and says Eric did the same, and I am sure that he will finish me off as quickly as anyone in England as well as doing the job properly—so he may well come cheaper in the end. I rather wish I'd talked it over with you before you went. I knew I had a 'growth'. But I wanted you to go away peacefully anyway, and I did *not* want to see Harvey Evers before the adoption was through in case it was cancer. I thought it just possible that the judge might make some enquiry about our health as we're old for parenthood and anyway it would have been an uneasy sort of thing to be producing oneself as an ideal parent a fortnight after being told that one couldn't live more than six months or something.

You may never get this letter but of course it's urgent about the house in the country. Inez [Holden]* thinks we might do something together with her cottage near Andover. It's quite big (6 rooms and kitchen) but it has disadvantages. The 25/– a week rent which she considers nominal I think big considering there is no sanitation whatever and only one tap, no electricity or gas, and expensive travelling to London. She and Hugh [Slater]* (incidentally they are more or less parting company at present but they might join up again I think) hire furniture for another 25/– a week which wouldn't be necessary if we were there, and it might be possible a) to get a long lease for a lower rent and b) to have modern conveniences installed. I am now so confident of being strong in a few months that I'm not actually frightened as I should have been of living a primitive life again (after all when you were ill soon after we were married I did clean out the whole of Wallington's sanitation and that was worse than emptying a bucket) but it does waste a lot of time. So we can consider that. Then George Kopp* has a clever idea. Apparently people constantly advertise in the *Times* wanting to exchange a house in the country for a flat in London. Most of these, probably all, would want something grander than N.1, but we might advertise ourselves—asking for correspondingly humble country accommodation. In the next few months people who have been living in the country for the war will be wanting somewhere in London and we might do well like that. Meanwhile there is a letter from the Ardlussa factor enclosing the contractor's estimate for repairing Barnhill[11]—which is £200. I found to my distress that George was not forwarding letters to you, although I gave him the address by telephone the day I got it, because he had not heard from you. I opened one from the Borough and found it was to say that the electricity supply would be cut off as soon as the man could get in to do it. I paid that bill and decided I'd better look at the rest of the mail. There was nothing else quite so urgent except perhaps a letter from the BBC Schools about your two broadcasts for them. They want the scripts as soon as possible! There's also a contract. I didn't send anything on at once because I thought you might be moving and in view of Ivor Brown's news of you I'm not sending them now, but I've written to say that you are abroad but expected home next month. The broadcasts aren't till June after all. If you don't come next month I'll have to think again, but there may be a firmer address to write to. I can do nothing with this except send it to the Hotel Scribe and hope they'll forward it. To get back to Barnhill. I'm going to write to the factor to say that you're away and I'm ill and will he wait till you get back. He's very apologetic about having kept us waiting and I'm sure they won't let the house to anyone else. I think this £200 can be very much reduced, but the house is quite grand—5 bedrooms, bathroom, W.C., H & C and all, large sitting room, kitchen, various pantries, dairies etc. and a whole village of 'buildings'—in fact just what we want to live in twelve months of the year. But we needn't have all this papered and painted. I put my hopes on Mrs. Fletcher.[12] The only thing that bothers me is that if it's thought worth while to spend £200 on repairs the kind of rent they have in mind must be much higher than our £25–£30, let alone David's £5. Incidentally I had a letter from David [Astor]* who just missed you in Paris.

It's odd—we have had nothing to discuss for months but the moment you leave the country there are dozens of things. But they can all be settled, or at least settled down, if you take this week's leave when you get back. I don't know about Garrigill.¹³ It depends when you come. But at worst you could come here couldn't you? If you were here we should stay mainly in my room, indeed I suppose I'll be there for some time after I get back in any case, and Richard will be available. Mary¹⁴ and Laurence both spend a lot of time with me now but they could be disposed of. Laurence by the way has improved out of recognition. He has three passions: farms, fairy tales, Richard. Not in that order—Richard probably comes first. So you ought to get on nicely. He has begun to invent fairy tales now, with magic cats and things in them, which is really a great advance. The pity is that the country isn't better but almost any country is good round about May and if I'm still at the pictur- esque stage of convalescence you could go out with Blackburn who knows every inch of the countryside or perhaps amuse yourself with Mr. Swinbank the farmer who would enjoy it I think. Or you could go over to Garrigill for a weekend's fishing on your own.

I liked hearing about Wodehouse.¹⁵ And I'm *very* glad you're going to Cologne. Perhaps you may get East of the Rhine before you come home. I have innumerable questions.

I think it's quite essential that you should write some book again. As you know, I thought *Tribune* better than the BBC and I still do. Indeed I should think a municipal dustman's work more dignified and better for your future as a writer. But as I said before I left London, I think you ought to stop the editing soon, as soon as possible, whether or not you think it worth while to stay on the editorial board or whatever it's called. And of course you must do much less reviewing and nothing but specialised reviewing if any. From my point of view I would infinitely rather live in the country on £200 than in London on any money at all. I don't think you understand what a nightmare the London life is to me. I know it is to you, but you often talk as though I *liked* it. I don't like even the things that you do. I can't stand hav- ing people all over the place, every meal makes me feel sick because every food has been handled by twenty dirty hands and I practically can't bear to eat anything that hasn't been boiled to clean it. I can't breathe the air, I can't think any more clearly that° one would expect to in the moment of being smothered, everything that bores me happens all the time in London and the things that interest me most don't happen at all and I can't read poetry. I never could. When I lived in London before I was married I used to go away certainly once a month with a suitcase full of poetry and that consoled me until the next time—or I used to go up to Oxford and read in the Bodleian and take a punt up the Cher if it was summer or walk in Port Meadow or to Godstow if it was winter. But all these years I have felt as though I were in a mild kind of concentration camp. The place has its points of course and I could enjoy it for a week. I like going to theatres for instance. But the fact of living in London destroys any pleasure I might have in its amenities and in fact as you know I never go to a theatre. As for eating in restaurants, it's the most barbarous habit and only tolerable very occasionally when one drinks enough to enjoy barbarity. And I can't drink enough beer. (George Mason took me out to dinner the night after I got to London and gave me to drink just what I would have drunk in peacetime—four glasses of sherry, half a bottle of claret and some brandy—and it did cheer me up I admit.) I like the Canonbury flat but I am suicidal every time I walk as far as the bread shop, and it would be very bad for Richard once he is mobile. Indeed if the worst comes to the worst I think he'd better go to Wallington for the summer, but it would be better to find somewhere with more space because you and Richard would be too much for the cottage very soon and I don't know where his sister[16] could go. And I think the cottage makes you ill—it's the damp and the smoke I think.

While this has been in progress I have read several stories to Laurence, dealt with Richard who woke up (he has just stopped his 10 o'clock feed), dealt with Mary who always cries in the evening, had my supper and listened to Mrs. Blackburn's distresses about Raymond[17] who has just got a motor bike. That's why it's so long. And partly why it's so involved. But I should like to see you stop living a literary life and start writing again and it would be much better for Richard too, so you need have no conflicts about it. Richard sends you this message. He has no conflicts. If he gets a black eye he cries while it hurts but with the tears wet on his cheeks he laughs heartily at a new blue cat who says miaow to him and embraces it with loving words. Faced with any new situation he is sure that it will be an exciting and desirable situation for him, and he knows so well that everyone in the world is his good friend that even if someone hurts him he understands that it was by accident and loses none of his confidence. He will fight for his rights (he actually drove Mary off the blue cat today, brandishing a stick at her and shouting) but without malice. Whether he can keep his certainties over the difficult second year I don't know of course but he's much more likely to if he has the country and you have the kind of life that satisfies you—and me. I think Richard really has a natural tendency to be sort of satisfied, balanced in fact. He demands but he demands something specific, he knows what he wants and if he gets it or some reasonable substitute he is satisfied; he isn't just *demanding* like Mary. I'm not protecting him. That is, he takes the troubles I think proper to his age. He gets no sympathy when his face is washed and very little when he topples over and knocks his head and I expect him to take in good part the slight sort of bumps he gets when the children play with him. But he can be tough only if he knows that it's all right really.

Now I'm going to bed. Before you get this you'll probably have the message about this operation and you may well be in England again if you keep what Ivor Brown calls on the move. What a waste that would be.

All my love, and Richard's.

E.

Mary calls Richard Which or Whicher or Which-Which. I suppose he'll call himself something like that too. Whicher I find rather attractive. She is better with him now and I must say I am proud to see that she is more apt to be frightened of him than he of her, sad though it is. I actually heard her say to him yesterday 'No no Whicher, no hurt Mamie.' She takes things from him but she runs away from him, relying on her mobility; once he can move himself I don't believe she'll dare to—she never stays within his reach once she has the thing in her hand. She tries to gain confidence for herself by saying *Baby wet* all the time—generally with truth because he has now got to the stage of rejecting his pot (this is the usual preliminary to being 'trained' and I hope we'll reach that stage soon though at present I see not the slightest indication of it), but when she dirtied her pants for the second time today I heard this conversation with Nurse: 'No cross with Mamie Nurse?' 'Yes I *am* cross this time' 'Iodine no cross?' '"Yes, Iodine's cross too.' 'Whicher cross?' 'Whicher says he'll have to lend you some nappies.' 'No. . . . Baby's.' And she began to cry—so she's not sure of her superiority even in this. She isn't so superior either. This has been a bad day, but she never gets through one with dry pants poor little wretch.

Dearest thank you very much for the books—*Psmith in the City*[18] has been making me laugh aloud. By the way, he arrived yesterday and the other three this afternoon although according to your letter you posted the three first. The oranges came too, and the fats.[19] I think you're being too generous but as the oranges *have* come I'm going to eat them. Blackburn got some the other day and I gave all mine and most of Richard's to the children so they're all right for the moment. Richard has the juice of half an orange every other day and Mary has his other half and Laurence a whole one.

This is being typed under difficulties as Mary is on my knee and trying to contribute.

Tomorrow I'm going to Newcastle, primarily to see the man in charge of Welfare Foods for the North of England. So far as I can see I can't get Richard's back orange juice as Stockton Food Office has stolen the coupons, but I hope to arrange that they won't bring off the same coup again. I now have some reason to think that they take orange juice out of stock on these extra coupons and sell it but of course I'm not proposing to mention this theory to Watkins. I'm also going to three food meetings and two infant welfare clinics with Nell.[20] If I stay the course. It will be very interesting and I hope profitable because I ought to lay hold of some Ostermilk[21] somewhere.

Don't bother about blankets. I've bought two from Binns' in Sunderland—

they cost 22/– each and are more like rugs than blankets but they'll do quite well. I hope to make one into a frock for myself. They're dark grey which isn't I think the colour of choice for blankets but they'll come in useful one way or another and they're certainly cheap. I hope you have enough at home and are not economising by leaving out the underblanket because without that you'll be cold if you have a dozen on top of you.

The playpen has come and all the children are entranced by it. Richard laughed heartily as soon as he was put in and then the others joined him and there was a riot. I don't know how he'll take to it when he is left alone but I think he'll be OK. I have made him some strings of beads which he passionately loves and he will now play by himself quite happily for as long as you like. He's had more trouble with his teeth but no more are through. He might have another couple by the 21st though. As for his appetite, he ate for his lunch the same food as Mary and very nearly the same quantity, but he didn't want his milk. I'd just announced that I was going to replace the midday milk by water so this came very aptly. But I've had to replace the cereal after his evening bath. I gave him Farex[22] for a couple of nights and the last two he has had MOF again made much thinner. When he had just milk he was restless at night and screaming for his late feed by nine o'clock. So I'm just going to risk his getting overweight—he's still below the average for his age and length I'm sure. He's beginning to drink cows' milk instead of Oster-milk but I can't go ahead with this as fast as I might because I'm terrified that he'll turn against the Ostermilk and we'll be dependent on that when we're in London. The other thing that doesn't progress well is his drinking. He's much worse at it since he had the teeth. But I think part of the trouble is that he can't manage the mug which he's supposed to use now. I'll try to buy one or two cups or mugs in Newcastle (I'm staying the night there and coming back on Friday to fit all these things in).

I've been dressed every day since you went away but I've done very little else except give Richard most of his food and have him for his social between five and six and play with Mary for half an hour or so after feeding Richard because she's so jealous of him, quite naturally. This morning

[*Handwritten*] At this point typing became impossible—I am now in the train but I got your wire last night (Wed). I hope you'll be able to do the Court[23] but of course you mustn't mess up the French trip.

Could you ring me up on Friday or Saturday evening? It's quite easy— Stillington, Co. Durham, 29. A trunk call of course—you dial TRU & ask for the number. Then we can talk about the plans. Unless of course you're coming up this weekend which would be nice. I'll be home at Greystone on Friday afternoon.

Eileen[24]

[XVII, 2638, pp. 95–103; typed and handwritten]

1. Greystone was the O'Shaughnessy family home. Joyce Pritchard, the O'Shaughnessys' nanny, told Ian Angus in a letter of 27 September 1967 that Eileen visited Greystone frequently between July 1944 (when the children were taken there) and March 1945.

2. Laurence (born 13 November 1938) was the son of Gwen* and Laurence O'Shaughnessy,* both doctors. Eileen was the sister of the elder Laurence.

3. George Kopp,* Orwell's commander in Spain, married Gwen O'Shaughnessy's half-sister Doreen Hunton. He and Doreen lived a few doors away from the Orwells in Canonbury Square so he had not got far to go to collect the mail, but he failed to forward it.

4. Raymond Blackburn was gardener and odd-job man at Greystone.

5. Harry Evers was Eileen's surgeon.

6. Gwen O'Shaughnessy's husband (see n. 2).

7. Eileen owned a house, Ravensden, at Harefield, Middlesex; this was let. See her letter of 25 March 1945 (XVII, 2642), and for a reference to its disposal, 11 January 1946 (XVIII, 2856, p. 33).

8. Evelyn Anderson, foreign editor of *Tribune*. She had studied at Frankfurt and came to England as a refugee. Orwell had 'volunteered Eileen's help . . . in correcting her English for a book' (Crick, p. 446). This was *Hammer or Anvil: The Story of the German Working-Class Movement*, reviewed by Orwell in the *Manchester Evening News*, 30 August 1945 (XVIII, 2734, pp. 271–3).

9. Presumably Miss Sparrow was a secretary at the Ministry of Food, where Eileen had worked until June 1944.

10. George Mason was a surgeon and one-time colleague of Laurence O'Shaughnessy.

11. In his Diary for 20 June 1940 Orwell writes, 'Thinking always of my island in the Hebrides' (see *Diaries*, pp. 257 and 258). This may have been prompted by his reviewing *Priest Island* by E.L. Grant Wilson on 21 June 1940 (XII, 640, pp. 190–1). Jura itself was doubtless chosen because it was recommended by David Astor who owned land there. He also suggested Barnhill which had been empty for several years. Avril describes Barnhill in her letter of **1.7.46.**

12. Margaret Fletcher (1917–; later Mrs Nelson) went to Jura with her husband, Robin, when he inherited the Ardlussa Estate, on which stood Barnhill.

13. Garrigill, a village near Alston, Cumbria, about midway between Penrith and Hexham.

14. Catherine Mary, Gwen O'Shaughnessy's adopted daughter, who was known as Mary until her cousin, Mary Kopp was born, when she took Catherine as her first name. She was also known as 'Mamie'.

15. Orwell had taken P.G. Wodehouse and his wife to a small restaurant near Les Halles in Paris.

16. Eileen and Orwell had hoped to adopt a little girl as a sister to Richard.

17. Raymond Blackburn, son of Mrs Blackburn, the housekeeper.

18. *Psmith in the City*, a novel by P.G. Wodehouse (1910) is discussed by Orwell in 'In Defence of P.G. Wodehouse' (XVII, 2624, pp. 51–63).

19. Oranges were unobtainable for most of the war and fats were severely rationed. A special allowance of concentrated orange juice was made available to children as a Welfare Food.

20. Not identified with certainty, but probably Nell Heaton, a friend of Eileen's. They met when they worked together at the Ministry of Food. In 1947 Nell Heaton published *The Complete Cook*, the foreword of which states: 'I owe a debt of gratitude . . . to George Orwell and Emily Blair, to whose sympathy and encouragement I owe so much.' Eileen was known as Emily at the Ministry of Food.

21. Ostermilk is a proprietary brand of milk powder for babies.

22. Farex is a proprietary brand of food for newly weaned babies.

23. This may possibly mean attend Court in connection with the final formalities for Richard's adoption, although Eileen, in her letter to Lettice Cooper (**23.3.45**), says 'Richard's adoption was through'. An alternative possibility is the kind of law court Orwell refers to in his report, 'Creating Order out of Cologne Chaos', *Observer*, 25 March 1945 (XVII, 2641, pp. 106–7).

24. The signature is an indecipherable scrawl.

Eileen Blair* to Lettice Cooper*

23 March 1945 or thereabouts
Greystone
Carlton

Dear Lettice,

I'm sorry about the paper and the typewriter but Mary got at both. You practically can't buy paper here so I can't waste that and although I could do something about the machine I am bored with it after about twenty minutes spent in collecting the ribbon and more or less replacing it. A typewriter ribbon is the longest thing in the world. It will go round every chair leg in a good sized house. So I've just discovered.

Richard was delighted with his coat and it will see him through the summer. He was just getting very short of jackets because he is so large. Mary's cast-offs will hardly go on, knitted things anyway. He took over her nightgowns the day after she inherited some pyjamas of Laurence's and even those aren't at all too big. He's still backward but has great charm which will be a lot more useful to him than talent. And he is not so stupid as Mogador[1] because he found out about pulling trucks by their strings before he was ten months old and is now investigating the principles of using one object to drag nearer or to pick up another. He's a hard worker.

I really would have written sooner but I came up to London about a fortnight ago to see my dentist so I thought I'd ring you up. Then I got ill and rang no one up and finished with all kinds of dramas at the Ministry. On the way up I went to see a Newcastle surgeon because as Richard's adoption was through I thought I might now deal with the grwoth° (no one could object to a grwoth) I knew I had. He found it or rather them without any difficulty and I'm going into his nursing home next week for the removal. I think the question about the hysterectomy is answered because there is hardly any chance that the tumours can come out without more or less everything else removable. So that on the whole is a very good thing. It was worth coming to the north country because there is to be none of the fattening up in hospital before the operation that I was to have in London. London surgeons love preparing their patients as an insurance against unknown consequences. I think they're all terrified of their knives really—probably they have a subconscious hope that the patient will die before getting as far as the theatre and then they can't possibly be blamed. In London they said I couldn't have any kind of operation without a preparatory month of blood transfusions etc.; here I'm going in next Wednesday to be done on Thursday. Apart from its other advantages this will save money, a lot of money. And that's as well. By the way, if you could write a letter that would be nice. Theoretically I don't want any visitors, particularly as I can't get a private room; in practice I'll probably be furious that no one comes—and no one can because such friends as I have in Newcastle will be away for the school holidays. So if you have time write a letter to Fernwood House, Clayton Road, Newcastle. It's a mercy George is away—in Cologne at the moment. George visiting the sick is a sight infinitely sadder than any disease-ridden wretch in the world.

[*Handwritten*] I hate to think that you are no longer at the Ministry & that this will be the last extract from Miss Tomkins' conversation. I clearly remember the sweetly pretty painting of snowdrops.

Tell me whether the flat materialises. It sounds perfect. Incidentally if you want somewhere to work or to live for that matter, use our flat which is rotting in solitude. Doreen Kopp², who lives at 14A Cannonbury° Square, has the key. Ours is 27B Cannonbury Square. And her telephone number is CAN 4901. She has a son, very large, with the hair and hands of a talented musician. I expected to be jealous but find that I didn't prefer him to Richard, preferable though he is. To return to the flat, Doreen can tell you whatever you don't know about its amenities, which don't include sheets. The last lot have disappeared since I came North. But you could have a peat fire which is a nice thing.

Raymond Blackburn is going to Stockton & he must carry this in his hand.

It has taken about a week to write . . .³ But all this time we have been thanking you for Richard's present, he & I.

> Lots of love
> Emily⁴

[XVII, 2640, pp. 104–5; typed and handwritten]

1. Unidentified, but possibly a grand form of 'Moggie' and therefore the blue cat Eileen refers to in her letter of **21.3.45**.
2. Doreen Kopp, half-sister of Doctor Gwen O'Shaughnessy, and wife of George Kopp*.
3. As in the original; nothing has been omitted.
4. 'Emily' was the pet-name by which Eileen was known at the Ministry of Food.

Eileen Blair* to her husband

25 March 1945
Greystone
Carlton

Dearest

I'm trying to get forward with my correspondence because I go into the nursing home on Wednesday (this is Sunday) & of course I shan't be ready. It's impossible to write or do anything else while the children are up. I finish reading to Laurence about a quarter to eight (tonight it was five to eight), we have supper at 8 or 8.15, the 9 o'clock news now must be listened to & lasts till at least 9.30 (the war reports the last two nights have been brilliant¹) & then it's time to fill hotwater bottles etc. because we come to bed early. So I write in bed & don't type. Incidentally I did while explaining the poaching laws as I understand them to Laurence make my will²—in handwriting because handwritten wills are nearly always valid. It is signed & witnessed. Nothing is less likely than that it will be used but I mention it because I have done an odd thing. I haven't left anything to Richard. You are the sole legatee if you survive me (your inheritance would be the Harefield house which ought to be worth a few hundreds, that insurance policy, & furniture). If you don't, the estate would be larger & I have left it to Gwen absolutely with a note that I hope she will use it for Richard's benefit but without any legal obligation. The note is to convince Richard that I was not disinheriting him. But I've done it that way because I don't know how to devise the money to Richard himself. For one thing, there has been no communication from the Registrar General so I suppose Richard's name is still Robertson. For another thing he must have trustees & I don't know who you want & they'd have to be asked. For another, if he is to inherit in childhood it's important that his trustees should be able to use his money during his minority so that he may have as good an education as possible. We must get all this straightened out properly when you come home but I thought I must cover the possibility that you might be killed within the next few days & I might die on the table on Thursday. If you're killed after I die that'll be just too bad but still my little testament will indicate what I wanted done. Gwen's results in child-rearing have not been encouraging so far but after the war she will have a proper house in the country containing both the children & herself, she loves Richard & Laurie adores him. And all the retainers love him dearly. I'm sure he would be happier in that household than with Marjorie though I think Marjorie would take him on. Avril I think & hope would not take him on anyway. That I couldn't bear.[3] Norah & Quartus[4] would have him & bring him up beautifully but you've never seen either of them. Quartus is in India & I can't arrange it. So in all the circumstances I thought you would agree that this would be the best emergency measure.

RICHARD HAS SIX TEETH. Also he got hold of the playpen rail when I was putting him in & stood hanging on to it without other support. But he doesn't really know at all how to pull himself up so don't expect too much. Yesterday Nurse & I took all three to the doctor for whooping cough injections. He lives about 2½–3 miles away, partly across fields. We got lost & had to cross ploughland. The pram wouldn't perambulate & neither would Mary. She sat in a furrow & bellowed until carried. Laurence cried to be carried too . . .[5] Laurence however didn't cry when the needle went in but Mary did *and* made an enormous pool on the surgery floor. Richard was done last. He played with a matchbox on my knee, looked at the doctor in some surprise when his arm was gripped & then turned to me in astonishment as though to say 'Why is this apparently nice man sticking needles into me? Can it be right?' On being told it was he looked up at the doctor again rather gravely—& then smiled. He didn't make a sound & he was perfectly good all day too, though his arm is sort of bruised. The other two unfortunately remembered that they'd been injected & screamed in agony if either arm was touched. It was a happy day.

But Richard did a *terrible* thing. He will *not* use his pot, nearly always goes into a tantrum when put on it & if he does sit on it does nothing more. The tooth upset his inside a bit too. After lunch I sent the other two to bed & left Richard in his playpen while I helped wash up. Then there were cries of agony. He had done what Mary calls tick-tocks for the third time, got his hands in it & *put his hands in his mouth*. I tried to wash his mouth out, hoping he'd be sick. But no. He seemed to swallow most of the water I poured in, so it was worse than useless. In the end I scoured his mouth with cotton wool, gave him some boiled water & hoped for the best. And he is very well. Poor little boy. And I was sorry for myself too. I *was* sick. Blackburn however says a lot of children do this every day – – – – –[6]

I haven't had a copy of *Windmill*[7] & I haven't had a proof. Surely you said they were sending a proof. And I failed to get the *Observer* one week which must have been the relevant one. I've also failed to get today's but shall get it I hope.

Your letter with the *Animal Farm* document came yesterday & I've sent the enclosure on to Moore. He will be pleased. This is much the quickest exchange we've had.

I suppose I'd better go to sleep. By the way the six teeth are 3 top & 3 bottom which gives rather an odd appearance, but I hope the fourth top one will be through soon.

All my love & Richard's

E.

[XVII, 2642, pp. 107–9; typed and handwritten]

1. On 23 March, Operation Plunder, the offensive across the Rhine, began; it may be reports of this to which Eileen refers.
2. Eileen's will can be read in XVII, 2643, pp. 109–10.
3. After Orwell had also died, it was Avril who took care of Richard, and he was very happy with her. Eileen's fears proved completely unfounded.
4. Norah Myles and her husband Quartus, a general practitioner. (See headnote to **3.11.36.**)
5. and 6. Nothing has been deleted at either of these points: the stops and dashes are Eileen's.
7. The journal *Windmill*, in which 'In Defence of P. G. Wodehouse' was to appear (XVII, 2624).

Eileen Blair* to her husband

29 March 1945
Fernwood House
Clayton Road
Newcastle-on-Tyne°

Dearest

I'm just going to have the operation, already enema'd, injected (with morphia in the *right* arm which is a nuisance), cleaned & packed up like a precious image in cotton wool & bandages. When its'° over I'll add a note to this &

it can get off quickly. Judging by my fellow patients it will be a *short* note. They've all had their operations. Annoying—I shall never have a chance to feel superior.

I haven't seen Harvey Evers since arrival & apparently Gwen didn't communicate with him & no one knows what operation I am having! They don't believe that Harvey Evers really left it to me to decide—he always 'does what he thinks best'! He will of course. But I must say I feel irritated though I am being a *model* patient. They think I'm wonderful, so placid & happy they say. As indeed I am once I can hand myself over to someone else to deal with.

This is a nice room—ground floor so one can see the garden. Not much in it except daffodils & I think arabis but a nice little lawn. My bed isn't next the window but it faces the right way. I also see the fire & the clock.

[XVII, 2647, pp. 112–3; handwritten]

The letter ends here. No note was added. Eileen suffered a heart attack and died under the anaesthetic. She was thirty-nine. Orwell was in Paris when he received the news that Eileen had died; he got to Greystone on Saturday, 31 March. Eileen was buried in St Andrew's and Jesmond Cemetery, Newcastle upon Tyne. The grave is number 145 in Section B. Orwell took Richard back with him to London, and Doreen Kopp took care of him when Orwell returned to France to complete his assignment.

To Lydia Jackson*

1 April 1945
at Greystone, Carlton

Dear Lydia,

I do not know whether you will have heard from anyone else the very bad news. Eileen is dead. As you know she had been ill for some time past and it was finally diagnosed that she had a growth which must be removed. The operation was not supposed to be a very serious one, but she seems to have died as soon as she was given the anaesthetic, and, apparently, as a result of the anaesthetic. This was last Thursday. I was in Paris and didn't even know she was to have the operation till two days before. It was a dreadful shock and a very cruel thing to happen, because she had become so devoted to Richard and was looking forward to living a normal life in the country again as soon as the war was over. The only consolation is that I don't think she suffered, because she went to the operation, apparently, not expecting anything to go wrong, and never recovered consciousness. It is perhaps as well that Richard wasn't a bit older, because I don't think he actually misses her, at any rate he seems in very good spirits as well as health. I am going to bring him back to London when I come, and for the time being he is going to stay with Doreen [Kopp] who lives in the same square and has a baby a month old herself. I think we shall be able to find a nurse whom we can share, and when the war stops I can probably get him a nurse of his own and make a proper home for him in the country. It is a shame Eileen should have died just when he is becoming so charming, however she did enjoy very much being with him during her last months of life. Please give my love to Pat. I don't know about my plans, but I think that if the *Observer* want me to I shall go back to France for a month or two when I have settled Richard.

Yours
George

[XVII, 2650, p. 118; typewritten]

To Anthony Powell*

13 April 1945
Hotel Scribe
Paris 9e

Dear Tony,

I tried to get in touch with you when I was in London last week, but failed. I don't know whether you will have heard from some other source about what has happened. Eileen is dead. She died very suddenly and unexpectedly on March 29th during an operation which was not supposed to be very serious. I was over here and had no expectation of anything going wrong, which indeed nobody seems to have had. I didn't see the final findings of the inquest and indeed don't want to, because it doesn't bring her back, but I think the anaesthetic was responsible. It was a most horrible thing to happen because she had had five really miserable years of bad health and overwork, and things were just beginning to get better. The only good thing is that I don't think she can have suffered or had any apprehensions. She was actually looking forward to the operation to cure her trouble, and I found among her papers a letter she must have written only about an hour before she died and which she expected to finish when she came round. But it was terribly sad that she should die when she had become so devoted to Richard and was making such a good job of his upbringing. Richard I am glad to say is very well and for the moment is provided for. He is staying with his sort of aunt[1] who lives in the same square as me and has a young baby of her own, and I hope within a fairly short time to find a good nurse whom I can take on as a permanency. As soon as I can get a nurse and a house I shall remove him to the country, as I don't want him to learn to walk in London. I just got him settled in and then came straight back here,

Orwell, his mother Ida, his sister Avril, and his father when on leave in 1916.

René-Noël Raimbault, Orwell's French translator.

Jacintha Buddicom leaving the solicitor's office where she had relinquished her daughter Michal (b. 1927) to her uncle and aunt, Dr and Mrs Hawley-Burke.

Jacintha 1948

Jacintha Buddicom in 1948, shortly before she renewed contact with Orwell.

Norah Myles (née Symes), a close friend of Eileen
from their Oxford days.

The Stores, 2 Kits Lane, Wallington, Herts., which Orwell rented from 1936.

Eileen on the Huesca Front, sitting to the right of the machine-gunner.
Orwell is the tall figure behind her.

At the Independent Labour Party Conference, 1937.
From left to right: John McNair, Douglas Moyle, Stafford Cottman, Orwell, and Jock Branthwaite.

Eileen sitting on the wall of the villa which she and Orwell
rented outside Marrakech, Morocco, 1938.

Orwell milking his goat in Morocco,
helped by Mahdjoub Mahommed.

Three of the five British and American French Foreign Legionnaires
who visited the Orwells in Marrakech.

Orwell's Home Guard section. Orwell is in the back row on the far right.

Eileen c. 1941.

Orwell with his son,
Richard, at their flat in
Canonbury Square, Islington.

Recording Voices, 5 at the BBC, 1 December 1942. *From left to right*:
Venu Chitale, M.J. Tambimuttu, T.S. Eliot, Una Marson, Mulk Raj Anand, Christopher
Pemberton, Narayana Menon; *standing*: Orwell, Nancy Parratt and William Empson.

Sonia Orwell in the *Horizon* office on her last day there, shortly after her marriage to Orwell on 13 October 1949. Also facing the camera is Lys Lubbock.

Barnhill, Jura. Orwell's large vegetable and fruit garden lies at the back of the house.

as I felt so upset at home I thought I would rather be on the move for a bit. I was in Germany for a few days recently and am now going back there for a week or two.

What I partly wrote for was to ask if you know Malcolm Muggeridge's address. He has left Paris and I have no idea how to get in touch with him. I vaguely heard there had been some kind of row in which l'affaire Wodehouse was mixed up, but have no idea what it is. Letters generally take about a fortnight, but the above address will find me. Please remember me to Violet.[2]

Yours
George

[XVII, 2656, p. 124; typewritten]

1. Doreen Kopp.
2. The Lady Violet Powell (1912–2002),* Anthony Powell's wife.

To Lydia Jackson*

11 May 1945
Hotel Scribe
Paris 9e

Dear Lydia,

I just had letters from you and Pat[1] about simultaneously. I don't want to relet the cottage, because for the time being I want to keep it on as a place to go down to for an occasional week end. I can however make either of the following arrangements with you. Either I will lend you the cottage for a month in the summer at any time you choose to name, or else you can continue to use the cottage at all times, but on the understanding that I can come and have it for a week or so any time I want to. In either case I don't want you to pay me anything. I should be back in London about May 25th and we can make any final arrangements then. You could have it for June or July or really whenever you like provided I know beforehand. At present it seems impossible to get a house in the country and for that reason I want to keep on the cottage so that Richard can get a few days of country air now and then. Eileen and I had hoped that it would not be necessary for him to learn to walk in London, but it seems unavoidable, so I am going to keep on the flat.

Gwen [O'Shaughnessy] says you borrowed a refrigerator of hers. Do you think we could have it back, because it is so hard to keep milk from going sour in the summer months and that makes it so difficult with the children.

I came straight back here after Eileen's death and have felt somewhat better for being at work most of the time. The destruction in Germany is terrifying, far worse than people in England grasp, but my trips there have been quite interesting. I am making one more trip, to Austria I hope, and then coming back about the end of next week. I get bulletins about Richard from Doreen and it seems he is doing very well and had tripled his birth weight at 11 months. The next thing is to find a nurse for him which is next door to impossible at present. I don't know how long this letter will take getting to you—sometimes they take only 4 days, sometimes about 3 weeks—but if it gets to you before I get back, and you want to go down to the cottage, you can do so. Looking forward to seeing you both.

Yours
George

[XVII, 2666, pp. 138–9; typewritten]

1.   Patricia Donoghue shared Orwell's cottage at Wallington with Lydia Jackson.

Unpublished letter to *Tribune*

This letter was set up in type but, according to Orwell's marginal note on the galley slip, 'withdrawn because Tribune *altered attitude in following week'.*

[26?] June 1945

POLISH TRIAL

I read with some disappointment your comment on the trial of the sixteen Poles in Moscow,[1] in which you seemed to imply that they had behaved in a discreditable manner and deserved punishment.

Early in the proceedings I formed the opinion that the accused were technically guilty: only, just what were they guilty of? Apparently it was merely of doing what everyone thinks it right to do when his country is occupied by a foreign power—that is, of trying to keep a military force in being, of maintaining communication with the outside world, of committing acts of sabotage and occasionally killing people. In other words, they were accused of trying to preserve the independence of their country against an unelected puppet government, and of remaining obedient to a government which at that time was recognised by the whole world except the U.S.S.R. The Germans during their period of occupation could have brought exactly the same indictment against them, and they would have been equally guilty.

It will not do to say that the efforts of the Poles to remain independent 'objectively' aided the Nazis, and leave it at that. Many actions which Left-wingers do not disapprove of have 'objectively' aided the Germans. How about E.A.M., for instance?[2] They also tried to keep their military force in being, and they, too, killed Allied soldiers—British in this case—and they were not even acting under the orders of a government which was recognised by anyone as legal. But what of it? We do not disapprove of their action, and if sixteen E.A.M. leaders were now brought to London and sentenced to long terms of imprisonment we should rightly protest.

To be anti-Polish and pro-Greek is only possible if one sets up a double standard of political morality, one for the U.S.S.R. and the other for the rest of the world. Before these sixteen Poles went to Moscow they were described in the Press as political delegates, and it was stated that they had been summoned there to take part in discussions on the formation of a new government. After their arrest all mention of their status as political delegates was dropped from the British Press—an example of the kind of censorship that is necessary if this double standard is to be made acceptable to the big public. Any well-informed person is aware of similar instances. To name just one: at this moment speakers up and down the country are justifying the Russian purges on the ground that Russia 'had no quislings,' at the same time as any mention of the considerable numbers of Russian troops, including several generals, who changed sides and fought for the Germans is being suppressed by cautious editors. This kind of whitewashing may be due to a number of different motives, some of them respectable ones, but its effect on the Socialist movement can be deadly if it is long continued.

When I wrote in your columns I repeatedly said that if one criticises this or that Russian action one is not obliged to put on airs of moral superiority. Their behaviour is not worse than that of capitalist governments, and its actual results may often be better. Nor is it likely that we shall alter the behaviour of the rulers of the U.S.S.R. by telling them that we disapprove of them. The whole point is the effect of the Russian mythos on the Socialist movement *here*. At present we are all but openly applying the double standard of morality. With one side of our mouths we cry out that mass deportations, concentration camps, forced labour and suppression of freedom of speech are appalling crimes, while with the other we proclaim that these things are perfectly all right if done by the U.S.S.R. or its satellite states: and where necessary we make this plausible by doctoring the news and cutting out unpalatable facts. One cannot possibly build up a healthy Socialist movement if one is obliged to condone no matter what crime when the U.S.S.R. commits it. No one knows better than I do that it is unpopular to say anything anti-Russian *at this moment*. But what of it? I am only 42, and I can remember the time when it was as dangerous to say anything pro-Russian as it is to say anything anti-Russian now. Indeed, I am old enough to have seen working class audiences booing and jeering at speakers who had used the word Socialism. These fashions pass away, but they can't be depended on to do so unless thinking people are willing to raise their voices against the fallacy of the moment. It is only because over the past hundred years small groups and lonely individuals have been willing to face unpopularity that the Socialist movement exists at all.

George Orwell

[XVII, 2685, pp. 193–5]

1. The British had called for a meeting of the leaders of the Polish underground to discuss the implementation of the Yalta decisions on the formation of a Polish Government of National Unity. The preliminary meeting was to be held in Moscow and a further meeting was planned for London. However, when the Poles reached Moscow they were put on trial.

2. E.A.M. (Ethnikon Apeleftherotikon Metopon), the National Liberation Front, was formed in Greece in 1941 after the German invasion. It started as a true resistance movement with nearly the whole population as members. By early 1942 it was discovered that it was in fact a Communist-organised movement. A national guerrilla army was then formed to fight the Germans, but found itself also fighting the E.A.M. When the British returned to Greece in 1945, they also found themselves fighting the E.A.M.

To C. E. de Salis

29 June 1945
27B Canonbury Square
Islington
London N 1

Dear Sir,

Your letter was sent on to me by the *Observer*. I am very sorry I made the bad slip of speaking of the scuttling of the ship in *Lord Jim*.[1] Of course I meant to say abandonment of the ship, and would probably have corrected this if I had sent the article in early enough to see a proof.

With regard to the other points in your letter. The rest of *Lord Jim* seems to me absurd, not because a young man who had behaved in that way would not seek redemption, but because the actual incidents of Jim's life among the Malays are of a kind I find incredible. Conrad could describe life in the Far East from a sailor's angle, with the emphasis on jungle scenery and the life of seaport towns, but if one has actually lived in one of those countries his descriptions of life inland are not convincing. As a whole, *Lord Jim* seems to me to be a very distinguished version of the type of book in which the hero is expelled from his club for cheating at cards and goes off to Central Africa to shoot big game. Even the Dorothy Lamour figure[2] comes in. When I made that remark about people who could have adventures and also appreciate them, I thought of T. E. Lawrence, whom you mention, but after all how common or typical are such people? Marlow himself seems to me quite incredible. A person like that would not be a sea captain. Conrad himself was perhaps rather like that, but then the point is that he left the sea and took to writing. That way of writing a book also seems to me unsatisfactory, because one is so often brought up by the thought, 'No one could possibly talk like this, or at such length.'

The *Observer* article rather deformed what I meant to say about Conrad, because as so often happens they had to cut out about 300 words from lack of space. I had written a paragraph or two in elaborating the point that with his Polish background Conrad had a remarkable understanding of the atmosphere of revolutionary movements—an understanding which very few Englishmen would have, and certainly no Englishman with anything resembling Conrad's political outlook. I especially praised *The Secret Agent*, and suggested that this book, which now seems quite difficult to get hold of, should be reprinted.

Yours truly
George Orwell

[XVII, 2690, pp. 200–1; typewritten]

1. This was in a review by Orwell published on 24 June 1945 (XVII, 2683, pp. 90–1).
2. Dorothy Lamour (Dorothy Kaumeyer, 1914–96) was first dressed by Hollywood in a sarong-like garment in *The Jungle Princess*, 1936, and came to typify exotic beauty, and especially so dressed in the 'Road' films to the point of self-parody. The film *Typhoon*, 1940, in which she appeared, had nothing to do with Conrad's novel of that title. Orwell very briefly reviewed her *Moon over Burma*, 5 July 1941 (XII, 828, p. 522), but devoted more attention to an elephant and a cobra than to Miss Lamour.

'Orwell and the Stinkers': A Correspondence

29 June 1945
Tribune

On 29 June 1945, Tribune *published a short review by Subramaniam[1] of* Million: Second Collection,[2] *edited by John Singer. This briefly summarised the contents and recommended the collection, but devoted half its length to an essay by J. E. Miller, 'George Orwell and Our Times,' which was said to deserve a separate paragraph:*

This article, which is as provocative as any of Orwell's, is analytical, stimulating and almost brilliant. Mr. Miller, however, fails in one respect. He does not give enough importance to the fact that Orwell is one of the few writers who give political writing a literary form. Instead, he seems to be primarily concerned as to how far George Orwell has correlated his beliefs with correct Socialist behaviour and submits a long indictment with several counts.

A lively correspondence followed, and Tribune *clearly played it for all it was worth. Twice letters were given headings as provocative as the argument: 'Orwell and the Stinkers' and 'More Views on Stinkers'. The first letter, from Paul Potts,³ was published on 6 July 1945:*

When reviewing *Million* last week Subramaniam mentioned an article on George Orwell by J. E. Miller. In this article Miller reiterates an old libel on Orwell, current at the time *The Road To Wigan Pier* first appeared, that Orwell said somewhere in that book that working-class folks stank. What he did say was that as a schoolboy at Eton he was brought up to believe they did. This error has been pointed out to Mr. Miller, who persists in circulating it. May one remind him that the particular version of socialism that he advocates is in no way aided by a mean untruth?

Further letters are included in XVII, pp. 202–3, and Orwell's letter to the Editor of Million *is to be found in* The Lost Orwell, *pp. 107–8. This is an extract from Orwell's response in* Tribune:

[...] what I was discussing in this chapter of *Wigan Pier* was the theory taught to us as children that the working classes are, as it were, smelly by nature. We were taught that the 'lower classes' (as it was usual to call them) had a different smell from ourselves, and that it was a nasty smell; we were taught just the same about Jews, Negroes and various other categories of human beings. In the book, I explained elaborately how I was taught this, how I accepted it, and how and why I afterwards got rid of it. Mr. Miller ignores all this and simply picks out isolated sentences which seem to support his thesis, a method by which anybody can be made to say anything.⁴

[XVII, 2691, pp. 201–205]

1. Unidentified.
2. *Million* ran for three issues. It was undated; they are assigned to 1943–45. It was published in Glasgow and carried one of two subtitles: 'New Left Writing' or 'The People's Review'.
3. For Paul Potts, see **1.7.46**, n. 5.
4. Orwell wrote, 'That was what we were taught—*the lower classes smell*' (V, p. 119); the italics are in the original. He then discussed this proposition on the

following four pages. It was Somerset Maugham who unequivocally stated that the working man stank. Orwell quoted a dozen lines from Maugham's *On a Chinese Screen*, the only book, Orwell said, he knew in which this issue 'is set forth without humbug'. Maugham wrote, and Orwell quoted, 'I do not blame the working man because he stinks, but stink he does.' Orwell concluded his discussion by saying, 'Actually people who have access to a bath will generally use it. But the essential thing is that middle-class people *believe* that the working class are dirty' (V, p. 122).

To Leonard Moore*

3 July 1945
27B Canonbury Square
Islington N 1

Dear Mr Moore,

I had a talk with Warburg about the contract position. He is quite satisfied with my assurance that I will bring him all my future work, subject to books of a special nature (eg. that Britain in Pictures book)[1] being allowed to go elsewhere. He is not pressing for a hard and fast contract, but he would no doubt prefer to have one when the other business is settled.

The real trouble is with Gollancz. The contract to bring him my next two novels is still extant, and as he refused to regard *Animal Farm* as working off one of these, it looks as if he wants to keep to it. At the same time I frankly would prefer not to give or offer him any more books if we can get out of it. I have no quarrel with him personally, he has treated me generously and published my work when no one else would, but it is obviously unsatisfactory to be tied to a publisher who accepts or refuses books partly on political grounds and whose own political views are constantly changing. When I wrote *Animal Farm* for instance, I knew in advance that it would be a very difficult book to find a publisher for, and having to submit it to Gollancz simply meant that much time wasted. This might happen over and over again, and judging by some of the things he has published during the past year or two, I doubt whether I could now write anything that Gollancz would approve of. For instance, I recently started a novel[2]. Considering how much work I have to do elsewhere I don't expect to finish it till some time in 1947, but I am pretty sure Gollancz would refuse it when the time comes, unless by that time his views have altered again. He might say that so far as novels go he does not mind what views they express, but it is a bad arrangement to take novels to one publisher and non-fiction to another. For example, that Spanish war book, which is about the best I have written, would probably have sold more if published by Gollancz, as by that time I was becoming known to the Gollancz public. With Warburg these difficulties don't arise. He is less interested in propaganda and in any case his views are near enough to mine to prevent serious disagreement. From Gollancz's own point of view I do not imagine I am a good proposition either. Having me on his list means that from time to time he will publish a book which neither he nor his friends can disapprove° of. It seems to me that if he will agree it would be better to scrap the contract. If he won't agree I will keep to the strict letter, ie. as regards two more novels, and I have no doubt I can make this all right with Warburg. Perhaps you could approach Gollancz about this. You can quote this paragraph if you wish.

I saw W. J. Turner the other day and asked him about the Britain in Pictures book. He said Edmund Blunden³ is writing the companion volume and the two will be published simultaneously. I said that as they had had the Ms a year I thought I ought to have some money. The agreed advance was £50 and I suggested they should give me £25 now. He said there would be no objection to this and I told him you would write to him, which you have perhaps done already.

Hamish Hamilton wrote to say Harper's would like to see something more of mine. I told him about the book of essays, and perhaps if the Dial Press people turn it down it might be worth showing it to Harpers,° though I shouldn't think it is much in their line.

Yours sincerely
Eric Blair

[XVII, 2694, pp. 207–8; typewritten]

1. *The English People*: see the penultimate paragraph. Turner was the general editor of the series.
2. *Nineteen Eighty-Four*.
3. Edmund Blunden (1896–1974; CBE), poet, editor, man of letters. He contributed to broadcasts to India for Orwell on English literature. His *English Villages* (1941) is No. 11 in the Britain in Pictures series.

To Lydia Jackson*

1 August 1945

Dear Lydia,

Of course use the cottage second half of August. Even if I did manage to go down there some time, it wouldn't be then.

I am still trying to take that cottage in the Hebrides. I don't know if it will materialise, but if it does, I shall send the Wallington furniture there. That wouldn't be until early next year, however.

I am frightfully busy, but I am glad to say I have got a good nurse who looks after Richard and cooks my meals as well. Richard is extremely well although he is teething rapidly. He is now 14½ months and weighs about 26 pounds. He can stand up without support but doesn't actually walk yet, and I don't want to hurry him as I am afraid he may be too heavy for his legs. He isn't talking yet, ie. he utters word-like sounds, but no actual words. He doesn't seem to have taken any harm from the many changes in his short life. When you are back, come over and see us both. I am nearly always at home in the afternoons. Richard has his tea about half past four and I have a high tea about seven.

My love to Pat.

Yours
Eric

[XVII, 2712, p. 236; typewritten]

Gleb Struve had written to Orwell on 28 August 1945, saying he had found Animal Farm *'delightful, even though I do not necessarily agree with what one of the reviewers described as your "Trotskyist prejudices." ' He was teaching in the Russian section of a Summer School at Oxford and students were queuing for the book. He had been very amused 'by the pudeur' of those reviewers who had praised the book but had avoided mentioning its real target. He wished to translate* Animal Farm, *not for the benefit of Russian émigrés, but for Russians abroad who could read the truth about their country only when outside it. He asked Orwell whether he had severed his connection with Tribune; he missed his articles. His own book, on Soviet literature, was soon to be published in French with a special preface emphasising the fact that there was no freedom of expression in the Soviet Union.*

To Gleb Struve*

1 September 1945
27B Canonbury Square
Islington N 1

Dear Mr Struve,

Many thanks for your letter of August 28th.

I will keep in mind your suggestion about translating *Animal Farm*, and naturally, if it could be in any way arranged, I should be highly honoured if it were you who made the translation. The thing is that I don't know what the procedure is. Are books in Russian published in this country, ie. from non-official sources? At about the same time as your letter a Pole wrote wanting to do the book into Polish. I can't, of course, encourage him to do so unless I can see a way of getting the book into print and recompensing him for his work, and ditto with yourself. If there is any way of arranging this that would allow a reasonable fee to the translators, I would be most happy to do it, as naturally I am anxious that the book should find its way into other languages. If translations into the Slav languages were made, I shouldn't want any money out of them myself.[1]

No, I haven't severed connection with *Tribune*, though I have stopped editing for them. I was away in France and Germany between February and May, and my affairs have been disorganised in other ways which obliged me to cut down my journalistic work for some time. However, I am going to start a weekly column again in *Tribune* in October, but not under the old title.

I am glad your book should be° translated into French. My impression in France was that the Soviet mythos is less strong there than in England, in spite of the big Communist party.

I am leaving London shortly for a holiday, but shall be back about the 25th. I would like to meet you if you are in London any time. My phone number is CAN 3751.

Yours sincerely
George Orwell

[XVII, 2737, pp. 274–5; typewritten]

1. Gleb Struve did translate *Animal Farm* into Russian, in conjunction with M. Kriger, as *Skotskii Khutor*. It first appeared as a serial in *Possev* (Frankfurt-am-Main), Nos. 7–25, 1949, and then in two book versions, one on ordinary paper for distribution in Western Europe and one on thin paper for distribution behind the Iron Curtain. Orwell's practice was never to benefit from his work distributed in Communist-dominated countries.

To Kay Dick*

26 September 1945
27B Canonbury Square
Islington N 1

Dear Kay,

I was very glad to get your letter because I had been trying to get in touch
with you. When I rang up *John o' London*°¹ they just said you had left, and I
had lost your home address.

I simply haven't any ideas for a story at this moment, and I don't want to
force one. Later on I don't know. I did one time contemplate a story about a
man who got so fed up with the weeds in his garden that he decided to have
a garden just of weeds, as they seem easier to grow. Then of course as soon
as he started to do this he would find the garden being overwhelmed with
flowers and vegetables which came up of their own accord. But I never got
round to writing it.

I note that you will be back in London about the 4th and will get in touch
with you after that. I'll try and not lose your address this time. I wish you
would come round here some time and see my little boy, who is now aged
nearly 17 months. If you come from Hampstead you have to go to the Angel
and then take a bus, or if you come from the City you come on the 4 bus to
Highbury Corner. I am almost always at home because I don't go to an office
now. The child goes to bed about 6 and after that I have high tea about 7.

You may be interested to hear that poor old Wodehouse was most
pathetically pleased about the article in the *Windmill*. I met him in Paris and
afterwards heard from him once or twice.

Looking forward to seeing you,

Yours
George Orwell

[XVII, 2754, p. 290; typewritten]

1.   *John O' London's Weekly* was a popular literary journal founded in 1919.

To Leonard Moore*

29 November 1945
27B Canonbury Square
London N 1

Dear Mr Moore,

I have just heard from Erval of Nagel Paris. He says that the contract you drew up for *Animal Farm* provides for publication in not less than a year, and says that this is an impossible condition. The main reason he gives is that it is not usual in France to publish two books by a foreign writer within 18 or 20 months of one another. *Burmese Days* is supposed to appear about February, so *Animal Farm* would clash with it if published in 1946. He also hints that from a political point of view this may not be a happy moment for producing a book like *Animal Farm* and says Nagel Paris would like to be able to judge the right moment. I fancy the second objection is the real one, as they are so short of books of any kind in France at present that the first consideration would not be likely to carry much weight.

I am going to tell him that I leave the matter in your hands. The point is that we don't want the publication of *A.F.* put off for 18–20 months if it is at all avoidable. I have no doubt that *now* such a book would be likely to get a hostile reception in France, but it would in any case be a question of publishing it some time late in 1946, by which time pro-Russian feeling may have worn thin as it seems to be doing here. I don't fancy the book would be suppressed while Malraux has the Ministry of Information. I met him when in Paris and found him very friendly, and he is far from being pro-Communist in his views. Could we at need take it to another French publisher? The Fontaine people asked for it, you may remember. How does the contract stand with Nagel? Have they an option on all my books? I should be glad to hear what you are doing about this.

I had to make a new will when my wife died, and I am just having it put into proper legal form. It is not that there is likely to be much to leave, but I must think of copyrights and reprints. I am naming Christy & Moore as my literary agents and Sir Richard Rees as my literary executor, and I am leaving it to him to sort out whatever unpublished or reprintable material I may leave behind and decide what is worth preserving. I am also leaving records of anything I publish in periodicals, as there might at any given moment be a good deal that was worth salvaging for some kind of reprint. It is just as well to get all this cleared up, what with atomic bombs etc.

Yours sincerely
Eric Blair

[XVII, 2806, pp. 401–2; typewritten]

To Michael Sayers

11 December 1945
27B Canonbury Square
London N 1

Dear Michael,

Please forgive delay in answering. I've been rather overwhelmed since I saw you.

I'd love to meet again, but I haven't many spare dates before Christmas. Dates I could manage would be Monday 17th or Friday 21st, for dinner either day. I can't arrange any lunch times at present, because I'm in the throes of getting a secretary[1], and when she starts I want to see how the time works out.

I don't think I could fairly be described as Russophobe. I am against all dictatorships and I think the Russian myth has done frightful harm to the leftwing movement in Britain and elsewhere, and that it is above all necessary to make people see the Russian regime for what it is (ie. what I think it is). But I thought all this as early as 1932 or thereabouts and always said so fairly freely. I have no wish to interfere with the Soviet regime even if I could. I merely don't want its methods and habits of thought imitated here, and that involves fighting against the Russianisers in this country. The danger as I see it is not our being conquered by Russia, which might happen but depends chiefly on geography. The danger is that some native form of totalitarianism will be developed here, and people like Laski, Pritt, Zilliacus, the *News Chronicle* and all the rest of them seem to me to be simply preparing the way for this. You might be interested in the articles I wrote for the first two numbers of *Polemic*.[2]

Looking forward to seeing you.

Yours
George

P.S. Nearly everyone calls me George now though I've never changed my name.[3]

1. Miss Siriol Hugh-Jones (see XVII, afternote to 2689, pp. 199–200).
2. 'Notes on Nationalism', *Polemic* 1, October 1945 (XVII, 2668, pp. 141–57) and 'The Prevention of Literature', *Polemic* 2, January 1946 (XVII, 2792, pp. 369–81). Orwell records payment for the former of £25 on 15 May 1945 and of £26 5s on 12 November 1945. 'The Prevention of Literature' was translated and published in French, Dutch, Italian and Finnish journals.
3. This important letter was one of two addressed to Michael Sayers discovered as this volume was in the press. The editor is extremely grateful to Michael Sayers (now aged 98 and living in New York) and his sons, Sean and Peter, for permission

to publish it. In his first letter of 29 November 1945, Orwell expresses pleasure in hearing from Mr Sayers and suggests meeting over lunch. Sayers, Rayner Heppenstall and Orwell had shared a flat in 1935 (see letter to Heppenstall, **24.9.35**, n. 1).

To G. H. Bantock

Late 1945–early 1946

These extracts are from a letter Orwell wrote to G. H. Bantock (1914–), who was then doing research for his L.H. Myers: A Critical Study, *published in 1956. Myers had died in 1944. (See **19.2.46**, n. 1).*

I was staying with him when war broke out. He spoke with the utmost bitterness of the British ruling class and said that he considered that many of them were actually treacherous in their attitude towards Germany. He said, speaking from his knowledge of them, that the rich were in general very class-conscious and well aware that their interests coincided with the interests of the rich in other countries, and that consequently they had no patriotism—'not even *their* kind of patriotism,' he added. He made an exception of Winston Churchill. . . .

. . . I didn't see Leo very frequently during the war. I was in London and he was generally in the country. The last time I saw him was at John Morris's flat.[1] We got into the usual argument about Russia and totalitarianism, Morris taking my side. I said something about freedom and Leo, who had got up to get some more whisky, said almost vehemently, 'I don't believe in freedom.' (NB. I think his exact words were 'I don't believe in liberty.') I said, 'All progress comes through heretics,' and Leo promptly agreed with me. It struck me then, not for the first time, that there was a contradiction in his ideas which he had not resolved. His instincts were those of a Liberal but he felt it his duty to support the USSR and therefore to repudiate Liberalism. I think part of his uncertainty was due to his having inherited a large income. Undoubtedly in a way he was ashamed of this. He lived fairly simply and gave his money away with both hands, but he could not help feeling that he was a person who enjoyed unjustified privileges. I think he felt that because of this he had no right to criticise Russia. Russia was the only country where private ownership had been abolished, and any hostile criticism might be prompted by an unconscious desire to protect his own possessions. This may be a wrong diagnosis, but that is the impression I derived. It was certainly not natural for such a sweet-natured and open-minded man to approve of a regime where freedom of thought was suppressed.

[XVII, 2825, p. 456; typewritten]

1. John Morris was one of Orwell's colleagues at the BBC. Their relations were rather sour. For an unfavourable account of Orwell by Morris, see his 'Some Are More Equal than Others,' *Penguin New Writing*, No. 40 (1950); as 'That Curiously Crucified Expression', in *Orwell Remembered*, pp. 171–76, and Crick's comments thereon, pp. 419–20.

Jura

1946 and 1947

Now that *Animal Farm* is seen as one of the greatest books of the twentieth century, it is remarkable how difficult it was to get it published in England and in the USA. There were simple physical problems in England – paper was in very short supply – but other forces conspired to ensure that Orwell became so desperate over rejections that he considered publishing the book himself. T. S. Eliot, for Faber & Faber, opined on behalf of the directors (of which he was one) that they had 'no conviction . . . that this is the right point of view from which to criticise the political situation at the present time' and later, 'your pigs are far more intelligent than the other animals . . . so that what was needed . . . was not more communism but more public-spirited pigs'. Warburg was willing but had no paper and when he eventually secured some could only initially print 4,500 copies. No US publisher saw the book's merits – there was no market, one publisher said, for animal stories – but eventually Harcourt, Brace took the risk and on 26 August 1946 published 50,000 copies. Then as a Book of the Month Club edition there were print runs of 430,000 and 110,000 and Orwell was suddenly earning major royalties: his first advance was $37,500. Foreign versions proliferated (although Orwell never took royalties from oppressed peoples), and sometimes there were comic side-effects. Thus, the French translation was to be *Union des Republiques Socialistes Animales – URSA,* The Bear. Because that might offend Communists, it was changed to *Les Animaux Partout!;* Napoleon became César. Misunderstanding abounded. Orwell subtitled his book, *A Fairy Story.* Only British and Telugu versions in Orwell's lifetime included this description. It was never acceptable in the USA. Yet one of the origins of *Animal Farm* is Beatrix Potter's *Pigling Bland,* a favourite of Orwell's and Jacintha Buddicom's childhood.

Orwell was still busy writing and this period saw the publication of 'The Prevention of Literature', 'Decline of English Murder', 'Politics and the English Language' (one of his most important essays), the delightful 'Some Thoughts on the Common Toad', 'Why I Write', 'Politics vs Literature', and 'How the Poor Die' (looking back to his time in a hospital in Paris in March 1929). He also wrote three radio plays: 'The Voyage of the *Beagle*', 'Little Red Riding Hood' for *Children's Hour*, and his own adaptation of *Animal Farm.*

From 23 May to 13 October 1946 Orwell rented Barnhill, Jura and started writing *Nineteen Eighty-Four*, completing about fifty pages that year. He was at Barnhill from 11 April to 20 December 1947 and although he was ill from time to time, it was also a very happy period. He cultivated his land, walked, went fishing, and played with Richard. Despite wishing to get on with *Nineteen Eighty-Four*, he found time to write 'Such, Such Were the Joys', which he sent to Warburg but which could not be published until after his death for fear of libel charges.

On 3 May 1946 his older sister, Marjorie, died and he travelled south to attend her funeral. His younger sister, Avril, came to share his life at Barnhill (see her letter, **1.7.46**), and he gave up The Stores in September 1947. By October he had become so ill he had to work in bed, and by the end of the year 'extensive' TB (see **23.12.47**) had been diagnosed and he left Jura for Hairmyres Hospital in East Kilbride, near Glasgow.

From Orwell's letter to his mother, 24 March 1912

To Dwight Macdonald*

3 January 1946
27 B Canonbury Square
Islington N 1

Dear Dwight,

Many thanks for your letter of December 31st. I'm so glad you read *Animal Farm* and liked it.[1] I asked Warburg to send you a copy, but knowing how desperately short he was of copies of the first edition, I wasn't sure whether you would get one. Neither he nor I now have a copy of that edition. A month or two back the Queen sent to Warburg's for a copy (this doesn't mean anything politically: her literary adviser is Osbert Sitwell* who would probably advise her to read a book of that type), and as there wasn't one left the Royal Messenger had to go down to the Anarchist bookshop run by George Woodcock*, which strikes me as mildly comic. However now a second edition of 10 thousand has come out, also a lot of translations are being done. I have just fixed up to have it done in the USA by a firm named Harcourt & Brace who I believe are good publishers. I had a lot of difficulty to place it in the USA. The Dial Press who had been pestering me for some time for a book rejected it on the ground that 'the American public is not interested in animals' (or words to that effect.) I think it will get a bit of pre-publicity in the USA as *Time* rang up saying they were going to review it and asking me for the usual particulars. I also had an awful fight to get it into print over here. No one except Warburg would look at it, and W. had to hold it up for a year for lack of paper. Even as it is he has only been able to print about half as many copies as he could have sold. Even the M[inistry] O[f] I[information] horned in and tried to keep it out of print. The comic thing is that after all this fuss the book got almost no hostile reception when it came out. The fact is people are fed up with this Russian nonsense and it's just a question of who is first to say 'The Emperor has no clothes on.'[2]

I feel very guilty that I still haven't done you that article on the 'comics.' The thing is that I am inconceivably busy. I have to do on average 4 articles a week and have hardly any energy left over for serious work. However I have roughly sketched out an article which I shall do *some* time. I am going to call it 'An American Reverie' and in it I shall contrast these papers with the American books and papers which I, like most people about my age, was partly brought up on.[3] I noticed with interest that the G.Is in Germany were mostly reading this kind of stuff, which seems to be aimed at children and adults indifferently.

I have another book coming out in the USA shortly, a book of reprinted articles, and I have included that one on 'Miss Blandish' which you printed. I'm afraid I didn't ask your permission, but I didn't suppose you'd mind. I have made the usual acknowledgements.

Did you see *Polemic*, the new paper Humphrey Slater* has started? I dare say it didn't get to you as they only did 3000 of the first number. The second number will be 5000 and then they hope to work up to 8000, but they can only become a monthly by stealth. One is not allowed to start new periodicals, but you can get hold of a little paper if you call yourself a publisher, and you have to start off by pretending that what you are publishing is a book or pamphlet. The first number was rather dull and very badly got-up, but I have great hopes of it because we have great need of some paper in which one can do long and serious literary-political articles.

David Martin[4] is over in Canada and was going to look you up if he is in New York. He has great schemes for starting an international review in several languages. Arthur Koestler* is also very anxious to start something like what the League for the Rights of Man used to be before it was stalinised. No doubt you will be hearing from him about this.

All the best and thanks for writing.

Yours
Geo. Orwell

[XVIII, 2839, pp. 11–13; typewritten]

1.   Macdonald had written to Orwell on 31 December 1945: '"Animal Farm" . . . is absolutely superb. The transposition of the Russian experience into farm equivalents is done with perfect taste and skill, so that what might have been simply a witty burlesque becomes something more—really a tragedy. The pathos of the Russian degeneration comes out more strongly in your fairy tale than in anything I've read in a long time. The ending is not a letdown, as I should have thought it would have had to be, but is instead one more triumph of inventiveness. Congratulations on a beautifully done piece of writing.' He asked if the book were to be published in America; he thought two or three hundred copies could be sold to readers of *Politics*.

2.   Macdonald reprinted the section of Orwell's letter from 'A month or two back' to 'has no clothes on' in *Politics*, March 1946, and then continued: 'What struck me about *Animal Farm*, in addition to the literary tact with which it is done so that

it never becomes either whimsical or boringly tendentious, was that I had rarely been made so aware of the pathos of the whole Russian experience. This fairy tale about animals, whose mood is reflective rather than indignant, conveys more of the terrible human meaning of Stalinism than any of the many serious books on the subject, with one or two exceptions.'

3. 'An American Reverie' was not published and no manuscript has been traced.
4. David Martin (1914–) was a Canadian airman whom Orwell befriended.

To Arthur Koestler*

10 January 1946
27B Canonbury Square
Islington N 1

Dear Arthur,

I saw Barbara Ward[1] and Tom Hopkinson[2] today and told them about our project. They were both a little timid, chiefly I think because they realise that an organisation of this type would in practice be anti-Russian, or would be compelled to become anti-Russian, and they are going through an acute phase of anti-Americanism. However they are anxious to hear more and certainly are not hostile to the idea. I said the next step would be to show them copies of the draft manifesto, or whatever it is, when drawn up. I wonder if you have seen Bertrand Russell, and if so, what he said. I have no doubt these two would help to the extent of passing our ideas on to others, but at some stage it might be more useful to contact Hulton[3] personally, which I could do. I haven't found out anything significant about the League for the Rights of Man. No one seems to have much about it in their files. All I can discover is that it is still in existence in France, and that it did exist in Germany up to Hitler, so it must have been an international organisation. There is something about it in Wells's *Crux Ansata*[4] (which I can't get hold of), so it is possible that it drew up the Declaration of the Rights of Man which Wells is always burbling about. But I am certain that some years before the war it had become a Stalinist organisation, as I distinctly remember that it refused to intervene in favour of the Trotskyists in Spain: nor so far as I remember did it do anything about the Moscow trials. But one ought to verify all this.

I hope you are all well. I am very busy as usual. I had lunch with Negrín[5] the other day, but couldn't get much information out of him. I never manage to see him quite alone. But I still feel fairly sure that he is *not* the Russians' man, as he was credited with being during the civil war. However I don't suppose it makes much difference, as I am afraid there is not much chance of Negrín's lot getting back when Franco moves out. I am also having lunch with Beaverbrook next week. If I get a chance to speak to him on equal terms at all I shall ask him about Stalin, whom after all he has seen at close quarters a number of times.

The French publisher who had signed a contract to translate *Animal Farm* has got cold feet and says it is impossible 'for political reasons.' It's really sad to think a thing like that happening in France, of all countries in the world. However I dare say one of the others will risk it. Did I tell you I had fixed an American edition?

The book of essays is printing and they say they can't make alterations in the text, but we are going to put in an erratum slip, at any rate about the German-English business.[6]

Please give my love to Mamaine.[7] Richard is very well. Celia came to tea on Tuesday and saw him have his bath.

Yours
George

P.S. I don't think I ever thanked you for our stay. I have a sort of inhibition about that, because as a child I was taught to say 'Thank you for having me' after a party, and it seemed to me such an awful phrase.

[XVIII, 2852, pp. 27–9; typewritten]

1. Barbara Ward (1914–81; DBE, 1974; Baroness Jackson of Lodsworth, 1976, economist and writer on politics; assistant editor *The Economist*, 1939–57. A Governor of the BBC, 1946–50. She was known for her concerns for individual freedom and civil rights.

2. Tom Hopkinson (1905–90; Kt. 1978), author, editor, and journalist. He was associated especially with *Picture Post* which he helped launch and edited 1940–50. He taught journalism at British and American universities, 1967–75 and wrote a British Council pamphlet on Orwell (1953). Of his two biographies, *Of This Our Time* (1982) is concerned with the period when Orwell was working.

3. Edward Hulton (1906–1988; Kt., 1957), lawyer, magazine publisher of liberal views, proprietor of *Picture Post* at this time. His *The New Age* was published in 1943 and reviewed by Orwell in the *Observer*, 15 August 1943 (XV, 2237, 201–2).

4. *Crux Ansata: An Indictment of the Roman Catholic Church* (Penguin Special, 1943). Orwell had got the wrong Penguin Special, however. In May 1940 Penguin Books published H.G. Wells's *The Rights of Man, Or, What Are We Fighting For?* Chapter X discussed a Complément à la Déclaration des Droits de l'homme, which had been passed by a congress of the Ligue des Droits de l'homme at Dijon in July 1936. Wells said this document was 'more plainly feminist and less simply equalitarian in sexual matters' than what was proposed in his book, and it made 'a distinction between "travail" and "loisirs" which we do not recognise'. He then gave the text.

5. Dr Juan Negrín (1889–1956), Socialist Prime Minister of Spain from September 1936 for much of the civil war. He went to France in 1939 and set up a Spanish government in exile; he resigned from its premiership in 1945 in the hope of uniting all exiles. (See Thomas, pp. 949–50.)
6. To Orwell's essay on Koestler.
7. Mamaine Koestler (née Paget, 1916–54), Koestler's wife and twin sister of Celia Kirwan.*

To Geoffrey Gorer*

22 January 1946
27B Canonbury Square
Islington N 1

Dear Geoffrey,

It was too good of you to send all those things. They were greatly appreciated here, especially by Richard, who had a big whack of the plum pudding and seemed none the worse afterwards. I was amused by the 'this is an unsolicited gift' on the outside, which I suppose is a formula necessitated by people over here writing cadging letters. I had quite a good Christmas. I went to Wales to stay with Arthur Koestler for a few days while the nurse went away with her own kid.[1] Richard went out to a lot of parties where he was the only child, and except for occasionally dirtying his trousers (I still can't get him house-trained) behaved with great aplomb and sat up to table in an ordinary chair. But of course the travelling just before and just after Xmas was fearful. To leave London you had to queue up 2 hours before the train left, and coming back the train was 4 hours late and landed one in town about half an hour after the undergrounds had stopped. However, fortunately Richard enjoys travelling, and I think when you are carrying a child you have a slightly better chance with porters.

It is foully cold here and the fuel shortage is just at its worst. We only got a ton of coal for the whole winter and it's almost impossible to get logs. Meanwhile the gas pressure is so low that one can hardly get a gas fire to light, and one can only get about 1½ gallons of lamp oil a week. What I do is to light the fires with a little of the coal I have left and keep them damped down all day with blocks of wet peat of which I happen to have a few. It's so much easier in the country where if you're absolutely forced to you can go out and scrounge firewood. Otherwise things aren't bad here. Food is about the same as ever. Yesterday I took Sillone[2] and his wife out to dinner. They were only here for a few days and were still in a state of being astonished at the food, all the English in Rome having told them we were starving over here. I am always ashamed when people come to England for the first time like that, and say to them 'Don't think England is like this in peacetime,' but the S.s. said that for cleanness and state of repair London was a dream compared with Rome. They said that in Rome you could get anything if you had enough money, but an overcoat, for instance, cost the equivalent of £120.

Didn't you tell me you met Dennis Collings* in Malaya? He was an anthropologist, and I think latterly was curator of the museum in Singapore. I used to know him very well. He got home recently and I heard from him the other day. He had been captured in Java and appeared not to have had absolutely too bad a time, having been a camp interpreter.

I forget if I'd started doing weekly articles for the *Evening Standard* before you left. In spite of—by my standards—enormous fees it doesn't do me much good financially, because one extra article a week just turns the scale and makes it necessary for me to have a secretary.[3] However, even with the extra article she takes a certain amount of drudgery off me, and I am using her to arrange and catalogue my collection of pamphlets.[4] I find that up to date I have about 1200, but of course they keep on accumulating. I have definitely arranged I am going to stop doing the *Evening Standard* stuff and most other journalism in May, and take six months off to write another novel. If the Jura place can be put in order this year I shall go there, otherwise I shall take a furnished house somewhere in the country, preferably by the sea, but anyway somewhere I can't be telephoned to. My book of reprints ought to be out soon and the American title is *Dickens, Dali and others*. Scribners[5] are doing that one, and Harcourt Brace (I think that is the name) are doing *Animal Farm*. I don't fancy that one will sell in the USA, though of course it *might* sell heavily, as with most books in America it seems you either sell 100,000 copies or nothing. I have arranged a lot of translations of *A.F.*, but the French publishers who signed the first contract have already got cold feet and say it's impossible at present 'for political reasons.' I think it's sad to think of a thing like that happening, in France of all countries.

I must knock off now as this is Susan's day off and I have to go out and do the shopping. Richard has been trying to help me with the typing of this letter. He is now 20 months old and weighs about 32 lbs. He still doesn't talk but is very alert in other ways and extremely active, in fact you can't keep him still for a moment. Three times in the last month he got all the radiants out of the gas fire and smashed them to bits, which is a nuisance because they're very difficult to buy. I think he could talk if he wanted to, but he hardly needs to as he can usually get what he wants by making an inarticulate noise and pointing—at least he does not exactly point but throws both arms out in the general direction of the thing he wants.

Let me hear how you are getting on and how things are in the USA. I hear they hate us more than ever now.

Yours
George

[XVIII, 2870, pp. 52–4; typewritten]

1. Susan Watson (1918–2001), was Orwell's housekeeper from early summer 1945 to autumn 1946 caring also for Richard. She had married a Cambridge University mathematician but they were in the process of being divorced. She had a seven-year-old daughter, Sally, who was at boarding school. (See her memoir in *Orwell Remembered*, pp. 217–25 and *Remembering Orwell*, pp. 156–62 and 175–78.)
2. Ignazio Silone (Secondo Tranquilli) (1900–1978), author and politician, was one of the founders of the Italian Communist Party but by the time of his exile in Switzerland after Mussolini's rise to power he had distanced himself from its aims but remained strongly anti-Fascist. He was at this time editor of *Avanti*, the organ of the Italian Socialist Party, but he resigned in July 1946. Orwell drama-tised his story, 'The Fox', for the BBC, broadcast 9 September 1943 (XV, 2270, pp. 230–42).
3. Siriol Hugh-Jones.
4. From 1935 onwards, Orwell had collected pamphlets representing minority views. These he left to the British Museum, and they are now in the British Library.
5. A curious error: *Critical Essays* was published in New York by Reynal & Hitchcock.

To Dorothy Plowman*

19 February 1946
27B Canonbury Square
Islington N1

Dear Dorothy,

I enclose cheque for £150 as a first instalment of repayment of that £300 anonymously lent to me in 1938[1]—it's a terribly long time afterwards to start repaying, but until this year I was really unable to. Just latterly I have started making money. I got your address from Richard Rees.* It's a long time since I heard from you, and I do not think I even wrote to you when Max died. One does not know what to say when these things happen. I reviewed Max's book of letters for the *Manchester Evening News*, which you may have seen.[2] My book *Animal Farm* has sold quite well, and the new one, which is merely a book of reprints,[3] also seems to be doing well. It was a terrible shame that Eileen didn't live to see the publication of *Animal Farm*, which she was particularly fond of and even helped in the planning of. I suppose you know I was in France when she died. It was a terribly cruel and stupid thing to happen. No doubt you know I have a little boy named Richard whom we adopted in 1944 when he was 3 weeks old. He was ten months old when Eileen died and is 21 months old now. Her last letter to me was to tell me he was beginning to crawl. Now he has grown into a big strong child and is very active and intelligent, although he doesn't talk yet. I have a nurse-housekeeper who looks after him and me, and luckily we are able to get a char as well. He is so full of beans that it is getting difficult to keep him in the flat, and I am looking forward to getting him out of London for the whole summer. I am not quite certain where we are going. I am supposed to be the tenant of a cottage in the Hebrides, but it's possible they won't have it in living order this year, in which case I shall probably take him to the east coast somewhere. I want a place where he can run in and out of the house all day with no fear of traffic. I am anxious to get out of London for my own sake as well, because I am constantly smothered under journalism—at present I am doing 4 articles every week—and I want to write another book which is impossible unless I can get 6 months quiet. I have been in London almost the whole of the war. Eileen was working for 4 or 5 years in government offices, generally for 10 hours a day or more, and it was partly overwork that killed her. I shall probably go back to the country in 1947, but at present it's impossible to get hold of unfurnished houses and so I daren't let go of my flat.

Richard Rees* is living in Chelsea and has kept his beard, although demobilised. Rayner Heppenstall* has a job in the BBC and seems to be quite liking it. It's funny that you should be at Royston, so near where we used to live.[4] I have got to go down some time to the cottage I still have there, to sort out the furniture and books, but I have been putting it off because last time I was there it was with Eileen and it upsets me to go there. What has become of Piers?[5] I hope all goes well with you both.

Yours
Eric Blair

[XVIII, 2903, pp. 115–6; typewritten]

1. L.H. Myers had, unknown to Orwell, financed his and Eileen's stay in Morocco. The Plowmans acted as intermediaries.
2. He did write at the time of Max's death (see **20.6.41**). Orwell reviewed *Bridge into the Future: Letters of Max Plowman* in the *Manchester Evening News*, 7 December 1944, (XVI, 2589, pp. 492–4).
3. *Critical Essays.*

4.   Wallington (where Orwell rented a cottage).
5.   The Plowmans' son.

To Arthur Koestler*

This letter lacks a strip torn off down its right-hand side. The missing words, conjecturally reconstructed, are given here in square brackets.

5 March 1946
27B Canonbury Square
Islington N 1

Dear Arthur,

It's funny you should send me Czapsky's°¹ pamphlet, which I have been trying for some time [to get] someone to translate and publish. Warburg wouldn't do it b[ecause] he said it was an awkward length, and latterly I gave it t[o the] Anarchist (Freedom Press) group. I don't know what decisi[on they've] come to. I met Czapsky° in Paris and had lunch with him. T[here is] no doubt that he is not only authentic but a rather exce[ptional] person, though whether he is any good as a painter I do[n't know. He] is the person who made to me a remark which I may or ma[y not have] retailed to you—I forget. After telling me something [of the priv-]ation and his sufferings in the concentration camp, he [said some-]thing like this: 'For a while in 1941 and 1942 there w[as much] defeatism in Russia, and in fact it was touch and go [whether the] Germans won the war. Do you know what saved Russia at [that time? In] my opinion it was the personal character of Stalin—I [put it down to] the greatness of Stalin. He stayed in Moscow when the [Germans nearly] took it, and his courage was what saved the situation.² [Considering] what he had been through, this seemed to me sufficie[nt proof of] Czapsky's reliability. I told him I would do what I [could about the] pamphlet here. If the Freedom Press people fall thro[ugh, what about] Arthur Ballard, who is now beginning to publish pamp[hlets? He might] take it.³ Do you want this copy back? The Anarchists [have mine] and it's a rather treasured item of my collection.

The Observer say, will you write for them some [reviews. I am] scouting round for people to do the main review, wh[ich must be done] by the same person every week—I do it every other [week and will] be stopping at the end of April. Apart from the mai[n review I] intend quite soon to start having essays of about 8[00 words on the] middle page under the main article. You would get a [good fee, I] think, for either of these jobs.

I'd love to come up to your place, but I dou[bt whether I can] get away. I have such a lot to do winding everythi[ng up, arranging for] the furniture to be sent and all sorts of things t[o do, almost like] stocking up a ship for an arctic voyage. Love to Ma[maine.]

Yours
George

[XVIII, 2919, pp. 136–8; typewritten]

1. Joseph Czapski (1896–1993), wrote to Orwell on 11 December 1945 at the suggestion of 'mon ami Poznanski' because he thought Orwell could find an English publisher for his pamphlet (a quite sizeable booklet) *Souvenirs de Starobielsk*. This had originally been published in Polish as *Wspomnienia Starobielskia* in 1944; Italian and French translations followed in 1945. Czapski, a Polish painter and author, but born in Prague, studied in St Petersburg, 1912–17, and witnessed the Russian Revolution; in 1920 he returned to Poland and from 1924 to 1931 he studied and worked as a painter in Paris, being shown there and in Geneva. He fought with the 8th Polish Lancers against the Germans and then the Russians in 1939, and was taken prisoner by the Soviets. He was one of 78 of nearly 4,000 prisoners at Starobielsk prison camp transferred to a prison camp at Gryazovets. He spent twenty-three months in these camps. When the Germans invaded Russia, he was allowed to join other Polish prisoners, many of whom had suffered terrible privations, in a Polish Army under General Anders to fight the Germans. It is known that some 15,700 Poles were murdered by the Russians at Katyn and other camps (Czapski's figures, *Souvenirs de Starobielsk*, 1945, p. 18). A further 7,000 from camps in the Komi Republic were packed into barges which were deliberately sunk in the White Sea, causing their deaths by drowning (*The Inhuman Land*, pp. 35–36). Czapski remained in Paris after the war and was one of the founders of the influential Polish cultural monthly journal, *Kultura*.

2. See **17.3.45** for the change to *Animal Farm* to reflect Stalin's staying in Moscow.

3. Orwell and Koestler were unsuccessful. Despite the booklet's having what Czapski called 'une certaine actualité' in the light of what was being presented in evidence at the Nuremberg Trial of War Criminals, *Souvenirs de Starobielsk* was not then translated into English and has never been published in Britain.

To Anne Popham*

15 March 1946
27B Canonbury Square
Islington N 1

Dear Andie,

I call you that because it is what I have heard other people call you—I don't know what you like to be called, really. It must be nearly a fortnight since you left. I would have written earlier, but I have been ill all this week with something called gastritis. I think a word like that tells you a lot about the medical profession. If you have a pain in your belly it is called gastritis, if it is in your head I suppose it would be called cephalitis and so on. Any way it is quite an unpleasant thing to have, but I am somewhat better and got up for the first time today. Richard has been quite offensively well and prancing all over the place. I have at last got one of those pens that don't have any ink in them,[1] so I have been able to suppress the inkpot, which he had got hold of three times in the last week or two. He has got a new waterproof cape in which he looks quite dashing, and when we go away for the summer he is going to have his first pair of boots.

I wonder what sort of journey you had and how bearable it is in Germany now. I think in that sort of life a lot depends on having a vehicle of your own and being able to get away from the others a bit. Write and tell me what it is like and any bits of gossip you hear about what the Germans are saying about us now. I think you said you would be back in England in July. I'm not sure where we shall be by then—I intend to get out of London for the whole summer, but we haven't yet fixed where. I have definitely arranged to drop all journalistic work for 6 months and am pining for that time to start. I've still got a few ghastly jobs, ie. outside my routine ones, hanging over my head, and being ill like this puts everything back. The rubbishy feature I was writing for the BBC got finished at last, but I now have to write a pamphlet for the British Council on English cookery. I don't know why I was such a fool as to let myself in for it—however it will be quite short so I can probably knock it off in a week.[2] After that I haven't any actual tripe to write. When I get away I am going to start on a novel. It is 6 years or so since I wrote any such thing and it will probably be an awful job to start, but I think with six clear months I could break the back of it.

I wonder if you were angry or surprised when I sort of made advances to you that night before you went away. You don't have to respond—what I mean is, I wouldn't be angry if you didn't respond. I didn't know till you told me about your young man.[3] I thought you looked lonely and unhappy, and I thought it just conceivable you might come to take an interest in me, partly because I imagined you were a little older than you are. But I fully realise that I'm not suited to someone like you who is young and pretty and can still expect to get something out of life. There isn't really anything left in my life except my work and seeing that Richard gets a good start. It is only that I feel so desperately alone sometimes. I have hundreds of friends, but no woman who takes an interest in me and can encourage me. Write and tell me what you think about all this. Of course it's absurd a person like me wanting to make love to someone of your age. I do want to, but, if you understand, I wouldn't be offended or even hurt if you simply say no. Any way, write and tell me what you feel.

I wonder if there is anything I can do for you or send you. Are there any books you want? Or any papers? Would you like to be sent *Tribune*, for instance? I should think some of your brother officers wouldn't approve of it much. Talking of books I have been able to get some of Henry Miller's books again—they seem to be reprinting them in Paris and a few copies get into this country illegally. I don't know what else of interest has appeared lately. Nearly all the books I get to review are such trash one doesn't know what to say about them. Would you like to be sent *Polemic*? The third number is supposed to appear towards the end of April, but lord knows whether it will, as there is always some mess-up about the printing. They now have some wild scheme of printing it in Eire, but then one might bump up against the censorship. Write to me soon and tell me whether there is anything you would like, and how you are getting on, and what you feel about things.

Yours
Geo. Orwell

P.S. I am not sure how to stamp this letter, but I suppose threepence is right?

[XVIII, 2931, pp. 153–4; typewritten]

1. A Biro. Orwell had first tried to buy one in February 1946. They were then quite hard to obtain and very expensive – about £3 (over half-a-week's wage for an unskilled worker). Orwell found them particularly useful because, when ill, he could write in bed. His use of a Biro can be a clue to when he wrote certain letters and documents.

2. The 'rubbishy feature' for the BBC was probably the dramatisation *The Voyage of the 'Beagle'*, broadcast 29 March 1946 (XVIII, 2953, pp. 179–201). The text of the booklet, *British Cookery*, is reproduced in XVIII, 2954, pp. 201–13. Although it was considered to be excellent it was decided not to publish it to avoid offending continental readers at a time of such stringency (though the recipes are hardly

exotic). Orwell was paid £31 10s for his script.

3.   He had been killed when serving in the RAF (Crick, p. 485).

To Arthur Koestler*

22 March 1946
27B Canonbury Square
Islington N 1

Dear Arthur,

The *Manchester Evening News* want to know whether, when I stop my review-ing for them (ie. end of April), you would like to take over my job for 6 months. I told them I didn't think it was awfully likely you would, but that I would ask you. It's rather hackwork, but it's a regular 8 guineas a week (that is what they pay me—I expect you could get a bit more out of them) for about 900 words, in which one can say more or less what one likes. The chief bore is reading the books; on the other hand one gets out of this from time to time by doing general articles or dealing with reprints which one knows already. One retains the second rights. You might let me know as soon as possible if this idea has any attraction for you, as otherwise they will have to scout round for someone else.

Love to Mamaine.

Yours
George

P.S. [*handwritten*] I've contacted Malory° Brown¹ who thinks he will probably be able to come up at Easter. I'm going to have lunch with him on April 3rd & talk it over. Meanwhile could you let me know exactly *what date* he should come up to your place?

[XVIII, 2941, pp. 164–5; typewritten with handwritten postscript]

Koestler replied on 23 March. He decided not to take on the work for the Manchester Evening News— *'for once I shall let puritanism get the upper hand over hedonism (dig)', a reference to Orwell's statement that there is 'a well-marked hedonistic strain in his writings' in the penultimate paragraph of Orwell's essay on Koestler.*

1.   Mallory Browne was then the London editor of the *Christian Science Monitor*. On 22 October 1944 he contributed 'The New Order in France' to the *Observer*.

To Arthur Koestler*

31 March 1946
27B Canonbury Square
Islington N 1

Dear Arthur,

I enclose a letter from the IRRC¹ people, about whom I wrote to you before, and a copy of their bulletin. The part of [it] about Jennie Lee* and Michael Foot² is rather vague and I am not sure what it is he wants me to do, but I hope to see Jennie Lee* tomorrow and will speak to her about it. Michael is in Teheran, I think.

I am seeing Malory° Brown on Wednesday and will tell him the Easter conference is off. Has anyone told Michael?

I think my Jura cottage is going to be ready by May and I am arranging to send my furniture up about the end of April and then, if all is well, go up there early in May. If anything falls through I shall go somewhere else, but in any case I shall leave London and do no writing or anything of the kind for two months. I feel desperately tired and jaded. Richard is very well and active but still not talking.

I have at last got hold of a book by that scientist I spoke to you of, John Baker.³ He is evidently one of the people we should circularise when we have a draft proposal ready. He could probably also be useful in telling us about other scientists who are not totalitarian-minded, which is important, because as a body they are much more subject to totalitarian habits of thought than writers, and have more popular prestige. Humphrey[Slater]* got Waddington,⁴ who is a borderline case, to do an article for *Polemic,* which I think was a good move, as it will appear in the same number as our opening volley against the *Modern Quarterly.*⁵ Unfortunately it was a very bad article.

Love to Mamaine. It is beautiful spring weather at last and daffodils out all over the place. Each winter I find it harder and harder to believe that spring will actually come.

Yours
George

[XVIII, 2955, pp.213–4; typewritten]

1.   International Rescue and Relief Committee.

2.   Michael Foot (1913–2010), politician, writer, and journalist, for much of his life on the extreme left of the Labour Party, was MP for Devonport, 1945–55; for Ebbw Vale, 1960–92 and Leader of the Labour Party (in Opposition), 1980–83. For *Trib-une* he was assistant editor, 1937–38; Managing Director, 1945–74; editor, 1948–52,

1955–60. His many books include *Guilty Men* (with Frank Owen and Peter Howard, 1940), *The Pen and the Sword* (1957), *The Politics of Paradise* (1988).

3. John Randal Baker (1900–1984), Reader in Cytology, Oxford University, 1955–67; joint editor of the *Journal of Microscopical Science*, 1946–64; Professorial Fellow, New College Oxford, 1964–67. He received the Oliver Bird Medal for researches into chemical contraception in 1958. Baker was an important influence on Orwell (see **19.3.47**).

4. Conrad Hal Waddington (1905–1975) was Buchanan Professor of Animal Genetics, University of Edinburgh. His publications include *The Scientific Attitude* (1941), and *The Ethical Animal* (1960). Orwell, while at the BBC, engaged him to broadcast talks to India.

5. The *Modern Quarterly*, founded 1938, aimed at contributing to a realistic, social revaluation of the arts and sciences, devoting special attention to studies based upon the materialistic interpretation of the universe. It lapsed during the war and was revived in December 1945, with Dr John Lewis as editor. Marxist in outlook, with many eminent scientists as contributors, it attacked, among other things, what it called 'persistent attempts to confuse moral issues', for example, Orwell's 'sophistries' in 'Notes on Nationalism' in *Polemic* (XVII, 2668, pp. 141–57), which was translated and published in French, Dutch, Italian, and Finnish journals.

To Yvonne Davet*

8 April 1946
27B Canonbury Square,
Islington, N 1

Chère Madame Davet,

I have just received your letter of the 6th. Two or three days ago I met Mademoiselle Odile Pathé, the publisher who is going to bring out *Animal Farm*. I didn't know she was in London, but she rang me up. I told her you had translated *Homage to Catalonia*, and that you had sent her the translation, but I suppose she won't be back in France until next week. She seemed to me to have a lot more courage than most publishers, and she explained that because she is in Monaco, she has less to fear[1] than the others, except for the paper. In any case *Homage to Catalonia* is a much less dangerous book than *Animal Farm*. It seems that the Communists now exert direct censorship on French publishers (I have heard they have 'prohibited' Gallimard publishing Hemingway's *For Whom the Bell Tolls*), and it's quite clear that they wouldn't let *Animal Farm* get through if they could find a way of suppressing it. If Mademoiselle Pathé has the courage to publish one book, she would have the courage to publish the other, if it seemed worth her while financially.

As for the essays, let me explain how things stand. In 1940 I published a book, *Inside the Whale*, which didn't sell very well, and shortly afterwards nearly all the copies were destroyed in the blitz. The book I've just published contains two of the original essays (there were only three), and eight others that I'd published in magazines in the last five years. One, or perhaps two, have a purely English interest. (One is on boys' weeklies, the other on comic postcards—which are after all pretty similar in France.) At the moment Nagel Paris have a copy of *Inside the Whale*—they asked for it before the publication of *Critical Essays*. I can't quite remember whether a copy of *Critical Essays* was sent to a French publisher,² but I'll ask my agent. If there was a question of translating one or the other, naturally it would be better to choose *Critical Essays*. Anyway, I'll send you a copy as soon as possible, but I haven't got one at the moment. The first edition is out of print, and the second edition hasn't come out. One could easily publish the book without the essays of purely local interest. I certainly think the essay on Dickens is worth translating.

Recently I had a letter from Victor Serge,³ who is in Mexico, and who is going to send me the manuscript of his memoirs. I hope my publisher, Warburg, will publish them.

At the end of April I'm going to leave London to spend six months in Scotland, but I'm not sure precisely when I'm going, as there will certainly be problems in sending on the furniture. My house is in the Hebrides, and I hope to be fairly quiet so that I can start a new novel. In the last few years I've been writing three articles a week, and I'm dreadfully tired. My little boy is very well. I'm sending a photograph of the two of us. It looks as if I'm giving him a good spanking, but really I'm changing his trousers.⁴ Before I go I'll send you my new address.

Très amicalement
George Orwell

[XVIII, 2963, pp. 226–8; typewritten; original in French]

1. From Communist pressure.
2. Three publishers were tried.
3. Victor Serge (pseudonym of Viktor Kibal'chiche, 1890–1947), edited *L'Anarchie*, Paris; imprisoned 1912–17 because of his political activities. He attempted to return to Russia in 1917 but was interned and only got to Russia in 1919. He worked with the International Secretariat until disillusioned following the Krondstadt incident, 1921 (see **15.12.46**, n. 3). He then worked in Berlin and Vienna for the Comintern. In 1926 returned to Russia and allied himself with Trotsky but was expelled from the Party and in 1933 internally exiled to Orenburg. He was expelled from the Soviet Union in 1936. He became Paris correspondent of the POUM during the

Spanish civil war. He settled in Mexico in 1941 where he died impoverished. His *Case of Comrade Tulayev* was published by Penguin (2004).

4. Presumably the photograph reproduced as plate 69 in *The World of George Orwell*, edited by Miriam Gross (1971).

To Inez Holden*

9 April 1946
27B Canonbury Square
Islington N 1

Dear Inez,

I'm sorry I didn't answer your earlier letter. I've been smothered under work as usual. Your second one, dated March 31st, reached me yesterday. You seem to be having quite an eventful time. I'm glad you got over your illness—I always say that being ill is part of the itinerary in a trip like that. It's due to draughts or the change of diet or something. I have wondered several times whether I detected some of your stuff in the *Observer*—or are you only collecting stuff to write when you come back? I thought you'd probably notice more about what people were eating and so on than the average observer, and I thought perhaps you had done part of 'Peregrine'[1] one week.

Not a great deal has happened here. I expect to go away about the end of the month, but there's still a lot of nightmares about repairs to the house and sending furniture. It's unfortunate that Susan has been ill and may have to go into hospital. If she does I shall have to park Richard at a nursery school for a couple of months, because I can't manage him singlehanded for that length of time and anyway I want to go up and get the Jura house livable as soon as the repairs are done. I'm going down to Wallington tomorrow to sort out the furniture and books, and then I hope Pickford's man will come along and tell me when he can remove the stuff. I've also got to buy a lot of stuff. This kind of thing is a complete nightmare to me, but I've no one I can shove it on to.

It's been quite nice spring weather here, on and off. Richard is extremely well, but is still not talking. He learned to blow a whistle lately, which was rather an affliction for a few days, however luckily he got tired of it. *Animal Farm* is being translated into 9 languages altogether and one or two of the translations have arrived. It is due to come out in the USA soon. I met the person who is publishing it in France, who turns out to be a woman who has her establishment in Monte Carlo, where she is a little safer than she would be in France. It seems the unofficial censorship in France itself is awful now.

I'll write and tell Karl[2] about his parents. I haven't seen him since you left. He was very down in the mouth about not being allowed to go back to

Germany—at the same time, of course, other people who don't want to go back to their own countries are being made to. You didn't say when you are coming back. As soon as we have the Jura house running I hope you'll come and stay. I think it could be very nice there in the summer once the house is in proper trim.

With love
George

P.S. Isn't it strange, we got a vacuum cleaner recently and Richard is terrified of it. He starts yelling as soon as he sees it, even before it is turned on, and in fact we can't use it when he is in the house. My theory is that he gets some kind of vibration from it which gives him an electric shock.

[XVIII, 2965, pp. 230–1; typewritten]

1. A gossip column.
2. Karl Schnetzler (1906–), German electrical research engineer. He worked in England, 1935–39, but was then interned (though a refugee) until 1943. He was naturalised British in 1948. He accompanied Eileen when she visited Orwell at Preston Hall Sanatorium. None of his letters to Orwell or those from Orwell to him have been traced. Orwell attempted, through Michael Foot, M P, to again permission for him to visit Germany to see his parents but this was unsuccessful. (See also **1.3.39**, n. 1.)

To Philip Rahv*

9 April 1946
27 B Canonbury Square
Islington N 1

Dear Rahv,

Thanks for your letter of April 4th. I note that you want the next 'London Letter' by about May 20th, and I will despatch it early in May. I am going to drop all my journalistic work here and go to Scotland for 6 months as from about the end of April, but I haven't definitely fixed the date of leaving yet. As soon as I do I'll send you my new address, but any way letters sent to the above would get to me.

Yes, I saw the article in *Time*,¹ which was a bit of good luck. I have no doubt the book² will be subject to some boycotting, but so far as this country is concerned I have been surprised by the unfriendly reactions it *didn't* get. It is being translated into 9 languages. The most difficult to arrange was French. One publisher signed a contract and then said it was 'impossible' for political reasons, others made similar answers—however, I have fixed it with a publisher who is in Monte Carlo and thus feels a bit safer. She is a woman, Odille Pathé, and worth keeping in mind for people who have unpopular books to translate, as she seems to have courage, which is not common in France these last few years. I have no doubt what Camus said was quite true. I am told French publishers are now 'commanded' by Aragon[3] and others not to publish undesirable books (according to my information, Hemingway's *For Whom the Bell Tolls* was one such). The Communists have no actual jurisdiction in the matter, but it would be in their power, eg., to set fire to a publisher's buildings with the connivance of the police. I don't know how long this kind of thing will go on. In England feeling has undoubtedly been growing against the C.P. In France a year ago I got the impression that hardly anyone cares a damn any longer about freedom of the press etc. The occupation seemed to me to have had a terrible crushing effect even upon people like Trotskyists: or maybe a sort of intellectual decadence had set in years before the war. The only Frenchman I met at that [time] to whom I felt I could talk freely was a man named Raimbaud, a hunchback, who was one of the editors of the little near-Trotskyist weekly *Libertés*. The queer thing is that with all this moral decay there has over the past decade or so been much more literary *talent* in France than in England, or than anywhere else, I should say.

I don't know whether you have seen *Polemic*, the new bi-monthly review. In the third number I have a long article on James Burnham which I shall reprint afterwards as a pamphlet.[4] He won't like it—however, it is what I think.

Yours
Geo. Orwell

[XVIII, 2966, pp. 231–2; typewritten]

1. The article appeared in *Time*, 4 February 1946, and was prompted by the publication of *Animal Farm* in England. Publication in the United States was more than six months later.

2. *Animal Farm.*

3. Louis Aragon (1897–1984), novelist, poet, journalist, and Communist activist, was a leading figure in the Surrealist school; see his first volume of poems, *Feu de joie* (1920), and his first novel *Le Paysan de Paris* (1926; English translation, *The Night-Walker*, 1950). He became a Communist following a visit to Russia in 1930 and he edited the Communist weekly *Les Lettres Françaises*, 1953–72.

4. 'Second Thoughts on James Burnham', *Polemic*, 3, May 1946, XVIII, 2989, pp. 268–84. As a pamphlet it was titled *James Burnham and the Managerial Revolution*, 1946.

The following letter, sent from Quakenbrück, Northern Germany, urges the need for a translation of Animal Farm *for the benefit of refugees, and particularly for those from the Ukraine, and vividly describes readings Ihor Szewczenko[1] gave in his own translation for Soviet refugees.*

Ihor Szewczenko* to Orwell

11 April 1946
c/o K. A. Jeleński, P40–OS, B.A.O.R.[2]

Dear Mr. Orwell,

About the middle of February this year I had the opportunity to read *Animal Farm*. I was immediately seized by the idea, that a translation of the tale into Ukrainian would be of great value to my countrymen.

Quite apart from the benefit it would bring to our intelligentsia, only too incidentally acquainted with modern English literary life, a condition due partly to a certain remoteness from the West, such a translation would have a broader 'moral' influence which cannot be too much stressed. It is a matter of fact, that the attitude of the Western World in many recent issues roused serious doubts among our refugees. The somewhat naïve interpretation of this attitude oscillated between two poles. For many it looked something like the famous 'tactics', a miscalculated and disastrous device, dictated subconsciously by fear. It seemed to be miscalculated, because the other side is much stronger in this sort of tactics. It was deemed disastrous, because it would lead to a disappointment on the part of the European masses, only too willing to identify the democratic principles with democratic acts.

By the others this attitude was attributed to the perfect skill with which English public opinion is influenced from outside, to the misconception of the Soviet state and institutions being to a great extent like those of the West, to the inability to penetrate a deliberately created state of confusion, caused by a lack of adequate information, or to something like this.

Whatever the roots of this alleged attitude might be, the predominance of such an opinion has had a disintegrating influence. The refugees always tend to 'lean against' and to localise their best hopes and their idea of what they consider 'moral perfection'. Such object lacking or failing to justify the expectations, purposelessness and cyni[ci]sm ensue.

This part° of our emigrants who found themselves in exile moved not purely by nationalistic considerations but by what they vaguely felt to be a search for 'human dignity' and 'liberty' were by no means consoled if some right-wing intellectual raised the so called warning voice. They were especially anxious to hear something of this sort from the Socialist quarters, to which they stood intellectually nearer. They wondered how it were possible that nobody 'knew the truth'. The task then was to prove that this assumption of the 'naïveté' was at least only partially true. Your book has solved the problem. I can judge it from my own feelings I had after having read it. I daresay the work can be savoured by an 'Eastern' reader in a degree equal to that accessible to an Englishman, the deformation a translation is bound to bring about being outweighed by the accuracy with which almost every 'traceable' sentence of the tale can be traced down to the prototype. For several occasions I translated different parts of *Animal Farm ex abrupto*. Soviet refugees were my listeners. The effect was striking. They approved of almost all of your interpretations. They were profoundly affected by such scenes as that of animals singing 'Beasts of England' on the hill. Here I saw, that in spite of their attention being primarily drawn on detecting 'concordances' between the reality they lived in and the tale, they very vividly reacted to the 'absolute' values of the book, to the tale 'types', to the underlying convictions of the author and so on. Besides, the mood of the book seems to correspond with their own actual state of mind.

For these and similar reasons I ask you for an authorisation to translate *Animal Farm* into Ukrainian, a task which is already begun.

I hear from Mr. Jeleński[3] that his mother[4] has already talked over with you the delicate question of publishing the translation in present conditions.[5] I must ask you therefore not to mention my name overmuch and to consider the whole business unofficial for the present.

Reading this kind of book one is often tempted to speculate about the 'real' opinions of the author. I myself confess to having indulged in this sort of guessing, and I have many questions to put to you, mainly related to your appreciation of certain developments in the USSR, but also many of more technical character, such as the translation of proper names. But this requires a separate letter. For the meantime I apologise for the long delay in addressing you. I was away in South Germany and your letter to Mme Jeleńska had not reached me until now.

Yours sincerely
Ihor Szewczenko

[XVIII, 2969, pp. 235–8]

1. Ihor Szewczenko was, in April 1946, commuting between Munich (where his then wife and mother-in-law, both Soviet-Ukrainian refugees, and he lived) and Quakenbrück in the British Zone of Germany, where a daily newspaper for the Second Polish, the Maczek, Division was published. Szewczenko, who was then twenty-five, had been 'found' after the war by one of its editors, André de Vincenz (a school friend from Warsaw), and, though Ukrainian, given work on

the newspaper. He was engaged to survey the British Press and paid particular attention to *Tribune* (picking out 'As I Please'). Another editor, Konstanty ('Kot') Jeleński, put him in touch, through his mother, with Orwell in order that he might ask permission to publish the Ukrainian translation of *Animal Farm*, upon which he worked every day after lunch in Quakenbrück and in the evenings in Munich.

2. B.A.O.R.: British Army of the Rhine.

3. Konstanty A. Jeleński was the son of a Polish diplomat. In April 1946 he held the rank of lieutenant. He was familiar with the English literary scene and later achieved some prominence in Paris, where he contributed to *Épreuves* and the important Polish monthly *Kultura*, which published four of Orwell's articles in Polish. The first three were translated by Teresa Jeleńska and the fourth by Teresa Skórzewska all 'with the author's authority'. Jeleński died about 1989.

4. Mme Teresa Jeleńska, Konstanty Jeleński's mother, was the intermediary who on Szewczenko's behalf broached with Orwell the possibility of the publication of a Ukrainian translation. No correspondence between her and Orwell has been traced. Mme Jeleńska made a translation into Polish of *Animal Farm* and that, with illustrations by Wojciecha Jastrzebowskiego, was published by the League of Poles Abroad, London, under the title *Folwark Zwierzecy*, in December 1946.

5. The translation into Ukrainian was published in Munich in November 1947; the translator's name was given as Ivan Cherniatync'kyi and the title as *Kolhosp Tvaryn*. It was intended for displaced persons. Orwell wrote a special Preface for this translation and it is printed as Appendix II of the *Complete Works* and Penguin Twentieth-Century Classics editions.

To Andrew S. F. Gow*

13 April 1946
27B Canonbury Square Islington N 1

Dear Mr Gow,

It was very nice to hear from you after all this time. I heard almost simultaneously from M. D. Hill,[1] who wrote to me appropos° of the *Gem* and *Magnet*[2] and George Lyttelton,[3] who is now editing a series for Home & Van Thal and wanted me to write something. To my sorrow I had to say no, at any rate for the time being, because I am just on the point of dropping all journalism and other casual work for six months. I may start another book during the period, but I have resolved to stop hackwork for a bit, because I have been writing three articles a week for two years and for two years previous to that had been in the BBC where I wrote enough rubbish (news commentaries and so on) to fill a shelf of books. I have become more and more like a sucked orange and I am going to get out of it and go to Scotland for six months to a place where there is no telephone and not much of a postal service.

A lot has happened to me since I saw you. I am very sorry to say I lost my wife a little over a year ago, very suddenly and unexpectedly although her health had been indifferent for some time. I have a little adopted son who is now nearly 2 and was about 10 months old when his mother, ie. my wife, died. He was 3 weeks old when we adopted him. He is a splendid child and fortunately very healthy, and is a great pleasure to me. I didn't do much in the war because I was class IV, having a disease called bronchiectasis and also a lesion in one lung which was never diagnosed when I was a boy. But actually my health has been much better the last few years thanks to M and B.[4] The only bit of war I saw apart from blitzes and the Home Guard was being a war correspondent for a little while in Germany about the time of the collapse, which was quite interesting. I was in the Spanish war for a bit and was wounded through the neck, which paralysed one vocal cord, but this doesn't affect my voice. As you gathered I had a difficult time making a living out of writing at the start, though looking back now, and knowing what a racket literary journalism is, I see that I could have managed much better if I had known the ropes. At present the difficulty with all writers I know is that whereas it is quite easy to make a living by journalism or broadcasting, it is practically impossible to live by books. Before the war my wife and I used to live off my books, but then we lived in the country on £5 a week, which you could do then, and we didn't have a child. The last few years life has been so ghastly expensive that I find the only way I can write books is to write long essays for the magazines and then reprint them. However all this hackwork I have done in the last few years has had the advantage that it gets me a new public, and when I do publish a book it sells a lot more than mine used to before the war.

You mentioned Freddie Ayer.[5] I didn't know you knew him. He is a great friend of mine. This new magazine, *Polemic*, has only made two appearances so far, but I have great hopes that it will develop into something good. Bertrand Russell is of course the chief star in the constellation. It was a bad job Bobby Longden[6] getting killed. I believe Wellington became very enlightened while he was there. A boy whom you may know called Michael Meyer,[7] who was in the RAF and is now I think back at Cambridge again, was at Wellington under Bobby and has a great regard for him.

I will certainly come and see you next time I am at Cambridge, but I don't quite know when that will be. I thought of you last time I was there about 2 years ago when I was lecturing to the London School of Economics which was evacuated there. About my name. I have used the name Orwell as a pen-name for a dozen years or more, and most of the people I know call me George, but I have never actually changed my name and some people still call me Blair. It is getting to be such a nuisance that I keep meaning to change it by deed poll, but you have to go to a solicitor etc. which puts me off.

Yours
Eric Blair

P.S. You couldn't be expected to read all the books your ex-pupils have produced, but I wonder whether you saw my last book but one, *Animal Farm*? If not I'd be happy to send you a copy. It is very short and might amuse you.

[XVIII, 2972, pp. 241–3; typewritten]

1. M. D. Hill was a master at Eton in Orwell's time.
2. 'Boys' Weeklies', *Horizon*, 1940, XII, pp. 57–79.
3. The Honorable George Lyttelton, a master at Eton who was also in correspondence with Orwell at this time. He was no longer at Eton and wrote to Orwell on 9 April 1946 to thank him for replying to an earlier letter and to invite him to write one of the biographies of great writers he was editing for Home & Van Thal. He said he suspected Orwell was 'committed kneedeep' but thought it worth asking. A year or two earlier, at £50 down and a royalty of 15% for 30,000 words, it might have been a chance to be seized. In a postscript he wrote, 'I am very glad you put in a word for that foolish old Wodehouse. The discovery made by all our patriots that, because he made an ass of himself in the war, none of his books was really at all funny was very absurd—& very English.'
4. May & Baker, drug manufacturers. Orwell is probably referring to a treatment for pneumonia.
5. Alfred Jules Ayer (1910–1989; Kt., 1970), philosopher. His *Language, Truth and Logic* (1936) was a revolutionary work, the first extensive presentation of Logical Positivism in English. After Eton and Christ Church (1932–44) he served in the Welsh Guards and was an attaché at the British Embassy in Paris. From 1946 to 1978 he held professional appointments at UCL and Oxford; he was a fellow of Wolfson College, 1978–83.
6. Robert P. ('Bobbie') Longden, a contemporary of Orwell's at Eton, had a brilliant academic career, became headmaster of Wellington, and was killed in 1940 by a German stray bomb that hit the school. Orwell's comment about Wellington becoming 'very enlightened while [Longden] was there' may reflect on his memories of the short time he spent at the school before going to Eton: he 'did not like Wellington at all. He found the militaristic spirit of this famous army school abhorrent' (Crick, p. 96).
7. Michael Leverson Meyer (1921–2000), writer, critic, and distinguished translator and biographer of Ibsen and Strindberg. He had written what he described as a 'timid letter' to Orwell when Orwell was at the BBC and had a friendly response (13 April 1943) and they became friends. He had served in Bomber Command, 1942–45, and was Lecturer in English Literature, Uppsala University, Sweden, 1947–50.

To Anne Popham*

18 April 1946
27 B Canonbury Square
Islington N 1

Dear Andy,

I must have got your letter about the 7th, and I have thought over it a long time, as you can see by the date. I wonder if I committed a sort of crime in approaching you. In a way it's scandalous that a person like me should make advances to a person like you, and yet I thought from your appearance that you were not only lonely and unhappy, but also a person who lived chiefly through the intellect and might become interested in a man who was much older and not much good physically. You asked me what attracted me to you in the first place. You are very beautiful, as no doubt you well know, but that wasn't quite all. I do so want someone who will share what is left of my life, and my work. It isn't so much a question of someone to sleep with, though of course I want that too, sometimes. You say you wouldn't be likely to love me. I don't see how you could be expected to. You are young and fresh and you have had someone you really loved and who would set up a standard I couldn't compete with. If you still feel you can start again and you want a handsome young man who can give you a lot of children, then I am no good to you. What I am really asking you is whether you would like to be the widow of a literary man. If things remain more or less as they are there is a certain amount of fun in this, as you would probably get royalties coming in and you might find it interesting to edit unpublished stuff etc. Of course there is no knowing how long I shall live, but I am supposed to be a 'bad life.' I have a disease called bronchiectasis which is always liable to develop into pneumonia, and also an old 'non-progressive' tuberculous lesion in one lung, and several times in the past I have been supposed to be about to die, but I always lived on just to spite them, and I have actually been better in health since M and B. I am also sterile I think—at any rate I have never had a child, though I have never undergone the examination because it is so disgusting. On the other hand if you wanted children of your own by someone else it wouldn't bother me, because I have very little physical jealousy. I don't much care who sleeps with whom, it seems to me what matters is being faithful in an emotional and intellectual sense. I was sometimes unfaithful to Eileen, and I also treated her very badly, and I think she treated me badly too at times, but it was a real marriage in the sense that we had been through awful struggles together and she understood all about my work, etc. You are young and healthy, and you deserve somebody better than me: on the other hand if you don't find such a person, and if you think of yourself as essentially a widow, then you might do worse—ie. supposing I am not actually disgusting to you. If I can live another ten years I think I have another three worth-while books in me, besides a lot of odds and ends, but I want peace and quiet and someone to be fond of me. There is also Richard. I don't know what your feelings are about him. You might think all this over. I have spoken plainly to you because I feel you are an exceptional person. And I wish when you come back you would come and stay on Jura. I think I should have made the house fairly comfortable by then, and Richard and Susan, and perhaps other people, will be there as chaperons. I am not asking you to come and be my mistress, just to come and stay. I think you would like it. It is a beautiful place, quite empty and wild.

I don't think there's much news here. It's been beautiful spring weather and the chestnut trees in the square are full out, ie. the leaves, such a vivid green as you don't expect to see in London. I am alone because Susan and Richard have gone down into the country for the Easter weekend. I stayed behind because I want to polish off odds and ends of work and to pack the stuff before sending it to Jura. Last week I went down to the cottage in Hertfordshire to sort out the furniture and books there before Pickfords came for it. I had been putting it off because I hadn't been down there since Eileen died and expected it to be horribly upsetting but actually it wasn't so bad except when I kept coming on old letters. I am sending what furniture I have there, but have also had to buy innumerable things, almost like stocking up a ship. Pickfords are supposed to remove everything next week, about the 25th, and they think it will take at least 10 days to get there, after which it has to travel to the house by lorry, so it's unlikely that I shall leave London before about May 10th, if then. Of course this move costs something fabulous[1]—on the other hand, once it's accomplished and the house got into running order, there is a nice summer residence at almost no rent. I particularly want it for Richard, because he's really getting too big to stay in a flat in the summer. It is a job now to keep him inside the garden, because he knows in principle how to open the gate and sometimes manages to do it. Next winter when we come back I shall send him to the nursery school. It's funny he doesn't seem to want to talk—he is so intelligent in every other way. He tries now to put on his own shoes and socks, and he knows how to drive in a nail, though he can't actually do it without hammering his fingers. He is still terrified of the vacuum cleaner and we can't use it while he is about.

You asked about a book of mine about France—I suppose *Down and Out in Paris and London*. I literally don't possess a copy, even of the Penguin edition. I suppose it will be re-issued some time. I think the American edition of the essays has just come out, and my other American publisher cabled to say

Animal Farm had been chosen by something called the Book of the Month Club. I think that must mean a sale of at least 20,000[2] and that even after paying the taxes at both ends, and even if I've signed a disadvantageous contract, which I probably did, it should bring in enough to keep me in idleness for several months. The only thing is that they won't publish it till the autumn and there's many a slip etc.

I wonder if you have heard the cuckoo. I think I did dimly hear it when I was in Germany this time last year, between 'Lili Marlene'[3] and the roaring of trucks and tanks. The year before that I was so tied to London I never heard a cuckoo at all, the first year in my life that this had happened to me, ie. in London. I haven't heard it this year yet because I was down in Wallington a few days too early, but I think I saw one sitting on a telegraph wire as I came back in the train. You often see them a few days before you hear them. After writing my article on toads for *Tribune*[4] I went up to the little disused reservoir in the village where we used to catch newts, and there were the tadpoles forming as usual. It was rather sad. We used to have a small aquarium made of a 7 pound pickle jar each year and watch the newts grow from little black blobs in the spawn to full-grown creatures, and we also used to have snails and caddis flies.

I shall have to stop because I have to wash up the breakfast things and then go out to lunch. Take care of yourself. I hope you're better. It's beastly being ill in those circumstances, so lonely and comfortless. You didn't say whether you want to be sent magazines or anything. And write as soon as you can. I hope you will come and stay on Jura. It would be wonderful walking over to the west side of the island which is quite uninhabited and where there are bays of green water so clear you can see about 20 feet down, with seals swimming about. Don't think I'll make love to you against your will. You know I am civilized.

With love
George

P.S. [*handwritten*] I'm taking you at your word & only putting 1½[d] on this, because it's Good Friday & these are all the stamps I can find.[5]

[XVIII, 2978, pp. 248–51; typewritten
with handwritten postscript]

1. Orwell's goods were valued at £250. The cost of transporting them (Pickfords, plus rail, plus ship as far as Craighouse, plus insurance) was £114 3s 8d. The goods had then to be conveyed from Craighouse to Barnhill.
2. The first printing for Book-of-the-Month Club was 430,000 copies and the second 110,000.

3. 'Lili Marlene' was a song popular with both German and Allied servicemen. It was played by chance by a German-operated station in Yugoslavia and heard, and enjoyed, by men of the British Eighth Army and Rommel's troops in North Africa. It tells of a woman waiting for her soldier-lover, and it was used by the British for propaganda purposes. It was made the subject of a propaganda film (with the same title) directed by Humphrey Jennings (1944).

4. 'Some Thoughts on the Common Toad', 12 April 1946 (XVIII, 2970, pp. 238–41) – one of Orwell's finest essays.

5. This was the correct amount for Forces' mail. Post Offices closed on Good Friday.

To Stafford Cottman*

25 April 1946
27B Canonbury Square
Islington N 1

Dear Staff,

It was very nice to hear from you. I didn't realise you were still in the RAF. Be sure and look me up if you're in London when I'm here (if I am the above telephone number¹ will always get me), but I'm shortly going away for 6 months. I've been doing too much hack journalism for several years past and have decided to drop it for a bit—for two months I mean to do nothing at all, then maybe I shall start another book, but any way, no journalism until next autumn. I have written three articles a week for two years, in addition to all the bilge I had to write for the BBC for two years before that. I have given up the cottage in Hertfordshire and taken another in the island of Jura in the Hebrides, and hope to go up there about May 10th if my furniture has arrived by that time. It's in an extremely un-get-atable place, but it's a nice house and I think I can make it quite comfortable with a little trouble, and then I shall have a nice place to retire to occasionally at almost no rent. My little boy whom I think you have never seen is now nearly 2 and extremely active, which is one of the reasons why I am anxious to get out of London for the summer. He was 10 months old when Eileen died. It was an awful shame—she had been so overworked for years and in wretched health, then things just seemed to be getting better and that happened. The only good thing was that I don't think she expected anything to go wrong with the operation. She died as a result of the anaesthetic almost as soon as they gave it her. I was in France at the time, as neither of us had expected the operation to be very serious. The child I think was just too young to miss her, and he has done very well in health and everything else. I have a good housekeeper who looks after him and me.

The other day I ran into Paddy Donovan in the Edgware Road.[2] He has a job cleaning windows and he said he would ring me up, but he hasn't done so yet. He was wounded in Germany about the time of the crossing of the Rhine. Don't forget to ring me up if you're in town this coming autumn.

Yours
Eric Blair

[XVIII, 2984, pp. 257–8; typewritten]

1. Orwell's telephone number has not been reprinted. It was CAN 3751.
2. John (Paddy) Donovan (1905–), a labourer who had served in World War I and was one of Orwell's colleagues in Spain. He, with Cottman and a number of others, had signed Orwell's refutation of F. A. Frankford's allegations in the *Daily Worker* against the ILP contingent (see Crick, pp. 346–47). Orwell was later to give him some work digging his Hertfordshire garden when Donovan was out of work (Crick, p. 354).

To Marjorie Dakin*

30 April 1946
27B Canonbury Square
Islington N 1

Dear Marj,

I have only just heard from Avril about your illness. Naturally I only got a brief account from her, but she said it was pernicious anaemia. I do hope you are going on all right and are being properly treated. I am sending simultaneously with this a few books, some of which I hope you may not have read.[1]

I am just on the point of going away to Jura for 6 months. The furniture has gone, but it's likely to take a long time getting there owing to the sea journey. I am letting this flat furnished, or rather am lending it to someone,[2] as we're not supposed to sublet. When the furniture arrives I shall go on ahead and get the house in order, and then bring Richard up later. Susan has to go into hospital for a treatment which will take about a month, and during that time I am going to park him in a nursery school. It seems rather ruthless, but I can't look after him singlehanded for that length of time, and he is such a social child that he is bound to get on all right. We intend to stay on Jura till about October and I am dropping all casual journalism during that time, though I hope to get started on another book once I've got the house straight. The move is of course very expensive, but once it's done we shall have a nice summer residence for almost no rent, and it will be a lovely place for children to stay.

Richard is extremely well and getting quite big. He weighs about 37 pounds and keeps growing out of his clothes. He will be 2 on the 14th of May. He doesn't speak, but is very forward in other ways and very enterprising. He loves tools and already understands how to do such things as hammering in nails. He also goes downstairs on his own initiative and tries to put on his own shoes and socks. I shall be very glad to get him into the country for the summer because he's getting too active for a flat. We have a garden here, but it's not possible to leave him alone in it because he gets out into the street.

Don't bother answering this. I am also writing to Humphrey. I am not certain what date I shall be leaving London (probably about May 10th), but my Jura address will be Barnhill, Isle of Jura, Argyllshire.

Love
Eric

[XVIII, 2987, pp. 262–3; typewritten]

1. Marjorie died on 3 May 1946. Orwell attended her funeral (see *Diaries*, p. 372). Writing later to her husband, Humphrey, he said, 'One cannot really say anything about Marjorie's death. I know what it is like and how it sinks in afterwards' (XVIII, 2998, p. 309). Her children would later stay at Barnhill.
2. Mrs Miranda Wood (then Miranda Christen) had returned from the Far East early in 1946 after 3½ years in Japanese-occupied territory. She was technically a German national by marriage and was pursuing protracted divorce proceedings. She stayed in Orwell's London flat during the summers of 1946 and 1947. She undertook typing for him including 'Such, Such Were the Joys' and sections of *Nineteen Eighty-Four*. (For fuller details see the long note, XIX, p. 228 and her memoir, XX, 3735, pp. 300–306.)

To Michael Meyer*

23 May 1946
Barnhill
Isle of Jura
Argyllshire

Dear Michael,

Thanks so much for your efforts. No, I haven't a licence[1] (there's no policeman on this island!) so don't worry about the black powder. I made some which is not as good as commercial stuff but will do. If you *could* get the percussion caps I'd be much obliged. Tell them the largest size they have, i.e. something about this size ☐ .

I'm just settling in here—up to my eyes getting the house straight, but it's a lovely house. Richard isn't coming till the end of June, because Susan has to have a minor operation & I couldn't cope with him singlehanded, so I've had to board him out. However the reports are that he is getting on well. Only difficulties at present are (a) that I can't yet get a jeep (hope to get one at the end of the month) & am having to make do with a motor bike which is hell on these roads, & (b) owing to the drought there's no water for baths, though enough to drink. However one doesn't get very dirty here. Come & stay sometime. It's not such an impossible journey (about 48 hours from London) & there's plenty of room in this house, though of course conditions are rough

> All the best
> George

[XVIII, 3002, p. 312; handwritten]

1.   A licence was needed to carry a gun. Presumably Orwell was seeking ammunition for his gun.

To Rayner Heppenstall*

16 June 1946
Barnhill   Isle of Jura   Argyllshire

Dear Rayner,

Do come about July 14th if that date suits you.[1] Try & let me have a week's notice, so as to arrange about meeting you, as posts here are somewhat infrequent. There are boats to Jura on Mondays, Wednesdays & Fridays. The itinerary is this (but better check it with the L.M.S.[2] in case any time is altered):—

> 8 am leave Glasgow Central Station for Gourock (GOUROCK)
> Join boat at Gourock
> Arrive East Tarbert about 12 noon
> Travel to West Tarbert by bus (runs in conjunction with boat)
> Join boat at West Tarbert
> Arrive Jura about 3 pm.[3]

You can book right [through] from Glasgow, or pay your fare on each boat. Fare Gourock–Jura is about £1. Bring any food you can manage, & bring a towel. You'll need thick boots & a raincoat.

> Looking forward to seeing you

> Yours
> Eric

[XVIII, 3015, p. 328; handwritten]

1. Heppenstall had written on 11 June 1946, saying he was pleased Orwell would do something for the BBC in the 'Imaginary Conversations' series in November or December. He expected to arrive in Jura about 14 July and (owing to the severe rationing) he would try to help with food: 'The comparative roughness does not in the least appal me.' He hoped Orwell's health was improving and looked forward to seeing him 'very beefy'.

2. Between 1923, when many individual railway companies were 'grouped,' and 31 December 1947, when the system was nationalised (as British Rail until its break up in the 1990s) there were four main companies, of which the London, Midland & Scottish was one.

3. Orwell's instructions for getting to Barnhill vary from time to time but are hereafter omitted.

Avril Blair* to Humphrey Dakin*

1 July 1946
Barnhill
Isle of Jura

Dear Humph

Glad to hear you & the family are progressing satisfactorily. Congratulate Henry[1] for me when next you write.

This is a lovely place. Why don't you come up for a bit if you are feeling browned off. The only snag is—no beer, so bring your own if you want any.

This is a very nice farmhouse with five bedrooms & bathroom, two sittingrooms & huge kitchen larders dairies etc. The house faces south & we have a lovely view over the Sound of Jura with little islands dotted here & there. Eric has bought a little boat & we go fishing in the evening which is the time the fish rise. They are simply delicious fresh from the sea. In fact, on the whole we live on the fat of the land. Plenty of eggs & milk & ½ lb butter extra weekly on to our rations. Our landlord[2] gave us a large hunk of venison a short while ago which was extremely good. Then there are local lobsters & crabs. Also the ubiquitous rabbit. Our nearest neighbours are a mile away. Then there is a strip of wild & remote country for eight miles to Ardlussa where our landlord the local estate owner & family live. This is a so called° village, but no shop. The only shop on the island is at Craighouse,[3] the port where the ship calls three times a week. We go to fetch our letters from Ardlussa twice a week in a very delapidated° Ford Van that E has bought. The roads are appalling.

I am really enjoying it all imenseley,° including cooking on a range, with which I had a tremendous battle at first. But having removed two buckets of soot from the flues it now cooks & heats the water a treat. One couldn't compare this place with Middlesmoor⁴ as it is quite different but next to it Middlesmoor seems like Blackpool. The country is lovely with rocky coastline & mountains all down the centre of the island. I am making a serious collection of pressed wild flowers. We have a friend of E's one Paul Potts staying here. He takes all my shafts of scintillating wit quite seriously & suffers from fits of temperament but I think I am welding him into a more human shape.⁵

With love
Avril

[XVIII, 3025, p.337–8; handwritten]

1. Avril's nephew, son of Humphrey and Marjorie Dakin.
2. Robin Fletcher, formerly an Eton housemaster; he inherited the Ardlussa Estate, which included Barnhill. He and his wife, later Margaret Nelson, set about restoring the estate and developing crofting. Mrs Nelson's interview with Nigel Williams for the BBC programme *Arena* in 1984 is reproduced in *Orwell Remembered*, pp. 225–29.
3. Craighouse is about sixteen miles south of Ardlussa and about three miles from the southern tip of Jura. It was therefore about twenty-three miles south of Barnhill as the crow flies, but Margaret Nelson gives the distance as twenty-seven miles (*Orwell Remembered*, p. 226). Orwell relied on Craighouse for a shop, a doctor, and a telephone.
4. A remote village in Nidderdale, Yorkshire, some fourteen miles west of Ripon as the crow flies. The Dakins had a cottage there, described by Marjorie as 'a magic cottage' (see **3.10.38**, n. 9).
5. Paul Potts (1911–90), Canadian poet whom Orwell befriended. His chapter, 'Don Quixote on a Bicycle' in his *Dante Called you Beatrice* (1960), partially reprinted in *Orwell Remembered*, pp. 248–60, describes Orwell affectionately. He recalls that 'The happiest years of my life were those during which I was a friend of his'. Avril had been a metal-worker during the war which might explain her use of 'welding'.

To Sally McEwan★

5 July 1946
Barnhill
Isle of Jura

Dear Sally,¹

So looking forward to seeing you on the 22nd. But I'm very sorry to say you'll have to walk the last 8 miles because we've no conveyance. However it isn't such a terrible walk if you can make do with rucksack luggage—for instance a rucksack and a couple of haversacks. I can tote that much on the back of my motor bike (only conveyance I have), but not heavy suitcases. Send the food on well in advance so that it is sure to arrive before you. For instance if you sent it off about Monday 15th it would get here on the Friday previous to your arrival. I think I've given you all the directions for the journey. Don't miss the train at Glasgow— it now leaves at 7.55, not 8. When you get to Jura, ask for the hired car at McKechnie's shop if it doesn't meet you on the quay. It will take you to Ardlussa where we will meet you. I may be able to arrange for it to take you another 3 miles to Lealt, but sometimes they won't take their cars past Ardlussa. Yesterday I brought Richard and Susan back (I rang you up when in town but it was your day at the printers), and in that case managed to bribe the driver to go within 2 miles of Barnhill, but he was appalled by the road and I don't think he'd do it again. I then carried Richard home from there and their luggage was brought on in the crofter's cart. It's really a quite pleasant walk if one takes it slowly. You don't need a great deal in the way of clothes if you have a raincoat and some stout boots or shoes. I hope by that time we shall have a spare pair of gum boots for use in the boat. I don't know what you'll do on the train, but on the boats from Gourock and Tarbert it pays to travel 3rd class because there's no difference in the accomodation° and the food is filthy any way.

With love
George

[XVIII, 3027, pp. 339–40; typewritten]

1.   Sally McEwan came to Barnhill with her child. She and Avril were united in dislike of Paul Potts. He left suddenly in the night. At first it was thought it was either because he was told to do so by Avril or because he chanced to see something hurtful about him written by Sally McEwan in a letter (Crick, pp. 512–14). This account was corrected by Sally McEwan and Susan Watson, interviewed by Ian Angus in February 1984. Susan Watson confirmed that Sally McEwan had not left anything hurtful about Paul Potts where he might read it. The reason for Potts's sudden departure was quite different: there was no newspaper left with which to get the fire started, so Susan Watson used what she took to be scrap paper; unfortunately, this turned out to be a draft of something Potts was writing.

To Sir Richard Rees*

5 July 1946
Barnhill
Isle of Jura

Dear Richard,

Thanks for your letter of the 1st. I have sometimes thought over the point you raise. I don't know if I would, as it were, get up to the point of having anything biographical written about me, but I suppose it could happen and it's ghastly to think of some people doing it. All I can say is, use your discretion and if someone seems a B.F., don't let him see any papers. I am going to include among my personal papers, in case of this happening, some short notes about the main events in my life, chiefly dates and places, because I notice that when people write about you, even people who know you well, they always get that kind of thing wrong. If I should peg out in the next few years, I don't really think there'll be a great deal for you to do except deal with publishers over reprints and decide whether or not to keep a few miscellaneous documents. I have named you as literary executor in my will, which has been properly drawn up by a lawyer, and Gwen O'Shaughnessy, who will be Richard's guardian if anything happens to me, knows all about it. Richard, I hope and trust, is well provided for. I had managed to save a little over the last year or two, and having had this stroke of luck with the American Book of the Month people, I can leave that money untouched, as it is so to speak over and above my ordinary earnings.

I have been up here since the middle of May and am now well settled in. I haven't done a stroke of work for two months, only gardening etc. My sister is here and does the cooking, and Susan and Richard came up a few days ago. I suppose I shall have to start work again soon, but I'm not going to do any journalism until October. This is a nice big farmhouse with a bathroom and we are making it quite comfortable. The only real snag here is transport— everything has to be brought over 8 miles of inconceivable road, and I've no transport except a motor bike. However it's only necessary to do the journey once a week, to fetch bread and the rations. We're well off for food. We get milk in any quantity and a fair amount of eggs and butter from a nearby crofter, our only neighbour within 6 miles, and we catch quantities of fish in the sea and also shoot rabbits. I've also got a few geese which we shall eat off by degrees. The house hadn't been inhabited for 12 years and of course the garden has gone back to wilderness, but I am getting it under by little and little,[1] and this autumn I shall put in fruit bushes etc. Getting the house running has cost a bit, but the rent is almost nothing and it's nice to have a retreat like this to which one can disappear when one likes and not be followed by telephone calls etc. At present it's about a 2-day journey from London, door to door, but one could do it in a few hours if one flew to the neighbouring island (Islay), which we shall be able to do another time because we shall leave clothes and so forth here. If you'd like to come and stay in for instance September we'd love to have you here. If so let me know and I'll tell you about how to do the journey.* It isn't really a very formidable one except that you have to walk the last 8 miles.

Yours
Eric

*P.S. You might find it rather paintable here.[2] The colours on the sea are incredible but they change all the time. You could do some studies of real Highland cattle. They're all over the place, just like in Landseer's pictures![3]

[XVIII, 3028, pp. 340–1; typed with handwritten postscript]

1. 'by little and little' means gradually; 'He that contemneth small things shall fall by little and little,' Ecclesiasticus, xix, 1.
2. Rees was living in Edinburgh at the time and painting. He made several oil paintings at Barnhill including one of Orwell's bedroom (now in the Orwell Archive, UCL).
3. Sir Edwin Landseer (1802–1873) was best known for his pictures of dogs and deer; his 'Monarch of the Glen' (1851) was highly regarded in its time. Although his pictures have now become more popular, they were less appreciated when Orwell referred to them. He sculpted the lions at the foot of Nelson's column (1867) in London. Orwell mentions them in *Nineteen Eighty-Four*, when Winston and Julia meet in Victory Square (p. 120).

To Yvonne Davet*

29 July 1946
Barnhill
Isle of Jura

Chère Madame Davet,

I would, of course, be very pleased if *Homage to Catalonia* were accepted by M. Charlot.[1] If it is, there are several mistakes (typographical errors etc.) which need correcting and which I'll point out to you. I also think that it would be better to add an introduction by someone (a Spaniard, if possible) who has a good knowledge of Spain and Spanish politics. When the book is reprinted in England, I plan to take out one or perhaps two chapters and put them at the end of the book as an appendix. It specially concerns the chapter giving a detailed picture of the May fighting, with quotations from the newspapers etc. It has a historic value, but it would be tedious for a reader with no special interest in the Spanish Civil War, and it could go at the end without damaging the text.[2] As for the title, it would probably be better to alter it. Even in English the title doesn't mean much. But perhaps you have some thoughts on the subject. I think it's impossible to choose a title in a foreign language.[3]

Unfortunately, I have no novel to give to M. Charlot. *Burmese Days*, *Animal Farm* and *Coming Up For Air* are all being translated,[4] and there aren't any more. That is, I did write two other novels, but I'm not very proud of them, and I made up my mind a long time ago to suppress them. As for the novel I'm beginning now, that will possibly be finished in 1947. I've only just started it. For nearly three months I've done nothing at all, that is, I've written nothing. After years of writing three articles a week, I was dreadfully tired, and I very much needed a long holiday. Here in Scotland we are living in a very primitive fashion, and we're quite busy shooting rabbits, catching fish etc. to get enough to eat. I've just started writing a long article for *Polemic*,[5] and after I've finished that, I hope to work on my novel for two months before I go back to London in October. In October I'll start doing journalism again, but if I've written at least a few chapters of the novel I'll probably be able to finish it sooner or later. The difficult thing is *starting* a new book when you're busy for five or six days a week.

I'm staying here till the beginning of October, or perhaps a few weeks later. After that my address in London will be as usual. The address of my publishers (for *Homage to Catalonia*) is Messrs. Secker and Warburg Publishers 7 John Street London W.C.1.

Très amicalement
Geo. Orwell

P.S. I enclose a copy of my pamphlet *James Burnham and the Managerial Revolution*, which first appeared as an article in *Polemic* with the title 'Second Thoughts on James Burnham.' I suppose it is possible that one of the monthlies might think it worth translating.

[XVIII, 3036, pp. 360–3; typewritten]

1. Charlot saw the French translation of *Homage to Catalonia* through the press.
2. These and other changes listed by Orwell were made for the *Collected Works* edition, Vol. VI.

3. The French edition (1955) simply translated the title *Homage to Catalonia* into French. For the changes made for the French edition, and Orwell's additional notes, see *CW*, VI, Textual Note.

4. The proposed translation of *Coming Up for Air* may be a reference to *La fille de l'air*.

5. 'Politics vs. Literature: An Examination of *Gulliver's Travels*', *Polemic*, No. 5, September–October 1946 (see XVIII, 3089, pp. 417–32).

To Lydia Jackson*

7 August 1946
Barnhill
Isle of Jura

Dear Lydia,

Thanks for your letter. If you'd like to come up here, there would be room in the house in the second half of August, say any time between the 15th and September 1st. Somebody else is coming on the latter date, I think. [*Details about travel: see* **16.6.46**][1] Try and give me several days° notice, won't you, so that I can arrange about hiring the car. I think Susan's little girl is coming up on Friday the 16th, in which case I shall go to Glasgow to meet her, but it's not certain yet.

Thanks so much for sending on the boots. We need all the footwear we can get here because of course one is constantly getting wet, especially when we go fishing. Latterly the weather has been foul but whenever it's decent we go out at night and catch a lot of fish which helps the larder.

As to the repairs.[2] As I am supposed to be the tenant, it might be best if you sent Keep's bill on to me and let me pay it, and I will then send the receipted bill to Dearman and see what I can get out of him. I don't suppose we'll get the whole amount, but anyway we can square up afterwards. I don't suppose Keep will charge an enormous amount from what I know of him.

Love to Pat.

Yours
Eric

[XVIII, 3044, pp. 369–70; typewritten]

1. Orwell also asked Lydia to bring 'some bread and/or flour'. The shortage of grain for bread grew worse during 1946 (partly because grain was needed for those near starvation in Continental Europe). The wheat content of bread was reduced in March 1946; in April the size of loaves was reduced from 2lbs to 1¾lbs – but the

price was *not* reduced – and there was a 15% cut in grain for brewing beer; in June bread was rationed despite the fact that that had not proved necessary throughout the war. Near the opening of *Nineteen Eighty-Four* (IX, p. 7) Winston Smith finds he has only 'a hunk of dark-coloured bread' to eat but that had to be saved for the next morning's breakfast. The draft manuscript is even more specific for it is there described as 'a single slab of bread three centimetres thick' (*Facsimile*, p. 15).

2.   The repairs are to The Stores, Wallington, not Barnhill. Mr Dearman was the landlord. (See Shelden, pp. 260–62.) Keep was, presumably, a local builder.

To Anne Popham*

7 August 1946
Barnhill
Isle of Jura

Dear Andy,

You see this time it's me who delays weeks or is it months before answering. You didn't have to be so apologetic—I know only too well how difficult it is to answer a letter and how they rise up and smite one day after day.

I thought over your letter a lot, and I expect you're right. You're young and you'll probably find someone who suits you. Any way° let's say no more about it.¹ I hope I shall see you when I am back in London (probably about October). I heard from Ruth² about a week ago, as she kindly took in and is looking after some books which were being sent and which I didn't want to follow me up here. We're all flourishing here and Richard is beginning to talk a little though he's still far more interested in doing things with his hands and is becoming very clever with tools. My sister is here and does the cooking, and Susan looks after Richard and looks after the house, while I do the gardening and carpentering. For two months I did no writing at all, then last month I did write an article,³ and I *may* begin a novel before returning to London but I'm not tying myself down. I had to have a good rest after years of hackwork, and it has done me a lot of good. So far I haven't even had a cold while here, in spite of getting wet to the skin several times a week. We have to catch or shoot a lot of our food, but I like doing that and as a matter of fact we feed better than one can do in London now. This is a nice big house, and if I can get a long lease which would make it worth while to furnish it more completely and instal an electric light plant, one could make it really comfortable. In any case I'm going to plant fruit trees this autumn and hope I shall be here to get the benefit of them. It's also a great treat to be in a place where Richard can run in and out of the house without being in any danger of getting run over. The only danger for him here is snakes, but I kill them whenever I see one anywhere near the house. This winter I shall send him to the nursery school if there is a vacancy.

Let me hear from you again if you can get round to writing.

Yours
George

[XVIII, 3045, pp. 370–1; typewritten]

1. For Anne Popham's reminiscences of this exchange, see *Remembering Orwell*, pp. 166–67.
2. Ruth Beresford, who shared the flat in Canonbury Square with Anne Popham immediately below Orwell's flat.
3. Possibly 'Politics vs. Literature', *Polemic* (XVIII, 3089, pp. 417–32.)

To Celia Kirwan*

17 August 1946
Barnhill
Isle of Jura

Dearest Celia,

How marvellous of you to get the brandy and send it off on your own initiative. I enclose cheque for £9–15–0. I hope you weren't put to any other expense about it—if so please let me know.

I forgot to say, I think one or two of the titles (of pamphlets and so on) in the Swift essay[1] are incorrect, as I was quoting them from memory, but so long as I see a galley proof it will be easy to put this right.

I am sorry you are pining away in London. It must be lousy being there at this time of year, especially if you have been having such marvellous weather as we have had here for the last week or two. I still haven't done any work to speak of, there always seems to be so much to do of other kinds, and the journeys one makes are quite astonishing. Susan's child came up here yesterday, and I was supposed to go to Glasgow to meet her. I set out the day before yesterday morning, but punctured my motor bike on the way and thus missed the boat. I then got a lift first in a lorry, then in a car, and crossed the ferry to the next island in hopes there would be a plane to Glasgow, however the plane was full up, so I took a bus on to Port Ellen, where there would be a boat on Friday morning. Port Ellen was full to the brim owing to a cattle show, all the hotels were full up, so I slept in a cell in the police station along with a lot of other people including a married couple with a perambulator. In the morning I got the boat, picked the child up and brought her back, then we hired a car for the first 20 miles and walked the last five home. This morning I got a lift in a motor boat to where my bike was, mended the puncture and rode home—all this in 3 days. I think we are going to get a motor boat, ie. a boat with an outboard engine, as it is the best way of travelling here when the weather is decent. At present we have only a little rowing boat which is good for fishing but which you can't go far out to sea in. We go fishing nearly every night, as we are partly dependent on fish for food, and we have also got two lobster pots and catch a certain number of lobsters and crabs. I have now learned how to tie up a lobster's claws, which you have to do if you are going to keep them alive, but it is very dangerous, especially when you have to do it in the dark. We also have to shoot rabbits when the larder gets low, and grow vegetables, though of course I haven't been here long enough to get much return from the ground yet, as it was simply a jungle when I got here. With all this you can imagine that I don't do much work—however I have actually begun my new book and hope to have done four or five chapters by the time I come back in October. I am glad Humphrey[2] has been getting on with his—I wonder how *The Heretics*[3] sold? I saw Norman Collins[4] gave it rather a snooty review in the *Observer*.

Richard now wears real shorts, which another child had grown out of, and braces, and I have got him some real farm labourer's boots. He has to wear boots here when he goes far from the house, because if he has shoes he is liable to take them off, and there are snakes here. I think you would like this place. Do come any time if you want to. But if you do, try and let me know in advance (it means writing about a week in advance, because we only get letters twice a week here), so that I can arrange about hiring a car. Also, don't bring more luggage than, say, a rucksack and a haversack, but on the other hand do bring a little flour if you can. We are nearly always short of bread and flour here since the rationing. You don't want many clothes so long as you have a raincoat and stout boots or shoes. Remember the boats sail on Mondays, Wednesdays and Fridays, and you have to leave Glasgow about 8 am. I expect to be here till about the 10th of October.

With love
George

PS. You might ask Freddie[5] from me, now that he has a chair in Mental Philosophy, who has the chair in non-mental philosophy.

[XVIII, 3051, pp. 375–7; typewritten]

1. 'Politics vs. Literature', *Polemic* (for which Celia Kirwan worked as an editorial assistant).
2. Humphrey Slater,* then editor of *Polemic*.
3. Orwell had written a reader's report for Fredric Warburg on Slater's *The Heretics*. It was published in April 1946. The report does not appear to have survived.
4. For Norman Collins see 17.3.36, n. 4.

5.   A. J. Ayer (1910–89), who had just been appointed Grote Professor of the Philoso-
      phy of Mind and Logic, University College London. (See also **13.4.46**, n. 5.)

To George Woodcock*

2 September 1946
Barnhill
Isle of Jura

Dear George,

Thanks ever so for the tea—it came just at the right moment because this
week the whole of the nearest village is being brought here in lorries to
get in the field of corn in front of our house, and of course tea will have
to flow like water while the job is on.[1] We have been helping the crofter
who is our only neighbour with his hay and corn, at least when rain hasn't
made it impossible to work. Everything is done here in an incredibly primitive way. Even when the field is ploughed with a tractor the corn is still sown
broadcast, then scythed and bound up into sheaves by hand. They seem to
broadcast corn, ie. oats, all over Scotland, and I must say they seem to get it
almost as even as can be done by a machine. Owing to the wet they don't get
the hay in till about the end of September or even later, sometimes as late as
November, and they can't leave it in the open but have to store it all in lofts.
A lot of the corn doesn't quite ripen and is fed to the cattle in sheaves like
hay. The crofters have to work very hard, but in many ways they are better
off and more independent than a town labourer, and they would be quite
comfortable if they could get a bit of help in the way of machinery, electrical
power and roads, and could get the landlords off their backs and get rid of
the deer. These animals are so common on this particular island that they are
an absolute curse. They eat up the pastures where there ought to be sheep,
and they make fencing immensely more expensive than it need be. The crofters aren't allowed to shoot them, and are constantly having to waste their
time dragging carcases of deer down from the hill during the stalking season.
Everything is sacrificed to the brutes because they are an easy source of meat
and therefore profitable to the people who own them. I suppose sooner or
later these islands will be taken in hand, and then they could either be turned
into a first-rate area for dairy produce and meat, or else they would support
a large population of small peasants living off cattle and fishing. In the 18th
century the population here was 10,000—now less than 300.

My love to Inge. I hope to be back in London about October 13th.

Yours
George

[XVIII, 3058, p. 385; typewritten]

1. In his study of Orwell, *The Crystal Spirit*, Woodcock explains this gift of tea and comments on Orwell's description of life on Jura: 'Knowing Orwell's passion for tea, my wife and I, coffee drinkers, would save up our rations and every now and again send him a packet of Typhoo Tips, which produced the dark, strong brew he liked. One of these packets . . . evoked a letter in which Orwell described existence on Jura; it reflected the intense interest he always took in the concrete aspects of life—particularly rural life—and also in its social overtones' (p. 36). The tea ration had been increased in July 1945 from 2 ounces a week to 2½, but it was still a meagre amount, especially for someone who drank as much strong tea as Orwell did. Although Orwell was desperate for tea, his first thought on receiving this gift was that he could share it with the harvesters.

To Rayner Heppenstall*

19 September 1946
Barnhill
Isle of Jura

Dear Rayner,

The version of *Boule de Suif* I was projecting would be a featurisation of the story, with a narrator but no critical talk or biographical material, so I suppose it would be 'drama.' If you can interest the relevant person, you might say that the way I would want to do it would be the way in which we did various stories for the Eastern Service in 1943, and also that version of *Little Red Riding Hood* which you kindly placed for me. In my experience the BBC, although making a minimum of 6 copies of everything, can never find a back number of a script, but the stories I would like to draw attention to are *Crainquebille* (Anatole France,) *The Fox* (Silone,) and *A Slip Under the Microscope* (H.G. Wells.) We did all these in featurised form sticking to the text of the story as closely as possible and not mucking it up with meaningless patches of music, but dramatising all the dialogue and using a number of different voices. If anyone is interested enough to look up these scripts, you might tell him I had to write them in desperate haste, as I was overwhelmed with administrative work, and in each case could give only a day to the job. I could do it better if I were doing it for the Home Service and had a bit more time.[1]

As to Pontius Pilate, I am not pining to write a script about him, but I have always felt he has had a raw deal and thought one might make a good dialogue out of it somehow.[2] *Boule de Suif* is a test of whether the C programme[3] is really nothing barred. Incidentally I don't believe it has ever been well translated into English (at least the only translation I have seen was damnable).

I expect to be back in London on October 13th. The weather here has been shocking for about a fortnight past and they are having a fearful job to get the harvest in. We stove in the bottom of our boat in the recent stormy weather. However we had had a good season's fun out of it and a lot of fish and lobsters, and next year I shall get a bigger one with a motor on it, which will help solve our transport problem. Transport is really the only big problem here, and wouldn't be a problem in normal times when one could lay in several months' stores at one go. Even as it is we have done better in food and fuel than one can in London, but at the expense of a good deal of labour and some terrifying journeys. Hoping to see you in town. My love to Margaret.

Yours
Eric

[XVIII, 3074, pp. 400–1; typewritten]

1. On Rayner Heppenstall's behalf, June Seligmann sent Orwell's suggestion to Laurance Gilliam, Director of Features, on 24 September 1946 who passed it on to the Drama Department. His memorandum is annotated, 'Sorry—no can do!' and the answer is marked for Heppenstall's attention. Except for *Little Red Riding Hood*, broadcast in BBC *Children's Hour*, the scripts to which Orwell refers were written when he was broadcasting to India.
2. In a letter to Heppenstall on 5 September 1946 (XVIII, 3059, p. 386–7), Orwell had in mind an imaginary conversation between Pontius Pilate and Lenin – for 'one could hardly make it J.C.'!
3. What was to become the Third Programme of the BBC, now Radio 3. Laurence Brander, the BBC's Intelligence Officer for India when Orwell worked for the BBC, wrote in 1954 that Orwell 'was the inspiration of that rudimentary Third Programme which was sent out to the Indian student' (*George Orwell*, pp. 8–9).

To Humphrey Slater*

26 September 1946
Barnhill
Isle of Jura

Dear Humphrey,

Can you come to lunch at the flat on Sunday October 13th, and if possible bring one of our mutual friends with you? I am getting back to town that morning, but my sister is arriving with Richard a day or two earlier. I think there'll be a goose for lunch, unless it somehow goes astray on the journey. We shall have one goose left when we leave, which we shall take with us or send on ahead, and if so we'll need someone to help eat it.

I sent the documents to Cyril[1] as requested in your wire, and hope he got them in time, but I couldn't send them very promptly because of the difficulty of there only being two posts a week here and a telegram not moving any faster than a letter once it gets on to the island. I hope he makes good use of them. It is all pretty tough but only what you would expect. I thought the most interesting feature was what you too pointed out—the ambivalence all the way through, the writers constantly complaining that literature is dull and unimaginative and then wanting to cure this by clipping the artist's wings a little shorter.

I haven't really done any work this summer—actually I have at last started my novel about the future, but I've only done about 50 pages and God knows when it will be finished. However it's something that it is started, which it wouldn't have been if I hadn't got away from regular journalism for a while. Soon I suppose I shall be back at it, but I am dropping some of it and am going to try and do mostly highly-paid stuff which I needn't do so much of. I have arranged to do some book reviewing for the *New Yorker* which of course pays well. Please give everyone my love. Looking forward to seeing you. If you can't come please reply to the flat, as it's possible a letter might miss me here.

Yours
George

[XVIII, 3084, p. 408; typewritten]

1. Possibly Cyril Connolly in connection with the 'Cost of Letters', published in *Horizon*, September 1946 (XVIII, 3057, pp. 382–4).

To George Woodcock*

28 September 1946
Barnhill
Isle of Jura

Dear George,

I was quite stunned on hearing from you about Colletts°[1] taking over the S.B.C.[2] How could it have happened? I thought they were doing quite well. And what happens about their publications, for instance the pamphlets they were issuing from time to time? There was one of mine they published a few months back,[3] and I don't even know how many copies it sold. It is simply calamitous if there isn't one large leftwing bookshop not under C[ommunist] P[arty] control. However, I shouldn't say it would be impossible to set up a successful rival, because any CP bookshop must be hampered as a shop by being unable to stock 'the wrong' kind of literature. We must talk it over when I get back. I have no idea what capital you need to set up a well-stocked bookshop, but I fancy it is several thousand pounds. It is not inconceivable that one might dig the money out of some well-intentioned person like Hulton,[4] if he saw his way to not making a loss on it. The thing is to have a shop which apart from selling all the leftwing stuff is a good *bookshop*, has a lending library and is managed by someone who knows something about books. Having worked in a bookshop I have got ideas on the subject, which I'll tell you about when I get back.

Of course it's very flattering to have that article in *Politics*.[5] I haven't a copy of *Keep the Aspidistra Flying*. I picked up a copy in a secondhand shop some months back, but I gave it away. There are two or three books which I am ashamed of and have not allowed to be reprinted or translated, and that is one of them. There is an even worse one called *A Clergyman's Daughter*. This was written simply as an exercise and I oughtn't to have published it, but I was desperate for money, ditto when I wrote *Keep the A*. At that time I simply hadn't a book in me, but I was half starved and had to turn out something to bring in £100 or so.

I'm leaving here on the 9th and shall reach London on the 13th. I'll ring you up then. Love to Inge. Richard is blooming.

Yours
George

[XVIII, 3087, pp. 410–11; typewritten]

1. Collet's bookshop specialised in Communist publications. It was still active in the early nineties with an 'International Bookshop', a 'Chinese Bookshop and Gallery', and a Penguin Bookshop, but was no longer listed in the London telephone directory in 1995.
2. Socialist Book Centre.
3. *James Burnham and the Managerial Revolution*.
4. Edward Hulton (1906–1988; Kt., 1957), magazine publisher of liberal views, at the time proprietor of *Picture Post*.
5. 'George Orwell, Nineteenth Century Liberal', by George Woodcock, *Politics*, December 1946. The essay forms chapter 7 of Woodcock's *The Writer and Politics* (1948).

To Dwight Macdonald*

15 October 1946
27B Canonbury Square
Islington N 1

Dear Dwight,

Thanks for your letter,[1] which I got just before leaving Jura (I'm at the above again until about April of next year.) I'm awfully sorry about not sending you anything as promised, but part of the reason is that I have written almost nothing for 5 months. I went to Scotland largely with that end in view, because I was most desperately tired and felt that I had written myself out.

While there I did write one article[2] and just started a new book (lord knows when it will be finished—perhaps by the end of 1947), but that was all. Now I'm starting up again, but I am going to do my best to keep out of ordinary daily and weekly journalism, except for *Tribune*. As to the *New Republic*, I gave them the reprint of that article because they cabled and asked for it. I would have gladly given it to you, but it didn't occur to me as a thing that would particularly interest you. Shortly after that the *New Republic* wrote asking whether they could take their pick of any articles I write for *Tribune*, with which they have a reciprocal arrangement for the exchange of articles. I told them they could, but I expect they won't often avail themselves of it, because when I start writing for *Tribune* again I shall probably take over the 'As I Please' column, which is mostly topical English stuff. I am well aware that the *N.R.* people are Stalino-Liberals, but so long as they have no control over what I write, as they wouldn't under this arrangement, I rather like to have a foot in that camp. Their opposite numbers over here, the *New Statesman*, won't touch me with a stick, in fact my last contact with them was their trying to blackmail me into withdrawing something I had written in *Tribune* by threats of a libel action.[3] Meanwhile I think I am going to write rather more for American papers when I start writing at all. I am going, I think, to do occasional book reviews for the *New Yorker*, and some agents called Mcintosh and Otis are very anxious for me to send copies of all my articles, a number of which they say they could market in the U.S. I have already arranged with *Polemic* that when I send them anything I shall simultaneously send a copy to the USA. Of course the agents' idea is to sell them to big-circulation magazines, but when there is anything that seems up your street I'll see that it gets to you first.

I suppose these letters aren't now opened by snoopers, and I want to ask you to do me a favour which I believe involves illegality (on my part, not yours.) Do you think you could get me some shoes? Or is it the same about clothes in the US as well? Even if you have the clothes coupons, which I never have, you simply can't get shoes in my size (twelves!) here. The last new pair I had were bought in 1941 and you can imagine what they are like now. I don't care what they cost, but I like stout heavy walking shoes and I would like two pairs if it's at all possible. I believe the American sizes are the same as the English.[4] Could you let me know whether you think you can do this and what it will cost? I can get the money to you because I have or shall have some dollars in the USA. Even if you can manage to get them it will need strategy to send them because things like that get pinched in the docks. I'll tell you about that later. I suppose this black-market business seems very sordid to you, but I have been almost ragged for years, and in the end it becomes irritating and even depressing, so I am doing my best to get hold of a few clothes by one route and another.

I was very flattered to learn that George Woodcock is writing an article on me for you. He wrote asking me for a copy of one of the books I have suppressed.[5] He was also very indignant about something I said about anarchism in *Polemic* and is writing a reply.[6] *Polemic* is making rather a speciality of 'reply' articles. I think it is now shaping better, and it is doing quite well from a circulation point of view. You'll be glad to hear that *Animal Farm* has been or is being translated into 10 languages besides various clandestine translations or ones made abroad by refugees from the occupied countries. All the best.

Yours
Geo. Orwell

[XVIII, 3097, pp. 449–51; typewritten]

1. Dwight Macdonald wrote on 10 September 1946 with particular reference to Orwell's article on James Burnham. He thought Orwell's points were akin to those Macdonald had made in his review of Burnham in 1942 and that Burnham was no longer taken seriously in America. He asked Orwell why he didn't write for *Politics* any more, and in particular why he had let *The New Republic* have 'Politics and the English Language'. He proposed to reprint Orwell's review of Koestler's 'The Yogi and the Commissar', which had been published in *C.W. Review*, November 1945 ('Catastrophic Gradualism', XVII, 2778, pp. 342–7) in the September issue of *Politics*.

2. Presumably 'Politics vs. Literature: An Examination of *Gulliver's Travels*' (XVIII, 3089, pp. 417–32).

3. It is possible that Orwell is referring to the response (especially Kingsley Martin's) to 'As I Please', 40 (XVI, 2541, pp. 371-2), in which he discussed the Warsaw Uprising and the reaction to it of the press and intellectuals. Martin, editor of the *New Statesman and Nation*, protested that Orwell was not justified in including it among

those which had 'licked the boots of Moscow'.

4. They are not the same. English 12 is US 12½.

5. *Keep the Aspidistra Flying*. Woodcock's article was 'George Orwell, Nineteenth Century Liberal', *Politics*, December 1946.

6. See afterword to 'Politics vs. Literature', p. 431, for a summary of Woodcock's article.

To Leonard Moore*

18 October 1946
27 B Canonbury Square
Islington N 1

Dear Moore,

Many thanks for your letter of 17th October. I am glad to hear about the Norwegian serialisation of *Animal Farm*.[1] You sent me recently some copies of the German edition, and it occurred to me that if the book sells well there may be some royalties over and above the amount Amstutz[2] paid in advance. If so, is there any way by which I could leave some francs in Switzerland? Everyone who comes back from there tells me about how easy it is to buy clothes in Switzerland, and after years of rationing I am in such desperate straits for shirts, underclothes etc. that I should like to be able to buy a few odds and ends. Or is one obliged to bring all foreign exchange back to this country? This matter isn't urgent, as even if extra royalties do accrue they won't be due for some months. But I should be glad to know how the position stands. With regard to possible future earnings in the USA, Mr Harrison[3] explained to me that by becoming a chartered company in the USA I could leave money there if I wished to, and so long as it was spent there and not here it would only be liable to American income tax. I told him I should like to do this, as if I ever go to the USA—I don't want to do so now, but I might some time in 1948—it would be convenient to have some money there and I might as well avoid the higher tax.

He also said that he was going to Hollywood, and could he make any attempt on my behalf to negotiate film rights. I told him to get in touch with you, and I suppose he did this before leaving.

Yours sincerely
Eric Blair

[XVIII, 3099, pp. 452–3; typewritten]

1. In addition to a serialisation in Norwegian, a cheap edition was published in October 1946 as *Diktatoren* by Brann Forlag, Oslo. Only a small number of the 5–6,000

    copies printed were sold, and when Brann Forlag was taken over, the new owners reduced the price (1948).

2.   Verlag Amstutz, Herdeg & Co, Zurich, publishers of *Farm der Tiere*, October 1946.

3.   Of Harrison, Son, Hill & Co., accountants. 'No one is patriotic about taxes' as Orwell remarked in his Wartime Diary on 9 August 1940. However, tax at the time he was earning anything like the just rewards for his labours amounted to 45% in the £ at the basic level and then rose to as much as 98% in the £.

To Leonard Moore*

23 October 1946
27 B Canonbury Square
Islington N 1

Dear Moore,

Many thanks for your letter of the 22nd. It doesn't matter sending those two copies of *Polemic* to America. I can get others. The great rarity is the first number, of which only a very few battered copies exist.

    As you know Warburg wants some time to do a uniform edition of my books, and would like in any case to re-issue one of the old ones some time in 1947, as I am not likely to have a new book ready for publication before 1948. The question therefore arises about copyright. To date, the books worth reprinting are—

> *Homage to Catalonia*
> *Animal Farm*
> *Critical Essays*
> *Down & Out*
> *Burmese Days*
> *Coming Up for Air.*[1]

The first three were originally published by Warburg himself, the other three by Gollancz. How does it stand about the re-issue of these three? Are the copyrights mine? My impression is that the copyrights reverted to me after two years, and I know that the copyright of the American edition of *Burmese Days* (actually the first edition of that book) is mine. The question arises first about *Coming Up for Air*, which has not been reprinted and which Warburg thinks it would be best to start with. Could you get in communication with him so that an agreement can be negotiated [?]

    I think you were keeping for me some copies of the American edition of the *Essays*.[2] If so I should be glad if you could send me them, as I have no copies of that book. Perhaps you could at the same time let me know the address of Harcourt Brace, to whom I want to write recommending a novel by a friend of mine which has been published here but not in the USA.

Yours sincerely
Eric Blair

[XVIII, 3100, pp. 453–4; typewritten]

1. Annotations made in Moore's office show that a letter was sent to Gollancz about the last three books on 29 October 1946. In the left-hand margin has been written 'R/R R/R their letter 21/4/43' against *Down & Out* and *Burmese Days*; and 'R.R. their 22/xi/41 letter' against *Coming Up for Air*. 'R/R' is also written in the margin against the reference to the American edition of *Burmese Days*. R.R. stands for Rights Reverted.
2. In the left-hand margin has been written '3 copies'.

Dwight Macdonald wrote to Orwell on 2 December 1946. He was still anxious to have something from Orwell for Politics, *the circulation of which was dropping enough (from 5,500 in spring 1946 to its present 5,000) to cause a financial crisis. He referred to George Woodcock's article on Orwell in the latest number of* Politics *–'neither flattering nor the reverse', which was how he imagined Orwell would like his work considered.[1] He had bought shoes for Orwell, at $8.95, which showed how the price had gone 'way up of late'. He wanted to know how they should be packed and whether Orwell needed shirts or sweaters, for example, into which they could be bundled and labelled as 'old clothes' to avoid pilfering. If they fitted, he would get him another pair; he feared American and English size twelves were not the same.[2] He also reported that anti-Stalinist intellectuals of his acquaintance claimed that the parable of* Animal Farm *meant that revolution always ended badly for the underdog, 'hence to hell with it and hail the status quo'. He himself read the book as applying solely to Russia and not making any larger statement about the philosophy of revolution. 'I've been impressed with how many leftists I know make this criticism quite independently of each other—impressed because it didn't occur to me when reading the book and still doesn't seem correct to me. Which view would you say comes closer to your own intentions?'*

To Dwight Macdonald*

5 December 1946
27B Canonbury Square,
Islington N 1

Dear Dwight,

I can't thank you enough about the shoes. I've written at once to my agent to see about getting the money to you. I suppose it would be better to see whether the first pair fits, though I think the American sizes are the same. Probably it would be all right if you did them up as old clothes as you said. But someone did tell me it was a good idea to send shoes in two separate parcels, then it's not worth anyone's while to pinch them, unless there happened to be a one-legged man on the dock.

Re. your query about *Animal Farm*. Of course I intended it primarily as a satire on the Russian revolution. But I did mean it to have a wider application in so much that I meant that *that kind* of revolution (violent conspiratorial revolution, led by unconsciously power-hungry people) can only lead to a change of masters. I meant the moral to be that revolutions only effect a radical improvement when the masses are alert and know how to chuck out their leaders as soon as the latter have done their job. The turning-point of the story was supposed to be when the pigs kept the milk and apples for themselves (Kronstadt.[3]) If the other animals had had the sense to put their foot down then, it would have been all right. If people think I am defending the *status quo*, that is, I think, because they have grown pessimistic and assume that there is no alternative except dictatorship or *laissez-faire* capitalism. In the case of Trotskyists, there is the added complication that they feel responsible for events in the USSR up to about 1926 and have to assume that a sudden degeneration took place about that date. Whereas I think the whole process was foreseeable—and was foreseen by a few people, eg. Bertrand Russell—from the very nature of the Bolshevik party. What I was trying to say was, 'You can't have a revolution unless you make it for yourself; there is no such thing as a benevolent dictat[or]ship.'[4]

I am at present struggling with a radio version of the book, which is a ghastly difficult job and will take a long time. But after that I shall get back to a long article I am doing for *Polemic*, and possibly it might interest you for *Politics*. Any way I'll see that a copy gets to you first. It's on Tolstoy's essay on Shakespeare, which I expect you have read. I dare say you won't approve of what I say. I don't like Tolstoy, much as I used to like his novels. I believe George Woodcock is writing an attack on me for something I wrote in *Polemic* about Tolstoy, Swift and anarchism.[5]

I'm sorry about the circulation of *Politics*. You *ought* to be able to dispose of more copies over here, but I don't know how one sets about the distribution. Did I previously send you lists of possible subscribers? One thing I found when trying to circularise the *Partisan Review* was that people don't know whether there is a regular channel for paying for American magazines, so if you are canvassing people you ought to make this clear to them. Of course everyone has felt the draught a bit. *Tribune*'s circulation has dropped over the past year, and I must say that during the last six months it has deserved to. However they've now got more paper and Kimche is back as editor, so I expect it will improve. The trouble was that with Labour in office they couldn't make up their minds whether to attack the government or not, especially as there are several Labour M.Ps on the board of directors. Also the paper had been given its main emphasis by Bevan who can now have nothing to do with it. By the way what you said about *Tribune*'s attitude to the squatters was not fair. Of course they didn't want squatters shot, but one must realise that that kind of action simply interferes with re-housing. The later part of the squatting campaign, ie. siezure° of flats, was 'got up' by the Communists in order to make trouble and also in hopes of winning popularity for the coming municipal elections. They therefore led on a lot of unfortunate people, representing to them that they could get them houses, with the result that all these people lost their places in the housing queue. I imagine the heavy defeat the CP had in the municipal elections was partly a result of this.

I have stopped sending my things to the *New Republic*, because what I am now doing is mostly topical English stuff that wouldn't interest them. I seldom see the *N.R.* and am not sure how far it is a fellow-traveller paper. From their frequently swapping articles with *Tribune*, and being anxious to have my stuff, I thought they couldn't be very much, but I was rather taken aback when I heard Wallace had become editor in chief.[6]

Yours
George

[XVIII, 3128, pp. 506–8; typewritten]

1. Woodcock described Orwell's reaction to this article in his study of Orwell, *The Crystal Spirit* (1967). He met Orwell in the Freedom Bookshop just as Orwell had bought this number of *Politics*. He felt apprehensive because on some points the essay was very critical. He had 'got into trouble with London literary friends over much less critical comments on their work'. That evening, Orwell telephoned him; 'he liked the essay and thought it was as good a first study as any writer could expect.' He objected only to Woodcock's accusation of political opportunism for arguing that conscription could not be avoided in wartime but thereafter must be ended because it infringed the liberties of the individual. 'But even here his protest

took a surprisingly mild form. "I have my reasons for arguing like that," he said, but he never explained them' (pp. 38–39).

2. English size 12 = American size 12½. The shoes did prove to be too small.

3. Kronstadt, a naval base guarding the approach to St Petersburg, a few miles from Finland, was established by Peter the Great in 1704. The turning point in *Animal Farm* is related to events that took place there early in 1921. Food shortages and a harsh regime prompted a series of strikes in Leningrad; in March the strikers were supported by sailors at the Kronstadt naval base. This was the first serious uprising not only by supporters of the Revolution against their government but by a city and by naval personnel particularly associated with ensuring the success of the 1917 Revolution. Trotsky and Mikhail Tukhachevsky (1893–1937) put down the rebellion, but the losses sustained by the rebels were not in vain. A New Economic Policy was enunciated shortly after which recognised the need for reforms. Tukhachevsky was made a Marshal of the Soviet Union in 1935, but two years later he was executed in one of Stalin's purges. The fact that Macdonald missed the significance of the 'turning-point' in *Animal Farm* may be the reason why Orwell strengthened this moment in his adaptation for radio, the script of which he was to deliver in a week or so. He added this little exchange:

> CLOVER: Do you think that it is quite fair to appropriate the apples?
> MOLLY: What, keep all the apples for themselves?
> MURIEL: Aren't we to have any?
> COW: I thought they were to be shared out equally. (VIII, p. 153)

Unfortunately, Rayner Heppenstall cut these from the script as broadcast.

4. When Yvonne Davet wrote to Orwell on 6 September 1946 (XVIII, 3063, pp. 390–1), she told him that the title initially chosen for the French translation of *Animal Farm* was to be *URSA – Union des Républiques Socialistes Animales* (= URSA, the Bear) but it was changed 'to avoid offending the Stalinists too much, which I think is a pity'.

5 See **15.10.46**, n. 6.

6. Henry Wallace (1888–1965), US Secretary of Agriculture, 1933–41; Vice-President, 1941–45. His very liberal views led to his replacement by Harry S. Truman as Vice-President, but he nevertheless served as Secretary of Commerce until, owing to his opposition to President Truman's policy toward the Soviet Union, he was forced to resign. He was editor of *New Republic*, 1946–47. In 1948 he stood as presidential candidate for the Progressive Party advocating closer co-operation with the Soviet Union. He received more than one million votes but none in the Electoral College.

To Mamaine Koestler

24 January 1947
27B Canonbury Square
Islington N 1

Dear Mamaine,

I can't thank you enough for the tea.[1] We always seem to drink more than we can legally get, and are always slightly inclined to go round cadging it, but I don't want to give you the impression that the shortage is calamitous.

As to books, I have only got a very little way with a novel which I hope to finish about the end of 1947, if too many things don't intervene. I don't really know how I stand about contracts with French publishers. Several books of mine are now being translated or have recently been translated, and I don't know whether I have exclusive agreements with any of the publishers. In any case, I don't like making arrangements before a book is written because I think it puts a hoodoo on it.

I have just read *Thieves in the Night*,[2] which I could not get hold of before. I enjoyed reading it, but you know my views, or at any rate Arthur knows my views about this terrorism business. You might just tell Arthur from me that his ideas about the prevalence of circumcision are quite incorrect. So far from stamping anyone as Jewish, this practice used at any rate to be so common, especially among the richer classes, that a boy at a public school felt embarrassed at swimming pools and so forth if he was not circumcised. I believe it is getting less common now, but is also commoner among the working classes. I have a good mind to put a piece about this in my column some time.[3]

I am glad you liked the radio version of *Animal Farm*. Most people seemed to, and it got quite a good press. I had the feeling that they had spoilt it, but one nearly always does with anything one writes for the air.

Richard is very well, and is talking distinctly more.

With love,
George

[XIX, 3159, pp. 27–8; typewritten]

1. The Koestlers preferred coffee, hence their being able to spare some of their tea ration for him.
2. A novel, about the Zionist struggle to set up an independent Jewish state in Palestine, by Mamaine's husband, Arthur Koestler, published in 1946.
3. There is no such discussion in the 'As I Please' columns.

To Rayner Heppenstall*

25 January 1947
27B Canonbury Square,
Islington N 1

Dear Rayner,

Thanks for your letter. Re. *Animal Farm*.[1] I had a number of people here to listen to it on the first day, and they all seemed to think it was good, and Porteous,[2] who had not read the book, grasped what was happening after a few minutes. I also had one or two fan letters and the press notices were good except on my native ground, ie. *Tribune*. As to what I thought myself, it's hard to get a detached view, because whenever I write anything for the air I have the impression it has been spoiled, owing to its inevitably coming out different to one's conception of it. I must say I don't agree about there being too much narrator. If anything I thought there should have been more explanation. People are always yearning to get rid of the narrator, but it seems to me that until certain problems have been overcome you only get rid of the narrator at the expense of having to play a lot of stupid tricks in order to let people know what is happening. The thing is to make the narrator a good turn in himself. But that means writing serious prose, which people don't, and making the actors stick to it instead of gagging and trying to make everything homey and naturalistic.

I can't write or promise to write anything more at present, I am too busy. I've still got ideas about fairy stories. I wish they would dig up and re-b'cast my adaptation of the *Emperor's New Clothes*. It was done on the Eastern and African services, but in those days I wasn't well-connected enough to crash the Home. I expect the discs would have been scraped,° however. I had them illicitly re-recorded at a commercial studio, but that lot of discs got lost. I've often pondered over 'Cinderella', which of course is the tops so far as fairy stories go but on the face of it is too visual to be suitable for the air. But don't you think one could make the godmother turn her into a wonderful singer who could sing a higher note than anyone else, or something of that kind? The best way would be if she had a wonderful voice but could not sing in tune, like Trilby, and the godmother cured this. One could make it quite comic with the wicked sisters singing in screeching voices. It might be worth talking over some time. Give my love to Margaret.

Yours
Eric[3]

[XIX, 3163, pp. 32–3; typewritten]

1. Heppenstall had written on 24 January 1947 asking for Orwell's conclusions about the broadcast of *Animal Farm*. He said that the opinion at the BBC, with which he agreed, was that 'there were too many lengthy pieces of narration—that in fact the adaptation was not sufficiently ruthless and complete'. He asked also whether Orwell had further ideas for the Third Programme, for instance, 'any Imaginary Conversation' and whether he wanted more scripts of *Animal Farm*.

2. Hugh Gordon Porteous (1906–1993), literary and art critic and sinologist. In 1933 he remarked, 'Verse will be worn longer this season and rather red,' blaming Auden for being the reddening agent (Valentine Cunningham, *British Writers of the Thirties*, 1988, p. 27). He reviewed extensively, especially for T. S. Eliot in *The Criterion* in the thirties and *The Listener* in the sixties.

3. Heppenstall replied on 29 January 1947. He was anxious to convince Orwell 'about this business of narration'. He did not agree that narration could be avoided only by resorting to 'a lot of stupid tricks'. Narration involved 'a very marked change of pace...straight reading and...dramatic presentation don't mix'. He said he would never allow an actor to gag (*ad lib*). He thought the fairy stories should 'follow Red Riding Hood to *Children's Hour*' unless Orwell had something more sophisticated in mind. His wife hoped Orwell would 'presently come to supper'. He had seen Richard Rees for the first time since the outbreak of the war and remarked how greatly he had aged. The second page of this letter has not been traced.

To Leonard Moore*

21 February 1947
27B Canonbury Square
Islington N 1

Dear Moore,

With reference to your two letters of the 18th and the 19th.

I don't think the offer to dramatise *Animal Farm* sounds very promising, in fact I don't see what we get out of it except that there would then be a dramatic version existing, which I suppose would make it slightly more likely to reach the stage. But we would also be tied down to that particular adaptor, at least for a year, and somebody else might make a more inviting offer in the mean time, though I am bound to say I do not think it is a suitable book to adapt for stage production. One doesn't, of course, know what sort of version he and his collaborator would make, but from the fact of his referring to the book as 'The' *Animal Farm* I assume he has not read it very attentively. I don't think I should close with him.[1]

I have meanwhile received a cable from some people in New York enquiring about film rights. I hope I shall have got you on the phone before this letter reaches you, but if not I will send the cable on with another letter.

As to Warburg. I want Warburg to become my regular publisher, because, although he may not sell the books so largely, I can trust him to publish whatever I write. At the same time we must settle this business about the uniform edition, as I don't see much point in simply re-issuing, in different formats, various books which have already appeared and therefore can't be expected to sell large numbers straight off. I had understood that what was intended was to produce all the books involved as paper became available in a uniform binding and at rather a low price—though I suppose not always the same price as some are much longer than others. But as to the variation in length, it is in most cases only between about 80,000 and about 50,000. The exception is *Animal Farm* (30,000), but I suppose he wouldn't work round to this till last, and one might put something else with it to bring it up to the right length. As to your query about cheap editions, I am not quite sure what is involved there. Is it a question of whether Warburg has all rights for cheap editions as well? I imagine the only reprint firm likely to do any of my books is the Penguin Library, which has already done two. I presume Warburg wouldn't object to a book being Penguinised, as I shouldn't think this cuts across ordinary sales much.

Do you think you could get this fixed up with Warburg as soon as possible[?] Tell him that I am fully ready for him to be my regular publisher, but that I want the following conditions:

(i) That though he may, if he wishes, issue ordinary editions of any books, he will also undertake to do a uniform edition which will include the six books we have agreed on and any suitable future books.

(ii) That though I will give him first refusal of all full-length books, I can if I choose do odd jobs for other publishers, such as introductions, contributions to miscellanies, etc.

Even if we can't draw up a full agreement immediately, I would like some settlement to be made as soon as possible about *Coming Up for Air*. Warburg proposed to do this as the first of the re-issues, and he says that if the matter can be settled quickly he might get it onto his March paper quota. I would like this to happen, because I shall not have anything ready to be published before 1948 and it would not be a bad idea to have something appearing this year. Also I think that book was rather sunk by appearing just before the outbreak of war, and it is now very completely out of print.[2]

Yours sincerely
Eric Blair

[XIX, 3173, pp. 47–9; typewritten]

1. Details of this proposal have not been traced. A dramatised version, with music and lyrics, directed by Peter Hall, was given with great success at the National Theatre on 25 April 1984. In 1985 it toured nine cities.
2. Moore wrote to Warburg on 27 February 1947 quoting much of this letter. Moore concludes with a reminder that Gollancz has an option on Orwell's next two novels: 'It may be, however, we can make some arrangement regarding this.' This was eventually agreed.

To Dwight Macdonald*

26 February 1947
27B Canonbury Square
Islington N 1

Dear Dwight,

Thanks awfully for sending the shoes which arrived today. I trust they have sent you the money for them—I wrote to my agent to remind him to do this and he said he had done so. I am sorry to say they were too small after all, however it doesn't matter because I recently managed to get another pair owing to somebody who takes the same size ordering a pair about a year ago and not wanting them when done. I shall send this pair on to Germany where doubtless they will be appreciated.

I wanted to ask, when you print the excerpt from the Tolstoy article,[1] if you're paying for it, could you pay the money to my American agents, Mcintosh & Otis. I'm trying to let any money I earn in the USA pile up over there in case I ever make a visit there. I don't know whether I shall do so, but even if I don't, I'm not short of money at present and might as well let it lie there as pay British income tax on it.

It's been a lousy winter here what with the fuel breakdown and this unheard-of weather. I suppose conditions here are now what would be normal postwar winter conditions in, say, Paris. *Polemic* were very pleased with the long note you gave them in *Politics*. I think the paper is now taking shape a bit, and it is doing fairly well from the point of view of circulation, though hampered by the usual organisational difficulties. I have now joined the editorial board, but I probably shan't do much on it as I am going back to Scotland in April and shall go on with a novel which I am doing and hope to finish by the end of 1947. While in London I have been snowed up with hackwork as usual. This two-weeks' closure of the weeklies[2] has meant an awful lot of nuisance and incidentally lost *Tribune* a lot of money it can ill afford.

Yours
George

[XIX, 3175, pp.49–50; typewritten]

1. Macdonald did not print an excerpt from 'Lear, Tolstoy and the Fool'.
2. Because of massive electricity power cuts.

To Fredric Warburg*

28 February 1947
27B Canonbury Square
Islington N 1

Dear Fred,

I said I would write to you following on our telephone conversation. I wrote to Moore some days back, asking him to expedite the business of *Coming Up for Air* and if possible to get the whole contract settled. I told him that I wanted you to be my regular publisher and to have first refusal of all my books, but there were some conditions, none of which I imagine are of a kind you would object to. One was that you should publish a uniform edition. The second was that I should have the right to do odd jobs for other publishers such as, for instance, introductions or contributions to miscellaneous publications, and the other was that you would not object to certain classes of cheap editions being done elsewhere, for instance, Penguins. Some of my books have been done as Penguins, and I suppose this might arise again.

Moore has just written again raising the point about my previous contract with Gollancz. Gollancz is still supposed to have an option on two works of fiction, though in my opinion it should be only one as he refused *Animal Farm* and then claimed that it was not a work of fiction of standard length. Moore is anxious to get this settled. I must say I was inclined to leave it hanging, because actually I can think of ways to evade the contract with Gollancz. However, if it must be settled it would probably be better if I saw Gollancz personally.[1] But meanwhile, need we let this hold up the republication of *Coming Up for Air*, the copyright of which is, I suppose, my own?[2]

Yours sincerely,
Geo. Orwell

[XIX, 3179, p. 53; typewritten]

1. This sentence had been annotated in the left-hand margin in Warburg's office: 'Go & see VG.'
2. The rights had reverted to Orwell on 22 November 1946 because the book had been allowed to go out of print for an agreed period of time.

On 7 March 1947, Ihor Szewczenko wrote to Orwell seeking a preface to Animal Farm. *The Ukrainian translation had been given to the publisher in the early autumn of 1946. On 19 February 1947, the publisher requested a preface, regarding it as essential to the satisfactory reception of the book in Ukrainian. Szewczenko explained that delays had arisen because he had moved from Munich to Belgium (where the book was being printed), although he still worked in Germany, and because of difficulties in sending letters to Germany. Although the printer and publisher of* Animal Farm *had been licensed by the occupying powers, Szewczenko did not know whether a licence to publish* Animal Farm *had been applied for by them. If Orwell could not send a preface, he was asked to provide biographical notes.*

Szewczenko then set out the political background of the publishers. They were, in the main, Soviet Ukrainians, many of them former members of the Bolshevik Party, but afterwards inmates of Siberian camps and who were 'genuinely interested' in the story. He reassured Orwell that 'AF is not being published by Ukrainian Joneses' – a reference to the farmer in Animal Farm.

To Ihor Szewczenko*

13 March 1947
27B Canonbury Square
Islington N 1

Dear Mr Szewczenko,

Many thanks for your letter of the 7th, which I received today.

I am frightfully busy, but I will try to send you a short introduction to A. F. and to despatch it not more than a week from hence. I gather that you want it to contain some biographical material, and also, I suppose, an account of how the book came to be written. I assume that the book will be produced in a very simple style with no illustrations on the cover, but just in case it should be wanted I will send a photograph as well.

I was very interested to hear about the people responsible for translating A.F.,[1] and encouraged to learn that that type of opposition exists in the USSR. I do hope it will not all end by the Displaced persons° being shipped back to the USSR or else mostly absorbed by Argentina. I think our desperate labour shortage may compel us to encourage a good many D.Ps to settle in this country, but at present the government is only talking of letting them in as servants etc., because there is still working-class resistance against letting in foreign workers, owing to fear of unemployment, and the Communists and 'sympathisers' are able to play on this.

I have noted your new address and presume you will be there till further notice. I shall be at the above address until April 10th, and after that at the

Scottish address. I think you have this, but in case you have not I will give it you:

    Barnhill Isle of Jura Argyllshire SCOTLAND.

Yours sincerely
Geo. Orwell

                             [XIX, 3187, 3188, pp. 72–4; typewritten]

1.   This seems to be a slight misunderstanding. Szewczenko was undertaking the translation (it appeared under the pen-name Ivan Cherniatync'kyi).

To Victor Gollancz

14 March 1947
27B Canonbury Square,
Islington N 1

Dear Gollancz,

I believe Leonard Moore has already spoken to you about the contract which I still have with you and about my wish to be released from it. I believe that the contract that still subsists between us is the one made for *Keep the Aspidistra Flying* in 1937, which provided that I would give you the first refusal of my next three novels. *Coming Up for Air* worked off one of these, but you did not accept *Animal Farm*, which you saw and refused in 1944, as working off another. So that by the terms of the contract I still owe you the refusal of two other novels.

I know that I am asking you a very great favour in asking that you should cancel the contract, but various circumstances have changed in the ten years since it was made, and I believe that it might be to your advantage, as it certainly would be to mine, to bring it to an end. The position is that since then you have published three books of mine¹ but you have also refused two others on political grounds,² and there was also another which you did not refuse but which it seemed natural to take to another publisher.³ The crucial case was *Animal Farm*. At the time when this book was finished, it was very hard indeed to get it published, and I determined then that if possible I would take all my future output to the publishers who would produce it, because I knew that anyone who would risk this book would risk anything. Secker & Warburg were not only ready to publish *Animal Farm* but are willing, when paper becomes available, to do a uniform edition of such of my books as I think worth reprinting, including some which are at present very completely out of print. They are also anxious to reprint my novel *Coming Up for Air* in an ordinary edition this year, but, not unnaturally, they are only willing to do all this if they can have a comprehensive contract giving them control of anything I write.

From my own point of view it is clearly very unsatisfactory to have to take my novels to one publisher and at the same time to be obliged, at any rate in some cases, to take non-fiction books elsewhere. I recognise, of course, that your political position is not now exactly what it was when you refused *Animal Farm*, and in any case I respect your unwillingness to publish books which go directly counter to your political principles. But it seems to me that this difficulty is likely to arise again in some form or other, and that it would be better if you are willing to bring the whole thing to an end.

If you wish to see me personally about this, I am at your disposal. I shall be at this address until about April 10th.

Yours sincerely,
Geo. Orwell

[XIX, 3191, pp. 77–9; typewritten]

1. The contract was not actually made 'for' *Keep the Aspidistra Flying* (which had been published on 20 April 1936), but it referred to it. The first clause of the draft contract (all that survives) states 'EB grants to G exclusive right to publish in English next 3 "new and original full-length novels" after Keep the A.' This was signed on Orwell's behalf – he was in Spain – by Eileen, who was empowered so to do. The three books published since then were *The Road to Wigan Pier*, *Coming Up for Air*, and *Inside the Whale*. Only the second is a novel, of course. Orwell could, perhaps, have mentioned that he had also collaborated with Gollancz on *The Betrayal of the Left*.

2. The two refused on political grounds were *Homage to Catalonia* and *Animal Farm*. Although there was no doubt that *Animal Farm* was refused on political grounds, Gollancz had a point that – whatever Orwell may have felt, it was hardly 'a work of fiction of standard length'. The contract – if it repeated the wording of the draft – did specifically refer to 'full-length novels '.

3. Presumably either *The Lion and the Unicorn* or *Critical Essays*, both published by Secker & Warburg.

It has long been accepted that, from his childhood, Orwell had shown an interest in science and had indicated he wanted one day to write a book like Wells's A Modern Utopia *(X, 29, p. 45). Sir Roger Mynors (see [?].8.20, n. 2) recalled how, when at Eton, he and Orwell had 'developed a great passion for biology and got permission to do extra dissection in the biology lab'. One day Orwell, who had remarkable skill with a catapult, shot and killed a jackdaw high on the roof of the College chapel. They then took it to the biology laboratory and dissected it. 'We made the great mistake of slitting the gall bladder and therefore flooding the place with, er . . . Well, it was an awful mess'* (Remembering Orwell, pp. 18–19).

Scholars have given much thought to when Orwell was prompted to set about writing Nineteen Eighty-Four. When The Lost Orwell was at proof stage, Ralph Desmarais, then undertaking doctoral research at Imperial College London, drew my attention to Orwell's correspondence with Dr C. D. Darlington. This showed how important was Orwell's attendance at a lecture given by John Baker at the PEN Conference, 22–26 August 1944 (see **19.3.47**, n. 3 below for the lecture). It was already known that Orwell was interested in Lysenko* and his notes for The Last Man in Europe make an obscure reference to 'The Swindle of Bakerism and Ingsoc' (XV, 2377, p. 368). We know that Orwell told Warburg that he first thought of the novel in 1943 and Orwell himself wrote that it was the Teheran Conference (28 November 1943) which led him 'to discuss the implications of dividing the world up into "Zones of influence"' (XIX, 3513, p. 487). So, whereas Orwell first thought of the novel in late 1943, this exchange of correspondence suggests it was hearing Baker and his citation of Lysenko that prompted Orwell to begin serious work on Nineteen Eighty-Four later in 1944. Lysenko rejected traditional hybridisation theories. Stalin backed his approach to such a degree that opposition to him was outlawed in 1948. He claimed he could vastly improve Soviet crop yield, but after the total failure of his methods they were finally discredited in 1964.

To Dr C. D. Darlington*

19 March 1947
27B Canonbury Square
Islington N 1

Dear Dr Darlington,

Very many thanks for the cutting of your article from Discovery,[1] which I read with great interest. I dare say someone had told you that I was interested in this story of Lysenko*, though I rather think we did meet once when I was at the B.B.C.[2]

I first heard about it in the speech given by John Baker at the PEN Conference in 1944, and afterwards read it at greater length in Baker's book Science and the Planned State.[3] I formed the opinion then that the story as told by Baker was true, and am very glad to get this confirmation. I would like to make use of the information supplied by you in my column some time, but I am no scientist and I hardly care to write about what is first and foremost a scientific matter. However, this persecution of scientists and falsification of results seems to me to follow naturally from the persecution of writers and historians, and I have written a number of times that British scientists ought not to remain so undisturbed when they see mere literary men sent to concentration camps.

I shall try to get hold of your obituary article on Vavilov in *Nature*.[4] I saw it stated in an American paper recently that he was definitely known to be dead.

Yours sincerely,
Geo. Orwell

[*LO*, pp. 128–31; XIX, 3192A, p. 79; typewritten]

1. C.D. Darlington, 'A Revolution in Russian Science', *Discovery*, vol 8, February 1947, pp. 33–43.

2. Orwell had asked Darlington to broadcast to India for university students on 'The Future of Science', 7 July 1942 (XIII, 1170, p. 321); on 'India and the Steel Age', 10 July 1942 (XIII, 1220, p. 361); and on 'Plant or Animal Breeding', 22 July 1943 (XV, 2088, p. 101).

3. In the lecture at the PEN Conference that Orwell heard Baker give, Baker reiterated his objection to scientific planning, specifying Trofim Denisovich Lysenko* as a case in point: 'A good example is provided by the appointment of one Lysenko to be an Academician in the U.S.S.R. and Director of the Soviet Academy of Agricultural Science'. After describing Lysenko's rejection of Western genetics and his insistence that Soviet researchers adopt his own beliefs, Baker concluded: 'The case of Lysenko provides a vivid illustration of the degradation of science under a totalitarian regime' (John R. Baker, 'Science, Culture and Freedom', in Herman Ould, ed., *Freedom of Expression: A Symposium* (1945), pp. 118–19 which Orwell reviewed, 12 October 1945, XVII, 2764, pp. 308–10). See also third paragraph from the end of 'The Prevention of Literature' (XVII, 2792, p. 379) for Orwell on the uncritical attitude of some scientists to the Soviet persecution of creative writers.

4. C.D. Darlington and SC Harland, 'Nikolai Ivanovich Vavilov, 1885–1942', *Nature*, 156 (1945), p. 621.

To Brenda Salkeld*

20 March 1947
27B Canonbury Square
Islington N 1

Dearest Brenda,

I tried to phone you last night but couldn't get any sense out of the phone.

In case this reaches you in time on Friday morning. I'm afraid Friday is hopeless for me. I'm going out to lunch, and, little as I want to, I believe I have got to go out to dinner as well. I shall be at home during the morning up to about 12.30, and during the afternoon. So ring if you get the chance.

I have now literally no fuel whatever. However it isn't quite so stinkingly cold, in fact we've distinctly seen the sun on more than one occasion, and I heard some birds trying to sing the other morning. I've been frantically busy but have now cleared off the more urgent stuff. I've only one more job to do and hope to get that out of the way before we leave for Barnhill, as I do so want not to have to take any bits and pieces of work with me. We have arranged to leave on April 10th, and if I can fix the tickets are going to fly from Glasgow to Islay, which ought to cut out about 6 hours of that dismal journey. Richard has had a nasty feverish cold and he had a temperature two days, but I think he's all right now. *Do* make sure to see me before we go, and try and fix up about coming to stay at Barnhill. I think after this stinking winter the weather ought to be better this year.

Take care of yourself and try and give me a ring tomorrow. Perhaps you could look in for a cup of tea, say about 3 or 4 in the afternoon?

Much love
Eric

[XIX, 3195, pp. 80–1; typewritten]

Arthur Koestler*

21 March 1947
27B Canonbury Square
Islington N 1

Dear Arthur,

Thanks for your letter. Ref. the Freedom Defence Committee. It is a very small organisation which does the best it can with inadequate funds. The sum they were appealing for on this occasion was £250, and they got somewhat more than that. Naturally they want an assured income to pay for premises and staff, and regular legal assistance. What they actually have at present is some small premises and one secretary, and the (I imagine) rather precarious aid of one lawyer who does not demand much in the way of fees. Of course one can do very little on such a tiny establishment, but they can hardly make it larger unless people do give them money. I think up to date they have done a certain amount of good. They have certainly taken up quite a few cases and bombarded secretaries of state etc. with letters, which is usually about all one can do. The point is that the N.C.C.L.[1] became a Stalinist organisation, and since then there has been no organisation aiming chiefly at the defence of civil liberties. Even a tiny nucleus like this is better than nothing, and if it became better known it could get more money, and so become larger. I think sooner or later there may be a row about the larger aims of the Committee, because at present the moving spirits in it are anarchists and there is a tendency to use it for anarchist propaganda. However, that might correct itself if the organisation became larger, because most of the new supporters would presumably be people of ordinary liberal views. I certainly think the Committee is worth £5 a year. If 9 other people have guaranteed the same sum, £50 a year assured is quite a consideration. It would cover stationary°, for example.

I am going back to Jura in April and hope then to get back to the novel I started last year. While in London I've been swamped with footling jobs as usual. The weather and the fuel shortage have been unbearable. For about a month one did nothing except try to keep warm. Richard is well and is talking rather more—in all other ways he seems fairly forward. Please give my love to Mamaine.

Yours
George

[XIX, 3196A, p. 84; typewritten]

1. National Council for Civil Liberties.

To Victor Gollancz*

25 March 1947
27B Canonbury Square
Islington N 1

Dear Gollancz,

I must thank you for your kind and considerate letter, and I have thought it over with some care. I nevertheless still think, if you are willing to agree, that it would be better to terminate our contract. It is not that anything in the book I am now writing is likely to lead to trouble, but I have to think of the over-all position. Neither Warburg nor anyone else can regard me as a good proposition unless he can have an option on my whole output, which is never very large in any case. It is obviously better if I can be with one publisher altogether, and, as I don't suppose I shall cease writing about politics from time to time, I am afraid of further differences arising, as in the past. You know what the difficulty is, ie., Russia. For quite 15 years I have regarded that regime with plain horror, and though, of course, I would change my opinion if I saw reason, I don't think my feelings are likely to change so long as the Communist party remains in power. I know that your position in recent years has been not very far from mine, but I don't know what it would be if, for instance, there is another seeming

raprochement° between Russia and the West, which is a possible development in the next few years. Or again in an actual war situation. I don't,
God knows, want a war to break out, but if one were compelled to choose
between Russia and America—and I suppose that is the choice one might
have to make—I would always choose America. I know Warburg and his
opinions well enough to know that he is very unlikely ever to refuse anything of mine on political grounds. As you say, no publisher can sign blind
an undertaking to print anything a writer produces, but I think Warbug is
less likely to jib than most.

I know that I am asking a great deal of you, since after all we have a contract which I signed freely and by which I am still bound. If you decide that
the contract must stand, of course I shall not violate it. But so far as my own
feelings go I would rather terminate it. Please forgive me for what must
seem like ungraciousness, and for causing you all this trouble.

Yours sincerely
Geo. Orwell

[XIX, 3200, pp. 90–1; typewritten]

To Victor Gollancz*

9 April 1947
27B Canonbury Square
Islington N 1

Dear Gollancz,

I should have written several days earlier, but I have been ill in bed. Very
many thanks for your generous action.[1]

Yours sincerely,
George Orwell

[XIX, 3211, p. 122; typewritten copy]

1.   Gollancz's generous action was to relinquish his right to publish Orwell's next two
     novels – in effect, *Nineteen Eighty-Four*.

To Sonia Brownell*

12 April 1947
Barnhill,
Isle of Jura

Dearest Sonia,

I am handwriting this because my typewriter is downstairs. We arrived O.K. & without incident yesterday. Richard was as good as gold & rather enjoyed having a sleeper to himself after he had got over the first strangeness, & as soon as we got into the plane at Glasgow he went to sleep, probably because of the noise. I hadn't been by plane before & I think it's really better. It costs £2 or £3 more, but it saves about 5 hours & the boredom of going on boats, & even if one was sick its° only three quarters of an hour whereas if one goes by sea one is sick for five or six hours, ie. if it is bad weather. Everything up here is just as backward as in England, hardly a bud showing & I saw quite a lot of snow yesterday. However it's beautiful spring weather now & the plants I put in at the new year seem to be mostly alive. There are daffodils all over the place, the only flower out. I'm still wrestling with more or less virgin meadow, but I think by next year I'll have quite a nice garden here. Of course we've had a nightmare all today getting things straight, with Richard only too ready to help, but it's more or less right now & the house is beginning to look quite civilized. It will be some weeks before we've got the transport problem fully solved, but otherwise we are fairly well appointed. I'm going to send for some hens as soon as we have put the hen house up, & this year I have been also able to arrange for alcohol so that we have just a little, a sort of rum ration, each day. Last year we had to be practically T.T. I think in a week everything will be straight & the essential work in the garden done, & then I can get down to some work.

I wrote to Genetta¹ asking her to come whenever she liked & giving instructions about the journey. So long as she's bringing the child, not just sending it, it should be simple enough. I want to give you the complete details about the journey, which isn't so formidable as it looks on paper. The facts are these:

There are boats to Jura on *Mondays, Wednesdays & Fridays*. You have to catch the boat train at Glasgow at 8 am, which means that it's safer to sleep the preceding night at Glasgow, because the all-night trains have a nasty way of coming in an hour or two hours late, & then one misses the boat train. [*Directions for travel, for similar details about travel see* **16.6.46**] If you want to go by plane, the planes run daily (except Sundays I think), & they nearly always take off unless it's very misty. The itinerary then is:

10.30 arrive at Scottish Airways office at St Enoch Station, Glasgow (the air office is in the railway station).

11.15 leave by plane for ISLAY. (Pronounced EYELY).

12 noon arrive Islay.

Hire a car (or take a bus) to the ferry that leads to Jura.

About 1 pm cross ferry.

Hired car to LEALT.

It's important to let us know in advance when you are coming, because of the hired car. There are only 2 posts a week here, & only 2 occasions on which I can send down to Craighouse to order the car. If you come by boat, you could probably get a car all right by asking on the quay, but if you come by air there wouldn't be a car at the ferry (which is several miles from Craighouse) unless ordered beforehand. Therefore if you proposed coming on, say, June 15th, it would be as well to write about June 5th because, according to the day of the week, it may be 4 or 5 days before your letter reaches me, & another 3 or 4 days before I can send a message. It's no use wiring because the telegrams come by the postman.

You want a raincoat & if possible stout boots or shoes—gum boots if you have them. We may have some spare gum boots, I'm not sure—we are fairly well off for spare oilskins & things like that. It would help if you brought that week's rations, because they're not quick at getting any newcomer's rations here, & a little flour & tea.

I am afraid I am making this all sound very intimidating, but really it's easy enough & the house is quite comfortable. The room you would have is rather small, but it looks out on the sea. I do so want to have you here. By that time I hope we'll have got hold of an engine for the boat, & if we get decent weather we can go round to the completely uninhabited bays on the west side of the island, where there is beautiful white sand & clear water with seals swimming about in it. At one of them there is a cave where we can take shelter when it rains, & at another there is a shepherd's hut which is disused but quite livable where one could even picnic for a day or two. Anyway do come, & come whenever you like for as long as you like, only try to let me know beforehand. And meanwhile take care of yourself & be happy.

I've just remembered I never paid you for that brandy you got for me, so enclose £3. I think it was about that wasn't it? The brandy was very nice & was much appreciated on the journey up because they can't get alcohol here at all easily. The next island, Islay, distills whisky but it all goes to America. I gave the lorry driver a large wallop, more than a double, & it disappeared so promptly that it seemed to hit the bottom of his belly with a click.

With much love
George

[XIX, 3212, pp. 122–4; handwritten]

1. Janetta Woolley (now Parladé) was a friend of those who ran *Horizon* and *Polemic*. She may have met Orwell through her former husband, Humphrey Slater* but it seems more likely it was through Cyril Connolly*. At this time she had changed her name by deed-poll to Sinclair-Loutit, whilst living with Kenneth Sinclair-Loutit: their daughter, Nicolette, then nearly four years old, is the child mentioned in this letter. Sonia Brownell had suggested to Orwell that Nicolette would be a suitable same-age companion for young Richard, hence Orwell's invitation, but in the event Janetta and Nicolette did not go to Jura. Kenneth Sinclair-Loutit also knew Orwell, having been in the Spanish civil war as a doctor in the International Brigade and had first met him in Spain.

The following letter is in reply to one from Dwight Macdonald of 9 April 1947. Macdonald said that since his last letter to Orwell he had decided to devote the May–June issue of Politics *to the USSR and the issue after that to France. There would therefore be no room for even an abridged version of Orwell's 'Lear, Tolstoy and the Fool' until September–October at the earliest. He would hold on to the article but would give it to someone else if Orwell wished. It was never published in* Politics. *He asked Orwell for help in compiling a reading list of 50–60 books and articles 'which might be called the basic ones for the layman if he wants to understand Russia today'. Had Orwell any 'pet discoveries'? What ten books would he recommend to a friend ignorant of Russia but seeking enlightenment? He also wanted another 50–60 titles of more specialised books on the best in Soviet art, movies, literature. He said he had no friendly contacts with the higher editors of* The New Republic. *His friends were being 'weeded out at a great rate', and he guessed that Orwell's column 'As I Please' would not be published now that 'the mag has become well-vulgarized by the Wallace crowd'. He suggested Orwell ask his agents to approach* The Nation. *Macdonald had airmailed his profile of Henry Wallace, because, since Wallace was now in England, Orwell might care to tell his readers about it. He confirmed that he had received payment for the shoes he had obtained for Orwell (the shoes which, unfortunately, proved too small).*

To Dwight Macdonald*

15 April 1947
Barnhill
Isle of Jura

Dear Dwight,

Many thanks for your very interesting and informative article on Wallace[1], which reached me yesterday—unfortunately a few days after I'd left London for the summer. I've sent it on to *Tribune*, as I should think they could well use parts of it, at least as background material. I left London the day before W[allace] had his big public meeting at the Albert Hall, but I heard him say a few words of welcome on arrival and got the impression that he meant to be very conciliatory and not make the sort of remarks about 'British imperialism' which he has been making in the USA. His visit here has been timed to do the maximum of mischief, and I was somewhat surprised by the respectful welcome given to him by nearly everyone, incidentally including *Tribune*, which has given him some raps over the knuckles in the past.

It doesn't matter about the Tolstoy article. If you feel you do want to use a piece of it sooner or later, hang on to it until then. Otherwise, could you be kind enough to send it on to my agents, Mcintosh & Otis, explaining the circumstances. It's possible they might be able to do something with it, though as they failed with another *Polemic* article (one on Swift), perhaps this one is no good for the American market either.

As to books on the USSR. It's very hard to think of a good list, and looking back, it seems to me that whatever I have learned, or rather guessed, about that country has come from reading between the lines of newspaper reports. I tried to think of 'pro' books, but couldn't think of any good ones except very early ones such as *Ten Days that Shook the World*[2] (which I haven't read through but have read *in*, of course.) The Webbs' *Soviet Communism*,[3] which I have not read, no doubt contains a lot of facts, but Michael Polanyi's little essay[4] on it certainly convicted the W.s of misrepresentation on some points. A nephew of Beatrice Webb[5] whom I know told me she admitted privately that there were things about the USSR that it was better not to put on paper. For the period round about the Revolution, Krupskaya's *Memories of Lenin* has some interesting facts. So does Angelica Balabanov's *My Life as a Rebel*.[6] The later editions of Krupskaya's book have been tampered with a little, at any rate in England. Of the same period, Bertrand Russell's *Theory and Practice of Bolshevism* (a very rare book which he will not bother to reprint) is interesting because he not only met all the tops but was able to foretell in general terms a good deal that happened later. Rosenberg's *History of Bolshevism* is said to be good and unprejudiced, but I haven't read it and his book on the German Republic seemed to me rather dry and cagey. A book that taught me more than any other about the general course of the Revolution was Franz Borkenau's *The Communist International*. This of course is only partly concerned with the USSR itself, and it is perhaps too much written round a thesis, but it is stuffed with facts which I believe have not been successfully disputed. As for books of 'revelations,' I must say I was doubtful of the authenticity of Valtin's book, but I thought Krivitsky's book[7] genuine although written in a cheap sensational style. In one place where it crossed with my own experiences it seemed to me substantially true. Kravchenko's book[8] is not out in England yet. For the concentration camps, Anton Ciliga's *The Russian Enigma*[9] is good, and more recently *The Dark Side of the Moon*[10] (now I think published in the USA) which is compiled from the experiences of many exiled Poles. A little book by a Polish woman, *Liberation, Russian Style*,[11] which appeared during the war and fell flat, overlaps with *The Dark Side* and is more detailed. I think the most important of very recent books is the Blue Book on the Canadian spy trials,[12] which is fascinating psychologically. As for literature, Gleb Struve's *Twenty-five Years of Soviet Russian Literature* is an invaluable handbook and I am told very accurate. Mirsky's *Russian Literature 1881–1927* (I think that is the title) takes in the earlier part of post-revolutionary literature. There is also Max Eastman's *Artists in Uniform*. You've probably read everything I have mentioned except perhaps the Blue Book. If you haven't read the latter, don't miss it—it's a real thriller.

I am up here for 6 months. Last year I was just taking a holiday after six years of non-stop journalism, but this year I am going to get on with a novel. I shan't finish it in six months but I ought to break its back and might finish it at the end of the year. It is very hard to get back to quiet continuous work after living in a lunatic asylum for years. Not that conditions are now any better than during the war—worse in many ways. This last winter has been quite unendurable, and even now the weather is appalling, but one is a little better off up here where it is a bit easier to get food and fuel than in London.

Yours
George

[XIX, 3215, pp. 126–9; typewritten]

1. For Henry Wallace see **5.12.46** n. 6.
2. John Reed, *Ten Days That Shook the World* (1919). Reed (1887–1920) was involved in setting up the Communist Party in the United States. He died of typhus and was buried in the Kremlin wall.
3. Sidney James Webb (1859–1947) and Beatrice Webb (1858–1943), *Soviet Communism: A New Civilisation?* (2 vols, London, 1935; New York, 1936). Republished in London in 1937, but without the question mark, and in 1941 with a new introduction by Beatrice Webb.
4. Michael Polanyi (1891–1976), *The Contempt of Freedom: The Russian Experiment and After* (1940). Includes his 'Soviet Economics – Fact and Theory' (1935), 'Truth and Propaganda' (1936), 'Collectivist Planning' (1940).
5. Malcolm Muggeridge (1903–90), author and journalist. In 1930, after three years as a lecturer at the Egyptian University, Cairo, he joined the *Manchester Guardian* and was its Moscow correspondent, 1932–3 (see his *Winter in Moscow*, 1934). He then worked on the *Calcutta Statesman* and, from 1935–6, on the *Evening Standard*.

He served throught the war (Major, Intelligence Corps) and afterwards was *Daily Telegraph* Washington correspondent, 1946–7, and its deputy editor 1950–2. From 1952–7 he edited *Punch*. His *The Thirties* (1940) is a useful account of that decade. Sonia Orwell asked him to write Orwell's biography; he agreed but never produced anything. The section of this letter from 'A nephew' to 'on paper' was marked in the margin, in Orwell's hand, 'Off the record.'

6. Nadezhda Krupskaya (1869–1939), wife of Lenin and active in his revolutionary programme. Her *Memories of Lenin* is quoted more than once by Orwell. Angelica Balabanov (1878–1965), associate editor with Mussolini of *Avanti*, worked with Lenin and Trotsky during the Russian Revolution and was the first secretary of the Third International. Her memoir was published in 1937.

7. Jan Valtin (pseudonym of Richard Krebs, 1904–1951), *Out of the Night* (New York, 1940; London and Toronto, 1941). He later became a war correspondent with the American forces in the Pacific. Walter G. Krivitsky (d. 1941), *In Stalin's Secret Service* (New York, 1939; *I Was Stalin's Agent*, London, 1963). He was head of the western division of the NKVD, but defected.

8. Victor Kravchenko (1905–1966), *I Chose Freedom: The Personal and Political Life of a Soviet Official* (New York, 1946; London, 1947). During the Spanish civil war, Kravchenko served as an aide to General Dimitri Pavlov (shot on Stalin's orders, 1941). (See Thomas, p. 588, n. 1.)

9. Anton Ciliga (1898–1991), a founder of the Yugoslav Communist Party. His *The Russian Enigma* was published in English in 1940 (in French, Paris, 1938). It is concerned chiefly with Russian economic policy, 1928–1932, and with its prisons. His *The Kronstadt Revolt* (Paris 1938; London, 1942) was described by Orwell as an 'Anarchist pamphlet largely an attack on Trotsky'.

10. Anonymous, *The Dark Side of the Moon* (London, 1946; New York, 1947), deals with Soviet-Polish relations. It has a preface by T. S. Eliot, a director of the book's English publishers, Faber & Faber.

11. Ada Halpern, *Liberation—Russian Style* (1945); it is listed by Whitaker as August 1945 and so published not during the war but just as it was ending.

12. In the left-hand margin, against one or both of *Liberation—Russian Style* and the Canadian Government Blue Book, is a marker arrow, presumably added by Macdonald. The Blue Book referred to reported on a Canadian Royal Commission which investigated Soviet espionage in Canada, 1946 and 1947. This found that a spy ring had been built up by the Soviet Military Attaché, Colonel Zabotin. Amongst those sentenced to terms of imprisonment was Fred Rose, the only Canadian Communist MP.

To Fredric Warburg*

31 May 1947
Barnhill
Isle of Jura

Dear Fred,

Many thanks for your letter. I have made a fairly good start on the book and I think I must have written nearly a third of the rough draft. I have not got as far as I had hoped to do by this time, because I have really been in most wretched health this year ever since about January (my chest as usual) and can't quite shake it off. However I keep pegging away, and I hope that when I leave here in October I shall either have finished the rough draft or at any rate broken its back. Of course the rough draft is always a ghastly mess having very little relation to the finished result, but all the same it is the main part of the job. So if I do finish the rough draft by October I might get the book done fairly early in 1948, barring illnesses. I don't like talking about books before they are written, but I will tell you now that this is a novel about the future— that is, it is in a sense a fantasy, but in the form of a naturalistic novel. That is what makes it a difficult job—of course as a book of anticipations it would be comparatively simple to write.

I am sending you separately a long autobiographical sketch[1] which I originally undertook as a sort of pendant to Cyril Connolly's *Enemies of Promise*, he having asked me to write a reminiscence of the preparatory school we were at together. I haven't actually sent it to Connolly or *Horizon*, because apart from being too long for a periodical I think it is really too libellous to print, and I am not disposed to change it, except perhaps the names. But I think it should be printed sooner or later when the people most concerned are dead, and maybe sooner or later I might do a book of collected sketches. I must apologise for the typescript. It is not only the carbon copy, but is very bad commercial typing which I have had to correct considerably—however, I think I have got most of the actual errors out.

Richard is very well in spite of various calamities. First he fell down and cut his forehead and had to have two stitches put in, and after that he had measles. He is talking a good deal more now (he was three a week or two ago.) The weather has cheered up after being absolutely stinking, and the garden we are creating out of virgin jungle is getting quite nice. Please remember me to Pamela and Roger.[2]

Yours
George

[XIX, 3232, pp. 149–50; typewritten]

1. In the margin there is a handwritten annotation (in Warburg's hand?): 'Such, Such were the Joys'. For the development of this essay and for the nature of the 'commercial typing', see headnote to the essay, XIX, 3408, pp. 353–6. Cyril Connolly's *Enemies of Promise* was published in 1938. Warburg wrote to Orwell on 6 June saying, 'I have read the autobiographical sketch about your prep. school and passed it to Roger.'

2. Fredric Warburg's second wife, formerly Pamela de Bayou (they married in 1933); and Roger Senhouse.

To Leonard Moore*

14 July 1947
Barnhill
Isle of Jura

Dear Moore,

I wonder if you could get in touch with the 'Britain in Pictures' people and find out what they are doing about a booklet, *The British People*, which I wrote for them 3 or 4 years ago. The history of it was this.[1]

In 1943 W. J. Turner,[2] who was editing the series, told me that they had had books on British scenery, British railways, etc., but none on the British people, and that they would like me to do one. I was not very keen on the idea, but as it was to be a short book (15,000) and Turner promised me I should have a free hand, I agreed. Before going to work I submitted a detailed synopsis, which was approved. I then wrote the book, and it was no sooner sent in than the reader for Collins's, who were publishing the series, raised a long series of objections which amounted, in effect, to a demand that I should turn the book into a much cruder kind of propaganda. I pointed out that I had closely followed the agreed synopsis, and said I was not going to change anything. Turner backed me up, and the matter seemed to be settled. About a year later, nothing having happened, I met Turner in the street and told him I thought I ought to have some money for the book, on which I had been promised an advance of £50. He said he could get me £25, and did so. About this time he told me it had been decided to get someone else to do a companion volume to mine, on the same subject, so as to give as it were two sides to the picture. They first got Edmund Blunden,[3] who made such a mess of it that his copy was unprintable, so there was another delay. They afterwards got someone else, I forget whom, to do the companion volume. Turner and his assistant, Miss Shannon, several times told me that the objections to my book had been over-ruled and that it would appear in due course. About a year ago I was sent the proofs and corrected them. I was told then, or shortly afterwards, that they were choosing the illustrations, and if I remember rightly Miss Shannon told me what the illustrations would be. During last winter Turner died suddenly, and Miss Shannon wrote to say that this would impose another short delay, but that the book would appear shortly. Since then nothing has happened. I think it must be more than 4 years since I submitted the manuscript.

I haven't the faintest interest in the book nor any desire that it should appear in print. It was simply a wartime book, part of a series designed to 'sell' Britain in the USA. At the same time I obviously ought to have some more money out of them, at least the other half of the £50 advance. £50 was incidentally rather a small advance, since these books, when once on the market, usually sold largely. Unfortunately I have not my copy of the contract, as this was one of the documents that were destroyed when my flat was bombed in 1944.[4] However, I suppose that wouldn't matter, and I am sure Miss Shannon, if she is still helping to run the series, would be cooperative.

Yours sincerely
Eric Blair

[XIX, 3248, pp. 172–3; typewritten]

1. Though he did not realise it when he wrote to Moore, *The English People* was about to be published, in August 1947 (XIX, 3253, p. 179). Collins had not bothered to inform the author.
2. W. J. Turner (1889–1946), poet, novelist, and music critic who did a variety of publishing and journalistic work, including acting as general editor of the Britain in Pictures series for Collins.
2. Edmund Charles Blunden (1896–1974), poet, critic, and teacher.
4. Orwell and his wife were bombed out on 14 July 1944.

To Lydia Jackson*

28 July 1947
Barnhill
Isle of Jura

Dear Lydia,

I have just received notice to quit the Wallington Cottage.[1] It was bound to happen sooner or later, and of course as it is only a weekly tenancy they can do it on very short notice. However the date given on the notice is August 4th, so that in theory your furniture ought to be removed by that date. I wrote off at once to the Solicitors explaining that you could hardly be expected to get out at such short notice, as you must find somewhere to put your furniture. If you want to write to them direct they are Balderston Warren & Co, Solicitors, Baldock, Herts. I have no doubt you could get more time, but of course if ordered to get out we have to do so, especially as I, the theoretical tenant, am not using the cottage at all, and you are only using it for week ends. I believe actually on a weekly tenancy they are supposed to give six week° notice. I am very sorry this should have happened.

If you'd like to come and stay any time, please do,[2] I shall be here till October, and there are always beds here. Just give me good notice, so that I can arrange about meeting you. The weather has been filthy but has lately turned nice again. Love to Pat.

Yours,
George

[XIX, 3250, p. 177; typewritten copy]

1.   The Stores, Wallington; Orwell moved there on 2 April 1936, and it was his home until May 1940. He seems to have used it rarely thereafter (most often for a few days in 1940 and 1941, and perhaps a Bank Holiday weekend in 1942).
2.   Lydia Jackson visited Barnhill 26 March to 2 April 1948. She might have retyped the final version of 'Such, Such Were the Joys' while she was there.

To Leonard Moore*

28 July 1947
Barnhill
Isle of Jura

Dear Moore,

Herewith the proofs.[1] It seems quite a good translation, so far as I am able to judge. I have made a few corrections, but mostly of punctuation etc.

Many thanks for your offices in connection with the 'Britain in Pictures' book.

I am getting on fairly well with the novel, and expect to finish the rough draft by October. I dare say it will need another six months° work on it after that, but I can't say yet when it is likely to be finished because I am not sure of my movements. I have to come back to London in October and shall probably stay at any rate a month, but we are thinking of spending most of the winter up here because I think it is not quite so cold here and fuel is a bit easier to get. If I do stay here I shall no doubt get on with the rewriting of the novel faster than if I am in London and involved in journalism. At any rate I have some hopes of finishing it fairly early next year.

Yours sincerely
Eric Blair

[XIX, 3251, pp. 177–8; typewritten]

1. Presumably proofs of the French translation of *Animal Farm*, published in October 1947.

To George Woodcock*

9 August 1947
Barnhill
Isle of Jura

Dear George,

I at last get round to answering your letter of 25th July. I am, as you say in principle prepared to do an article in the series you mention, but 'in principle' is about right, because I am busy and don't want to undertake any more work in the near future. I am struggling with this novel which I hope to finish early in 1948. I don't even expect to finish the rough draft before about October, then I must come to London for about a month to see to various things and do one or two articles I have promised, then I shall get down to the rewriting of the book which will probably take me 4 or 5 months. It always takes me a hell of a time to write a book even if I am doing nothing else, and I can't help doing an occasional article, usually for some American magazine, because one must earn some money occasionally.

I think probably I shall come back in November and we shall spend the winter here. I can work here with fewer interruptions, and I think we shall be less cold here. The climate, although wet, is not quite so cold as England, and it is much easier to get fuel. We are saving our coal as much as possible and hope to start the winter with a reserve of 3 tons, and you can get oil by the 40 gallon drum here, whereas last winter in London you had to go down on your knees to get a gallon once a fortnight. There are also wood and peat, which are a fag to collect but help out the coal. Part of the winter may be pretty bleak and one is sometimes cut off from the mainland for a week or two, but it doesn't matter so long as you have flour in hand to make scones. Latterly the weather has been quite incredible, and I am afraid we shall be paying for it soon. Last week we went round in the boat and spent a couple of days on the completely uninhabited Atlantic side of the island in an empty shepherd's hut—no beds, but otherwise quite comfortable. There are beautiful white beaches round that side, and if you do about an hour's climb into the hills you come to lochs which are full of trout but never fished because too ungetatable. This last week of course we've all been breaking our backs helping to get the hay in, including Richard, who likes to roll about in the hay stark naked. If you want to come here any time, of course do, only just give me a week's notice because of meeting. After September the weather gets pretty wild, though I know there are very warm days even in mid winter.

I got two copies of the FDC[1] bulletin. I am not too happy about following up the Nunn May case, ie, building him up as a well-meaning man who has been victimised. I think the Home Secretary can make hay of this claim if he wants to. I signed the first petition, not without misgivings, simply because I thought 10 years too stiff a sentence (assuming that *any* prison sentence is ever justified.) If I had had to argue the case, I should have pointed out that if he had communicated the information to the USA he would probably have got off with 2 years at most. But the fact is that he was an ordinary spy—I don't mean that he was doing it for money—and went out to Canada as part of a spy ring. I suppose you read the Blue Book[2] on the subject. It also seems to me a weak argument to say that he felt information was being withheld from an ally, because in his position he must have known that the Russians never communicated military information to anybody. However, in so far as the object is simply to get him out of jail somewhat earlier, I am not against it.

Yours
George

[XIX, 3256, pp. 188–9; typewritten]

1. This was *Freedom Defence Committee Bulletin*, 5, July–August 1947. This issue outlines action taken to have Nunn May's sentence reduced, achieving, if possible, 'early release'. Dr Allan Nunn May (1911–2003) was found guilty of spying on behalf of the Soviets. Conor Cruise O'Brien defended him in the *Daily Telegraph*, 10 February 2003, as someone who thought it was his 'moral duty' to help the Soviet Union. He told O'Brien that on his release his communist colleagues cut him dead because he had pleaded guilty. He should, he said, 'have pleaded *not* guilty, thereby enabling the Soviet Union to accuse the British Government of having framed' him – it was, said Nunn May, 'an instructive experience'.
2. Issued by the Canadian government (see Orwell's letter to Dwight Macdonald, **15.4.47**, n. 12).

To Brenda Salkeld*

1 September 1947
Barnhill
Isle of Jura

Dearest Brenda,

At last I get round to answering your letter. We have had unheard-of weather here for the last six weeks, one blazing day after another, and in fact at present we're suffering from a severe drought, which is not a usual complaint in these parts. There has been no water in the taps for nearly a fortnight, and everyone has had to stagger to and fro with buckets from a well about 200 yards away. However there have been plenty of people to do it as the house was very full with people staying. We made several expeditions round to Glengarrisdale and slept a couple of nights in the shepherd's cottage—no beds, only blankets and piles of bracken, but otherwise quite comfortable. Unfortunately on the last expedition we had a bad boat accident on the way back and 4 of us including Richard were nearly drowned. We got into the [Corryvreckan] whirlpool, owing to trying to go through the gulf at the wrong state of the tide, and the outboard motor was sucked off the boat. We managed to get out of it with the oars and then got to one of the little islands, just rocks covered with sea birds, which are dotted about there. The sea was pretty bad and the boat turned over as we were getting ashore, so that we lost everything we had including the oars and including 12 blankets. We might normally have expected to be there till next day, but luckily a boat came past some hours later and took us off. Luckily, also, it was a hot day and we managed to get a fire going and dry our clothes. Richard loved every moment of it except when he went into the water. The boat which picked us up put us off at the bay we used to call the W bay,[1] and then we had to walk home over the hill, barefooted because most of our boots had gone with the other wreckage.[2] Our boat luckily wasn't damaged apart from the loss of the engine, but I'm trying to get hold of a bigger one as these trips are really a bit too unsafe in a little rowing boat. I went fishing in the lochs near Glengarrisdale both times (I've got to continue in pen because the wire of the typewriter has slipped) & caught quite a lot of trout. Several of these lochs are full of trout but never fished because however you approach them it's a day's expedition to get there.

We're going to spend the winter up here, but I shall be in London roughly for November—I haven't fixed a date because it partly depends on when I finish the rough draft of my novel. I'll let you know later just when I am coming up.[3]

Love
Eric

[XIX, 3262, pp. 195–6; typed and hadwritten]

1. Presumably the adjacent bays of Glentrosdale and Gleann nam Muc at the north-western tip of Jura which, on a map, with a headland separating the bays, looks like the letter W. Eilean Mór lies opposite the centre point of the 'W'.
2. This would involve a walk of at least three miles over rough country.
3. Orwell was to lecture at the Working Men's College, Crowndale Road, London, NW1, on 12 November 1947. However, he was too ill to leave Jura and so could not give his lecture.

To Arthur Koestler*

20 September 1947
Barnhill
Isle of Jura

Dear Arthur,

I think a Ukrainian refugee named Ihor Sevcenko° may have written to you—he told me that he had written and that you had not yet answered.

What he wanted to know was whether they could translate some of your stuff into Ukrainian, without payment of course, for distribution among the Ukrainian D.Ps, who now seem to have printing outfits of their own going in the American Zone and in Belgium. I told him I thought you would be delighted to have your stuff disseminated among Soviet citizens and would not press for payment, which in any case these people could not make. They made a Ukrainian translation of *Animal Farm* which appeared recently, reasonably well printed and got up, and, so far as I could judge by my correspondence with Sevcenko°, well translated. I have just heard from them that the American authorities in Munich have siezed° 1500 copies of it and handed them over to the Soviet repatriation people, but it appears about 2000 copies got distributed among the D.Ps first. If you decide to let them have some of your stuff, I think it is well to treat it as a matter of confidence and not tell too many people this end, as the whole thing is more or less illicit. Sevcenko °asked me simultaneously whether he thought Laski¹ would agree to let them have some of his stuff (they are apparently trying to get hold of representative samples of Western thought.) I told him to have nothing to do with Laski and by no means let a person of that type know that illicit printing in Soviet languages is going on in the allied zones, but I told him you were a person to be trusted. I am sure we ought to help these people all we can, and I have been saying ever since 1945 that the DPs were a godsent opportunity for breaking down the wall between Russia and the west. If our government won't see this, one must do what one can privately.

[*Final paragraph omitted: will visit London but stay at Barnhill for winter.*]

Yours
George

[XIX, 3275, pp. 206–7; typewritten]

1.   Harold J. Laski (1893–1950), political theorist, Marxist, author, and journalist, was connected with the London School of Economics from 1920 and Professor of Political Science in the University of London from 1926, member of the Fabian Executive, 1922 and 1936, member of the Executive Committee of the Labour Party, 1936–49. Although critical of Laski, Orwell had appealed for support for him after Laski lost an action for libel; see 'As I Please', 67, 27 December 1946, (XVIII, 3140, p. 523).

To David Astor*

29 September 1947
Barnhill
Isle of Jura

Dear David,

I wonder how things are going with you and the family. I am going to be in London for November to see to some odds and ends of business, but after that we intend spending the winter here. I think it will be easier to keep warm here, as we are better off for coal etc., also I am struggling with this novel and can work more quietly here. I hope to finish it some time in the spring. I have got on fairly well but not so fast as I could have wished because I have been in wretched health a lot of the year, starting with last winter. We have got the house a lot more in order and some more garden broken in, and I am going to send up some more furniture this winter. I think the Barnhill croft is going to be farmed after all, which eases my conscience about living here. A chap I don't think you have met named Bill Dunn,¹ who lost a foot in the war, has been living with the Darrochs all the summer as a pupil, and in the spring he is going to take over the Barnhill croft and live with us. Apart from the land getting cultivated again, it is very convenient for us because we can then share implements such as a small tractor which it [is] not worth getting for the garden alone, and also have various animals which I have hitherto hesitated to get for fear a moment should come when nobody was here. We have had a marvellous summer here, in fact there was a severe drought and no bath water for ten days. Four of us including Richard were nearly drowned in Corrievrechan,° an event which got into the newspapers even as far away as Glasgow. Richard is getting enormous and unbelievably destructive, and is now talking a good deal more. I expect your baby will have grown out of recognition by this time. I don't know if you're going to be up here any time in the winter but if so do look in here. There's always a bed and food of sorts, and the road is I think slightly better as it's being drained in places. Your friend Donovan came over riding on Bob and bearing incredible quantities of food, evidently sure he would find us starving. Actually we do very well for food here except bread, because we buy huge hunks of venison off the Fletchers whenever they break up a deer, also lobsters, and we have a few hens and can get plenty of milk.

Please remember me to your wife.

Yours
George

P.S. Do you want Bob wintered again by any chance? I got hay for him last year and he seemed to me in pretty good condition when I took him back, though I'm no judge. Till the day I took him back I had never mounted him, because the Darrochs had built up a picture of him as a sort of raging unicorn, and I was in such poor health I felt I was getting past that sort of thing. Actually he was as good as gold even when ridden bareback.

[XIX, 3277, p. 209–10; typewritten]

1. Bill Dunn (1921–92), had been an officer in the army but after the loss of a leg had been invalided out. He came to Jura in 1947 and later entered into a partnership with Sir Richard Rees to farm Barnhill. He married Avril, Orwell's sister, in 1951. See *Orwell Remembered*, pp. 231–5, and *Remembering Orwell*, pp. 182–5. Richard Blair has contributed a very interesting memoir about Avril and Bill Dunn to the *Eric & Us* website (www.finlay-publisher.com).

To Roger Senhouse*

22 October 1947
Barnhill
Isle of Jura

Dear Roger,

I'm returning the proofs of *Coming Up for Air*.

There are not many corrections. In just one or two cases I've altered something that had been correctly transcribed, including one or two misprints that existed in the original text. I note that on p. 46 the compositor has twice altered 'Boars' to 'Boers,' evidently taking it for a misprint. 'Boars' was intentional, however (a lot of people used to pronounce it like that.)

What about dates? On the title page it says '1947,' but it isn't going to be published in 1947. And should there not somewhere be a mention of the fact that the book was first published in 1939?

Did you know by the way that this book hasn't got a semicolon in it? I had decided about that time that the semicolon is an unnecessary stop and that I would write my next book without one.¹

I'm coming up to London on November 7th and shall be there for about a month. I have various time-wasting things to do, lectures and so on. I *hope* before I arrive to have finished the rough draft of my novel, which I'm on the last lap of now. But its° a most dreadful mess and about two-thirds of it will have to be rewritten entirely besides the usual touching up. I don't know how long that will take—I hope only 4 or 5 months but it might well be longer. I've been in such wretched health all this year that I never seem to have much spare energy. I wonder if Fred will be back by November.² I hope to see you both then.

> Yours
> George

[XIX, 3290, pp. 216–17; typewritten]

1. See Textual Note to *Coming Up for Air*, VII, pp. 249–50. Despite Orwell's clearly expressed wishes, the proofs and Uniform Edition include three semi-colons. Whether Orwell missed these (and they do make for easier reading than do the commas he wished to have used) or whether his instructions were ignored is not known.

2. Warburg had gone on his first of a dozen visits to the United States. Orwell had written to him on 1 September 1947 asking him, if he had time, to buy him a pair of shoes.

To Anthony Powell*

> 29 November 1947
> Barnhill
> Isle of Jura

Dear Tony,

Thanks so much for your letter. I'm still on my back, but I think really getting better after many relapses. I'd probably be all right by this time if I could have got to my usual chest specialist, but I dare not make the journey to the mainland while I have a temperature. It's really a foul journey in winter even if one flies part of the way. However I've arranged for a man to come from Glasgow & give me the once-over, & then maybe I'll get up to London later, or perhaps only as far as Glasgow. I think I'll have to go into hospital for a bit, because apart from treatment there's the X-raying etc., & after that I might have a stab at going abroad for a couple of months if I can get a newspaper assignment to somewhere warm. Of course I've done no work for weeks—have only done the rough draft of my novel, which I always consider as the halfway mark. I was supposed to finish it by May—now, God knows when. I'm glad the Aubrey book[1] is coming along at last. I think in these days besides putting the date of publication in books one also ought to put the date of writing. In the spring I'm reprinting a novel which came out in 1939 & was rather killed by the war, so that makes up a little for being late with my new one.

Apparently Mrs Christen has just sailed. What I partly wrote about was this: have you got, or do you know anyone who has got, a saddle for sale? Good condition doesn't matter very much so long as it has a sound girth & stirrups. It's for a horse only about 14 h[ands] but on the stout side, so very likely a saddle belonging to a big horse would do. It's the sort of thing someone might have kicking round, & you can't buy them for love or money. The farm pony we have here is ridden for certain errands to save petrol, & it's so tiring riding bareback. I am ready to pay a reasonable price.

Richard is *offensively* well & full of violence. He went through whooping cough without noticing that he had it. My love to everyone. I hope to see you all some day.

Yours
George

[XIX, 3308, pp. 227–8; handwritten]

1. Powell published *John Aubrey and His Friends* in 1948, and *Brief Lives and Other Selected Writings of John Aubrey* in 1949.

To Leonard Moore*

7 December 1947
Barnhill
Isle of Jura

Dear Moore,

Thanks for your letter of the 1st. I have of course no objection to the arrangement with the F[oreign] O[ffice] about *A.F.*[1] I had already written to the U.S. Information Service to tell them they could broadcast it free of charge.

I have seen a chest specialist, &, as I feared, I am seriously ill. As soon as there is a bed vacant, I think in about 10 days, I shall have to go into a sanatorium—for how long I don't know of course, but I gather probably something like 4 months. It's T.B., as I suspected. They think they can cure it all right, but I am bound to be *hors de combat* for a good while. Could you inform all the publishers etc. concerned. Could you also thank very kindly Harcourt Brace for getting & sending me a pair of shoes (just arrived) & find out from Fred Warburg who paid for them, ie. whom I should repay. I believe Warburg paid.

Yours sincerely
Eric Blair

P.S. I'll send you the address of the hospital as soon as I'm there, but any way this address will find me.

[XIX, 3313, pp. 233–4; handwritten]

1.   Probably for the Persian-language version, *Enqelāb Hayvānāt*, arranged by the Central Office of Information and translated by Ali Javāherkālām, 1947.

To Frederick Tomlinson, *The Observer*

23 December 1947
Ward 3
Hairmyres Hospital
East Kilbride
Nr. Glasgow
[*Tel:*] East Kilbride 325

Dear Tomlinson,

I'm afraid it's all off about Africa so far as I'm concerned, much as I'd like to have done the trip. As you see I'm in hospital & I think likely to remain here 3–4 months. After being really very ill for about 2 months I got a chest specialist to come from the mainland, & sure enough it was T.B. as I feared. I've had it before, but not so badly. This time it's what they call 'extensive' but they seem confident they can patch me up in a few months. For some time I've been far too ill even to attempt any work, but I'm beginning to feel somewhat better, & I was wondering whether the *Obs.* would like to start letting me have some books to review again. I suppose this isn't your department, but perhaps you could be kind enough to shove the suggestion along to Ivor Brown.*[1]

I haven't heard from David [Astor]* so don't know if he's back yet. Please give all the best to everybody from me.

Yours
Geo. Orwell

[XIX, 3315, p. 235; handwritten]

Hairmyres and Jura

1948

In November 1947 Frederick Tomlinson, news editor of the *Observer*, had suggested to Orwell that he might like a three-month assignment to cover the progress of what would prove to be a disastrous groundnut scheme in East Africa, and the South African elections. Orwell was tempted but by the end of the year he had become so ill that he had to turn down the offer. Instead he had to move to Hairmyres Hospital, East Kilbride, near Glasgow. He was there until almost the end of July when he was able to return to Barnhill. Through David Astor, streptomycin (then a new drug) was obtained from the USA but although it was beneficial at first, Orwell proved allergic to it. Nevertheless, by May his health was improving and he was getting a little stronger. He thought 'Such, Such Were the Joys' was important enough to devote time and energy to making final revisions to it even though he knew the essay could not be published for many years for fear of libel actions. He also started the second draft of *Nineteen Eighty-Four*. He wrote several essays, including one on an author he greatly admired, George Gissing. It was intended for *Politics and Letters* but that failed before the essay could be published. It finally appeared in the *London Magazine* ten years after Orwell's death.

Orwell's thoughts were very much at Barnhill and with Richard. He was terrified that contact with his son could entail his passing on his TB. From the references in his letters it is clear that he closely followed Richard's development. He also describes the Christmas they had had at Barnhill, glad to have got away before the day so that he was not 'a death's head', and contrasts the inevitably hollow jollity of Christmas in hospital. He suffered the painful treatment he underwent, dreading it but never complaining: 'we all noticed how much self-control he had', as one of the surgeons put it.

Although very much the invalid, he was able to enjoy a final few months at Barnhill, but was too weak to make even slight exertions – apart, that is, from slogging away at *Nineteen Eighty-Four*. By early November he had finished the final draft and hoped that a typist could be induced to come to Barnhill to produce a fair copy of what the facsimile shows was a very much altered and overwritten text. But no one could be found to make the journey and Orwell suffered agonies typing the final copies (a very difficult task on a mechanical typewriter, with carbon copies to make and correct). Much of the time he typed in bed. By 4th December the final copies were completed and he posted them to Leonard Moore, his literary agent, for Warburg and for consideration in the USA. He was by now very ill indeed, but not so ill that he could not take Roger Senhouse to task for his proposed blurb for the book: it was not, as Senhouse seemed to suggest, 'a thriller mixed up with a love story'. The year ended with his arranging to go to a private sanatorium and, almost as significantly, giving up his lease on his flat in Canonbury Square, Islington.

From Orwell's letter to his mother, 1 December 1912

To Gwen O' Shaughnessy*

1 January 1948
Hairmyres Hospital
East Kilbride

Dear Gwen,

I thought you'd like to hear how I was getting on. I believe Mr Dick* sent you a line about my case. As soon as he listened to me he said I had a fairly extensive cavity in the left lung, & also a small patch at the top of the other lung—this, I think, the old one I had before. The X-ray confirms this, he says. I have now been here nearly a fortnight, & the treatment they are giving me is to put the left lung out of action, apparently for about 6 months, which is supposed to give it a better chance to heal.[1] They first crushed the phrenic nerve, which I gather is what makes the lung expand & contract, & then pumped air into the diaphragm, which I understand is to push the lung into a different position & get it away from some kind of movement which occurs automatically. I have to have 'refills' of air in the diaphragm every few days but I think later it gets down to once a week or less. For the rest, I am still really very ill & weak, & on getting here I found I had lost 1½ stone, but I have felt better since being here, don't sweat at night like I used & have more appetite. They make me eat a tremendous lot. At present I am not allowed out of bed because apparently one has to get adjusted to having the extra air inside. It is a nice hospital & everyone is extremely kind to me. I have also got a room to myself, but I don't know whether that will be permanent. I have of course done no work for 2–3 months, but I think I may be equal to some light work soon & I am arranging to do a little book-reviewing.

Richard was tremendously well when I came away. After I was certain what was wrong with me I tried to keep him out of my room, but of course couldn't do so entirely. When Avril goes up to London in Jan. or Feb. to do some shopping I am going to take the opportunity of having Richard thoroughly examined to make sure he is O.K. We boiled his milk ever since you warned us, but of course one can forget sometimes. I am trying to buy a T B.-tested cow, & I think we are on the track of one now. With Bill Dunn in the house it is easier about animals, as he is going to pay part of his board by looking after our cows, which means that at need we can go away. I must say Richard doesn't look very T.B, but I would like to be sure. I think they had quite a good Christmas at Barnhill. There were 4 of them including Richard, & there was a nice goose we bought off the Kopps. I was glad to get away before Xmas so as not to be a death's head. I am afraid I didn't write any Xmas letters or anything & it's now a bit late even for New Year wishes. I hope by the summer I shall be well enough to go back to Barnhill for a bit & you & the kids will come again. Maybe there'll be a pony to ride this time—we have got one at present but he is only borrowed. They had a New Year party for the patients here, all the beds dragged into one ward & there were singers & a conjuror. I hope you had a good Christmas. Love to the kids.

Yours
George

[XIX, 3324, pp. 247–8; handwritten]

1. In *Remembering Orwell*, pp. 197–8, Professor James Williamson, who was a junior doctor in the Thoracic Unit at Hairmyres Hospital when Orwell was a patient, describes Orwell's condition and treatment:

It was a fairly trivial operation: you could do it in five minutes. You just pull the muscle aside, expose the nerve, and tweak it with a pair of forceps. The patient would get one sudden pain, and the diaphragm would jump, and that was the diaphragm paralysed for three to six months, until the nerve recovered again. Then we pumped air into his abdomen. The diaphragm was pushed up by this, and the lungs were collapsed. You put anything from four hundred to seven hundred cc of air in, under low pressure, with a special machine, through a needle which was a fairly elephantine-looking thing, a hollow needle about three inches long, actually. The first time you did it, you used a local anesthetic,° because you had to go very cautiously and advance it very slowly. But after that you just stuck it in, because patients agreed that if it was done expertly, one sharp jab was better than all this fiddling about with anesthetics and things.

I remember he used to dread each 'refill' and couldn't relax at all when he was on the table. But he never complained. In fact we all noticed how much self-control he had. There was never a gasp, or any kind of noise from him when we did this.

I don't think he would ever have been terribly infectious. The person who is highly infectious is the person who is coughing a lot, whose sputum has a lot of TB bacilli in it. He wasn't coughing a lot, nor was his sputum, as I remember it, terribly strongly positive. But he would still be a potential danger to other people, particularly to young people like his son.

Most patients made much use of sputum mugs but Orwell's tuberculosis was not of that kind, and Williamson did not recall his having a sputum mug on his bedside locker: 'Mind you, I don't think there was any room for anything on his bedside locker because there were always books everywhere.'

To Julian Symons*

2 January 1948
Hairmyres Hospital
East Kilbride

Dear Julian,

Thanks ever so for sending the pen, which as you see I'm using. Of course it'll do just as well as a Biro & I prefer the colour of the ink. My other was just on its last legs & you can't use ink in bed.

I think I'm getting a bit better. I don't feel quite so deathlike & am eating a lot more. They stuff food into me all the time here. I don't know whether my weight is going up, because I'm kept strictly in bed at this stage of the treatment. They have put the affected lung out of action, which involves pumping air into one's diaphragm. I have this done every few days. It's a nice hospital & everyone is very kind to me. I was recommended to come here by my London chest specialist, & did so rather than go to London simply to avoid the long journey. It wasn't much fun coming even here in that state, but I could do most of it by car. It's funny you always think Scotland must be cold. The west part isn't colder than England, & the islands I should think decidedly warmer on average, though probably the summer isn't so hot. When I'm well enough to leave hospital I shall have to continue with this air-pumping business, so shall stay either in Glasgow or London for some months & just dodge up to Jura when I can. I have arranged things fairly well there. We, ie. my sister & I, have the house, & a young chap who lost a foot in the war & is taking up farming lives with us & farms the croft. Another friend of mine acts as a sort of sleeping partner,¹ financing the croft & coming to help at the busy times. So I don't have bad conscience about living in a farmhouse & keeping someone else off the land, & at the same time can go away whenever I want to as our animals will be looked after in our absence. I'm just going to embark on cows, just one or two, because I'm in terror of Richard getting this disease & the safest thing is to have a T.T cow. I'm also going to get him thoroughly examined when my sister goes up to London. Of course I kept him off me once I was certain what was wrong with me, but he has certainly been exposed to infection. He has got such a splendid physique & I don't want him to wreck it.

About book reviewing. I had no thoughts of going back to the M[anchester] E[vening] News. I am merely arranging to do a review once a fortnight for the *Observer*, & I think I shall try & fix one once a fortnight for someone else, as I'm probably up to doing one article a week now. I think that shows I'm better, as I couldn't have contemplated that a few weeks ago. I can't do any serious work—I never can do in bed, even when I feel well. I can't show you the part-finished novel. I never show them to anybody, because they are just a mess & don't have much relationship to the final draft. I always say a book doesn't exist until it is finished. I am glad you finished the life of your brother.[2] It is such a ghastly effort ever to finish a book nowadays.

I agree with you about *Tribune*, though I think it's probably Fyvel* rather than Kimche[3] who is responsible for the over-emphasis on Zionism. They would have done better when Labour got in to label themselves frankly a government organ, *a.* because in all major matters they *are* in agreement with the government, *b.* because Labour has no weekly paper definitely faithful to it & is in fact on the defensive so far as the press goes. The evil genius of the paper has I think been Crossman,[4] who influences it through Foot & Fyvel. Crossman & the rest of that gang thought they saw an opening for themselves in squealing about foreign policy, which in the circumstances was bound to go badly, & so *Tribune* has been in the position of coming down on the side of the government whenever there is a major issue, eg. conscription, & at the same time trying to look fearfully left by raising an outcry about Greece etc. I really think I prefer the Zilliacus lot, since after all they do have a policy, ie. to appease Russia. I started writing an open letter to *Tribune* about this, but was taken ill before I finished it.[5] I particularly hate that trick of sucking up to the left cliques by perpetually attacking America while relying on America to feed & protect us. I even get letters from American university students asking why *Tribune* is always going for the USA & in such an ignorant way.

Well, this is quite a long letter. So my thanks again for sending the pen. I'll send my old Biro sometime when I've got a bit of paper & perhaps you'd be kind enough to get it refilled. My best respects to your wife.

Yours
George

[XIX, 3325, pp. 249–51; handwritten]

1.   Bill Dunn* and Sir Richard Rees*.
2.   *A. J. A. Symons: His Life and Speculations* (1950).
3.   Jon Kimche (1909–1994), author and journalist, was acting editor of *Tribune*, 1942–46, editor, 1946–1948; and editor of the *Jewish Observer*, 1952–67. He and Orwell worked together at Booklovers' Corner, 1934–35. He contributes several reminiscences to *Remembering Orwell*.
4.   R. H. S. Crossman (1907–1974), scholar, journalist, and left-wing politician (Labour

MP, 1945–55); assistant editor of the *New Statesman*, 1938–55. Strenuous efforts were made to stop the publication of his political diaries (4 vols., 1975–81).

5. Konni Zilliacus (1894–1967), left-wing Labour MP, 1945–50 and 1955–67. He was frequently at odds with the Labour Party because of his extreme pro-Soviet opinions and was expelled in 1949. (See Orwell's 'In Defence of Comrade Ziliacus', XIX, 3254, pp. 179–84.)

To George Woodcock*

4 January 1948
Hairmyres Hospital
East Kilbride

Dear George,

I'd been meaning to write for some time to explain I wouldn't be coming down to London after all. As I feared, I am seriously ill, T.B. in the left lung. I've only been in the hospital about a fortnight, but before that I was in bed at home for about 2 months. I'm likely to be here for some time, because the treatment, which involves putting the lung out of action, is a slow one, & in any case I'm so pulled down & weak that I wouldn't be able to get out of bed for a couple of months or so. However, they seem confident they can patch me up all right, & I have felt a bit less like death since being here. It's a nice hospital & everyone is very kind. With luck I may be out for the summer & then I think I'll try & get a correspondent's job somewhere warm next winter. I have [had] this disease before, but not so badly, & I'm pretty sure it was the cold of last winter that started me off.[1]

I hope the F.D.C.[2] is doing something about these constant demands to outlaw Mosley & Co. *Tribune*'s attitude I think has been shameful, & when the other week Zilliacus wrote in demanding what amounts to Fascist legislation & creation of 2nd-class citizens, nobody seems to have replied. The whole thing is simply a thinly-disguised desire to persecute someone who can't hit back, as obviously the Mosley lot don't matter a damn & can't get a real mass following. I think it's a case for a pamphlet, & I only wish I felt well enough to write one. The central thing one has [to] come to terms with is the argument, always advanced by those advocating repressive legislation, that 'you cannot allow democracy to be used to overthrow democracy—you cannot allow freedom to those who merely use it in order to destroy freedom'. This of course is true, & both Fascists & Communists do aim at making use of democracy in order to destroy it. But if you carry this to its conclusion, there can be no case for allowing any political or intellectual freedom whatever. Evidently therefore it is a matter of distinguishing between a real & a merely theoretical threat to democracy, & no one should be persecuted for expressing his opinions, however anti-social, & no political organisation suppressed, unless it can be shown that there is *a substantial threat to the stability of the state.* That is the main point I should make any way. Of course there are many others.

I've done no work whatever for 2–3 months. In this place I couldn't do serious work even if I felt well, but I intend shortly to start doing an occasional book review, as I think I'm equal to that & I might as well earn some money. Richard was blooming when I came away, but I'm going to have him thoroughly examined, as he has of course been subjected to infection. All the best to Inge.

Yours
George

[XIX, 3329, pp. 254–5; handwritten]

1. When snow began to fall on 24 January 1947 it was the start of the bitterest cold experienced in the UK in the twentieth century. It led, for example, to electricity cuts for five hours a day, suspension of the Third Programme and TV, cuts in radio transmission and suspension of many journals coupled with paper rationing, and an increase in unemployment from 400,000 in mid January to 1,750,000. (See David Kynaston, *Austerity Britain, 1945–51* (2007; pb, 2008, pp. 189–200).

2. The Freedom Defence Committee, of which Orwell was vice-chairman; George Woodcock, secretary; and Herbert Read, chairman. The FDC's Bulletins for Spring and Autumn 1948 (Nos. 6 and 7), though reporting efforts to help other unpopular causes—deserters, Polish 'recalcitrants' (its quotes), Dr Allan Nunn May, and Norman Baillie-Stewart (a British Fascist) – make no mention of 'Mosley & Co'.

To Helmut Klöse

12 January 1948
Hairmyres Hospital
East Kilbride

Dear Klöse,[1]

I am ashamed I have not written earlier to thank you for those apples you sent, also for your long letter of advice about the tractors. But as I dare say you know I have been seriously ill for about 3 months. It is TB of the left lung. I was brought to this hospital some weeks ago, & I am glad to say I am feeling definitely better. Of course I'm frightfully weak & have lost a great deal of weight, but I don't feel sick & giddy all the time as I did at first, & have got some appetite back. I imagine I shall be under treatment for a long time, as it is a slow cure which involves disabling the defective lung so as to let it heal without having to work. However they seem quite confident of being able to patch me up, & they say this disease is not so dangerous at my age as if I was younger. Of course I've done not a stroke of work for months past, but I am going to start doing a little book-reviewing soon.

In your letter you were inclined to think the BMB was the best light tractor. However, after getting all the specifications from a firm which deals in these tractors, I finally decided on the one you told me of first, the Iron Horse. From the photographs I thought it was a bit more solidly constructed than the other, which would be an advantage in a place like Jura, & also you can hitch horse-drawn implements on to it, which would be a great help because one could then use it for cutting the hay & even the oats. It also has a 5-cwt trailer which would be useful for potatoes, manure & so on. I am getting a circular saw, but I believe at present it's almost impossible to get blades. I will take your advice & not try to run a dynamo off the tractor. Actually we find we can light the house quite satisfactorily with paraffin lamps. We use the Tilly incandescent lamps which are very powerful & don't use much oil.

Karl[2] & David Astor* came & visited me here yesterday, bringing loads of food with them. It was very kind of them to make the long uncomfortable journey. The weather has turned absolutely filthy, snow & fog alternating, making me quite glad to be in bed. There was marvellous weather in Jura all the time before I came away, brilliant sunshine on the snow & the sea as blue & smooth as the Mediterranean. The average winter temperature there is very mild & the grass seems to be quite nourishing up till about Christmas. The blackfaced sheep remain out all the winter without being fed, & the highland cattle can get through the winter without feeding, though of course it's better to feed them.

My little boy, now 3½, is getting enormous. We are trying to get hold of an attested cow so as to make sure that he doesn't get this disease of mine. I hope I shall see you again some time.

Yours
Geo. Orwell

[XIX, 3330, pp. 255–6; handwritten]

1. Helmut Klöse was described by Orwell as 'the German anarchist who was on the same part of the front as me in Spain and was imprisoned for a long time by the Communists'. He would later visit Orwell in Cranham Sanatorium. Orwell usually omits the umlaut; it is added silently here.
2. Karl Schnetzler (see 1.3.39, n. 1 and 9.4.46 to Inez Holden, n. 2).

To Celia Kirwan*

20 January 1948
Hairmyres Hospital
East Kilbride

Dearest Celia,

How delightful to get your nice long letter. I've been here about a month after being ill for about two months at home. I thought I'd told you what was wrong with me. It is TB, which of course was bound to get me sooner or later, in fact I've had it before, though not so badly. However I don't think it is very serious, & I seem to be getting better slowly. I don't feel so death like as I did a month ago, & I now eat quite a lot & have started to gain weight slowly, after losing nearly 2 stone. Today when I was X-rayed the doctor said he could see definite improvement. But I'm likely to be here a long time, as it's a slow treatment, & I don't think I shall even be fit to get out of bed for about 2 months. Richard is tremendously well & growing enormous. Of course I'm going to have him thoroughly examined when Avril takes him up to London shortly, but by the look of him I don't think he's caught this disease. I was very glad to be able to get away just before Christmas, so as not to be a death's head. There were 4 of them at Barnhill & a nice fat goose & plenty to drink, so I expect they had quite a good Christmas. This is the second Christmas I've spent in hospital.[1] It's always rather harrowing, with the 'parties' they have—all the beds dragged into one ward, & then a concert & a Christmas tree. This is a very nice hospital & everyone is most kind to me, & I have a room to myself. I'm starting to attempt a very little work, ie. an occasional book review, after doing nothing for 3 months.

Yes, I remember the Deux Magots.[2] I think I saw James Joyce there in 1928, but I've never quite been able to swear to that because J. was not of very distinctive appearance. I also went there to meet Camus who was supposed to have lunch with me, but he was ill & didn't come. I suppose Paris has cheered up a bit since I was there at the beginning of 1945. It was too gloomy for words then, & of course it was almost impossible to get anything to eat & drink, & everybody was so shabby & pale. But I can't believe it is what it used to be. It's lucky for you you're too young to have seen it in the 'twenties, it always seemed a bit ghostlike after that, even before the war. I don't know when I'll see France again, as at present one can't travel because of this currency business,[3] but if one of my books *did* strike it lucky I'd get them to keep some of the francs in France so that I could go & spend them. If I'm cured & about by then as I assume I shall be, I am going to try & wangle a correspondent's job this winter so as to winter in a warm place. The winter of 1946-7 in London was really a bit too thick, & I think it was probably what started me on this show. In Jura it's a bit better, because it isn't quite so cold & we get more coal, also more food, but it's a bit awkward if one needs medical attention at a time when one can't get to the mainland. Early last year my sister dislocated her arm & was nearly drowned going across to the doctor in a tiny motor boat. Inez [Holden]* exaggerated our later adventure a bit, but we did have a very nasty accident in the famous whirlpool of Corrievrechan° (which comes into a film called *I know where I'm going*) & were lucky not to be drowned. The awful thing was having Richard with us, however he loved every moment of it except when we were in the water. I think Jura is doing him good except that he doesn't see enough of other children & therefore is still very backward in talking. Otherwise he is most enterprising & full of energy, & is out working on the farm all day long. It's nice to be able to let him roam about with no traffic to be afraid of. Write again if you get time. I love getting letters.

With much love
George

[XIX, 3332, pp. 257–8; handwritten]

1. The first time was when Orwell went into Uxbridge Cottage Hospital just before Christmas 1933 with pneumonia.
2. The Café aux Deux Magots, much frequented by writers, on the Boulevard Saint-Germain.
3. At the end of August 1947, because of the grave financial crisis, the Labour government reduced food rations, and banned pleasure motoring and holidays abroad. Clement Attlee, the Prime Minister, said, 'I have no easy words for the nation. I cannot say when we shall emerge into easier times.' On 29 September, the Midlands was deprived of power for one day a week to cut fuel costs. On 9 October 1947, to reduce foreign indebtedness, especially in dollars, the government cut the bacon ration to one ounce a week. The following month the potato ration was cut to 3 pounds a week.

To Eugene Reynal

28 January 1948
Hairmyres Hospital
East Kilbride

Dear Mr. Reynal,¹

I must thank you very kindly for the food parcel which you so kindly sent me & which reached me here about a week ago. It was a very pleasant surprise. I was particularly thrilled to find in it a tin of olive oil, a thing we have not seen for years.

I expect Leonard Moore told you I was ill, as I asked him to let anyone in the USA with whom I had any connections know I should be out of action for some months. It is TB of the left lung. I have been ill for three months or more, but actually I think ever since that vile winter of 1946–47. I feel better & I think I have just about turned the corner, but the cure is a slow one at best. Of course I can't do any serious work till I'm in good health, but I am beginning to do just a little journalism. After months of idleness, I'm afraid my handwriting is getting a bit funny, but that is because I have my right arm in plaster² & haven't got used to this yet.

Thank you so much again.

Yours sincerely,
George Orwell

[XIX, 3335, p. 260; handwritten copy]

1. Of Reynal & Hitchcock, New York, publishers of *Dickens, Dali & Others* (1946).
2. Why Orwell's arm was in plaster is not known. He was confined to bed so could hardly have fallen. However, the phrenic nerve, crushed as part of the procedure described in his letter to his sister (see **1.1.48**), affects the arms, and it might have been related to that.

To David Astor*

1 February 1948
Hairmyres Hospital
East Kilbride

Dear David,

Thanks so much for your letter. Before anything else I must tell you of something Dr Dick* has just said to me.

He says I am getting on quite well, but slowly, & it would speed recovery if one had some streptomycin (STREPTOMYCIN).¹ This is only obtainable in the USA, & because of dollars the B.O.T.² (or whoever it is) won't normally grant a licence. One can however buy it there if one has some dollars. He suggested that you with your American connections might arrange to buy it & I could pay you. He wants 70 grammes, & it costs about £1 a gramme. I would be awfully obliged if you could put this transaction through for me, as no doubt you can do it quicker than I could myself. There is no twist or illegality about this, Dr Dick says, & the stuff is not difficult to send. I suppose it will mean paying out about 300 dollars. If you want to be repaid in dollars, I think I have enough, as I had started building up a reserve of dollars in the US, otherwise I can pay you in sterling. I must in either case pay you, as it is a considerable sum & of course the hospital can't pay it.

I received from McIntyre³ a parcel of butter & eggs, & he told me you had instructed him to send this weekly. It is awfully kind, but I am going to ask him not to send the eggs, as I can't use them in those numbers & I expect the hens aren't laying too well now. I know ours at Barnhill are still doing very badly. I feel we ought to pay for Bob if we have him 10 months of the year—however. He only gets hay in the winter—of course he'd get oats if he were doing harder work—but he was in excellent condition when I came away. Our new cow has just arrived & my sister can't leave until it has calved. I'm afraid my writing is awful, but I have my arm in plaster. It's much better that way, as it doesn't hurt but it is awkward for certain purposes such as writing & eating. I also have to shave left-handed. Dr Dick says he will write to you. I suppose it will be best to have the drug sent to him. His correct designation is Mr Bruce Dick.

Yours
George

[XIX, 3337, pp. 262–3; handwritten]

1. Streptomycin was discovered in the United States in 1944 and was at this time being tested in Britain by the Medical Research Council.
2. Board of Trade, which controlled imports, and at this time refused to allow as many as it could, especially if payment was in dollars.
3. Presumably one of the Astor estate staff on Jura.

To Fredric Warburg*

4 February 1948
Hairmyres Hospital
East Kilbride

Dear Fred,

Thanks so much for your letter.¹ As you inferred, my beginning to do articles in the *Observer* is a sign of partial revival, though even that is an effort, especially as I now have my right arm in plaster. I can't attempt any serious work while I am like this (1½ stone under weight) but I like to do a little to keep my hand in & incidentally earn some money. I've been definitely ill since about October, & really, I think, since the beginning of 1947. I believe that frightful winter in London started it off. I didn't really feel well all last year except during that hot period in the summer. Before taking to my bed

I had finished the rough draft of my novel all save the last few hundred words, & if I had been well I might have finished it by about May. If I'm well & out of here by June, I might finish it by the end of the year—I don't know. It is just a ghastly mess as it stands, but the idea is so good that I could not possibly abandon it. If anything should happen to me I've instructed Richard Rees, my literary executor, to destroy the Ms. without showing it to anybody, but it's unlikely that anything like that would happen. This disease isn't dangerous at my age, & they say the cure is going on quite well, though slowly. Part of the cure is to put the affected lung out of action for six months, which gives it a better chance to heal. We are now sending for some new American drug called streptomycin which they say will speed up the cure.

Richard is getting enormous & is very forward in everything except talking. I'm going to have him thoroughly examined when my sister goes up to town, but I really don't think he's T.B. to judge by the look of him. It's sad that I can't see him again till I'm non-infectious. Please remember me to Pamela and Roger.

Yours
George

[XIX, 3339, pp. 264–5; handwritten]

1. Warburg wrote to Orwell on 2 February 1948 saying that Orwell's review of *India Called Them* by Lord Beveridge in the *Observer* (1 February, XIX, 3336, pp. 261–2), 'gave me heart to write and enquire how you are getting on'. He said there was nothing they needed to consult about but he would be greatly cheered by 'a line, however brief, as to how you are and how soon you hope to come out of that wretched hospital'.

To David Astor*

Monday [9 February 1948]

Dear David,

Just a hurried note to say thanks awfully your seeing about the streptomycin. Meanwhile you'll have had a telegram[1] which crossed your letter & which I hope you didn't bother to answer. Just having heard I got time to ring up last night, & as you were down in the country I then wired, as I did think it conceivable my original letter hadn't gone off. We get them posted in a rather sketchy way here.

Of course I must pay you for the stuff. But I'll try & think of something else you'd like, or your little girl.

I've just heard the Darrochs[2] are 'definitely leaving' Kinuachdrach[d], but I still can't find out what the row was about. It's a sad business after D.D. has broken his back reclaiming the farm, & awkward for the Fletchers[3] too. However, they'll have to get another tenant if only to look after their cattle.

All well here. They pump me so full of air once a week that I feel like a balloon for two days afterwards.

Yours,
George

[XIX, 3342, pp. 265–6; handwritten]

1.   Not traced.
2.   Donald Darroch and his sister, Katie, had a croft a mile or so from Barnhill at Kinuachdrachd. Orwell went there every day for milk until he bought a cow. He and Donald, who worked on a profit-sharing basis with Orwell's laird, Robin Fletcher, were very friendly. Donald and Katie are very frequently mentioned in Orwell's diaries. In *Remembering Orwell* (pp. 174–5) Katie contributes a brief but telling memoir. She describes Orwell as 'cheery and happy in his own way' – and a great fan of her scones!
3.   Robin Fletcher inherited the Ardlussa Estate some eight miles south of Barnhill. He had formerly been a housemaster at Eton. He and his wife, Margaret, set about restoring the estate and developing crofting. Margaret in *Orwell Remembered* (pp. 225–9) vividly describes Orwell: 'how ill, how terribly ill, he looked – and drawn: a sad face he had . . . I think he very much missed his wife . . . He was devoted to Richard.'

To David Astor*

Saturday [14 February 1948][1]

Dear David,

Did you really not want the pens? They're very useful, as my Biro was out of action & also lost, & my Rollball not functioning very well. This is yours I'm writing with.

The Van Gogh exhibition apparently begins on the 21st.

I'd certainly love to come down to your Abingdon place in the summer for a weekend, if I'm about by then. It would be lovely having the river at your door. Probably in June or July there'd be good fishing, dace & chub. The Thames fishing can be quite good. I caught some good fish at Eton, but hardly anybody outside College knew the place, as it was in the backwater joining on College field.

I still haven't got to the bottom of the row at Kinuachdrach[d], but I gather it was between Bill & Donald. I assume Donald won't leave immediately. The Fletchers are advertising for another tenant. They'll have to have someone to look after their herd of Highlands.

By the way, I think you said poor old Niel° Darroch might want to sell his boat—do you remember whether it was petrol or paraffin?

Yours
George

[XIX, 3344, p. 267; handwritten]

1.   Dated only 'Sat.' The Van Gogh Exhibition opened at the Tate Gallery, London, on 10 December 1947 and ran to 14 January 1948; it visited Birmingham, 24 January to 14 February 1948, and Glasgow—near where Orwell was in hospital—20 February to 14 March 1948. This letter is so fresh with hope that it must surely have been written before the course of streptomycin began: that, he would write to Middleton Murry on 20 February 1948, had 'just started'. Saturday, 14 February, is, therefore, the most likely date for this letter. That must place the next letter, here dated **16.2.48**, to that particular Monday.

To David Astor*

Monday [16 February 1948]

Dear David,

I've had 2 letters from you today. I'll take the business one first. I'm perfectly willing to do the reviews for the U.S., in fact I'd like it, as they will probably want them rather longer than yours, & I prefer that. I presume that they will be for papers more or less on a level with the *Observer* & similar in tone. The only caveat is, that I might have a relapse or something, & any way I can only do about 2 hours work each day. They will be starting with the streptomycin soon, & though I don't suppose so, it *may* have unpleasant effects, like M. & B.[1] But anyway, up to capacity I'll certainly do the reviews.

As to the streptomycin. Thanks awfully for getting it on the wing so quickly.[2] I suppose it will get here in only a few days. If you really don't want to be paid for it O. K., I won't press it. But I really could easily have paid, not only in £s but even in dollars, because I remember now, I have at least 500 lying by in New York. I don't need [to] tell you I am grateful. Let's hope it does its stuff. I gather they aren't very satisfied with my case at present. I haven't gained weight for 2 weeks, & I have a feeling I am getting weaker, though mentally I am more alert. Dr Dick* seems anxious to start in with the strepto as early as possible.

I'm sorry A[rthur] K[oestler]* has blown up. He's a bit temperamental. I thought his fi[rst] despatch from France was very good. The 'London Letters' he has been doing in P[artisan] R[eview] are shocking & I have been meaning to have a row with him about them—just one long squeal about basic petrol[3] etc.

I'll let you know how the strepto goes.

Yours
George

[XIX, 3349, p. 272; handwritten]

1.   May and Baker, manufacturers of pharmaceuticals; their initials were a shorthand means of referring to sulphonamides.
2.   David Astor wrote to Dr Dick* on 19 February 1948 thanking him for encouraging Orwell to get the streptomycin and offering to help in getting anything else that would aid Orwell's recovery. He made it clear that he wished to pay for any drugs that would help and said he was 'in communication with Blair on this' and trying to convince him to accept help. He asked Dick not to discuss payment with Orwell, 'as I think the only possibility of persuading him to be reasonable is that it should be a very private matter between him and me.' He could make another visit to Hairmyres Hospital, he said, 'this coming Sunday [22 February] or on Sunday, 7th March', the latter being slightly more convenient. Was Orwell doing too much work, he asked; he could either increase or decrease it as would prove desirable.
3.   'Basic' petrol was the amount allowed before supplements for special purposes were added. Writing to Anthony Powell on 8 March (XIX, 3360, p. 283) Orwell said he was allowed six gallons of petrol a month and that his car did only ten miles to the gallon 'on a highland road'.

To Ivor Brown*

20 February 1948
Hairmyres Hosp.

Dear Ivor Brown,

I'm sorry, but it was an *awful* book.[1] It had all the marks of an amateur's writing, everything jammed in indiscriminately, a sort of matey facetious manner that failed to come off, & a most irritating trick of giving everything its Faeroese name, which meant one had to look up the glossary every few lines. Its only merit was that it was informative about a little-known subject, which I think I indicated. Linklater's introduction didn't impress me as sincere. I thought of saying that the book was stodgy, or heavy going, or words to that effect, but didn't want to be unkind to an amateur.

I am not prepared to give praise on literary grounds to books of this type. One sinks one's standards below zero by pretending that they exist in a literary sense at all. This kind of book (eg.° another you have sent me, about caves in France²) are simply bits of topography, or travel diary set down by people who have no idea how to select or to write, & they get boosted because of local patriotism. If one is to review them, I do not see what we can do except to give an exposition.³

Yours sincerely
George Orwell

[XX, 3351A, p. 564; handwritten]

1. On 18 February 1948, an unsigned letter from Ivor Brown of the *Observer* questioned Orwell about the review he had submitted of Kenneth Williamson's *The Atlantic Islands*. He had noted that high claims had been made for the book and that Eric Linklater 'puts it very high'. Orwell, he said, had taken no line at all about the book but merely reported what Williamson said. Readers, publishers and authors 'like to see signs of enthusiasm and encouragement for good work, if it is good'. He himself had not read Williamson's book. He asked Orwell if he could 'give a bit more colour to your notice of it should you feel this is justified'. Eric Linklater (Robert Russell; 1899–1974), Scottish novelist (*Juan in America*, 1931), who wrote several war pamphlets (e.g., *The Highland Division*, 1942). Orwell's review appeared on 29 February 1948 (XIX, 3356, pp. 277–8).
2. *My Caves* by Norbert Casteret reviewed 14 March 1948 (XIX, 3356, pp. 283–4).
3. Ivor Brown replied on 24 February saying he quite understood how Orwell felt.

To John Middleton Murry*

5 March 1948
Hairmyres Hospital
East Kilbride

Dear Murry,

Thanks very much for the book,¹ which I read with interest. I agree with your general thesis, but I think that in assessing the world situation it is very rash to assume that the rest of the world° would combine against Russia. We have a fearful handicap in the attitude towards us of the coloured races, & the under-privileged peoples generally (eg. in S. America), which we possibly don't deserve any longer but which we have inherited from our imperial past. I also think it is rash to assume that most orientals, or indeed any except a few westernised ones, would prefer democracy to totalitarianism. It seems to me that the great difficulty of our position is that in the coming show-down we must have the peoples of Africa & the Middle East—if possible of Asia too, of course—on our side, & they will all look towards Russia unless there is a radical change of attitude, especially in the USA. I doubt whether we can put things right in Africa, at least in some parts of it, without quite definitely siding with the blacks against the whites. The latter will then look [to] the USA for support, & they will get it. It can easily turn out that we & America are alone, with all the coloured peoples siding with Russia. Perhaps even then we could win a war against Russia, but only by laying the world in ruins, especially this country.

I'm sorry to hear about your illness. My own seems to be getting better rapidly. They can't say yet whether the streptomycin is doing its stuff, but I certainly have been a lot better the last week or so. I imagine however that I shall be in bed for another month or two, & under treatment at any rate until the summer. The lung has been collapsed, which is supposed to give it a better chance to heal, but of course it takes a long time, & meanwhile they have to keep on pumping air into one's diaphragm. Fortunately this is a very nice hospital & very well run. Everyone is extraordinarily kind to me. It is sad I cannot see my little boy until I am non-infectious, however he will be able to come & visit me when I am allowed out of doors. He is getting on for 4 & growing enormously, though he is a bit backward about talking, because we live in such a solitary spot that he doesn't see enough of other children. I have got our place in Jura running pretty well now. I myself couldn't farm the land that went with the house, but a young chap who was wounded in the war lives with us & farms it. We are pretty well found there, & better off for fuel & food than one is in London. The winters also are not quite so cold, funnily enough. The chief difficulties are that in bad weather one is sometimes cut off from the mainland, & that one is chronically short of petrol. However one can use a horse if one is obliged to. Of course I have to go up to London occasionally, but the journey only takes 24 hours, less if one flies. I was half way through a novel when I took to my bed. It ought to have been finished by May—possibly I might finish it by the end of 1948 if I get out of here by the summer.

Please remember me to your wife.

Yours sincerely
Geo. Orwell

[XIX, 3358, pp. 279–80; handwritten]

1.   *The Free Society.* In this Murry comes close to approving war against the Soviet Union, contrary to his long-held pacifist views and hence E.L. Allen's *Pacifism and the Free Society: A Reply to John Middleton Murry* (1948).

To Dwight Macdonald*

7 March 1948
Hairmyres Hospital
East Kilbride

Dear Dwight,

Thanks so much for sending me your book on Wallace, which I have read with the greatest interest. Have you done anything about finding an English publisher? In case you haven't, I am writing to Victor Gollancz bringing the book to his attention.[1] If you're not already in touch with some other publisher, I would write to Gollancz & send him a copy. In spite of the awful paper shortage etc., the book should find a publisher here, as people are naturally interested in Wallace, as the man who is likely to cause 'our' candidate to lose the election.[2] (It's difficult to keep up with American politics here, but it does look as though Wallace is making great strides lately. I'm afraid he may get the whole anti-war vote, as Chamberlain did before the war.) And I think Gollancz is your man, as he is politically sympathetic & is able to bring a book out quickly, as Warburg, for instance, can't. I suppose you know his address—17 Henrietta St. Covent Garden, London WC.2. The book might do with some minor modifications for the English public, but you could fix all that with G.

There's another instance of Wallace's habit of issuing garbled versions of his speeches, which might be worth putting in. When he was over here, Wallace of course played down the Palestine issue, or at least didn't make mischief about it. He was no sooner in France than he referred to the Jewish terrorists as a 'maquis' fighting against a British occupation. This appeared in French reports of his speech, but not in any English-language paper (except one, I think the *Christian Science Monitor*, which somehow got hold of it), presumably having been cut out from versions issued to them. The *Manchester Guardian* documented the facts at the time.

As you see I'm in hospital. [*Reference to illness omitted.*] I'm starting my uniform edition this year & shall start off by reprinting a novel which was published in 1939 & rather killed by the war. I believe Harcourt Brace are going to reprint my Burma novel. They were BFs not to do so immediately after having that bit of luck with *Animal Farm*.

What's happened to *Politics*? I haven't seen it for months. I told my agent in New York to take out a subscription for me, but she seemed rather reluctant to do so, evidently thinking I ought to get all the American papers free.

Isn't it funny how surprised everyone seems over this Czechoslovakia business?[3] Many people seem really angry with Russia, as though at some time there had been reason to expect different behaviour on the Russians' part. Middleton Murry has just renounced his pacifism & written a book (practically) demanding a preventive war against the USSR! This after writing less than 10 years ago that 'Russia is the only inherently peaceful country.'

Excuse bad handwriting

Yours
Geo. Orwell

[XIX, 3359, pp. 281–2; handwritten]

1. Letter not traced.
2. In the 1948 election Henry Wallace (see **5.12.46**, n. 6) was a candidate of the left-wing Progressive Party, which received over one million popular votes. Thomas E. Dewey was expected to win the election (and a famous headline prematurely showed him as doing so), but Truman won with a two-million majority of the popular vote.
3. On 27 February 1948, Klement Gottwald (1896–1953), Communist Prime Minister of Czechoslovakia, announced that the resignation of twelve centre and right-wing ministers had been accepted by President Edvard Beneš (although a week earlier Beneš had stated that there would be no Communist takeover of Czechoslovakia). Jan Masaryk (son of Czechoslovakia's 'founding father') remained Foreign Minister, and attention (and hopes) were focused on him as the means whereby a total victory for the Communists might be averted. However, on 10 March 1948 he was found dead in the courtyard beneath his flat in Prague. The Communist line was that Masaryk had committed suicide in 'a moment of nervous breakdown'. Those who opposed the Communist takeover, which had become complete, interpreted his death as murder.

To Leonard Moore*

19 March 1948
Hairmyres Hospital
East Kilbride

Dear Moore,

Thank you for your letter. I didn't object to the jacket, & it had 'Uniform Edition' on it, which I wanted to make sure of. But I did think the light green cover was unsuitable & asked Warburg whether he could manage to change the cloth for something darker.[1] I favour dark blue, or any dark colour except red, which always seems to come off on one's fingers. I thought the format was all right. Of course the price is fearful for a reprint, but I suppose subsequent volumes need not be so expensive.

I see that *Burmese Days* is supposed to come out in the same edition only a few months later. I believe the Penguin edition is still in print, as you sent me an account of sales recently. I suppose the Penguin people won't print many more, otherwise it may damage the Warburg edition.

Warburg suggested that I should bring out another volume of essays in the fairly near future. I think it would be better not to do this for another 2–3 years, as people feel rather cheated if they buy a book & find it contains things which they have read in magazines only a year or so earlier.

Yours sincerely
Eric Blair

[XIX, 3362, pp. 285–6; handwritten]

1.   Fredric Warburg had visited Orwell, probably on 10 March, bringing a specimen binding case (or cloth) for the Uniform Edition. Warburg took note of Orwell's wish that a darker colour be selected. Orwell had some of his own books rebound in dark blue; these included a presentation copy of *Animal Farm* for his son, Richard. Warburg wrote to Orwell on 15 March, expressing 'real pleasure' at finding him 'in better shape and better spirits than I had anticipated'. He realised that Orwell would require all his patience and control 'to overcome the obstacles to a complete restoration of health', but he did not doubt that Orwell could do that 'since you still have many books you still wish to write'.

To Sally McEwan*

27 March 1948
Hairmyres Hospital
East Kilbride

Dear Sally,

It seems literally years since I have heard from you, or of you? How are things going? I am going to send this to the Nature Clinic, hoping they'll forward it if you aren't still there. How is your young man? Are you married? And how is little Sally? Excuse this filthy pen. It is all I have, as my other one is being refilled.

I dare say you heard I am suffering from T.B. [*Details of illness; progress of novel; Richard*]

We have got more furniture at Barnhill now, & the place is running quite well. Transport is still the chief difficulty. We have got a car now, but the headache is tyres, apart from the everlasting petrol difficulty. However, we also have a horse which can be used in moments of emergency. A friend now lives with us & farms the croft, which is a good arrangement, because we don't then feel guilty about occupying land & not using it, & also when we like we can go away, because there is someone to look after our animals. We have got a cow now, also of course hens, & am thinking of pigs. We've also got more of a garden now, & have made an end of all those awful rushes. I have planted a lot of fruit trees & bushes, but I am not sure yet whether trees will do much good in such a windy place.

Write some time & let me know how everything is going. The above address will find me for some time, I am afraid.

Yours
George

[XIX, 3373, pp. 305–6; handwritten]

To Mrs David Astor

5 April 1948
Hairmyres Hospital
East Kilbride

Dear Mrs Astor,

I believe it was you who sent me a 7 lb. bag of sugar from Jamaica, also a tin of pears & some guava jelly. It was extremely kind of you to think of it. I was especially delighted to get the sugar, which my sister will use for making jam. I have been getting on pretty well, but just this last week have been feeling rather bad with a sore throat & various other minor ailments which are probably secondary effects of the streptomycin I am having. I think they are probably going to stop the injections for a few days & then go on again when these effects have worn off.[1]

I haven't seen Richard, my little boy, since before Christmas, as I can't see him while I am infectious. However I have had him photographed & can see that he is growing fast & is in good health. My sister says he is learning to talk better. I had been rather worried about that, though he is not backward in any other way.

Please forgive bad handwriting. My writing is bad enough at the best of times, but whatever is wrong with me has affected my fingernails & it is difficult to hold on to the pen. With many thanks again.

Yours sincerely
Geo. Orwell

[XIX, 3376, p.309; handwritten]

1. Professor James Williamson, who was a junior doctor at Hairmyres Hospital when Orwell was a patient, remembers the arrival of the streptomycin and its adverse effect on Orwell (*Remembering Orwell*, p. 200). In a note for Professor Crick, written many years later, Dr Williamson said that Orwell's TB was 'pretty "chronic"... It was not the type that would have largely cleared with effective drug treatment and he would always have been breathless and incapacitated' (Crick, p. 602).

To David Astor*

[14 April 1948]

Dear David,

I thought you'd like to hear that Bobbie is making himself useful. Part of the field behind the house was too steep a slope for the small tractor, so they harnessed Bobbie into the harrow & he behaved 'like a lamb,' Bill says. So perhaps now they can use him in the trap, which is as well, as the car needs new wheels as well as tyres.

They've stopped the streptomycin for a few days & the unpleasant symptoms have practically disappeared. Shortly they will continue with the strepto, which has about 3 weeks to go. It's evidently doing its stuff as my last 3 tests were 'negative,' ie no TB germs. Of course that doesn't necessarily mean they're all dead, but at any rate they must have taken a pretty good beating. I have felt better the last day or two & have nearly finished the article I promised for the *Observer* [1] The weather has at last improved, & I'm longing to go out, which I think they may soon let me do, in a chair, of course.

Yours
George

[XIX, 3379, p. 311; handwritten]

1. Probably his review of Wilde's *The Soul of Man under Socialism* (XIX, 3395, pp. 333–4).

To Julian Symons*

20 April 1948
Hairmyres Hospital
East Kilbride

Dear Julian,

Thanks so much for sending the pen, & prospectively for some chocolate you mentioned. I am so glad to hear you are going to have a baby. They're awful fun in spite of the nuisance, & as they develop one has one's own childhood over again. I suppose one thing one has to guard against is imposing one's own childhood on the child, but I do think it is relatively easy to give a child a decent time nowadays & allow it to escape the quite unnecessary torments that I for instance went through. I'm not sure either that one ought to trouble too much about bringing a child into a world of atomic bombs, because those born now will never have known anything except wars, rationing etc., & can probably be quite happy against that background if they've had a good psychological start.

I am a lot better, but I had a bad fortnight with the secondary effects of the streptomycin. I suppose with all these drugs it's rather a case of sinking the ship to get rid of the rats. [*Passage regarding progress of illness and Richard.*]

It's funny you should have mentioned Gissing. I am a great fan of his (though I've never read *Born in Exile*, which some say is his masterpiece, because I can't get hold of a copy), & was just in the act of re-reading two reprints, which I promised to review for *Politics & Letters*. I think I shall do a long article on him, for them or someone else.[1] I think *The Odd Women* is one of the best novels in English. You asked about my uniform edition. They're starting with a novel called *Coming Up for Air*, which was published in 1939 & rather killed by the war, & doing *Burmese Days* later in the year. I just° corrected the proofs of the latter, which I wrote more than 15 years ago & probably hadn't looked at for 10 years. It was a queer experience— almost like reading a book by somebody else. I'm also going to try & get Harcourt Brace to reprint these two books in the USA but even if they do so they'll probably only take 'sheets', which never does one much good. It's funny what BFs American publishers are about re-prints. Harcourt Brace have been nagging me for 2 years for a manuscript, any kind of manuscript, & are now havering with the idea of doing a series of reprints, but when I urged them to reprint *Burmese Days* immediately after they had cleaned up on *Animal Farm*, they wouldn't do so. Nor would the original publishers of *B.D*, though they too were trying to get something out of me. Apparently reprints in the USA are done mostly by special firms which only take them on if they are safe for an enormous sale.

Yes, I thought the last number of *Politics* quite good, but I must say that in spite of all their elegies I retain dark suspicions about Gandhi,[2] based only on gossip, but such a lot of gossip that I think there must be something in it. Please remember me to your wife.

Yours
George

[XIX, 3386, pp. 321–3; handwritten]

1. The typescript of Orwell's article on George Gissing only surfaced in the summer of 1959. It was published in the *London Magazine*, June 1960. (See XIX, 3406, pp. 346–52.)
2. Mahatma (Mohandas Karamchand) Gandhi (1869–1948), a major figure in the struggle for Indian independence and a continuing force in Indian life after his death. He was fatally shot on 30 January 1948 by a Hindu fanatic. See Orwell's 'Reflections on Gandhi', *Partisan Review*, January 1949, (XX, 3516, pp. 5–12).

To Gleb Struve*

21 April 1948
Hairmyres Hospital
East Kilbride

Dear Struve,

I'm awfully sorry to have to send this[1] back, after such a long delay, having finally failed to find a home for it. But as you see by the above, I am in hospital (tuberculosis), & at the time of receiving your letter I wasn't able to do very much. I am better now, & hope to get out of here some time during the summer, but of course the treatment of this disease is always a slow job.

I have arranged to review *We* for the *Times Lit. Supp.*, when the English translation comes out.[2] Did you tell me that Zamyatin's widow is still alive & in Paris? If so, & she can be contacted, it might be worth doing so, as there may be others of his books which some English publisher might be induced to take, if *We* is a success. You told me that his satire on England, *The Islanders*, had never been translated, & perhaps it might be suitable.[3]

I hope you will forgive me for my failure to find an editor for Mandelstam's sketches. There are so few magazines in England now. *Polemic* died of the usual disease, & the other possible one *Politics & Letters*, was no good.

You asked about my novel, *Burmese Days*. I think it is still in print as a

Penguin, but there won't be many copies left. It is being reprinted about the end of this year, as I am beginning a uniform edition, & that is second on the list. I *may* succeed in getting some of these books reprinted in the USA as well.

Yours sincerely
Geo. Orwell

P.S. This address will find me for some months, I'm afraid.

[XIX, 3387, pp. 323–4; handwritten]

1. Presumably the Mandelstam sketches mentioned later in the letter.
2. An English translation, by Gregory Zilboorg, was, in fact, published in New York by E. P. Dutton in 1924 and reprinted the following year. Although Orwell knew of the US edition, he had not seen it. The French translation, *Nous autres*, which Orwell reviewed in *Tribune*, 4 January 1946 (see XVIII, 2841, pp. 13–17), was published in Paris in 1929.
3. Yevgeny Zamyatin came to England in 1916 to supervise the building of Russian icebreakers in the northeast of England and Scotland. He wrote two amusing satires on English life, *The Islanders*, written in England in 1917, and *The Fisher of Men*, written in 1918 on his return to Russia. The first is set in Jesmond, near Newcastle upon Tyne and the second in Chiswick. A translation by Sophie Fuller and Julian Sacchi was published in 1984.

To John Middleton Murry*

28 April 1948
Hairmyres Hospital
East Kilbride

Dear Murry,

Thank you for your letter. I'm very sorry to hear the *Adelphi* is coming to an end.[1] At any rate it's had a long run for its money, longer than most magazines. I could do you a review, but I'm not keen on doing the Joad book. I looked at it recently, & it didn't seem to me to be *about* anything. How about the third volume of Osbert Sitwell's autobiography,[2] which has come out recently & which I think is very good in a way? You wouldn't need to send a copy, as I have one already. It would be better to do more than 1000 words if you have the space. I note that you want the copy by May 15, but perhaps you could let me know whether you think this a suitable book.

[*Brief account of illness and Barnhill*] I would like to see what is going on [*at Barnhill*], also to see my little boy, whom I haven't seen since Christmas for fear of infection. I get photographs of him, & he is evidently growing enormous.

Yours
Geo. Orwell

[XIX, 3390, pp. 326–7; handwritten]

1.   It survived until 1955.
2.   Orwell reviewed Sitwell's *Great Morning* in the July–September 1948 issue of *The Adelphi* (see XIX, 3418, pp. 395–8).

To Dwight Macdonald*

2 May 1948
Hairmyres Hosp
East Kilbride

Dear Dwight,

Thanks so much for your letter, and prospectively for sending the books.[1] Yes, I got *Politics*, as a matter of fact 2 copies, as you sent one to me direct here. It set me thinking again about Gandhi, whom I never met but whom I know a certain amount about. The funny thing is that though he was almost certainly used by the British for their own ends over a long period, I'm not certain that in the long run he failed. He was not able to stop the fight[ing] between Moslems and Hindus, but his major aim of getting the British out of India peacefully did finally come off. I personally would never have predicted this even five years ago, and I am not sure that a good deal of the credit should not go to Gandhi. Of course a Conservative government would never have got out without a fight, but the fact that a Labour government did so might indirectly be due to Gandhi's influence. One might say that they only agreed to dominion status because they knew they couldn't hold on to India much longer, but this doesn't apply for instance to Burma, a country which was extremely profitable to us and easy enough to hold down. I think, *pace tua*, that Gandhi behaved abominably, or at any rate stupidly, in 1942 when he thought the Axis had won the war, but I think also that his prolonged effort to keep the Indian struggle on a decent plane may have gradually modified the British attitude.

Incidentally, this business of assassinating important individuals[2] is something one has to take account of. In the same number I see you note regretfully that Walter Reuther[3] has a bodyguard, but I also see that he has just been seriously wounded—the second attempt, I believe. I notice also that you speak more or less approvingly of the *Esprit*⁴ crowd. I don't know if you know that some at any rate of these people are fellow travellers of a peculiarly slimy religious brand, like Macmurray⁵ in England. Their line is that Communism and Christianity are compatible, and latterly that there is no choice except Communism or Fascism and one must therefore regretfully choose the former. But this is all right, because Communism will presently shed certain unfortunate characteristics such as bumping off its opponents, and if Socialists join up with the CP they can persuade it into better ways. It's funny that when I met Mounier⁶ for only about 10 minutes in 1945 I thought to myself, that man's a fellow traveller. I can smell them. I believe Sartre has been latterly taking the same line.

I'm sorry Gollancz fell through.⁷ I don't know if it's any use trying Warburg. He read the book and was impressed by it, but of course he is chronically short of paper and takes years to get a book out. The binding is the real trouble here. I must say I feel envious when I see American books now, their solidity and so on. The way British books are printed now makes one ashamed to be associated with them. I asked them to send you a copy of the first book in my uniform edition, coming out in a fortnight or so. I must say I wish I could have started this edition at a time when one could get hold of decent bindings. I feel that a uniform edition which in any case is a sign of approaching senility ought to be very chaste-looking in buckram covers. Have you got an agent over here, or an agent with connections here? It's worth while I think.

Yes, I think Lanarkshire was where Owen⁸ flourished. It's rather an unpleasant industrial county with a lot of coal mines, and its chief ornament is Glasgow. Out here it's quite pleasant though. I am longing to go out of doors, having barely done so for six months. They now let me up an hour a day and I think they would let me out a little if it were warmer. It's been a horrible spring, however not so bad as last year.

I'm in sympathy with the Europe-America leaflet you sent,⁹ but I don't know if there's anything I personally can do about it. Thanks for your query, but there is honestly not anything I want. We are well cared for here and people have been very kind about sending me food etc.

Yours
George

[XIX, 3392, pp. 328–90; typewritten]

1. Macdonald had written on 23 April 1948 and he sent a parcel of books by separate mail. He mentions two of these in his letter: Joseph Wood Krutch, *Samuel Johnson* (1944) and T. Polner, *Tolstoy and His Wife*, translated by N. Wreden (1945). These, he wrote, 'are two of the best modern biographies I know', especially the first.

He asked Orwell if he shared his 'private enthusiasm for Dr. Johnson'. Orwell did not respond to this in his reply. Krutch (1893–1970) was drama critic to *The Nation*, 1924–51.

2. Gandhi had been assassinated on 30 January 1948.

3. Walter Philip Reuther (1907–1970), President of the United Automobile Workers of America, 1946–70; President of the Congress of Industrial Organizations, 1952–55. He was one of those instrumental in the merger of the CIO with the American Federation of Labor in 1955 and served as Vice-President of the AFL-CIO until, in disagreement with the President of the organisation, he took out the UAW. He had worked in a Soviet car factory for two years in the 1930s, but later was critical of the Soviets. He was killed when his plane crashed in fog.

4. *Esprit* was a periodical launched in 1932 by Emmanuel Mounier (see n. 6) 'to close the gap between communist and non-communist Frenchmen'. At the same time, Mounier inaugurated 'the Personalist movement, a non-party philosophy between Marxism and Existentialism' (J. F. Falvey, *The Penguin Companion to Literature* (1969), II, p. 553).

5. John Macmurray (1891–1976), Grote Professor of the Philosophy of Mind and Logic, University of London, 1929–44; Professor of Moral Philosophy, University of Edinburgh, 1944–58. His many books include *The Philosophy of Communism* (1933) and *Constructive Democracy* (1943). In Orwell's pamphlet collection is a copy of his Peace Aims Pamphlet, *Foundations of Economic Reconstruction* (1942).

6. Emmanuel Mounier (1905–1950), writer, literary critic, intellectual leader in the French Resistance, was a Roman Catholic and Marxist sympathiser and the founder of the journal *Esprit*. He was influenced by Bergson and Péguy, and, with others, published *La Pensée de Charles Péguy* (1931), several books on Personalism, and some 170 articles. He advocated economic revolution, a new socialist system, respect for the individual, and an active Roman Catholic Church in order to implement ethical values appropriate to the age. He particularly addressed the needs of apathetic and disorientated post-war youth (J. F. Falvey, see n. 4).

7. Orwell had suggested to Gollancz that he publish Macdonald's *Henry Wallace: The Man and the Myth*. Macdonald told Orwell that, though Gollancz was at first enthusiastic, he had written later saying he could not get the book out in time. Despite good reviews the book had sold only 3,500 copies in two months in the USA. However, Macdonald was having 'a lot of fun' speaking at colleges exposing Wallace's 'lies and demagogy, and the almost 100% Commie entourage which writes his speeches'.

8. The text of Macdonald's letter that has survived is a carbon copy. It contains no reference to Owen, so that may well have been in a postscript added only to the top copy. Robert Owen (1771–1858), born and died in Wales, a successful Lancashire cotton manufacturer, established the model industrial town of New Lanark in Scotland, with good living conditions for the employees complete with non-profitmaking shops.

9. A leaflet issued in connection with a proposed series of meetings – the first had by then been held – 'on the Russian culture purge. Speakers: Nicolas Nabokov, Meyer Schapiro, Lionel Trilling, and myself. It was a success—about 400 people, $300 profit, and solid speeches.'

To Julian Symons*

10 May 1948
Hairmyres Hospital
East Kilbride

Dear Julian,

Thanks ever so much to yourself and your wife for the chocolate and the tea and rice, which got here last week. I'd been meaning to write. You see I've organised a typewriter at last. It's a bit awkward to use in bed, but it saves hideous misprints in reviews etc. caused by my handwriting. As you say, the ball-bearing pen is the last stage in the decay of handwriting, but I've given mine up years ago. At one time I used to spend hours with script pens and squared paper, trying to re-teach myself to write, but it was no use after being taught copperplate and on top of that encouraged to write a 'scholarly' hand. The writing of children nowadays is even worse than ours used to be, because they will teach them this disconnected script which is very slow to write. Evidently the first thing is to get a good simple cursive script, but on top of that you have to teach hand control, in fact learning to write involves learning to draw. Evidently it can be done, as in countries like China and Japan anyone who can write at all writes more or less gracefully.

I am glad E[yre] and S[pottiswoode] are pleased with the biography, but don't let them get away with *The Quest for AJA Symons* as a title. It is true that if a book is going to sell no title can kill it, but I am sure that is a bad one. Of course I can't make suggestions without seeing the book, but if they insist on having the name, something like *A.J.A. Symons: a Memoir* is always inoffensive.[1]

Coming Up for Air isn't much, but I thought it worth reprinting because it was rather killed by the outbreak of war and then blitzed out of existence, so thoroughly that in order to get a copy from which to reset it we had to steal one from a public library.[2] Of course you are perfectly right about my own character constantly intruding on that of the narrator. I am not a real novelist anyway, and that particular vice is inherent in writing a novel in the first person, which one should never do. One difficulty I have never solved is that one has masses of experience which one passionately wants to write about, eg. the part about fishing in that book, and no way of using them up except by disguising them as a novel. Of course the book was bound to suggest Wells watered down. I have a great admiration for Wells, ie. as a writer, and he was a very early influence on me. I think I was ten or eleven when Cyril Connolly* and I got hold of a copy of Wells's *The Country of the Blind* (short stories) and were so fascinated by it that we kept stealing it from one another. I can still remember at 4 o'clock on a midsummer morning, with the school fast asleep and the sun slanting through the window, creeping down a passage to Connolly's dormitory where I knew the book would be beside his bed. We also got into severe trouble (and I think a caning—I forget) for having a copy of Compton Mackenzie's *Sinister Street*.³

They now tell me that I shall have to stay here till about August. [*State of health; worries about Richard*] I don't know who put that par in the *Standard*⁴—someone who knew me, though there were the usual mistakes. I don't think they ought to have given my real name.

Please remember me to your wife.

Yours
George

[XIX, 3397, pp. 335–7; typewritten]

1. Julian Symons's biography of his brother was called *A. J. A. Symons: His Life and Speculations* (1950).
2. Whether or not the copy was 'permanently stolen' is not known.
3. Cyril Connolly recalls the incident less painfully. He and Orwell alternately won a prize given by Mrs Wilkes, the headmaster's wife, for the best list of books borrowed from the school library. However, 'we were both caught at last with two volumes of *Sinister Street* and our favour sank to zero' (*Enemies of Promise*, 1948, chapter 19).
4. On 5 May 1948, in the 'Londoner's Diary', a gossip column in the *Evening Standard*, there was a paragraph about Orwell which referred to Eileen's death.

To Leonard Moore*

12 May 1948
Hairmyres Hospital
East Kilbride

Dear Moore,

On going through my books I see that I wrote an introduction for a book of collected pamphlets for Allan Wingate more than a year ago. I don't know why the book hasn't come out,¹ but I think it is time they paid me for the introduction. If I remember rightly, I was promised £50 and was paid £10 in advance: or it may have been that I was promised £40—anyway, I think £40 is the sum involved. Perhaps you could communicate with them about it.

I am a lot better and the infection has evidently been quelled, but the doctors think I should remain here till about August. However, I feel so much better that I think I can get back to a little serious work and am starting on the second draft of my novel. I don't know how far I shall [get] as it is awkward working in bed, but if I can get well started before leaving hospital I should get the book done before the end of the year.

Yours sincerely
Eric Blair

[XIX, 3398, p. 336; typewritten]

1. *British Pamphleteers*, edited with Reginald Reynolds. Volume 1 was published 15 November 1948. The second volume, in which Orwell was not involved, appeared in 1951.

To Mrs Jessica Marshall*

19 May 1948
Hairmyres Hospital
East Kilbride

Dear Mrs Marshall,

Many thanks for your letter. It has been on my conscience for a long time that you once sent me a pot of jam for which I never thanked you. I was rather distraught all through the war years and left a lot of letters unanswered. My wife I am sorry to say died three years ago, leaving me with a little adopted son who was not then a year old. He has just had his fourth birthday and is now of enormous size and full of vigour and mischief, though I haven't seen him since Christmas because of the danger of infection. Of course all these events have put back my work a great deal, and, as you say, I have not published a full-length book since before the war. I was about half way through a novel when I was taken ill, and if I had not been ill I should have finished it by the spring. As it is I hope to finish it before the end of the year, which I suppose means it would not come out before the autumn of 1949. It takes about a year to get a book through the press now.[1]

I have been here since before Christmas, but I was ill at home for some months before that. However I am now much better, thanks largely to the streptomycin, and hope to get out of hospital some time during the summer.

They have evidently succeeded in killing the infection, but of course it takes a long time for the damaged lung to heal up. I imagine that I shall have to take things very easily for about a year, so far as physical effort goes. But I am now able to do a little work, though I find it very tiresome to write in bed. When I get out I may have to attend for out-patient treatment, in which case I shall have to make my headquarters in Edinburgh, otherwise I can go back to Jura where we have been installed for the last two years. It is a completely wild place and a bit un-getatable, but it is quite easy to live there if you have a cow and hens, and you are better off for food and fuel than in England. Also, contrary to what people think, that side of Scotland is not at all cold. It is damp, but the winter is mild and you get beautiful weather in the summer. The only thing that worries me is that my little boy only sees other children about once a week, except when people are staying with us, and I think this has made him a bit backward in his talking. However I shall have to arrange for him to go to school in about a year's time, and Jura will be a good place for him to spend his holidays. He is tremendously healthy and didn't seem much affected even when he had measles and whooping cough. I am terrified of his getting this disease that I have, but actually I don't think he is the type that would get it, and we now have tuberculin-tested cows, so the likeliest source of infection is shut off. I think it is good for him to grow up among farm animals and boats, in a place where there are no 'trespassers will be prosecuted' boards.

I agree with you about Priestley – he is awful, and it is astonishing that he has actually had a sort of come-back in reputation during the last year or two. What you say of Wells is of course true, but that has never stopped me enjoying at any rate his early work. I have just read the third volume of Osbert Sitwell's autobiography, in fact I reviewed it for the last number of the *Adelphi,* which is now packing up after 25 years of moribund existence. Evidently there will be more volumes, as this one only goes up to 1914. I am a great admirer of his novel *Before the Bombardment,* and the only time I met him I liked him very much. I have also been re-reading some books of George Gissing, on whom I am going to write a long essay for a magazine. I always say he is one of the best English novelists, though he has never had his due, and they always seem to reprint the wrong books. His two best ones, *New Grub Street* and *The Odd Women,* can't now be got, even secondhand. I also re-read recently George Moore's *Esther Waters,* which is a marvellous straightforward story in spite of being very clumsily written. While in bed I have been making one of my periodical attacks[2] on Henry James, but I never can really get to care for him.

Half way through writing this letter I have been out for my usual half-hour walk in the grounds. It leaves me very out of breath, in fact I can't go more than about 100 yards without stopping for a rest. However, they are now going to let the lung which they have collapsed return to its normal shape, so I suppose breathing will become easier. This is a nice hospital and everyone has been very good to me. Thanks so much for writing.

Yours sincerely
Geo. Orwell

[*LO*, pp. 113–5; XIX, 3401A, p. 339; typewritten]

1. Orwell was contrasting pre-war practice. Thus, he posted the ms of *The Road to Wigan Pier* to his agent on 15 December 1936. On the 19th he saw Victor Gollancz and it was decided to illustrate the book. It was published twelve weeks later on 8 March 1937 with 32 pages of plates.
2. attacks = attempts to read

To George Woodcock*

24 May 1948

Dear George,

I received another letter from Charles Davey, drawing my attention to the fact that E. M. Forster has resigned from the NCCL. I then sat down, or sat up rather, with the idea of writing that article on the F.D.C., but on second thoughts I really don't think I can do it. To begin with I have two long articles on hand and I can't do much yet, but what is more to the point, I don't know enough factually about the F.D.C. for the purpose. Do you think you could do the article? I think you said Davey had written to you. Perhaps you could ring him up. I don't know if you know him—he is a very nice chap. I don't know exactly what they want, but I assume they would want an account of the Committee and its activities, in general terms, with some remarks on the threat to individual liberty contained in the modern centralised state. I don't like shoving this off on to you, on the other hand if they are willing for you to write the article they'll pay you quite well for it.

I hadn't yet thanked you for the copy of the book of essays. Of course I was delighted to see the one on myself appearing in book form. I liked the one on Bates whose book I read years ago.[1] All nineteenth-century books about S. America have a wonderful Arcadian atmosphere, though I think I was always more attracted by the pampas than by the forest. I suppose you've read *The Purple Land*. And the one on hymns, which I'd always been meaning to write something about myself. I think you're wrong in saying that people respond to a hymn like 'Abide with me' (by the way shouldn't it be 'the darkness deepens,' not 'gathers')[2] chiefly because of wars, unemployment etc. There is a great deal of inherent sadness and loneliness in human life that would be the same whatever the external circumstances. You don't mention two of the best hymns, 'praise° to the holiest' and 'Jerusalem my happy home'—this one, I think, however, must be a great deal earlier than the other groups you were studying. In *Ancient and Modern*[3] if I remember rightly it's heavily expurgated to get the Catholic imagery out. [*Paragraph on health, Richard.*]

Please give all the best to Inge. I've gone and lost your new address, but I will think of someone to send this care of. I will write to Charles Davey about the article.

Yours
George

[XIX, 3403, pp. 341–3; typewritten]

1. Henry Walter Bates (1825-92), visited South America in 1848. He wrote *The Naturalist on the River Amazons* °(1863).
2. Orwell is correct.
3. The first edition of *Hymns Ancient and Modern* was published in 1861. Ironically in the light of his comments about Roman Catholicism 'Praise to the Holiest in the height' was by Cardinal John Henry Newman.

To Celia Kirwan*

27 May 1948
Hairmyres Hospital
East Kilbride

Dearest Celia,

Thanks ever so much for your letter. I must say, anything to do with UNESCO sounds pretty discouraging. Any way, I should knock all the money you can out of them, as I don't suppose they'll last much longer. [*Paragraph on health; Richard, now aged four.*]

How I wish I were with you in Paris, now that spring is there. Do you ever go to the Jardin des Plantes? I used to love it, though there was really nothing of interest except the rats, which at one time overran it & were so tame that they would almost eat out of your hand. In the end they got to be such a nuisance that they introduced cats & more or less wiped them out. The plane trees are so beautiful in Paris, because the bark isn't blackened by smoke the way it is in London. I suppose the food & so on is still pretty grisly, but that will improve if the Marshall plan[1] gets working. I see you have to put a 10 franc[2] stamp on your letter, which gives one an idea of what meals must cost now.

I can't help feeling that it's a bit treacherous on Arthur's part if he does settle down in the USA.[3] He was talking about doing it before. I suppose he is furious about what is happening in Palestine, though what else was to be expected I don't know. His lecture tour seems to have been quite a success. I wonder if he has got back yet, & what he will do about his place in Wales. It seems a pity to start sending roots down somewhere & then tear them up again, & I can imagine Mamaine not liking it.

[*His book put back* 'frightfully'] – now it can't be finished before the end of the year, which means not coming out till the end of 1949. However it's something to be capable of working again. Last year before they brought me here I really felt as though I were finished. Thank Heaven Richard looks as if he is going to have good health. We have got 2 tested cows now, so at any rate he won't get this disease through milk, which is the usual way with children. Take care of yourself & write to me again some time.

With love
George

[XIX, 3405, pp. 344–5; handwritten]

1.   The Marshall Plan, properly the European Recovery Program, was the outcome of the Paris Economic Conference, July 1947, to aid post-war recovery in a number of European countries. It was financed by the United States ($17 billion in grants and loans over four years) and was named after US Secretary of State George C. Marshall (1880–1959), whose advocacy of such aid was instrumental in bringing the scheme to fruition. In 1953 General Marshall was awarded the Nobel Peace Prize in recognition of his work in this field.

2.   Ten francs was about one old penny in mid-1948.

3.   Arthur Koestler, who had been living with his wife, Mamaine, in Wales, decided he would like to move to the United States, and they lived there for a short time.

To Anthony Powell*

25 June 1948
Hairmyres Hospital
East Kilbride

Dear Tony,

I received a letter from your friend Cecil Roberts[1] asking me if he could have my flat. I had to write and tell him it was impossible. I am awfully sorry about this, but they have already been riding me like the nightmare for lending it to Mrs Christen, and threatening to let the Borough take it away from me. I don't want this to happen because I must have *a* pied à terre in London, and also I have a little furniture still there and a lot of papers which it's awkward to store elsewhere. Even if I gave up the flat they won't let you transfer the lease and of course they have their own candidates ready many deep, with bribes in their hands.[2]

If you happen to see Graham Greene, could you break the news to him that I have written a very bad review of his novel[3] for the *New Yorker*. I couldn't do otherwise—I thought the book awful, though of course don't put it as crudely as that. I am going to review Kingsmill's book[4] for the *Obs.* as soon as possible, but I still have another book to get out of the way first.[5] I seem to be getting quite back into the journalistic mill, however I do tinker a little at my novel and no doubt shall get it done by the end of the year.

I am a lot better and now get up for three hours a day. I have been playing a lot of croquet, which seems quite a tough game when you've been on your back for 6 months. In the ward below me the editor of the *Hotspur*[6] is a patient. He tells me their circulation is 300,000. He says they don't pay very good rates per thou, but they can give people regular work and also give them the plots so that they only have to do the actual writing. In this way a man can turn out 40,000 words a week. They had one man who used to do 70,000, but his stuff was 'rather stereotyped.' I hope to get out in August, but the date isn't fixed because it depends on when my lung resumes its normal shape after the collapse therapy has worn off. Richard is coming to see me early in July. He couldn't before because of infection. I suppose I shall hardly know him after six months.

It's my birthday to day—45, isn't it awful. I've also got some more false teeth, and, since being here, a lot more grey in my hair. Please remember me to Violet.

Yours
George

[XIX, 3416, pp. 393–4; typewritten]

1. Cecil A. ("Bobby") Roberts, sometime manager of Sadler's Wells Theatre, had recently been demobilised from the Royal Air Force.

2. Accommodation was hard to find in the years immediately after the war. Most leases included a clause forbidding the lessee to sub-let or 'part with possession' in whole or in part, whether or not money changed hands, for example as a 'premium'.

3. *The Heart of the Matter*, see 17 July 1948 (XIX, 3424, pp. 404–7).

4. *The Dawn's Delay*; see 18 July 1948 (XIX, 3425, pp. 407–8).

5. Probably *Mr. Attlee: An Interim Biography*; see 4 July 1948 (XIX, 3419, pp. 398–9).

6. A weekly paper for boys published from 1933 to 1959. In a letter to Ian Angus, 17.9.96, Professor Williamson said this man shared a room with Orwell for a while and that Professor Dick was interested to see how they got on. 'In the event they got on well together (as I think almost anyone would have . . .).'

To Julian Symons*

10 July 1948
Hairmyres Hospital
East Kilbride

Dear Julian,

I must thank you for a very kind review in the M[anchester] E[vening] News[1] which I have just had a cutting of. I hope your wife is well and that everything is going all right. I thought you would like to hear that I am leaving here on the 25th. They seem to think I am pretty well all right now, though I shall have to take things very quietly for a long time, perhaps a year or so. I am only to get up for six hours a day, but I don't know that it makes much difference as I have got quite used to working in bed. My sister brought Richard over to see me this week, the first time I had seen him since Christmas. He is tremendously well and almost frighteningly energetic. His talking still seems backward, but in other ways I should say he was forward. Farm life seems to suit him, though I am pretty sure he is one for machines rather than animals. [References to Hotspur and Gissing] I also wasn't so up in the air as most people about Evelyn Waugh's The Loved One, though of course it was amusing. Unlike a lot of people I thought Brideshead Revisited was very good, in spite of hideous faults on the surface. I have been trying to read a book of extracts from Leon Bloy,[°2] whose novels I have never succeeded in getting hold of. He irritates me rather, and Peguy,[°3] whom I also tried recently, made me feel unwell. I think it's about time to do a new counterattack against these Catholic writers. I also recently read Farrell's Studs Lonigan[4] for the first time, and was very disappointed by it. I don't know that I've read much else.

The weather here was filthy all June but now it's turned at last and they are getting the hay in with great speed. I am longing to go fishing, but I suppose I shan't be able to this year, not because fishing in itself is much of an exertion, but because you always have to walk five or ten miles and end up by getting soaked to the skin. Please remember me to your wife. After the 25th my address will be as before, ie. Barnhill, Isle of Jura, Argyllshire.

Yours
George

[XIX, 3420, pp. 400–1; handwritten]

1. Symons had reviewed the reprint of Coming Up for Air in the Manchester Evening News, 19 May 1948.
2. Leon Marie Bloy (1846–1917), French novelist whose work attacks the bourgeois

conformism of his time. He expected the collapse of that society and became increasingly influenced by Roman Catholic mysticism, expressed particularly in his Journal, 1892–1917.

3. Republican and socialist, he founded *Cahiers de la Quinzaine* (1900–14). This set out 'To tell the truth, the whole truth, nothing but the truth, to tell flat truth flatly, dull truth dully, sad truth sadly'—that was its doctrine and method, and, above all, its action (Péguy, quoted by Daniel Halevy, *Peguy and 'Les Cahiers de la Quinzaine'*, 1946, 52). In the course of his editing, his Roman Catholicism and his patriotism were intensified. A favourite story of Orwell's, which he dramatised for the BBC, was Anatole France's *L'Affaire Crainquebille* (11 August 1943, XV, 2230, pp. 186-97), first published by Péguy in *Les Cahiers*.

4. James Thomas Farrell (1904–1979), prolific and successful US novelist and a forthright social and literary critic (for example, *The League of Frightened Philistines*, 1945).

Fredric Warburg* to Orwell

19 and 22 July 1948

On 19 July 1948, Warburg wrote to Orwell saying he had heard that Orwell was looking very much better and he mentioned Orwell's interest in getting more of Gissing's novels back into print. The main burden of the letter concerned Nineteen Eighty-Four:

I was of course specially pleased to know that you have done quite a substantial amount of revision on the new novel. From our point of view, and I should say also from your point of view, a revision of this is far and away the most important single undertaking to which you could apply yourself when the vitality is there. It should not be put aside for reviews or miscellaneous work, however tempting, and will I am certain sooner rather than later bring in more money than you could expect from any other activity. If you do succeed in finishing the revision by the end of the year this would be pretty satisfactory, and we should publish in the autumn of 1949, but it really is rather important from the point of view of your literary career to get it done by the end of the year, and indeed earlier if at all possible.

On 22 July, he told Orwell of the great interest aroused in Japan by Animal Farm. *The Americans had submitted 50–75 titles of Western books to Japanese publishers and invited them to bid for them.* Animal Farm *received the most bids; forty-eight Japanese publishers were anxious to publish it. It was 'finally knocked down to an Osaka firm who are paying 20 cents or 20 yens° per copy, I am not sure which'. It would not make Orwell wealthy and the yen could be spent only in Japan: 'Perhaps a trip one Spring in cherry time might be practicable for you, if and when the world clears up a bit.'*

[XIX, 3426, pp. 408–9]

Avril Blair★ to Michael Kennard[1]

29 July 1948
Barnhill
Isle of Jura

…[2] Eric returned yesterday & looks much better. He has got to take it very easy but is interested in how things are going & has been going round the estate today; practically everything is new or different since he was last at home. Richard Rees is also here for a day or two & we all (not E) bravely went down & had a bathe this afternoon. The water was icy despite the fact that we are in the midst of a terrific heat wave…

We have just been erecting a large tent in the garden for the overflow of visitors who start arriving tomorrow…

So glad you enjoyed your holiday. Do come up again if you ever have any more time off.

Yours
Avril

[XIX, 3429, pp. 410–11; handwritten]

1. Michael Kennard (= Koessler) a Jewish refugee who came to England in 1938; the Warburgs looked after him. He visited Jura two or three times and visited Orwell in hospital. Orwell left him his fishing rods. Kennard designed several dust-jackets for Secker & Warburg including those for *Animal Farm* and *Nineteen Eighty-Four* (see also XIX, p. 304–5).

2. The ellipses in this passage indicate the editor's cuts and are not original to Avril's letter.

To David Astor*

9 October 1948
Barnhill
Isle of Jura

Dear David,

Thanks so much for your letter. A little before getting it I had written to Mr Rose,¹ sending him a short review of one book and making suggestions for some others. I think I had put on the list of books I should like to have one called *Boys will be Boys*² (about thrillers etc.), of which the publishers have now sent me a copy: so even if he would like to have me review it, there is no need to send it to me.

You were right about my being not very well. I am a bit better now but felt very poorly for about a fortnight. It started funnily enough with my going back to Hairmyres to be examined, which they had told me to do in September. Mr Dick seemed to be quite pleased with the results of his examination, but the journey upset me. Any kind of journey seems to do this. He told me to go on as at present, ie. spending half the day in bed, which I quite gladly do as I simply can't manage any kind of exertion. To walk a mile or pick up anything in the least heavy, or above all to get cold, promptly upsets me. Even if I go out in the evening to fetch the cows in it gives me a temperature. On the other hand so long as I live a senile sort of life I feel all right, and I seem to be able to work much as usual. I have got so used to writing in bed that I think I prefer it, though of course it's awkward to type there. I am just struggling with the last stages of this bloody book, which is supposed to be done by early December, and will be if I don't get ill again. It would have been done by the spring if it had not been for this illness.

Richard is tremendously well and is out of doors in all weathers. I am sorry to say he took to smoking recently, but he made himself horribly sick and that has put him off it. He also swears. I don't stop him of course, but I am trying to improve my own language a bit. The weather has been absolutely filthy, except for three or four days just recently. Bill Dunn managed to get all his hay and corn in early, but a lot must have been spoiled elsewhere. The farm is building up. He has now got about 50 sheep and about 10 head of cattle, some of which are my property. We have also got a pig which will go to be baconed shortly. I had never kept one before and shan't be sorry to see the last of this one. They are most annoying destructive animals, and hard to keep out of anywhere because they are so strong and cunning. We have built up a bit of a garden here now. Of course a lot of it has gone back owing to my not being able to do anything, but I hope to get an Irish labourer³ to do some digging this winter and even this year we had quite a few flowers and lashings of strawberries. Richard seems interested in farm and garden operations, and he helps me in the garden and is sometimes quite useful. I would like him to be a farmer when he grows up, in fact I shouldn't wonder if anyone who survives will have to be that, but of course I'm not going to force him.

I don't know when I'm coming up to London. First I must finish this book, and I'm not keen on London just before Xmas. I had thought of coming in January, but I must wait till I feel up to travelling. I'm a bit out of touch with the news, partly because the battery of my wireless is getting weak, but everything looks pretty black. I don't personally believe an all-out shooting war could happen now, only perhaps 'incidents' such as used to occur all the time between Russia and Japan, but I suppose the atomic war is now a certainty within not very many years. This book I am writing is about the possible state of affairs if the atomic war *isn't* conclusive. I think you were right after all about de Gaulle being a serious figure. I suppose at need we shall have to back the swine up rather than have a Communist France, but I must say I think this backing-up of Franco, which now appears to be the policy is a mistake. In France there doesn't seem to be an alternative between de Gaulle and the Communists, because apart from the CP there has never been a mass working-class movement and everyone appears to be either pro-CP or *bien pensant*. But I shouldn't have said from what little knowledge I have that things were the same in Spain. No doubt it is the American Catholics who saved Franco from being turfed out in 1945. I am still worried about our policies in Africa and South Asia. Is Crankshaw⁴ still going to Africa for you, I wonder? It's all most depressing. I keep thinking, shall I get such and such a book done before the rockets begin to fly and we go back to clay tablets.

There is an eagle flying over the field in front. They always come here in windy weather.

Yours
George

P.S. [*handwritten*] Do you happen to know anyone who restores pictures. A picture of mine has been damaged (a slit in the canvas) & though it isn't worth anything I should like to have it repaired.

[XIX, 3467, pp. 450–2; typed with handwritten postscript]

1. Jim Rose, a member of the literary editor's staff of the *Observer*.
2. *Boys Will be Boys: The Story of Sweeney Todd, Deadwood Dick, Sexton Blake, et al.*, by E. S. Turner (1948; revised, 1957). Orwell did not review it.
3. Francis (Francey) Boyle, a road-worker (see Crick, p. 525).

4. Edward Crankshaw (1909–1984), novelist and critic, member of diplomatic staff on the *Observer* from 1947; British Military Mission to Moscow, 1941–43. In *David Astor and 'The Observer'*, Richard Cockett states: 'Orwell was instrumental in making David aware of the post-war problem of decolonization in Africa. The *Observer* was thus the first, and for a long time the only, British paper to focus on the problems of decolonization in Africa and in particular the plight of Africans on their own continent' (p. 126).

To Fredric Warburg*

22 October 1948
Barnhill
Isle of Jura

Dear Fred,

You will have had my wire by now, and if anything crossed your mind I dare say I shall have had a return wire from you by the time this goes off. I shall finish the book, *D.V.*,[1] early in November, and I am rather flinching from the job of typing it, because it is a very awkward thing to do in bed, where I still have to spend half the time. Also there will have to be carbon copies, a thing which always fidgets me, and the book is fearfully long, I should think well over 100,000 words, possibly 125,000. I can't send it away because it is an unbelievably bad MS and no one could make head or tail of it without explanation. On the other hand a skilled typist under my eye could do it easily enough. If you can think of anybody who would be willing to come, I will send money for the journey and full instructions. I think we could make her quite comfortable. There is always plenty to eat and I will see that she has a comfortable warm place to work in.

I am not pleased with the book but I am not absolutely dissatisfied. I first thought of it in 1943. I think it is a good idea but the execution would have been better if I had not written it under the influence of TB. I haven't definitely fixed on the title but I am hesitating between *Nineteen Eighty-Four* and *The Last Man in Europe*.

I have just had Sartre's book on antisemitism, which you published, to review. I think Sartre is a bag of wind and I am going to give him a good boot.[2]

Please give everyone my love.

Yours
George

[XIX, 3477, pp. 456–7; typewritten]

1. D.V.: *Deo volente* = God willing.
2. *Portrait of the Anti-Semite, Observer,* 7 November 1948, XIX, 3485, pp. 464–5.

To Julian Symons*

29 October 1948
Barnhill
Isle of Jura

Dear Julian,

I can't thank you enough for the tea, which I do hope you could spare. My sister, who keeps house for me, was enchanted to see it and asked me to say she will pack up a little butter for you next churning day. I am so glad to hear that all is well with your wife and daughter and that you enjoy having a baby. They're really great fun, so much so that I find myself wishing at each stage that they could stay like that. I suppose you are on the steady grind of 5 bottles and 15 nappies a day. It's funny that they are so insatiably greedy when they are small babies and then between about 2 and 6 it is such a fight to get them to eat, except between meals. I wonder which milk you are using. We brought up Richard on Ostermilk, which seemed to be better than National Dried.[1] His cousin was brought up on Cow and Gate and became grossly fat on it. You've got a big battle ahead when it comes to weaning time.

I was very well for some time after leaving hospital but have been very poorly again for the last month. [*Effect of visit to Hairmyres Hospital.*] Even to walk half a mile is upsetting. I was going to come down to London in January, but I am consulting with my doctor and if he thinks it best I shall go into a private sanatorium, if I can find one, for the worst of the winter, ie. Jan–Feb. I could go abroad perhaps, but the journey might be the death of me, so perhaps a sanatorium would be best. I think I am going to give up my London flat, as I never use it at present and it costs me about £100 a year and a lot of nuisance. Of course I shall have to get another London place later. I shall finish my book, *D.V.*, in a week or ten days, but I am rather flinching from typing it, which is a tiring job and in any case can't be done in bed where I have to be half the day. [*Attempting to get a typist to come to Jura.*]

I am rather surprised to hear of John Davenport associating himself with a CP or near-CP paper.[2] He used not to be that way inclined, that I knew of. *Politics & Letters* I am sorry to say has disappeared and is supposed to be reappearing next year as a monthly, rather to my annoyance as they had an article of mine. It is nonsense what Fyvel said about Eliot being antisemitic. Of course you can find what would now be called antisemitic remarks in his early work, but who didn't say such things at that time? One has to draw a distinction between what was said before and what after 1934. Of course all these nationalistic prejudices are ridiculous, but disliking Jews isn't intrinsically worse than disliking Negroes or Americans or any other block of people. In the early twenties, Eliot's antisemitic remarks were about on a par with the automatic sneer one casts at Anglo-Indian colonels in boarding houses. On the other hand if they had been written after the persecutions began they would have meant something quite different. Look for instance at the Anglophobia in the USA, which is shared even by people like Edmund Wilson. It doesn't matter, because we are not being persecuted. But if 6 million Englishmen had recently been killed in gas vans, I imagine I should feel insecure if I even saw a joke in a French comic paper about Englishwomen's teeth sticking out. Some people go round smelling after antisemitism all the time. I have no doubt Fyvel* thinks I am antisemitic.³ More rubbish is written about this subject than any other I can think of. I have just had Sartre's book on the subject for review, and I doubt whether it would be possible to pack more nonsense into so short a space. I have maintained from the start that Sartre is a bag of wind, though possibly when it comes to Existentialism, which I don't profess to understand, it may not be so.

Richard is blooming. [*His progress; winters milder in Jura than England.*] For the first time in my life I have tried the experiment of keeping a pig. They really are disgusting brutes and we are all longing for the day when he goes to the butcher, but I am glad to see they do well here. He has grown to a stupendous size purely on milk and potatoes, without our buying any food for him from outside. In another year or so I shall have to be thinking about Richard's schooling, but I am not making any plans because one can't see far ahead now. I am not going to let him go to a boarding school before he is ten, and I would like him to start off at the elementary school. If one could find a good one. It's a difficult question. Obviously it is democratic for everyone to go to the same schools, or at least start off there but when you see what the elementary schools are like, and the results, you feel that any child that has the chance should be rescued from them. It is quite easy, for instance, to leave those schools at 14 without having learned to read. I heard on the wireless lately that 10 per cent of army recruits, aged 19, have to be taught to read after they join the army. I remember in 1936 meeting John Strachey⁴ in the street—then a CP member or at least on the staff of the [*Daily*] *Worker*—and him telling me he had just had a son and was putting him down for Eton. I said 'How can you do that?' and he said that given our existing society it was the best education. Actually I doubt whether it is the best, but in principle I don't feel sure that he was wrong. However I am taking no decisions about Richard one way or the other. Of course we may all have been blown to hell before it becomes urgent, but personally I don't expect a major shooting war for 5 or 10 years. After the Russians have fully recovered and have atomic bombs,[5] I suppose it isn't avoidable. And even if it is avoided, there are a lot of other unpleasantnesses blowing up.

Please remember me to your wife and give my best regards to your daughter.

Yours
George

[XIX, 3481, pp. 460–2; typewritten]

1. National Dried was a milk powder, akin to proprietary brands such as Ostermilk, made available by the government through Baby Clinics to mothers of young babies.
2. John Davenport (1906–1966), critic and man of letters, a friend of many writers and painters. The paper was probably *Our Time*, to which he was a contributor. In the autumn of 1948 it was edited by Frank Jellinek and in 1949 by Randall Swingler.
3. Tosco Fyvel*, a long-standing friend of Orwell's, comments on Orwell's remark that he, Fyvel, doubtless thought him anti-Semitic in *George Orwell: A Personal Memoir*, pp. 178–82: 'I would never have said that,' though he reported that Malcolm Muggeridge thought Orwell 'at heart strongly anti-Semitic'. Fyvel went on, 'Put baldly like that, I would not agree. . . . It was unthinkable that he should ever have been openly anti-Semitic. But his ideological views concerning the assimilation into British culture of a strong Jewish ethnic minority were a different matter.'
4. John Strachey (1901–1963), politician and political theorist; Labour MP, 1929–31, 1945–63. In 1946 he became a prominent member of the Labour government.
5. Soviet Russia tested its first atomic bomb in September 1949.

To David Astor*

19 November 1948
Barnhill
Isle of Jura

Dear David,

Thanks so much for your letter. If you'd really like to give Richard something for Christmas, I wonder whether one can still get Meccano sets? I should think he is about ripe for one of the lower grades. Of course he'll lose all the bolts, but still that is the kind of thing he likes. He is tremendously active about the farm and household, has to take part in all operations such as chopping firewood, filling lamps etc., and even insists on pouring out my ration of gin for me every evening. He goes fishing with the others and caught several fish the other day. I am so glad your little girl is going on well. I suppose at 20 months she will be talking a bit, as well as walking. Julian Symons, whom I think you met at lunch once, has just got a baby and seems very absorbed in it. Margie Fletcher is over on the mainland having her fourth.

It's very kind of Charoux¹ to help about restoring the picture. When I can get round to doing so I'll make a crate and send it to him direct. I never can remember his address but I expect I have a letter of his somewhere. It's only a very small picture, about 20" by 16", so it won't be difficult to pack. In sending it here those bloody fools Pickfords succeeded in making a slit in the canvas and also chipping it in two places, but I don't imagine it would be difficult to mend. It's of no value, but it has sentimental associations and I think is quite a good painting. There was also that picture which you gave me and which got blitzed.² I was going to have that restored, but it's a more extensive job as it got scratched all over. It was thrown right across the room by the blast.

I am on the grisly job of typing out my book which I have at last finished after messing about with it ever since the summer of 1947. I tried to get a ste-nog. to come here and do it for me, but it's awkward to get anyone for such a short period so I am doing it myself. I feel somewhat better now, but I was in absolutely lousy health for about a month and I have decided if I can arrange it to go into a private sanatorium for Jan–Feb, which is the worst of the winter. Dr. Dick thinks it would be a good idea. I seem to be all right so long as I stay in bed till lunch time and then spend the rest of the day on a sofa, but if I walk even a few hundred yards or pull up a few weeds in the garden I promptly get a temperature. Otherwise everything is going well here and the farm has had quite a good first year in spite of the vile weather. There is now a bull, which is very good and quiet and I trust will remain so, as I can't run very fast these days. Bobbie, your pony, is still at Tarbert, and I am not sure whether McIntyre° wants us to winter him or not. I had a talk with your brother about it when I met him at the sports about August, but subsequently there was some mix-up and nobody from here has been down as far as Tarbert for some months. Anyway, if they would like us to winter Bobbie, we are pleased to do so, as he is useful to us in several ways and also makes a companion for the other horse. I do not know whether I shall be in London at any time in the near future—I suppose some time next year, but I must try and get my health right.

I am so glad the *Obs.* is taking up Africa so to speak. Also that O'Donovan³ is going on reporting Asia for you. He is really a great acquisition. Your friend de Gaulle seems to be bent on making mischief all round. However it rather looks now as if there won't be war for some years.

Yours
George

[XIX, 3490, pp. 468–9; typewritten]

1.   A picture-framer and restorer; his address is given in Orwell's address book as 65 Holland Park Road, [London] W.14.
2.   A flying bomb fell close by the Orwells' flat in Mortimer Crescent on 28 June 1944.
3.   Patrick O'Donovan, who had joined the *Observer* in 1946 and worked with distinction as a roving correspondent abroad. (See his *A Journalist's Odyssey*, 1985.)

To Gleb Struve*

22 November 1948
Barnhill
Isle of Jura

Dear Struve,

Thanks so much for your letter of November 6th (only just got here.) I have written to Warburg, explaining the circumstances about *We,* and suggesting that if interested he should write either to you or to the people handling Westhouse's affairs. Of course if Warburg isn't interested there are plenty of others.

Yes, of course it's all right about the Russian translation of *Animal Farm.*[1] Naturally I don't want any money from D.Ps, but if they ever do produce it in book form I should like a copy or two of that. Did I tell you it was done into Ukrainian by the D.Ps in the American Zone about a year ago? I understand that the American authorities seized about half the copies printed and handed them over to the Soviet repatriation people, but that about 3000 copies got distributed.

I'll look out for your Turgenev translation in *Politics.*[2] [*Is typing his book.*]

Yours sincerely
Geo. Orwell

[XIX, 3496, pp. 472–3; typewritten]

1.   The Russian translation of *Animal Farm*, *Skotskii Khutor*, was made by M. Kriger and Gleb Struve; it appeared in *Possev*, a weekly social and political review, Nos. 7–25, 1949, which published it as a book in 1950. *Possev* means the sowing of seed and outlasted the Soviet Union.
2.   *Politics* ceased publication before the translation could be published.

To Leonard Moore*

30 November 1948
Barnhill
Isle of Jura

Dear Moore,

I am afraid there has been a mix-up about this typing business and that you and perhaps the typing agencies you applied [to] have been put to unnecessary trouble. What happened was this. I wrote first to Warburg, asking him to engage a typist in London, but he and Senhouse apparently decided that it would be easier to arrange it in Edinburgh, because of the journey, although, of course, the tiresome part of the journey is not between London and Scotland but between Jura and the mainland. I waited for a bit, and then Roger Senhouse said he was putting his niece in Edinburgh on to the job of finding a typist. Meanwhile in case nothing materialised I had started doing it myself. Then apparently Warburg rang you up and I got two letters from you, suggesting the names of two people in London, but I couldn't close with this in case Senhouse's niece suddenly produced somebody. I have never heard from her, and now I hear from Senhouse that in fact she couldn't get anybody. Meanwhile I have almost finished the typing and shall send it off probably on the 7th December, so you should get it in about a week. I do hope the two women whose names you suggested have not been inconvenienced or put off other engagements or anything like that. It really wasn't worth all this fuss. It's merely that as it tires me to sit upright for any length of time I can't type very neatly and can't do many pages a day.

These copies I am sending you are only carbons, and not first-class typing. If you think bad typing might prejudice the MS. with the American publishers, it would be worth having it redone by a commercial agency. But if you do decide on that, can you see that they don't make mistakes. I know what these agencies are like. As the thing is typed already, and I don't *think* I have left any errors in it, it should be easy enough, but it is wonderful what mistakes a professional typist will make, and in this book there is the difficulty that it contains a lot of neologisms.

Yours sincerely
Eric Blair

[XIX, 3501, p. 477; typewritten]

To David Astor*

21 December 1948
Barnhill
[Isle of Jura]

Dear David,

I am really very unwell indeed, & have been since about September, & I am arranging to go into a private sanatorium early in January & stay there at least 2 months. I was going to go to a place called Kingussie, reccommended° by Dr. Dick, but they were full up & I have made arrangements to go to a place in Glostershire.° I suppose there might be some slip-up, but if not my address as from 7th Jan. will be The Cotswold Sanatorium, CRANHAM, GLOS.

I tell you this chiefly because I feel I simply must stop working, or rather trying to work, for at least a month or two. I would have gone to a sana-torium two months ago if I hadn't wanted to finish that bloody book off, which thank God I have done. I had been messing about with it for 18 months thanks to this bloody disease. I have polished off all the reviews I promised for the *Observer* except two [*details and apologies to Mr Rose*]. I'm afraid I[vor] B[rown] will mark this as another black mark against me, but I just must have a good rest for a month or two. I just must try & stay alive for a while because apart from other considerations I have a good idea for a novel.¹

Everything is flourishing here except me. [*Life at Barnhill; has a stationary engine for Richard's Meccano.*] We sent our pig to be slaughtered a week or two ago. He was only nine months old & weighed 2 cwt. *after* removal of the head & trotters.

I hope your little girl is well. Margie Fletcher's new baby had something wrong intestinally, but it seems to be better now. It's another boy.

Yours
George

[XIX, 3510, pp. 485–6; handwritten]

1. Perhaps 'A Smoking-Room Story' (see XX, 3723–4, pp. 193–200).

To Fredric Warburg*

21 December 1948
Barnhill
[Isle of Jura]

Dear Fred,

Thanks for two letters. [*Is really very unwell indeed & arranging to go into The Cotswold Sanatorium.*] But better consider Barnhill my address till I confirm the other. I ought to have done this 2 months ago but I wanted to get that bloody book finished.

About photos. I have none here, but I'm pretty certain I had a number at my flat, which my sister has just been closing up & dismantling. The photos will have been in a file which will be coming up here, but I suppose not for ages, as anything sent by rail takes months. I'll send you any photos I can when they arrive, but meanwhile could you try first Moore, who I *think* has one or two, & then Vernon & Marie-Louise Richards' who took a lot 3 years ago. [*How to find them.*] At need we could bring a photographer to the sanatorium, but I am really a deathshead at present, & I imagine shall be in bed for a month or so.

I'm glad you liked the book. It isn't a book I would gamble on for a big sale, but I suppose one could be sure of 10,000 any way. It's still beautiful weather here, but I never stir out of doors & seldom off the sofa. Richard is offensively well, & everything else flourishing except me. I am trying to finish off my scraps of book-reviewing etc. & must then just strike work for a month or so. I can't go on as at present. I have a stunning idea for a very short novel which has been in my head for years, but I can't start anything until I am free from high temperatures etc.

Love to all.

George

[XIX, 3511, pp. 486–7; handwritten]

1. Vernon Richards* (1915–2001) and Marie-Louise Richards (1918–49) were very active in the Anarchist movement. They both took photographs of Orwell at his request for use in newspapers and magazines and, in 1946, photographed him with his adopted son, Richard. (See *George Orwell at Home (and Among the Anarchists): Essays and Photographs*, Freedom Press, 1998.)

To Roger Senhouse*

26 December 1948
Barnhill   Isle of Jura   Argyll

Dear Roger,

Thanks so much for your letter. As to the blurb. I really don't think the approach in the draft you sent me is the right one. It makes the book sound as though it were a thriller mixed up with a love story, & I didn't intend it to be primarily that. What it is really meant to do is to discuss the implications of dividing the world up into 'Zones of influence' (I thought of it in 1944 as a result of the Teheran Conference), & in addition to indicate by parodying them the intellectual implications of totalitarianism. It has always seemed to me that people have not faced up to these & that, eg., the persecution of scientists in Russia[1] is simply part of a logical process which should have been foreseeable 10–20 years ago. When you get to the proof stage, how would it be to get some eminent person who might be interested, eg. Bertrand Russell[2] or Lancelot Hogben,[3] to give his opinions about the book, & (if he consented) use a piece of that as the blurb? There are a number of people one might choose from.

I am going into a sanatorium as from 6th Jan., & unless there is some last-minute slip-up my address will be, The Cotswold Sanatorium, Cranham, Glos.

Love to all

George

[XIX, 3513, pp. 487–8; handwritten]

1.   See **19.3.47**.
2.   Bertrand Russell (1872–1970; 3rd Earl Russell), philosopher, mathematician, lecturer, and writer. Among the many causes for which he fought perhaps the most important was that for nuclear disarmament. (See his 'George Orwell', *World Review*, new series 16, June 1950.)
3.   Lancelot Hogben (1895–1975), scientist and author, first achieved distinction as a geneticist and endocrinologist but later became known to a very wide public for a series of books that introduced science and language to the general reader, especially *Mathematics for the Million* (1936), and *Science for the Citizen* (1938).

Cranham, University College Hospital, and Orwell's Death

Dr Bruce Dick* to David Astor*

5 January 1949
as from The Peel, Busby [south of Glasgow]

Dear Mr David,°

I am sorry for the delay in reply to your letter.

I was for a time in correspondence with Eric Blair. It was obvious° a relapse story, presumably of fairly acute onset. When we saw him in Sept. we thought he was as good as when he left us.

I had offered to take him into our hospital or this one. However he had a hankering for the less rigorous south. He had decided on Mundesley[1] I expect the delay in getting fixed up made him decide on the Cotswold Sanatorium.[2] I have not been in touch with the Superintendent personally, but one of my assistants sent a detailed history.

I believe the disease will respond again to a course of streptomycin. It can now be procured more easily at home. Certainly no other form of treatment is available.

It is all bad luck for such a fine character & gifted man. I know he gets great heart from your continued comradeship & kindness.

I hope the poor fellow will do well. It is now obvious that he will need to live a most sheltered life in a sanatorium environment. I fear the dream of Jura must fade out.

If I can be of the least help, I will. If he was to come north later we would give him refuge.

With kind regards.

Yours sincerely,
Bruce Dick

[XX, 3518, pp. 13–14; handwritten]

1. On the east coast of England about 20 to 22 miles northeast of Norwich. It is not known why he did not go there. Gwen O'Shaughnessy helped him find a place at Cranham.
2. Orwell was admitted to The Cotswold Sanatorium on 6 January 1949. Richard Rees drove Orwell on the first stage of the long journey from Barnhill to Cranham

(*George Orwell: Fugitive from the Camp of Victory*, p. 150). He notes that at Barnhill, Orwell 'was certainly happy. . . . He felt that he was at last putting down roots. But in reality it was obvious that he had chosen a too rocky soil' (p. 149). Orwell completed his journey by train.

To David Astor*

12 January 1949
The Cotswold Sanatorium[1]
Cranham, Glos.

Dear David,

Thanks so much for your two wires & the offer about the streptomycin. But at present they aren't treating me with strepto, & in any case it appears that it is now easier to get & comparatively cheap. They are giving me something called P.A.S.[2] which I gather stands for para-amino-salicylic acid. This sounds rather as if it was just aspirin in disguise, but I assume it isn't. We will give it a trial any way. If it doesn't work I can always have another go of strepto. This seems quite a nice place & comfortable. If you can come any time I should love it, though of course don't put yourself out. I can even arrange meals for you if I get notice. I have felt better the last week or so but I am not going to attempt any work for at least a month.

Yours
George

P.S. Looking at the map this isn't so very far from your Abingdon place by road. I've never been in Glos. before but I think it must be rather like the Oxfordshire country I knew as a little boy.

[XX, 3520, pp. 15–16; handwritten]

1.   Cranham was a private sanatorium 900 feet up in the Cotswold hills between Stroud and Gloucester with views across the Bristol Channel to the mountains of Wales. It is only a mile or two from Slad, described in *Cider with Rosie* (1959) by Laurie Lee. The patients were in individual chalets with central heating; rest, altitude and fresh, cold air were then believed to be appropriate treatments for tuberculosis (Crick, p. 553). The resident physicians were Geoffrey A. Hoffman BA, MB, TC, Dublin, and Margaret A. Kirkman, MB, BS, London. But see **18.1.49** to Fredric Warburg.

2.   P.A.S. was a chemotherapeutic drug introduced in 1946 for the treatment of tuberculosis. It was only slightly effective used alone and was usually combined with isoniazid or streptomycin. Such a combination delayed the development of the

disease. Shelden notes that these drugs were so new that no doctors 'had enough experience with them to understand the best way to use them in treating advanced cases such as Orwell's. He might have benefited from smaller doses or from a combination of drugs and other forms of treatment. Unfortunately, the most potent drug—isoniazid—was not developed for use in tuberculosis cases until 1952. . . . But the fact that he was given PAS at the sanatorium in Cranham shows that he was receiving the latest treatment for the disease. The doctors there seem to have made every effort to achieve an improvement in his condition' (pp. 466–7).

To Leonard Moore*

17 January 1949
The Cotswold Sanatorium
Cranham

Dear Moore,

I enclose the 6 contracts,[1] duly signed. Thanks also for sending the copies of *Burmese Days*, & the magazine with that cartoon.

I am glad the new book is fixed up for the USA. I assume it does no harm for it to have a different title here & there.[2] Warburg seems to prefer the title *1984*, & I think I prefer it slightly myself.[3] But I think it would be better to write it *Nineteen Eighty-four*, but I expect to see Warburg shortly & I'll talk to him about that. It's possible that the American publishers will want to cut out the Appendix,[4] which of course is not a usual thing to have in something purporting to be a novel, but I would like to retain it if possible.

The above address will, I am afraid, find me for the next 2 or 3 months. It is a nice place & I am quite comfortable. I am trying to do no work whatever, which I think is the wisest thing at the moment. So, with reference to your other letter, could you tell *Harper's Bazaar* that I would have liked to do the article, but have been seriously ill & cannot undertake anything. I dare say in a month or so I shall be fit to begin working again, but for the moment I do not want to make any commitments.

Yours sincerely
Eric Blair

[XX, 3525, pp. 19–20; handwritten]

1. Unidentified. Possibly contracts for foreign-language versions of *Animal Farm*.
2. *Nineteen Eighty-Four* was used in the United Kingdom; *1984* in the USA.
3. The facsimile of the draft shows clearly that the novel was first set in 1980; then, as time passed in the writing of the book, 1982, and finally 1984. This is particularly plain on page 23 of the facsimile, but the consequential changes occur at various

points. It is arguable that, in setting the novel in, successively, 1980, 1982, and 1984, Orwell was projecting forward his own age, 36, when World War II started, from the time when he was planning or actually writing the novel. Thus, 1944 + 36 = 1980; 1946 + 36 = 1982; 1948 + 36 = 1984. It is not, perhaps, a coincidence that in 1944, when the idea for the novel might reasonably be said to be taking shape, Richard was adopted. It would be natural for Orwell to wonder at that time (as many people did) what prospects there would be for war or peace when their children grew up. By choosing *Nineteen Eighty-Four*, Orwell set his novel in both present *and* future. Had Orwell only been writing about the present, there would have been no need for him to have advanced the year beyond 1980, and preserving the interval he did – of 36 years – must have had significance for him. Inverting the final digits of 1980 and 1982 would have been meaningless; the inversion of those for 1984 was probably coincidental.

4. The appendix, 'The Principles of Newspeak', was included in English and US editions.

To Sir Richard Rees*

18 January 1949
The Cotswold Sanatorium
Cranham

Dear Richard,

I hope you got home all right & were not too exhausted by all your journeyings on my behalf. I am well settled in here & quite comfortable. The 'chalet' isn't as grim as I had feared—quite warm, with central heating & hot & cold water, & the food is quite good. My appetite has definitely improved. The Tawneys[1] came in & saw me, but now have left for London. Karl Schnetzler also came, & Warburg is coming on Friday. I'll send back your book *In Parenthesis*[2] when I can. I think it's very good in a way, but it's what I call mannered writing, a thing I don't approve of. I haven't heard from Barnhill yet, but trust Avril has got properly over her cold. I don't know how the weather has been there, but here it has been as mild & sunny as early April, & the birds have even been trying to sing. My book has been accepted for the USA & they've also agreed to reprint a number of earlier ones on quite good terms, which is unusual in an American publisher. Actually I'm somewhat against this, as they're sure to lose money on the reprints & this may sour them on later books.

They are giving me something called P.A.S., which I believe stands for para-amino-salicylic acid. They say it is good. It's very expensive, though not so expensive as streptomycin. You take it by mouth, which I must say I prefer to those endless injections. I have been thinking things over, & have decided that even if I am reasonably well by the summer, I must from now on spend my winters within reach of a doctor—where, I don't know yet, but possibly somewhere like Brighton. If, therefore, it is impossible for me to be at Barnhill in the winter, can we fix things somehow so that Bill is looked after during those months? I don't in the least wish to sever my connection with Barnhill, because it is a marvellous place to be at, & in any case we have now sent down fairly respectable roots there, but I think it would be wiser to do as I first intended, when I took the place in 1946, & use it only for the summers. I must try & stay alive for 5–10 years, which involves having medical attention at hand when necessary, & in addition I am just a nuisance to everybody when I am ill, whereas in a more civilized place this doesn't matter. In the summers no doubt I shall generally be well enough to potter about, provided that this present infection is got under. In more reasonable times we might arrange to live every winter in Sicily or somewhere, but nowadays I suppose it will have to be somewhere in England.[3] In the beginning we took the house on the understanding that we should only stay there April–November, but now there is Bill. It is a question of finding a housekeeper for him. Have you got any ideas about this? I'll also write to Avril setting forth the problem.

Gleb Struve sent me a translation of some remarks about me in a Russian magazine.[4] They're really very annoying, but disquieting in a way because the whole thing is somehow so *illiterate*.

Yours
Eric

[XX, 3529, pp. 22–4; handwritten]

1. Professor R. H. Tawney (1888–1962), historian, author of *Religion and the Rise of Capitalism* (1926), joint editor of *Economic History Review*, 1926–33, and of *Studies in Economic and Social History* from 1934. He and his wife were very old friends of Richard Rees, who had asked them to visit Orwell at Cranham, as they were on holiday nearby at their country home.

2. *In Parenthesis* (1937) by David Jones (1895–1974), poet, novelist, and artist. It combines free verse with an account of his World War I experience. It won the Hawthornden Prize.

3. Travel abroad was made difficult because the government limited severely the amount of money that could be taken out of the country.

4. With his letter to Orwell of 1 January 1949, Gleb Struve had enclosed two articles by Ivan Anisimov attacking Arthur Koestler and Orwell, 'typical of the literary xenophobia now raging in the Soviet Union'.

To Fredric Warburg*

18 January 1949
Telegram

LOOK FORWARD TO SEEING YOU FRIDAY DO BRING PAMELA CAR WILL MEET
YOU
GEORGE

[XX, 3530, p. 24]

The visit was arranged for Friday, 21 January 1949. Warburg went with his wife, Pamela, and in All Authors are Equal *(1973) he gives a vivid account of Cranham (which horrified them) and of Orwell's distressing state. Warburg, confirming the visit in a letter to Orwell of 19 January, asked his permission to have a frank discussion with his doctors: 'Your future is important to more people than yourself.' In reply to their questions, Orwell told Pamela Warburg that 'a woman doctor [presumably Margaret Kirkman] visits me every morning. . . . I think she's thoroughly competent and kind, and asks me how I feel and all that.' However, in response to Mrs Warburg's questions, it transpired that no chest examination by stethoscope had taken place. 'I expect they're understaffed here, you know,' Orwell told her, 'she probably hasn't got time,' to which Mrs Warburg angrily replied: 'It's monstrous, absolutely shocking' (p. 109). Nevertheless, Orwell thought the doctors knew what they were doing, and Warburg remarks, 'The reply was so typical of him—he couldn't bear to make a fuss—and so heartrending that I could hardly believe my ears, but at least it made it easy for Pamela to beg him to see a London specialist.' She persuaded Orwell to promise to let them know if he would like Dr Andrew Morland (a leading specialist in the field who had treated D. H. Lawrence) to see him and, if necessary, to get him into University College Hospital, London. Warburg also recounts how at this time, Louis Simmonds, a bookseller with whom Orwell dealt and who was a warm admirer of Orwell, told Warburg that he and one or two friends would raise £500—a very large sum in those days—to enable Orwell to go to Switzerland for treatment because 'he is far too precious to lose' (pp. 107–9).*

To Julian Symons*

2 February 1949
The Cotswold Sanatorium
Cranham

Dear Julian,

I wonder how you & family are getting on. I have been in this place about a month. [*Progress of his treatment – P.A.S.*] During the last month my weight has only increased 4 ounces, but actually I do feel better & I am well looked after here, though the doctors don't strike me as very brilliant.

Your baby must be getting quite a size & must be cutting teeth & eating solid food. I wonder if you had the battle over weaning that we had with Richard. It's like Machiavelli says about government, you can't do it except by force or fraud. Richard is getting [on] for 5 now & is enormous & very healthy, though still not interested in learning his letters. He likes to be read to, but doesn't see that as a reason for learning to read himself. I suppose this coming winter he will have to start going to school, which he is certain to enjoy as he is very gregarious.

My new book is supposed to come out in July (Warburg said May or June, which means July in publisher's language) but maybe the American edition will be out first. Any way I'll see you get a copy. I must thank you for some friendly references in the *M[anchester] E[vening] News*, including one to that ghastly book of pamphlets in which I reluctantly collaborated. I am having another try to get Warburg to reprint some of Gissing's books, to which I would write introductions. They reprinted (I forget which publishers) those 3 last year, but of course the wrong ones.[1] Meanwhile I am still trying to get hold of a copy of *New Grub Street*, & am now trying in New York. Somewhat to my annoyance that paper *Politics & Letters* got me to write an essay on Gissing & then died, & have never sent my article back or answered my queries about it, though it appears distinctly unlikely that the magazine will re-appear. What a calamity that we can't find a way of financing *one* decent magazine in this country. I suppose it's only a question of losing about £2000 a year. The *Partisan Review* have either increased their sales or got hold of some money from somewhere, as I notice they now pay one quite decently. For all those articles I did during the war for them I got only 10 dollars a time.[2]

I don't know this part of the country but it's supposed to be a beauty spot. Professor Tawney lives nearby, but unfortunately he's had to go back to London as the L.S.E. term had started. The weather is quite incredible, bright sunshine & birds singing as though it were April. Please remember me to your wife & excuse this bad handwriting.

Yours
George

[XX, 3538, pp. 31–2; handwritten]

1. *In the Year of the Jubilee* and *The Whirlpool* were published by Watergate Classics; the former had an introduction by William Plomer, and the latter, one by Myfanwy Evans.
2. Ten dollars was then approximately £2.50.

To Sir Richard Rees*

4 February 1949
The Cotswold Sanatorium
Cranham

Dear Richard,

I enclose cheque for what I owed you. You will notice I have added £3. Do you think you could be kind enough to get your wine merchant to send me 2 bottles of rum, which I suppose will come to about that. I assume he will know how to pack them so as not to get them broken.

I have heard from Avril who says she and Bill both think it would be better to move to a farm on the mainland. I think they are right, but can't help feeling bad about it as I feel my health is the precipitating factor, though the state of the road is a good second. I think you would be rash to sink more money in any non-removable improvements etc.,¹ because such a place might of its nature become untenable at some time. I trust it will be possible to move without selling off the stock and losing on the transaction. I am afraid the actual move will be a godawful° business from which I shall probably absent myself whenever it happens. I have asked Avril to tell Robin [Fletcher] that unless he happens on a tenant who would actually farm the place, I would like to keep on the lease of the house. I don't see why we shouldn't have it as a summer holiday place, and one could leave camp beds etc. there. Of course I may never be strong enough for that kind of thing again even in the summer, but others may be and the rent is next to nothing.

I am reading B. Russell's latest book, about human knowledge.² He quotes Shakespeare, 'Doubt that the stars are fire, Doubt that the earth doth move' (it goes on I think, 'Doubt truth to be a liar, But never doubt I love.') But he makes it 'Doubt that the *sun* doth move,' and uses this as an instance of S.'s ignorance. Is that right? I had an idea it was 'the earth.' But I haven't got

Shakespeare here and I can't even remember where the lines come (must be one of the comedies I think.) I wish you'd verify this for me if you can remember where it comes.[3] I see by the way that the Russian press has just described B. R. as a wolf in a dinner jacket and a wild beast in philosopher's robes.

I don't know really that I'd be very interested in that book about the cards etc. I had heard of that chap before,[4] but I can't get very interested in telepathy unless it could be developed into a reliable method.

I've been reading *The First Europe*[5] (history of the Dark Ages), very interesting though written in a rather tiresome way. For the first week or two here I hadn't got my book supply going and had to rely on the library, which meant reading some fearful trash. Among other things I read a Deeping[6] for the first time—actually not so bad as I expected, a sort of natural novelist like A. S. M. Hutchinson.[7] Also a Peter Cheyney.[8] He evidently does well out of his books as I used often to get invites from him for slap-up parties at the Dorchester. I have sent for several of Hardy's novels[9] and am looking at them rather unenthusiastically.

Yours
Eric

[XX, 3540, pp. 33–5; typewritten]

1. Rees had invested £1,000 in developing Barnhill.
2. *Human Knowledge: Its Scope and Limits* (1948). In his list of what he read in 1949, Orwell wrote against this book, 'Tried & failed.'
3. Russell was almost textually correct. The passage is from *Hamlet*, 2.2.116–19; the first line should read: 'Doubt thou' not 'Doubt that'. Russell takes the meaning at its simple, face value—that the earth does not move. If that is correct, Shakespeare (or Hamlet) cannot be accused of ignorance because, as the cosmos was still almost uniformly then understood, that was correct according to Ptolomaic theory. Copernicus and Galileo were challenging that theory (Galileo and Shakespeare were born in the same year), and their theory was regarded as heretical, as the Inquisition pointedly explained to Galileo. However, this passage is usually interpreted as hinting that the earth does move; Shakespeare was more subtle than either Russell or Orwell seems to have realised, and Hamlet, perhaps, more devious.
4. Professor J. B. Rhine, Director of the Parapsychology Laboratory at Duke University.
5. By Cecil Delisle Burns; Orwell lists it under March and annotates it, 'Skimmed.'
6. Warwick Deeping (1877–1950), a prolific novelist who trained as a doctor. His most successful book was *Sorrell and Son* (1925), based on his work in the Royal Army Medical Corps during World War I. Orwell does not list which book he read. He

expressed some scorn for 'the Dells and Deepings', although he admits in *Keep the Aspidistra Flying*, p. 34: 'Even the Dells and Deepings do at least turn out their yearly acre of print.'

7. Arthur Stuart-Menteith Hutchinson (1879–1971), born in Uttar Pradesh, India; a prolific novelist whose *If Winter Comes* had earlier attracted Orwell's attention; see 'Good Bad Books', *Tribune*, 2 November 1945 (XVII, 2780, p. 348).

8. Peter Cheyney (1896–1951), prolific author, chiefly of detective stories and thrillers, though he also published poems and lyrics. He served in World War I, rose to the rank of major, and in 1916 was severely wounded. Orwell had read his *Dark Hero*.

9. Orwell records reading *Jude the Obscure* and *Tess of the D'Urbevilles* in February 1949.

To Julian Symons*

> 4 February 1949
> The Cotswold Sanatorium
> Cranham

Dear Julian,

Thanks so much for your letter. Do send me a copy of your thriller.¹ I'm sure I should enjoy it. I do nothing now except read anyway, and I'm rather an amateur of detective stories, although, as you know, I have old-fashioned tastes in them. I recently by the way read for the first time *The Postman always Rings Twice*²—what an awful book. [*Arrangements for a proposed visit.*]

My new book is a Utopia in the form of a novel. I ballsed it up rather, partly owing to being so ill while I was writing it, but I think some of the ideas in it might interest you. We haven't definitively fixed the title, but I think it will be called *Nineteen Eighty-four*. Tony says Malcolm Muggeridge has a novel coming out about the same time.³

Please remember me to the family.

Yours
George

> [XX, 3541, p. 35; typewritten]

1. *Bland Beginning*; read by Orwell in February 1949.
2. By James M. Cain, published in 1934; read by Orwell in January 1949.
3. *Affairs of the Heart* (1949). It was the last book listed by Orwell as read in 1949.

In her book Eric and Us, *Jacintha Buddicom explains that after Orwell—to her then, Eric Blair—'had slipped away without trace' after his visit in 1927, they had no contact. Then, on 8 February 1949, she received a letter from her Aunt Lilian (with whom they had all stayed in 1927) to say that George Orwell was Eric Blair. She telephoned Martin Secker to find where Orwell was and wrote to him on 9 February. The following two letters arrived on 17 February enclosed in the same envelope. (See* Eric and Us, *pp. 143–45 and 146–58, and especially her letter of 4 May 1972 to her cousin on page 8 of this book.)*

To Jacintha Buddicom*

14 February 1949
The Cotswold Sanatorium
Cranham

Dear Jacintha,

How nice to get your letter after all these years. I suppose it really must be 30 years since the winter holidays when I stayed with you at Shiplake, though I saw Prosper and Guinever a good deal later, in 1927, when I stayed with them at Ticklerton after coming back from Burma. After that I was living in various parts of the world and often in great difficulties about making a living, and I rather lost touch with a lot of old friends. I seem to remember Prosper got married about 1930. I am a widower. My wife died suddenly four years ago, leaving me with a little (adopted) son who was then not quite a year old. Most of the time since then Avril has been keeping house for me, and we have been living in Jura, in the Hebrides, or more properly the Western Isles. I think we are going in any case to keep on the house there, but with my health as it now is I imagine I shall have to spend at least the winters in some get-at-able place where there is a doctor. In any case Richard, my little boy, who will be 5 in May, will soon have to start going to school, which he can't satisfactorily do on the island.

I have been having this dreary disease (T.B.) in an acute way since the autumn of 1947, but of course it has been hanging over me all my life, and actually I think I had my first go of it in early childhood. I spent the first half of 1948 in hospital, then went home much better after being treated with streptomycin, then began to feel ill again about September. I couldn't go for treatment then because I had to finish off a beastly book which, owing to illness, I had been messing about with for eighteen months. So I didn't get to this place till about the beginning of the year, by which time I was rather sorry for myself. I am trying now not to do any work at all, and shan't start any for another month or two. All I do is read and do crossword puzzles. I am well looked after here and can keep quiet and warm and not worry about anything, which is about the only treatment that is any good in my opinion. Thank goodness Richard is extremely tough and healthy and is unlikely, I should think, ever to get this disease.

I have never been back to the Henley area, except once passing through the town in a car. I wonder what happened to that property your mother had which we used to hunt all over with those 'saloon rifles,'¹ and which seemed so enormous in those days. Do you remember our passion for R. Austin Freeman?² I have never really lost it, and I think I must have read his entire works except some of the very last ones. I think he only died quite recently, at a great age.

I hope to get out of here in the spring or summer, and if so I shall be in London or near London for a bit. In that case I'll come and look you up if you would like it. Meanwhile if you'd care to write again and tell me some more news I'd be very pleased. I am afraid this is rather a poor letter, but I can't write long letters at present because it tires me to sit up for long at a time.

    Yours
    Eric Blair

                                [XX, 3550, pp. 42–3; typewritten]

1. Small-bore rifles used in shooting galleries – at fairs, for example.
2. Richard Austin Freeman (1862–1943), author of many novels and short stories, particularly featuring the pathologist-detective John Thorndyke, the first of which, written after his enforced retirement as a physician and surgeon in what is now Ghana, *The Red Thumb Mark* (1907), established Freeman (and Thorndyke). His novels and stories were characterised by their scientific accuracy. In 'Grandeur et décadence du roman policier anglais' ('The Detective Story'), *Fontaine*, 1944 (XV, 2357, pp. 309–20)), Orwell describes his *The Eye of Osiris* and *The Singing Bone* as 'classics of English detective fiction'.

To Jacintha Buddicom*

                                [15 February] 1949
                                Cranham

Hail and Fare Well, my dear Jacintha,

You see I haven't forgotten. I wrote to you yesterday but the letter isn't posted yet, so I'll go on to cheer this dismal day. It's been a day when everything's gone wrong. First there was a stupid accident to the book I was reading, which is now unreadable. After that the typewriter stuck & I'm too poorly to fix it. I've managed to borrow a substitute but it's not much better. Ever since I got your letter I've been remembering. I can't stop thinking about the young days with you & Guin & Prosper, & things put out of mind for 20 and 30 years. I am so wanting to see you. We must meet when I get out of this place, but the doctor says I'll have to stay another 3 or 4 months.

I would like you to see Richard. He can't read yet & is rather backward in talking, but he's as keen on fishing as I was & loves working on the farm, where he's really quite helpful. He has an enormous interest in machinery, which may be useful to him later on. When I was not much more than his age I always knew I wanted to write, but for the first ten years it was very hard to make a living. I had to take a lot of beastly jobs to earn enough to keep going & could only write in any spare time that was left, when I was too tired & had to destroy a dozen pages for one that was worth keeping. I tore up a whole novel once[1] & wish I now hadn't been so ruthless. Parts of it might have been worth re-writing, though it's impossible to come back to something written in such a different world. But I'm rather sorry now. ("'An w'en I sor wot 'e'd bin an' gorn an' don, I sed coo lor, wot 'ave you bin an' gorn an' done?"[2]) I think it's rather a good thing Richard is such an entirely practical child.

Are you fond of children? I think you must be. You were such a tender-hearted girl, always full of pity for the creatures we others shot & killed. But you were not so tender-hearted to me when you abandoned me to Burma with all hope denied. We are older now, & with this wretched illness the years will have taken more of a toll of me than of you. But I am well cared-for here & feel much better than I did when I got here last month. As soon as I can get back to London I do so want to meet you again.

As we always ended so that there should be no ending.

Farewell and Hail.
Eric

[XX, 3551, pp. 43–4; typewritten]

1. In the Introduction to the French edition of *Down and Out in Paris and London*, Orwell says he wrote two novels when living in Paris.
2. In *Eric & Us* Jacintha Buddicom refers to this 'old favourite joke from *Punch*' which they both enjoyed: a sailor had knocked over a bucket of tar onto a deck newly scrubbed for an admiral's inspection. Another sailor gave this explanation to the petty officer in charge. She comments, 'That old joke alone, together with the ever-constant beginning and ending, would hallmark that letter as Eric' (p. 152).

Wiadomości, a Polish émigré literary weekly published in London, sent a question-naire on Joseph Conrad to several English writers asking them two questions:
'First, what do you believe to be his permanent place and rank in English letters?

When Conrad died, some critics were uncertain of his final position, and Virginia Woolf, in particular, doubted whether any of his later novels would survive. Today, on the occasion of a new edition of his collected writings, Mr Richard Curle wrote in Time and Tide *that Conrad's works now rank among the great classics of the English novel. Which of these views, in your opinion, is correct?*

'The other question to which we would like to have your answer, is whether you detect in Conrad's work any oddity, exoticism and strangeness (of course, against the background of the English literary tradition), and if so, do you attribute it to his Polish origin?'

To [the Editor], *Wiadomości*

25 February 1949
The Cotswold Sanatorium
Cranham

Dear Sir,

Many thanks for your letter dated the 22nd February. I cannot answer at great length, as I am ill in bed, but I am happy to give you my opinions for what they are worth.

[1.] I regard Conrad as one of the best writers of this century, and— supposing that one can count him as an English writer—one of the very few true novelists that England possesses. His reputation, which was somewhat eclipsed after his death, has risen again during the past ten years, and I have no doubt that the bulk of his work will survive. During his lifetime he suffered by being stamped as a writer of 'sea stories,' and books like *The Secret Agent* and *Under Western Eyes* went almost unnoticed. Actually Conrad only spent about a third of his life at sea, and he had only a sketchy knowledge of the Asiatic countries of which he wrote in *Lord Jim*, *Almayer's Folly*, etc. What he did have, however, was a sort of grown-upness and political understanding which would have been almost impossible to a native English writer at that time. I consider that his best work belongs to what might be called his middle period, roughly between 1900 and 1914. This period includes *Nostromo*, *Chance*, *Victory*, the two mentioned above, and several outstanding short stories.

2. Yes, Conrad has definitely a slight exotic flavour to me. That is part of his attraction. In the earlier books, such as *Almayer's Folly*, his English is sometimes definitely incorrect, though not in a way that matters. He used I believe to think in Polish and then translate his thought into French and finally into English, and one can sometimes follow the process back at least as far as French, for instance in his tendency to put the adjective after the noun. Conrad was one of those writers who in the present century civilized English

literature and brought it back into contact with Europe, from which it had been almost severed for a hundred years. Most of the writers who did this were foreigners, or at any rate not quite English—Eliot and James (Americans), Joyce and Yeats (Irish), and Conrad himself, a transplanted Pole.

Yours truly
Geo. Orwell

[XX, 3553, pp. 47–8; typewritten]

To Roger Senhouse*

2 March 1949
The Cotswold Sanatorium
Cranham

Dear Roger,

I'm awfully sorry I haven't yet dealt with your queries, but the reason is that I lent my spare copy of proofs to Julian Symons, who was in here last week, and haven't had them back yet. [*Answers one or two queries.*] As to 'onto.' I know this is an ugly word, but I consider it to be necessary in certain contexts. If you say 'the cat jumped on the table' you may mean that the cat, already on the table, jumped up and down there. On the other hand, 'on to' (two words) means something different, as in 'we stopped at Barnet and then drove on to Hatfield.' In some contexts, therefore, one needs 'onto.' Fowler, if I remember rightly, doesn't altogether condemn it.[1]

I'm afraid there is going to be a big battle with Harcourt Brace, as they want to alter the metric system measurements all the way through the book to miles, yards etc., and in fact have done so in the proofs. This would be a serious mistake. I've already cabled in strong terms, but I don't like having to fight these battles 3000 miles from my base.

Yours
George

[XX, 3557, pp. 50–1; typewritten]

1. Orwell was allowed to use 'onto': see IX, p. 13, line 27. He had used the one-word form in earlier novels, although, as the Gollancz editions show, that usage is not always systematic. He won his battle with Harcourt Brace.

To Sir Richard Rees*

3 March 1949
Cranham

Dear Richard,

Thanks so much for your letter, with the cuttings, which I thought gave quite a good exposition of C.P. policy. I always disagree, however, when people end by saying that we can only combat Communism, Fascism or what-not if we develop an equal fanaticism. It appears to me that one defeats the fanatic precisely by *not* being a fanatic oneself, but on the contrary by using one's intelligence. In the same way, a man can kill a tiger because he is *not* like a tiger and uses his brain to invent the rifle, which no tiger could ever do.

I looked up the passage in Russell's book.[1] If the antithesis to a 'some' statement is always an 'all' statement, then it seems to me that the antithesis of 'some men are tailless' is not 'all men have tails,' but 'all men are tailless.'[2] Russell seems, in that paragraph, to be citing only pairs of statements of which one is untrue, but clearly there must be many cases when both 'some' and 'all' are true, except that 'some' is an understatement. Thus 'some men are tailless' is true, unless you are implying by it that some men have tails. But I never can follow that kind of thing. It is the sort of thing that makes me feel that philosophy should be forbidden by law.

I have arranged to write an essay on Evelyn Waugh and have just read his early book on Rossetti and also *Robbery under Law* (about Mexico.) I am now reading a new life of Dickens by Hesketh Pearson, which I have to review.[3] It isn't awfully good. There doesn't seem to be a perfect life of Dickens—perverse and unfair though it is, I really think Kingsmill's book is the best.[4] You were right about Huxley's book[5]—it is awful. And do you notice that the more holy he gets, the more his books stink with sex. He cannot get off the subject of flagellating women. Possibly, if he had the courage to come out and say so, that is the solution to the problem of war. If we took it out in a little private sadism, which after all doesn't do much harm, perhaps we wouldn't want to drop bombs etc. I also re-read, after very many years, *Tess of the D'Urbervilles*, and *Jude the Obscure* (for the first time). *Tess* is really better than I had remembered, and incidentally is quite funny in places, which I didn't think Hardy was capable of.

The doctor says I shall have to stay *in bed* for another 2 months, i.e. till about May, so I suppose I shan't actually get out till about July. However I don't know that it matters except for being expensive and not seeing little R[ichard]. I am so afraid of his growing away from me, or getting to think of me as just a person who is always lying down and can't play. Of course children can't understand illness. He used to come to me and say 'Where have you hurt yourself?'—I suppose the only reason he could see for always being in bed.[6] But otherwise I don't mind being here and I am comfortable and well cared-for. I feel much better and my appetite is a lot better. (By the way I never thanked you for sending that rum. Did I pay you enough for it?) I hope to start some serious work in April, and I think I could work fairly well here, as it is quiet and there are not many interruptions. Various people have been to see me, and I manage to keep pretty well supplied with books. Contrary to what people say, time seems to go very fast when you are in bed, and months can whizz by with nothing to show for it.

Yours
Eric

[XX, 3560, pp. 52–3; handwritten]

1. *Human Knowledge: Its Scope and Limits*, by Bertrand Russell (1948).
2. "all men are tailless" is underlined, and, written in the margin by Rees, is 'But this is *not* what Russell says!'
3. Orwell's review of *Dickens: His Character, Comedy and Career* by Hesketh Pearson, appeared in *The New York Times Book Review*, 15 May 1949 (see XX, 3625, pp. 113–16).
4. *The Sentimental Journey: A Life of Charles Dickens*, by Hugh Kingsmill (1934).
5. *Ape and Essence* by Aldous Huxley (New York, 1948; London, 1949).
6. Richard Blair later recalled his relationship with his father: 'He was very concerned about not being able to see me as much as he ought to. His biggest concern was that the relationship wouldn't develop properly between father and son. As far as he was concerned, it was fully developed, but he was more concerned about son-to-father relationships. He'd formed a bond with me, but it wasn't as strong the other way around.' Lettice Cooper described the problems posed for Orwell in establishing this bond when he became severely ill and the effect Orwell's illness and Eileen's early death had had. Orwell 'was terrified to let Richard come near him, and he would hold out his hand and push him away—and George would do it very abruptly because he was abrupt in his manner and movements. And he wouldn't let the child sit on his knee or anything. And I suppose Richard had never asked [if his father loved him]. Children don't, do they? And he said, did they love him? And I said they both did, so much. It was very hard, that, wasn't it?' (*Remembering Orwell*, pp. 196–97.)

To Michael Meyer*

12 March 1949
The Cotswold Sanatorium
Cranham

Dear Michael,

Thanks ever so much for sending all that food, which arrived a day or two ago, and for your letter. You really shouldn't have sent the food, but I take your word that you could spare it, and of course I am delighted to receive it. As a matter of fact I'm sending most of it on to Jura, where food is always welcome as there's usually someone staying.

[*Paragraph about his sedentary life and Richard.*]

I always thought Sweden[1] sounded a dull country, much more so than Norway or Finland. I should think there would probably be very good fishing, if you can whack up any interest in that. But I have never been able to like these model countries with everything up to date and hygienic and an enormous suicide rate. I also have a vague feeling that in our century there is some sort of interconnection between the quality of thought and culture in a country, and the *size* of the country. Small countries don't seem to produce interesting writers any longer, though possibly it is merely that one doesn't hear about them. I have ideas about the reason for this, if it is true, but of course only guesswork. I hope your novel gets on.[2] Even if one makes a mess of it the first time, one learns a great deal in making the attempt, also if you once have a draft finished, however discouraging it is, you can generally pull it into shape. I simply destroyed my first novel after unsuccessfully submitting it to one publisher, for which I'm rather sorry now. I think Thomas Hood[3] is a very good subject. He is incidentally no longer as well known as he should be, and very thoroughly out of print. I have only a selection of his poems and have for a long time been trying in vain to get the rest. I want particularly the one where he is writing a poem on the beauties of childhood but can't get on with it because the children are making such a noise (I remember it has the beautiful line, 'Go to your mother, child, and blow your nose.'[4]) I don't know whether one could call him a serious poet—he is what I call a good bad poet. I am glad you like Surtees. I think after being so long abandoned to the hunting people, who I don't suppose read him, he is beginning to be appreciated again. I haven't however read much of his works, and am trying to get hold of several now.[5] At present I do nothing except read—I'm not going to try and start any work till some time next month. [*He had read some Hardy, Pearson's* Dickens, *and Huxley.*] Koestler's new book I haven't seen yet.[6] I am going to do an essay on Evelyn Waugh for the *Partisan Review*, and have been reading his early works, including a quite good life of Rossetti.[7] My novel is supposed to come out in June. I don't know whether the American edition may come out before the English, but I should think not. I hope to hear from you again some time. This place will be my address till about July, I'm afraid.

Yours
George

[XX, 3570, pp. 61–3; typewritten]

1. Meyer was then a lecturer in English at Uppsala University, 1947–50.
2. *The End of the Corridor*, published in 1951.
3. Thomas Hood (1799–1845), poet and journalist. His comic poetry was marked by gallows humour, and he could write with great bitterness (for example, 'The Song of the Shirt,' 1843, on sweated labour), and splendid wit.
4. From 'A Parental Ode to My Son, Aged Three years and Five Months'. Orwell has 'blow' for 'wipe', so is doubtless (as so often) quoting from memory.
5. Orwell recorded having read *Mr Sponge's Sporting Tour* in April 1949.
6. *Insight and Outlook*.
7. *Rossetti: His Life and Works* (1928).

To Sir Richard Rees*

16 March 1949
Cranham

Dear Richard,

I hope all is going well with you. I have heard once or twice from Barnhill and things seem to be fairly prosperous. Avril says Bill is going to plant about an acre of kale. Ian M'Kechnie is there at present, working on the road, and Francis Boyle[1] has done some work in the garden. Bill suggested we should sell off the milch cows, as some of his own cows will be calving and will have surplus milk, and of course it would make more room in the byre. On the other hand there is the question of overlapping, so I suggested keeping one Ayrshire. The boat is apparently in good order and they have been over to Crinan in her. Avril says Richard has found out about money, ie. has grasped that you can buy sweets with it, so I expect I had better start giving him pocket money, though at present he hasn't any opportunity to spend it. Incidentally, getting pocket money would probably teach him the days of the week.

I have been feeling fairly good, though of course they won't dream of letting me up. Most of the time it has been beautiful spring-like weather.

[*Reading Evelyn Waugh and Hesketh Pearson on Dickens.*] Also re-reading Israel Zangwill's *Children of the Ghetto*, a book I hadn't set eyes on for very many years. I am trying to get hold of the sequel to it, *Grandchildren of the Ghetto*,[2] which I remember as being better than the other. I don't know what else he wrote, but I believe a whole lot. I think he is a very good novelist who hasn't had his due, though I notice now that he has a very strong tinge of Jewish nationalism, of a rather tiresome kind. I sent for Marie Bashkirtseff's diary, which I had never read, and it is now staring me in the face, an enormous and rather intimidating volume.[3] I haven't seen Koestler's new book, which I think has only been published in the USA, but I think I shall send for it. My book is billed to come out on June 15th. It is going to be the *Evening Standard* book of the month, which I believe doesn't mean anything in particular.

Have you torn up your clothing book?[4] The reaction of everybody here was the same—'it must be a trap.' Of course clothes are now sufficiently rationed by price. I think I shall order myself a new jacket all the same.

> Yours
> Eric

[XX, 3574, pp. 65–6; typewritten]

1. Ian M'Kechnie was an estate worker at Ardlussa; Francis Boyle, a roadworker on Jura. Both helped at Barnhill from time to time.
2. Israel Zangwill (1864–1926), English novelist and playwright who was one of the first to present the lives of immigrant Jews in fictional form in English literature. He was for a time a Zionist and later served as President of the Jewish Territorial Organization for the Settlement of the Jews within the British Empire, 1905–25.
3. Marie Bashkirtseff (1860–1884), Russian-born diarist and painter. Her *Journal* was published posthumously in 1887 and became very fashionable.
4. Clothes were rationed during the war. Clothes rationing ended on 15 March 1949.

To Leonard Moore*

17 March 1949
The Cotswold Sanatorium
Cranham

Dear Moore,

You will have had Robert Giroux's letter, of which he sent me a duplicate.

I can't possibly agree to the kind of alteration and abbreviation suggested. It would alter the whole colour of the book and leave out a good deal that is essential. I think it would also—though the judges, having read the parts that it is proposed to cut out, may not appreciate this—make the story unintelligible.

There would also be something visibly wrong with the structure of the book if about a fifth or a quarter were cut out and the last chapter then tacked on to the abbreviated trunk. A book is built up as a balanced structure and one cannot simply remove large chunks here and there unless one is ready to recast the whole thing. In any case, merely to cut out the suggested chapters and abridge the passages from the 'book within the book' would mean a lot of re-writing which I simply do not feel equal to at present.

The only terms on which I could agree to any such arrangement would be if the book were published definitely as an abridged version and if it were clearly stated that the English edition contained several chapters which had been omitted. But obviously the Book of the Month people couldn't be expected to agree to any such thing. As Robert Giroux says in his letter they have not promised to select the book in any case, but he evidently hopes they might, and I suppose it will be disappointing to Harcourt & Brace° if I reject the suggestion. I suppose you, too, stand to lose a good deal of commission. But I really cannot allow my work to be mucked about beyond a certain point, and I doubt whether it even pays in the long run. I should be much obliged if you would make my point of view clear to them.[1]

Yours sincerely
Eric Blair

[XX, 3575, pp. 66–7; typewritten]

1. The 'book within the book' suggests Goldstein's The Theory and Practice of Oligar-chical Collectivism was to be cut.

Orwell and the Information Research Department

When Celia Kirwan* worked for the IRD, she was, so far as her relationship with Orwell was concerned, far more a close friend than merely a government official. Much of the information here and for 6.4.49 is based on documents in Foreign Office files released by the Public Record Office on 10 July 1996 under the Government's 'open government policy'. The permission of the Controller of Her Majesty's Stationery Office to reproduce Crown copyright material is gratefully acknowledged.

The IRD was set up by the Foreign Office in 1948. 'Its creation was prompted by the desire of Ministers of Mr Attlee's Labour Government to devise means to combat Communist propaganda, then engaged in a global and damaging campaign to undermine Western power and influence. British concern for an effective counter-offensive against Communism was sharpened by the need to rebut a relentless Soviet-inspired campaign to undermine British institutions, a campaign which included direct personal attacks on the Prime Minister and members of the Cabinet and divisive criticism *of government policies.' Among the activities in which it engaged, it commissioned* *special articles and circulated books and journals to appropriate posts abroad. Thus,* Tribune, *because of its anti-Stalin stance, was widely distributed. Much fuller details* *relative to* **30.3.49** *and* **6.4.49** *will be found in XX, 3590A, pp. 319, 321, 323-5.*

On 29 March 1949, Celia Kirwan went to see Orwell at Cranham at the IRD's *request. This report, written the following day, and Orwell's letter of 6 April, are the* *outcome of that meeting.*

30 March 1949

Yesterday I went to visit George Orwell, who is in a sanatorium in Glouces- tershire. I discussed some aspects of our work with him in great confidence, and he was delighted to learn of them, and expressed his wholehearted and enthusiastic approval of our aims. He said that he could not agree to write an article himself at present, or even to re-write one, because he is too ill to undertake any literary work at all; also because he does not like to write 'on commission', as he feels he does not do his best work that way. However I left some material with him, and shall send him photostats of some of his articles on the theme of Soviet repression of the arts, in the hope that he may become inspired when he is better to take them up again.

He suggested various names of writers who might be enlisted to write for us, and promised to think of more in due course and to communicate them to us. The ones he thought of while I was there were:–

D'Arcy Gillie, the *Manchester Guardian* Paris correspondent, who he says is a serious opponent of Communism, and an expert on Poland as well as on French politics;

C. D. Darlington,[*1] the scientist. Mr Orwell considers that the Lysenko case should be fully documented, and suggested that Darlington might undertake this;

Franz Borkenau, the German professor, who wrote a History of the Comintern, and has also written some articles recently in the *Observer*.[2]

Mr Orwell said that undoubtedly Gollancz would be the man to publish such a series of books as we had in mind. He would have been very willing to act as a go-between if he had been well enough; as it was, he would try to think of someone else who would do so, and he suggested that a glance at a list of Gollancz writers would probably recall to our minds someone who would be able to help us. He says, however, that Gollancz has a one-track mind, and at present it is running along the track of Arab refugees, so it might be a good plan to allow him to get these out of his system before try- ing to interest him in our plan. He said that Gollancz books always sell well, and that they are well displayed and given the widest publicity.

As Mr Orwell was for two° years in the Indian Police stationed in Burma, and as he ran a B.B.C. service to the Indians during the war, I asked him what in his view would be the best way of furthering our aims in India and Burma. He said that whatever was the best way, the *worst* was undoubtedly broadcasting, since hardly any of the natives had radio sets, and those who did (who were mostly Eurasians) tended only to listen in to local stations. He thought that one plane-load of leaflets probably did more good than six months broadcasting.

Indeed he did not think that there was a great deal of scope for propaganda in India and Pakistan, where Communism meant something quite different from what it did in Europe—it meant, on [t]he whole, opposition to the ruling class, and he thought that more good would be done by maintaining the closest possible links with these countries, through trade and through the interchange of students. He thought this latter aspect of Anglo-Indian relations very important, and was of the opinion that we ought to offer far more scholarships to Indian and Pakistan° students.

In Burma, he thought that propaganda should avoid 'atrocity' stories, since the Burmese were 'rather apt to admire that kind of thing', or, if they did not actually admire it, to think 'If that's what the Communists are like, better not oppose them.'

Incidentally, he said that the Commander Young,[3] whose wife committed suicide the other day, is a Communist, and is the Naval equivalent, on a more modest scale, of the Archbishop of Canterbury[4]—that is, he is called in to confirm the Soviet point of view about matters relating to the Navy. Also, his wife was a Czech; and Mr Orwell wonders whether there is any connection between these two facts and Mrs Young's suicide.

[XX, 3590A, pp. 318–21]

1. See **19.3.47**.
2. For Franz Borkenau, see **31.7.37**, n. 3.
3. Orwell included Cdr. Edgar P. Young in his list of crypto-communists. He wrote, 'Naval expert. Pamphlets'; under 'Remarks', 'F. T.? Active in People's Convention. Quite possibly an underground member I should think. Wife (Czech) committed suicide (in slightly doubtful circumstances) 1949.' Mrs Ida Young was found hanged in their flat on 23 March 1949.
4. 'Archbishop' has been mistakenly written for Dean Hewlett-Johnson, the 'Red Dean'.

To Sir Richard Rees*

31 March 1949
Cranham

Dear Richard,

Thanks so much for your letter. I send herewith a copy of P[artisan] R[eview] with the article I spoke of.¹ I'd have sent it before, as I thought it would interest you, but I was under the impression that you took in PR. Celia Kirwan was here the other day & she will send me a copy of that number of Polemic which I lost & which has the essay on Tolstoy in it. It really connects up with the Gandhi article.

Yes, I must get this will business sewn up. I had my will properly drawn up by a solicitor, then, as I wanted to make some alterations, re-wrote it myself, & I dare say this second draft, though duly witnessed etc., is not legal. Have you got a solicitor in Edinburgh? I am out of touch with my London ones. It is important to get the literary executorship sewn up properly, & also to be quite sure about Richard's position, because there is some legal difference, I forget what, in the case of an adopted child. In addition I must bring up to date the notes I left for you about my books, which editions to follow, etc. When Avril came back from town she brought some box files marked 'Personal' which I *think* have all the relevant stuff in them. Do you think when you are at Barnhill you could go through these files & send the relevant papers to me. I want my will, ie. the second will, dated about the beginning of 1947 I think, the notes I left for you, & a notebook marked 'Reprintable Essays'² which wants bringing up to date. It's important that your powers should be made clear, ie. that you should have the final say when any definitely literary question is involved. For example. The American Book of the Month people, though they didn't actually promise, half promised to select my present book if I would cut out about a quarter of it. Of course I'm not going to do this, but if I had died the week before, Moore & the American publishers would have jumped at the offer, ruining the book & not even benefiting my estate much, because whenever you make a large sum you are in the surtax class & it is all taken away again.

I have been very poorly, spitting up quantities of blood. This doesn't necessarily do any harm, indeed Morlock, the specialist I went to before the war, said it might even do good, but it always depresses & disgusts me, & I have been feeling rather down. There is evidently nothing very definite they can do for me. They talked of doing the 'thora' operation, but the surgeon wouldn't undertake it because you have to have one sound lung which I haven't. Evidently the only thing to do is to keep quiet. It worries me not to see little R., but perhaps later I can arrange somehow for him to visit me. If I do get up this year I want to take him for a trip to London.

Yours
Eric

Excuse this writing. They've forbidden me to use a typewriter at present because it is tiring!

[XX, 3584, pp. 73–4; handwritten]

1. 'Reflections on Gandhi' (see XX, 3516, pp. 5–12).
2. See XX, 3728, pp. 223–31, which includes a section on 'Reprintable Essays'.

Orwell's letter to Celia Kirwan, which follows, should be read in the context of what the Information Research Department was seeking: those who might reliably represent British interests in writing on its behalf to counteract Soviet propaganda designed to undermine democratic institutions. The copious notes and annotations relevant to this letter will be found in XX, 3590B, pp. 323–7.

To Celia Kirwan*

6 April 1949
Cranham

Dear Celia,

I haven't written earlier because I have really been rather poorly, & I can't use the typewriter even now, so I hope you will be able to cope with my handwriting.

I couldn't think of any more names to add to your possible list of writers except FRANZ BORKENAU (the *Observer* would know his address) whose name I think I gave you, & GLEB STRUVE* (he's at Pasadena in California at present), the Russian translator and critic. Of course there are hordes of Americans, whose names can be found in the (New York) *New Leader*, the Jewish monthly paper *Commentary*, & the *Partisan Review*. I could also, if it is of any value, give you a list of journalists & writers who in my opinion are crypto-Communists, fellow-travellers or inclined that way & should not be trusted as propagandists. But for that I shall have to send for a notebook which I have at home, & if I do give you such a list it is strictly confidential, as I imagine it is libellous to describe somebody as a fellow-traveller.[1]

Just one idea occurred to me for propaganda not abroad but in this country. A friend of mine in Stockholm[2] tells me that as the Swedes don't make many films of their own one sees a lot of German & Russian films, & some of the Russian films, which of course would not normally reach this country, are unbelievably scurrilous anti-British propaganda. He referred especi[ally] to a historical film about the Crimean war. As the Swedes can get hold of these films I suppose we can: might it not be a good idea to have showings of some of them in this country, particularly for the benefit of the intelligentsia?

I read the enclosed article[3] with interest, but it seems to me anti-religious rather than anti-semitic. For what my opinion is worth, I don't think anti-anti-semitism is a strong card to play in anti-Russian propaganda. The USSR must in practice be somewhat anti-semitic, as it is opposed both to Zionism within its own borders & on the other hand to the liberalism and internationalism of the non-Zionist Jews, but a polyglot state of that kind can never be officially anti-semitic, in the Nazi manner, just as the British Empire cannot. If you try to tie up Communism and anti-semitism, it is always possible in reply to point to people like Kaganovich[4] or Anna° Pauker,[5] also to the large number of Jews in the Communist parties everywhere. I also think it is bad policy to try to curry favour with your enemies. The Zionist Jews everywhere hate us & regard Britain as the enemy, more even than Germany. Of course this is based on misunderstanding, but as long as it is so I do not think we do ourselves any good by denouncing anti-semitism in other nations.

I am sorry I can't write a better letter, but I really have felt so lousy the last few days. Perhaps a bit later I'll get some ideas.

With love
George

[Postscript] I did suggest DARCY GILLY,° (Manchester Guardian) didn't I? There is also a man called CHOLLERTON (expert on the Moscow trials) who could be contacted through the Observer.[6]

[XX, 3590B, pp. 322–7; handwritten]

1. Orwell's Lists of Crypto-Communists and Fellow-Travellers are to be found in XX, 3732, pp. 240–59; supplemented in LO, pp. 149–51; and in LO, pp.140–9 is the list of names Orwell sent to Celia Kirwan, 2 May 1949. Orwell wrote that the list wasn't very sensational but 'it isn't a bad idea to have the people who are probably unreliable listed'. There is a very serious aspect to the list. It includes, for example, two on the NKVD payroll (Tom Driberg, Labour MP (codename 'Lepage') and Peter Smollet, OBE (= Smolka, codename 'Abo' and probably the man who persuaded Cape not to publish Animal Farm). There is also a jokey element – Orwell's income tax inspector is listed. The project has raised considerable comment, some unfavourable, some ill-informed.
2. Michael Meyer.*
3. Not identified.

4. Lazar Moiseyevich Kaganovich (1893–1991), a Jew, originally a shoemaker, who became Secretary of the Central Committeee of the Commuist Party. He managed the Soviet Union's transport system during the war.
5. Ana Pauker (1894–1960), daughter of a Jewish butcher, spent some time in the USA, served as a Colonel in the Red Army and became a leader of the Romanian Communist Party when the Soviets occupied Romania in 1944.
6. Darsie Gillie, the *Guardian*'s Paris correspondent, told Adam Watson (one of Celia's colleagues) that Chollerton was 'an expert on Russia, & would be useful in various ways'. A.T. Chollerton was the *Daily Telegraph*'s correspondent in Moscow in 1939 when the Soviet Union was in alliance with Germany.

To Sir Richard Rees*

8 April 1949
Cranham

Dear Richard,

I thought you'd all like to know that I have just had a cable saying that the Book of the Month Club have selected my novel after all, in spite of my refusing to make the changes they demanded. So that shows that virtue is its own reward, or honesty is the best policy, I forget which. I don't know whether I shall ultimately end up with a net profit, but at any rate this should pay off my arrears of income tax.

I've had the sanatorium cable the magazines to which I had promised articles saying I am unfit to do any work, which is the truth. Don't depress the others too much with this, but the fact is I am in a bad way at present. They are going to try streptomycin again, which I had previously urged them to do & which Mr Dick* thought might be a good idea. They had been afraid of it because of the secondary effects, but they now say they can offset these to some extent with nicotine, or something, & in any case they can always stop if the results are too bad. *If* things go badly—of course we'll hope they won't, but one must be prepared for the worst—I'll ask you to bring little Richard to see me before I get too frightening in appearance. I think it would upset you less than it would Avril, & there may be business deals to talk over as well. If the stuff works, as it seemed to do last time, I shall take care this time to keep the improvement by leading an invalid life for the rest of the year.

I forgot to say, I wish some time you'd have a look at my books & see they're not getting too mildewy (I asked Avril to light a fire from time to time for that reason) & that the magazines in the bottom shelf are in some sort of order. I want to keep all the magazines that are there, as some of them have

articles of mine that I might want to reprint. The books are piling up here &
I'm going to start sending them home some time, but I can't do up parcels at
present.

Love to all
Eric

[XX, 3594, pp. 82–3; handwritten]

To Tosco Fyvel*

Fyvel lost the original of this letter after most of it had been printed in Encounter,
January 1962. It is reproduced here as printed in Encounter.

15 April 1949
[The Cotswold Sanatorium]
Cranham

Dear Tosco,

Thanks so much for sending Ruth Fischer's book.¹ I had intended buying it,
but perhaps after reading a borrowed copy I shan't need to. I'll see you get
it back. I read Margarete Neumann's book² with some interest. It wasn't a
particularly good book but she struck me as a sincere person. Gollancz also
has a quite remarkable novel about the forced-labour camps coming along,
by someone calling himself pseudonymously 'Richard Cargoe'³—a Pole I
should say—how authentic I couldn't be sure, but quite a striking book, in
the Slav manner.

There were several points in your articles that I had been meaning to take
up with you. One is about Graham Greene. You keep referring to him as an
extreme Conservative, the usual Catholic reactionary type. This isn't so at
all, either in his books or privately. Of course he is a Catholic and in some
issues has to take sides politically with the church, but in outlook he is just a
mild Left with faint CP leanings. I have even thought that he might become
our first Catholic fellow-traveller, a thing that doesn't exist in England but
does in France, etc. If you look at books like *A Gun for Sale, England Made
Me, The Confidential Agent* and others, you will see that there is the usual left-
wing scenery. The bad men are millionaires, armaments manufacturers etc.,
and the good man is sometimes a Communist. In his last book there is also
the usual inverted colour-feeling. According to Rayner Heppenstall, Greene
somewhat reluctantly supported Franco during the Spanish civil war, but *The
Confidential Agent* is written from the other point of view.

The other thing is that you are always attacking novelists for not writing
about the contemporary scene. But can you think of a novel that ever was

written about the strictly contemporary scene? It is very unlikely that any novel, *i.e.* worth reading, would ever be set back less than three years at least. If you tried, *in* 1949, to write a novel about 1949 it would simply be 'reportage' and probably would seem out of date and silly before you could get it into print. I have a novel dealing with 1945 in my head now, but even if I survive to write it I shouldn't touch it before 1950.[4] The reason is not only that one can't see the events of the moment in perspective, but also that a novel has to be lived with for years before it can be written down, otherwise the working-out of detail, which takes an immense time and can only be done at odd moments, can't happen. This is my experience and I think it is also other people's. I have sometimes written a so-called novel within about two years of the original conception, but then they were always weak, silly books which I afterwards suppressed. You may remember that nearly all the worthwhile books about the 1914 war appeared 5, 10 or even more years after it was over, which was when one might have expected them. I think books about the late war are about due to appear now, and books about the immediate post-war at some time in the fifties.

I've been horribly ill the last few weeks. I had a bit of a relapse, then they decided to have another go with streptomycin, which previously did me a lot of good, at least temporarily. This time only one dose of it had ghastly results, as I suppose I had built up an allergy or something. I'm a bit better now, however, but I can't work and don't know when I shall be able to. I've no hope of getting out of here before the late summer. If the weather is good I might then get up to Scotland for a few weeks, but not more, and then I shall have to spend the autumn and winter somewhere near a doctor, perhaps even in some kind of residential sanatorium. I can't make plans till my health takes a more definite turn one way or the other. Richard is blooming, or was when I last saw him. He will be five in May. I think he will go to the village school this winter, but next year I shall have to remove him to the mainland so that he can go to a proper day school. He is still backward about talking but bright in other ways. I don't think he will ever be one for books. His bent seems to be mechanical, and he is very good at farm work. If he grew to be a farmer[5] I should be pleased, though I shan't try to influence him. . . .[6]

Yours
George

[XX, 3598, pp. 85–7; handwritten]

1. *Stalin and German Communism*, by Ruth Fischer; Orwell lists it as read in April.
2. *Under Two Dictators*, by Margarete Buber-Neumann; Orwell lists it as read in April.
3. *The Tormentors*; listed by Orwell as read in February. Cargoe's real name was Robert

Payne (1911–1983). Orwell apparently did not know him by his pseudonym, but he may have known him as Payne when he was a war correspondent in Spain in 1938 (the year after Orwell fought there). In 1941–42 he worked for the British Ministry of Information in Chungking, China.

4. This was the second of the two books Orwell had in mind at his death.

5. Richard Blair did initially take up farming as a career. In 1964 he married Eleanor Moir, a schoolteacher; they have two sons.

6. The letter was cut here by *Encounter*.

To Sir Richard Rees*

17 April 1949
[The Cotswold Sanatorium]
Cranham

Dear Richard,

Thanks so much for sending on the things. It doesn't matter much about the book marked Essays. I can remember most of the items I wanted to note down, and I dare say the book itself will turn up among the papers which were sent to Pickfords. You might ask Avril whether, when she cleaned out my papers at Canonbury, she threw any notebooks away. There was another one, a dirty old red book,¹ which had notes that I might need some time.

I am somewhat better I think. The streptomycin after only one dose had the most disastrous results, so they dropped it promptly. Evidently I had built up an allergy or something. However I've now got over that, and today for the first time I was allowed to sit out in a deck chair for an hour or two. When I'll get to the point of putting some clothes on, lord knows. However, I've ordered myself a few new clothes, just to keep my morale up. I have discovered that there is a stream just near here with trout in it, so when I am somewhere near the point of getting up I'll ask Avril to send me my fishing things. I do hope I'll be able to get up to Jura for a few weeks some time in the summer, perhaps in August or so, and that the motor boat will be running then. I can't make plans till I know more about my health, but I suppose I'll have to spend this winter in some kind of institution, or at any rate near a doctor, and conceivably abroad. Probably somewhere like Brighton would be better, but in case of going abroad I'm taking steps to get my passport renewed. And after that I'm going to look about for a flat somewhere. It's evident that from now on I must spend the winters in civilized places, and in any case Richard will soon have to spend most of his time on the mainland, because of schooling. But I needn't remove anything from Barnhill, except perhaps my books, or some of them, because I think I could afford to furnish a second establishment now.

Inez [Holden] is coming to see me next week and Brenda [Salkeld] the week after. I asked Inez to get me a birthday present for R., or at least to go to Gamage's and see what they've got. I can't think what to get him. I suppose he's almost ripe for a pocket knife, but somehow I don't fancy the idea.

I get visits occasionally from the people at Whiteway, [which] seems to be some sort of Anarchist colony run, or financed, by the old lady whose name I forget[2] who keeps the Freedom Bookshop. One of them is old Mat Kavanagh, whom you perhaps know, an old Irish I.R.A. Anarchist hairdresser, a figure at meetings for many years, who used to cut my hair in Fleet Street. He now tells me, what I hadn't known, that when a person with my sort of hair comes into the shop there is a sort of competition not to deal with him. He said he always used to cut my hair because the others pushed me off onto him, feeling that I wasn't the sort of person they could do themselves credit with.

Re. the cryptos and fellow travellers. I don't think Laski[3] is a fellow traveller, much as he has aided them by his boosting of Russia. *In this country* he loathes the CP, because they menace his job. I suppose he imagines they are different elsewhere. I also think he is too integrally a part of the L[abour] P[arty], and too fond of being in an official position, to go over to the enemy if, for instance, we were at war with the USSR. The thing one can't imagine Laski doing is breaking the law. Cole[4] I think should probably not be on the list, but I would be less certain of him than of Laski in case of a war. Martin[5] of course is far too dishonest to be outright a crypto or fellow-traveller, but his main influence is pro-Russian and is certainly intended to be so, and I feel reasonably sure he would quislingise in the case of a Russian occupation, if he had not managed to get away on the last plane. I think there *must* be two Niebuhrs.[6] I saw an unmistakeable fellow-traveller statement over that name, quoted in the *New Leader* about two years ago. The whole business is very tricky, and one can never do more than use one's judgement and treat each case individually. I feel reasonably sure that Zilliacus,[7] for instance, is a crypto, but I would concede perhaps a twenty-five percent chance that he is not, whereas about Pritt[8] I feel completely certain. I feel less sure about John Platt-Mills[9] than about Z., but I feel pretty sure of Lester Hutchinson[10] after meeting him once. Mikardo[11] is I should say simply a fool, but he is also one of those who think they see a chance of self-advancement in making mischief and are quite ready to flirt with the cryptos.

I'm just reading Ruth Fischer's enormous book, *Stalin and German Communism*. It's extremely good—not at all the sort of doctrinaire Trotskyism I would have expected. Have you seen the new Catholic magazine, the *Month*? It's lousy. I also read Margarete Neumann's book (the woman who gave evidence for Kravchenko), but it's about the Russian and German concentration camps, not about the party squabbles in Germany. I must send some books home soon. They're piling up fast here. Ask Avril to wipe the books now and then, will you, and to light a fire in those rooms. Otherwise the covers end by bending.

Love to all
Eric

[XX, 3600, pp. 87–90; typewritten]

1. Described, with contents, and reproduced at XX, 3729, pp. 231–3.
2. Lilian Wolfe (1875–1974), born in London, worked for twenty years as a Post Office telegraphist. She became a socialist and women's suffragist in 1907, and in 1913 an anarcho-syndicalist. She was active in the anti-war movement, 1914–16, and was imprisoned, as was her companion, Thomas Keell (1866–1938). After the war she ran health-food shops in London and Stroud, living in the main at the anarchist colony at Whiteway, some five miles from Cranham; Richard stayed there when visiting his father. She earned enough to keep her husband and son and support the anarchist journal, *Freedom*. In 1966 the anarchist movement gave her a holiday in the United States as a ninetieth birthday present. After a lifetime devoted to anarchism she died at her son's home in Cheltenham at ninety-eight (Nicolas Walter's account of her life, *Freedom*, Centenary Number, 1986, 23–24).
3. Harold Laski (see **20.9.47,** n. 1). Re list of crypto-Communists and fellow-travellers, see **6.4.49,** n. 1.
4. G. D. H. Cole (1889–1959), economist and prolific author; his books include *The Intelligent Man's Guide to the Post-War World* (1947) and *The Meaning of Marxism* (1948), based on his *What Marx Really Meant* (1934).
5. Kingsley Martin (1887–1969), then editor of the *New Statesman* (see **9.2.38**, n. 1).
6. One was presumably Reinhold Niebuhr (1892–1971), American theologian and professor at Union Theological Seminary, 1930–60, for a time a socialist and pacifist; later a supporter of the war against Hitler. Regarding a second Niebuhr, it is possible that there is confusion between Reinhold and his brother, Helmut Richard (1894–1962), ordained a minister of the Evangelical & Reformed Church in 1916 and from 1931 pursued a distinguished career at Yale. He was involved in the union of the Congregational and the Evangelical & Reformed churches.
7. Konni Zilliacus (see **2.1.48** n. 5).
8. Dennis Noel Pritt (1887–1972), Labour and then Independent Labour MP and chairman of the Society for Cultural Relations with the USSR.
9. John Platt-Mills (1906–2001), a New Zealander and unshakeable apologist for Stalin; he disbelieved the Soviets committed atrocities even after Khrushchev denounced Stalin in 1956. Expelled from the Labour Party, 1948.
10. Hugh Lester Hutchinson (1904–1950), journalist and author, studied in Switzerland

and at Edinburgh University, and served in the Navy, 1942–44. He was elected Labour MP in 1945 but was expelled in 1949 for his criticism of the Labour government's foreign policy.

11. Ian Mikardo (1908–1993), management consultant, author of *Centralised Control of Industry* (1942), and politician. He was a left-wing Labour MP, 1945–59 and 1964–87, and was a prominent follower of Aneurin Bevan and a rumbustious debater with a strong sense of comedy. He was often considered to be unduly sympathetic to Communism, but his passionate Zionism ensured that he never forgot or forgave Stalin for his treatment of Jews. He was much appreciated by fellow MPs of all parties in his role as 'unofficial bookmaker' to Parliament, offering odds on contentious issues and the fortunes of political figures.

To Dr Gwen O'Shaughnessy*

17 April 1949
The Cotswold Sanatorium
Cranham

Dear Gwen,

I have been meaning for ages to write to you. Among other things I owe you money for some things you got for Richard. I can't remember what they were but I have an idea they included an overcoat. Please let me know and I'll pay you.

I have been here since January and am getting a little better I think. I was really very ill in December, and again recently. I had a relapse and they decided to try another go of streptomycin, with dreadful results after only one dose. I suppose I had built up a resistance to it or something. However the last few days I have felt better and have even been sitting out in a deck chair a little. They can't really do much for me except keep me quiet. They can't do the 'thora' operation (somewhat to my relief I must say) because you need one reliable lung which I haven't got. It looks as though I shall be here till well into the summer, and if I do get up to Jura this year it will only be for a week or two in August or September. [*Must be surer about his health – shall have to spend the winter somewhere warmer; Richard's schooling; Barnhill.*]

I have remade my will,[1] or rather I have sent the will I made some years ago to a solicitor to be redrafted, as it occurred to me it might not be in proper legal order. I have made you my executor, which I don't think will involve much nuisance, as Richard Rees is my literary executor and he will see to all the business of dealing with publishers etc. I have also requested— this is one of the things that I want the solicitor to put in good order—that you and Avril shall decide between you about Richard's upbringing, but that if there is any dispute the decision shall lie with you. I don't suppose any disagreement is likely to arise between you. Avril is very fond of him and I know will want to bring him up, but if anything should happen to her, or if she should wish to live in any place where he can't go to school, I wish you would take charge of him. I don't think you would be financially out of pocket. I have put aside enough to see him through his childhood in a modest way. If I should die in the near future, there are considerable income tax claims to be met, but there is also a good deal of money coming in and I think the 'estate' would be easily cleared without encroaching on my savings. There should also be at any rate a small income from royalties for some years to come. I trust that all this won't become urgent yet awhile, but after these two illnesses I don't imagine I can last very many years, and I do want to feel that Richard's future is assured. When I am able to get up to London I shall go and see Morlock² or somebody and get an expert opinion on how long I am likely to live. It is a thing doctors usually will not tell you, but it affects my plans, for future books as well as for Richard.

Richard was extremely well when I came away, and is evidently enjoying himself with the spring ploughing etc. He really seems quite fond of farm work. I have been trying to think what to give him for his birthday next month. I suppose he is almost old enough to have a pocket knife, but somehow I don't fancy the idea. Avril says he has found out about money, ie. knows you can get sweets³ for it, so I have started him on regular pocket money, which I hope may teach him the days of the week. I am going to get her to bring him down here to see me, but it is no use till I am out of bed.

I am not doing any work at present. I have cancelled everything, but I hope to start again next month. My new book is coming out in June, here and in the USA. I had a line from Doreen and George [Kopp*] announcing their new baby, but otherwise haven't heard from them. Please remember me to the kids.

Yours
George

[XX, 3601, pp. 90–2; typewritten]

1. Orwell made a new will on 18 January 1950, before the flight he hoped to make to Switzerland. At probate Orwell's estate was valued at £9,908 14s 11d. He was owed £520 he had lent to friends. Of course his royalties proved to be – and continue to be – considerable. For his will and estate (see XX, 3730, pp. 235–7).

2. Dr H. V. Morlock, the specialist whom Orwell had consulted before the war.

3. Sweets and chocolate were still rationed when Orwell wrote, but just one week later restrictions were lifted. Unfortunately, this freedom did not last long.

Confectionery was rationed again (4 ounces per week) on 14 July, the sugar ration was cut to 8 ounces, and tobacco imports were reduced.

To Sir Richard Rees*

25 April 1949
[The Cotswold Sanatorium]
Cranham

Dear Richard,

Thanks for your letter. I have been sort of up & down in health but on the whole am a little better, I think. I still can't make any plans, but if I am up & about for the winter, I thought it might not be a bad idea to go abroad somewhere, & Orlando¹ (I don't know if you know him, he writes for the *Observer* sometimes) suggested Capri as a good place to stay. It sounds as if it would have good food & wine, & Silone,² who is a friend of mine & lives there, would no doubt be able to arrange somewhere for me to stay. Any way it's worth thinking over. The Tawneys came in the other day. I think they're going back to London almost immediately, so I'm afraid I may not see them again. For little Richard's birthday, Inez [Holden] is going to try & get me one of those children's typewriters you see advertised now, if not too impossibly expensive. I thought if he could be kept from smashing it, it would come in useful when he begins to learn his letters in earnest, & it would also keep him off my typewriter. The Tawneys took that book of yours³ I had & are going to send it to you. When Brenda [Salkeld] comes I am going to get her to make up some parcels for me & send home some of the books, which are piling up fearfully. I still can't do any work. Some days I take pen & paper & try to write a few lines, but it's impossible. When you are in this state you have the impression that your brain is working normally until you try to put words together, & then you find that you have acquired a sort of awful heaviness & clumsiness, as well as inability to concentrate for more than a few seconds. I am reading *Mr Sponge's Sporting Tour*, which I had never read before. I don't think it's as good as *Handley Cross*. I also recently re-read *Little Dorrit*⁴ for the first time in a good many years. It's a dull book in a way, but it contains a really subtle character, William Dorrit, quite unlike most of Dickens's people. Someone in the USA has managed to get me a copy of Gissing's *New Grub Street* at last. Don't lose *The Odd Women*, will you.

Yours
Eric

[XX, 3607, pp. 97–98; handwritten]

L. Ruggiero Orlando (1907–1994), journalist, broadcaster, poet, and critic. His passionate, slightly anarchic political views led to his fleeing Italy in 1939 for Britain. He was engaged by the BBC to broadcast in its external service and did so with great success, achieving a legendary status with colleagues and listeners. After the war he worked for RAI, the Italian state broadcasting service, and was its correspondent in the United States for eighteen years. He returned to Italy in 1972 and was elected to the Chamber of Deputies. He was, when in England, a frequent contributor to *Poetry Today*, and he translated Dylan Thomas into Italian.

2. Ignazio Silone (1900–1978), Italian novelist. In his essay on Arthur Koestler, Orwell claimed that there had been nothing in English writing to resemble Silone's *Fontamara* (1933; English translation, 1934) or Koestler's *Darkness at Noon* (1940): 'there is almost no English writer to whom it has happened to see totalitarianism from the inside.'

3. Probably David Jones's *In Parenthesis*. (See letter to Sir Richard Rees, **18.1.49**, n. 2.)

4. Orwell's list of his reading for April 1949 includes Dickens's *Little Dorrit* and Surtees's *Mr Sponge's Sporting Tour*.

To S. M. Levitas

2 May 1949
The Cotswold Sanatorium,
Cranham

Dear Mr Levitas,[1]

Many thanks for your letter of the 21st April. I will do something for you later when I can, but I really am most deadly ill & quite unable to work, & I don't know how soon this state of affairs will change. I don't want any payment & certainly not Care packages – the truth is I have no appetite & can't eat the food I am given already. But next time I do something for you I'll ask you to pay me by sending one of the books I see advertised in American papers & which one can't get over here.

The above address will continue to find me, I'm afraid.

Yours sincerely
Geo. Orwell

[XX, 3616, p. 104; handwritten]

1. S. M. Levitas (1894–1961) was the editor of the long-running left-wing periodical, *The New Leader*, New York. It closed down in 2006. He replied to Orwell on 3 June saying how willing he was to get 'any and every book which you would like'. However, he seemed oblivious to Orwell's repeated protestations that he was very

ill and continued to harass him. On this occasion, despite Orwell's description of his sickness, he asked for 'an original piece' and also to write a 'Guest Columnist Editorial' of one thousand words 'on any subject you desire'.

To Sir Richard Rees*

2 May 1949
[The Cotswold Sanatorium]
Cranham

Dear Richard,

I have to hand-write because there is a patient further down the row who is *in articulo mortis*,[1] or thinks she is, & the typewriter worries her.

About this business of Barnhill etc. I cannot make any real plans until I know if & when I shall get out of bed, but the governing facts are:
1. I can't in future spend the winters in Jura.
2. Richard must go to school next year, which means somebody being with him, as I don't want him to go to a boarding school till he is at any rate 10.
3. I don't want to disrupt the Barnhill ménage.
4. Avril will probably want to stay on at Barnhill, & Bill in any case couldn't get on without her, or without some female helper.

All this being so, it seems to me that if I am in circulation again later this year, I had best go abroad or somewhere like Brighton for the winter, & then next spring set up a second establishment in London or Edinburgh where I can have Richard with me & where he can go to day-school. He can spend his holidays in Jura, & I hope I shall be able to spend my summers there as well. This will mean having another nurse-maid or housekeeper or something. However, *provided* I can work I can easily earn enough money for this; in any case it was agreed between Avril & me that if she stopped looking after R. I should reduce the amount I paid her. If I remain bedridden, or at any rate have to remain under medical care, which I suppose is a possibility, I shall move to a sanatorium somewhere near London, where it is easier for friends & business associates to come & see me, & set up an establishment for Richard near there, with a housekeeper or something. That is as much as I can plan at present.

Thanks so much for drying off all the books. I don't agree with you about *The Great Gatsby*—I was rather disappointed by it. It seemed to me to lack point,[2] & *Tender is the Night*, which I read recently, even more so.[3] I've just read Geoffrey Gorer's book on the Americans—very amusing & shallow, as usual. I've at last got hold of May Sinclair's *The Combined Maze*—a forgotten good bad novel which I've been trying to get a copy of for years. I must get some more books rebound before long. Re my unsuccessful efforts to get Gissing reprinted, it's struck me that the Everyman Library might do one of them. They have no Gissing on their list. I wonder how one approaches them, & whether there is a string one can pull.

In spite of his chumminess with 'Zilli'[4] (who he of course thinks can help him in his political career), I don't believe Mikardo is a crypto. Apart from other things, if he were a crypto, Michael Foot[5] would probably know it & wouldn't have him on *Tribune*. They got rid of Edelmann°[6] for that reason. It's of course true that 'objectively' people like Laski[7] are a lot more useful to the Russians than the overt Communists, just as it is true that 'objectively' a pacifist is pro-war & pro-militarist. But it seems to me very important to attempt to gauge people's *subjective* feelings, because otherwise one can't predict their behaviour in situations where the results of certain actions are clear even to a self-deceiver. Suppose for example that Laski had possession of an important military secret. Would he betray it to the Russian military intelligence? I don't imagine so, because he has not actually made up his mind to be a traitor, & the nature of what he was doing would in that case be quite clear. But a real Communist would, of course, hand the secret over without any sense of guilt, & so would a real crypto, such as Pritt. The whole difficulty is to decide where each person stands, & one has to treat each case individually.

The weather has rather gone off here. I sat outside in a deck chair one or two days, but latterly it's been too cold. A man came from the *E[vening]. Standard* to 'interview' me,[8] rather an intimidating experience, also Paul Potts,[9] who has just got back from Palestine, together with the wife of A. J. P. Taylor,[10] the chap who turned traitor at the Wroclaw conference. I gather from her that Taylor has since turned a good deal more anti-CP.

Yours
Eric

[XX, 3617, pp. 104–6; handwritten]

1. 'at the moment of death'.
2. Orwell's letter has been annotated here, 'NO!'
3. Orwell's letter has been annotated here, 'Yes.'
4. Konni Zilliacus (see **2.1.48**, n. 5).
5. Michael Foot (see **31.3.46**, n. 2).
6. Maurice Edelman (1911–1975), educated at Trinity College, Cambridge, entered the plywood business which led to visits to the USSR, about which he then wrote. He was a war correspondent in North Africa and in Normandy and a Labour MP in 1945, re-elected in 1950.
7. Harold Laski (see **20.9.47**, n. 1).

8.   Charles Curran, who 'tired me so . . . arguing about politics' (see **16.5.49**).

9.   Paul Potts (see letters to Humphrey Dakin of **1.7.46**, n. 5 and to Sally McEwan of **5.7.46**, n. 1).

10. A. J. P. Taylor (1906–1990), historian and journalist. At this time he was Tutor in Modern History, Magdalen College, Oxford (to 1963); Fellow, 1938–76. He wrote prolifically and authoritatively (if not always uncontroversially), especially on Germany and World Wars I and II. The Wroclaw Conference was a Communist-front Conference of Intellectuals, August 1948, attended by scientists, writers, and cultural leaders from forty countries. It passed a resolution condemning the revival of Fascism. The conference backfired on the organisers; some participants saw through the proceedings, Taylor among them, and walked out.

To Fredric Warburg*

16 May 1949
Cranham

Dear Fred,

Thanks so much for your letter. As she may have told you, I had to put Sonia Brownell* off. I am in most ghastly health, & have been for some weeks. I am due for another X-ray picture, but for some days I have been too feverish to go over to the X-ray room & stand up against the screen. When the picture is taken, I am afraid there is not much doubt it will show that both lungs have deteriorated badly. I asked the doctor recently whether she[1] thought I would survive, & she wouldn't go further than saying she didn't know. If the 'prognosis' after this photo is bad, I shall get a second opinion. Can you give me the name of that specialist you mentioned? Then I will suggest either him or Dr. Morlock, another specialist whom I consulted before the war. They can't *do* anything, as I am not a case for operation, but I would like an expert opinion on how long I am likely to stay alive. I do hope people won't now start chasing me to go to Switzerland, which is supposed to have magical qualities. I don't believe it makes any difference where you are, & a journey would be the death of me. The one chance of surviving, I imagine, is to keep quiet. Don't think I am making up my mind to peg out. On the contrary, I have the strongest reasons for wanting to stay alive. But I want to get a clear idea of *how long* I am likely to last, & not just be jollied along the way doctors usually do.

Yes, do come & see me. I hope & trust by the beginning of June I may be a bit better, at any rate less feverish. I am glad *1984* has done so well before publication. The *World Review* published a most stupid extract, abridged in such a way as to make nonsense of it.[2] I wouldn't have let Moore arrange this if I'd known they meant to hack it about. However I suppose it's advertisement.

That *Evening Standard* man, Mr. Curran, came to interview me, & had arranged to come again, but I'm thinking of putting him off, because he tired me so last time, arguing about politics. Please give everyone my love.

Yours
George

[XX, 3626, pp. 116–17; handwritten]

1. Dr Margaret Kirkman, one of the two resident physicians at Cranham.
2. 'A Look into the Future: 1984 and *Newspeak*', an insensitive abridgement of the Appendix to *Nineteen Eighty-Four*, *World Review*, May 1949.

To David Astor*

20 May 1949
Cranham Lodge[1]
Cranham
Gloucester

Dear David,

Thanks so much for your letter. Do come on Sunday the 29th. I'll look forward to seeing you both. If you can, let me know beforehand time of arrival, so that I can arrange for the car. Better have lunch here, if you arrive in time (it's quite eatable.)

I have been absolutely ghastly. I am getting a second opinion, a London specialist, supposed to be very good. Of course they can't actually do anything but I don't want to feel I'm letting my case go by default, also a specialist called in for one consultation might be willing to give an expert opinion on whether I'm likely to stay alive, the thing most doctors will only hum & haw about.

I'm arranging for Richard to come & stay near here, near Stroud. I suppose it will take weeks to fix up, but it's quite a good arrangement, the people he is going to stay with have 2 children, & he can go to kindergarten with them & come over & see me in the afternoons sometimes.

Yours
George

[XX, 3628, p. 118; handwritten]

1. Orwell was writing on headed notepaper that referred to the sanatorium as Cranham Lodge.

To Jacintha Buddicom*

22 May 1949
Cranham Lodge
Cranham

Dear Jacintha,

Thanks so much for your letter, I'd have written before, but I've been most horribly ill & am not very grand now. I can't write much of a letter because it tires me to sit up. Thanks awfully for the offer, but I am generally pretty well supplied with books & things. It looks as if I am going to be in bed for months yet. I have sent for my little boy to come & stay with friends near by. I think he'll like it, & as he is now 5 he can perhaps start going to day school. I hope to see you when I am in Town if I ever am.

Yours
Eric

[XX, 3631, pp. 119–20; handwritten]

This is the last of Orwell's letters to Jacintha Buddicom to survive. She replied on 2 June, and he wrote again on the 8th. Both letters have been lost, but she describes Orwell's letter in Eric & Us: *'My diary records: "Letter from Eric about Nothing Ever Dies." As I remember . . . it defined his faith in some sort of after-life. Not necessarily, or even probably, a conventional Heaven-or-Hell, but the firm belief that "nothing ever dies", and that we must go on somewhere. And it ended with our old ending,* Farewell and Hail. *He probably wrote it because I had told him that my mother was ill: though I had not stressed this unduly, since he was in such poor health himself' (p. 157).*

To Sonia Brownell*

24 May 1949
Cranham Lodge
Cranham

Dear Sonia,

I was so very sorry to put you off, but at the time I was in a ghastly state. Now I seem to be somewhat better. I do hope you'll come & see me soon. Any day would suit me except the day you think Cyril [Connolly*] might be coming, on the 29th, when I think someone else is coming. But any way when & if you can come let me know in advance because of ordering a car.

I've just had what is called a 'second opinion', incidentally the doctor who attended D. H. Lawrence in his last illness.[1] He says I'm not so bad & have a good chance of surviving, but it means keeping quiet & doing no work for a long time, possibly a year or more. I don't mind very much if I could then get well enough to do say another 5 years° work. Richard is coming down soon to stay near here. He will start going to kindergarten school in the mornings, & can sometimes come over & see me in the afternoons.

Please give everyone my love. By the way I cut the enclosed out of the *N. Y. Times*. If you see Stephen [Spender*] tell him to get another photo taken, for the honour of English letters. Looking forward to seeing you.

With love
George

[XX, 3633, p. 120; handwritten]

1.   Dr Andrew Morland.

To Sir Richard Rees*

1 June 1949
Cranham Lodge
Cranham

Dear Richard,

Thanks so much for your letter. Avril & R[ichard] arrived on Saturday & I think he's settling in all right. I hope to see him once or twice this week. He seemed to me to have grown (his weight is now 3st 5lb.) & to be extremely fit.[1] I think Avril returns to Jura on today's boat, but I am not certain.

I have been a good bit better this last week, & after seeing my last plate they decided I am not so bad as they thought. Dr. Morland said the same, but he said I shall have to keep still for a long time, possibly as long as a year (I trust it won't be so long as that) & not attempt to work till I am definitely better. Another doctor[2] whom David Astor brought along, although a psychologist, said much the same as the others.

I enclose a copy of that article I wanted you to read.[3] The magazine itself seemed quite unprocurable, but someone managed to get it typed out. Actually some of what I said in it I also said appropos° of Gandhi. I've just read the 4th vol. of Osbert Sitwell's memoirs—not so good as some of the others, I think. I know nothing about Goethe, nor indeed about any German writer. I'm trying to read Henry James's *The Spoils of Poynton*, but it bores me unbearably. Also read a short book by Rex Warner *Why was I killed?*—very silly, I thought.

So looking forward to seeing you.

Yours
G

[XX, 3638, pp. 124–5; handwritten]

1. Richard stayed at Whiteway (see letter to Sir Richard Rees of **17.4.49**, n. 2). In *Remembering Orwell*, Richard Blair recalls: 'When I saw my father at Cranham I used to say, "Where does it hurt, Daddy?" because I couldn't understand why he said it didn't hurt, but he was in bed. I couldn't relate to that at all' (p. 203).
2. Unidentified.
3. 'Lear, Tolstoy and the Fool', *Polemic*, March 1947 (XIX, 3181, pp. 54–67).

To Anthony Powell*

6 June 1949
Cranham Lodge
Cranham

Dear Tony,

Thanks ever so for sending me the 'Aubrey' book. I'm so glad you *did* put in my favourite Mrs Overall after all, also the story about Sir W. Raleigh & his son. I was so sorry about Hugh Kingsmill.² If they are trying to get a pension for his widow, if my signature would be useful in any way, of course include me. I'm a good deal better, & trust this will continue. I had a specialist from London, who said much the same as the people here, ie. that if I get round *this* corner I could be good for quite a few years, but that I have got to keep quiet & not try to work for a long time, possibly as long as a year or two years—I trust it won't be as long as that. It's a great bore, but worth while if it means I can work again later. Richard is staying nearby for the summer, & comes over & sees me once or twice a week. Please remember me to everybody. I hope you & Malcolm [Muggeridge] will come & see me some time—but of course don't put yourselves out. I know what a tiresome journey it must be.

Yours
George

P.S. I'm reading Dante! (with a crib of course.)

[XX, 3641, p. 126; handwritten]

1. *Brief Lives and Other Selected Writings of John Aubrey*, edited by Anthony Powell (1949).

2.   Hugh Kingsmill (= Hugh Kingsmill Lunn, 1889–1949), critic, editor and anthol-
ogist. In his *Progress of a Biographer* (1949), Kingsmill wrote that *Animal Farm*
'revealed the poetry, humour and tenderness' of Orwell.

To William Phillips

8 June 1949
Cranham Lodge
Cranham

Dear Mr Phillips,[1]

I received your letter of the 2nd today. I need hardly tell you that I am
delighted as well as very much astonished at your picking me out for the
Partisan Review Award. It is the kind of honour I am quite unused to. Perhaps
you will convey my thanks to the rest of the Advisory Board. I will not tell
anyone about it until you make the announcement.

I will send you something when I can, but I have done no work since
December & may not be able to work for a long time to come. The doctors
tell me the best chance of recovery is to lie in bed & do nothing, possibly for
as long as another year—I hope it won't be as long as that, of course.

With very many thanks again, & best wishes to everybody.

Yours sincerely
Geo. Orwell

[XX, 3644, p. 130; handwritten]

1.   Co-editor with Philip Rahv* of *Partisan Review*.

To Julian Symons*

16 June 1949
Cranham Lodge
Cranham

Dear Julian,

I think it was you who reviewed *1984* in the *T.L.S.*[1] I must thank you for such a
brilliant as well as generous review. I don't think you could have brought out
the sense of the book better in so short a space. You are of course right about
the vulgarity of the 'Room 101' business. I was aware of this while writing it,
but I didn't know another way of getting somewhere near the effect I wanted.

I have been horribly ill since last seeing you, but a lot better in the last few
weeks, & I hope perhaps now I have turned the corner. The various doctors

I have seen are all quite encouraging but say I must remain quiet & not work for a long time, possibly as much as a year—I hope it won't be so long, of course. It's a bore, but worth while if it means recovering. Richard is staying nearby for the summer & comes & sees me every week. He has started kindergarten school & this winter is going to the village school in Jura, I don't know for how long. I have been thinking about Westminster for him when he is older. They have abandoned their top hats, I learn. It is a day school, which I prefer, & I think has other good points. Any way I'm going to make enquiries & put his name down if it seems suitable. Of course god° knows what will have happened by then, say 1956, but one has to plan as though nothing would change drastically.

Have you any news of the Empsons,[2] who were in Pekin°? I don't know whether you knew them. There have been various rumours, & I am trying to get some news from Empson's American publishers.

Did you read Ruth Fischer's book *Stalin & German Communism*? She's coming to see me tomorrow, I think.

Hope all is well & baby flourishing. Please remember me to your wife.

Yours
George

[XX, 3647, p. 137; handwritten]

1. The review had appeared in *The Times Literary Supplement* on 10 June 1949.
2. William Empson (see **11.7.43**, n. 7).

To Jordi Arquer*

22 June 1949
Cranham Lodge
Cranham

Dear Comrade,

Please forgive me for writing in English. Very many thanks for sending the press-cuttings.

I am & have been for a long time seriously ill with tuberculosis, & the doctors forbid me to do any work for a time to come, possibly as long as a year. In connection with the Federacion Española de Internados y Deportados, therefore, I cannot give more than my nominal support. If you wish merely to use my <u>name</u>, you are at liberty to do so, & I could manage a small subscription, say £10,[1] if you can indicate someone in England where I can pay it to. But I cannot do any work such as writing letters, organising, speaking, etc. I am sorry, but I must try to recover from this disease, & the only way of doing so is to rest. I imagine that I shall not even be allowed to leave my bed for some months to come.

I am instructing my agent to send you copies of the Italian translation of *Homage to Catalonia* & of the *Observer* of the 27th February. Please let me know if they do not arrive, & forgive me for not being more helpful. Please forgive also the bad handwriting, but I am writing this in bed.

Yours fraternally
Geo. Orwell.

[*LO*, p. 121; XX, 3650A, p. 140; handwritten]

1.   £10 may not sound very much but its present-day value is roughly twenty-five times greater than in 1949. In that year I was paid just under £5 a week for editing a magazine about railways.

To David Astor*

18 July 1949
Cranham Lodge
Cranham

Dear David,

I wonder how you are getting on. I was slightly dismayed to hear from Charoux[1] that you were getting along 'as well as can be expected.' I had thought the operation you were having was something very minor.[2] Let me know how you are when you get a chance to write.

Richard went back to Jura yesterday, as he is going to the village school at Ardlussa for the Xmas term & it starts at the end of this month. He enjoyed himself at the kindergarten & had a good report, I am glad to say, though I didn't notice that he learned very much.

I have been so-so, up & down. I get what they call flare-ups, ie. periods with high temperatures & so on, but on the whole I am better I think. I have got Morland, the specialist, coming to see me again next week. When I am well & about again, some time next year perhaps, I intend getting married again. I suppose everyone will be horrified, but it seems to me a good idea. Apart from other considerations, I think I should stay alive longer if I were married & had someone to look after me. It is to Sonia Brownell, the sub-editor of *Horizon*, I can't remember whether you know her, but you probably do.

It is evident that I shall be under medical care for a long time yet, & I shan't even be able to get out of bed until I stop being feverish. Later on I might move to a sanatorium nearer London, & Morland may have some ideas about that, but at present I don't think I could face a journey.

Have you read *The Naked & the Dead*?[3] It's awfully good, the best war book of the last war yet.

Write when you can.

Yours
George

[XX, 3661, pp. 147–8; handwritten]

1. Charoux was a picture-framer and restorer (see **19.11.48**).
2. Astor's operation was relatively minor but very painful.
3. By Norman Mailer (1948).

To Leonard Moore*

20 July 1949
Cranham Lodge
Cranham

Dear Moore,

Recently some Russian DPs who run a Russian-language paper called POSSEV in Frankfurt sent me a file of the papers containing a Russian translation of *Animal Farm*.[1] They want to issue it as a booklet and say, what is no doubt true, that it would be quite easy for them to get a few thousand copies of it through the Iron Curtain, I suppose via Berlin and Vienna. Of course I am willing enough for them to do this, but it will cost money, ie. for the printing and binding. They want 2000 deutsch° marks, which represents about £155. This is more than I can pay out of my own pocket, but I wouldn't mind contributing something. As a start it occurs to me that the American army magazine *Der Monat* must owe me something.[2] There was their serialisation of *A.F.*, but in addition there was a mix-up about a previous article (reprinted from *Commentary*) which I believe has never been paid for. They sent some kind of official form which I thought was the cheque, and I believe I incorrectly told Melvyn Lasky, the editor, that I had received the cheque. Their bank account would show whether the money has actually been paid over. But any way, if *Der Monat* do owe me something which they have not yet paid to you, it would be a convenient way of financing the Russian translation of *A.F.* if they paid the money over in marks which wouldn't have to leave Germany. I can't remember whether there is anything else of mine appearing in Germany, but at any rate, could you let me know how many marks you think I could realise there? In the case of our carrying through any transaction of this kind, naturally you will draw your commission as usual.[3]

I am also trying to pull a wire at the Foreign Office to see if they will subscribe a bit. I'm afraid it's not likely. They will throw millions down the drain on useless radio propaganda,[4] but not finance books.

If all this comes to anything we shall have to make sure that these *Possev* people are O.K. and not just working a swindle. Their notepaper etc. looks all right, and I know the translation must be a good one as it was made by Gleb Struve whom I know well. They gave me as the address of their English agent Mr Lew Rahr, 18 Downs Road, Beckenham, Kent, and suggested he should come and see me. I don't think I want to see him at this stage, but do you think you could write to him, say tentatively that we are trying to get this scheme financed and see from his answer whether he seems O.K. I have also asked a friend who is I think in Frankfurt[5] to contact the *Possev* people.

Yours sincerely
Eric Blair

[XX, 3662, pp. 148–9; typewritten]

1. Vladimir Gorachek, who described himself as the 'Authorized DP-Publisher' of *Possev* (the subtitle of which was 'Social and Political Review in Russian Language. Germany'), wrote to Orwell on 16 July 1949 with proposals for publishing *Animal Farm* in Russian for distribution gratis among Russian readers behind the Iron Curtain. It was planned to distribute the books through Berlin and Vienna 'and other channels further E[a]st'. The cost of distribution was to be met from selling 1,000 to 1,200 copies in West Germany. Gorachek apologised for the fact that an earlier letter had been written in Russian: 'We thought that such a perfect understanding of all events occurred° in our country after the revolution and of the very substance of the regime now established there could not be acquired without the knowledge of Russian language.'

2. Annotated in Moore's office: 'Paid £50 for *A.F.*'

3. Annotated in Moore's office: '£250 owing from U.S. Army 1984.' This was money due for the serialisation of *Nineteen Eighty-Four* in *Der Monat*, November 1949 to March 1950.

4. The Foreign Office made no contribution; 'useless radio propaganda' is doubtless based on Orwell's experience during his 'two wasted years' at the BBC.

5. Ruth Fischer.

To Leonard Moore*

21 July 1949[1]
Cranham Lodge,
Cranham

Dear Moore,

Thank you for two letters date the 19th, with various enclosures.

I enclose the photostats of the McGill article. I don't object to its being published in this form *provided it is stated that this is an abridgement* (they needn't of course say why it has been abridged.)[2] Could you please make this clear to Harcourt Brace?

I am of course very pleased about the NBC broadcast of *1984*,[3] & the serialisation in *Der Monat*. This last would at need solve the difficulty I wrote to you about yesterday, of getting some marks to pay for the Russian translation of *Animal Farm*. Of course I'm not going to pay this myself if I can help it, but I haven't very great hopes of the government coming to my aid. Meanwhile, could you ask the editor of *Der Monat* to hold over the necessary sum (2000 deutsch° marks) in case we want to disburse it in Germany. The editor, Melvyn Lasky, would be sympathetic to this idea & can no doubt make the necessary arrangements. As I said before, your commission will not be affected by this.

Yours sincerely
Eric Blair[4]

[XX, 3663, pp. 149–50; handwritten]

1. This letter was dated 20.9.49 but is date-stamped as having been received in Moore's office on 22 July 1949. The month is clearly incorrect, and Orwell seems also to have misdated the day of the month, since he refers to 'the difficulty I wrote to you about yesterday'.

2. 'The Art of Donald McGill', *Horizon*, September 1941 (XX, 850, pp. 23-31), was published in an abridged form in *A Writer's Reader*, edited by P. W. Souers and others (New York, 1950).

3. Broadcast 27 August 1949 in NBC University Theatre with David Niven as Winston Smith. The excellent dramatisation was by Milton Wayne. The novelist, James Hilton (1900–54), provided an interval commentary. The presenter described it as the 'current and widely discussed novel'. A CD of the broadcast was made available by the Old Time Radio Club, 2007.

4. A postscript refers to two slight proof corrections.

To Jack Common*

27 July 1949
Cranham Lodge
Cranham

Dear Jack,

Herewith cheque for £50—reply if when° you can, no hurry.

This place is a sanatorium. I've been under treatment for TB for the better part of 2 years, all of this year here, & half of last year in a hospital near Glasgow. Of course I've had it coming to me all my life. The only real treatment, it seems, is rest, so I've got to do damn-all, including not trying to work for a long time, possibly as long as a year or two, though I trust it won't be quite as bad as that. It's an awful bore, but I am obeying orders, as I do want to stay alive at least 10 years, I've got such a lot of work to do besides Richard to look after.

Richard is now 5 & very big & strong. He's been spending the summer here, so that I can see him every week, & going to kindergarten school, but shortly he's going back home so that he can start attending the village school in the winter term. We've lived since 1946 in Jura,¹ but I'm afraid I personally shall only be able to spend the summers there from now on, because it's too remote & inconvenient in the winter for a semi-invalid. I suppose Richard, too, will have to start going to school on the mainland before long, as you can imagine what a village school in the Hebrides is like. So I shall probably have to have some sort of establishment in London or Edinburgh or somewhere— however, I can't make plans till I know when I shall be on my feet again. I'm glad to hear you've been so philoprogenitive, or at any rate, progenitive.

I haven't ever remarried, though I sometimes think I would if I could get some of my health back.² Richard Rees spends part of each year with us in Jura as he is sort of partner with the chap who farms the croft our house is on. Otherwise he is more & more wrapped up in painting.³

All the best
Eric

[XX, 3666, pp. 151–2; handwritten]

1. Common had evidently not been in contact with Orwell for some time. The amount lent to Common remained unpaid at Orwell's death.
2. Orwell suggests, contrary to what happened, that he might remarry if his health improved.
3. One of Rees's paintings of Barnhill is held in the Orwell Archive.

To Sir Richard Rees*

27 July 1949
Cranham Lodge
Cranham

Dear Richard,

Thanks so much for your letter, with cutting. Do you think you could get your Mr Roberts to make me a bookcase, same dimensions as yours but 5' feet° wide, if he can manage it. If, as I assume, it will be of white wood, I suppose it should be stained or painted, I don't much mind which, except that if painted I think off-white is the best colour. I'd be much obliged if you could get him to do this & send it up to Barnhill.

I think you'll find at Barnhill one novel by Charles Williams, called *The Place of the Lion*[1] or something like that (published by Gollancz.) He's quite unreadable, one of those writers who just go on & on & have no idea of selecting. I think Eliot's approval of him must be purely sectarian (Anglo-Catholic). It wouldn't surprise me to learn that Eliot approves of C.S. Lewis as well. The more I see the more I doubt whether people ever really make aesthetic judgements at all. Everything is judged on political grounds which are then given an aesthetic disguise. When, for instance, Eliot can't see anything good in Shelley or anything bad in Kipling, the real underlying reason must be that the one is a radical & the other a conservative, of sorts. Yet evidently one does have aesthetic reactions, especially as a lot of art & even literature is politically neutral, & also certain unmistakeable° standards do exist, e.g. Homer is better than Edgar Wallace. Perhaps the way we should put it is: the more one is aware of political bias the more one can be independent of it, & the more one claims to be impartial the more one is biassed.

1984 has had good reviews in the USA, such as I have seen of them, but of course also some very shame-making publicity. You'll be glad to hear *Animal Farm* has been translated into Russian at last, in a D.P. paper in Frankfurt. I'm trying to arrange for it to be done in book form.

Yours
Eric

[XX, 3669, p. 154; handwritten]

1. Charles Williams (1886–1945), poet, novelist, dramatist, and writer on theological subjects. He worked for the Oxford University Press for much of his life.

To Fredric Warburg*

22 August 1949
Cranham Lodge
Cranham

Dear Fred,

Could you please send one copy each of *Burmese Days* & *Coming Up for Air* to Sonia Brownell, care of *Horizon*.

I have Morland coming to see me again this evening. On & off I have been feeling absolutely ghastly. It comes & goes, but I have periodical bouts of high temperatures etc. I will tell you what Morland says. Richard has just gone back to Jura & is going to the village school for the winter term. Beyond that I can't make plans for the moment. I have put him down for Westminster, but he wouldn't be going there till 1957, heaven knows what may have happened by then. As I warned you I might do, I intend getting married again (to Sonia) when I am once again in the land of the living, if I ever am. I suppose everyone will be horrified, but apart from other considerations I really think I should stay alive longer if I were married.

I have sketched out the book of essays I would like to publish next year, but I want it to include two long new essays, on Joseph Conrad and George Gissing, & of course I can't touch those till I am definitively better.

Love to all
George

[XX, 3678, p.159–60; handwritten]

To Sir Richard Rees*

30 August 1949
Cranham Lodge
Cranham

Dear Richard,

I am removing to a London hospital on September 3rd, and my address will be: Private Wing, University College Hospital, Gower Street, London, W.C.1. This is Morland's own hospital and the idea is that I shall go there probably for about two months. I don't think you need fear my having too many visitors—in fact it may be easier to keep them off in London where people don't have to come for the whole day.

Of course its° perfectly O.K. about the old Austin. Anything you can get for her should go towards the jeep. As to the motor boat it seems to me that it would be a good idea to leave her in the boat-yard at Ardrishaig for the winter unless they need her at Barnhill. I suppose you can do that with boats like leaving a car in a garage, and then next year it would be in good order when we picked it up.

I am going to send on the remaining books I have here. Could you be kind enough to see that the magazines etc., go in the right place. There are various bundles of papers which I have asked Avril to put in my desk upstairs.

I hope the harvest is going O.K. Avril told me she had started, or was starting another pig. If nothing has been decided yet you might suggest to Avril to think seriously about a sow which I am very in favour of, and would willingly pay the initial costs of. The only difficulty is about getting her to a hog once a year. I suppose one would buy a gravid sow in the Autumn to litter about March, but one would have to make very sure that she really was in pig the first time.

Do make Bill go to the dentist. It is nonsense to put it off when they can come across in the boat and go to Lochgilphead. He was already having trouble with that tooth when I came away in January, and at the last moment refused to go to Glasgow.

Love to all,
Eric

[XX, 3684, pp. 163–4; typewritten]

To David Astor*

5 September 1949
U.C.H.[1]

Dear David,

Thanks ever so for sending those beautiful crysanths° & the box of peaches that actually met me on my arrival here. I feel ghastly & can't write much, but we had a wonderful journey down yesterday in the most ritzy ambulance you can imagine. This beastly fever never seems to go away but is better some days than others, & I really quite enjoyed the drive down.

What a bastard that doctor[2] must have been. It seems that there's a regular tradition of withholding anaesthetics & analgesics & that it is particularly bad in England. I know Americans are often astonished by the tortures people are made to go through here.

I hope you're feeling better & that soon you will be able to meet Sonia. Morland says I mustn't see people much, but here in London it's easier for people to just look in for half an hour, which they hardly can at Cranham. Sonia lives only a few minutes away from here. She thinks we might as well get married while I am still an invalid, because it would give her a better status to look after me especially if, eg., I went somewhere abroad after leaving here. It's an idea, but I think I should have to feel a little less ghastly than at present before I could even face a registrar for 10 minutes. I am much encouraged by none of my friends or relatives seeming to disapprove of my remarrying, in spite of this disease. I had had an uneasy feeling that 'they' would converge from all directions & stop me, but it hasn't happened. Morland, the doctor, is very much in favour of it.

I remember visiting you when you had the sinus but I didn't know it was this hospital. It seems very comfortable & easy-going here. Can't write more.

Yours
George

[XX, 3686, p. 165; handwritten]

1. University College Hospital, a major teaching hospital in London, WC1.
2. The doctor attending Astor.

To Sir Richard Rees*

17 September 1949
Room 65 Private Wing
U.C. Hospital
Gower St WC 1

Dear Richard,

Thanks so much for seeing about the boat & for re-arranging my books. I suppose by the way they'll send on the bill for the bookcases to you—if so, forward it to me, won't you.°

It's all right about the literary executorship. You & Sonia wouldn't quarrel about anything. Some time I'll have to make another will, & then I'll regularise it.

I am getting on quite well & have felt distinctly better since being here. The only new treatment they have done to me is to make me lie all night & part of the day with my feet higher than my head. Sonia comes & sees me for an hour every day & otherwise I am allowed one visitor for 20 minutes. Sonia thinks that when I am a little better it would be a good idea for us to get married while I am still in hospital, which would make it easier for her to accompany me wherever I have to go afterwards. Someone, I think Fred Warburg, told the press about this & there was some rather nasty publicity.[1]

I'm afraid I haven't a copy of Trilling's review of 1984.[2] The only copy I had was among some press cuttings I sent up to Barnhill. I've just had back that picture that went to be restored.[3] He's made a beautiful job of it, & it is almost like a new picture. Apparently they can lift a picture right off & stick it onto a new piece of canvas. I have another old picture which I thought was past praying for, as the canvas is sort of moth eaten, but perhaps this chap could do something with it. He also put the picture in a quite nice new frame, & only charged 12 guineas for the whole job.

Things seem to be going O.K. at Barnhill. R[ichard] evidently hasn't started going to school yet, as Mrs Angus [4] was ill. He sent me a 'letter' which showed that he knows at any rate 12 letters of the alphabet. Unless I am out of England by then, I will have him down for the Xmas holidays, & then he can start getting to know Sonia a bit better. I do not think there need be any complications about his upbringing. We have agreed that if I should die in the near future, even if I were already married, Avril shall be his guardian. Beyond that I can't make plans at present.

Yours
Eric

[XX, 3692, pp. 168–9; handwritten]

1.   In *The Star* (one of the then three London evening papers) and *Daily Mail,* 17 September 1949.
2.   The review by Lionel Trilling (1905–1975) appeared in *The New Yorker,* 18 June 1949. He praised the 'intensity and passion' of this 'momentous book' (Crick, p. 564).
3.   Mr Charoux, the picture-restorer recommended by Rees. (See **19.11.48.**)
4.   Presumably the teacher on Jura.

Arthur Koestler* to Orwell

24 September 1949

My dear George,

I thought that Mamaine had written to you and Mamaine thought that I had written to you, hence the delay. I was extremely happy to hear that you are going to marry Sonia. I have been saying for years that she is the nicest, most intelligent and decent girl that I met during my whole stay in England. She is precisely for this reason also very lonely in that crowd in which she moves and she will become a changed person when you take her out of it. I think I had a closer view of the Connolly set-up than you did; it has a steady stultifying effect which left its mark even on a tough guy like me. If a fairy had granted me three wishes for Sonia, the first would have been that she should be married to you, the second some dough for her, and the third a child – adopted or not makes little difference.

If you don't resent the advice of a chronically meddlesome friend, get through with it, the sooner the better, without waiting until your health is entirely restored. Delay is always a bore and as an amateur psychologist I have a feeling that having this settled will to a surprising extent speed up your recovery.

I hardly dare to hope of having you both down here in the near future, but whenever it is feasible it will be a great treat for me to see you both again and pop champagne corks into the Seine.

[*No valediction or signature*]

[XX, 3695A, p. 329; typewritten carbon copy]

Nancy Heather Parratt, Orwell's secretary at the BBC, wrote from Geneva. As she says in her letter, she had telephoned Orwell early in November, and he apparently asked her for a photograph, which she was now enclosing. This shows her rowing and is dated August 1949. Her description of life in the United States has been omitted here. Despite many inquiries, and the help of the Ministry of Defence and Navy News, *it was not possible to trace her.*

Nancy Parratt* to Orwell

8 December 1949

Dear George,

Just a line to send you the enclosed [photograph]. I wonder which will amuse you most. It must be a pretty strange sensation to be quoted so approvingly by men who, a couple of years ago, would have been on very different ground from you. I must say I at least find it strange to see you turning up so often in such respectable places! You presumably know that the *Philadelphia Inquirer* is serializing *1984* in its Sunday supplement starting 4 December. I wonder if it is the only one or if a whole gang of them are doing it.

Bill[1] told me after I talked to you at the beginning of Nov. that he had sat next to a very pretty girl at a Hallow'en° party who told him she was reading a v.g. book—*1984*, but it was too strong meat for her. She couldn't remember the name of the author but Bill happened to know it, and she said—Yes, he just got married recently. So Bill knew you were married before I did! *And* he forgot to tell me. . . .

You see I have one of these new fangled ball point pens—I only just succumbed to the fashion last week—it seems quite good, only cost $1[2] but sometimes I get carried away by it and it writes funny things!

I hope you are getting on well and not finding the time goes too slowly.

If you are allowed visitors being in London must have its compensations I should think. Next time we come we hope to stay at least twice as long. By that time I am sure you will be moved on to the country or to some mountains or other.

All the best
Nancy

I don't really talk American but it was such a lousy line I had to talk loudly & then I do sound a bit peculiar! If I can mutter I can usually get away with it!

[XX, 3713, pp. 183–4]

1. Nancy's husband.
2. Orwell had started using a Biro early in 1946. He found it particularly useful when writing in bed where liquid ink was not allowed. Even by the end of 1947 he was paying £3 for a new pen.

Sonia Orwell* to Yvonne Davet*

6 January 1950
18 Percy Street
London W1

Chère Madame Davet,

I'm writing to you on behalf of my husband, George Orwell, who is rather ill at the moment and so isn't strong enough to write himself. He has asked me to apologise for his long delay in replying to your letter, but it only reached him two days ago.

I think you will have heard about my husband from our friends Alexei and John Russell[1]—he is still ill etc. We hope to go to Switzerland soon, as it really isn't possible to get over this disease in England.

My husband asks me to thank you most sincerely for all the trouble you have taken on his behalf. He hopes as much for your sake as for his own that the translation of *Homage to Catalonia* will finally appear.[2] As for your article, he has absolutely nothing interesting to say about his life, but in any case this letter will probably arrive too late to be of much help.

He asks me to send you his best wishes for the New Year, and hopes very much to be able to come and see you when he is in Paris again.

Je vous prie de croire, chère Madame, a l'expression de mes sentiments les meilleurs.

Sonia Orwell

[XX, 3716, pp. 185-6; handwritten; translation of French original]

1. John Russell (1919–2008; CBE, 1975), art critic, then married to Alexandrine Appo-nyi (dissolved 1950), worked at the Ministry of Information, 1941–43, and for Naval Intelligence, 1943–46. He was art critic of the *Sunday Times*, 1949–74, and later for the *New York Times*. In 1958, he was a witness at Sonia's marriage to Michael Pitt-Rivers.

2. Madame Davet's translation of *Homage to Catalonia* was published in 1955. It included Orwell's corrections and the re-arrangement of chapters as he had requested. The changes were only made in the English text in 1986 (see VI, pp. 251–61).

Orwell's Death

Having married Sonia Brownell on 13 October 1949, Orwell hoped to be well enough to recuperate in Switzerland, and friends (especially booksellers) raised funds to enable him to make the journey. However, early on Saturday 21 January 1950 he died, his beloved fishing rods standing in the corner of his hospital room. His funeral service was arranged by Malcolm Muggeridge at Christ Church, Albany Street, London, NW1. He had asked to be buried, not cremated, and David Astor arranged for that to take place at All Saints, Sutton Courtney, Berkshire. His headstone is inscribed simply: 'Here Lies Eric Arthur Blair' with his dates of birth and death.

New Textual Discoveries

Proof copy of *A Clergyman's Daughter*

When I edited *A Clergyman's Daughter* in 1982–3, it was known that a proof copy of the novel existed but attempts to see it failed. It recently came to light and is now in the possession of Mr Richard Young. I am deeply grateful to him for allowing me to see it and for providing the following commentary and readings:

The proof appears to be a late stage of the novel's development. It would seem that most of the re-writing of this work was done in manuscript prior to the production of the extant proof. Nevertheless the proof does contain a number of late changes. The most significant of these is to change the character of Mr Blifil-Gordon, the Conservative candidate, so as to remove any trace that he is a Jew who had converted to Roman Catholicism. This was undoubtedly for fear of libel. Below I give the location of this proof text by page and line (e.g. 13/19) followed by the proof's reading in bold; then after the square bracket the equivalent *Collected Works* reading. Pagination and lineation are the same for the *Complete Works* and Penguin Twentieth-Century Classics editions.

13/19: **Catkin Palm**] Catkin and Palm
19/21: **But Mr Blifil-Gordon the proprietor of the sugar beet refinery**] But Mr Cameron the Secretary of the Knype Hill Conservative Club
33/27: **Even more Jewish in appearance than his father**] Given to the writing of sub-Eliot vers libre poems
38/29: **And to think that that scum of the ghetto**] And to think that that low born hound
38/31: **For the beastliest type the world has yet produced give me the Roman Catholic Jew**] And that suit he is wearing is an offence in itself
123/26: **Lord Snowdon**] Lord Snowden
125/22: **Consideration of your a**] Consideration, your a
232/2: *Peg's Paper*] Get hold of – all these filthy (*Peg's Paper* goes between 'of' and 'all')
289/31: *English Review*] *London Mercury*

Proof Copy of *Keep the Aspidistra Flying*

As for *A Clergyman's Daughter,* when editing the *Complete Works* in 1982–3, I was unable to inspect this proof and I am very grateful to Mr Richard Young, who now owns these proofs, for generously providing this commentary and information:

It is both known and obvious that many changes were made to this novel at the proof stage (more so than for *A Clergyman's Daughter* – see **10.1.35**). A large number of these changes were restored in the preparation of the *Collected Works* edition by examination of the files of Victor Gollancz. This proof reveals significant further changes relating mainly to the quoting of product names and contemporary adver-tisements in the novel which were obviously changed or omitted at a late stage. As Orwell was very sensitive to this 'mutilation' it would be good if these readings could be restored. Below I give the locations of this proof text by pages and lines (e.g. 19/22) followed by the proof's reading in bold; then after the square bracket the equivalent *Collected Works* reading. Pagination and lineation are the same for the *Complete Works* and Penguin Twentieth-Century Classics editions.

19/22 *and* 21/19: **Q.T. Sauce**] QT Sauce
25/1, 26/10, 57/6 *and* 26, 271/7 *and* 28: **Rose of Sharon Toilet Requisites Co.**]
Queen of Sheba Toilet Requisites Co.
26/14 *and* 27/12: **Kissprufe Naturetint**] Sexapeal Naturetint
144/32, 145/7 *and* 20, *and* 146/1: **Riverside Hotel**] Ravenscroft Hotel
222/27: **The shop was in the desolate stretch of road south of Waterloo Bridge**]
The shop was in the Waterloo Road
224/29: **A cut-price undertaker**] A smartish undertaker
262/18: **Have a Camel**] *deleted after* Flick, flick
263/1: *the following paragraph appears after* Flick, flick. Guinness is good for you!
Night-starvation – let Horlick's be your guardian. She *said* **'Thanks awfully
for the lift' but she** *thought* **'Poor boy, why doesn't somebody tell him?' How a
woman of thirty-two stole her young man from a girl of twenty. Silkyseam – the
smooth sliding bathroom tissue. Halitosis is ruining his career. Now I'm school-
girl complexion all over. Kiddies clamour for their Breakfast Crisps. Pyorrhea?
Not me! Are you a Highbrow? Dandruff is the reason.**
This proof version contains the Horlick's night-starvation line and the other ads are in a different order to the *CW* text. I guess that the order given here is the original reading.

Chronology

7 January 1857: Orwell's father, Richard Walmesley Blair born at Milborne St Andrew, Dorset. His father, Thomas Arthur Blair, was Vicar of Milborne St Andrew.

19 May 1875: Orwell's mother, Ida Mabel Limouzin, born at Penge, Surrey.

15 June 1897: Richard Blair, an officer in the Opium Department of the Indian Civil Service and Ida Limouzin married at St John in the Wilderness, Naini Tal, India (Bowker, p. 8).

21 April 1898: Marjorie Francis Blair born, Gaya, Bengal.

25 June 1903: Eric Arthur Blair born, Motihari, Bengal.

1904: Ida Blair returns to live in England with Marjorie and Eric at Henley-on-Thames.

Summer 1907: Richard Blair spends three months' leave at Henley.

6 April 1908: Avril Nora Blair born.

1908–1911: Attends a Roman Catholic day-school run by Ursuline nuns, as did his sisters (Bowker, pp. 21–2).

September 1911–December 1916: Boards at St Cyprian's private preparatory school, Eastbourne.

1912: Richard Blair retires as sub-deputy agent in the Opium Department and returns to England. The family moves to Shiplake, Oxfordshire, probably early in December.

Summer 1914: Makes friends with the Buddicom family, especially Jacintha.

2 October 1914: Poem: 'Awake! Young Men of England' published in *Henley and South Oxfordshire Standard* – Orwell's first appearance in print (as Eric Blair).

1915–autumn 1917: The Blairs move back to Henley-on-Thames.

1 July 1916: The Battle of the Somme was launched at 7.30 a.m. On that day 19,240 men were killed or died of wounds; 35,493 wounded; 2,152 missing; and 585 taken prisoner; Total: 57,470 for virtually no advance [Martin Middlebrook, *The First Day of the Somme* (1971; 2001), p. 263].

21 July 1916: Poem: 'Kitchener' (which Orwell himself submitted) published in *Henley and South Oxfordshire Standard*.

Lent Term 1917: At Wellington College as a scholar.

May 1917–December 1921: At Eton as a King's Scholar. Contributes to *The Election Times* and *College Days*.

13 September 1917: Orwell's father commissioned as 2nd Lieutenant; posted to 51st (Ranchi) Indian Pioneer Company, Marseilles. He soon became the youngest 2nd Lieutenant in the British Army. Orwell's mother starts work for the Ministry of Pensions in London.

October–November 1917: Battle of Passchendaele (Third Battle of Ypres) in which Fredric Warburg, Orwell's later publisher and member of his HG platoon, fought.

9 December 1919: Orwell's father relinquishes his commission and returns to London.

December 1921: The Blairs move to Southwold on the Suffolk coast.

October 1922–December 1927: Orwell serves in the Indian Imperial Police, Burma.

Autumn 1927: First expeditions into the East End of London whilst on leave from Burma.

Spring 1928: About this time lives for a while as a tramp.

Spring 1928 to late 1929: Lives in working-class district of Paris; five articles published in French journals; writes one or two novels (he gives both figures); he destroys both.

March 1929: Admitted to Hôpital Cochin, Paris with 'une grippe'. (See 'How the Poor Die', *Now*, 1946.)

Autumn 1929: Works as kitchen porter and dishwasher, probably at Hôtel Lotti or Crillon.

1930–31: Lives with his parents at Southwold but goes off tramping with down-and-outs in London. Starts writing what will become *Down and Out in Paris and London*.

April 1931: 'The Spike' published in *The Adelphi*.

August 1931: 'A Hanging' published in *The Adelphi*.

September 1931: Revised version of *Down and Out* rejected by Jonathan Cape.

Autumn 1931: Picks hops in Kent (see *A Clergyman's Daughter*). Starts *Burmese Days*.

17 October 1931: 'Hop-Picking' published in *New Statesman & Nation*.

14 December 1931: Revised version of *Down and Out* (now called 'A Scullion's Diary') submitted to Faber & Faber but rejected by T.S. Eliot, 15 February 1932.

26 April 1932: Orwell writes to Leonard Moore following submission to him of *Down and Out* by Mrs Mabel Fierz; Moore becomes his literary agent.

April 1932–July 1933: Teaches at The Hawthorns, a private school at Hayes, Middlesex.

Christmas 1932: Writes and directs a school play, *Charles II*.

3 September 1932: 'Common Lodging Houses' published in *New Statesman & Nation*.

19 November 1932: Submits pen-names under which his first book will be published; for a time writes both as Eric Blair (until December 1936) and George Orwell.

January 1933: *Down and Out in Paris and London* by George Orwell (first use of the name) published by Victor Gollancz Ltd. Published in New York on 30 June 1933.

March 1933: Poem: 'Sometimes in the middle autumn days', *The Adelphi*.

May 1933: Poem: 'Summer-like for an instant the autumn sun bursts out', *The Adelphi*.

Autumn 1933: Teaches at Frays College, Uxbridge. Finishes *Burmese Days*.

December 1933: In hospital with pneumonia. Gives up teaching.

October 1933: Poem: 'On a Ruined Farm near His Master's Voice Gramophone Factory', *The Adelphi*.

January–October 1934: Lives with his parents at Southwold; writes *A Clergyman's Daughter*.

25 October 1934: *Burmese Days* published by Harper & Brothers, New York.

October 1934 – March 1935: Takes a room at 3 Warwick Mansions, Hampstead.

October 1934–January 1936: Part-time assistant (with Jon Kimche) at Booklovers Corner, 1 South End Road, Hampstead.

11 March 1935: *A Clergyman's Daughter* published by Gollancz.

May 1935: *Down and Out* published as *La vache Enragée,* translated by R.N. Raimbault.

24 June 1935: *Burmese Days* published by Gollancz, London, with modified text.

August 1935: Moves to Kentish Town, London.

23 January 1936: 'Rudyard Kipling', *New English Weekly*.

31 January–30 March 1936: In North of England collecting material for *The Road to Wigan Pier*. Makes detour by Lake Rudyard following Kipling's death; stays in hostel overlooking the lake (see his *Diary,* 3–4 February 1936).

2 April 1936: Moves to The Stores, Wallington, Hertfordshire.

20 April 1936: *Keep the Aspidistra Flying* published by Gollancz.

May 1936: Starts writing *The Road to Wigan Pier*; begins reviewing for *Time and Tide*.

9 June 1936: Marries Eileen O'Shaughnessy.

Autumn 1936: 'Shooting an Elephant', *New Writing*.

November 1936: 'Bookshop Memories', *Fortnightly*.

December 1936: Poem: 'A happy vicar I might have been', *The Adelphi*.

15 December 1936: Delivers MS of *The Road to Wigan Pier* to Victor Gollancz.

Christmas 1936: Leaves to fight for the Republicans in Spanish Civil War.

January–June 1937: Serves with POUM Militia on the Aragón Front.

8 March 1937: *The Road to Wigan Pier* published in trade and Left Book Club editions.

c. **28 April–10 May 1937**: On leave in Barcelona when Communists violently suppress POUM and other revolutionaries ('The May Events').

20 May 1937: Wounded through the throat by a Fascist sniper at Huesca.

23 June 1937: Escapes from Spain with Eileen, John McNair, and Stafford Cottman.

1–7 July 1937: Arrives back in Wallington and begins writing *Homage to Catalonia*.

July 1937: *New Statesman and Nation* refuses to publish Orwell's article on the POUM or his review of Borkenau's *Spanish Cockpit*.

13 July 1937: Report to Tribunal for Espionage and High Treason, Valencia, charging the Orwells as 'rabid Trotskyists' and agents of the POUM. In the ensuing trial, October–November 1938, his friend Jordi Arquer, was sentenced to 11 years in prison.

29 July and 2 September 1937: 'Spilling the Spanish Beans', *New English Weekly*.

August 1937: 'Eye-Witness in Barcelona', *Controversy.*

5 August 1937: Addresses ILP Conference, Letchworth, Herts, on his experiences in Spain.

12 November 1937: Invited to join *The Pioneer*, Lucknow.

Mid-January 1938: Completes *Homage to Catalonia*.

8 March 1938: Ill with tubercular lesion in one lung and so forced to abandon *Pioneer* offer.

15 March–1 September 1938: Patient at Preston Hall Sanatorium, Aylesford, Kent.

25 April 1938: *Homage to Catalonia* published by Secker & Warburg after rejection by Gollancz.

June 1938: Joins the Independent Labour Party.

24 June 1938: 'Why I Join the I.L.P.', *New Leader.*

2 September 1938–26 March 1939: On 2 September the Orwells left Tilbury on board the P&O liner SS *Stratheden* bound for Gibraltar. They arrived in Morocco on 11 September. On 26 March 1939 they left Casablanca on board the NYK liner, SS *Yasukunimaru* homeward bound. For details of their stay (mainly near Marrakech) see his Domestic and Morocco diaries (*Orwell: Diaries*, 2009). Whilst there he wrote *Coming Up for Air*.

30 September 1938: Munich Agreement signed; Chamberlain returns to London waving the notorious piece of paper assuring 'peace in our time'.

December 1938: 'Political Reflections on the Crisis', *The Adelphi*.

11 April 1939: Back in Wallington.

May–December 1939: Writes *Inside the Whale and Other Essays*.

12 June 1939: *Coming Up for Air* published by Gollancz.

28 June 1939: Orwell's father dies of cancer aged 82. Orwell was at his bedside.

24–31 August 1939: Stays with L.H. Myers in Hampshire. Orwell never knew that Myers had, through an intermediary, Dorothy Plowman, paid for his and Eileen's stay in Morocco. Orwell believed he had been loaned £300.

September 1939: 'Democracy in the British Army', *Left Forum*.

1 September 1939: Germany invades Poland.

3 September 1939: UK and France declare war on Germany. Shortly thereafter, Orwell leaves the Independent Labour Party because of its opposition to the war.

Christmas 1939: 'Marrakech', *New Writing*.

February 1940: Orwell makes his first contribution to *Horizon* ('Lessons of War', a review).

March 1940: 'Boys' Weeklies', *Horizon*.

1 March 1940: *Inside the Whale and Other Essays* published by Gollancz.

29 March 1940: Orwell makes his first contribution to *Tribune*.

April 1940: Projects long novel in three parts (probably not started).

May 1940: Joins the Local Defence Volunteers (later the Home Guard) as platoon commander.

18 May 1940: First of 25 theatre reviews for *Time & Tide* (until 9 August 1941).

25 May 1940: Lecture on Dickens to the Dickens Fellowship.

June 1940: Eileen's dearly-loved brother, Laurence O'Shaughnessy, a Major in the RAMC, killed in Flanders tending the wounded during the retreat to Dunkirk. According to Lydia Jackson (pen-name Elisaveta Fen), Eileen's 'grasp on life loosened considerably' thereafter.

August–October 1940: Writes *The Lion and the Unicorn*.

17 August 1940: 'Books in General' (on Charles Reade), *New Statesman*.

Autumn 1940: 'My Country Right or Left', *Folios of New Writing*.

5 October 1940: First of 27 film reviews for *Time & Tide* (until 23 August 1941).

December 1940: 'The Ruling Class', *Horizon*.

6 December 1940: BBC broadcast (with Desmond Hawkins): 'The Proletarian Writer'.

20 December 1940: 'The Home Guard and You', *Tribune*.

January 1941: 'Our Opportunity', *Left News* (see 3 March 1941 on page 497).

3 January 1941: Writes 'London Letter', first of 15, *Partisan Review* (published March/April 1941).

19 February 1941: *The Lion and the Unicorn* published by Secker & Warburg, the first of the 'Searchlight Books' edited by Orwell and T. R. Fyvel.

3 March 1941: 'Fascism and Democracy' and 'Patriots and Revolutionaries (= 'Our Opportunity') as chapters 8 and 10 of *Betrayal of the Left*, published by Gollancz.

Early April 1941: They move to St John's Wood, London.

23 May 1941: 'Literature and Totalitarianism', Oxford University Democratic Socialist Club.

May–June 1941: Series of four talks broadcast by BBC Overseas Service published in *The Listener* as 'Frontiers of Art and Propaganda', 29 May 1941; 'Tolstoy and Shakespeare', 5 June 1941; 'The Meaning of a Poem', 12 June 1941; and 'Literature and Totalitarianism', 19 June 1941.

August 1941: 'Wells, Hitler, and the World State', *Horizon*.

17 August 1941: 'London Letter', *Partisan Review*.

18 August 1941: Joins the BBC Eastern Service Indian section as Talks Assistant.

18 August 1941–24 November 1943: Talks Assistant, later Talks Producer, Indian Section, BBC Eastern Service.

September 1941: 'The Art of Donald McGill', *Horizon*.

21 November 1941: First of Orwell's weekly newsletters for broadcast to India and S.E. Asia. He wrote 104 or 105 to be broadcast in English and 115 or 116 for translation into Gujarati, Marathi, Bengali, Tamil, or Hindustani. Of those in English, most were broadcast to India, 30 to Malaya, and 19 to Indonesia. Orwell only read his scripts from 21 November 1942.

22 November 1941: Talk: 'Culture and Democracy', Fabian Society.

1 January 1942: 'London Letter', *Partisan Review*.

8 January 1942: Radio talk: 'Paper is Precious'. (Radio talks are for the BBC's Eastern Service.)

15 January 1942: Radio talk: 'The Meaning of Scorched Earth'.

20 January 1942: Radio talk: 'Money and Guns'.

22 January 1942: Radio talk: 'Britain's Rations and the Submarine War'.

29 January 1942: Radio talk: 'The Meaning of Sabotage'.

February 1942: 'Rudyard Kipling', *Horizon*.

8 March 1942: First contribution to *Observer*.

10 March 1942: Radio talk: 'The Re-discovery of Europe' (*The Listener*, 19.3.42).

8 May 1942: 'London Letter', *Partisan Review*.

15 May 1942: 'Culture and Democracy', *Victory or Vested Interest*, George Routledge & Sons.

Summer 1942: They move to Maida Vale, London.

11 August 1942: 'Voice 1', first of six radio literary magazines for India.

29 August 1942: 'London Letter', *Partisan Review*.

9 September 1942: Lectures at Morley College, Lambeth.

9 October 1942: Orwell writes first instalment of a story by five authors broadcast to India. Later instalments by L.A.G. Strong, Inez Holden, Martin Armstrong, and E.M. Forster.

2 November 1942: Imaginary radio interview with Jonathan Swift (*The Listener*, 26.11.42).

29 November 1942: 'In the Darlan Country', *Observer*.

3 January 1943: 'London Letter', *Partisan Review*.

9 January 1943: 'Pamphlet Literature', *New Statesman & Nation*.

22 January 1943: Radio talk: 'George Bernard Shaw'.

23 February 1943: First (anonymous) contribution to 'Forum' (on India), *Observer*.

March 1943: 'Looking Back on the Spanish Civil War' (written autumn 1942), *New Road*.

5 March 1943: Radio talk: 'Jack London'.

19 March 1943: Ida Blair, Orwell's mother, dies with Orwell at her bedside.

2 April 1943: 'Not Enough Money: A Sketch of George Gissing', *Tribune*.

9 May 1943: 'Three Years of Home Guard', *Observer*.

c. **23 May 1943**: 'London Letter', *Partisan Review*.

4 June 1943: 'Literature and the Left', *Tribune*.

13 June 1943: Radio talk: 'English Poetry since 1900'.

18 June 1943: Verse: 'As One Non-Combatant to Another: A Letter to "Obadiah Hornbrooke" [= Alex Comfort]', *Tribune*.

11 August 1943: Radio: featurised story: *Crainquebille* by Anatole France.

22 August 1943: 'I am definitely leaving it [the BBC] probably in about three months'.

September 1943: Review: 'Gandhi in Mayfair', *Horizon*.

9 September 1943: Radio play adapted from *The Fox* by Ignazio Silone.

6 October 1943: Radio: featurised story: 'A Slip Under the Microscope' by H.G. Wells.

17 October 1943: Radio talk: *Macbeth*.

18 November 1943: Radio dramatization: *The Emperor's New Clothes* by Hans Christian Andersen.

18 November 1943: *Talking to India*, Allen & Unwin, ed. and introduced by Orwell.

21 November 1943: Radio talk: *Lady Windermere's Fan*.

23 November 1943: Leaves the BBC and joins *Tribune* as Literary Editor. Leaves Home Guard on medical grounds.

November 1943–February 1944: Writes *Animal Farm*.

26 November 1943: 'Mark Twain – The Licensed Jester', *Tribune*.

3 December 1943: First of 80 personal columns entitled 'As I Please', *Tribune*, 59 published to 16.2.45; remainder 8.11.46 to 4.4.47.

24 December 1943: 'Can Socialists be Happy?' as by 'John Freeman', *Tribune*.

15 January 1944: 'London Letter', *Partisan Review*.

21 January 1944: Poem: 'Memories of the Blitz', *Tribune*.

13 February 1944: 'A Hundred Up' (centenary of *Martin Chuzzlewit*], *Observer*.

17 April 1944: 'London Letter', *Partisan Review*.

May 1944: Finishes *The English People*; published by Collins, August 1947.

14 May 1944: The Orwells' son (adopted June 1944) born; christened Richard Horatio Blair.

Summer 1944: Visits Jura and sees Barnhill.

'Propaganda and Demotic Speech', *Persuasion*.

28 June 1944: The Orwells' flat bombed; move to Inez Holden's flat near Baker St, London.

16 July 1944: 'The Eight Years of War: Spanish Memories', *Observer*.

24 July 1944: 'London Letter', *Partisan Review*.

7 September 1944: 'How Long is a Short Story?', *Manchester Evening News*.

22 September 1944: 'Tobias Smollett: Scotland's Best Novelist', *Tribune*.

October 1944: 'Raffles and Miss Blandish', *Horizon*.

Early October 1944: They move to 27b Canonbury Square, Islington, London, N1.

October (?) 1944: 'London Letter', *Partisan Review*.

19 October 1944: 'Home Guard Lessons for the Future', *Horizon*.

October/November 1944: 'Benefit of Clergy: Some Notes on Salvador Dali', *Saturday Book*, 4. Orwell's article is physically sliced out – though its title is still indexed.

22 December 1944: 'Oysters and Brown Stout' (on Thackeray), *Tribune*.

15 February–end March 1945: War Correspondent for the *Observer* and *Manchester Evening News*, France, Germany, and Austria.

25 February 1945: 'Paris Puts a Gay Face on her Miseries', *Observer*; mentions visiting the rue de Pot de Fer where he lodged in 1928–29.

28 February 1945: 'Inside the Papers in Paris', *Manchester Evening News*.

March 1945: 'Poetry and the Microphone', *New Saxon Pamphlets* (written autumn 1943).

4 March 1945: 'Occupation's Effect on French Outlook', *Observer*.

7 March 1945: 'The Political Aims of the French Resistance', *Manchester Evening News*.

11 March 1945: 'Clerical Party may Re-emerge in France: Educational Controversy', *Observer*.

18 March 1945: 'De Gaulle Intends to Keep Indo-China: But French Apathetic on Empire', *Observer*.

20 March 1945: 'The French Believe we have had a Revolution', *Manchester Evening News*.

25 March 1945: Eileen Blair signs her Will.

25 March 1945: 'Creating Order out of Cologne Chaos: Water Supplied from Carts', *Observer*.

29 March 1945: Eileen Blair dies under anaesthetic. Orwell returns to England.

31 March 1945: Signs first of his 'Notes for my Literary Executor'.

April 1945: 'Antisemitism in Britain', *Contemporary Jewish Chronicle*.

8 April–24 May 1945: Returns to France, Germany and Austria as War Correspondent.

8 April 1945: 'Future of a Ruined Germany: Rural Slum Cannot Help Europe', *Observer*.

15 April 1945: 'Allies Facing Food Crisis in Germany: Problem of Freed Workers', *Observer*.

16 April 1945: 'The French Elections will be Influenced by the Fact that Women will have First Vote', *Manchester Evening News*.

22 April 1945: 'Bavarian Peasants Ignore the War: Germans Know They are Beaten', *Observer*.

29 April 1945: 'The Germans Still Doubt Our Unity: The Flags do not Help', *Observer*.

4 May 1945: 'Now Germany Faces Hunger', *Manchester Evening News*.

6 May 1945: 'France's Interest in the War Dwindles: Back to Normal is the Aim', *Observer*.

8 May 1945: VE Day: end of war in Europe.

13 May 1945: 'Freed Politicians Return to Paris: T.U. Leader sees de Gaulle', *Observer*.

20 May 1945: 'Danger of Separate Occupation Zones: Delaying Austria's Recovery', *Observer*.

27 May 1945: 'Obstacles to Joint Rule in Germany', *Observer*.

5 June 1945: 'London Letter', *Partisan Review*.

8 June 1945: Broadcast for Schools: *Erewhon*, BBC Home Service.

10 June 1945: 'Uncertain Fate of Displaced Persons', *Observer*.

15 June 1945: Broadcast for Schools: *The Way of All Flesh*, BBC Home Service.

24 June 1945: 'Morrison and Bracken Face Stiff Fights: Heavy Poll Expected', *Observer*.

25 June 1945: Warburg reports that Orwell has written 'the first twelve pages of his new novel'. This would eventually become *Nineteen Eighty-Four*.

July 1945: 'In Defence of P. G. Wodehouse', *Windmill* (written February 1945).

1 July 1945: 'Liberal Intervention Aids Labour', *Observer*.

5 July 1945: 'Authors Deserve a New Deal', *Manchester Evening News*.

21 July 1945: 'On Scientifiction', *Leader Magazine*.

28 July 1945: 'Funny but not Vulgar', *Leader Magazine*.

August 1945: Elected Vice-Chairman of the Freedom Defence Committee.

15 August 1945: VJ Day: end of war in Far East.

15–16 August 1945: 'London Letter', *Partisan Review*.

17 August 1945: 4,500 copies of *Animal Farm* published by Secker & Warburg.

10–22 September 1945: Stays in fisherman's cottage on Jura.

October 1945: 'Notes on Nationalism', *Polemic*.

8 October 1945: Forces Educational Broadcast: 'Jack London', BBC Light Programme.

14 October 1945: 'Profile: Aneurin Bevan'; anon., chiefly by Orwell, *Observer*.

19 October 1945: 'You and the Atom Bomb', *Tribune*.

26 October 1945: 'What is Science?', *Tribune*.

November 1945: 'The British General Election', *Commentary*.

2 November 1945: 'Good Bad Books', *Tribune*.

9 November 1945: 'Revenge is Sour', *Tribune*.

23 November 1945: 'Through a Glass Darkly', *Tribune*.

14 December 1945: 'The Sporting Spirit', *Tribune*.

15 December 1945: 'In Defence of English Cooking', *Evening Standard*.

21 December 1945: 'Nonsense Poetry', *Tribune*.

January 1946: 'The Prevention of Literature', *Polemic*.

4 January 1946: 'Freedom v. Happiness' (review of Zamyatin's *We*), *Tribune*.

12 January 1946: 'A Nice Cup of Tea', *Evening Standard*.

18 January 1946: 'The Politics of Starvation', *Tribune*.

24, 31 January, 7, 14 February 1946: Four related articles: '1: The Intellectual Revolt'; '2. What is Socialism?'; '3. The Christian Reformers'; '4. Pacifism and Progress', *Manchester Evening News*.

1 February 1946: 'The Cost of Radio Programmes', *Tribune*.

8 February 1946: 'Books v. Cigarettes', *Tribune*.

9 February 1946: 'The Moon under Water' (the ideal pub), *Evening Standard*.

14 February 1946: *Critical Essays* published by Secker & Warburg (as *Dickens, Dali and Others: Studies in Popular Culture*, by Reynal & Hitchcock, New York, 29 April 1946).

15 February 1946: 'Decline of the English Murder', *Tribune*.

8 March 1946: 'Do Our Colonies Pay?', *Tribune*.

29 March 1946: Radio Play: 'The Voyage of the *Beagle*', BBC Home Service.

29 March 1946: 'British Cookery', unpublished British Council booklet (XVIII, 2954 201–13).

April 1946: 'Politics and the English Language', *Horizon*.

12 April 1946: 'Some Thoughts on the Common Toad', *Tribune*.

26 April 1946: 'A Good Word for the Vicar of Bray', *Tribune*.

Mid-April 1946: Gives up journalism for six months to concentrate on *Nineteen Eighty-Four*.

May 1946: 'Second Thoughts on James Burnham', *Politics*.

3 May 1946: Death of Marjorie Dakin, Orwell's elder sister.

3 May 1946: 'Confessions of a Book Reviewer', *Tribune*.

Early May 1946: Last 'London Letter', *Partisan Review*.

23 May–13 October 1946: Rents Barnhill on Jura.

Summer 1946: 'Why I Write', *Gangrel*.

9 July 1946: Radio Play: 'Little Red Riding Hood', BBC *Children's Hour*.

14 August 1946: 'The True Pattern of H.G. Wells', *Manchester Evening News*.

26 September 1946: Has 'only done about fifty pages [of *Nineteen Eighty-Four*]'.

September–October 1946: 'Politics vs. Literature', *Polemic*.

14 October 1946–10 April 1947: At 27b Canonbury Square, London.

29 October 1946: BBC Pamphlets No 2: *Books and Authors* (containing Orwell's 'Bernard Shaw's *Arms and the Man*') and No 3: *Landmarks in American Literature* (containing Orwell's 'Jack London'), published by Oxford University Press, Bombay.

November 1946: Introduction to Jack London, *Love of Life and Other Stories*, Paul Elek.

November 1946: 'How the Poor Die', *Now*.

22 November 1946: 'Riding Down from Bangor' (review of *Helen's Babies*), *Tribune*.

January 1947: 'Arthur Koestler', *Focus* (written September 1944).

14 January 1947: Radio play: Orwell's adaptation of *Animal Farm*, BBC Third Programme.

March 1947: 'Lear, Tolstoy and the Fool', *Polemic*.

4 April 1947: 80th and last 'As I Please' column, *Tribune*. Orwell intended only to suspend his column.

11 April–20 December 1947: At Barnhill, Jura, writing *Nineteen Eighty-Four*. Often ill.

31 May 1947: Sends Warburg version of 'Such, Such Were the Joys'; finalised about May 1948.

July/August 1947: 'Towards European Unity', *Partisan Review*.

August 1947: *The English People* published by Collins in the series *Britain in Pictures*.

September 1947: Gives up lease of The Stores, Wallington.

31 October 1947: So ill that he has to work in bed.

7 November 1947: First draft of *Nineteen Eighty-Four* completed.

30 November 1947: 'Profile: Krishna Menon' by David Astor, with Orwell, *Observer.*

20 December–28 July 1948: Patient in Hairmyres Hospital, East Kilbride, Glasgow, with TB.

March 1948: Writes 'Writers and Leviathan' for *Politics and Letters*; when that fails it is published in *New Leader,* New York, 19 June 1948.

May 1948: Starts second draft of *Nineteen Eighty-Four.*
Writes 'Britain's Left-Wing Press' for *The Progressive.*
Writes 'George Gissing' for *Politics and Letters*, published *London Magazine,* June 1960. About this time makes final amendments to typescript of 'Such, Such Were the Joys'.

13 May 1948: *Coming Up for Air* published as first volume of Secker's Uniform Edition.

28 July 1948–c. 2 January 1949: At Barnhill, Jura.

28 August 1948: 'The Writer's Dilemma' (review of *The Writer and Politics* by George Woodcock), *Observer.*

Autumn 1948: Writes 'Reflections on Gandhi', published in *Partisan Review*, June 1949.

October 1948: 'Britain's Struggle for Survival: The Labour Government after Three Years', *Commentary.*

Early November 1948: Finishes writing *Nineteen Eighty-Four* and sets about typing manuscript.

15 November 1948: Introduction to *British Pamphleteers*, vol. 1 (written spring 1947), Allan Wingate.

4 December 1948: Completes typing fair copy of *Nineteen Eighty-Four* and posts typescript. Has serious relapse.

December 1948: Gives up lease of his flat in Canonbury Square, Islington.

January 1949: *Burmese Days* published as second volume of Secker's Uniform Edition.

c. 2 January 1949: Leaves Jura for the last time.

6 January–3 September 1949: TB patient at Cotswold Sanatorium, Cranham, Glos.

Mid-February 1949: Starts but does not complete article on Evelyn Waugh.

March 1949: Corrects proofs of *Nineteen Eighty-Four.*

9 April 1949: Sends off his last completed review – of Winston Churchill's *Their Finest Hour* for *New Leader,* New York.

April 1949 onwards: Plans novel set in 1945 (*not written*).
Writes synopsis and four pages of long short-story: 'A Smoking-Room Story'.
Makes notes for an essay on Conrad.

May 1949: 'The Question of the [Ezra] Pound Award', *Partisan Review.*

8 June 1949: *Nineteen Eighty-Four* published by Secker & Warburg.

8 June 1949: Given the first *Partisan Review Annual Award.*

13 June 1949: *1984* published by Harcourt, Brace, New York.

Post June 1949: Signs second 'Notes for my Literary Executor'.

July 1949: *1984* made American Book of the Month.

August 1949: Plans a volume of reprinted essays.

3 September 1949: Transferred to University College Hospital, London.

13 October 1949: Marries Sonia Brownell in hospital by special licence.

18 January 1950: Signs his Will on eve of his proposed journey to Switzerland which had been recommended for his health's sake.

21 January 1950: Orwell dies in University College Hospital following a massive haemorrhage of the lungs.

26 January 1950: Orwell's funeral held at Christ Church, Albany Street, London, NW1. Later that day he is buried at All Saints, Sutton Courtney, Berkshire.

A Short List of Further Reading

All Orwell's writings – and, with their accompanying notes, they take up some 9,000 pages – are to be found in *The Complete Works of George Orwell*, ed. Peter Davison, assisted by Ian Angus and Sheila Davison, 1998; second paperback edition, 2000–2. The books take up the first nine volumes and are published by Penguin with the same pagination of the texts. *The Facsimile of the Manuscript of 'Nineteen Eighty-Four'* was published in 1984; a supplementary volume, *The Lost Orwell*, was published in 2006. Penguin Books have also published four collections of essays, edited by Peter Davison, which have notes additional to those in the *Complete Works*. These are:

Orwell in Spain (includes *Homage to Catalonia*); 393 pages
Orwell's England (includes *The Road to Wigan Pier*); 432 pages with its 32 pages of plates
Orwell and the Dispossessed (includes *Down and Out in Paris and London*); 424 pages
Orwell and Politics (includes *Animal Farm*); 537 pages

Reference might also be made to the companion volume to *A Life in Letters: Orwell: Diaries*, Harvill Secker, 2009 (referred to as *Diaries* with page number).

Footnote references

References to the *Complete Works* are given by volume number + item number + page(s), e.g. XX, 3612, pp. 100–2. References to *The Lost Orwell* are given by *LO* + page number; a link to the location of the item in *Complete Works* follows. References to books listed below are given by the author's name + page number – e.g. Crick, p. 482, except for *Orwell Remembered* and *Remembering Orwell*, which are so designated + their page number(s).

There are very many critical studies of George Orwell and his writings. It might be most helpful if only details of recent biographies and half-a-dozen very recent critical studies are listed here. From these it will be fairly straightforward to seek out earlier biographies and studies.

Biographies

Gordon Bowker, *George Orwell*, Little Brown, 2003 (as *Bowker*).
Jacintha Buddicom, *Eric & Us* (1974), with an important Postscript by Dione Venables, Finlay Publishing, Chichester, 2006.

Audrey Coppard and Bernard Crick, *Orwell Remembered,* Ariel (BBC), 1984 (as *Orwell Remembered*).

Bernard Crick, *George Orwell: A Life*, Secker and Warburg, 1980; Penguin, 1992 edition with important new Appendix (as *Crick*).

Scott Lucas, *Orwell*, Haus Publishing, 2003.

Jeffrey Meyers, *Orwell: Wintry Conscience of a Generation*, Norton, 2000.

Michael Shelden, *Orwell: The Authorised Biography*, Harper Collins, New York, 1991; William Heinemann, 1991, London (which is quoted as *Shelden*).

Hilary Spurling, *The Girl from the Fiction Department: A Portrait of Sonia Orwell*, Hamish Hamilton, 2002.

D. J. Taylor, *Orwell: The Life*, Chatto & Windus, 2003 (as *Taylor*).

John Thompson, *Orwell's London* (with many photographs by Philippa Scoones), Fourth Estate, 1984 (as *Thompson*).

Stephen Wadhams, *Remembering Orwell*, Penguin Canada, 1984 (as *Remembering Orwell*).

Critical Studies

Thomas Cushman and John Rodden, *George Orwell: Into the Twenty-first Century*, Paradigm Publishers, Boulder, Colorado, 2004.

Christopher Hitchens, *Orwell's Victory*, Allen Lane, 2002 (as *Why Orwell Matters* in USA).

Douglas Kerr, *George Orwell*, Northcote House: Writers and their Work, 2003.

Emma Larkin, *Secret Histories: Finding George Orwell in a Burmese Teashop*, John Murray, 2004.

Daniel J. Leab, *Orwell Subverted: The CIA and the Filming of 'Animal Farm'*, Pennsylvania State UP, 2007.

The Cambridge Companion to George Orwell, edited by John Rodden, CUP, 2007.

John Rodden, *Every Intellectual's Big Brother: George Orwell's Literary Siblings*, University of Texas, Austin, 2006. This gives a valuable account of the Centenary Conference, 'George Orwell: An Exploration of His World and Legacy', held at Wellesley College, near Boston, Massachusetts in May 2003. In many ways it takes further John Rodden's, *The Politics of Literary Reputation: The Making and Claiming of 'St. George' Orwell*, Oxford University Press, Oxford and New York, 1989.

Loraine Saunders, *The Unsung Artistry of George Orwell: The Novels from 'Burmese Days' to 'Nineteen Eighty-Four'*, Ashgate, Aldershot and Burlington VT, 2008.

Hugh Thomas, *The Spanish Civil War* (1961), third Penguin edn. 1977 (as *Thomas*).

Internet Websites

www.finlay-publisher.com – this is the website of *Eric & Us*. This publishes essays by leading scholars every two months together with comments from readers. It is run by Dione Venables who wrote the Postscript to the second edition to Jacintha Buddicom's book of that title (2006).

www.orwelldiaries.wordpress.com – which not only gives details of events related to the annual Orwell Prize, but also details of many other events. It reproduces some of the articles from the *Eric & Us* website and is currently reproducing Orwell's diary entries day by day seventy years on. Associated with that is an excellent Google map showing where Orwell was when he wrote his diary entries. It is run by Professor Jean Seaton and Gavin Freeguard.

Biographical Notes

An asterisk after a name in the text indicates an entry here.

Mulk Raj Anand (1905–2004), novelist, essayist and critic. He was born in India, fought for the Republicans in the Spanish Civil War (although he did not meet Orwell in Spain). He wrote scripts and broadcast for the BBC from 1939–45 and did much work for Orwell whilst he was there. After the war he lectured in various Indian universities and became Professor of Fine Arts, University of Punjab in 1963. He and Orwell were frequent companions, especially at the BBC. He told W.J. West that Orwell had a predilection for quoting often and at length from the *Book of Common Prayer*, which he clearly knew well.

Jordi Arquer i Saltó (1906–81), a Catalan, was one of Orwell's comrades in the POUM. He was a defendant in the 'POUM trial', October–November 1938, a trial in which Orwell and his wife, Eileen, might also have appeared had they not left Spain (see XI, 374A). Arquer was charged with espionage and desertion but the charges collapsed because of the transparent absurdity of the evidence. He was instead charged with organising a meeting in Lérida in preparation for the May Events in Barcelona. He insisted on speaking only in Catalan at the trial and was sentenced to eleven years imprisonment; on his release he went to live in Paris.

The Hon. David Astor (1912–2001) served in the Royal Marines, 1940–45, and was successively foreign editor (1946–48), editor (1948–75), and a director (1976–81) of the *Observer*, doing much to improve its content and increase its circulation. He and Orwell were very good friends. Astor was instrumental in finding him somewhere to live on Jura, obtained streptomycin for him in his final illness, and arranged for him to be buried as Orwell wished. Despite Orwell's reputation for being gloomy, Astor told the editor that when he felt depressed, he would seek out Orwell because Orwell's humour so cheered him up.

Avril Blair (1908–1978), Orwell's younger sister. She came to live with her brother at Barnhill and worked very hard caring for him, the house, and their smallholding. She married Bill Dunn in 1951 and cared for Orwell's son, Richard, after her brother died. Richard Blair has contributed a valuable essay on Avril to the *Eric & Us* website (www.finlay-publisher.com) where the essay has been archived.

Eileen Blair *née* O'Shaughnessy (1905–45) married Orwell on 9 June 1936. She was born in South Shields and graduated from Oxford in 1927. When she met Orwell she was reading for a master's degree in psychology at University College London. During the war she first worked (ironically) in a Whitehall Censorship Department, and then at the Ministry of Food. Lettice Cooper worked with her at the Ministry of Food. Eileen, she recalls, was 'of medium height, a little high-shouldered, she was very pretty, and had what George called a cat's face, blue eyes and near black hair. She moved slowly, she always looked as if she was drifting into a room with no particular purpose there. She had small, very shapely hands and feet. I never saw her in a hurry, but her work was always finished up to time. . . . Eileen's mind was a mill that ground all the time slowly but independently. Diffident and unassuming in manner she had a quiet integrity that I never saw shaken' (X, p. 394).

Ida Blair *née* Limouzin (1875–1943), Orwell's mother. She was born at Penge in Surrey to an English mother and a French father but brought up and lived in India. She was a lively and independent woman and, as her diary shows, led an active social and sporting life on her return to England in 1904. Her family had connections with Burma. She was adept at arranging for her son and Avril to be cared for by others in school holidays.

Richard Horatio Blair (1944–), adopted by Eric and Eileen Blair in June 1944. His middle name is a Blair family name. As was common in the early twentieth century, children were, so far as possible, kept away from those with tuberculosis. Thus Richard and his father saw far less of each other than either wished, especially when Orwell was in Hairmyres Hospital and Cranham Sanatorium. After his father's death he was cared for by Orwell's sister, Avril, and her husband, Bill Dunn. He was educated at Loreto and Wiltshire Farm School, Lackham, and finally at the North of Scotland College of Agriculture, Aberdeen. He married Eleanor Moir in 1964 and farmed in Herefordshire before joining Massey-Fergusson in 1975. See his memoir, 'Life with my Aunt Avril Blair', www.finlay-publisher.com.

Richard Walmsley Blair (1857–1939), Orwell's father. He joined the Opium Department of the Indian Civil Service in 1875 and rose to the rank of sub-deputy agent, retiring in 1912. For reasons unknown he took sick leave for fifteen months from 20 August 1885. In 1917 he was commissioned as a 2nd Lieutenant in the 51st (Ranchi) Indian Pioneer Company, Marseilles, serving as one of the oldest, and for a time the oldest, lieutenants in the army until 9 December 1919. The Blairs retired to Southwold, Suffolk, in December 1921. Although Jacintha Buddicom describes the Blairs as a united and happy family, she also tellingly describes Mr Blair as 'not unkind'.

Zulfaqar Ali Bokhari, Indian Programme Organiser for the BBC from the foundation of its Indian Section and Orwell's superior officer. After the war he became director-general of Pakistan Radio.

Henry Noel Brailsford (1873–1958), socialist intellectual, author, political journalist and leader writer for several newspapers including the *Manchester Guardian*. He edited the ILP's weekly journal, *The New Leader*, 1922–26.

Laurence Brander (1903–) was BBC Eastern Intelligence Officer when Orwell worked for that section. His report on the BBC's Indian service graphically describes the difficulties faced by the service and also its shortcomings. See XV, 2374, pp. 343–56. In this he states that 'our most damaging failure' has been English programmes for Indians. His *George Orwell* was published in 1954 and in it he wrote that Orwell 'was the inspiration of that rudimentary Third Programme which was sent out to the Indian student'. He wrote many studies of literary figures including Tobias Smollett, William Thackeray, Aldous Huxley and E.M. Forster.

Ivor Brown (1891–1974), author, critic, editor, drama critic and leader writer for the *Manchester Guardian*, 1919–35. He was also drama critic for the *Observer* and its editor from 1942–48, (XVII p. 313). If Orwell wrote a review that troubled him he did not hesitate to write for external advice, e.g. as to whether his correspondent thought 'the whole tone of [the review] breathes a distaste for christianity' (*The Lost Orwell*, p. 104).

Sonia Brownell (1918–80), Orwell's second wife. A short memoir by Ian Angus (who knew her well and worked with her in the production of the four-volume *Collected Essays, Journalism & Letters* (1968) which did so much to establish Orwell's wider reputation) will be found in XX, pp. 170–1. Despite her widely acknowledged generosity, she has been subjected to much unfair adverse criticism. Only with Hilary Spurling's *The Girl from the Fiction Department: A Portrait of Sonia Orwell* (2002) did a balanced account become available. Curiously, she was born at Ranchi, Bihar, only some 230 miles from Orwell's birthplace at Motihari. She was the innocent victim in a boating accident on a Swiss lake in 1936. She and three other teenagers were caught in a vicious squall; she was the only one who could swim and the others drowned. Sonia never wholly recovered from this tragedy. She worked on *Horizon* where Cyril Connolly introduced her to Orwell. She and Orwell married in University College Hospital, on 13 October 1949. When Arthur Koestler heard of their wedding, he told Orwell how happy he and his wife, Mamaine, were, and that the first of his three wishes for Sonia had been 'that she should be married to you' (XX, p. 329). It was Sonia who established the Orwell Archive which has done so much to preserve Orwelliana.

Jacintha Buddicom (1901–93) was the eldest child of Laura and Robert Buddicom. Her father had been curator of Plymouth Museum but moved to Shiplake-on-Thames to take up market gardening. Her brother, Prosper (1904–68) and sister, Guinever (1907–2002) were Orwell's childhood companions when he was at home. She and Orwell exchanged poems and her vivid memoir, *Eric & Us* (1974), describes how they played together. See the second edition with its very informative postscript by Dione Venables (2006), and Jacintha's letter of 4 May 1972 on page 8 of this book.

Dennis Collings (1905–2001) was a friend of Orwell's from the time the Blair family moved to Southwold in 1921. Collings's father became the Blairs' family doctor. He read anthropology at Cambridge and was appointed assistant curator of the Raffles Museum, Singapore in 1934. He was taken prisoner by the Japanese but survived the war. Also in 1934 he married Eleanor Jaques, a close friend of Orwell's.

Alex Comfort (1920–2000), poet, novelist, medical biologist. He wrote a number of books including *No Such Liberty* (1941), a miracle play (*Into Egypt*, 1942) and, most famously, *The Joy of Sex* (1972). He also co-edited *Poetry Folios*, nos 1–10, 1942–46.

Jack Common (1903–68), a working man from Tyneside who worked for *The Adelphi* from 1930 to 1936, first as a circulation pusher, then as assistant editor, and from 1935–36 as co-editor with Sir Richard Rees. He wrote several books and Crick called him 'one of the few authentic English proletarian writers. In 1938 Orwell reviewed his *The Freedom of the Streets* (XI, pp. 162–3). He and his wife, Mary, lived in the Orwells' cottage at Wallington whilst the latter were in Morocco.

Cyril Connolly (1903–74) was with Orwell at St Cyprian's and Eton. They met again in 1935 after Connolly had reviewed *Burmese Days*. They were associated in a number of literary activities, particularly the journal *Horizon* which Connolly edited with great distinction. See his *Enemies of Promise* (1938), which has references to Orwell; and *The Rock Pool* (1936), which Orwell reviewed (X, pp. 490–1) and which includes the critique, 'A more serious objection is that even to want to write about so-called artists who spend on sodomy what they have gained by sponging betrays a kind of spiritual inadequacy', a world that it is clear the author 'rather admires'.

Lettice Cooper (1897–1994), novelist and biographer. She worked during the war at the Ministry of Food with Eileen, who looked after the 'Kitchen Front' radio broadcasts. Her novels include *The Lighted Room* (1925), and *Black Bethlehem* (1947), in which the character Ann is said to be based on Eileen. In her touching memoir of Eileen (recorded for the Orwell Archive) she tells how Orwell read each instalment of *Animal Farm* to her every evening 'and she used to come in and tell us next morning how it was getting on, she knew at once it was a winner' (see *Remembering Orwell*, pp. 116–17, 130–2, 144–5, and 196–7). She underwent psychoanalysis and Orwell's knowledge of this may have come from her.

Stafford Cottman (1918–99) was the youngest member of the ILP unit which fought with the POUM in the Spanish Civil War. He and Orwell fought alongside each other and escaped together. He was initially pro-Communist but rejected Communism after the May Events in Barcelona in 1937. On his return home to Bristol he was expelled from the Young Communist League as an enemy of the working class and his house was 'shadowed' by its members. There is an excellent obituary of Cottman in the *Independent*, 3 November 1999.

Humphrey Dakin (1896–1970) married Orwell's older sister, Marjorie in July 1920. He was a civil servant and worked for the National Savings Committee. Orwell stayed with them from time to time in Leeds when he was examining conditions in the Distressed Areas. Humphrey seemed to resent his brother-in-law, considering him a 'work-shy drop-out' (*Orwell Remembered*, pp. 127–30).

Marjorie Dakin *née* **Blair** (1898–1946), Orwell's elder sister. She served as motorcycle despatch rider for the Women's Legion during the First World War. She married

Humphrey Dakin (1896–1970). Their children, Henry, Jane and Lucy, all stayed with Orwell on Jura.

C.D. Darlington (1903–81), Director of the John Innes Horticultural Institution, 1939–53, Professor of Botany and Keeper of the Botanic Garden, Oxford University, 1953–71. He pubished *The Conflict of Science and Society* (1948), which Orwell read in May 1949. Although associated with J.D. Bernal and J.G. Crowther he was an anti-communist. He and Orwell were both concerned about the damage done to science (and the Soviet people) by the work of Trofim Denisovich Lysenko, Director of the Soviet Academy of Agricultural Science, who rejected Western genetics and was favoured by Stalin. Hearing John Baker lecture on Lysenko at the PEN Conference, 22–26 August 1944, was one of the motivating factors in Orwell's writing *Nineteen Eighty-Four*. When Orwell was working at the BBC, he engaged Darlington to give three talks to India.

Yvonne Davet (c. 1895–?) was for many years secretary to André Gide. She and Orwell did not meet but corresponded before and after the war. Her translation of *Homage to Catalonia* was completed before the war and read and commented upon by Orwell. Orwell's instructions were later applied to the *Complete Works* edition. Her translation was not published until 1955, after Orwell's death. She also translated the work of Jean Rhys, Graham Greene, and Iris Murdoch.

E. Rowan Davies When Orwell joined the BBC in 1941 Davies was listed as a Transcription Assistant in the Eastern Service. On 21 August 1943 he was shown on a staff list as Schools Broadcasting Manager in the Home Service.

R.R. Desai was a postgraduate student at Cambridge whose department had been evacuated to Aberystwyth. He translated into Gujerati forty-two English texts written by Orwell and re-cast two others. He would travel each Sunday night to London to read his versions, the BBC paying his rail fare and giving him £1 14s subsistence together with a fee of £5 5s. Later he wrote the newsletters himself. He was still living in London in 2004.

Dr Bruce Dick, specialist in charge of the Thoracic Unit at Hairmyres Hospital. Much to Orwell's amusement, he thought that Dick had served with Franco's forces in the Spanish Civil War. However, his junior doctor at the time, Dr James Williamson thought that 'bunkum'. Williamson's description of Orwell's treatment is reproduced in *Remembering Orwell*, pp. 197–202. In 1996 Professor Williamson told Ian Angus that for a while Orwell shared a room with the editor of the boys' comic *Hotspur* and Professor Dick had been interested to see how they got on. 'In the event they got on well together (as I think almost anyone would have . . .).'

Kay Dick (1915–2001), under the pen-name Edward Lee, was co-editor with Reginald Moore of *The Windmill*, nos 1–12, which ran from 1944–48.

Sergei Dinamov (1901–39), chief editor of *International Literature*, Moscow. He was an authority on Western literature and a leading Shakespeare scholar. He was arrested in 1938 and died in a Gulag, probably having been shot.

Charles Doran (1894–1974) was born in Dublin but moved to Glasgow in 1915. He served in the First World War and then became active in the Anti-Parliamentary Communist Federation. He joined the ILP in the 1930s and served with Orwell in the POUM in Spain. His widow, Bertha, said her husband classed Orwell 'as a rebel – not a revolutionary – who was dissatisfied with the Establishment, while remaining part of it.' In 1983 Mrs Doran told Dr James D. Young that her late husband was impressed with Orwell's modesty and sincerity. 'I remember Charlie saying that Orwell was not an argumentative sort of person. He [Charlie] might voice an opinion about something, hoping to provoke Orwell into agreeing or disagreeing, but Orwell would just say: "You might be right, Doran!" '

T.S. Eliot (1888–1965), poet and critic. Orwell commissioned Eliot to make half-a-dozen broadcasts to India and he reviewed *The Four Quartets* in 1944 (XVI, pp. 420–3). As a reader for Faber, he rejected *Down and Out in Paris and London,* and *Animal Farm.*

Roy Fuller (1912–91), although a solicitor for the Woolwich Building Society, he was also a prolific poet. He became Professor of Poetry at Oxford in 1968, the year in which he was awarded the Duff Cooper Memorial Prize. In 1969 he became Vice-President of the Building Societies Association.

Tosco Fyvel (1907–85), his parents had emigrated to Palestine (as it then was) from Vienna and he became associated with the Zionist movement, working with Golda Meir. Orwell met him with Fredric Warburg in January 1940 the outcome of which was the Searchlight series of books, which Fyvel and Orwell edited. (Orwell contributed *The Lion and the Unicorn.*) Fyvel's *George Orwell: A Personal Memoir* (1982) is particularly helpful especially on the subject of anti-Semitism and Zionism (see pp. 178–82).

Victor Gollancz (1893–1967), Orwell's first publisher. After Oxford he taught at Repton for two years where his introduction of a class on civics brought him into conflict with the headmaster, Dr Geoffrey Fisher, who would later become Archbishop of Canterbury. He was sacked in 1918, worked on minimum-wage legislation, and after working for OUP joined Benn Brothers, publishers of trade journals. His success there led to his establishing his own publishing house in 1927. In his first year he published sixty-four books. Although a member of the Labour Party and born into an orthodox Jewish family he would later describe himself as a Christian socialist. His major achievement was the formation of the Left Book Club, which brought out *The Road to Wigan Pier*. He was well-known for offering modest advances to authors ensuring the likelihood that there would be more to follow after publication.

Geoffrey Gorer (1905–85), social anthropologist and author of many books including *Africa Dances* (1935), *The American People* (1964), and *Death Grief and Mourning in*

Contemporary Britain (1965). He wrote to Orwell about *Burmese Days*, 'it seems to me you have done a necessary and important piece of work as well as it could be done'. They met and remained lifelong friends.

A.S.F. Gow (1886–1978), Orwell's tutor at Eton. He was later appointed to a fellowship at Trinity College, Cambridge. He and Orwell corresponded occasionally. His name was inverted to 'Wog' at Eton and Orwell wrote a doggerel verse when there starting, "Then up waddled Wog and he squeaked in Greek: / "I've grown another hair on my cheek"' (X, p. 52).

Rayner Heppenstall (1911–81), novelist, critic and crime historian. He shared a flat with Orwell in 1935 but the arrangement was not an unqualified success; they even came to blows. Nevertheless they remained friends and Heppenstall produced some of Orwell's work for the BBC, notably his script for *The Voyage of the Beagle* and a radio adaptation of *Animal Farm*. Orwell is one of those featured in his *Four Absentees* (1960), extracts from which are reproduced in *Orwell Remembered*.

Inez Holden (1906–74), novelist, short-story writer, journalist and broadcaster, was a cousin of Celia Kirwan, twin sister of Arthur Koestler's wife, Mamaine. She proved a good friend to the Orwells lending them her flat in Portman Square after they had been bombed out. She and Orwell considered publishing their war diaries as a joint venture. The project fell through because she wanted to change anything Orwell wrote with which she disagreed. Her diary was published as *It Was Different at the Time* (1943).

Lydia Jackson *née* Jiburtovich (1899–1983), psychologist, writer and translator (using the pen-name Elisaveta Fen). She was born in Russia and came to England in 1925. She met Eileen at University College London in 1935 and they remained friends. She stayed at the Orwell's Wallington cottage when they were not there and visited Orwell at Barnhill and Hairmyres Hospital. She translated Chekhov's plays for Penguin, 1951–54. Her *A Russian's England*, 1976, gives good accounts of Eileen, Wallington, and Eileen and Orwell's relationship.

Eleanor Jaques (?–1962) arrived in Southwold from Canada in 1921 shortly before the Blair family. They were for a time the Blairs' next-door-neighbours in Stradbroke Road. Eleanor and Orwell became friends. She is first mentioned in Orwell's letter to Dennis Collings of 12 October 1931 saying she might be allowed to read Orwell's 'narrative of my adventures' when hop-picking.

Revd Iorwerth Jones, Minister of Pan-teg Congregational Church, Ystalyfera, Swansea. He wrote to Malcolm Muggeridge on 4 May 1955 enclosing Orwell's letter of 8 April, 1941. He had written to Orwell to 'raise queries about his comments on pacificism'. The minister thought this letter might be helpful to Muggeridge in writing Orwell's biography – a biography he did not, in the event, get round to writing.

Dr Thomas Jones, CH (1870–1955), described by Crick as 'Lloyd George's famous Cabinet Secretary'. He was a prime mover in the establishment of CEMA, the forerunner of the Arts Council. Orwell had written to him about 20 March 1942 regarding the abysmal delay in the issue of ammunition to the Home Guard in a surprise call-out (XIII, p. 236).

Denys King-Farlow (1903–82), a fellow Colleger in Orwell's Election at Eton. They produced *The Election Times* and co-edited *College Days*, nos. 4 and 5. He won scholarships to Cambridge and Princeton and worked for Royal Dutch Shell in Canada. For his reminiscences of Orwell, see *Orwell Remembered*, pp. 54–60.

Celia Kirwan (1916–2002) was the twin sister of Mamaine Koestler. The sisters both suffered badly from asthma. She and Orwell first met when they travelled together (with Richard) to spend Christmas 1945 with the Koestlers at Bwylch Ocyn near Blaenau Ffestiniog. Orwell proposed marriage to her after Eileen's death. Although she 'gently refused him' they remained close friends. She worked as an editorial assistant for *Polemic* (which published 'Politics vs. Literature', 1946) but when that collapsed moved to Paris to work on *Occident*, a tri-lingual magazine. When she worked for the Information Research Department, she was, so far as her relationship with Orwell was concerned, far more a close friend than a government official. She visited Orwell at Cranham to ask him to write for the Information Research Department. He did not feel well enough to do so but suggested names of those who might help and also gave a list of those whom he thought could not be trusted. See XX, pp. 318–27 and *The Lost Orwell*, pp. 140–51.

Arthur Koestler (1905–83), born in Budapest, joined the Communist Party in 1931, leaving in the late 1930s, and spent a year in the USSR. He worked as a reporter during the Spanish Civil War, was captured and condemned to death. He escaped and was interned in France in 1940 and then imprisoned as an alien by the British but later released. Among books describing his experiences are *Spanish Testament* (1937), *Scum of the Earth* (1941), and *Darkness at Noon* (1940), which Orwell reviewed (XII, pp. 357–9). He became a British citizen in 1945. Orwell's essay, 'Arthur Koestler', was published in 1946; see XVI, pp. 391–402. His first wife, Mamaine, was the twin sister of Celia Kirwan). He and his third wife, Cynthia, both committed suicide in 1983 although she was much younger than was Koestler.

George(s) Kopp (1902–1951) was born in Petrograd and was Orwell's commandant in Spain. They remained friends thereafter. Kopp was a mysterious figure. He lived for a significant part of his life in Belgium and created various fictions about himself. It was certain that he was brave and skilful in war. He seems to have served for the Vichy Secret Service and also for MI5 (his handler being Anthony Blunt). Various claims have been made that he and Eileen had an affair, but Eileen's letter of New Year's Day, 1938, explodes that theory. He died in Marseilles. Bert Govaerts has done much to discover the truth of Kopp's background: see *The Lost Orwell*, pp. 83–91.

Jennie Lee (1904–88; Baroness Lee of Ashridge, 1970), daughter of a Scottish miner who was chairman of his local ILP branch. She served in the Labour governments of 1964–70 and was appointed as the first Minister of the Arts, making a profound impression in that role. She married Aneurin Bevan in 1934.

Captain Sir Basil Henry Liddell Hart (1895–1970) wrote more than thirty books including *History of the Second World War* (1970). He had been military correspondent to the *Daily Telegraph*, 1925–35, and to *The Times*, 1935–39. In 1937 he was personal adviser to the Minister of War. Orwell wrote of him, 'The two military critics most favoured by the intelligentsia are Captain Liddell Hart and Major-General Fuller, the first of whom teaches that the defence is stronger than the attack, and the second that the attack is stronger than the defence. This contradiction has not prevented both of them from being accepted as authorities by the same public. The secret reason for their vogue in left-wing circles is that both of them are at odds with the War Office' ('Notes on Nationalism', 1945, XVII, p. 143).

Trofim Denisovich Lysenko (1989–1976), Soviet advocate of Lamarckism (roughly, the ability in nature to develop acquired characteristics). His views were supported by Stalin. They dominated Soviet biology from the 1930s leading to the elimination of rival, and far sounder, biologists. In 1948 the Central Committee of the Soviet Union decreed that 'Lysenkoism' was correct. Lysenko and his theories were totally discredited following the fall of Khrushchev. The penultimate book Orwell read in 1949 was Julian Huxley's *Soviet Genetics and World Science: Lysenko and the Meaning of Heredity* (1949). Orwell was interested in Lysenko to the last. He pasted a cutting from the *News Chronicle* for 16 December 1949 into his Last Literary Notebook which quoted Lysenko as maintaining that 'Wheat can become Rye' (XX, 3725, p. 214).

Dwight Macdonald (1906–82), libertarian critic, pamphleteer, and scholar. He was an associate editor of *Partisan Review* and later founded *Politics* of which he was editor 1944–49 and to which Orwell contributed, November 1944 and September 1946.

Sally McEwan (?–1987) was Orwell's secretary when he was literary editor of *Tribune*. She stayed at Barnhill with her daughter in 1946 and Michael Shelden records that over forty years later she still had happy memories of her time there (Shelden, p. 449).

John McNair (1887–1968), a Tynesider and indefatigable worker for socialism all his life. He left school when he was twelve, ran into trouble with employers because of his left-wing views, and went to France to find work. He stayed there for twenty-five years, becoming a leather merchant, founding a football club with eight teams, and lecturing on English poets at the Sorbonne. He returned to England in 1936, rejoined the ILP and was its General Secretary, 1939–55. He was the first British worker to go to Spain and was the ILP representative in Barcelona.

Jessica Marshall (*née* Browne) lived at Byfleet, Surrey. She heard Orwell give a lecture and thereafter read all he wrote. They seem to have had no personal contact. It is typical of Orwell's generous spirit that, even though he was ill, he took the trouble to write to her at such length.

Michael Meyer (1921–2000), author and translator (most notably of Ibsen and Strindberg). In 1943 he wrote what he later described as a 'timid letter' to Orwell and received an invitation to lunch (see XV, p. 65). They met and became good friends. Meyer describes Orwell in *Remembering Orwell*, pp. 132–7.

Henry Miller (1891–1980), American author who lived in Paris from 1930–39. His fictionalised autobiographies, such as *Tropic of Cancer* (1934), and *Tropic of Capricorn* (1938), were banned in the USA until 1961 for their explicit treatment of sex. For Orwell's essay on Miller, see 'Inside the Whale' (XII, pp. 86–115).

Leonard Moore (?–1959), of Christy & Moore, became Orwell's literary agent in 1932 at the suggestion of Mabel Fierz. He succeeded in placing *Down and Out in Paris and London* and was throughout Orwell's life a patient and skilful supporter of Orwell and his work.

Raymond Mortimer, CBE (1895–1980), critic and literary editor of the *New Statesman and Nation* and one of the best that paper had.

John Middleton Murry (1889–1957) was nominally the editor of *The Adelphi* (which he founded in June 1923) for some fourteen years but much of the editing was undertaken by Max Plowman and Sir Richard Rees. Despite his unorthodox Marxism, deeply entrenched pacifism, and later entry to the church, he and Orwell remained good friends, although crossing swords from time to time. In 1948 he renounced pacifism and demanded a preventive war against the USSR despite, as Orwell reminded Dwight Macdonald, writing less than ten years earlier that 'Russia is the only inherently peaceful country' (XIX, p. 282).

Norah Myles *née* Symes (1906–94) and Orwell's wife Eileen became friends when they read English at St Hugh's College, Oxford. Her father and husband were physicians in Bristol. Eileen gave no addressee to the letters she wrote and signed them simply as 'E' or by a pet-name, 'Pig'. Norah only met Orwell once or twice and found him 'rather intimidating'. Eileen thought of her and her husband, Quartus, as carers for Richard Blair should she die under anaesthetic (as she did) but slightly confusingly said, 'you have never seen either of them'.

C.K. Ogden (1889–1957), psychologist and teacher. In the 1920s he developed Basic English, in part as a result of discussions with the critic, I.A. Richards. BASIC stands for British American Scientific International Commercial. It comprises 850 words: 400 nouns, 200 picturable objects, 100 general qualities, 50 opposites, and 100 operators such as adverbs and particles. Winston Churchill formed a Cabinet Committee on Basic English in 1943 and in June 1946 Ogden assigned his copyright to the Crown for £23,000. A Basic English Foundation was established by the Ministry of Education in 1947. Reading in Basic proved fairly easy but writing clearly much more difficult.

Gwen O'Shaughnessy, a doctor and Eileen's sister-in-law. She lived at 24 Croom's Hill, Greenwich, SE 10. Her son, Laurence, went to Canada by ship in June 1940 in an evacuation scheme to save children from bombing. The scheme ended after the most successful German submarine, the U-48, sank *City of Benares* on 17 September 1940 on its way to Canada. Of about 300 adults on board, 175 were drowned; 87 of the 100 children were drowned.

Dr Laurence (Eric) O'Shaughnessy (1900–40), Eileen's much-loved brother. He was proving an outstanding chest and heart surgeon, being appointed Hunterian Professor at the Royal College of Surgeons, 1933–35. In 1937 he won the Hunter Medal Triennial Prize for research work in surgery of the thorax. He joined the Royal Army Medical Corps at the outbreak of war and served at a casualty clearing station in Flanders where he was killed. Her brother's death greatly affected Eileen (see Fyvel, pp. 105–6 and 136).

Marie O'Shaughnessy, Eileen's mother.

Nancy Parratt (1919–) joined the BBC on 13 June 1941 and worked for Orwell. She can be seen standing next to Orwell in a photograph of those participating in a 'Voice' programme – including T.S. Eliot and Mulk Raj Anand (Crick, plate 22). She left on 15 March 1943 to join the WRNS. She served in the USA, married there and was demobilised in May 1946.

Dorothy Plowman (1887–1967), wife of Max Plowman. When Orwell was advised to winter in a warm climate, L.H. Myers (1881–1944), the novelist, wished to finance this anonymously and gave Mrs Plowman £300 to enable him to do so. She never told Orwell the source of the money, although he realised that she was acting as an intermediary.

Max Plowman (1883–1941) worked on *The Adelphi* from 1929 until his death. He was Warden of the Adelphi Centre, 1938–41, an ardent supporter of the Peace Pledge Union from its foundation in 1934 and its General Secretary 1937–38. His publications include *Introduction to the Study of Blake* (1927), *A Subaltern on the Somme* (as Mark VII, 1928) a product of his experiences in the front line, and *The Faith Called Pacifism* (1936). He and his wife, Dorothy, remained lifelong friends of Orwell.

Anne Popham studied the history of art and joined the Arts Council. She married Virginia Woolf's nephew, Quentin Bell in 1952, and, as Anne Olivier Bell, edited Virginia Woolf's *Diaries 1915–41* with Andrew McNeillie (1977–85). In 1946 she had a flat on the floor below Orwell's at 27b Canonbury Square.

Anthony Powell, CH (1905–2000), novelist and editor, famous for the novel series, *A Dance to the Music of Time* (1951–75). He served from 1939–45 in the Welch Regiment and the Intelligence Corps.

Lady Violet Powell (1912–2002), when Lady Violet Pakenham she married Anthony Powell.

Philip Rahv (1908–1973; born Ivan Greenberg), prominent Marxist literary critic and member of the John Reed Club. With William Phillips he founded *Partisan Review* and earlier was a contributor to *New Masses*.

R.N. Raimbault (1882–1962), a distinguished wood engraver, painter, writer and translator. He taught French Literature, Greek and Latin at the Lycée du Mans. He was a particularly distinguished translator of American literature, especially of William Faulkner. He was the first translator of Orwell, who greatly admired his work.

Sir Herbert Read (1893–1968), poet, critic, educator and interpreter of modern art. He served in the First World War being awarded the DSO and MC. He was particularly influential in the thirties and forties. His major works include *Form in Modern Poetry* (1932), *Art Now* (1933), *Art and Society* (1936), and *Poetry and Anarchism* (1938) – reprinted as *Anarchy and Order* (1954). His *Education through Art*, 1943, had an important post-war influence. He was the most influential British intellectual to support anarchism before World War II and was closely associated with anarchism until he was knighted.

Sir Richard Rees (1900–70), editor, painter and critic. He was an attaché at the British Embassy in Berlin, 1922–23, a lecturer for the Workers' Educational Association, 1925–27, and editor of *The Adelphi*, 1930–37. He introduced a more political and less-consciously literary tone to the journal. He gave much encouragement to Orwell from this period until his death. Ravelston of *Keep the Aspidistra Flying* owes something to his generous nature. He partnered Orwell on Jura and showed him great kindness throughout his life. He became Orwell's literary executor jointly with Sonia Orwell and wrote *George Orwell: A Fugitive from the Camp of Victory* (1961).

Vernon Richards (born Vero Recchione, 1915–2001), edited *Spain and the World* and its successor, *Revolt!*, 1936–39, which presented the Spanish Civil War from an anti-Stalinist stance. He was then one of the editors of *Freedom through Anarchism*, 1939–49. Born in Soho, London, he was a civil engineer, journalist, and anarchist. Orwell met him through the International Anti-Fascist Solidarity Committee to which Emma Goldman had introduced Orwell in 1938. He took many photographs of Orwell and his son: see *George Orwell at Home* (1998).

Sir Steven Runciman (1903–2000) was a King's Scholar at Eton in the same Election as Orwell. He became a distinguished historian and published *A History of the Crusades*, 3 volumes (1951–4), *The Sicilian Vespers* (1958), and *The Fall of Constantinople* (1965). To celebrate his 97th birthday he managed a visit to Mount Athos to observe the consecration of a monastery which he had helped pay to be restored.

L.F. Rushbrook Williams, CBE (1890–1978), BBC Eastern Service Director, one-time Fellow of All Souls' College, Oxford; Professor of Modern History, Allahabad

University, 1914–19, and Director of the Central Bureau of Information, India, 1920–26. Director of the BBC Indian Service, 1941 to November 1944 then joined *The Times* to 1955. His enlightened attitude to India is well expressed in *India*, an Oxford Pamphlet on World Affairs, 1940. In papers prepared for Sir Stafford Cripps comments on him include 'has spent his life in the service of Indian Princes . . . Sails with the wind'.

Balraj Sahni (1913–1973), was educated at Harvard and worked with Gandhi in 1938. He was an Indian Programme Assistant when Orwell joined the BBC. His wife, Damyanti, who died in 1947, was working at the Shakespeare Memorial Theatre, Stratford-upon-Avon. Orwell brought them together with Norman Marshall for the programme series, 'Let's Act it Ourselves'. On their return to India they worked for the Indian People's Theatre Association. He then became an outstanding film actor. Damyanti starred in two films in 1946 and 1947. Did his work with Gandhi influence Orwell's writing on Gandhi?

Brenda Salkeld (1903–99), a clergyman's daughter, and gym mistress at St Felix Girls' School, Southwold. She met Orwell at Southwold and, although they did not agree on many issues – literary and personal – she remained a loyal friend to the end. She visited Orwell at Canonbury Square to see young Richard, on Jura, and at Cranham. Orwell sent her a dedicated copy of *Down and Out in Paris and London*. This has sixteen valuable annotations (see X, pp. 299–300). For her reminiscences of Orwell see *Orwell Remembered*, pp. 67–8, and *Remembering Orwell*, pp. 39–41.

John Sceats (1912–), an insurance agent who wrote articles for the socialist monthly, *Controversy*. Orwell admired these and asked Sceats to visit him at Preston Hall Sanatorium shortly after the publication of *Homage to Catalonia*.

Roger Senhouse (c.1900–65) joined Martin Secker Ltd in 1936 and remained a director until he retired in 1962. His last year at Eton overlapped with Orwell. He processed Orwell's work at Secker. Warburg in *All Authors are Equal* describes him as 'larger than life . . . His rages . . . were uninhibitedly magnificent . . . Physically brave as a lion, he was something of a moral coward. He had a real appreciation of literature, coupled with a fabulous memory. . . . one of the best copy-editors and proof readers I have ever known' (pp. 2–3).

Sir Osbert Sitwell (1892–1969), poet, essayist, novelist and a particularly engaging author of autobiography. He was brother to Edith and Sacheverell Sitwell and a fervent fighter against philistinism. He was educated at Eton and served in the Grenadier Guards from 1912 to 1919. In his review of *Great Morning* (XIX, 3416, 395–8) Orwell described Sitwell's first three autobiographies as among 'the best of our time'. The fourth, *Laughter in the Next Room*, as 'not so good'(see **1.6.49**).

Sir Sacheverell Sitwell (1897–1988), poet and critic; younger brother of Edith and Osbert Sitwell; educated at Eton. He served in the Grenadier Guards in World War I. Orwell reviewed his book, *Poltergeists* in September 1940 (XII, pp. 246–8).

Hugh (Humphrey) Slater (1905–58), painter and author. He was at one time a Communist and involved in anti-Nazi politics in Berlin in the early thirties. He fought for the Republicans in Spain, 1936–38, becoming Chief of Operations for the International Brigade. He put this experience to practical use (with Tom Wintringham) at the unofficial Osterley Park Training School which they ran to instruct members of the Home Guard in guerrilla tactics and street fighting. Orwell's lecture notes on street fighting, field fortifications, and smoke mortars survive (XII, pp. 328–40).

Sir Stephen Spender (1909–95), prolific poet, novelist, critic and translator. He edited *Horizon* with Cyril Connolly, 1940–41. He was co-editor of *Encounter*, 1953–65, remaining on the editorial board until 1967, when it was discovered that it was partially financed by the US Central Intelligence Agency. Orwell originally included him amongst the parlour Bolsheviks and 'fashionable successful persons' whom he castigated from time to time. After his letter of 15 April 1938 they became friends.

Gleb Struve (1898–1985), born St Petersburg, very prolific author. Fought in the anti-Bolshevik Volunteer Army in 1918 and then fled to Finland and England. Studied at Balliol College and later taught at the School of Slavonic and East European Studies, London University, 1932–47. He then became Professor of Slavic Languages and Literature, University of California, Berkeley, until 1965. He was the author of *25 Years of Soviet Russian Literature, 1918–43* (1944) and *Soviet Literature 1917–50* (1951).

Julian Symons (1912–94), editor of *Twentieth Century Verse*, 1937–39, and *Anthology of War Poetry* (1942); author of critical books and biographies among them *Charles Dickens* (1951), *Thomas Carlyle* (1952), and *Horatio Bottomley* (1955). He is perhaps best remembered today for his detective stories for which he won several awards. His *Bloody Murder: from the Detective Story to the Crime Novel* (1972) won the Edgar Allan Poe Award. He took over from Orwell as guest critic of the *Manchester Evening News*, 28 November 1946 (and though inexperienced, was paid £9 per contribution compared to Orwell's £8 8s). When Orwell died he wrote a personal memoir for *Tribune*, 27 January 1950.

Ihor Szewczenko (1922– ; now as Ševčenko), very distinguished scholar of Byzantine and Slavic Studies. When he and Orwell corresponded he commuted between Munich, where members of his family were living as Soviet-Ukrainian refugees, and Quakenbrück in the British Zone of Germany, where he worked on a daily newspaper for the Second Polish, the Maczek, Division (he was born in Poland). He emigrated to the United States and became Dumbarton Oaks Professor of Byzantine History and Literature at Harvard University. His translation of *Animal Farm* stands out strangely from his many Byzantine and Slavic studies. He still has one link with Orwell: his hobby is trout fishing.

Geoffrey Trease (1909–98), prolific author, most of whose 113 books were written for children. His study, *Tales Out of School* (1949) was an innovative survey of children's literature. His stories, very different in style from those of G.A. Henty in the nineteenth century and Percy F. Westerman in the early twentieth, eschewed jingoism and appealed equally to girls and boys. In 1935 he and his wife, Marian, travelled for five months in Soviet Russia to benefit from his royalties frozen there. He was a member of the Labour Party and wrote 'I myself never seriously considered joining the Communist Party . . . I noticed early what happened to individuals who left the Party on a sincere difference of opinion'. During the war he served in the Army Education Corps.

Richard Alexander Usborne (1910–2006) was the author of a groundbreaking study, *Clubland Heroes: a nostalgic study of some recurrent characters in romantic fiction* (1953), which discussed such fictional characters as Bulldog Drummond and Richard Hannay. He also wrote much on, and adapted for radio, the stories of P.G. Wodehouse (e.g. *A Wodehouse Companion*, 1981). Like Orwell he was born in India and his father was also a member of the Indian Civil Service. The *Strand* (which he edited) ran from January 1891 to March 1950 when it was incorporated in *Men Only*.

Fredric Warburg (1898–1980), Orwell's second publisher. He began his career with George Routledge & Sons in 1922 when he came down from Oxford, 'fit for practically nothing or, perhaps more accurately, for nothing practical'. He joined Martin Secker in 1936 and, as Harvill Secker, the house still flourishes. When Gollancz turned down *Homage to Catalonia*, he took it and then, when several publishers refused to publish *Animal Farm* he took that – and became Orwell's publisher. He and his wife were very supportive of Orwell in his final illness. See *Orwell Remembered*, pp. 193–9. Warburg fought at Passchendaele in 1917. Though a commissioned officer, he was happy to serve in Orwell's platoon in the Home Guard as a corporal in World War II. They are illustrated together in *The Lost Orwell*, plate 18.

Francis and Myfanwy Westrope, Francis had been a conscientious objector in World War I; Myfanwy was an active suffragette and joined the ILP in 1905. Orwell's employers at Booklovers' Corner, Hampstead from the end of 1934 to January 1936. Gollancz's lawyer was anxious lest the bookshop owner in *Keep the Aspidistra Flying* might lead to a libel or defamation action from the Westropes. Orwell reassured him he was very different in character and no action resulted. Orwell and Eileen ordered books from them when they were in Morocco.

Tom Wintringham (1898–1949), served in the Royal Flying Corps in World War I, and edited *Left Review*, 1934–36. He went to Spain as a war correspondent in 1936 and commanded the British Battalion of the International Brigade near Madrid in 1937. He was a founder member of the British Communist Party but left after his service in Spain. He wrote on weapons, tactics, and the new methods of warfare and was a founder, with Hugh Slater, of the Osterley Park Training Centre for the Home Guard.

George Woodcock (1912–95), author, anarchist, editor of *Now,* 1940–47, and later Professor of English, University of British Columbia. After a controversy with Orwell in 1942 (XIII, pp. 393–400), they corresponded and became close friends. They worked closely together on The Freedom Defence Committee. His books include *The Crystal Spirit: A Study of George Orwell,* 1967, and *Orwell's Message: 1984 and the Present* (1984).

Index

This is an index chiefly of names. It is a selective index. Thus, 'money' is not indexed; if it were it, or a related word, would appear in almost one page in three. The brief biographical notes are indexed first, in **bold,** that page number being given immediately after the name; their contents are *not* indexed. Place names within addresses are not indexed. Because the great majority of letters were written by Orwell, they are not indexed under his name but are indexed under the recipient's name with the page number(s) after the letter 'L' and a colon, e.g.: 'L: 66'. Letters sent by Eileen and other correspondents are indicated by italic *'L'* and a colon after the sender's name followed by the recipient's name and page number(s); a semicolon follows the last page reference to a letter after which pages with significant references are indexed in roman; significant footnotes are indexed in italic. The Chronology and Reading List are not indexed. Mac, Mc, and M' are indexed as 'Mac', the order thereafter being by the ensuing letter; St is indexed as 'Saint'. Titles are not given in the index unless there is no first name. Orwell's misspellings of names are ignored in the index.

Thus: Blair, Eileen, **509;** L: 74; *L: to* Jack Common, 103; 221, 261 *etc.*